# HARCOURT SCHOOL PUBLISHERS
# STORYtown

## Reach for the Stars

# TEACHER EDITION

### Senior Authors
Isabel L. Beck • Roger C. Farr • Dorothy S. Strickland

### Authors
Alma Flor Ada • Roxanne F. Hudson • Margaret G. McKeown
Robin C. Scarcella • Julie A. Washington

### Consultants
F. Isabel Campoy • Tyrone C. Howard • David A. Monti

## Harcourt
SCHOOL PUBLISHERS

www.harcourtschool.com

3 4 5 6 7 8 9 10    030    17 16 15 14 13 12 11 10 09 08 07

# Program Authors

## SENIOR AUTHORS

**Isabel L. Beck**
Professor of Education and Senior Scientist at the Learning Research and Development Center, *University of Pittsburgh*

RESEARCH CONTRIBUTIONS:
Reading Comprehension, Vocabulary, Beginning Reading, Phonics

**Roger C. Farr**
Chancellor's Professor Emeritus of Education and Former Director for the Center for Innovation in Assessment, *Indiana University, Bloomington*

RESEARCH CONTRIBUTIONS:
Instructional Assessment, Reading Strategies, Reading in the Content Areas

**Dorothy S. Strickland**
Samuel DeWitt Proctor Professor of Education and The State of New Jersey Professor of Reading, *Rutgers University, The State University of New Jersey*

RESEARCH CONTRIBUTIONS:
Early Literacy, Elementary Reading/Language Arts, Writing, Intervention

## AUTHORS

**Alma Flor Ada**
Professor Emerita, *University of San Francisco*

RESEARCH CONTRIBUTIONS:
Literacy, Biliteracy, Multicultural Children's Literature, Home-School Interaction, First and Second Language Acquisition

**Roxanne F. Hudson**
Assistant Professor, Area of Special Education *University of Washington*

RESEARCH CONTRIBUTIONS:
Reading Fluency, Learning Disabilities, Interventions

**Margaret G. McKeown**
Senior Scientist at the Learning Research and Development Center, *University of Pittsburgh*

RESEARCH CONTRIBUTIONS:
Vocabulary, Reading Comprehension

**Robin C. Scarcella**
Professor, Director of Academic English and ESL, *University of California, Irvine*

RESEARCH CONTRIBUTIONS:
English as a Second Language

**Julie A. Washington**
Professor, College of Letters and Sciences, *University of Wisconsin*

RESEARCH CONTRIBUTIONS:
Understanding of Cultural Dialect with an emphasis on Language Assessment, Specific Language Impairment and Academic Performance; Early Childhood Language and Early Literacy of African American Children

## CONSULTANTS

**F. Isabel Campoy**
President, Transformative Educational Services

RESEARCH CONTRIBUTIONS:
English as a Second Language, Applied Linguistics, Writing in the Curriculum, Family Involvement

**Tyrone C. Howard**
Associate Professor Urban Schooling, *University of California, Los Angeles*

RESEARCH CONTRIBUTIONS:
Multicultural Education, The Social and Political Context of Schools, Urban Education

**David A. Monti**
Professor Emeritus Department of Reading and Language Arts, *Central Connecticut State University*

RESEARCH CONTRIBUTIONS:
Reading Comprehension, Alternative Assessments, Flexible Grouping

# Theme: Wild and Wonderful

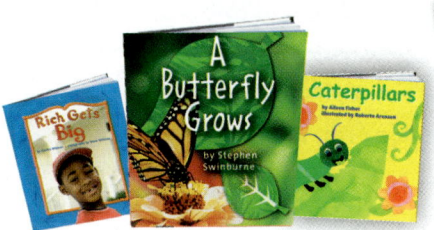

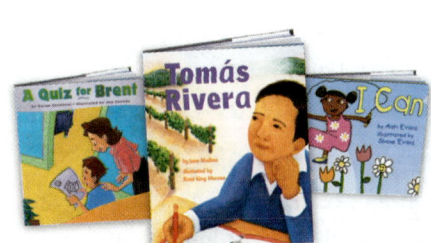

# Reference Materials

## Additional Resources

# Data-Driven Instruction

 **ASSESS**

Use assessments to track student progress.

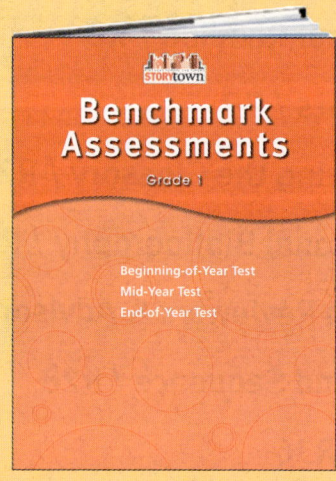

▲ **Weekly Lesson Tests (grades 1–6)**

▲ **Theme Tests**

▲ **Benchmark Assessments**
- Beginning-of-Year
- Mid-Year
- End-of-Year

 StoryTown Online Assessment

 **TEACH**

Provide instruction in key areas of reading.

◀ **Suggested Lesson Planner**

Online TE and Planning Resource

# 3 DIFFERENTIATE INSTRUCTION

Use daily Monitor Progress notes to inform instruction.

## MONITOR PROGRESS

### Fluency

| **IF** children need more support in fluency-building, | **THEN** have them echo-read with you, paying close attention to punctuation marks. |

**Small-Group Instruction, pp. S54–S55:**

- **BELOW-LEVEL: Reteach**
- **ON-LEVEL: Reinforce**
- **ADVANCED: Extend**

▲ **Suggested Small-Group Planner**

# 4 ASSESS, REMEDIATE, AND EXTEND

Use assessment results to remediate instruction.

**INTENSIVE INTERVENTION PROGRAM**

▲ **Strategic Intervention Resource Kit**

▲ **Challenge Resource Kit**

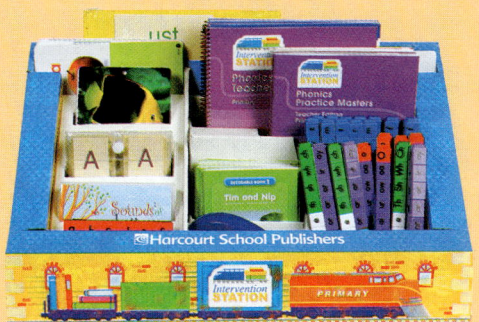

▲ **Intervention Station, Primary**

- Phonemic Awareness
- Phonics
- Vocabulary
- Comprehension
- Fluency

# Overview of a Theme

CORE LESSONS

- **Explicit, Systematic Instruction**

- **Spiraled Review of Key Skills**

- **Abundant Practice and Application**

- **Point-of-Use Progress Monitoring**

- **Support for *Leveled Readers***

- **Digital Support for Teachers and Students**

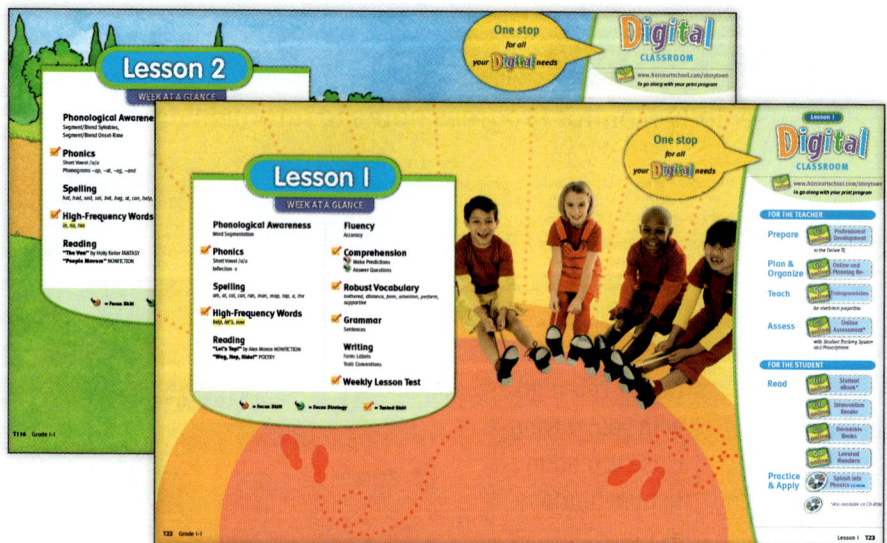

## READING-WRITING CONNECTION

- **Reading-Writing Connection in *Student Edition***

- **Instruction in *Teacher Edition***

- **Focus on the Traits of Good Writing**
  - Organization
  - Ideas
  - Sentence Fluency
  - Word Choice
  - Voice
  - Conventions

- **Develop Writing Forms Through the Writing Process**
  - Sentences About Us (Shared Writing)
  - Describing an Event (Shared Writing)
  - Respond to a Selection (Shared Writing)
  - Description (Independent Writing)
  - Personal Narrative (Independent Writing)

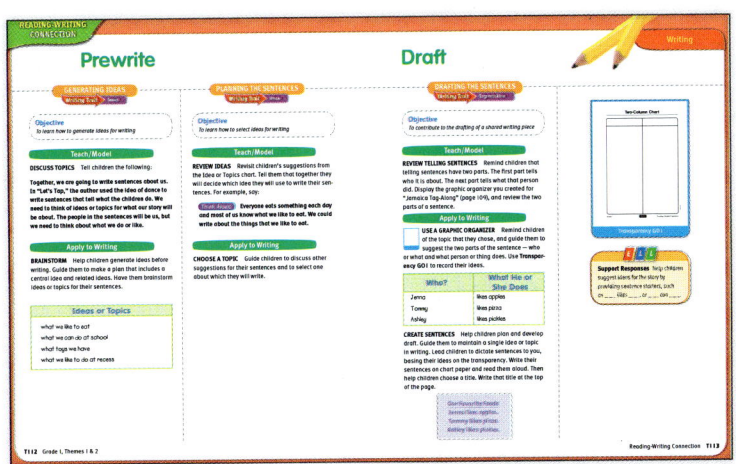

# Overview of a Lesson

- ● **Lesson Resources**

- ● **Suggested Lesson Planner**

- ● **Suggested Small-Group Planner**

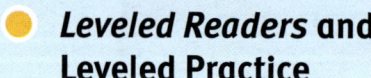

- ● *Leveled Readers* and **Leveled Practice**

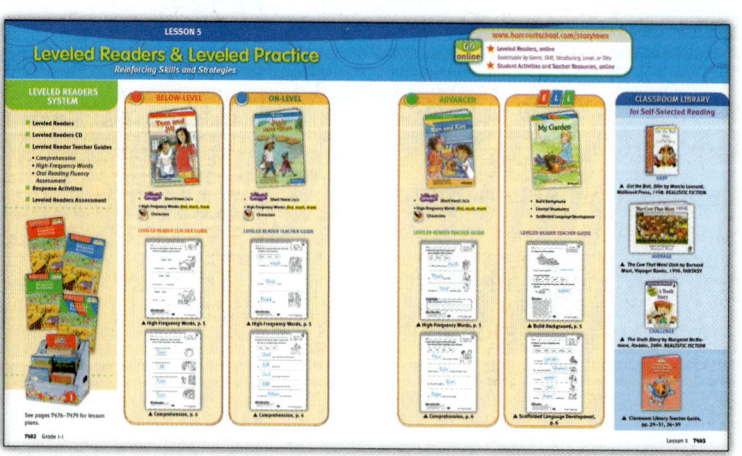

## ROUTINES

- **Oral Language**
- **Read Aloud**
- **Word Wall**
- **Phonemic Awareness**

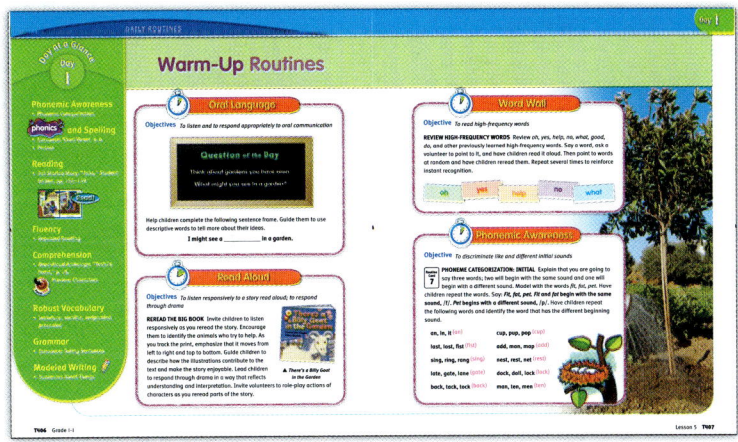

## PHONICS/SPELLING

- **Connect Letter to Sound**
- **Word Blending**
- **Word Building**
- **Spelling Pretest and Posttest**
- **Introduce and Review Structural Elements**

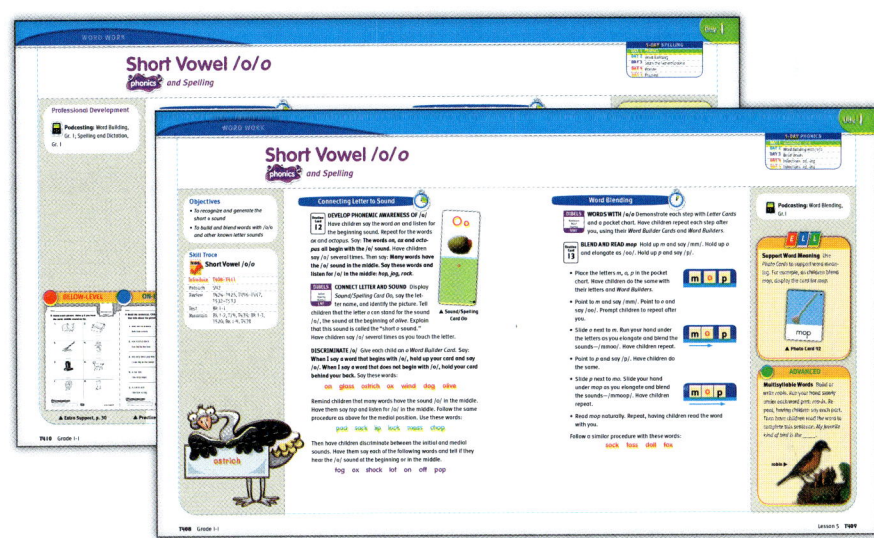

## HIGH-FREQUENCY WORDS

- **New Words for Each Lesson**
- **Instructional Routines**
- **Apply in the *Student Edition***
- **Spiraled Review**

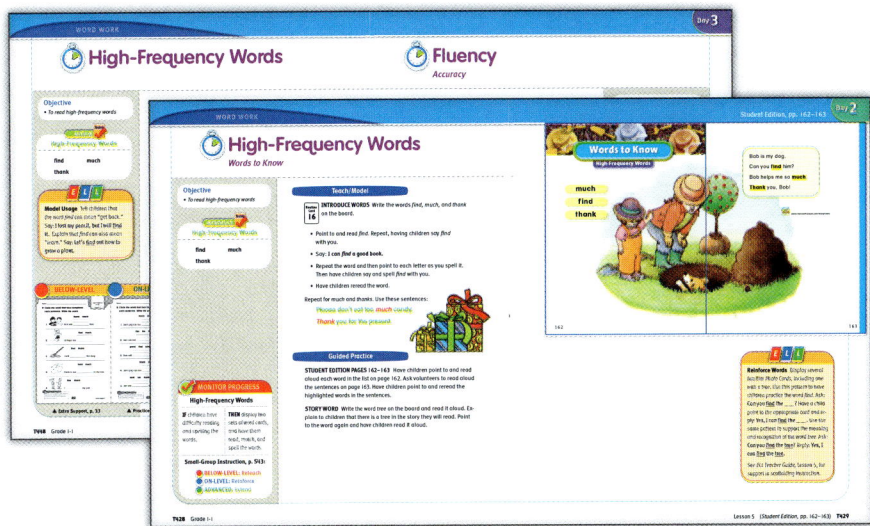

# *Overview of a Lesson (continued)*

## READING

- **Get Started Stories**
- **Main Selections**
- **Paired Selections**

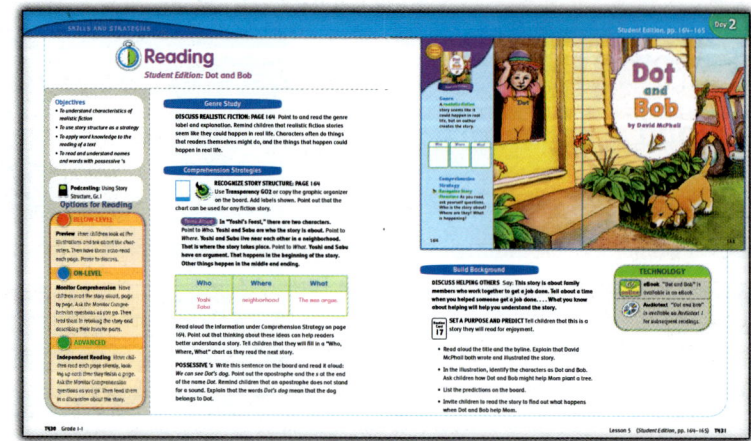

## FLUENCY

- **Explicit Introduction of Skills**
- **Repeated Readings**
- **Readers' Theater**

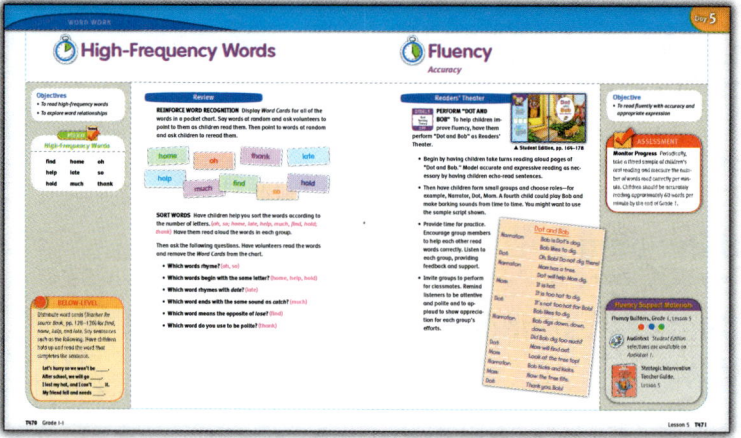

## COMPREHENSION

- **Focus Skills**
- **Focus Strategies**
- **Listening Comprehension**

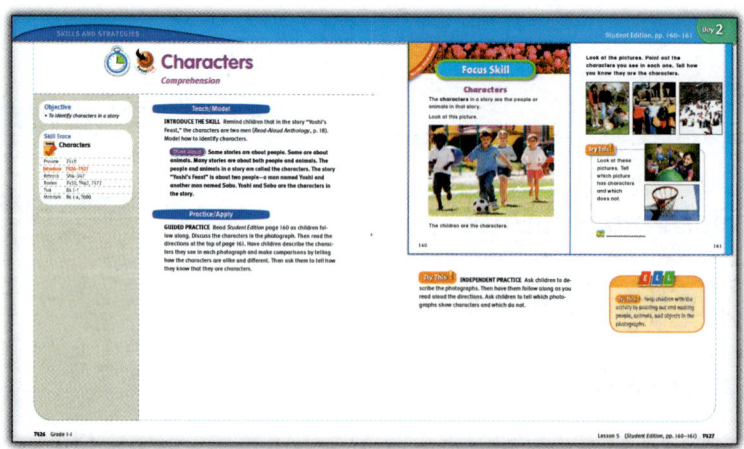

## ROBUST VOCABULARY

- **Listening/Speaking Vocabulary**
  - Tier-Two Words

- **Instructional Routines**

- **Student-Friendly Explanations**

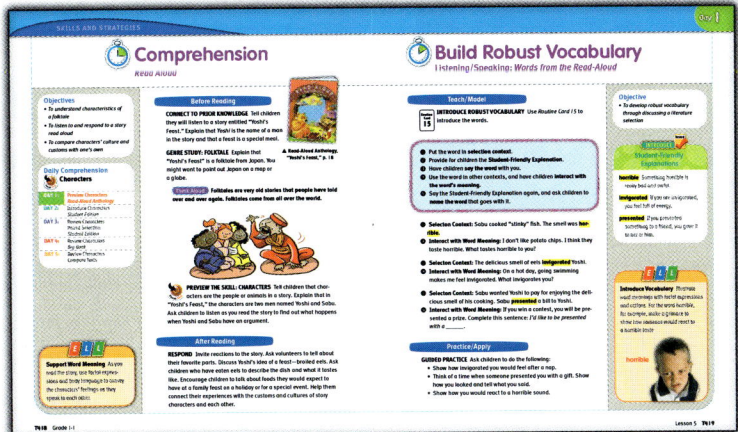

## LANGUAGE ARTS

- **Grammar**

- **Writing**

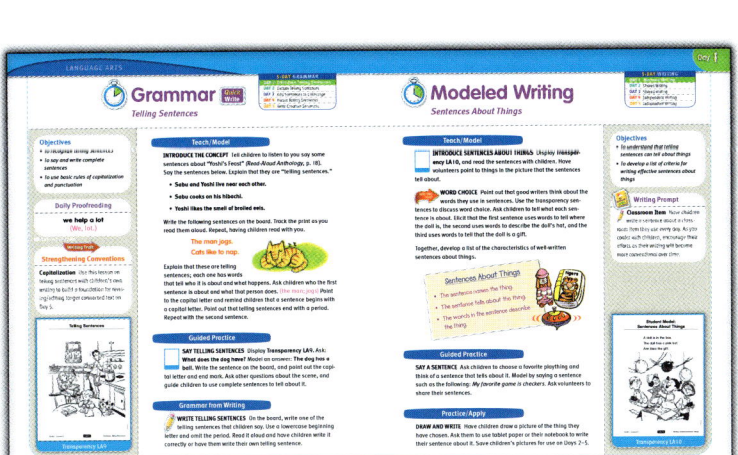

## LEVELED READERS

- **Reinforce Skills and Strategies**

- **Review High-Frequency Words**

- **Build Background and Concept Vocabulary**

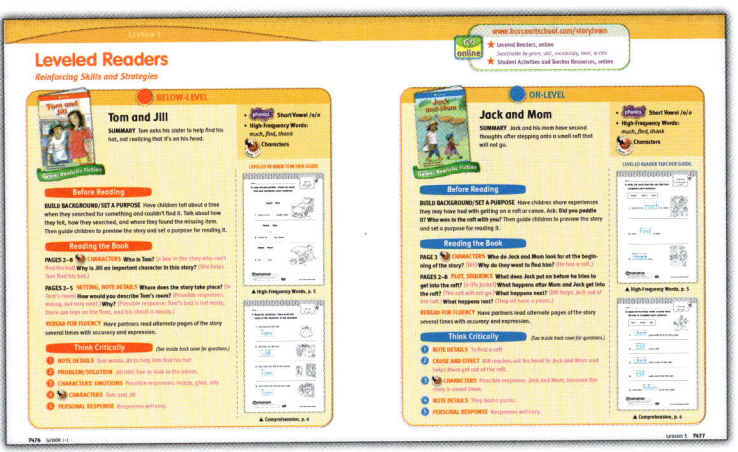

# Introducing the Book

## Discuss the Book's Organization

Have children turn to each of the following features in the *Student Edition*. Briefly discuss how each part helps readers use the book and understand the selections.

- **Contents** Shows titles, authors, and page numbers.

- **Comprehension Strategies** Describes tools readers can use to read well.

- **Theme Overview** Shows theme-related artwork and lists selections, skills, and strategies in that theme.

- **Lesson Overview** Lists selections, focus skill, and focus strategy in that lesson.

- **Get Started Story** Provides practice reading a decodable selection that reflects the target phonics skill.

- **Focus/Phonics Skill** Provides instruction in skills related to the selection.

- **Words to Know** Introduce new high-frequency words from the selection.

- **Genre Study** Describes the characteristics of the selection's genre.

- **Focus Strategy** Tells how to use strategies during reading.

- **Paired Selection** Presents poetry and other selections connected to the main selection.

- **Connections** Provides questions and activities related to both selections.

- **Reading-Writing Connection** Connects the selection to a good model of student writing.

- **Glossary** Provides example sentences and pictures to explain high-frequency words from the selections.

## Introduce Strategies

**USING *STUDENT EDITION* PAGES 8–11** Have children open their *Student Editions* to page 8, and explain to them that these pages will help them think about ways to better understand what they read. Tell them that these ways are called "strategies," and that they can use strategies before they read, while they read, and after they read.

**BEFORE YOU READ** Tell children that before they read, they can think about what they already know about a topic to help them understand. They can also set a purpose for reading.

**Think Aloud** If I was going to read a book about frogs, I could look at the pictures and think about what I already know about frogs. I could also think about why I'm reading. These would help me understand the book better.

**WHILE YOU READ** Model strategies children can use while they read as follows:

**Think Aloud** Asking questions about what I'm reading helps me know if I'm understanding it. If I'm not understanding, I can go back and reread parts of the book. When I answer questions about a book, I can be sure that I understood it.

**AFTER YOU READ** Explain how retelling or summarizing and making connections can help children understand what they read. Say:

**Think Aloud** After I read something, I tell myself what I just read. This helps me remember and understand. I also think about other things I have read, heard, or learned. Sometimes I can make connections between two different books.

## Comprehension Strategies

### Before You Read

Look at the pictures. Think about what you already know.

Set a purpose.

I want to find out about frogs.

8

9

### While You Read

Ask questions.

What do frogs eat?

Reread.

I'll read this page again.

Answer questions.

Oh! Some frogs eat bugs.

### After You Read

Summarize.

First, tadpoles hatch from eggs. Then, they begin changing into frogs. Last, they are full-grown frogs.

Make connections.

This is like another book I read. I learned about how butterflies change.

10

11

# Wild and Wonderful

# Theme Resources

 **Go online** **eBook STUDENT EDITION**

## STUDENT EDITION LITERATURE

### Lesson 13

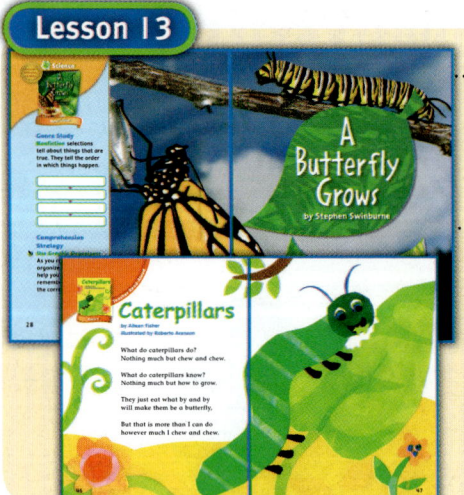

**GET STARTED STORY**

"Rich Gets Big,"
pp. 16–23

**PAIRED SELECTIONS**

"A Butterfly Grows,"
pp. 28–45
NONFICTION

"Caterpillars"
pp. 46–47
POETRY

### Lesson 14

**GET STARTED STORY**

"Ann's Trip to the Stars,"
pp. 54–61

**PAIRED SELECTIONS**

"Mark's Big Day,"
pp. 66–87
REALISTIC FICTION

"Putting on a Play,"
pp. 88–89
NONFICTION

### Lesson 15

**GET STARTED STORY**

"A Quiz for Brent,"
pp. 94–101

**PAIRED SELECTIONS**

"Tomás Rivera,"
pp. 106–123
BIOGRAPHY

"I Can,"
pp. 124–125
POETRY

### Lesson 16

**GET STARTED STORY**

"A Perfect Lunch,"
pp. 130–137

**PAIRED SELECTIONS**

"One More Friend,"
pp. 142–158
FANTASY

"Good Friends,"
pp. 160–161
NONFICTION

### Lesson 17

**GET STARTED STORY**

"Jungle Fun,"
pp. 166–173

**PAIRED SELECTIONS**

"Can Elephants Paint?"
pp. 178–198
NONFICTION

"An Elephant's Three T's,"
pp. 200–201
NONFICTION ARTICLE

### Lesson 18

**GET STARTED STORY**

"Shadow in the Snow,"
pp. 206–213

**PAIRED SELECTIONS**

"Snow Surprise,"
pp. 218–239
REALISTIC FICTION

"The Snowflake Man,"
pp. 240–245
NONFICTION

*Literature selections are available on Audiotext 3.*

## THEME 4 CLASSROOM LIBRARY

▲ **Hello, House!,** *by Linda Hayward*

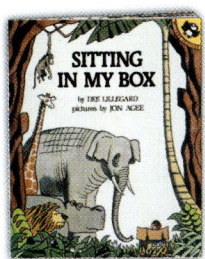

▲ **Sitting in My Box,** *by Dee Lillegard*

▲ **Classroom Library Books Teacher Guide**

## BIG BOOKS

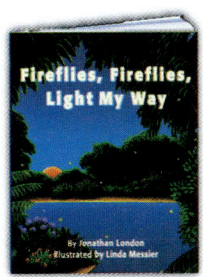

▲ **Fireflies, Fireflies, Light My Way**

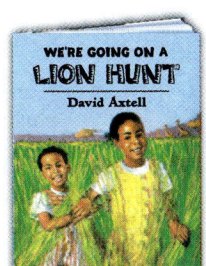

▲ **We're Going on a Lion Hunt**

## READ-ALOUD ANTHOLOGY

▲ **Read-Aloud Anthology, pp. 52–71**

## DECODABLE BOOKS

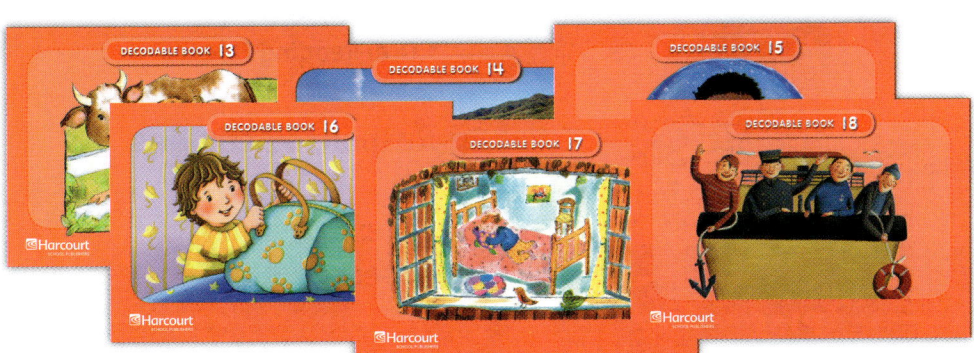

Decodable Book 13: **"Ranch Pals,"** Digraphs /ch/*ch*, *tch*

Decodable Book 14: **"Charming Carmel,"** *r*-Controlled Vowel /är/*ar*

Decodable Book 15: **"Quint and the Squids,"** Digraph /kw/*qu*

Decodable Book 15: **"Which Animal Is It,"** Digraph /hw/*wh*

Decodable Book 15: **"Whack! Wham!,"** Digraph /hw/*wh*

Decodable Book 16: **"Helping a Bird,"** *r*-Controlled Vowels /ûr/*er, ir*

Decodable Book 16: **"King Curtis and Shirl,"** *r*-Controlled Vowel /ar/*ur*

Decodable Book 16: **"Burt's Bag,"** *r*-Controlled Vowel /ûr/*ur*

Decodable Book 17: **"Little Ann's Nap,"** Syllable /əl/-*le*

Decodable Book 18: **"The Little Yellow Tugboat,"** Long Vowel /ō/*ow, oa*

## ADDITIONAL RESOURCES

- Reading Transparencies
- Language Arts Transparencies
- Literacy Center Kit
- Spelling Practice Book
- Grammar Practice Book
- Phonics Practice Book
- Audiotext Grade 1, CD 3 and 6
- Writer's Companion
- Routine Cards
- Photo Cards
- Big Book Audiotext CD

PROFESSIONAL DEVELOPMENT

- Professional Development Book

-  Videos for Podcasting

# Leveled Resources

 **BELOW-LEVEL**

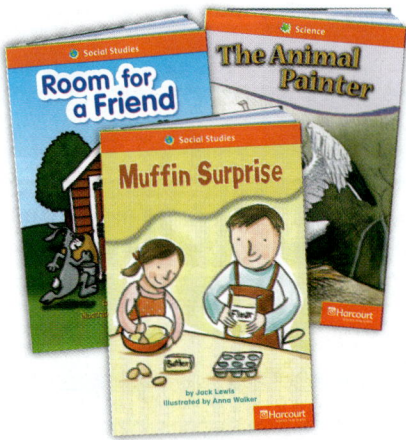

-  Phonics
- High-Frequency Words
- Focus Skills

 **ON-LEVEL**

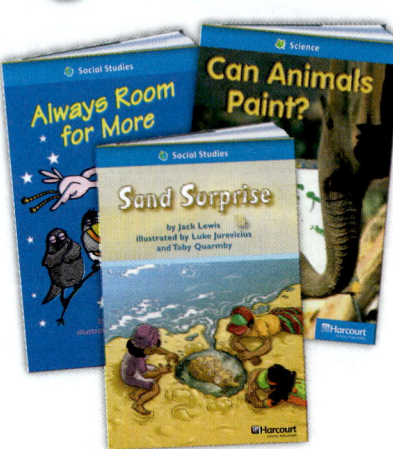

- phonics Phonics
- High-Frequency Words
- Focus Skills

 **ADVANCED**

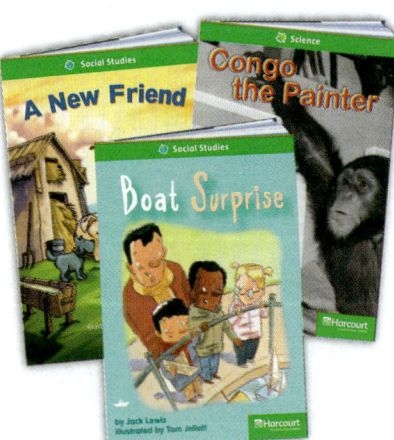

- phonics Phonics
- High-Frequency Words
- Focus Skill

 **E L L**

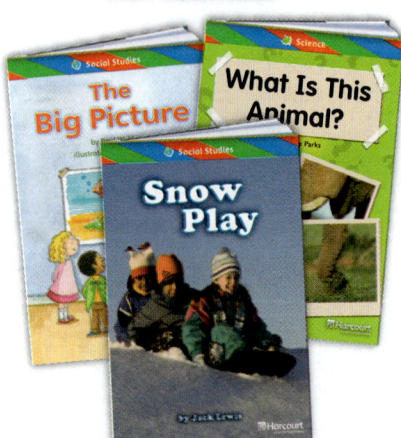

- Build Background
- Concept Vocabulary
- Scaffolded Language Development

*Teaching suggestions for the Leveled Readers can be found on pp. T104–T107, T202–T205, T288–T291, T374–T377, T462–T465, T552–T555*

## Leveled Readers System

- **Leveled Readers**
- **Leveled Readers CD**
- **Leveled Reader Teacher Guides**
  - High-Frequency Words
  - Comprehension
  - Oral Reading Fluency
- **Response Activities**
- **Leveled Readers Assessment**

## TECHNOLOGY

 www.harcourtschool.com/storytown

✔ **Leveled Readers,** *Online Database* Searchable by Genre, Skill, Vocabulary, Level or Title

✔ **Student Activities and Teacher Resources,** *online*

## Strategic Intervention Resource Kit,
### Lessons 13–18

*Strategic Intervention Interactive Reader: What a Thrill!*

- "How many?"
- "Star"
- "Tom's Book"
- "Please Get In!"
- "Paint Your Dog!"
- "First Snow"

*Also available:*

- Strategic Intervention Teacher Guide
- Strategic Intervention Practice Book
- Audiotext CD
- Teacher Resource Book
- Strategic Intervention Assessment Book

-  *Strategic Intervention Interactive Reader eBook*

 ## ELL Extra Support Kit,
### Lessons 13–18

- ELL Teacher Guide
- ELL Student Handbook
- ELL Copying Masters

 ## Challenge Resource Kit,
### Theme 4

- Challenge Book Pack
- Challenge Student Activities
- Challenge Teacher Guide

## Leveled Practice

 **BELOW-LEVEL**
Extra Support Copying Masters

 **ON-LEVEL**
Practice Book

 **ADVANCED**
Challenge Copying Masters

### INTERVENTION STATION, PRIMARY

**GRADES K–3** Sets of intervention material providing targeted instruction in:

- Phonemic Awareness
- Phonics
- Comprehension
- Vocabulary
- Fluency

# Digital Classroom
## To Go Along with Your Print Program

 **Go online**

**www.harcourtschool.com/storytown**

---

## FOR THE TEACHER

### Prepare

**Go online** Professional Development

*in the Online TE*

📱 Videos for Podcasting

PROFESSIONAL DEVELOPMENT

### Plan & Organize

**Go online** Online TE & Planning Resources*

### Teach

**Go online** Transparencies

*access from the ePlanner*

### Assess

**Go online** Online Assessment

*StoryTown Online Assessment with Student Tracking System and Prescriptions*

---

## FOR THE STUDENT

### Read

**Go online** Student eBook*

**Go online** Strategic Intervention Interactive Reader

**Go online** Leveled Readers

🔴 **BELOW-LEVEL**
🔵 **ON-LEVEL**
🟢 **ADVANCED**
**E L L**

### Practice & Apply

💿 Splash into Phonics CD-ROM

---

 *\* Also available on CD-ROM*

 # Monitor Progress

 **Plan Ahead**

## To Inform Instruction for Theme 4

## MONITOR PROGRESS

### Looking Back to Theme 3

| IF performance is | THEN, in addition to core instruction, use these resources: |
|---|---|
| ● **BELOW-LEVEL:** Reteach | • Below-Level Leveled Readers<br>• Leveled Readers System<br>• Extra Support Copying Masters<br>• Strategic Intervention Resource Kit<br>• Intervention Station, Primary |
| ● **ON-LEVEL:** Reinforce | • On-Level Leveled Readers<br>• Leveled Readers System<br>• Practice Book |
| ● **ADVANCED:** Extend | • Advanced Leveled Readers<br>• Leveled Readers System<br>• Challenge Copying Masters<br>• Challenge Resource Kit |

## ONLINE ASSESSMENT

✔ Prescriptions for Reteaching

✔ Weekly Lesson Tests

✔ Theme Test

✔ Benchmark Assessments

✔ Student Profile System to track student growth

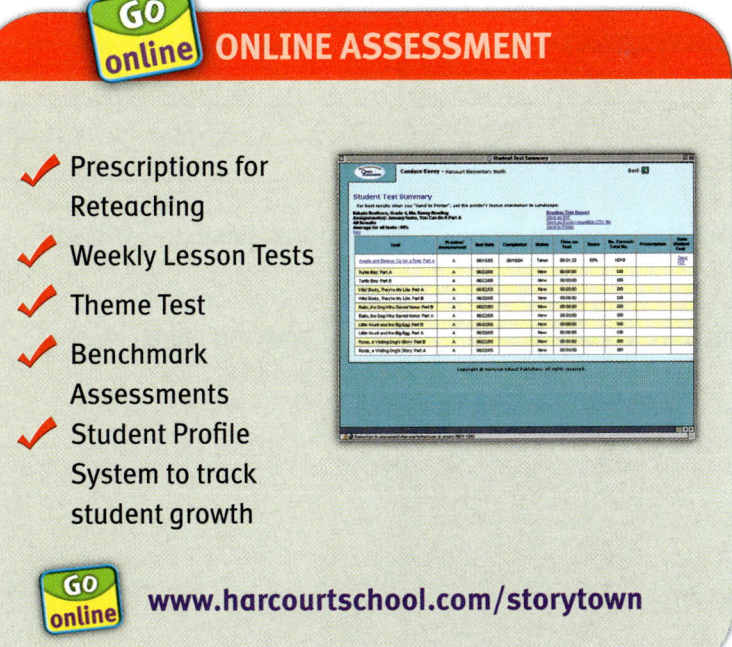

**GO online** www.harcourtschool.com/storytown

---

**Tested**

## TESTED SKILLS

| Domain | Skills |
|---|---|
| **PHONICS/SPELLING** | • Digraphs /ch/*ch, tch*<br>• *r*-Controlled Vowel /är/*ar*<br>• Digraphs /kw/*qu*, /hw/*wh*<br>• *r*-Controlled Vowels /ûr/*er, ir, ur*<br>• Long Vowel /ō/*ow, oa*<br>• Syllable /əl/*-le* |
| **HIGH-FREQUENCY WORDS** | • Words from Lessons 13–18 |
| **VOCABULARY** | • Robust Vocabulary |
| **FLUENCY** | • Oral Reading Fluency |
| **COMPREHENSION** | • 🐚 Sequence<br>• 🐚 Author's Purpose/Point of View<br>• 🐚 Sequence<br>• 🐚 Main Idea<br>• 🐚 Main Idea<br>• 🐚 Author's Purpose/Point of View |
| **GRAMMAR** | • Names of Days and Months<br>• Names of Holidays<br>• Using *I* and *Me*<br>• Using *He, She, It,* and *They*<br>• Possessives ('s and pronouns)<br>• Troublesome Words: Homophones |

# Theme at a Glance

| | **LESSON 13** pp. T22–T107  | **LESSON 14** pp. T118–T205 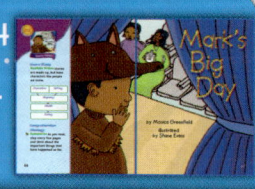 | **LESSON 15** pp. T206–T291 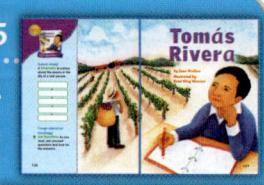 |
|---|---|---|---|
| • **Phonemic Awareness** | **PHONEME DELETION (INITIAL AND MEDIAL)** | **REVIEW BLENDING AND DELETION** | **REVIEW SEGMENTATION AND DELETION** |
| • **Phonics/ Spelling** | ✓ **DIGRAPHS** /ch/ch, tch<br><br>**INFLECTION** -es | ✓ **r-CONTROLLED VOWEL** /är/ar<br><br>✓ **INFLECTIONS** -s, -ed, -ing (no spelling changes) | ✓ **DIGRAPHS** /kw/qu, /hw/wh<br><br>✓ **INFLECTIONS** -ed, -ing (double final consonant) |
| • **Reading** | **PAIRED SELECTIONS** "A Butterfly Grows," NONFICTION "Caterpillars" POETRY | **PAIRED SELECTIONS** "Mark's Big Day" REALISTIC FICTION "Putting on a Play," NONFICTION | **PAIRED SELECTIONS** "Tomás Rivera," BIOGRAPHY "I Can," POETRY |
| • **Comprehension** | ✓ Sequence<br>Use Graphic Organizers | ✓ Author's Purpose/Point of View<br>Summarize | ✓ Sequence<br>Ask Questions |
| • **High-Frequency Words** | ✓ **HIGH-FREQUENCY WORDS** *air, fly, friends, grew, need, play, rain, watch* | ✓ **HIGH-FREQUENCY WORDS** *again, feel, house, know, loud, Mrs., put, say* | ✓ **HIGH-FREQUENCY WORDS** *about, books, family, name, read, work, writing, people* |
| • **Robust Vocabulary** | ✓ **ROBUST VOCABULARY** *astonishing, continue, doubt, transform, examine, devour* | ✓ **ROBUST VOCABULARY** *approached, energetic, pace, blunder, reassure, excel* | ✓ **ROBUST VOCABULARY** *cozily, interrupted, triumphantly, accomplishment, admire, ambition* |
| • **Fluency** | ✓ **FLUENCY:** INTONATION | ✓ **FLUENCY:** INTONATION | ✓ **FLUENCY:** INTONATION |

**Theme Writing** | **Reading-Writing Connection** | Respond to a Selection, pp. T108–T117

| | | | |
|---|---|---|---|
| • **Grammar** | ✓ **GRAMMAR:** Names of Days and Months | ✓ **GRAMMAR:** Names of Holidays | ✓ **GRAMMAR:** Using *I* and *Me* |
| • **Writing** | **WRITING FORM:** Sequence Story<br><br>**WRITING TRAIT:** Organization | **WRITING FORM:** E-mail<br><br>**WRITING TRAIT:** Conventions | **WRITING FORM:** Personal Narrative<br><br>**WRITING TRAIT:** Voice |

**THEME 4**

**Theme Project: Construction with Found Objects**

 = Focus Skill   = Focus Strategy   ✓ = Tested Skill

## LESSON 16
pp. T292–T377

**REVIEW BLENDING, DELETION AND SEGMENTATION**

- ✓ **r-CONTROLLED VOWEL** /ûr/er, ir, ur
- ✓ **INFLECTIONS** -er, -est

**PAIRED SELECTIONS**
"One More Friend," FANTASY
"Good Friends," NONFICTION

- ✓ Main Idea
- Summarize

- ✓ **HIGH-FREQUENCY WORDS**
  *always, by, Cow's, join, nice, please, room*

- ✓ **ROBUST VOCABULARY**
  *captured, mercy, struggling, compatible, amiable, relax*

- ✓ **FLUENCY:** READING RATE

---

## LESSON 17
pp. T378–T465

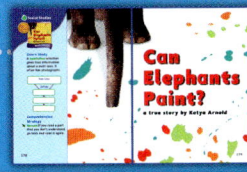

**PHONEME SUBSTITUTION (INITIAL AND MEDIAL)**

- **SYLLABLE** əl -le
- ✓ **INFLECTIONS** -ed, -ing (double final consonant)

**PAIRED SELECTIONS**
"Can Elephants Paint?" NONFICTION
"An Elephant's Three T's," NONFICTION ARTICLE

- ✓ Main Idea
- Monitor Comprehension: Reread

- ✓ **HIGH-FREQUENCY WORDS**
  *buy, carry, money, other, paint, paper, would*

- ✓ **ROBUST VOCABULARY**
  *agreement, unnoticed, unthinkable, rejoice, predicament, extraordinary*

- ✓ **FLUENCY:** INTONATION

---

## LESSON 18
pp. T466–T555

**REVIEW BLENDING AND SUBSTITUTION**

- ✓ **LONG VOWEL** /ō/ow, oa
  **PHONOGRAMS** -ow, -oat, -own, -oast

**PAIRED SELECTIONS**
"Snow Surprise," REALISTIC FICTION
"The Snowflake Man," NONFICTION

- ✓ Author's Purpose/Point of View
- Monitor Comprehension: Make Inferences

- ✓ **HIGH-FREQUENCY WORDS**
  *mouse, our, over, pretty, surprise, three*

- ✓ **ROBUST VOCABULARY**
  *bulged, jostled, argue, command, labored, wary*

- ✓ **FLUENCY:** READING RATE

---

**Writing Traits** → Organization, Conventions, Voice, Ideas, Word Choice

---

- ✓ **GRAMMAR:** Using *He, She, It,* and *They*

-  **WRITING FORM:** Invitation

- **WRITING TRAIT:** Ideas

---

- ✓ **GRAMMAR:** Possessives ('s and pronouns)

- **WRITING FORM:** Friendly Letter

- **WRITING TRAIT:** Voice

---

- ✓ **GRAMMAR:** Troublesome Words: Homophones

-  **WRITING FORM:** Thank-You Letter

- **WRITING TRAIT:** Word Choice

# Planning for Reading Success

| Tested Skill | Teach/Model | ✅ Monitor Progress | Additional Support |
|---|---|---|---|
| **DIBELS FLUENCY** | | | |
| • Intonation | Lessons 13, 14, 17, pp. T77, T175, T435 | Lessons 13, 14, 17, pp. T77, T175, T435 | Small-Group Instruction, pp. S4–S5, S14–S15, S44–S45 |
| • Reading Rate | Lessons 15, 16, 18, pp. T261, T347, T523 | Lessons 15, 16, 18, pp. T261, T347, T523 | Small-Group Instruction, pp. S24–S25, S34–S35, S54–S55 |
| **DIBELS PHONEMIC AWARENESS/ PHONICS/SPELLING** | | | |
| • Digraphs /ch/*ch, tch* | Lesson 13, pp. T36–T39 | Lesson 13, p. T39 | Small-Group Instruction, p. S2 |
| • *r*-Controlled Vowel /är/*ar* | Lesson 14, pp. T132–T135 | Lesson 14, p. T135 | Small-Group Instruction, p. S12 |
| • Digraphs /kw/*qu*, /hw/*wh* | Lesson 15, pp. T220–T223 | Lesson 15, p. T223 | Small-Group Instruction, p. S22 |
| • *r*-Controlled Vowels /ûr/*er, ir, ur* | Lesson 16, pp. T306–T309 | Lesson 16, p. T309 | Small-Group Instruction, p. S32 |
| • Syllable /əl/-*le* | Lesson 17, pp. T392–T395 | Lesson 17, p. T395 | Small-Group Instruction, p. S42 |
| • Long Vowel /ō/*ow, oa* | Lesson 18, pp. T480–T483 | Lesson 18, p. T483 | Small-Group Instruction, p. S52 |
| **HIGH-FREQUENCY WORDS** | Lessons 13–18, pp. T56–T57, T152–T153, T240–T241, T326–T327, T412–T413, T500–T501 | Lessons 13–18, pp. T56, T152, T240, T326, T412, T500 | Small-Group Instruction, pp. S3, S13, S23, S33, S43, S53 |
| **ROBUST VOCABULARY** | Lessons 13–18, pp. T47, T81, T143, T179, T231, T265, T317, T351, T403, T439, T491, T529 | Lessons 13–18, pp. T101, T199, T285, T371, T459, T549 | Small-Group Instruction, pp. S8–S9, S18–S19, S28–S29, S38–S39, S48–S49, S58–S59 |
| **COMPREHENSION** | | | |
| 🔥 Sequence | Lesson 13, pp. T46, T54–T55 Lesson 15, pp. T230, T238–T239 | Lesson 13, p. T90 Lesson 15, p. T274 | Small-Group Instruction, pp. S6–S7, S26–S27 |
| 🔥 Author's Purpose/Point of View | Lesson 14, pp. T150–T151 | Lesson 14, p. T188, T538 | Small-Group Instruction, pp. S16–S17, S56–S57 |
| 🔥 Main Idea | Lesson 16, pp. T324–T325 | Lesson 16, p. T360, T448 | Small-Group Instruction, pp. S36–S37, S46–S47 |
| **GRAMMAR** | Lessons 13–18, pp. T48, T144, T232, T318, T404, T492 | Language Arts Checkpoints, pp. T102, T200, T286, T372, T460, T550 | Reteach Activities, pp. S10–S11, S20–S21, S30–S31, S40–S41, S50–S51, S60–S61 |

🔥 = Focus Skill

| Review |  Assess |
|---|---|
| Lesson 13, pp. T45, T68, T89, T99<br>Lesson 14, pp. T141, T166, T187, T197<br>Lesson 15, pp. T229, T252, T273, T283<br>Lesson 16, pp. T315, T338, T359, T369<br>Lesson 17, pp. T401, T426, T447, T457<br>Lesson 18, pp. T489, T514, T537, T547 | Weekly Lesson Tests<br>Theme Reading Fluency Tests<br>Benchmark Assessment, Mid-Year |
| Lesson 13, pp. T52–T53, T74–T75, T87, T97<br>Lesson 14, pp. T148–T149, T172–T173, T185, T195<br>Lesson 15, pp. T236–T237, T258–T259, T271, T281<br>Lesson 16, pp. T322–T323, T344–T345, T357, T367<br>Lesson 17, pp. T408–T409, T432–T433, T445, T455<br>Lesson 18, pp. T496–T497, T520–T521, T535, T545 | Weekly Lesson Tests<br>Theme Tests<br>Benchmark Assessments, Mid-Year |
| Lessons 13–18, pp. T76, T88, T98, T174, T186, T196, T260, T272, T282, T346, T358, T368, T434, T446, T456, T522, T536, T546 | Weekly Lesson Tests<br>Theme Tests<br>Benchmark Assessment, Mid-Year |
| Lessons 13–18, pp. T69, T91, T101, T167, T179, T189, T199, T253, T275, T285, T339, T361, T371, T427, T449, T459, T515, T539, T549 | Weekly Lesson Tests<br>Theme Tests<br>Benchmark Assessment, Mid-Year |
| Lesson 13, pp. T78, T90, T100<br>Lesson 15, pp. T238–T239<br>Lesson 14, pp. T176, T188, T198<br>Lesson 18, pp. T499, T524, T538, T548<br>Lesson 16, pp. T348, T360, T370<br>Lesson 17, pp. T410–T411, T436, T448, T458 | Weekly Lesson Tests<br>Theme Tests<br>Benchmark Assessment, Mid-Year |
| Lesson 13, pp. T48, T70, T82, T92, T102; Lesson 14, pp. T144, T168, T180, T190, T200; Lesson 15, pp. T232, T254, T266, T276, T286; Lesson 16, pp. T318, T340, T352, T362, T372; Lesson 17, pp. T404, T428, T440, T450, T460; Lesson 18, pp. T492, T516, T530, T540, T550 | Weekly Lesson Tests<br>Theme Tests |

## INTEGRATED TEST PREP

- Short Response, pp. T103, T201, T287, T373, T461, T551

## ⏱ TEST PREP MINUTES

For early finishers, beginning of class, or anytime:

- **SEQUENCE** **Think about how our class gets ready for lunch.** Write some sentences about the order in which each action is done. (Possible response: We all clean off our tables. Each table lines up at the door. The line leader takes us down the hall to the cafeteria.)

- **VOCABULARY** **Draw a picture of the kind of animal with which you are most compatible.** Write a sentence that explains in what way you are compatible with this animal. (Possible response: I am very compatible with cats because we both like to nap in sunny places.)

- **WRITING** **Think about a time when you were very energetic.** Write a few sentences about how you felt and what you did. Responses will vary.

# Setting the Stage with Big Books
## *Fireflies, Fireflies, Light My Way*

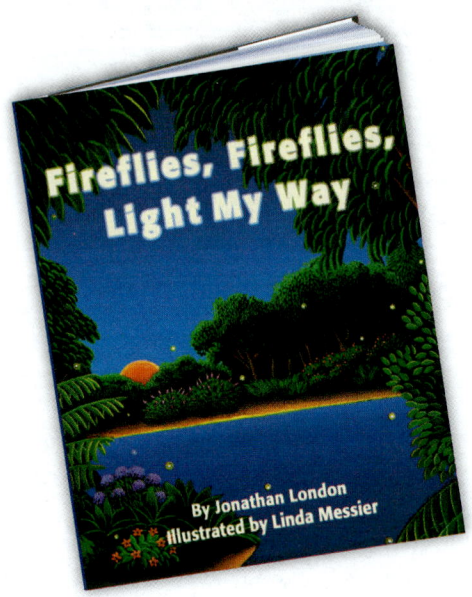

▲ Big Book

## Modeling Fluency

- Stimulate by reading rich literature
- Develop vocabulary
- Model reading strategies
- Develop the concept of making predictions

## Theme Connection

**FIREFLIES, FIREFLIES, LIGHT MY WAY** presents in rhythmic language how forest creatures live. The story follows various animals throughout the woods and tells us, through either rhyme or illustration, about an animal's characteristics or habitat. Point out that the story informs us that otters slide and frogs leap. Discuss with children how the rhyming lines and creative illustrations tell facts about the animals.

## Ideas for Sharing Literature

**CHORAL RECITING** Before reading *Fireflies, Fireflies, Light My Way*, have children use picture clues to tell what kinds of animals they are going to read about. Read the story aloud, having children join in on the repeated phrase "Lead me to the place."

**RHYMING WORDS** Point out to children that many of the lines in this story end with rhyming words. Have children listen for and identify the rhyming pairs *deep* and *leap*, *best* and *nest*, *chance* and *dance*. Ask them what other rhyming pairs they hear.

### OPPORTUNITIES TO SHARE

**FIREFLIES, FIREFLIES, LIGHT MY WAY**
- Lesson 13, page T34
- Lesson 13, page T90
- Lesson 13, page T100

- Lesson 15, page T218
- Lesson 15, page T274
- Lesson 15, page T284
- Lesson 15, page T286

- Lesson 17, page T390
- Lesson 17, page T448
- Lesson 17, page T458

 **Audiotext** Big Books are available on the *Big Book Audiotext CD,* Grade 1.

... where the muskrats play.
Muskrats, muskrats, paddle far.

Lead me to the place . . .

... where the raccoons are.
Raccoons, raccoons, sniff away.

Lead me to the place . . .

... where the crawdads stay.
Crawdads, crawdads, scuttle away.

Lead me to the place . . .

... where the otters play.
Otters, otters, slide some more.

Lead me to the place . . .

... Yikes! Where the alligators ROAR?
Alligators, alligators, give me a chance!

Chase me to the place . . .

... where the fireflies dance.
Fireflies, fireflies, light my way.

Lead me to the place . . .

... where the turtles dive
bullfrogs leap
beavers gnaw
catfish swim
wood ducks squawk
muskrats paddle
raccoons sniff
crawdads scuttle
otters slide

... and no alligators chase me away!

Everybody, everybody, sing HURRAY!

# Setting the Stage with Big Books
## *We're Going on a Lion Hunt*

▲ Big Book

## Modeling Fluency

- Stimulate by reading rich literature
- Develop vocabulary
- Model reading strategies
- Develop the concept of making predictions

## Theme Connection

**WE'RE GOING ON A LION HUNT** tells about two sisters' playful adventures as they imagine what they would encounter if they were hunting lion. Through the use of rhythmic language and illustrations, we follow the girls' journey through long grass, a lake, a swamp, and a dark cave to find a lion. Discuss with children what the two girls see and encounter on their imaginary journey. Ask them how they know this story is make believe.

## Ideas for Sharing Literature

**MAKING PREDICTIONS** After reading about the long grass and the lake that the girls encounter on their way to find a lion, have children predict what challenges or adventures they think the girls will encounter next.

**APPRECIATING LANGUAGE** As you reread *We're Going on a Lion Hunt*, call attention to some of the colorful action words in the story, such as *splish*, *splash* and *swish*, *swash*. Encourage children to talk about and act out the meaning of each word.

### OPPORTUNITIES TO SHARE

**WE'RE GOING ON A LION HUNT**

- Lesson 14, page T130
- Lesson 14, page T188
- Lesson 14, page T198

- Lesson 16, page T304
- Lesson 16, page T360
- Lesson 16, page T370
- Lesson 16, page T372

- Lesson 18, page T478
- Lesson 18, page T532
- Lesson 18, page T538
- Lesson 18, page T548

  **Audiotext** Big Books are available on the *Big Book Audiotext CD,* Grade 1.

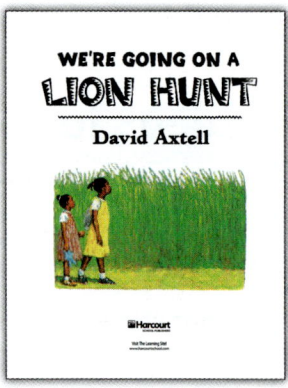

**WE'RE GOING ON A**
# LION HUNT

**David Axtell**

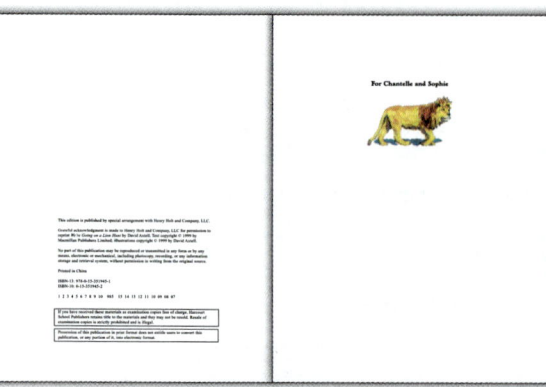

For Chantelle and Sophie

We're going on a lion hunt.
We're going to catch a big one.
We're not scared.
Been there before.

We're going on a lion hunt.
We're going to catch a big one.
We're not scared.
Been there before.
**Oh, no . . .**
**Long grass!**
Can't go *over* it.
Can't go *under* it.
Can't go *around* it.
Have to go *through* it.
**Swish, swash, swish, swash.**

We're going on a lion hunt.
We're going to catch a big one.
We're not scared.
Been there before.
**Oh, no . . .**
**A lake!**
Can't go *over* it.
Can't go *under* it.
Can't go *around* it.
Have to go *through* it.
**Splish, splash, splish, splash.**

We're going on a lion hunt.
We're going to catch a big one.
We're not scared.
Been there before.
**Oh, no . . .**
**A swamp!**
Can't go *over* it.
Can't go *under* it.
Can't go *around* it.
Have to go *through* it.
**Squish, squash, squish, squash.**

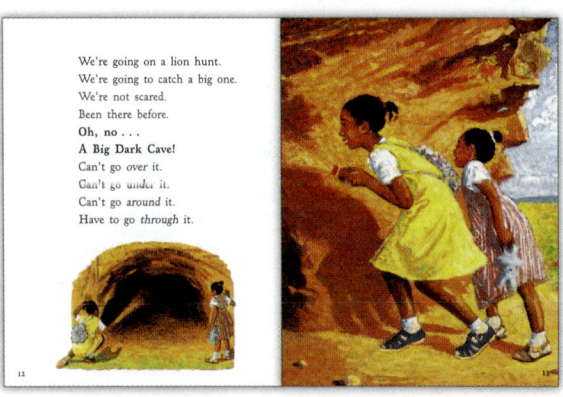

We're going on a lion hunt.
We're going to catch a big one.
We're not scared.
Been there before.
**Oh, no . . .**
**A Big Dark Cave!**
Can't go *over* it.
Can't go *under* it.
Can't go *around* it.
Have to go *through* it.

In we go,
Tiptoe, tiptoe.

But what's that?

One shiny wet **nose!**

One big shaggy **mane!**

Four big furry **paws!**

**It's a lion!**

Back through the cave.
Back we go.

Tiptoe, tiptoe.

Back through the swamp.

Squish, squash, squish, squash.

Back through the lake.

Splish, splash, splish, splash.

Back through the long grass.

Swish, swash, swish, swash.

All the way home.
Slam the door—
CRASH!

We're all tired now.
Tired and sleepy.

Better catch a lion tomorrow instead!

# Theme Project
## Construction with Found Objects

### Objective
- *To create a construction using ordinary objects*

### Materials
- found objects, such as small boxes, egg cartons, paper plates or cups, lunch bags, yarn, or craft sticks
- art supplies, such as paint, markers, glue, and scissors
- shoe box lid or cardboard for base
- paper and pencil

See **Project Ideas from The Bag Ladies, pages 8–9.**

### Getting Started

Explain that a construction is an artwork that an artist puts together out of various materials. Tell children they will be creating constructions using found objects, or ordinary materials that are usually used for other purposes, such as paper cups, plastic lids, or rubber bands.

### Along the Way

**1 Brainstorm**  Have children think about some ordinary objects and ways they could put them together to make something new. You may want to show examples of artworks created by artists out of everyday materials. Explain that creative people often enjoy finding new purposes for ordinary objects.

**2 Research**  Have children find and collect objects for their construction. Have them think about ways they can change their objects before attaching them to a base. For example, they could cut pictures out of an old magazine and glue them onto a paper bag, crush a paper cup and paint it, or glue several plastic lids together and then decorate.

**3 Plan**  Have children gather all their found objects and begin experimenting with ways they can put them together on the base. Have them compose a storyboard with pictures that shows how they transformed their ordinary objects into a new creation.

**4 Complete the Construction**  Have children complete their constructions. Then have groups present their constructions and storyboards that show how their ordinary objects were transformed to extraordinary constructions.

## LISTENING AND SPEAKING

Working in groups affords children opportunities to develop their listening and speaking skills. As they work on their theme project, help them do the following:

- **Respond appropriately and courteously to directions and questions, making contributions to group discussions**
- **Use language, volume, and rate appropriate for the audience, purpose, and occasion**
- **Use nonverbal communication effectively to clarify and support what they say, using props and pictures**

## SUGGESTIONS FOR INQUIRY

The theme project can be a springboard for inquiry into a variety of topics and ideas. Help children formulate questions about how people think of new ideas, such as

- **Where do inventors get their ideas?**
- **What would you like to invent?**

Invite children to speculate about what they would invent and then research how some inventions were created. As they generate questions, have them decide which questions are most relevant to the topic. Then have them focus on those questions. After they complete their research, invite them to share with the class what they learned.

**Build Learning** Make word cards for some of the found objects so children can become familiar with words for everyday objects.

   **BELOW-LEVEL**

**Work Together** If children are not confident with making their own storyboard, have them work with a partner for extra support.

   **School-Home Connection**

Invite family members to visit the classroom to see the constructions. Besides pointing out and naming features of the construction, children can tell family members how they made their creation and what makes it special. Rehearse with children how to respond courteously to questions. Invite family members to share their own experiences about their creative use of an everyday object.

# Build Theme Connections
## *Wild and Wonderful*

### Relate to Personal Experience

**DISCUSS USING IMAGINATION**   Ask children to tell about a time when they used their imagination to solve a problem, such as making a toy out of an everyday object or creating a picture from unusual materials. Ask children to tell how they felt while they were being creative and using their imagination. You may wish to use the following poem to help children explore and elaborate on feelings associated with being creative.

## Keep a Poem in Your Pocket

Keep a poem in your pocket
And a picture in your head
And you'll never feel lonely
At night when you're in bed.
The little poem will sing to you
The little picture bring to you
A dozen dreams to dance to you
At night when you're in bed.
So—
Keep a poem in your pocket
And a picture in your head
And you'll never feel lonely
At night when you're in bed.

—BEATRICE SCHENK DE REGNIERS

| | Lesson 13 ▶ | Lesson 14 ▶ | Lesson 15 ▶ | Lesson 16 ▶ | Lesson 17 ▶ | Lesson 18 ▶ |
|---|---|---|---|---|---|---|
| Selection Titles | Rich Gets Big **A Butterfly Grows** Caterpillars | Ann's Trip to the Stars **Mark's Big Day** Putting on a Play | A Quiz for Brent **Tomás Rivera** I Can | A Perfect Lunch **One More Friend** Good Friends | Jungle Fun **Can Elephants Paint?** An Elephant's Three T's | Shadow in the Snow **Snow Surprise** The Snowflake Man |
| Comprehension Strategies | Use Graphic Organizers | Summarize | Ask Questions | Summarize | Reread | Make Inferences |
| Focus Skills | Sequence | Words with *ar* | Sequence | Main Idea | Main Idea | Words with *ow* and *oa* |

Theme **4** Wild and Wonderful

*Boy Playing with Toys*, Steve Dininno

READING-WRITING CONNECTION

12

13

# Talk About the Theme

**BUILD BACKGROUND**  Read aloud the theme title, "Wild and Wonderful," and ask what it means. Discuss ways that children can display their creativity.

**CONNECT IDEAS**  Have children page through the stories in the theme. Talk about the characters and what is happening in various illustrations. Discuss what the stories might be about and how the characters might demonstrate creativity.

# Talk About Fine Art

**LOOK CLOSER**  Discuss with children how the illustration reflects the theme title, "Wild and Wonderful." Ask *How does this picture show creativity? What do you think this boy is pretending? What kinds of things do you pretend with your toys?*

# Lesson 13

## WEEK AT A GLANCE

### Phonemic Awareness
Phoneme Deletion

### ✔ Phonics
Digraphs /ch/*ch*, *tch*
Inflection *-es*

### ✔ Spelling
*chip, chin, inch, such, catch, match, wish, shop, saw, were*

### ✔ High-Frequency Words
*air*, *fly*, *friends*, *grew*, *need*, *play*, *rain*, *watch*

### Reading
**"A Butterfly Grows"** by Stephen Swinburne
NONFICTION
**"Caterpillars"** POETRY

### ✔ Fluency
Intonation

### ✔ Comprehension
 Sequence
 Use Graphic Organizers

### ✔ Robust Vocabulary
*astonishing, continue, doubt, transform, examine, devour*

### ✔ Grammar
Names of Days and Months

### Writing
Form: Sequence Story
Trait: Organization

### Weekly Lesson Test

 = Focus Skill     = Focus Strategy    ✔ = Tested Skill

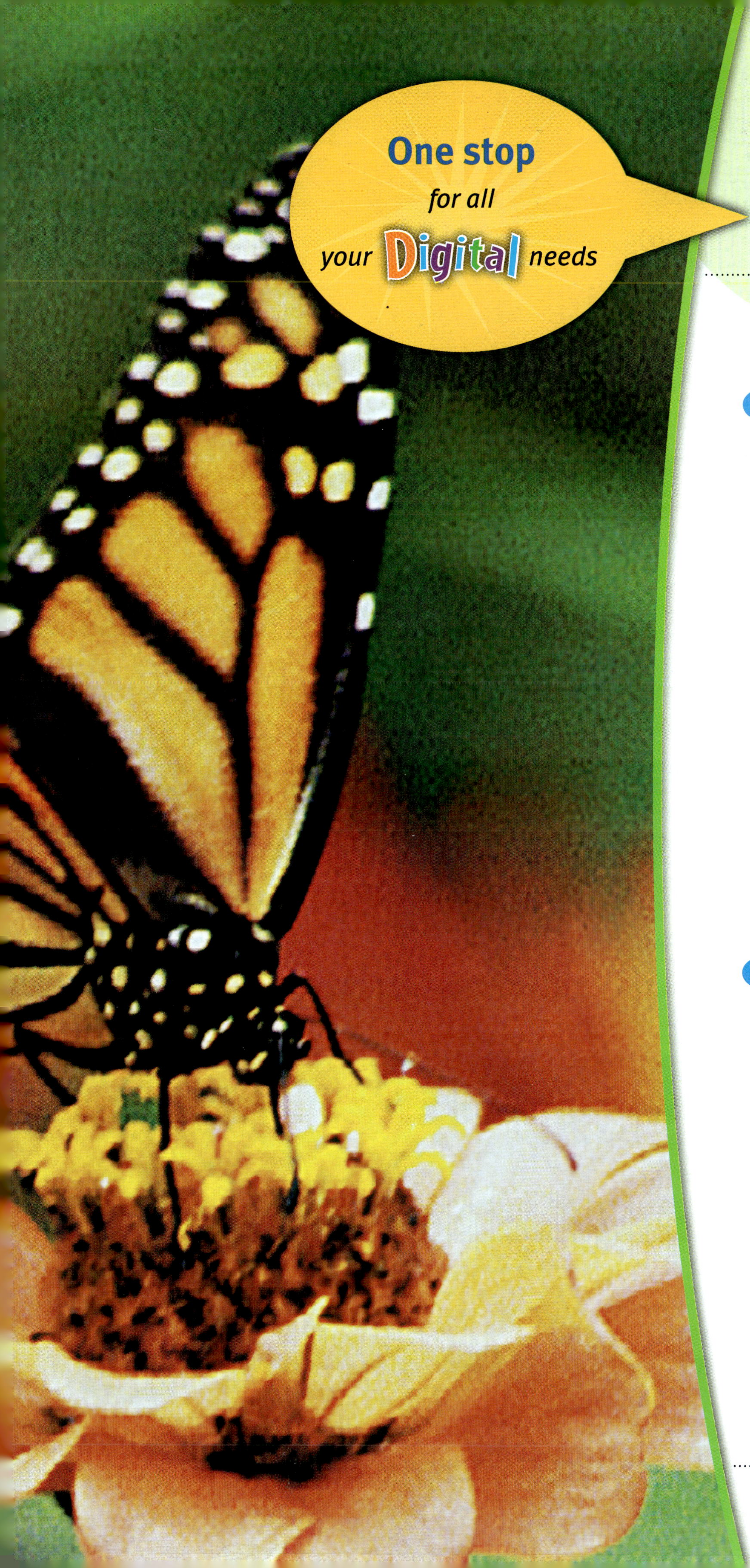

**One stop** *for all* *your* **Digital** *needs*

# Digital
## CLASSROOM

 www.harcourtschool.com/storytown
*To go along with your print program*

## FOR THE TEACHER

**Prepare**
 Professional Development
*in the Online TE*

 *Videos for Podcasting*

**Plan & Organize**
 Online TE & Planning Resources*

**Teach**
 Transparencies
*for electronic projection*

**Assess**
 Online Assessment*
*with Student Tracking System and Prescriptions*

## FOR THE STUDENT

**Read**
 Student eBook*

 Strategic Intervention Interactive Reader

 Leveled Readers

**Practice & Apply**
 Splash into Phonics CD-ROM

 *Also available on CD-ROM*

# LESSON 13

# Literature Resources

## STUDENT EDITION

 **eBook STUDENT EDITION**

**Get Started Story**

**Rich Gets Big, pp. 16–23**

**Genre: Nonfiction**

**Paired Selections**

 **SCIENCE** **A Butterfly Grows, pp. 28–45**

*by Stephen Swinburne* A caterpillar tells about his life, including his transformation into a beautiful butterfly.

**Accelerated Reader™**

*Practice Quizzes for the Selection*

 **Audiotext** *Student Edition selections are available on Audiotext Grade 1, CD 3 and 6.*

◀ **Reading Across Texts** **Comparing Nonfiction and Poetry**

**Genre: Poetry**

## ADDITIONAL READING

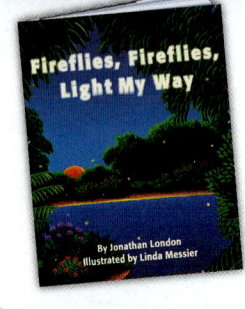

**Big Book**
*Fireflies, Fireflies, Light My Way*

**Decodable Book**
"Ranch Pals"
★ Applies Digraphs /ch/ch, tch

# Support for Differentiated Instruction

 **LEVELED READERS**

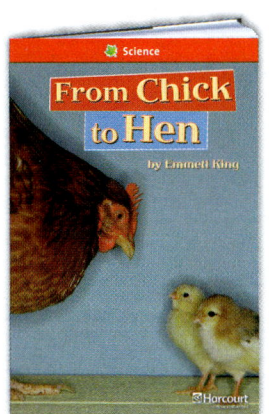

**BELOW-LEVEL**

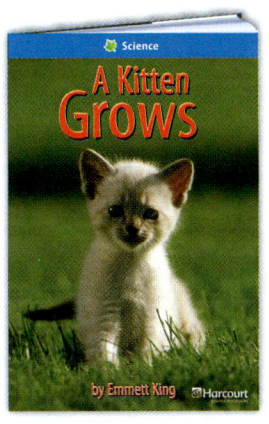

**ON-LEVEL**

**ADVANCED**

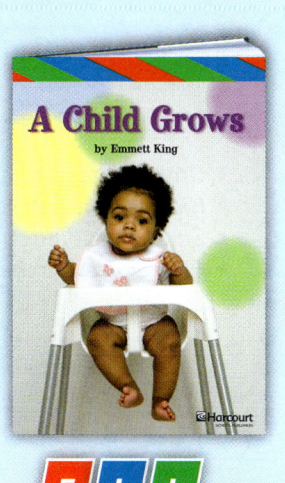

**ELL**

## LEVELED PRACTICE

◄ **Strategic Intervention Resource Kit, Lesson 13**

◄ **Strategic Intervention Interactive Reader, Lesson 13**
Strategic Intervention Interactive Reader Online

◄ **ELL Extra Support Kit, Lesson 13**

◄ **Challenge Resource Kit, Lesson 13**

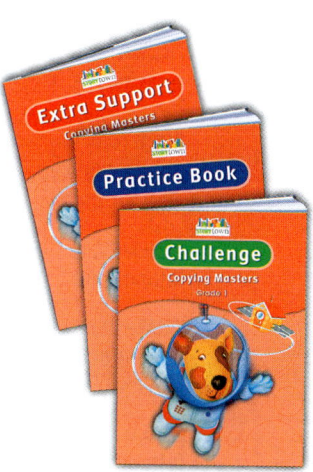

**BELOW-LEVEL**
Extra Support Copying Masters, pp. 2–7

**ON-LEVEL**
Practice Book, pp. 2–8

**ADVANCED**
Challenge Copying Masters, pp. 2–7

## ADDITIONAL RESOURCES

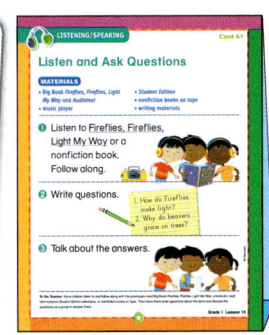

• Spelling Practice Book, pp. 43–45
• Grammar Practice Book, pp. 49–52
• Reading Transparencies R25–R26
• Language Arts Transparencies LA25–LA26
• Test Prep System
◄ **Literacy Center Kit, Cards 61–65**
◄ **Sound/Spelling Card**
• Fluency Builders
◄ **Photo Cards**
• Read-Aloud Anthology, p. 52

## ASSESSMENT

✓ **Weekly Lesson Tests**
• Comprehension
• Phonics and Spelling
• Focus Skill
• Robust Vocabulary
• High-Frequency Words
• Grammar
• Fluency

 **www.harcourtschool.com/storytown**
• Online Assessment
*Also available on CD-ROM—ExamView®*

  # Suggested Lesson Planner

## Day 1

## Day 2

 **Step 1  Whole Group**

### Daily Language
- *Oral Language*
- *High-Frequency Words*
- *Shared Reading*
- *Phonemic Awareness*

**QUESTION OF THE DAY,** p. T34
*What does a firefly look like? What does it do?*

**READ ALOUD,** p. T34
*Big Book: Fireflies, Fireflies, Light My Way*

**WORD WALL,** p. T35

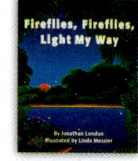
▲ Big Book

**PHONEMIC AWARENESS,** p. T35
Phoneme Deletion

**QUESTION OF THE DAY,** p. T50
*What does an inchworm look like? How does it move?*

**SHARED READING,** p. T50
*Big Book of Rhymes and Poems, "The Inchworm"*

**WORD WALL,** p. T51

**PHONEMIC AWARENESS,** p. T51
Phoneme Deletion

### Word Work
-  **phonics**
- *Spelling*
- *High-Frequency Words*

 **phonics**, p. T36
Introduce: Digraphs /ch/*ch, tch*

**SPELLING,** p. T39
Pretest: *chip, chin, inch, such, catch, match, wish, shop, saw, were*

**HIGH-FREQUENCY WORDS,** p. T41
Review: *be, grow, was*

**phonics**, p. T52
Review: Digraphs /ch/*ch, tch*

**SPELLING,** p. T52
Word Building

**HIGH-FREQUENCY WORDS**
Words to Know, p. T56
Introduce: *air, fly, friends, grew, need, play, rain, watch*

### Skills and Strategies
- *Reading*
- *Fluency*
- *Comprehension*
- *Build Robust Vocabulary*

**READING,** p. T40
Get Started Story, "Rich Gets Big"
Decodable Text
*Options for Reading*

▲ Student Edition

**FLUENCY,** p. T45
Intonation

**COMPREHENSION,** p. T46
Read-Aloud: "Hurry and the Monarch"
Preview: Sequence

**BUILD ROBUST VOCABULARY,** p. T47
Introduce: *astonishing, continue, doubt*

**READING,** p. T58
"A Butterfly Grows"
*Options for Reading*

**COMPREHENSION,** pp. T54, T58
Introduce: Sequence
Introduce: Use Graphic Organizers

▲ Student Edition

**RETELLING/FLUENCY,** p. T68
Intonation

**BUILD ROBUST VOCABULARY,** p. T69
Review: *astonishing, continue, doubt*

 **Step 2  Small Groups**

**Suggestions for Differentiated Instruction (See pp. T28–T29.)**

 **Step 3  Whole Group**

### Language Arts
- *Grammar*
- *Writing*

**GRAMMAR,** p. T48
Introduce: Names of Days and Months

*Daily Proofreading*
Mom made lunc on Sunday (lunch, Sunday.)

 **MODELED WRITING,** p. T49
Introduce: Sequence Story
Writing Trait: Organization

 **Writing Prompt**  *Write and draw a picture about what you do before you go to sleep each night.*

**GRAMMAR,** p. T70
Review: Names of Days and Months

*Daily Proofreading*
i went on a trip in march. (I, March)

 **SHARED WRITING,** p. T71
Review: Sequence Story
Writing Trait: Organization

 **Writing Prompt**  *Write and draw a picture about something you know how to make.*

 = Focus Skill      = Focus Strategy      = Tested Skill

**Skills at a Glance**

 **phonics**
- Digraphs /ch/ch, tch
- Inflection –es

**Comprehension**

FOCUS SKILL
Sequence

FOCUS STRATEGY Use
Graphic Organizers

**Phonemic Awareness**
Phoneme Deletion

**Fluency**
Intonation

**Vocabulary**

HIGH-FREQUENCY: *air*, *fly*, *friends*, *grew*,
*need*, *play*, *rain*, *watch*

ROBUST: *astonishing, continue, doubt,
transform, examine, devour*

# Day 3

**QUESTION OF THE DAY,** p. T72
*Inchworms move slowly. When do you move slowly? Why?*

**SHARED READING,** p. T72
*Big Book of Rhymes and Poems,* "The Inchworm"

**WORD WALL,** p. T73

✔ **PHONEMIC AWARENESS,** p. T73
Phoneme Deletion

✔ 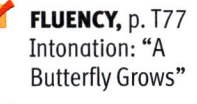, p. T74
Review: Digraphs /ch/*ch*, *tch*, /sh/*sh*

✔ **SPELLING,** p. T75
State the Generalization

✔ **HIGH-FREQUENCY WORDS,** p. T76
Review: *air*, *fly*, *friends*, *grew*, *need*, *play*, *rain*, *watch*

✔ **FLUENCY,** p. T77
Intonation: "A Butterfly Grows"

✔ **COMPREHENSION,** p. T78
Review: Sequence
Paired Selection: "Caterpillars"

**CONNECTIONS,** p. T80

✔ **BUILD ROBUST VOCABULARY,** p. T81
Introduce: *transform, examine, devour*

▲ Student Edition

✔ **GRAMMAR,** p. T82
Review: Names of Days and Months

*Daily Proofreading*
it was raining on monday. (It, Monday)

✔ **SHARED WRITING,** p. T83
Review: Sequence Story
Writing Trait: Organization

**Writing Prompt** *Write about what you did yesterday at school.*

# Day 4

**QUESTION OF THE DAY,** p. T84
*Pretend you are holding a caterpillar or a butterfly in your hand. How does it look and feel?*

**SHARED READING,** p. T84
*Big Book of Rhymes and Poems,* "Fuzzy, Wuzzy, Creepy, Crawly"

**WORD WALL,** p. T85

✔ **PHONEMIC AWARENESS,** p. T85
Phoneme Deletion

✔ , p. T86
Introduce: Inflection –es

✔ **SPELLING,** p. T87
Review Spelling Words

✔ **HIGH-FREQUENCY WORDS,** p. I88
Review: *air*, *fly*, *friends*, *grew*, *need*, *play*, *rain*, *watch*

✔ **FLUENCY,** p. T89
Intonation: "A Butterfly Grows"

✔ **COMPREHENSION,** p. T90
Review: Sequence
*Big Book: Fireflies, Fireflies, Light My Way*

✔ **BUILD ROBUST VOCABULARY,** p. T91
Review: *transform, examine, devour*

▲ Student Edition

✔ **GRAMMAR,** p. T92
Review: Names of Days and Months

*Daily Proofreading*
We go to skool in april. (school, April)

✔ **INDEPENDENT WRITING,** p. T93
Review: Sequence Story
Writing Trait: Organization

**Writing Prompt** *Draw and write about your favorite vacation.*

# Day 5

**QUESTION OF THE DAY,** p. T94
*Would you rather be a caterpillar or a butterfly? Why?*

**SHARED READING,** p. T94
*Big Book of Rhymes and Poems,* "Fuzzy, Wuzzy, Creepy, Crawly"

**WORD WALL,** p. T95

✔ **PHONEMIC AWARENESS,** p. T95
Phoneme Deletion

✔ , p. T96
Review: Inflection –es

✔ **SPELLING,** p. T97
Posttest

✔ **HIGH-FREQUENCY WORDS,** p. T98
Review,: *air*, *fly*, *friends*, *grew*, *need*, *play*, *rain*, *watch*

✔ **FLUENCY,** p. T99
Intonation: "A Butterfly Grows"

✔ **COMPREHENSION,** p. T100
Review: Sequence

✔ **BUILD ROBUST VOCABULARY,** p. T101
Review

▲ Student Edition

✔ **GRAMMAR,** p. T102
Review: Names of Days and Months

*Daily Proofreading*
saturday is the first day of march. (Saturday, March)

✔ **INDEPENDENT WRITING,** p. T103
Review: Sequence Story
Writing Trait: Organization

**Writing Prompt** *Look at pictures to get an idea of a topic, and then write about it.*

 **BELOW-LEVEL**  **ON-LEVEL**  **ADVANCED**

# Suggested Small Group Planner

  45–60+ Minutes

## Day 1

## Day 2

  15+ Min. each

🔴 **BELOW-LEVEL**

### Day 1
**Teacher-Directed**
*Student Edition:*
Get Started Story,
"Rich Gets Big," p. T40

**Independent**
 ⭐ Listening/Speaking
Center, p. T32
Extra Support Copying Masters, p. 2

▲ Student Edition

### Day 2
**Teacher-Directed**
*Student Edition:*
"A Butterfly Grows," p. T58

**Independent**
 ⭐ Reading Center, p. T32
Extra Support Copying
Masters, p. 4

▲ Student Edition

  15+ Min. each

🔵 **ON-LEVEL**

### Day 1
**Teacher-Directed**
*Student Edition:*
Get Started Story,
"Rich Gets Big," p. T40

**Independent**
 ⭐ Reading Center, p. T32
Practice Book, p. 2

▲ Student Edition

### Day 2
**Teacher-Directed**
*Student Edition:*
"A Butterfly Grows," p. T58

**Independent**
 ⭐ Letters and Sounds
Center, p. T33
Practice Book, p. 4

▲ Student Edition

🟢 **ADVANCED**

### Day 1
**Teacher-Directed**
Leveled Reader:
"A Frog's Life," p. T106
Before Reading

**Independent**
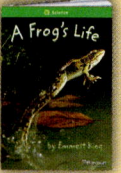 ⭐ Letters and Sounds
Center, p. T33
Challenge Copying Masters, p. 2

▲ Leveled Reader

### Day 2
**Teacher-Directed**
Leveled Reader:
"A Frog's Life," p. T106
Read the Book

**Independent**
 ⭐ Word Work Center,
p. T33
Challenge Copying Masters, p. 4

▲ Leveled Reader

 E L L

## English-Language Learners

*In addition to the small-group suggestions above, use the ELL Extra Support Kit to promote language development.*

### Day 1
**LANGUAGE DEVELOPMENT SUPPORT**
**Teacher-Directed**
ELL TG, Day 1
**Independent**
ELL Copying Masters, Lesson 13

### Day 2
**LANGUAGE DEVELOPMENT SUPPORT**
**Teacher-Directed**
ELL TG, Day 2
**Independent**
ELL Copying Masters, Lesson 13

## Intervention

 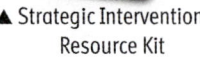

▲ Strategic Intervention Resource Kit    ▲ Strategic Intervention Interactive Reader

### Day 1
Strategic Intervention TG, Day 1
Strategic Intervention Practice Book, Lesson 13

### Day 2
Strategic Intervention TG, Day 2
Strategic Intervention Interactive Reader, Lesson 13

▲ Strategic Intervention Interactive Reader

 ⭐ = **Literacy Center Cards**

**MONITOR PROGRESS**

**Small-Group Instruction**

| Phonemic Awareness/ Phonics | High-Frequency Words | Fluency | Comprehension | Robust Vocabulary | Language Arts Checkpoint |
|---|---|---|---|---|---|
| Digraphs /ch/*ch, tch* p. S2 | *air, fly, friends, grew, need, play, rain, watch* p. S3 | Intonation pp. S4–S5 | **Focus Skill** Sequence pp. S6–S7 | *astonishing, continue, doubt, transform, examine, devour* pp. S8–S9 | **Grammar:** Names of Days and Months **Writing:** Organization pp. S10–S11 |

# Day 3

**Teacher-Directed**
Leveled Reader:
"From Chick to Hen," p. T104
Before Reading; Read the Book

**Independent**
⭐ Word Work Center, p. T33
Extra Support Copying Masters, p. 5

▲ Leveled Reader

**Teacher-Directed**
Leveled Reader:
"A Kitten Grows," p. T105
Before Reading; Read the Book

**Independent**
⭐ Writing Center, p. T33
Practice Book, p. 5

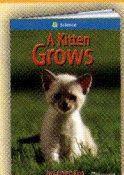
▲ Leveled Reader

**Teacher-Directed**
Leveled Reader:
"A Frog's Life," p. T106
Think Critically

**Independent**
⭐ Listening/Speaking Center, p. T32
Challenge Copying Masters, p. 5

▲ Leveled Reader

**LANGUAGE DEVELOPMENT SUPPORT**
**Teacher-Directed**
Leveled Reader:
"A Child Grows," p. T107
Before Reading; Read the Book
ELL TG, Day 3
**Independent**
ELL Copying Masters, Lesson 13

▲ Leveled Reader

Strategic Intervention TG, Day 3
Strategic Intervention Interactive Reader, Lesson 13
Strategic Intervention Practice Book, Lesson 13

▲ Strategic Intervention Interactive Reader

# Day 4

**Teacher-Directed**
Leveled Reader:
"From Chick to Hen," p. T104
Reread for Fluency

**Independent**
⭐ Letters and Sounds Center, p. T33
Cut-Out/Fold-Up Book, Practice Book, pp. 45–46

▲ Leveled Reader

**Teacher-Directed**
Leveled Reader:
"A Kitten Grows," p. T105
Reread for Fluency

**Independent**
⭐ Word Work Center, p. T33
Cut-Out/Fold-Up Book: Practice Book, pp. 45–46

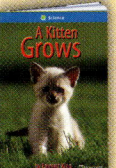
▲ Leveled Reader

**Teacher-Directed**
Leveled Reader:
"A Frog's Life," p. T106
Reread for Fluency
Self-Selected Reading: Classroom Library Collection

**Independent**
⭐ Writing Center, p. T33
Cut-Out/Fold-Up Book: Practice Book, pp. 45–46

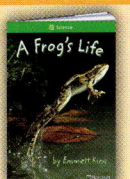
▲ Leveled Reader

**LANGUAGE DEVELOPMENT SUPPORT**
**Teacher-Directed**
Leveled Reader:
"A Child Grows," p. T107
Reread for Fluency
ELL TG, Day 4
**Independent**
ELL Copying Masters, Lesson 13

▲ Leveled Reader

Strategic Intervention TG, Day 4
Strategic Intervention Interactive Reader, Lesson 13

▲ Strategic Intervention Interactive Reader

# Day 5

**Teacher-Directed**
Leveled Reader:
"From Chick to Hen," p. T104
Think Critically

**Independent**
⭐ Writing Center, p. T33
Leveled Reader: Reread for Fluency
Extra Support Copying Masters, p. 7

▲ Leveled Reader

**Teacher-Directed**
Leveled Reader:
"A Kitten Grows," p. T105
Think Critically

**Independent**
⭐ Listening/Speaking Center, p. T32
Leveled Reader: Reread for Fluency
Practice Book, p. 7

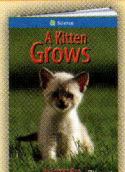
▲ Leveled Reader

**Teacher-Directed**
Leveled Reader:
A Frog's Life," p. T106
Reread for Fluency
Self-Selected Reading: Classroom Library Collection

**Independent**
⭐ Reading Center, p. T32
Leveled Reader: Reread for Fluency
Challenge Copying Masters, p. 7

▲ Leveled Reader

**LANGUAGE DEVELOPMENT SUPPORT**
**Teacher-Directed**
Leveled Reader:
"A Child Grows," p. T107
Think Critically
ELL TG, Day 5
**Independent**
Leveled Reader:
Reread for Fluency
ELL Copying Masters, Lesson 13

▲ Leveled Reader

Strategic Intervention TG, Day 5
Strategic Intervention Interactive Reader, Lesson 13

▲ Strategic Intervention Interactive Reader

# Leveled Readers & Leveled Practice
## *Reinforcing Skills and Strategies*

## LEVELED READERS SYSTEM

- **Leveled Readers**
- **Leveled Readers CD**
- **Leveled Reader Teacher Guides**
  - *Comprehension*
  - *High-Frequency Words*
  - *Oral Reading Fluency Assessment*
- **Response Activities**
- **Leveled Readers Assessment**

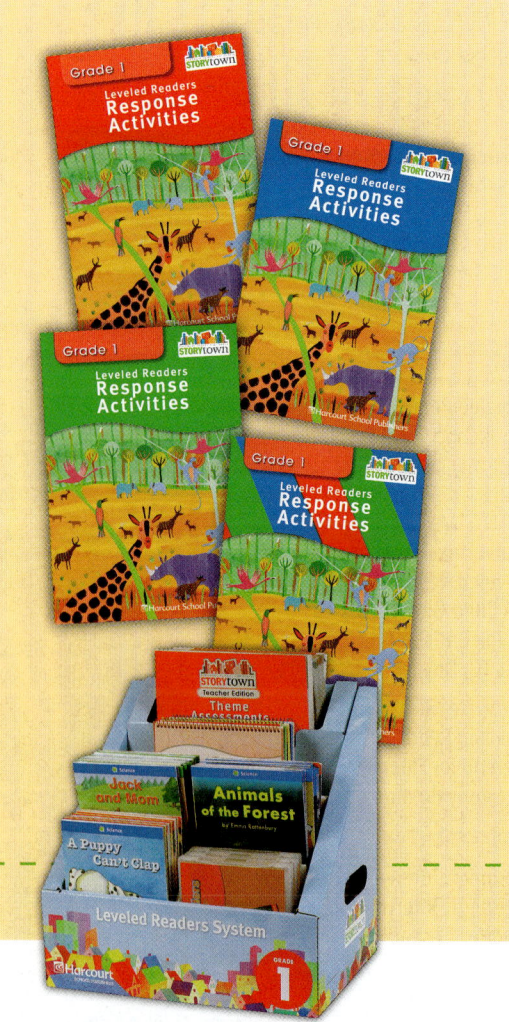

See pages T104–T107 for lesson plans.

### BELOW-LEVEL

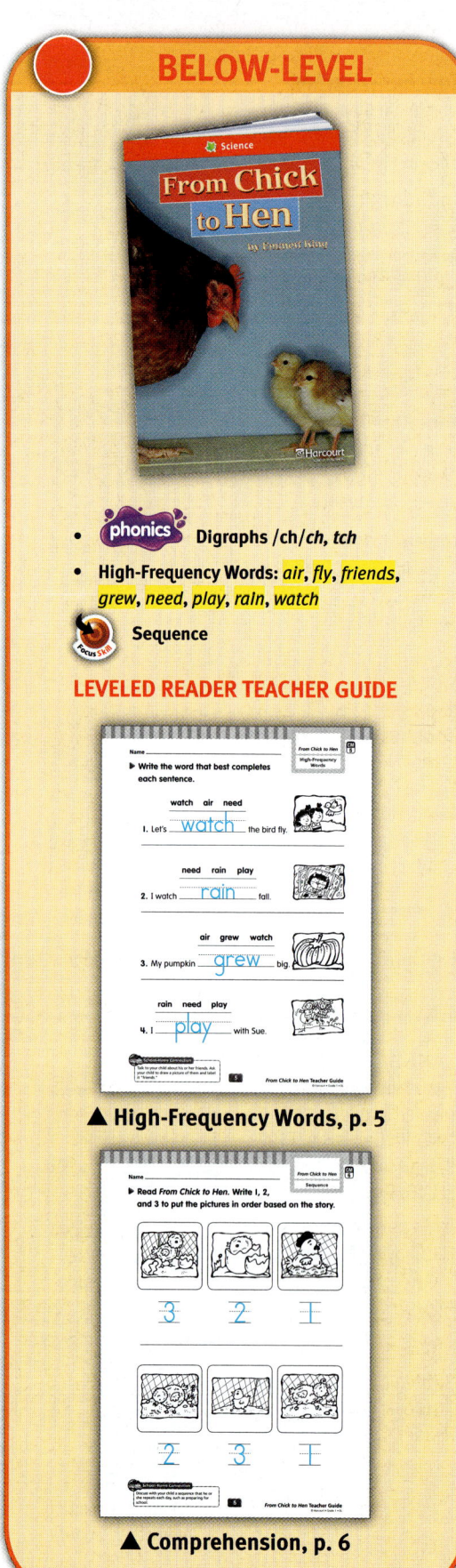

- **phonics** Digraphs /ch/*ch*, *tch*
- **High-Frequency Words:** *air*, *fly*, *friends*, *grew*, *need*, *play*, *rain*, *watch*
- **Focus Skill** Sequence

**LEVELED READER TEACHER GUIDE**

▲ High-Frequency Words, p. 5

▲ Comprehension, p. 6

### ON-LEVEL

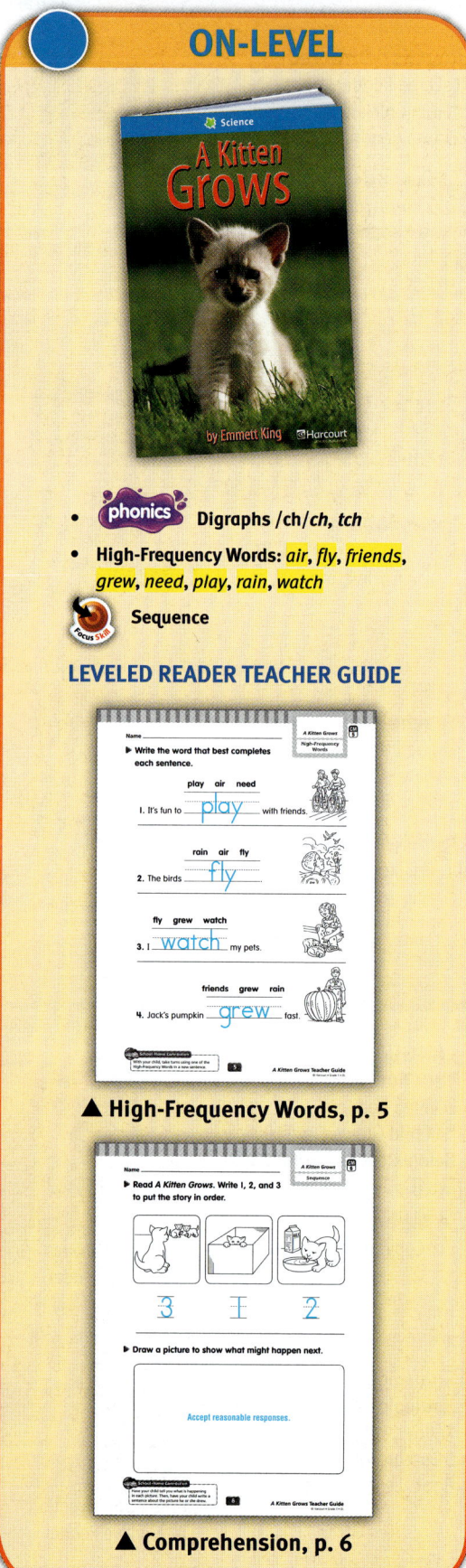

- **phonics** Digraphs /ch/*ch*, *tch*
- **High-Frequency Words:** *air*, *fly*, *friends*, *grew*, *need*, *play*, *rain*, *watch*
- **Focus Skill** Sequence

**LEVELED READER TEACHER GUIDE**

▲ High-Frequency Words, p. 5

▲ Comprehension, p. 6

## www.harcourtschool.com/storytown

**Go online**

★ **Leveled Readers, online**
*Searchable by Genre, Skill, Vocabulary, Level, or Title*
★ **Student Activities and Teacher Resources, online**

## ADVANCED

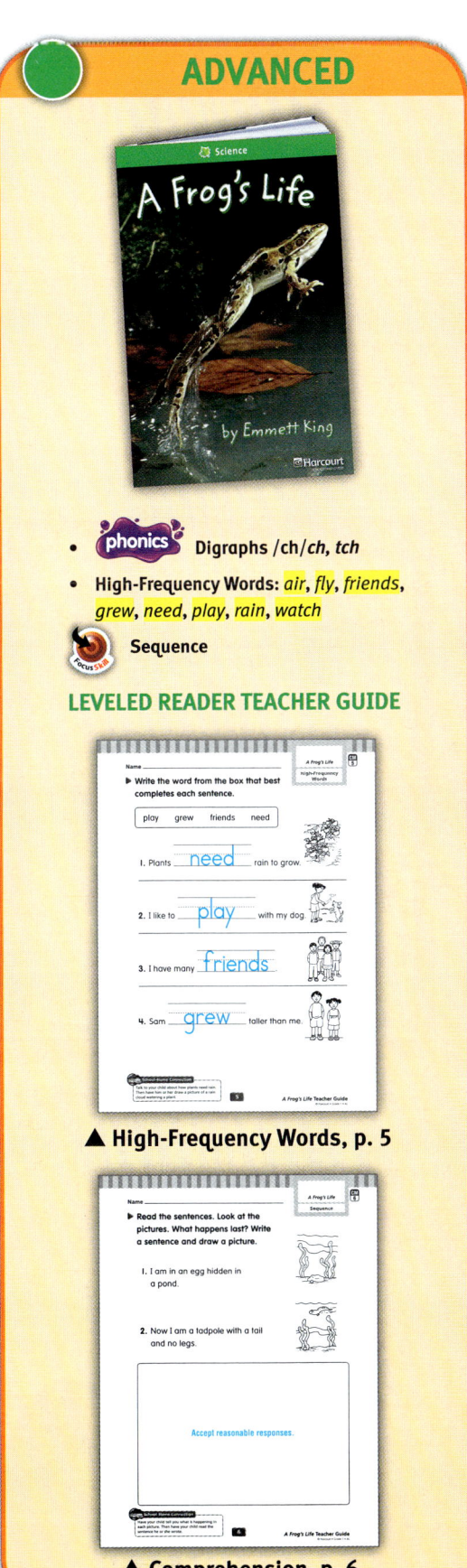

- **phonics** Digraphs /ch/*ch, tch*
- **High-Frequency Words:** *air, fly, friends, grew, need, play, rain, watch*
- **Focus Skill** Sequence

### LEVELED READER TEACHER GUIDE

▲ **High-Frequency Words, p. 5**

▲ **Comprehension, p. 6**

## ELL

- **Strong Picture Support**
- **Concept Vocabulary**
- **Scaffolded Language Development**

### LEVELED READER TEACHER GUIDE

▲ **Build Background, p. 5**

▲ **Scaffolded Language Development, p. 6**

## CLASSROOM LIBRARY
### for Self-Selected Reading

**EASY**
▲ *Maxwell Mouse* by Sharon Gordon.
**FANTASY**

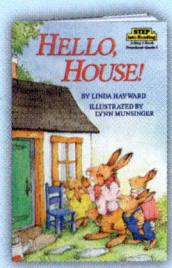

**AVERAGE**
▲ *Hello, House!* by Linda Hayward.
**FOLKTALE**

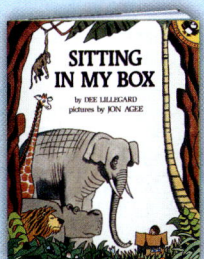

**AVERAGE**
▲ *Sitting in My Box* by Dee Lillegard.
**FANTASY**

▲ **Classroom Library Books Teacher Guide, pp. 16–19, 40–47**

# Literacy Centers

15 Min. each

## Management Support

While you provide direct instruction to individuals or small groups, other children can work on literacy center activities.

▲ Literacy Centers Pocket Chart

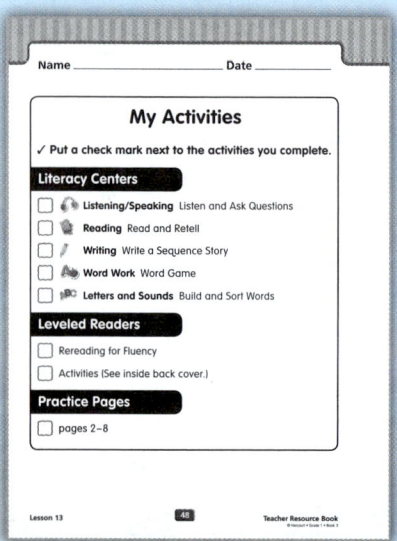

▲ Teacher Resource Book, p. 48

## Homework for the Week

**TEACHER RESOURCE BOOK, PAGE 17**
The *Homework Copying Master* provides activities to complete for each day of the week.

**GO online**
www.harcourtschool.com/storytown

---

### LISTENING/SPEAKING

## Listen and Ask Questions

**Objectives** To listen to a story or a nonfiction selection, to write question about the selection, and to discuss it

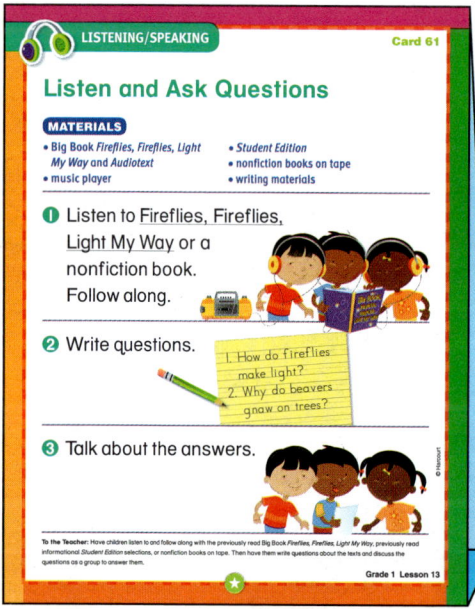

⭐ **Literacy Center Kit • Card 61**

How do fireflies make light? Why do beavers gnaw on trees?

---

### READING

## Read and Retell

**Objective** To identify and recall events from a story in the correct order

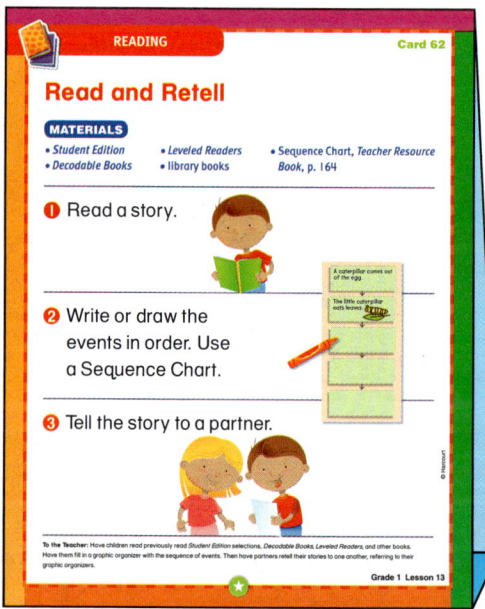

⭐ **Literacy Center Kit • Card 62**

Sequence Chart

---

Go online

www.harcourtschool.com/storytown

★ Additional Literacy Center Activities
★ Resources for Parents and Teachers

Differentiated
for Your Needs

 WRITING

## Write a Sequence Story

**Objective** To practice writing a narrative story with a clear sequence of events

---

 WORD WORK

## Word Game

**Objective** To read and write high-frequency words and use them in oral sentences

---

**ABC** LETTERS AND SOUNDS

## Build and Sort Words

**Objective** To build, read, and sort words spelled with ch and tch

---

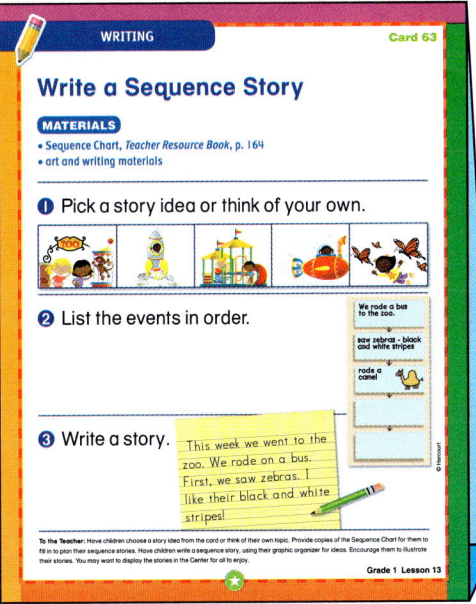

**Literacy Center Kit** • Card 63

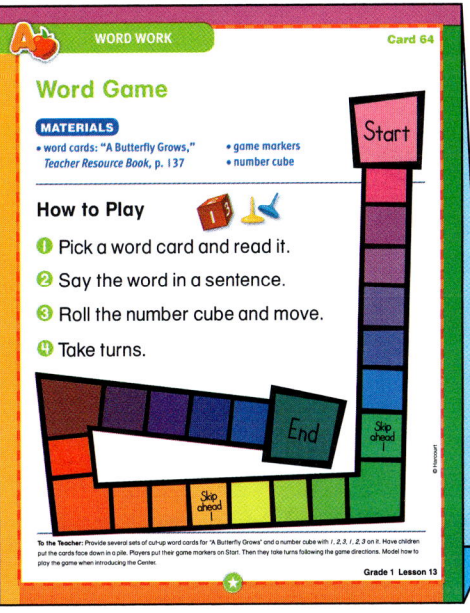

**Literacy Center Kit** • Card 64

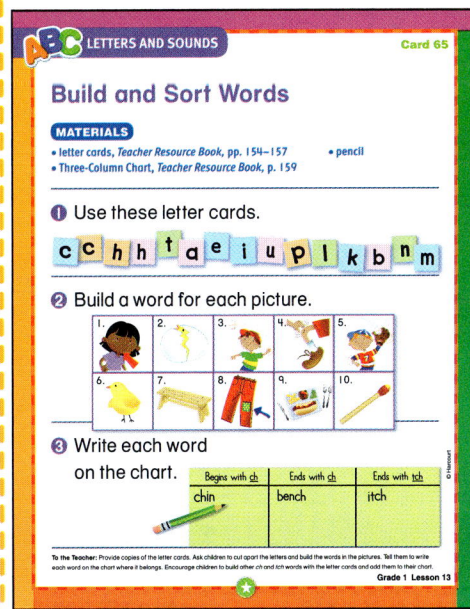

**Literacy Center Kit** • Card 65

## Day at a Glance

### Day 1

**Phonemic Awareness**
- Phoneme Deletion

 **and Spelling**
- Introduce: Digraphs /ch/*ch, tch*
- Pretest

**Reading**
- Get Started Story: "Rich Gets Big," *Student Edition*, pp. 16–23

**Read!**

**Fluency**
- Intonation

**Comprehension**
- *Read-Aloud Anthology:* "Hurry and the Monarch"
 Preview: Sequence

**Robust Vocabulary**
- Introduce: *astonishing, continue, doubt*

**Grammar**
- Introduce: Names of Days and Months

**Modeled Writing**
- Sequence Story

# Warm-Up Routines

## Oral Language

**Objective** *To listen and respond appropriately to oral communication*

### Question of the Day

**What does a firefly look like?**

**What does it do?**

Talk with children about what they know about fireflies. Then write the following sentence frames and help children complete them.

**A firefly is _____.** **A firefly likes to _____.**

## Read Aloud

**Objective** *To listen for a purpose*

**Routine Card 7** **BIG BOOK** Share *Fireflies, Fireflies, Light My Way* with children. Have a volunteer point to the title and names of the author and illustrator as you read them aloud. Tell children that the title comes from a Native American lullaby. Share information about the Mesaquakie people from the author's note on the copyright page.

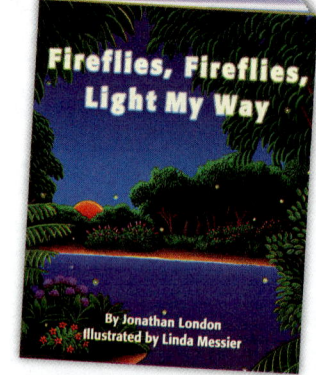
▲ Big Book: *Fireflies, Fireflies, Light My Way*

**Set a purpose, read, and respond.** Tell children to listen to find out where the fireflies lead. As you read, invite children to join in on the refrain. Then have them identify their favorite part and tell why they liked it.

# Word Wall

**Objective** *To read high-frequency words*

**REVIEW HIGH-FREQUENCY WORDS** Review *saw, were, be, of, was, too, grow,* and other previously learned high-frequency words. Say each word, ask a volunteer to point to it, and have children read it aloud. Then point to words at random and have children reread them. Repeat several times to reinforce instant recognition.

saw    were    be    of    was

# Phonemic Awareness

**Objective** *To delete initial phonemes from words*

**Routine Card 9**

**PHONEME DELETION** Tell children you will say some words and ask them to remove the beginning sound in each word. Model by saying: *Cat* without the /k/ is *at.* Say the following words and have children delete the first sound to form a new word.

*hill* without /h/ (ill)       *ran* without /r/ (an)       *glad* without /g/ (lad)

*hitch* without /h/ (itch)    *tall* without /t/ (all)      *branch* without /b/ (ranch)

*chin* without /ch/ (in)      *pat* without /p/ (at)       *chart* without /ch/ (art)

*hand* without /h/ (and)     *cheer* without /ch/ (ear)    *bride* without /b/ (ride)

*chart* without /ch/

art

# Digraphs /ch/ *ch, tch*

**phonics** *and Spelling*

## Objectives

- *To recognize and generate the sound of /ch/ch, tch*
- *To build and blend words with /ch/ch, tch and other known letter-sounds*
- *To use /ch/ch, tch and other known letter-sounds to spell words*
- *To spell known high-frequency words*

## Skill Trace

**Tested** Digraphs /ch/*ch, tch*

| | |
|---|---|
| Introduce | T36–T39 |
| Reteach | S2 |
| Review | T52–T53, T74–T75, T87 |
| Test | Bk 1-3 |
| Maintain | Bk 1-4, T76–T77 |

 Refer to *Sounds of Letters CD* Track 12 for pronunciation of /ch/.

hatch

---

## Connecting Letter to Sound

**Routine Card 12**

**DEVELOP PHONEMIC AWARENESS OF /ch/** Say the word *cherry*. Have children say the word. Repeat for the words *check* and *chain*. Say: **The words *cherry*, *check*, and *chain* begin with the /ch/ sound.** Have children say /ch/ several times.

**CONNECT LETTER AND SOUND** Display *Sound/ Spelling Card ch, tch,* and say the letter names in each spelling. Explain that the letters *c* and *h* together stand for the /ch/ sound, the sound at the beginning of *cherry*. Have children say /ch/ several times as you touch the letters. Then explain that the letters *tch* at the end of a word also stand for the /ch/ sound, as in the word *patch*. Have children say /ch/ several times as you touch the letters *tch*.

**DISCRIMINATE /ch/** Give each child a *c* and an *h* Word Builder Card. Say: **When I say a word that begins with /ch/, hold up your cards and say /ch/. When I say a word that does not begin with /ch/, hold the cards in your lap.** Say:

chick    drip    child    chill    back    gruff    chain

Tell children that some words have the /ch/ sound at the end, as in the word *lunch*. Follow the same procedure for the final position with these words:

touch    much    last    bunch    duck    bench

Then give each child a *t* Word Builder Card and have them form *tch*. Say: **Now when I say a word that ends with /ch/, it will end with the letters *tch*, so hold up your cards and say /ch/. When I say a word that does not end with /ch/, hold the cards in your lap.** Say these words:

match    fetch    fat    hatch    latch    rash

ch
■tch

▲ Sound/Spelling Card

**5-DAY PHONICS**

| DAY 1 | Introduce Digraphs /ch/*ch, tch* |
|-------|----------------------------------|
| DAY 2 | Word Building with Digraphs /ch/*ch, tch* |
| DAY 3 | Word Building |
| DAY 4 | Inflection *-es* |
| DAY 5 | Inflection *-es* |

## Word Blending

**DIBELS** Nonsense Word Fluency **NWF**

**WORDS WITH /ch/*ch, tch*** Demonstrate each step with *Letter Cards* and a pocket chart. Have children repeat each step after you, using their *Word Builder Cards* and *Word Builders*.

**Routine Card 13**

**BLEND AND READ *CHOP*** Hold up the *c* and *h* together and say /ch/. Hold up *o* and say /o/. Hold up *p* and say /p/.

- Place the letters *c, h, o, p* in the pocket chart. Make sure the letters *c* and *h* touch. Have children do the same with their letters and *Word Builders*.

- Point to *ch* and say /ch/. Point to *o* and say /o/. Have children do the same.

- Slide the *o* next to *ch*. Run your hand under the letters as you blend the sounds by elongating them—/cho/. Have children repeat.

- Point to *p* and say /p/. Have children do the same.

- Slide the *p* next to *cho*. Slide your hand under *chop* as you blend the sounds by elongating them—/chop/. Have children repeat.

- Read *chop* naturally. Repeat, having children read the word with you.

Follow the same procedures for *chug, chat, lunch,* and *pinch.* Then use similar procedures to lead children in blending words with *tch,* such as *itch, pitch,* and *patch.*

### Professional Development

 **Podcasting:** Word Blending, Grade 1

**E L L**

**Support Word Meaning** Use *Photo Cards* to support word meaning for words with /ch/*ch.* Display *Photo Cards 17* (branch), *76* (inch), and *87* (lunch). Point to and read aloud each word with children and ask them what sound they hear at the end.

▲ Photo Cards 17, 76, 87

 **ADVANCED**

**Medial /ch/*tch*** Have children read the word to complete this sentence: *I like to put ketchup on hot dogs.* Have children read the word again as you run your hand under each syllable: ketch • up.

# Digraphs /ch/ch, tch
 **phonics** *and Spelling*

## Professional Development

 **Podcasting:** Word Building, Gr. 1; Spelling and Dictation, Gr. 1

## Word Building

**Routine Card 14**

**BUILD SPELLING WORDS** Use *Letter Cards* and a pocket chart. Have children use their *Word Builder Cards* and *Word Builders*.

Place the *Letter Cards c, h, i,* and *p* in the pocket chart. Say the sounds the letters stand for. Then read the word naturally—*chip.*

Have children build and read new words. As they build each word, write it on the board. Say:

- **Change *p* to *n*. What word did you make?**

- **Move the *in* to the beginning. What word did you make?**

- **Take away *in*. Put *s* and *u* at the beginning. What did you make?**

Have children read the words on the board.

c h i p

c h i n

i n c h

s u c h

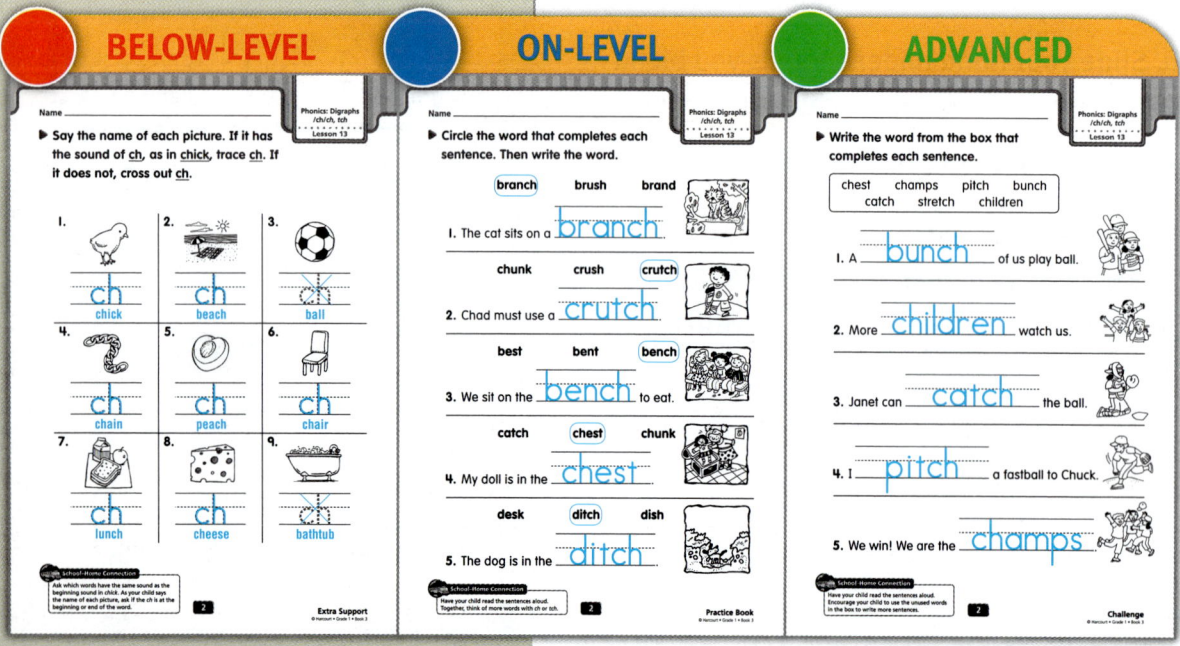

▲ Extra Support, p. 2    ▲ Practice Book, p. 2    ▲ Challenge, p. 2

## ELL

- Group children according to academic levels, and assign one of the pages on the left.

- Clarify any unfamiliar concepts as necessary. See *ELL Teacher Guide*, Lesson 13, for support in scaffolding instruction.

**5-DAY SPELLING**

| | |
|---|---|
| **DAY 1** | Pretest |
| **DAY 2** | Word Building |
| **DAY 3** | State the Generalization |
| **DAY 4** | Review |
| **DAY 5** | Posttest |

## Introduce Spelling Words

**PRETEST** Say the first word and read the dictation sentence. Repeat the word as children write it. Write the word on the board and have children check their spelling. Tell them to circle the word if they spelled it correctly or write it correctly if they did not. Repeat for words 2–10.

### Words with /ch/*ch, tch*

1. chip — There is a **chip** on this broken cup.
2. chin — Your **chin** is below your mouth.
3. inch — The paper clip is about one **inch** long.
4. such — That is **such** a nice car!
5. catch — Let's play **catch** with the ball.
6. match — Can you **match** the words and pictures?

### Review

7. wish — I **wish** we could go to the movies.
8. shop — That **shop** sells books.

### High-Frequency

9. saw — I **saw** him at school.
10. were — There **were** toys in the box.

### Spelling Words

| | |
|---|---|
| 1. **chip** | 6. **match** |
| 2. **chin** | 7. **wish** |
| 3. **inch** | 8. **shop** |
| 4. **such** | 9. **saw** |
| 5. **catch** | 10. **were** |

 **MONITOR PROGRESS**

### Phonics: Digraphs /ch/*ch, tch*

**IF** children have difficulty building and reading words with /ch/*ch, tch,*

**THEN** remind them that both *ch* and *tch* spell /ch/, so they can try both spellings and see which one looks correct.

**Small-Group Instruction, p. S2:**

 **BELOW-LEVEL:** Reteach

 **ON-LEVEL:** Reinforce

 **ADVANCED:** Extend

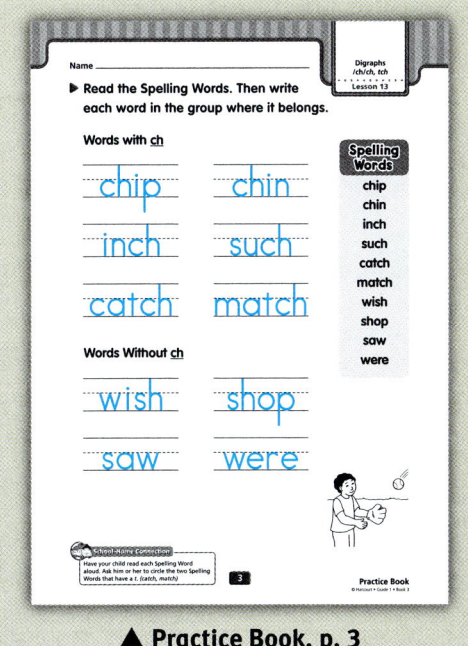

▲ Practice Book, p. 3

Lesson 13 **T39**

#  Reading

## *Get Started Story:* Rich Gets Big

### Objectives
- *To read decodable text*
- *To review high-frequency words*
- *To develop fluency*

### Professional Development

 **Podcasting:** Reading Decodable Text, Gr. 1

## Options for Reading

 **BELOW-LEVEL**

**Echo-Reading** Have children echo-read each sentence. Pause to discuss it, using the Monitor Comprehension questions. Have children frame and read /ch/*ch, tch* words.

 **ON-LEVEL**

**Monitor Comprehension** Have children read the story aloud, page by page. Ask the Monitor Comprehension questions as you go. Then lead them in retelling the story.

 **ADVANCED**

**Independent Reading** Have children read each page silently, looking up each time they finish a page. Ask the Monitor Comprehension questions as you go. Then lead them in a discussion about whether Rich gets his wish.

### Apply Digraphs /ch/*ch, tch*

**READ DECODABLE TEXT** Write the following sentences on the board. Tell children they will read a story about a boy named Rich.

> **Rich stands to get a branch.**
> **"Grow just an inch more!" Mom calls.**

- Have children read the first sentence silently and then aloud as you track the print.
- Have a volunteer frame and read the words that include the letters *ch*.
- Repeat for the second sentence.
- Tell children that many words in the story have the /ch/ sound.

**Routine Card 17** **INTRODUCE THE STORY** Have children look at the first page and read aloud the title. Ask them to point to the names of the author and the illustrator as you read them aloud. Discuss the picture and identify Rich. Tell children they will read the story to find out about a wish Rich has.

 **ELL**

**Preview** Preview the story with a picture walk. Use the illustrations to develop meaning for the text. Then guide children through the story, using the Monitor Comprehension questions.

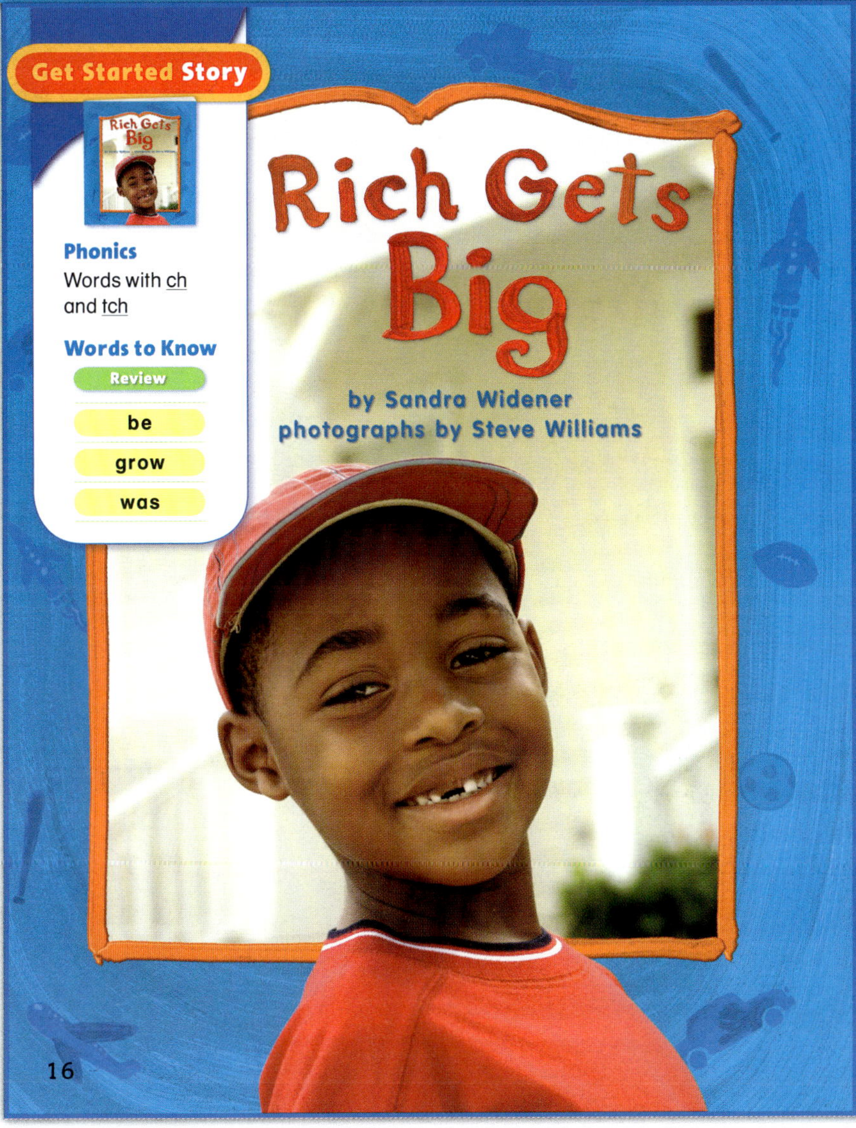
Get Started Story
Phonics
Words with ch and tch
Words to Know
Review
be
grow
was
Rich Gets Big
by Sandra Widener
photographs by Steve Williams
16

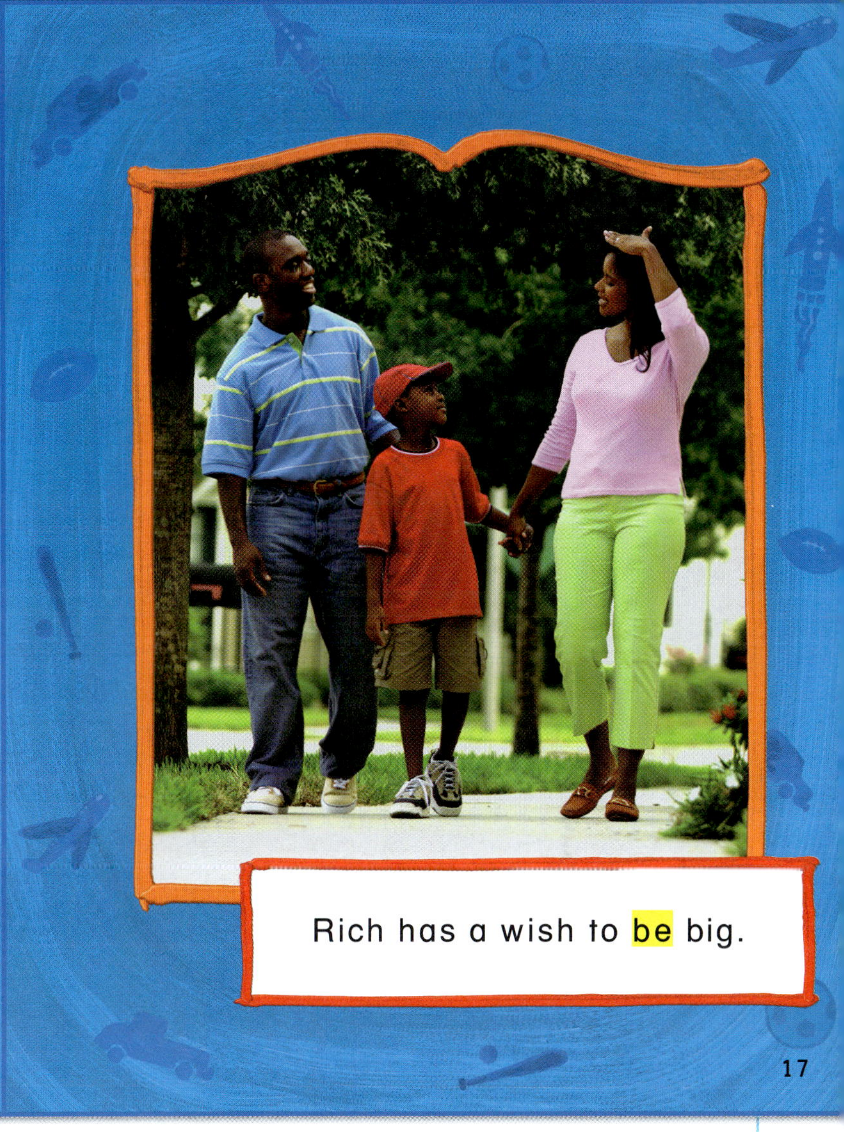
Rich has a wish to be big.
17

# Monitor Comprehension

**PAGES 16–17** Have children look at the title page and the first page of the story. Say: **What do you think Rich is talking to his parents about? Why? Let's read to find out.**

1 **NOTE DETAILS** **What does Rich wish for?** (He wants to be big.)

## TECHNOLOGY

Go online **eBook** "Rich Gets Big" is available in an eBook.

**Audiotext** "Rich Gets Big" is available on *Audiotext Grade 1*, CD 6 for subsequent readings.

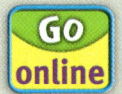

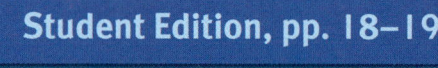

Rich stands to get a branch. He cannot get it.

"Grow just an inch more!" Mom calls.

18

19

# Monitor Comprehension

**PAGES 18–19** Say: **I see Rich. I wonder what he is trying to do. I also see a person who looks like his mom. Let's read to find out what she is saying.**

1 **APPLY PHONICS/NOTE DETAILS** What is Rich trying to get? Read the word that tells. *(branch)*

2 **PERSONAL RESPONSE** How do you feel when you cannot reach things? *(Possible response: I feel upset because I am not tall enough to get some things that I want.)*

**E L L**

**Clarify Meaning** Display *Photo Card 17* (branch), and tell children that a *branch* is a part of a tree. Explain that *branch* can also mean a section of a big business. Clarify the meaning of the word in this story.

▲ **Photo Card 17**

Rich wants to pitch and catch. He cannot see the mitt on his shelf. Mom tells Rich, "You will not be small for long."

Rich sits on his porch with his cat Patch. He thinks he will not grow.

20

21

# Monitor Comprehension

**PAGES 20–21** Say: **I noticed that Rich is on his tiptoes in this picture. Why do people get on their tiptoes? Let's read to find out why Rich is doing this.**

1. **SEQUENCE** **What does Rich reach for after he has reached for the branch?** (Rich reaches for his mitt next.)

2. **APPLY PHONICS** **Where are Rich and his cat sitting?** (on the porch) **Point to the word *porch* and read it.**

3. **MAKE INFERENCES** **How do you think Rich is feeling in this part of the story? Why?** (He is sad because he thinks he will not grow bigger.)

## STRATEGIC READING

**Words with /ch/*ch*** Remind children that this story includes many words with the /ch/ sound. Ask them to count and read the words with the /ch/ sound on these pages.

Mom brings Rich a chest with snapshots. Mom was small. Now she is big.

22

"I will grow!" thinks Rich.
Will Rich get that branch? Yes!
Will Rich get that mitt? Yes!

23

# Monitor Comprehension

**PAGES 22-23** Say: **Rich looks happier now. Why do you think he does? Let's read to find out.**

① **DETERMINE CHARACTERS' EMOTIONS** **How do Rich's feelings change when he sees the snapshots? Why?** (Rich becomes very happy and excited because he sees that his mom grew bigger and now he knows that he will too.)

② **DRAW CONCLUSIONS** **When Rich grows, will he be able to reach and do more things?** (Possible response: Yes, Rich will be taller and will be able to do the things his mom can do.)

③ **MAKE INFERENCES** **Does Rich really get big?** (No, not yet.) **Why do you think the story has this title?** (because Rich will get big someday and he knows it)

## HIGH-FREQUENCY WORDS

**Review** Remind children that they have already learned to read the high-frequency words *was, now,* and *grow*. Have them frame and read those words on these two pages.

# Check Comprehension
## *Retelling*

### Retell

**DIBELS**
Oral Reading Fluency
**ORF**

**RETELL "RICH GETS BIG"** Ask children to name the main character. Ask: **What things did Rich try to reach? What happened?** Then have volunteers retell in order the important events that happened. Write children's responses in a sequence chart such as the one shown here.

> Rich cannot reach the branch.
> ↓
> Rich cannot reach his mitt.
> ↓
> Rich is sad and sits on the porch.
> ↓
> Mom shows Rich pictures of herself.
> ↓
> Rich is happy. He knows he will grow.

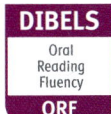

# Fluency

### Repeated Reading

**DIBELS**
Oral Reading Fluency
**ORF**

**READ WITH A PARTNER** Have partners reread "Rich Gets Big" three or four times. Emphasize to children that they should read aloud in a way that sounds like people do when they speak. Listen to partners read, and provide feedback on effective intonation. Model how to stress the appropriate words in a sentence, such as certain nouns and verbs, to convey the meaning of the text.

## Objectives
- *To practice retelling a story*
- *To read fluently in a manner that sounds like natural speech*

### RETELLING RUBRIC

| | |
|---|---|
| 4 | Uses details to clearly retell the story |
| 3 | Uses some details to retell the story |
| 2 | Retells the story with some inaccuracies |
| 1 | Is unable to retell the story |

### Professional Development

 **Podcasting:** Auditory Modeling

# Comprehension
## *Read Aloud*

▲ Read-Aloud Anthology, "Hurry and the Monarch," p. 52

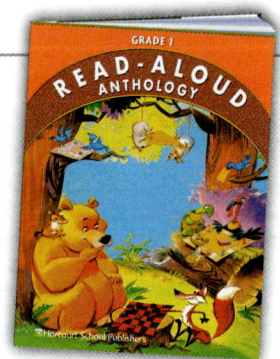

### Objective
• *To understand characteristics of narrative nonfiction*

### Daily Comprehension

**Sequence**

| DAY 1: | Preview Sequence *Read-Aloud Anthology* |
|---|---|
| DAY 2: | Introduce Sequence *Student Edition* |
| DAY 3: | Paired Selection Review Sequence *Student Edition* |
| DAY 4: | Review Sequence *Big Book* |
| DAY 5: | Review Sequence Comparing Texts |

**E L L**

**Connect to Prior Knowledge**
Display *Photo Cards 32* (caterpillar) and *24* (butterfly). Explain that a caterpillar looks similar to a worm. It grows and changes and turns into a butterfly. Encourage children to describe caterpillars and butterflies that they have seen, and invite them to pantomime how they move.

## Before Reading

**CONNECT TO PRIOR KNOWLEDGE** Tell children that they will listen to a story about a tortoise named "Hurry" and a monarch butterfly. Ask them to share what they know about caterpillars and butterflies.

**GENRE STUDY: NARRATIVE NONFICTION**
Explain that "Hurry and the Monarch" is a make-believe story that has a lot of true information. Model your thinking by saying:

**Think Aloud** **Some stories are nonfiction. They give true information. Sometimes the author will add animals that talk or other make-believe parts to the story. These imaginative parts make the story fun and interesting. You can still learn a lot of facts, or true information, from a story like this.**

 **PREVIEW THE SKILL: SEQUENCE** Tell children that the events in a story happen in a certain order and that one event leads to the next. This is called the **sequence**. Model the skill by describing the sequence of events in "Rich Gets Big." Say: **First, Rich tries to reach the branch. Next, he tries to reach his mitt. After that, he feels sad. His mom shows him some pictures to cheer him up. Finally, Rich feels happier because he knows he will grow.** Tell children that they will discuss the sequence of events in "Hurry and the Monarch" later in the week. Then read the story to children.

## After Reading

**RESPOND** Ask volunteers to tell facts, or true information, they learned from "Hurry and the Monarch." Have others tell which parts of the story are make-believe. List their ideas and discuss them.

# Build Robust Vocabulary

## Listening/Speaking: *Words from the Read-Aloud*

### Teach/Model

Routine Card 15

**INTRODUCE ROBUST VOCABULARY** Use *Routine Card 15* to introduce the words.

❶ Put the word in **selection context.**
❷ Provide the **Student-Friendly Explanation** for children.
❸ Have children **say the word** with you.
❹ Use the word in other contexts, and have children **interact with the word's meaning.**
❺ Say the Student-Friendly Explanation again, and ask children to **name the word** that goes with it.

❶ **Selection Context:** Hurry believed that his garden was a place filled with ==astonishing== things.
❹ **Interact with Word Meaning:** I would find it astonishing to see a caterpillar turn into a butterfly. Which would astonish you—to see a caterpillar crawl or a caterpillar turn into a butterfly?

❶ **Selection Context:** The butterflies ==continue== their journey south toward Sweetwater and on to Mexico.
❹ **Interact with Word Meaning:** If I were hiking up a mountain, I'd walk until I reached the top. If you were swimming across a pool, would you continue until you reached the other side?

❶ **Selection Context:** When the butterfly suggests that Hurry might grow wings and fly away, Hurry says, "I ==doubt== it."
❹ **Interact with Word Meaning:** I doubt that a butterfly could grow a shell like Hurry. What do you doubt a butterfly could do?

### Practice/Apply

**GUIDED PRACTICE** Ask children to do the following:
• Imagine seeing something very surprising walk into the room. Have a look on your face that shows you are astonished.
• Continue clapping until you see the lights go off and on.

### Objective
• *To develop robust vocabulary through discussing a literature selection*

**INTRODUCE** **Tested** ✓
**Student-Friendly Explanations**

**astonishing** If something is astonishing, it amazes and surprises you.

**continue** If you continue to do something, you keep doing it.

**doubt** If you doubt something, you do not believe it is true.

E L L

**Introduce Vocabulary** Act out the meaning of each word. For example, show how your face might look when you are astonished.

astonished

# Grammar
## Names of Days and Months

**5-DAY GRAMMAR**

| | |
|---|---|
| **DAY 1** | Introduce Names of Days and Months |
| **DAY 2** | Dictate Names of Days and Months |
| **DAY 3** | Add Days and Months to Sentences |
| **DAY 4** | Revise Names of Days and Months |
| **DAY 5** | Write Names of Days and Months |

## Objectives

- *To recognize names of days of the week and months of the year*
- *To identify and use the names of days and months in sentences*

## Daily Proofreading

**Mom made lunc on Sunday**
(lunch, Sunday.)

### Names of Days and Months

**Days of the Week**

| | |
|---|---|
| Sunday | Thursday |
| Monday | Friday |
| Tuesday | Saturday |
| Wednesday | |

**Months of the Year**

| | | |
|---|---|---|
| January | May | September |
| February | June | October |
| March | July | November |
| April | August | December |

Grade 1, Lesson 13    **LA25**    Grammar: Names of Days and Months

**Transparency LA25**

## Teach/Model

**INTRODUCE NAMES OF DAYS AND MONTHS** Read aloud sentences from "Hurry and the Monarch" (*Read-Aloud Anthology,* pages 52–55), and have children listen for the names of months.

- **Hurry the Texas tortoise is starting to think about winter when out of the bright October sky a Monarch butterfly lands on his back.**

- **On and on she flies until finally, one November evening, she finds it.**

Display a calendar. Point out the names of the days and the months. Tell children that these names always begin with a capital letter. Then write the following sentences on the board, inserting the day and the month. Read them to children and then with them.

**Today is (day).**
**This month is (month).**

Have a volunteer underline the day and month. Ask children how each word begins. (with a capital letter)

## Guided Practice

**SAY NAMES OF DAYS AND MONTHS** Display **Transparency LA25.** Have volunteers point to each word as you read aloud the names of the days and the months. Repeat, and ask children to echo-read each word. Ask children to tell what letter begins the name of each day and each month. Make sure children respond with "capital *J*," for example.

## Practice/Apply

**DICTATE SENTENCES WITH DAYS AND MONTHS** Have children share sentences about their favorite day or month. Record several, using a lowercase beginning letter in the name of the day or month. Read the sentences aloud. Have children tell how to correct them.

#  Modeled Writing
## *Sequence Story*

| 5-DAY WRITING | |
| --- | --- |
| **DAY 1** | Modeled Writing |
| **DAY 2** | Shared Writing |
| **DAY 3** | Shared Writing |
| **DAY 4** | Independent Writing |
| **DAY 5** | Independent Writing |

## Teach/Model

**INTRODUCE SEQUENCE STORY** Display **Transparency LA26** and explain that this a sequence story. It tells what a boy and his mother did one rainy afternoon. Read the passage to children, and discuss what they learned about the experience. Together, develop a list of the characteristics of a well-written sequence story.

> ### Sequence Story
> - It tells events in order.
> - It uses words such as <u>first</u>, <u>next</u>, and <u>last</u>.
> - It has a beginning, a middle, and an ending.

 **ORGANIZATION** Tell children that the words *first, next,* and *last* will help them to write the events in their stories in the correct order. Guide them to decide what belongs at the beginning, middle, and ending of their story.

## Guided Practice

**DRAFT A SEQUENCE STORY** Model saying sentences about what you did this morning. Say: **Today I woke up at six o'clock. First, I got dressed. Next, I ate breakfast. Last, I packed my things and drove to school.** Talk about how the words *first, next,* and *last* help make the order of events clear. Have volunteers say sentences to add.

## Practice/Apply

**TELL A SEQUENCE STORY** Together, decide on a topic for a sequence story, such as a class trip. Use the Sequence Chart, **Transparency GO7,** to sketch or write notes about the events in the correct order. Then ask volunteers to take turns telling the story in order. Ask them to use the words *first, next,* and *last* and to refer to the graphic organizer for ideas. Save the organizer for Days 2–3.

## Objectives
- *To understand sequence words*
- *To develop a list of criteria for an effective sequence story*
- *To choose a focus for writing and to generate ideas*

## Writing Prompt

**Write and Draw** Have children write and draw about what they usually do before they go to bed each night.

---

**Student Model: Sequence Story**

It was raining on Saturday. I had to stay inside. Mom said, "Let's make sock puppets!" First, we found old socks and added bits of cloth and string to make the puppets. Next, we drew faces on the socks. Last, we made up a puppet show. We added some songs and put on the show for Dad. Sock puppets are fun!

Grade 1, Lesson 13    LA26    Writing: Sequence Story

**Transparency LA26**

# Warm-Up Routines

## Day at a Glance

### Day 2

**Phonemic Awareness**
- Phoneme Deletion

 **phonics** and Spelling
- Review: Digraphs /ch/*ch*, *tch*
- Build Words

**Comprehension**
Introduce: Sequence

**High-Frequency Words**
- Introduce: air, fly, friends, grew, need, play, rain, watch

**Reading**
- "A Butterfly Grows," *Student Edition*, pp. 28-45

**Read!**

**Fluency**
- Intonation

**Robust Vocabulary**
- Review: *astonishing, continue, doubt*

**Grammar**
- Review: Names of Days; Months

**Shared Writing**
- Sequence Story

## Oral Language

**Objective** *To listen and respond appropriately to oral communication*

### Question of the Day

**What does an inchworm look like?**
**How does it move?**

Pinch your pointer finger and thumb together repeatedly, moving them along a surface to model how an inchworm moves, and have children do the same. Discuss inchworms, and have children help complete these sentences:

**An inchworm is _____. It moves _____.**

## Read Aloud

**Objective** *To identify the characteristics of concrete poetry*

**BIG BOOK OF RHYMES AND POEMS** Display the *Big Book* and discuss with children the purpose of the cover, title page, and table of contents. Read each, and discuss the information. Have children direct you in using the table of contents to find "The Inchworm," and turn to that page. Then tell children that in a **concrete** poem, the words form a picture that adds meaning to the poem. Have children look at the shape the words make as you read "The Inchworm." Ask them to listen for clues that will help them to confirm the picture the poet made with words. (an inchworm)

▲ Big Book of Rhymes and Poems, p. 25

## Word Wall

**Objective**  *To read high-frequency words*

**REVIEW HIGH-FREQUENCY WORDS**  Review *came, could, gold, happy, made, night, saw, were,* and other previously learned high-frequency words. Say each word, ask a volunteer to point to it, and have children read it aloud. Then point to words at random and have children reread them. Repeat several times to reinforce instant recognition.

came could gold happy

made night saw were

## Phonemic Awareness

**Objective**  *To delete initial phonemes from words*

**Routine Card 9**

**PHONEME DELETION**  Tell children you are going to sing a song that tells them to delete the beginning sound in a word. They should then say the new word. Model the song for them.

*(Sung to the tune of "The Farmer in the Dell.")*

**Say *hat* without the /h/. Say *hat* without the /h/. Hi-ho, the derrio. Say *hat* without the /h/.** (at)

Continue singing the song, using the words below.

*cheer* **without the** /ch/ (ear)          *cloud* **without the** /k/ (loud)

*stop* **without the** /s/ (top)          *branch* **without the** /b/ (ranch)

*flap* **without the** /f/ (lap)          *mat* **without the** /m/ (at)

*pitch* **without the** /p/ (itch)          *fin* **without the** /f/ (in)

# Digraphs /ch/ *ch, tch*

 phonics *and Spelling*

## Objectives

- *To blend sounds into words*
- *To spell four- and five-letter short-vowel words and high-frequency words*

## Skill Trace

 **Tested** **Digraphs /ch/ *ch, tch***

| | |
|---|---|
| Introduce | T36–T39 |
| Reteach | S2 |
| **Review** | **T52–T53, T74–T75** |
| Test | Bk 1-3 |
| Maintain | Bk 1-4, T76–T77 |

## Spelling Words

| | | | |
|---|---|---|---|
| 1. | chip | 6. | match |
| 2. | chin | 7. | wish |
| 3. | inch | 8. | shop |
| 4. | such | 9. | saw |
| 5. | catch | 10. | were |

## Word Building

**DIBELS**
Nonsense Word Fluency
NWF

**Routine Card 14**

**BUILD AND READ A SPELLING WORD** Place the *Letter Cards c, h, i, p* in the pocket chart. Arrange the cards so that *c* and *h* are touching. Ask children to say the name and sound of each letter, keeping the letters *ch* together. Then read the word naturally—*chip*. Have children do the same.

**BUILD SPELLING WORDS** Ask children which letter you should change to make *chip* become *chin*. (Change *p* to *n*.) Ask them what you should change to make *chin* become *inch*. (Move the *ch* from the beginning to the end of the word.) Continue building spelling words 4–6 in this manner. Have children repeat each step after you and then read the words.

| c | h | i | p |
|---|---|---|---|
| c | h | i | n |
| i | n | c | h |
| s | u | c | h |
| c | a | t | c | h |
| m | a | t | c | h |

 **BELOW-LEVEL**

**Build Spelling Words** Write the words on the board. Point to each word, one at a time, and read it aloud. Have children repeat it and trace it with a finger for kinesthetic reinforcement.

**ADVANCED**

**Multiple-Meaning Words** Tell children that several spelling words can be used as both naming words and action words; for example, a cup can have a chip on the rim, and a person could chip a cup by bumping it on the counter. Challenge children to use the words *match, catch,* and *shop* as both naming words and action words in oral sentences.

**5-DAY** PHONICS/SPELLING

| | |
|---|---|
| **DAY 1** | Pretest |
| **DAY 2** | **Word Building** |
| **DAY 3** | State the Generalization |
| **DAY 4** | Review |
| **DAY 5** | Posttest |

## Read Words in Context

**APPLY PHONICS** Write the following sentences on the board or on chart paper. Have children read each sentence silently. Then track the print as children read the sentence aloud.

> The cup has a small <u>chip</u> on the rim.
>
> I fell and hit my <u>chin</u>.
>
> That is <u>such</u> a little dog!
>
> That bug is one <u>inch</u> long.
>
> I <u>wish</u> I could <u>catch</u> the ball.
>
> She will <u>shop</u> for a hat to <u>match</u> the dress.

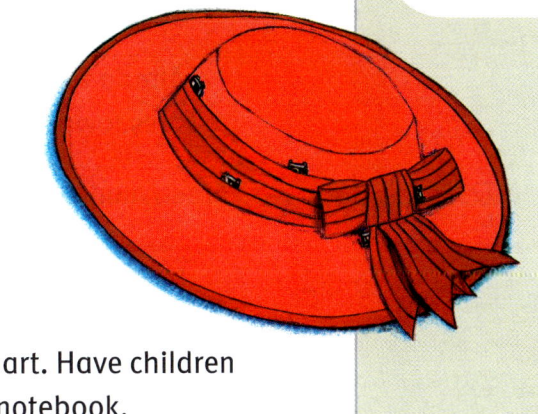

**WRITE** Dictate several words from the pocket chart. Have children write the words on a dry-erase board or in their notebook.

**phonics** Resources

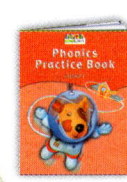

Phonics Practice Book, pp. 67–70

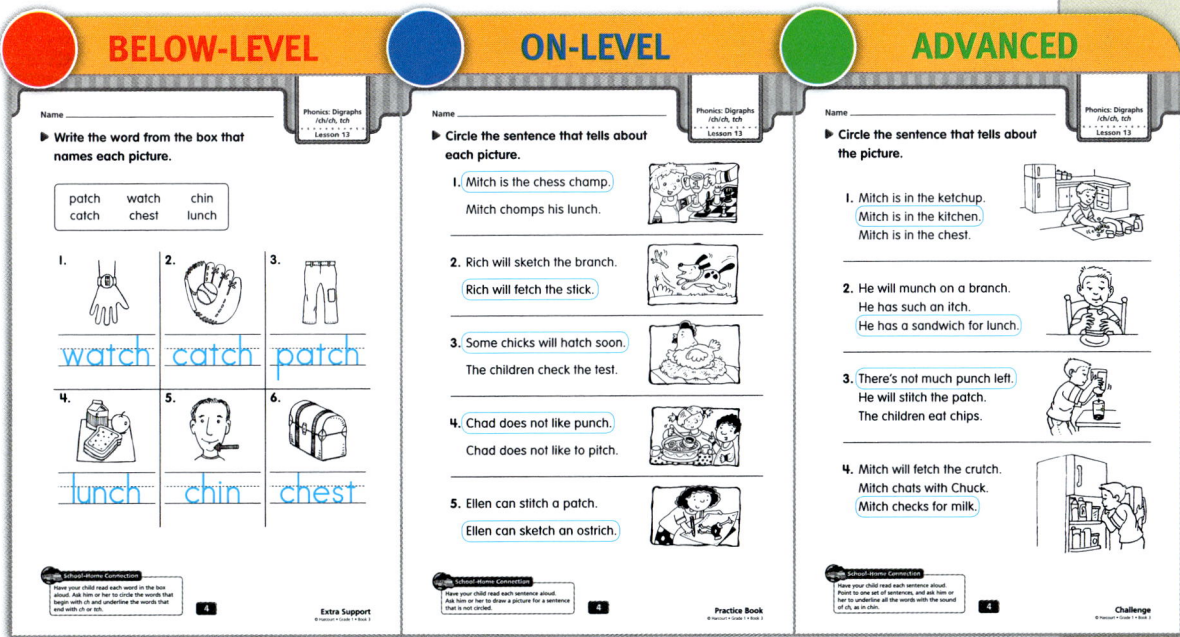

▲ Extra Support, p. 4    ▲ Practice Book, p. 4    ▲ Challenge, p. 4

**E L L**

- Group children according to academic levels, and assign one of the pages on the left.

- Clarify any unfamiliar concepts as necessary. See *ELL Teacher Guide*, Lesson 13, for support in scaffolding instruction.

# Sequence
## *Comprehension*

### Objective
- *To identify and describe a sequence of events*

### Skill Trace
 **Tested** **Sequence**

| | |
|---|---|
| Preview | T46 |
| **Introduce** | **T54–T55** |
| Reteach | S6–S7, S26–S27 |
| Review | T78, T90, T100, T230, T238–T239, T262, T274, T284 |
| Test | Bk 1–3 |
| Maintain | Monitor Comprehension, Bks 1–4, 1–5 |

## Teach/Model

**INTRODUCE THE SKILL** Tell the children that the sequence is the order in which things happen in a story. Have them listen carefully to recall events in the following excerpts from "Hurry and the Monarch" (*Read-Aloud Anthology,* p. 52).

> **Then one morning, the monarch also returns.**
>
> **After a few hours, the monarch spreads his strong new wings and flies toward Hurry. . . .**

Then model how to recognize sequence.

**Think Aloud** **The words *then* and *after* help me understand that one event happens after another event. These words help show the sequence of events, or the order in which things happen. I can use these words and other words, such as *first, next,* and *last,* to help understand the sequence of events in a story.**

## Practice/Apply

**GUIDED PRACTICE** Read *Student Edition* page 24 to children, and remind them of what *sequence* means. Then have children look at the series of pictures on page 25 and follow along as you read the sentence and questions. Ask children if the pictures show a sequence, or things happening in a certain order. (Yes, they all show the same bird hatching from an egg.) Ask them to tell what happens *first, next,* and *last*. (First, the egg begins to crack. Next, the bird pushes partway out of the shell. Last, the bird has hatched.)

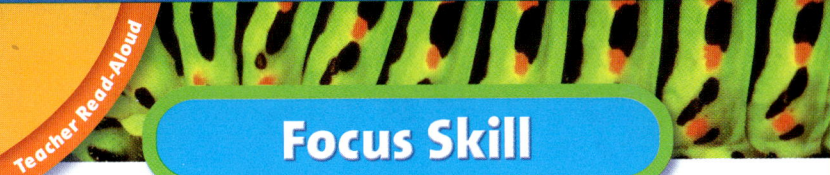

## Focus Skill

 **Sequence**

Many stories and nonfiction selections tell about things in the order in which they happen—first, next, and last. This order is called the **sequence**.

Look at the pictures.

They show a sequence of first, next, and last.

Look at the pictures. Do the pictures show a sequence? What happens first, next, and last?

**Try This!**

Look at these pictures. Put the pictures in order. Tell what happens first, next, and last.

 www.harcourtschool.com/storytown

24

25

**Try This!** **INDEPENDENT PRACTICE** Discuss the pictures and have children follow along as you read aloud the sentences. Ask children to point to the pictures in the correct sequence to show what happens as a baby grows, and have them describe what happens first, next, and last.

**E L L**

**Try This!** Help children with the Try This! activity by providing similar photographs that children can manipulate to put into a logical sequence.

#  High-Frequency Words
## *Words to Know*

###  Tested
### INTRODUCE

## Objective
• *To read high-frequency words*

### High-Frequency Words

| | |
|---|---|
| air | need |
| fly | play |
| friends | rain |
| grew | watch |

### ✓ MONITOR PROGRESS

#### High-Frequency Words

| **IF** children have difficulty reading and spelling words, | **THEN** display two sets of word cards, and have them read and match the words. |
|---|---|

**Small-Group Instruction, p. S3:**

● **BELOW-LEVEL:** Reteach
● **ON-LEVEL:** Reinforce
● **ADVANCED:** Extend

---

## Teach/Model

**Routine Card 16** **INTRODUCE WORDS** Write the words *air, fly, friends, grew, need, play, rain,* and *watch* on the board.

• Point to and read *air.* Repeat it, having children say it with you.

• Say: **I like to smell the fresh *air.***

• Point to each letter as you spell the word. Have children spell the word with you.

• Have children reread the word.

Repeat for the remaining words. Use the following sentences:

I wish I could *fly* like a bird.

We have many *friends* in this classroom.

I am sure you *grew* taller this year.

Do you *need* a drink of water?

What will you *play* at recess?

The *rain* has made the ground muddy.

Can you *watch* me dance?

## Guided Practice

**STUDENT EDITION PAGES 26–27** Have children point to and read aloud each of the highlighted words. Talk about the artwork. Then ask volunteers to read aloud the sentences.

**STORY WORDS** List *caterpillar, chrysalis,* and *butterfly* and display Photo Cards 24 and 32. Read the words aloud. Repeat, having children read the words with you. Point out that these words tell about a butterfly's life, which they will read about in "A Butterfly Grows." Have children reread the words aloud.

▲ Photo Card 24, 32

## Words to Know

**High-Frequency Words**

grew

fly

air

friends

play

need

watch

rain

26

I **grew** from a small egg. Now I **fly** in the **air** with all my **friends**. Wings help us fly and **play**.

We **need** to drink water. We **watch** for **rain**. Then we sip drops on the plants.

 www.harcourtschool.com/storytown

27

**ELL**

**Reinforce Story Words** Display *Photo Card butterfly* and read the word with children. Remind them that some long words are made by putting two shorter words together. Write *butterfly* on the board. Point to the word, and ask children to find one of the new high-frequency words in the word. *(fly)* Underline *fly,* and ask a volunteer to underline the other word that makes up this word. *(butter)*

See *ELL Teacher Guide*, Lesson 13, for support in scaffolding instruction.

# Reading

## Student Edition: A Butterfly Grows

### Objectives

- *To understand genre: nonfiction*
- *To use graphic organizers as a strategy for comprehension*
- *To apply word knowledge to the reading of a text*

 **Podcasting:** Using Story Structures, Gr. I

## Options for Reading

 **BELOW-LEVEL**

**Preview** Have children preview the selection by looking at the illustrations. Guide them to predict what they will learn about butterflies. Read each page of the selection, and have them read it after you.

 **ON-LEVEL**

**Monitor Comprehension** Have children read the selection aloud, page by page. Ask the Monitor Comprehension questions. Then lead them in retelling the selection and describing their favorite parts.

 **ADVANCED**

**Independent Reading** Have children read the selection silently, looking up each time they finish a page. Ask the Monitor Comprehension questions as you go. Then discuss how the caterpillar changed.

### Genre Study

**DISCUSS NONFICTION: PAGE 28** Point to the genre label on *Student Edition* page 28 and tell children that this selection is *nonfiction*. Explain that nonfiction selections include facts, or true information, about real things. Point out that many nonfiction selections have photographs and that the information is given in a certain order, or sequence. Then use **Transparency GO7** or copy the graphic organizer from page 28 onto the board. Tell children that they can fill it in for any nonfiction text they read.

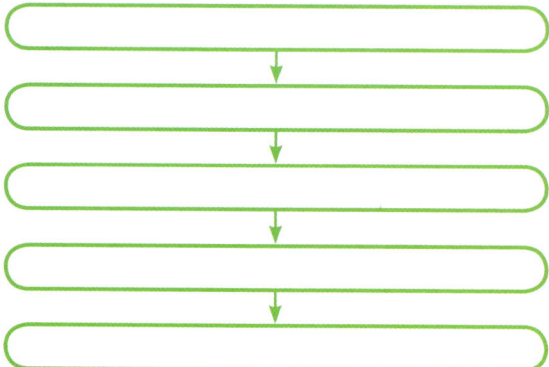

### Comprehension Strategies

**USE GRAPHIC ORGANIZERS: PAGE 28** Tell children that good readers use graphic organizers to help them understand and remember what they read.

**Think Aloud** In "A Butterfly Grows," you will read about what a caterpillar needs to live and also how it grows up. The events happen in sequence, or in a certain order. Writing the events in order in a graphic organizer is a good way to remember the information.

Then read aloud the text under Comprehension Strategy on page 28. Explain that they will work together to fill in a Sequence Chart as they read "A Butterfly Grows."

**Genre Study**
**Nonfiction** selections tell about things that are true. They tell the order in which things happen.

**Comprehension Strategy**
**Use Graphic Organizers**
As you read, use a graphic organizer like this to help you understand and remember information in the correct order.

A **Butterfly** Grows

by Stephen Swinburne

28

29

## Build Background

**DISCUSS BUTTERFLIES** Invite children to tell what they know about butterflies. Explain that they will read a selection about a butterfly who begins its life as a caterpillar.

**Routine Card 17**

**SET A PURPOSE AND PREDICT** Tell children that they will read this selection to become informed about butterflies. Ask them what they think they will learn.

- Read the title to children.

- Identify the butterfly as a monarch butterfly. Have children share questions they have about this butterfly and tell what they would like to learn.

- List children's questions on the board.

- Invite children to read to find out about a butterfly's life.

## TECHNOLOGY

 **eBook** "A Butterfly Grows" is available in an eBook.

 **Audiotext** "A Butterfly Grows" is available on *Audiotext Grade 1*, CD 3 for subsequent readings.

Can you see me on the plant?

30

I am a little caterpillar!
I **grew** in an egg.
Then I hatched!

31

# Monitor Comprehension

**PAGES 30–31** Say: **Let's look at the photographs. What do you see? Let's read to find out what is on the plant.**

**①** **NOTE DETAILS** **What is on the plant?** (a little caterpillar)

**②** **DRAW CONCLUSIONS** **Who is telling this story? What makes you think this?** (The caterpillar; the words *me* and *I* make it seem as if the caterpillar is talking.)

**③** **COMPARE AND CONTRAST** **How is this caterpillar like other caterpillars you have seen? How is it different?** (Possible responses: It is the same size and shape as most caterpillars; it has yellow, black, and white stripes, while most caterpillars I have seen are green.)

## Apply
### Comprehension Strategies

**Focus Strategy** **Use Graphic Organizers** Demonstrate how to use the graphic organizer to begin recording important information.

**Think Aloud** As I read, I use a graphic organizer to help me understand and remember information. This graphic organizer helps me put information in order. I will write the first thing that happens to the caterpillar at the beginning of the selection.

A baby caterpillar hatches out of an egg.

Wind fills the **air**. I hang onto a branch so I don't fall.

32

**Rain** falls. It plips and plops.
I **need** to drink water.
I drink the small drops.

33

# Monitor Comprehension

**PAGES 32–33** Say: **Look at what the weather is like in the pictures. Let's read to find out how weather affects the caterpillar.**

**1** **CAUSE AND EFFECT** **What might happen if the caterpillar lets go of the branch?** (The wind might blow the caterpillar away.)

**2** **NOTE DETAILS** **How does rain help the caterpillar?** (The rain gives the caterpillar the water that it needs to live.)

**3** **AUTHOR'S CRAFT** **What do the words *plips* and *plops* remind you of? Why do you think the author uses these words?** (The words *plips* and *plops* make the same sound as rain when it falls. By using these words, the author helps me know what the rain sounds like.)

## Use Multiple Strategies

**Generate Questions** Say: Asking questions about a selection helps me think about what I read. I ask myself, "What else does a caterpillar need to live?" I will read on to find out.

 **Use Graphic Organizers**
Add information.

**Think Aloud** The next thing I learn is that caterpillars need to drink water to live and how they get water.

> It needs water to live.
> It drinks raindrops.

This plant is my food. I need food so I can grow.

I eat this plant for lunch. Chomp, chomp! Crunch, munch!

34

35

# Monitor Comprehension

**PAGES 34–35** Ask: **What do you think the caterpillar is doing? Let's read to find out.**

**1** **NOTE DETAILS** **What is the caterpillar doing?** (The caterpillar is eating the plant.)

**2** **CAUSE AND EFFECT** **Why does it need food?** (The caterpillar needs food so it can grow.)

**3** **MAKE INFERENCES** **Are plants and leaves good for the caterpillar?** (yes) **What happens when you eat food that is good for you?** (Possible response: I grow.)

I eat and grow,
eat and grow.
Now I am big!
My skin is snug.

36

I look for a spot to rest.
Soon I will shed my skin.

37

# Monitor Comprehension

**PAGES 36–37** Say: **How has the caterpillar changed since the beginning of the story? Now, let's read to find out what happens as the caterpillar continues to eat.**

1. **NOTE DETAILS** **What happens as the caterpillar eats?** (The caterpillar grows.)

2. **CAUSE AND EFFECT** **What do you think the word *snug* means? How do you know?** (It means "tight." Its skin would be tight since its body got bigger from eating a lot of plants. The caterpillar in the picture has snug skin.) **What causes the caterpillar's skin to become snug?** (The caterpillar's skin becomes snug because the caterpillar has grown so much.)

3. **SEQUENCE** **What will happen after the caterpillar finds a spot to rest?** (The caterpillar will shed its skin.)

**Apply**
**Comprehension Strategies**

**Use Graphic Organizers** Work with children to add to the graphic organizer. Continue throughout the selection.

**Think Aloud** I want to write some more important information on the chart. The caterpillar eats plants and grows. Then it rests and sheds its skin. I'll add these facts.

The caterpillar eats plants and grows.

At last I am a chrysalis.
I'm an inch long.
Then in ten days, out I come!

38

Look at me now!
I am an insect.
I have six legs.

39

# Monitor Comprehension

**PAGES 38–39** Say: **I wonder where the caterpillar is. Before we read on, let's predict what will happen next.**

**①** **CONFIRM PREDICTIONS** **What did you think would happen? Were you correct?** (Responses will vary.)

**②** **NOTE DETAILS** **How big is the chrysalis?** (an inch long) **Find and read the words that tell this.** (*I am a chrysalis. I'm an inch long.*)

Explain to children that *I'm* is a contraction, which is a short way to write the two words *I am.*

**③** **SEQUENCE** **We are reading about things that happen in a certain order. What word on page 38 gives us a signal that something happens *after* something else?** *(then)* **What do you think will happen next?** (Responses will vary.)

*Focus Skill*

---

**SCIENCE**

## SUPPORTING STANDARDS

**Butterflies' Food** Tell children that this is a monarch butterfly. This kind of butterfly lays its eggs on the leaves of milkweed plants because that is the food the baby caterpillars need after they hatch. Explain that when the caterpillars eat milkweed leaves, their bodies make a liquid that is poisonous to other animals, and this helps to keep them from being eaten. It is one way that monarch caterpillars and butterflies are protected as they grow. Ask children to retell this information in their own words.

My wings help me **fly**.
**Watch** me fly!

40

I like to fly with all my **friends**.
Wings help us **play**.
Wings help us to go find plants
for food.

41

# Monitor Comprehension

**PAGES 40–41** Ask: **I see a lot of butterflies. I wonder where they are going. Let's read to find out.**

**1** **NOTE DETAILS** **How does the butterfly get around?** (It uses its wings to fly.)

**2** **MAKE INFERENCES** **Why is flying so important to the butterfly?** (Flying is the way a butterfly moves around. A butterfly flies to get food.)

Watch me eat now!
I sip and sip.

42

I am a butterfly!
I'm a beautiful butterfly!

43

# Monitor Comprehension

**PAGES 42-43** Ask: **I see the butterflies on the flowers. What do you think they are doing? Let's read to the end of the selection to learn more.**

1. **NOTE DETAILS** **How does a butterfly eat?** (A butterfly sips from a flower.)

2. **COMPARE AND CONTRAST** **How are a caterpillar and a butterfly alike? How are they different?** (They are alike because they both need to eat; they are different in the way they look, the way they move, and the way they eat.)

3. **SPECULATE** **Imagine that you could talk to this butterfly. What questions would you ask it?** (Possible response: I would ask it where it goes at night.)

**SCIENCE**

## SUPPORTING STANDARDS

**Butterfly Adaptations** Discuss the meaning of *sip* on page 42. Explain that *sipping* usually means "drinking a liquid in small amounts." Have children name drinks they might sip. Then explain that a butterfly has a body part called a *proboscis*, which is a hollow tube almost like a straw. It uses its proboscis to sip a liquid, called *nectar*, from flowers. Nectar is food. Invite children to act out sipping nectar.

**proboscis**

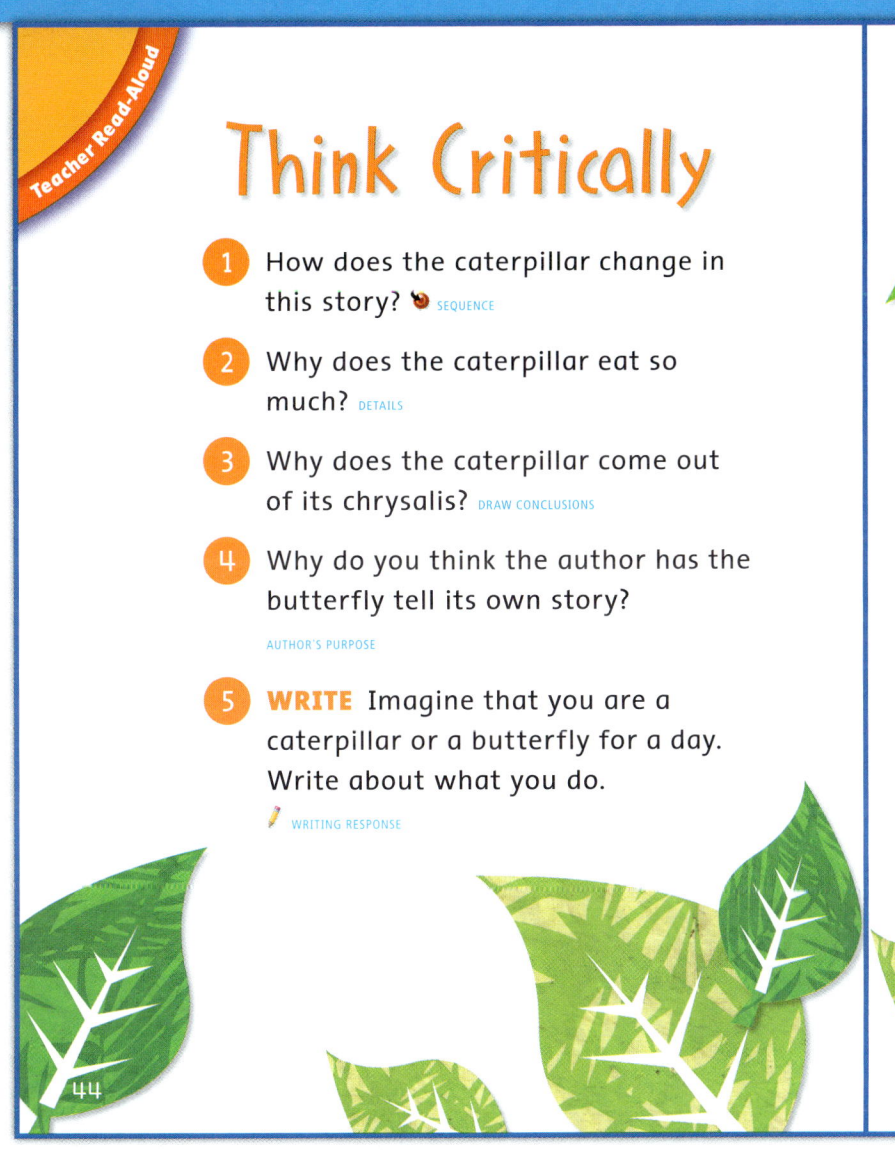

Teacher Read-Aloud

# Think Critically

1. How does the caterpillar change in this story? **SEQUENCE**

2. Why does the caterpillar eat so much? **DETAILS**

3. Why does the caterpillar come out of its chrysalis? **DRAW CONCLUSIONS**

4. Why do you think the author has the butterfly tell its own story? **AUTHOR'S PURPOSE**

5. **WRITE** Imagine that you are a caterpillar or a butterfly for a day. Write about what you do. **WRITING RESPONSE**

44

## Meet the Author/Photographer
## Stephen Swinburne

Stephen Swinburne loves nature—especially butterflies! He planted a garden at his house filled with flowers that butterflies like. He took many of the pictures for "A Butterfly Grows" in his garden. He hopes you enjoy learning about butterflies!

**Go online** www.harcourtschool.com/storytown

45

# Think Critically

## Respond to the Literature

1. Possible responses: The caterpillar grows and changes into a butterfly. It starts as an egg. Then it hatches and the baby caterpillar grows. It turns into a chrysalis and then into a butterfly. **SEQUENCE**

2. It eats so much because it is growing. **DETAILS**

3. It comes out because it is a big butterfly now. **DRAW CONCLUSIONS**

4. Possible response: I think the author has the butterfly tell its story because it is more interesting and easier to understand. **AUTHOR'S PURPOSE**

5. **WRITE** Possible response: I fly from flower to flower looking for nectar. I fly and play tag with my friends. **WRITING RESPONSE**

# Meet the Author/ Photographer

**PAGE 45** Explain that this page tells about the person who wrote "A Butterfly Grows." Identify Stephen Swinburne in the photograph. Point out that Mr. Swinburne is the author *and* the illustrator of the selection because he wrote the words and took the photographs. Read page 45 aloud. Encourage children to follow along as you read.

 # Check Comprehension
## *Summarizing*

## Objectives
- *To practice summarizing a selection*
- *To read with fluency in a manner that sounds like natural speech*

### SUMMARIZING RUBRIC

| | |
|---|---|
| 4 | Uses details to summarize the selection clearly |
| 3 | Uses some details to summarize the selection |
| 2 | Summarizes the selection with some inaccuracies |
| 1 | Is unable to summarize the selection |

### Summarize

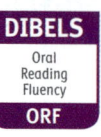  **DIBELS** Oral Reading Fluency **ORF** **SEQUENCE** Ask children to tell the sequence of important events in this selection. Guide them with *who, what, when, where, why,* and *how* questions.

**REVISIT THE GRAPHIC ORGANIZER** Display completed **Transparency GO7.** Guide children to use the Sequence Chart to summarize the story.

**STORY RETELLING CARDS** The cards for "A Butterfly Grows" can be used for a retelling or as an aid to completing the graphic organizer.

▲ Story Retelling Cards 1–6, "A Butterfly Grows"

 # Fluency

### Teach/Model

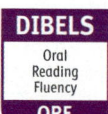 **DIBELS** Oral Reading Fluency **ORF** **READING WITH INTONATION** Have children open to pages 30–31 of "A Butterfly Grows." Tell children that good readers make their reading sound like someone talking. Explain that their voices usually go up at the end of questions and that some words in a sentence are spoken more strongly than others. Have children track the print as you model reading, first without intonation and then with appropriate intonation.

### Practice/Apply

**ECHO-READ** Read aloud the rest of the selection, one page at a time. Model appropriate intonation and have children echo-read this familiar text.

### BELOW-LEVEL

**Fluency Practice** For fluency practice, have children read *Decodable Book 13*, the appropriate *Leveled Reader* (pp. T104–T107), or "How Many?" in the *Book 1-3 Strategic Intervention Interactive Reader.*

# Build Robust Vocabulary

**Listening/Speaking:** *Words from the Read-Aloud*

## Review Robust Vocabulary

**USE VOCABULARY IN DIFFERENT CONTEXTS** Remind children of the Student-Friendly Explanations of *astonishing, continue,* and *doubt.* Then discuss each word using the following examples:

**astonishing**

- What might you find astonishing in a grocery store?
- What is something you might hear about that would astonish you?
- Tell about something that would NOT be astonishing.

**continue**

- Would you continue watching a very exciting movie? Why?
- Would you continue on a hike if the sun suddenly came out from behind a cloud?
- Would you continue to play if your mother asked you to set the table?

**doubt**

- If I told you that school was closed for a month, would you say, "I believe it" or "I doubt it"? Why?
- Would you doubt or believe a weather report that says it will rain tomorrow?
- Tell about something that you would NOT doubt if your best friend told you that it was true.

### Objective

- *To review robust vocabulary to describe ideas*

**REVIEW** Tested

### Student-Friendly Explanations

**astonishing** If something is astonishing, it amazes and surprises you.

**continue** If you continue to do something, you keep doing it.

**doubt** If you doubt something, you do not believe it is true.

 **ADVANCED**

Ask children to imagine that a friend showed them an egg. What might they say if their friend told them it was a dinosaur egg? Then have them describe something astonishing that might come out of the egg. Would they continue to doubt their friend if it turned out to be a baby dinosaur?

# Grammar
## Names of Days and Months

**5-DAY GRAMMAR**

| | |
|---|---|
| DAY I | Introduce Names of Days and Months |
| DAY 2 | Dictate Names of Days and Months |
| DAY 3 | Add Days and Months to Sentences |
| DAY 4 | Revise Names of Days and Months |
| DAY 5 | Write Names of Days and Months |

## Objectives
- *To dictate sentences with names of days and months*
- *To use basic capitalization skills to capitalize proper nouns*

### Daily Proofreading

**i went on a trip in march.**
(I, March.)

**Reinforce Days and Months** Reinforce names of days or months by showing children a calender. Help them to recognize the patterns that occur week by week and year after year. Recite the days of the week and the months of the year with children several times.

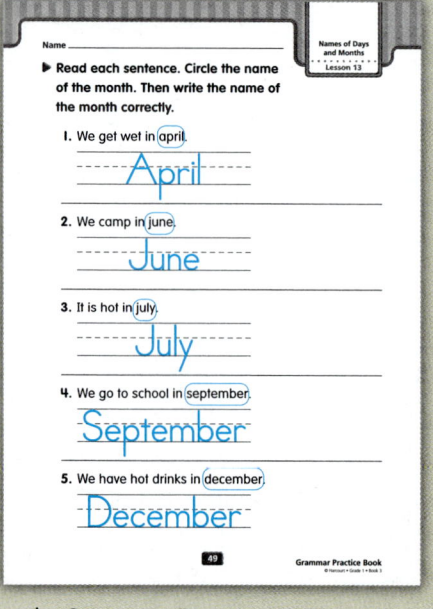

▲ Grammar Practice Book, p. 49

### Review

**USE A LITERATURE MODEL** Sing the traditional song, "The Mulberry Bush," with children. Have them listen for the names of the days of the week.

> Here we go 'round the mulberry bush,
>
> The mulberry bush, the mulberry bush.
>
> Here we go 'round the mulberry bush, so early in the morning.
>
> This is the way we wash our clothes, . . . so early Monday morning.

Repeat, having children "iron our clothes" on Tuesday, "mend our clothes" on Wednesday, "scrub the floor" on Thursday, "sweep the house" on Friday, "bake our bread" on Saturday, and "rest ourselves" on Sunday.

Review the song and ask children to name the days of the week. Write them on chart paper. Track the print and read the words with children. Ask what kind of letter starts each word. (capital letter) Make a similar list of the months. Display the lists.

### Practice/Apply

**GUIDED PRACTICE** Have children dictate sentences telling what they do on certain days or during certain months, using sentences from the song as a model. Record the sentences on the board and read them with children, tracking the print.

**This is the way we go to gym, so early Monday morning.**

**INDEPENDENT PRACTICE** Ask children to copy one of the sentences. Have them read aloud the sentence and identify the name of the day or month and the capital letter.

# Shared Writing
## Sequence Story

| 5-DAY WRITING | |
|---|---|
| DAY 1 | Modeled Writing |
| DAY 2 | Shared Writing |
| DAY 3 | Shared Writing |
| DAY 4 | Independent Writing |
| DAY 5 | Independent Writing |

### Write Together

**REVIEW SEQUENCE STORY** Write on the board the sentences *Last, we rode the bus back to school. We were tired, but happy!* Talk about what may have happened before and after these events. Ask children if the sentences would make sense in the group's sequence story.

**GENERATE IDEAS** Review with children the graphic organizer they helped complete on Day 1. Work with them to add and change the order of ideas as needed.

**MODEL WRITING** Have volunteers refer to the graphic organizer and dictate sentences to tell the sequence story as you write it on chart paper, using the Step-by-Step Writing Instruction as a guide. Then track the print and read the story with children. Save it for Day 3.

## Step-by-Step Writing Instruction

| | | |
|---|---|---|
| 1 | Say a sentence to tell what our story is about. | *In January, we went to the Science Center.* |
| 2 | Each sentence begins with a capital letter. How do I write the first word? | In |
| 3 | Say the sentence again. Let's write the rest of it. How does the name of the month begin? How does the name of a special place begin? | In January, we went to the Science Center. |
| 4 | **WRITING TRAIT** What is the first thing that happens in our story? Which word can we use to show that it is the first event? How do I write that word? | First |
| 5 | Say the sentence again. Let's write it. Notice the comma after *First*. What mark do I use at the end of the sentence? | First, we looked at a beehive with real bees. |
| 6 | Let's read together the two sentences that begin our story. | |

### Objectives

- *To compose sentences that tell a story in sequence*
- *To understand and use sequence signal words*
- *To generate ideas before writing on assigned tasks*

### Writing Prompt

**Draw and Write** Have children draw and write about something they know how to make.

▲ Writer's Companion, Lesson 13

**Use Sentence Frames** If children need help forming sentences, display the following frames and guide children in using them:

First, we _____.

Next, we _____.

After that, we _____.

Last, we _____.

## Day at a Glance

### Day 3

#### Phonemic Awareness
- Phoneme Deletion

**phonics** and Spelling
- Review: /ch/*ch, tch;* /sh/*sh*
- State the Generalization

#### High-Frequency Words
- Review: *air, fly, friends, grew, need, play, rain, watch*

#### Fluency
- Intonation
- "A Butterfly Grows," *Student Edition*, pp. 28–45

#### Comprehension
 Review: Sequence

#### Reading
- "Caterpillars," *Student Edition*, pp. 46–47

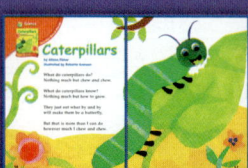

#### Robust Vocabulary
- *transform, examine, devour*

#### Grammar
- Review: Names of Days; Months

#### Shared Writing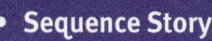
- Sequence Story

---

# Warm-Up Routines

## Oral Language

**Objective** *To listen attentively and respond appropriately to oral communication*

> ### Question of the Day
> Inchworms move slowly. When do you move slowly? Why?

Help children brainstorm times they move slowly and carefully, and have them tell why they move this way. Have them help complete the following sentence frame: **I move slowly when I _____ because _____.**

## Read Aloud

**Objectives** *To recognize and appreciate rhyme; to understand alliteration*

**BIG BOOK OF RHYMES AND POEMS** As you read the poem, have children raise their hand each time they hear a word with the /ch/ sound. Explain that many poets repeat words and sounds to create a rhythm, or beat, in a poem. Read aloud the first seven words again, and ask children what they hear repeated. (I, /ch/) Read the rest of poem and have them tell what other words or sounds they hear repeated. Then reread the poem. Ask them to identify rhyming words. (arch/march, pinch/inch, along/long, thickets/tickets)

▲ Big Book of Rhymes and Poems, p. 25

# Word Wall

**Objective** *To read high-frequency words*

**REVIEW HIGH-FREQUENCY WORDS** Review *air, fly, friends, grew, need, play, rain, watch,* and other previously learned high-frequency words. Say each word, ask a volunteer to point to it, and have children read it aloud. Then point to words at random and have children reread them. Repeat several times to reinforce instant recognition.

| | | | |
|---|---|---|---|
| air | fly | friends | grew |
| need | play | rain | watch |

# Phonemic Awareness

**Objective** *To delete medial phonemes to form new words*

**Routine Card 9** **PHONEME DELETION** Tell children you will say some words and ask them to take out a middle sound in each word to make a new word. Model by saying: **The sounds in *past* are /p/ /a/ /s/ /t/. *Past* without the /s/ is /p/ /a/ /t/—*pat*.** Say the following words and have children delete the identified middle sound to form a new word.

*fast* without /s/ (fat)          *west* without /s/ (wet)

*best* without /s/ (bet)          *cast* without /s/ (cat)

*plan* without /l/ (pan)          *trap* without /r/ (tap)

*trick* without /r/ (tick)          *lend* without /n/ (led)

*play* without /l/ (pay)          *fist* without /s/ (fit)

*spend* without /p/ (send)          *stand* without /t/ (sand)

# Build Words

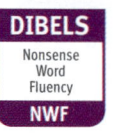 **phonics** *and Spelling*

**5-DAY PHONICS**

| | |
|---|---|
| **DAY 1** | Introduce Digraphs /ch/*ch*, *tch* |
| **DAY 2** | Word Building with Digraphs /ch/*ch*, *tch* |
| **DAY 3** | Word Building |
| **DAY 4** | Inflection -*es* |
| **DAY 5** | Inflection -*es* |

## Objectives

- *To discriminate between the letter-sound associations /ch/ch, tch and /sh/sh*
- *To use /ch/ch, tch, /sh/sh, and other known letter-sounds to de-code words*

## Skill Trace

 **Tested**

### Digraphs

| | /ch/*ch, tch* | /sh/sh |
|---|---|---|
| Introduce | T36–T39 | Bk 1-2 T482–T485 |
| Reteach | S2 | Bk 1-2, S52 |
| Review | T52–T53, T74–T75 | T498–T499 T522–T523 |
| Test | Bk 1-3 | Bk 1-2 |
| Maintain | Bk 1-4 T76–T77 | T74–T75 |

---

**Digraphs /ch/*ch, tch***

Mitch the chimp was in the kitchen.
"What's for lunch?" Mitch asked.
Rich said, "We have mush, chips, and chicken."
"We'll eat fish and shrimp, too."
Munch, crunch! Chomp, chomp!
"Yum!" said Mitch. "Thanks, Rich!"

Grade 1, Lesson 13    R25    Phonics: Digraphs /ch/*ch, tch*; /sh/sh*

**Transparency R25**

---

## Word Building

**DIBELS** Nonsense Word Fluency **NWF**

**Routine Card 14**

**BUILD AND READ WORDS** Use a pocket chart and *Letter Cards.* Have children repeat each step with their *Word Builders* and *Word Builder Cards.*

Build the word *much.* Then have children say the word naturally—*much.* Lead children in building another word that ends with a consonant digraph by saying:

- **Add an *n* after the *u*. Read the word.**
- **Take away the *n* and change *ch* to *sh*. Read the word.**
- **Change *u* to *a*. Read the word.**
- **Change *sh* to *tch*. Read the word.**

Continue, having children change consonant digraphs to build and read these words: *chap, champ, chimp, chip, ship.*

**BUILD AND READ TWO-SYLLABLE WORDS** Use a pocket chart and *Letter Cards.* Build words like the ones below. After each word is built, slide your hand under each syllable and say it with children. Then point to the word, read it naturally, and have children read it aloud.

| | | |
|---|---|---|
| **children** | **kitchen** | **shamrock** |
| **sandwich** | **ketchup** | **selfish** |

## Read Words in Context

**READ SENTENCES** Display **Transparency R25** or write the sentences on the board or on chart paper. Have children choral-read the story as you track the print. Then ask volunteers to read each sentence aloud. Call on volunteers to underline or frame words that have the sound /ch/ or /sh/.

**5-DAY SPELLING**

| DAY 1 | Pretest |
| DAY 2 | Word Building |
| DAY 3 | State the Generalization |
| DAY 4 | Review |
| DAY 5 | Posttest |

## Review Spelling Words

**STATE THE GENERALIZATION** List spelling words 1–6 on chart paper or the board and have children read them. Ask: **What is the same about words 1–4?** (They all have the /ch/ sound; they have *c, h*.) Discuss what is the same about words 5–6. (Both words have the /ch/ sound; they have *t,c,h*.) Have volunteers read each word and underline the letters that stand for the /ch/ sound. Tell children that the letter combinations *ch* and *tch* are used to spell the /ch/ sound.

**REVIEW WORDS** Follow a similar procedure for words 7–8. Talk about how both words are alike. (Both have the /sh/ sound spelled with the letters *sh*.) Have children read and spell the words.

**HIGH-FREQUENCY WORDS** List spelling words 9–10. Remind children that they have seen and read these words many times. Run your hand under *saw* as you read it, and ask children to look carefully at the letters. Ask them to close their eyes, picture the word in their minds, and spell it with you. Repeat for *were*.

**WRITE** Have children write the spelling words in their notebook. Remind them to use their best handwriting and to use the list to check their spelling.

# Handwriting

**LETTER FORMATION** Have children write the spelling words in their notebook. Guide them in correct letter formation, if they need help, and provide handwriting models (pp. R2–R7) for them to use to check their handwriting.

chip — match
chin — wish
inch — shop
such — saw
catch — were

### Spelling Words

1. chip
2. chin
3. inch
4. such
5. catch
6. match
7. wish
8. shop
9. saw
10. were

### Decodable Book

- **Phonics** Digraphs /ch/*ch, tch*
- **Decodable Words** Decodable Book 13 ▲

See the list on page R11. Have children who need additional decoding practice read "Ranch Pals" in *Decodable Book 13*. See also *Decodable Books* online (Take-Home Version).

▲ Spelling Practice Book, p. 44

#  High-Frequency Words

## Objective
• *To read high-frequency words*

**REVIEW** Tested

### High-Frequency Words

| | |
|---|---|
| air | need |
| fly | play |
| friends | rain |
| grew | watch |

**Model Usage** Tell children *grew* is the past tense of *grow: The tree* grew *very tall* tells that the growing already happened. Guide children to use *grew* and *grow* in oral sentences.

## Review

**DISPLAY THE WORDS** Write the word *air*. Have a volunteer read it. Erase the word, and ask children to spell it. Repeat the routine for *fly, friends, grew, need, play, rain,* and *watch.*

## Practice/Apply

**GUIDED PRACTICE** Give each child a set of word cards (*Teacher Resource Book*, p. 137), and have children spread the cards out so they can read them. Call out one of the words, and have children hold up and read aloud the matching word card. Continue until children can read the words automatically.

| air | fly | friends | grew |
|---|---|---|---|

**INDEPENDENT PRACTICE** Have partners practice reading the word cards to one another. Then have them take turns using the words in sentences. Finally, have children practice writing the words in their notebook.

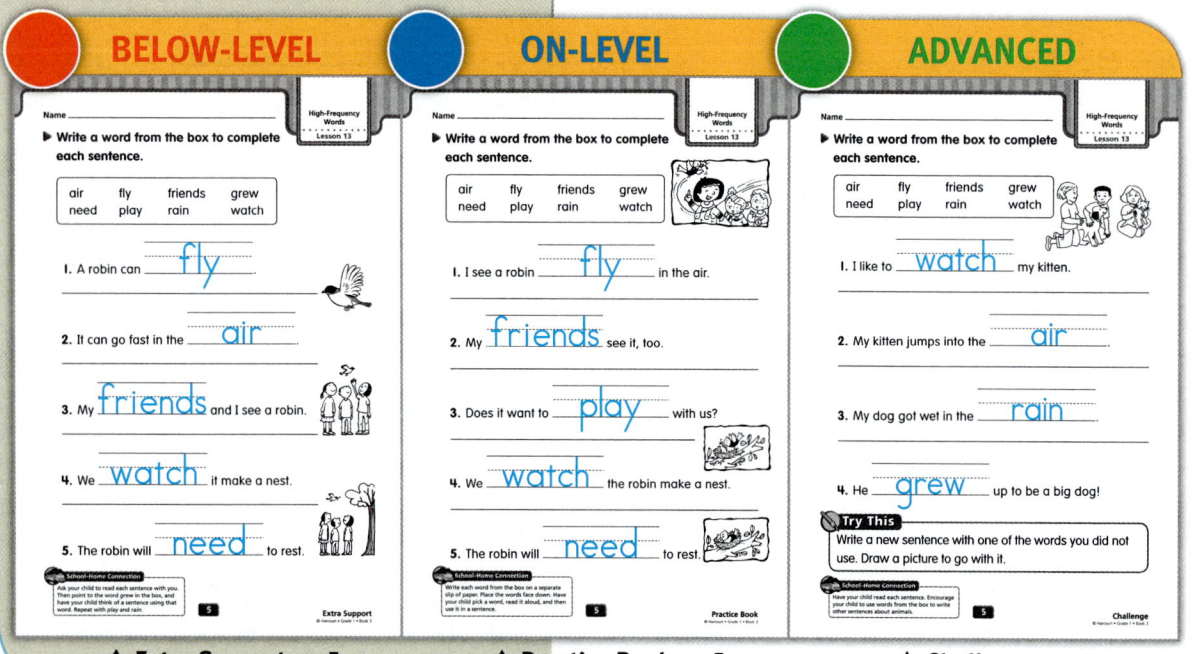

▲ Extra Support, p. 5    ▲ Practice Book, p. 5    ▲ Challenge, p. 5

**E L L**

• Group children according to academic levels, and assign one of the pages on the left.

• Clarify any unfamiliar concepts as necessary. See *ELL Teacher Guide,* Lesson 13, for support in scaffolding instruction.

# Fluency
*Intonation*

## Review

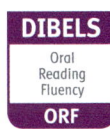

**DIBELS** Oral Reading Fluency **ORF**

**REVIEW INTONATION** Write the following sentence on the board.

### Where would you like to go?

Review that we say some words more strongly than others when we speak and read aloud. Words that name people, places, things, and actions are usually more important and so are said a little louder. "Little words" like *of, the, to,* and *for,* are said more softly. Have children listen and identify the word you stress as you read the sentence on the board: **Where would *you* like to go?** Tell them to listen again and say: **Where would you like to *go?*** Talk about how the meaning changed when you said *go* more strongly. Also, point out how your voice goes up at the end of the question.

Have children turn to page 35 in the *Student Edition* and read silently as you read **I eat this *plant* for lunch.** Have children repeat. Then read like this: **I eat *this* plant for lunch,** and have children repeat. Talk about how reading the sentence in different ways makes it mean different things.

## Practice/Apply

**GUIDED PRACTICE** Read aloud pages 30–31 with correct intonation, and have children echo-read. Ask them to notice which words are said more strongly and how their voices go up and down in each sentence.

**INDEPENDENT PRACTICE** Have each child choose a page from the selection and practice reading it with correct intonation. Allow children an opportunity to read aloud for classmates. Encourage listeners to give positive feedback by telling what the readers did well.

### Objective
• *To read with correct intonation in a manner that sounds like natural speech*

**Echo-Read** Have children echo-read the selection with you. Ask them to listen carefully to how your voice goes up and down in each sentence and which words you say a little louder. Ask them to read each sentence just as you have read it.

### MONITOR PROGRESS

#### Fluency

| **IF** children have difficulty reading with correct intonation, | **THEN** model reading with correct intonation as children track the print. Have them repeat. |
|---|---|

**Small-Group Instruction, pp. S4–S5:**

🔴 **BELOW-LEVEL:** Reteach
🔵 **ON-LEVEL:** Reinforce
🟢 **ADVANCED:** Extend

# Sequence
## *Comprehension*

## Objectives

- *To identify and describe the sequence of a selection*
- *To listen to a poem being read aloud for information and for enjoyment*
- *To respond to a poem through drama in a way that reflects understanding and interpretation*

## Skill Trace

 **Sequence**

| | |
|---|---|
| Preview | T46 |
| Introduce | T54–T55 |
| Reteach | S6–S7, S26–S27 |
| **Review** | **T78, T90, T100, T230, T238–T239, T262, T274, T284** |
| Test | Bk 1-3 |
| Maintain | Monitor Comprehension Bks 1–4, 1–5 |

## Review

**REVIEW SEQUENCE** Remind children that the events in a story or nonfiction selection happen in a certain order, called the sequence. Help them recall the sequence of events in "Hurry and the Monarch" from the *Read-Aloud Anthology*. You may want to work with children to fill in a Sequence Chart, **Transparency GO7,** with the important events from this story. Have them answer *who, what, when, where, why,* and *how* questions to help them retell the sequence of events.

## Practice/Apply

**GUIDED PRACTICE** Guide children to recall the sequence of events in "A Butterfly Grows."

**INDEPENDENT PRACTICE** Have children apply their knowledge of sequence by completing *Practice Book* page 6 and when responding to the poem "Caterpillars" that they will listen to.

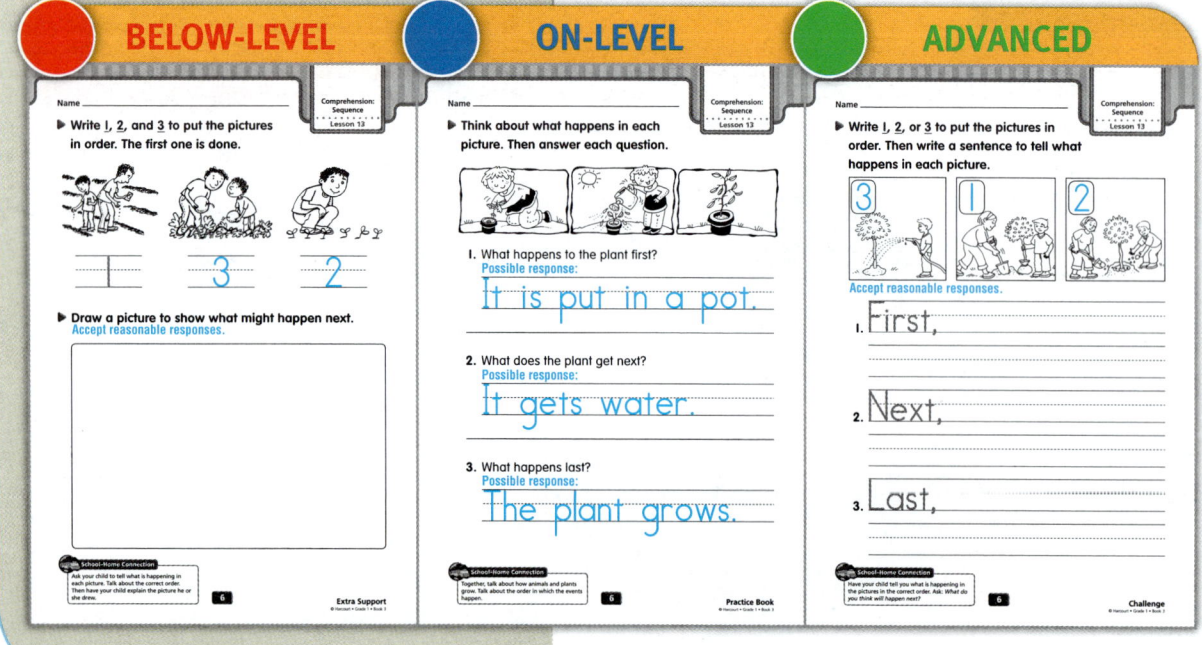

▲ Extra Support, p. 6    ▲ Practice Book, p. 6    ▲ Challenge, p. 6

**ELL**

- Group children according to academic levels, and assign one of the pages on the left.
- Clarify any unfamiliar concepts as necessary. See *ELL Teacher Guide,* Lesson 13, for support in scaffolding instruction.

Science

Caterpillars
by Aileen Fisher
Illustrated by Roberta Arenson

Teacher Read-Aloud

Poetry

# Caterpillars

by Aileen Fisher
illustrated by Roberta Arenson

What do caterpillars do?
Nothing much but chew and chew.

What do caterpillars know?
Nothing much but how to grow.

They just eat what by and by
will make them be a butterfly,

But that is more than I can do
however much I chew and chew.

46

47

# Reading

## Student Edition: Paired Selection

### Read Aloud

**Routine Card 17**

**USE PRIOR KNOWLEDGE/SET A PURPOSE** Guide children to use prior knowledge and set a purpose for listening.

**MONITOR LISTENING COMPREHENSION** As you read, monitor listening comprehension by using the following questions:

> **SEQUENCE What happens after caterpillars eat a lot?** (They grow.)

- **GENRE How can you tell this is a poem?** (It has rhyming words; words are used over and over in a creative way.)

**ON-LEVEL**

**Respond** Lead children to respond to the poem through drama in a way that reflects understanding and interpretation. Ask children to create simple movements and hand gestures to act out the poem. Then reread it, and have children interpret it through their actions. Encourage them to chime in, especially on the repeated words.

## Connections

### Comparing Texts

**1** What do the story and the poem say a caterpillar must do to grow?
Possible Responses: A caterpillar must eat.

**2** Tell about a butterfly or another bug you have seen. What did it do?
Accept reasonable responses.

**3** How have you changed as you have grown? Accept reasonable responses.

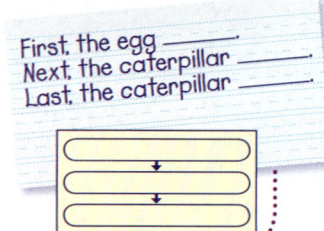

### Writing

Think about the story. Write three sentences to tell how a butterfly grows.

First, the egg _____.
Next, the caterpillar _____.
Last, the caterpillar _____.

48

### Phonics

Make and read new words.

Start with **chin**.

Switch [c] [h] and [i] [n].

Add [p] in front of [i].

Change [n] to [t].

Change [i] to [a].

### Fluency Practice

Read the story aloud with a partner. Make your voice go up or down. Make it loud or soft to sound as if the butterfly is really talking.

I am a butterfly!

I'm a beautiful butterfly!

49

# Connections

### WRITING

**Write Sentences** Guide children to recall the steps in a butterfly's growth described in "A Butterfly Grows." Have children respond to the story through writing in a way that reflects understanding and interpretation by writing three sentences that tell how a caterpillar grows and changes into a butterfly.

*First, the egg hatches.*

### PHONICS

**Word Building** Distribute to children *Word Builder Cards a, c, h, i, n, p,* and *t.* Have children practice manipulating the cards to build and read *chin, inch, pinch, pitch,* and *patch.*

### FLUENCY

**Partner Reading** Ask one partner to read what the caterpillar says and the other child to read what the butterfly says. Ask children to read it so that it sounds as if someone is really talking. You may want to model reading a few pages, using correct intonation, before children begin.

Then in ten days, out I come!

Look at me now!

# Build Robust Vocabulary

## Listening/Speaking: *Words About the Selection*

### Teach/Model

**Routine Card 15**

**INTRODUCE ROBUST VOCABULARY** Use *Routine Card 15* to introduce the words.

❶ Put the word in **selection context.**
❷ Provide the **Student-Friendly Explanation** for children.
❸ Have children **say the word** with you.
❹ Use the word in other contexts, and have children **interact with the word's meaning.**
❺ Say the Student-Friendly Explanation again, and ask children to **name the word** that goes with it.

❶ **Selection Context:** Caterpillars **transform** themselves into butterflies.

❹ **Interact with Word Meaning:** I read a story about how a frog could transform itself into a prince. Is it more likely that a caterpillar can transform itself into a butterfly or that a frog can transform itself into a prince?

❶ **Selection Context:** The author had to **examine** many caterpillars to find out how they eat.

❹ **Interact with Word Meaning:** I would find it interesting to examine how other insects grow and change. Which would you rather examine—a plain piece of paper or a butterfly?

❶ **Selection Context:** Caterpillars **devour** many leaves.

❹ **Interact with Word Meaning:** When I am very hungry, I devour everything on my plate. Which would you rather devour—spinach or an apple?

### Practice/Apply

**GUIDED PRACTICE** Ask children to do the following:
• Describe how to transform a messy room into a clean room.
• Show how to examine your finger to see if you have a splinter.

### Objective
• *To develop robust vocabulary through describing ideas*

**INTRODUCE** Tested ✓

### Student-Friendly Explanations

**transform** If you transform something, you totally change it.

**examine** If you examine something, you look at it closely.

**devour** If you devour something, you eat it all up very quickly.

**E L L**

**Introduce Vocabulary** Act out the meaning of each word. For example, demonstrate how you might devour one of your favorite foods if you had not eaten all day. Then say the word and have children repeat it after you.

#  Grammar

## Names of Days and Months

**5-DAY GRAMMAR**

| DAY 1 | Introduce Names of Days and Months |
| DAY 2 | Dictate Names of Days and Months |
| **DAY 3** | **Add Days and Months to Sentences** |
| DAY 4 | Revise Names of Days and Months |
| DAY 5 | Write Names of Days and Months |

### Objectives
- *To identify names of days and months*
- *To apply knowledge of basic rules of capitalization*

### Daily Proofreading

**it was raining on monday.**

(It, Monday)

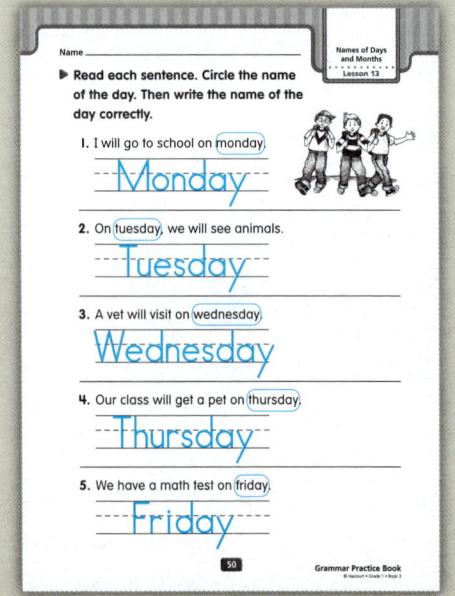

▲ Grammar Practice Book, p. 50

### Review

**DICTATE SENTENCES** Model sentences about school using the name of a day or a month, such as **We have a class birthday party on the last Friday of each month.** Ask children to dictate other sentences that include the name of a day or a month. Record their sentences without capitalizing these proper nouns. Read the sentences to children.

> We have a class birthday party on the last friday of each month.
>
> We plan the party on thursday.
>
> Last september, we had a party for Alberto.
>
> Pam and Kim had a birthday party in october.
>
> We played fun games in november.

### Practice/Apply

**GUIDED PRACTICE** Reread the first sentence to children, tracking the print. Model how to rewrite it correctly by capitalizing the name of the day of the week. Explain: **The word *Friday* is the name of the day of the week. We always capitalize the first letter of the names of days and months.**

Follow a similar procedure to guide children to correct the other sentences. Have a volunteer identify the word that names a day or a month. Then track the print and read the corrected sentences, asking children if the capital letters are correct.

**INDEPENDENT PRACTICE** Have children write another sentence that could be added to the story. Remind them to include the name of a day or month. Ask partners to read their sentences to one another and check that they capitalized words correctly.

# Shared Writing

*Sequence Story*

| **5-DAY** WRITING | |
| --- | --- |
| **DAY 1** | Modeled Writing |
| **DAY 2** | Shared Writing |
| **DAY 3** | **Shared Writing** |
| **DAY 4** | Independent Writing |
| **DAY 5** | Independent Writing |

## Write Together

**REVIEW A LITERATURE MODEL** Have children open their *Student Edition* to "A Butterfly Grows" and read aloud these sentences with you.

p. 36: **I eat and grow, eat and grow. Now I am big!**

p. 38: **At last I am a chrysalis. I'm an inch long.
Then in ten days, out I come!**

After reading, discuss the sequence of events in these sentences. Ask what happened first and what happened next.

 **PRACTICE WRITING** Have children look again at the graphic organizer they completed on Day 1. Continue helping them, modeling how to write the sentences they dictate in their sequence story. Guide children to use sequence words when writing. Add the sentences to the story written on Day 2.

**WRITING TRAIT** **ORGANIZATION** Explain that good writers tell about the events in their stories in an order that makes sense. They use words like *first, next,* and *last* to make it clear when things happen.

## Share

**DISCUSS THE SEQUENCE STORY** Read the finished story with children, tracking the print. Then ask children to

- identify the events in the beginning, middle, and ending of the story.

- identify words that signal sequence.

- identify capital letters in names of days and months.

Display the sequence story. Children can use the story as a writing model for Days 4 and 5.

### Objectives

- *To compose a story that has a clear sequence of events*
- *To identify sequence words*
- *To understand the basic rules of punctuation and capitalization*

### Writing Prompt

**Write About School** Have children write about what they did yesterday at school.

## Day at a Glance

### Day 4

**Phonemic Awareness**
- Phoneme Deletion

 **and Spelling**
- Introduce: Inflection *-es*

**High-Frequency Words**
- Review: *air, fly, friends, grew, need, play, rain, watch*

**Fluency**
- Intonation
- "A Butterfly Grows," *Student Edition,* pp. 28–45

**Comprehension**

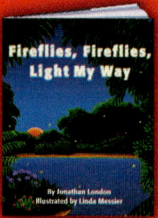 Review: Sequence

- Big Book: *Fireflies, Fireflies, Light My Way*

**Robust Vocabulary**
- Review: *transform, examine, devour*

**Grammar**
- Review: Names of Days; Months

**Independent Writing**
- Sequence Story

# Warm-Up Routines

## Oral Language

**Objectives** *To listen attentively and respond appropriately to oral communication; to use sensory words in a description*

**Question of the Day**

Pretend you are holding a caterpillar or a butterfly in your hand.

How does it look and feel?

Help children brainstorm sensory words that describe a caterpillar and butterfly. Help children complete the following sentence frames.

**A caterpillar is _____. A butterfly is _____.**

## Read Aloud

**Objective** *To identify the rhythm of a poem*

**BIG BOOK OF RHYMES AND POEMS** Display the poem and read the title and the poet's name. Tell children to listen for the rhythm, or beat, of the poem and to find out what creature the poem is about. Read the poem, keeping the beat by clapping your hands. Then ask children what the poem is about. Reread the poem, asking children to clap along with the beat and to chime in. Have children tell what they noticed about the beat. Elicit that the poem has a strong rhythm—it's easy to clap the beat. Ask children to tell what they liked about this poem.

▲ Big Book of Rhymes and Poems, p. 26

# Word Wall

**Objective** *To read high-frequency words*

**REVIEW HIGH-FREQUENCY WORDS** Review *air, fly, friends, grew, be, of, too, grow, was, now,* and other previously learned high-frequency words. Say each word, ask a volunteer to point to it, and have children read it aloud. Then point to words at random and have children reread them. Repeat several times to reinforce instant recognition.

# Phonemic Awareness

**Objective** *To delete medial phonemes to form new words*

**PHONEME DELETION** Tell children they will sing a song and delete one of the middle sounds that they hear in a word. Model the first example for them. *(Sing to the tune of "The Farmer in the Dell.")*

*Cast* without /s/ is *cat*. *Cast* without /s/ is *cat*.
Hi-ho, the derrio. *Cast* without /s/ is *cat*.

Continue singing the song, using the words below. Have children clap as they sing each new word.

*mast* without /s/ (mat)    *dusk* without /s/ (duck)

*mint* without /n/ (mitt)    *task* without /s/ (tack)

*hint* without /n/ (hit)    *fact* without /k/ (fat)

*plants* without /l/ (pants)    *tracks* without /r/ (tacks)

# Inflection -es

phonics

| 5-DAY PHONICS | |
|---|---|
| DAY 1 | Introduce Digraphs /ch/ch, tch |
| DAY 2 | Word Building with Digraphs /ch/ch, tch |
| DAY 3 | Word Building |
| DAY 4 | Inflection -es |
| DAY 5 | Inflection -es |

## Objectives

- *To recognize root words*
- *To read the inflectional form* -es

## Skill Trace

**Inflection -es**

| Introduce | T86 |
|---|---|
| Review | T96 |

 **phonics** Resources

Phonics Practice Book,
pp. 71–72

### Inflection -es

Fran pitches the ball.
It swishes! Rich swings and misses.
Fran scratches her chin.
Then she tosses a fast ball.
It swishes! The pitch is a good one.
Rich swings and smashes the ball with his bat.
Fang fetches the ball from the porch.
Rich dashes home.

Grade 1, Lesson 13      R26      Phonics: Inflection -es

**Transparency R26**

## Teach/Model

**INTRODUCE -es** Write the following words on the board:

| foxes | bushes | bunches | catches |
|---|---|---|---|
| buses | dresses | buzzes | classes |

As you read each word, underline the root word and point out the -es ending. Have children repeat each word. Ask: **How are all these words alike?** (They all have the ending -es.) Explain that -es, rather than -s, is added when a word ends in *x, s, ss, ch, tch, sh,* or *zz.*

## Guided Practice

**ADD -es** Make a chart as shown. Model reading the parts of each word separately and then together. Have children repeat after you. For example, say: **box, -es, boxes.** Tell children that adding -es adds another word part, or syllable, to the word. Also point out the nouns that name more than one when -es is added. Save the chart for Day 5.

| Root Word | + Ending = | New Word |
|---|---|---|
| box | es | boxes |
| toss | es | tosses |
| porch | es | porches |
| match | es | matches |
| rush | es | rushes |
| fizz | es | fizzes |
| bus | es | buses |

## Practice/Apply

**READ WORDS IN CONTEXT** Display **Transparency R26.** Have children read each sentence silently. Then ask volunteers to read each sentence aloud. Point to the word (s) with the inflection *es,* and have children identify the root word and the ending. Then track the print as you lead children in choral-reading the sentences.

# Digraphs /ch/ *ch, tch*
**phonics** *and Spelling*

| 5-DAY SPELLING | |
|---|---|
| **DAY 1** | Pretest |
| **DAY 2** | Word Building |
| **DAY 3** | State the Generalization |
| **DAY 4** | Review |
| **DAY 5** | Posttest |

## Build Words

**MAP LETTERS TO SOUNDS** Use *Letter Cards* and a pocket chart to form words. Have children listen to your directions and change one letter in each word to spell a spelling word. Have them write the word on a sheet of paper or in their notebook. Then have a volunteer change the *Letter Card* in the pocket chart so that children can self-check their spelling.

- Form *chap* in the pocket chart and have children read it. Ask: **Which spelling word can you make by changing the third letter?** *(chip)*

- Leave *chip* in the pocket chart. Ask: **Which spelling word can you make by changing the last letter?** *(chin)*

- Leave *chin* in the pocket chart. Ask: **Which spelling word can you make by switching the first two letters with the last two letters?** *(inch)*

Follow a similar procedure with the following words: *much (such)*, *patch (match)*, *match (catch)*, *dish (wish)*, and *chop (shop)*.

**HIGH-FREQUENCY WORDS** Remind children that there are some other words they have to remember how to spell. Tell them that *saw* is one such word. Tell children to picture the word and then write it. Continue with *were*.

### Objectives
- *To use /ch/ch, tch and other known letter-sounds to spell and write words*
- *To spell and write known high-frequency words*

### Spelling Words

| | | | |
|---|---|---|---|
| 1. | chip | 6. | match |
| 2. | chin | 7. | wish |
| 3. | inch | 8. | shop |
| 4. | such | 9. | saw |
| 5. | catch | 10. | were |

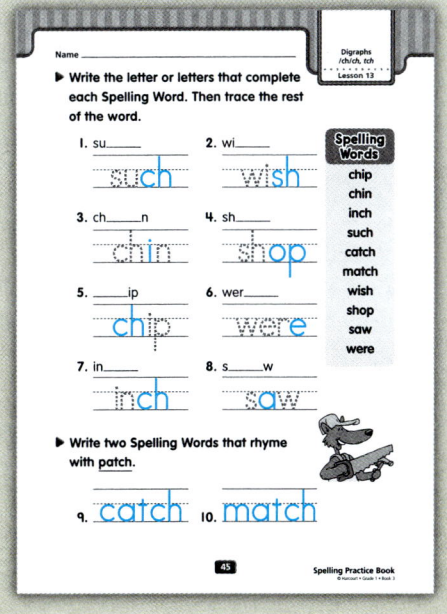

▲ Spelling Practice Book, p. 45

### BELOW-LEVEL

**Map Letters to Sounds** Display *Letter Cards* for each word in random order. For each word, help children make a connection between each sound and its letter or letters by saying it one phoneme at a time. Arrange the letters to spell the word. Then have children write the word.

#  High-Frequency Words

## Objective
- *To read high-frequency words*

**REVIEW** Tested

### High-Frequency Words

| | |
|---|---|
| air | need |
| fly | play |
| friends | rain |
| grew | watch |

## Review

**READ AND WRITE WORDS** Duplicate and distribute to each child an uncut story strip page (*Teacher Resource Book,* p. R223). Then do the following:

- Have children read the story title in the first strip. Explain that the sentences tell the story, but that some have missing words.

- Display *Word Cards* for the high-frequency words, or list the words on the board. Have children read each word.

| air | fly | friends | grew |
|---|---|---|---|

## Practice/Apply

**GUIDED PRACTICE** Direct children to read all the story strip sentences and to write the missing words in the blanks.

> **I drink small drops of <u>rain</u>.**

**INDEPENDENT PRACTICE** After children complete the story strips page, have them cut apart the strips. Have partners work together to read and match their story strips and then to arrange the events in the order in which they happen. Have children take the story strips home to share with family members.

Children read the words in context in the Cut-Out/Fold-Up Book.

**Review Story Events** Have children cut apart the completed story strips and glue each one at the bottom of a sheet of paper. Guide children to illustrate each sentence. Then have children use the captioned pictures to retell the story to a small group.

◄ "A Hen and Her Chicks" Practice Book, pp. 45–46

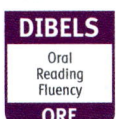 # Fluency
## *Intonation*

### Review

**DIBELS**
Oral Reading Fluency
**ORF**

**MODEL READING WITH APPROPRIATE INTONATION** Remind children that when good readers read, they make it sound the way it does when someone is talking. Model using correct intonation for children. Have children open to page 30 in "A Butterfly Grows."

▲ **Student Edition, pp. 28–45**

**Think Aloud** **I'm going to read "A Butterfly Grows" one page at a time. As I read, I'm going to make sure that my voice goes up and down and that I say some words more strongly than others so it sounds as if I am the caterpillar or butterfly really talking. Read each page after me, just the way I read it.**

### Practice/Apply

**GUIDED PRACTICE** Have partners read "A Butterfly Grows" aloud three or four times. Listen to partners read. Correct intonation errors by modeling the correct stresses and having the child repeat after you.

**INDEPENDENT PRACTICE** Have children take the parts of the caterpillar and the butterfly and practice reading their parts of "A Butterfly Grows" fluently with appropriate intonation. Then have partners make stick puppets using character cutouts, *Teacher Resource Book,* p. 192, and use them to act out the selection as they read it aloud for the group. Have children read aloud with fluency in a manner that sounds like natural speech.

### Objectives

- *To build fluency through rereading a story*
- *To read in a manner that sounds like natural speech*

### ● BELOW-LEVEL

**Fluency Practice** Have children reread for fluency, using "How Many?" in the *Book 1-3 Strategic Intervention Interactive Reader, Decodable Book 13,* or the appropriate *Leveled Reader.* (See pages T104–T107.) Guide them to select a small portion of a story and practice reading it several times.

### Additional Related Reading

Guide children to self-select related books, such as these:

- ***Beautiful Bugs*** by Ana Larrañaga. Polka Dot, 2000. **EASY**
- ***It's a Good Thing There Are Insects*** by Allan Fowler. Children's Press, 1991. **AVERAGE**
- ***Waiting for Wings*** by Lois Ehlert. Harcourt, 2001. **CHALLENGE**

# Sequence
*Comprehension*

## Objective
- *To identify the sequence of events*

### Skill Trace
 **Tested Sequence**

| Preview | T46 |
|---|---|
| Introduce | T54–T55 |
| Reteach | S6–S7, S26–S27 |
| **Review** | **T78, T90, T100, T230, T238–T239, T262, T274, T284** |
| Test | Bk 1-3 |
| Maintain | Monitor Comprehension Bks 1-4, 1-5 |

###  MONITOR PROGRESS

 **Comprehension: Sequence**

| **IF** children do not understand sequence, | **THEN** use familiar texts to discuss the order of events in a story. |
|---|---|

**Small-Group Instruction, p. S6–S7:**

- ● **BELOW-LEVEL:** Reteach
- ● **ON-LEVEL:** Reinforce
- ● **ADVANCED:** Extend

**Sequence Cards** Photocopy pictures of the animals from the *Big Book* or have children draw them on cards. Have children mix up the cards and then put them in the sequence in which they appear in the story.

## Review

**TALK ABOUT SEQUENCE** Review what the sequence of a story or nonfiction selection is. (The sequence is the order of the events.) Point out that in the *Big Book,* the storyteller meets the animals in a certain order.

**USE PRIOR KNOWLEDGE/SET A PURPOSE** Display the *Big Book.* Invite children to tell what they recall about the story. Guide them to set a purpose for listening. Tell them to listen for the order in which the author meets the animals.

**EXAMINE CONCEPTS OF PRINT** As you read, point out the ellipses. Explain that they signal the reader to pause briefly. Point out that by using ellipses, the author invites readers to guess what will come next. Have children participate actively when you read the patterned selection *Fireflies, Fireflies, Light My Way.* Invite them to chime in on reading the repeated line "Lead me to the place . . . ."

## Practice/Apply

**GUIDED PRACTICE** Monitor listening comprehension as you read, using the following questions:

- **RECOGNIZE STORY STRUCTURE** **What pattern do you see in this story? What do the characters do?** (The storyteller meets animals that lead him to new groups of animals.)

-  **Page 30: SEQUENCE** **What page helps you recall the sequence in which the storyteller meets the animals?** (the page that lists all the animals) **Why do you think that the storyteller meets the alligators last?** (The alligators are the most dangerous and exciting. They chase the storyteller.)

**INDEPENDENT PRACTICE** Have children identify the sequence of the events in the *Big Book.* Page through the illustrations and have children identify the animals in sequence. List their ideas on the board, and then check the list against the one at the end of the story.

# Build Robust Vocabulary

## Listening/Speaking: *Words About the Selection*

### Review Robust Vocabulary

**USE VOCABULARY IN DIFFERENT CONTEXTS** Remind children of the Student-Friendly Explanations of *transform, examine,* and *devour.* Then discuss each word, using the following examples:

**transform** Tell children that you will name some things that might transform themselves. If children think this could happen, they should raise a hand. If not, they should do nothing.

| | |
|---|---|
| **a worm** | **a book** |
| **a stack of paper** | **a seed** |
| **a flower** | **a caterpillar** |

**examine** Tell children that you will name some things, and if they think they could examine a thing, they should point to their eyes. If not, they should do nothing.

| | |
|---|---|
| **a colorful butterfly** | **a beautiful song** |
| **water** | **a large caterpillar** |
| **a nice smell** | **a book** |

**devour** Tell children that you will name some foods, and if they would want to devour the food, they should point to their mouths. If not, they should do nothing.

**muffins**

**pizza**

**steak**

**onions**

**peas**

**chocolate cake**

**broccoli**

**sandwich**

### Objective
- *To review robust vocabulary*

**Tested**

**REVIEW** ✓

### Student-Friendly Explanations

**transform** If you transform something, you totally change it.

**examine** If you examine something, you look at it closely.

**devour** If you devour something, you eat it all up very quickly.

### ADVANCED

**Create Clues for Vocabulary**
Invite children to create clues for the Vocabulary Words. Have them say their clues and challenge their classmates to guess the word.

# Grammar
## Names of Days and Months

**5-DAY GRAMMAR**

| | |
|---|---|
| **DAY 1** | Introduce Names of Days and Months |
| **DAY 2** | Dictate Names of Days and Months |
| **DAY 3** | Add Days and Months to Sentences |
| **DAY 4** | **Revise Names of Days and Months** |
| **DAY 5** | Write Names of Days and Months |

### Objective
- *To use knowledge of basic rules of capitalization*

### Daily Proofreading

**We go to skool in april.**
(school, April)

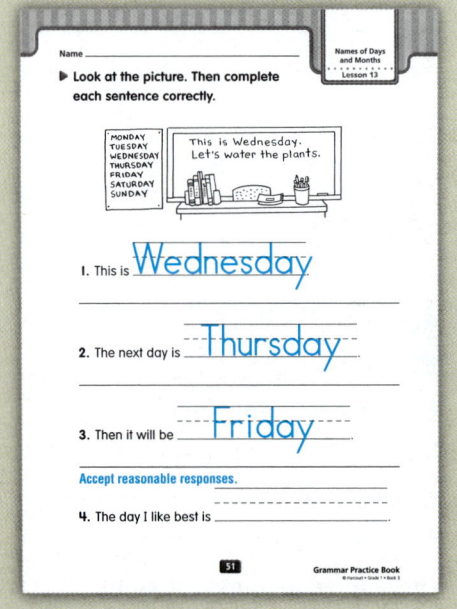

▲ Grammar Practice Book, p. 51

### Review

**IDENTIFY NAMES OF DAYS AND MONTHS** Display a one-year calendar, or use **Transparency LA25,** and lead children in reciting the names of the days of the week and the months of the year. Then ask the following and record children's answers on the board: **What day of the week is today? How do we write it? What month of the year is it? How do we write it?**

### Practice/Apply

**GUIDED PRACTICE** Write the following sentence frames on the board and read them aloud to children.

Today is _____.
The day I like best is _____.
This month is _____.
The month I like best is _____.

Work with children to add words to complete the sentences.

**INDEPENDENT PRACTICE** Write these sentences on the board and read them aloud to children. Explain that the names of the days and months are not written correctly. Have children choose two sentences and write them correctly by adding capital letters. Guide children to use basic capitalization skills, such as capitalizing the first word in a sentence, the pronoun *I,* and proper nouns.

1. the first day of the school week is monday.

2. the last day of the school week is friday.

3. i did not go to school on saturday and sunday.

4. the first month of the year is january.

5. the last month of the year is december.

6. the shortest month is february.

**5-DAY** WRITING
| DAY 1 | Modeled Writing |
| DAY 2 | Shared Writing |
| DAY 3 | Shared Writing |
| **DAY 4** | **Independent Writing** |
| DAY 5 | Independent Writing |

# Independent Writing
## *Sequence Story*

## Write a Story

**GENERATE IDEAS** Tell children they will write their own sequence story to tell about a sequence of events. Have them decide on a topic for a sequence story, such as a family trip. Have them fill in a Sequence Chart (*Teacher Resource Book,* p. 164) with sketches or notes about the events in the order in which they happened.

**REVIEW CHARACTERISTICS** Display the list of characteristics of a well-written sequence story from Day 1, and read it with children.

**ORGANIZATION** Remind children that they should write their story in an order that makes sense. Explain that they can look at their graphic organizer to know what to write next and use words like *first, next,* and *last* to show the order of events.

**WRITE** Ask children to begin writing their sequence stories, using their graphic organizers for ideas. Remind them to capitalize the names of days and months. Guide children to write with more proficient spelling of inflectional endings by reminding them to add the ending *-es* when a word ends in *ch, tch, sh, x, s,* or *zz.* Save the drafts to have children add to and revise on Day 5.

### Sequence Story
- It tells events in order.
- It uses words such as <u>first, next,</u> and <u>last.</u>
- It has a beginning, a middle, and an ending.

*On Saturday, I went to my friend Dan's house. First, we played hide and seek in his yard. That's when I found a turtle!*

### Objectives
- *To choose a focus for writing*
- *To generate ideas about a topic*
- *To write a story in a logical order*
- *To use sequence words in writing*

### Writing Prompt
**Vacation Sentences** Have children draw and write about their favorite vacation.

### ADVANCED
**Use Signal Words** Have children write detailed sentences that describe the sequence of events. Encourage them to use unique signal words to show the sequence, such as *in the morning, after that,* and *finally.*

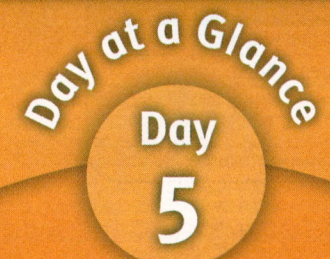

## Day at a Glance

### Day 5

**Phonemic Awareness**
- Phoneme Deletion

 **and Spelling**
- Review: Inflection *-es*
- Posttest: Digraphs /ch/*ch, tch*

**High-Frequency Words**
- Review

**Fluency**
- Intonation
- "A Butterfly Grows," *Student Edition*, pp. 28-45

**Comprehension**

 Review: Sequence

**Robust Vocabulary**
- Review

**Grammar**
- Review: Names of Days and Months

**Independent Writing**
- Sequence Story

# Warm-Up Routines

## Oral Language

**Objectives** *To listen attentively and respond appropriately to oral communication; to express personal preferences*

### Question of the Day

Would you rather be a caterpillar or a butterfly? Why?

Write the following sentence frame and help children complete it.

**I would rather be a _____ because _____.**

## Read Aloud

**Objectives** *To distinguish genre; to use drama to show understanding and interpretation*

**BIG BOOK OF RHYMES AND POEMS** Reread the poem. Ask: **How can you tell that this is a poem?** (Words rhyme; it has a strong rhythm; words are used in a creative way.)

Invite children to use drama to demonstrate their understanding of the poem by moving their bodies in ways that interpret the meaning of the poem as you reread it. Encourage them to join in on the words they know.

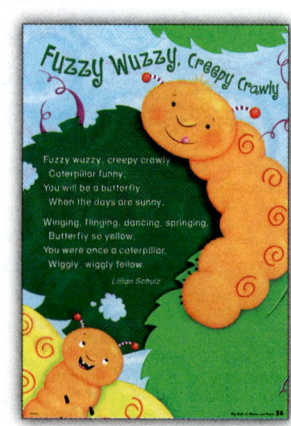

▲ **Big Book of Rhymes and Poems, p. 26**

## Word Wall

**Objective** *To read high-frequency words*

**REVIEW HIGH-FREQUENCY WORDS** Review *need, play, rain, watch, saw,* and *were*. Point to the words at random several times, and have children read them. Then point to all the words displayed, one at a time, and have children read them.

need
play
rain
watch
saw

## Phonemic Awareness

**Objective** *To delete initial and medial phonemes from words*

**PHONEME DELETION** Tell children they will sing a song and delete a sound that they hear in a given word. Explain that this sound can be either the first sound or the middle sound of the word. Model:

*(Sing to the tune of "The Farmer in the Dell.")*

*Hill* without /h/ is *ill. Hill* without /h/ is *ill.*
Hi-ho, the derrio. *Hill* without /h/ is *ill.*

Continue singing the song, using the words below. Have children participate by clapping as they sing each new word.

| | |
|---|---|
| trail without /t/ (rail) | slap without /s/ (lap) |
| wall without /w/ (all) | stalk without /s/ (talk) |
| truck without /r/ (tuck) | flat without /l/ (fat) |
| clap without /l/ (cap) | past without /s/ (pat) |
| lost without /s/ (lot) | stack without /t/ (sack) |

# Inflection -es
**phonics**

**5-DAY PHONICS**

| | |
|---|---|
| DAY I | Introduce Digraphs /ch/ch, tch |
| DAY 2 | Word Building with Digraphs /ch/ch, tch |
| DAY 3 | Word Building |
| DAY 4 | Inflection -es |
| DAY 5 | Inflection -es |

## Objectives
- To recognize root words
- To read inflectional forms with no spelling changes

## Skill Trace
**Inflection -es**

| | |
|---|---|
| Introduce | T86 |
| Review | T96 |

### Review

**ROOT WORDS AND ENDINGS** Remind children that when a word ends in *ch, tch, sh, x, s, ss,* or *zz,* the ending -es is added. Write *hatch.* Ask children how to spell *hatches.* Write *hatches.* Ask volunteers to use both words in sentences. Repeat with *fox* and *foxes.* Explain how *foxes* is plural.

### Work with Patterns

**ADDING ENDINGS** Display the chart from Day 4. Ask volunteers to read each new word. Have children add more words.

| Root Word | + Ending = | New Word |
|---|---|---|
| box | es | boxes |
| toss | es | tosses |
| porch | es | porches |
| match | es | matches |
| rush | es | rushes |
| fizz | es | fizzes |
| bus | es | buses |

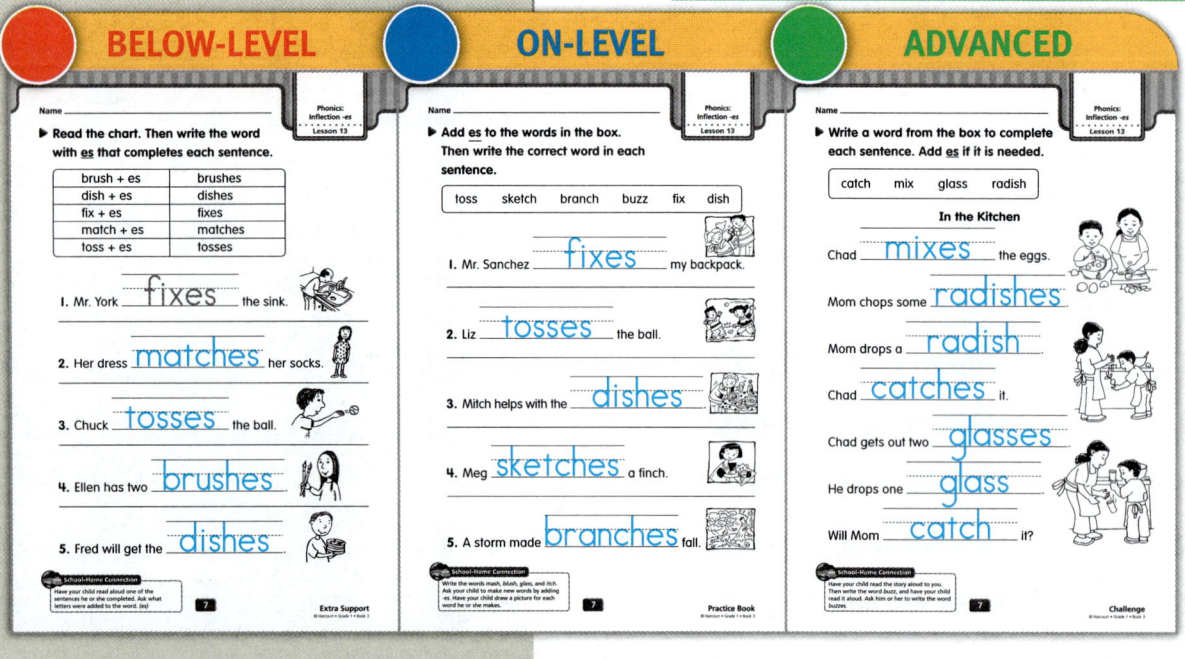

▲ Extra Support, p. 7        ▲ Practice Book, p. 7        ▲ Challenge, p. 7

- Group children according to academic levels, and assign one of the pages on the left.
- Clarify any unfamiliar concepts as necessary. See *ELL Teacher Guide,* Lesson 13, for support in scaffolding instruction.

# Digraphs /ch/ ch, tch

**phonics** *and Spelling*

**5-DAY SPELLING**

| | |
|---|---|
| **DAY 1** | Pretest |
| **DAY 2** | Word Building |
| **DAY 3** | State the Generalization |
| **DAY 4** | Review |
| **DAY 5** | Posttest |

## Assess

**POSTTEST** Assess children's progress. Use the dictation sentences from Day 1.

**Words with /ch/ ch, tch**

1. chip — There is a **chip** on this broken cup.
2. chin — Your **chin** is below your mouth.
3. inch — The paper clip is about one **inch** long.
4. such — That is **such** a nice car!
5. catch — Let's play **catch** with the ball.
6. match — Can you **match** the words and pictures?

**Review**

7. wish — I **wish** we could go to the movies.
8. shop — That **shop** sells books.

**High-Frequency**

9. saw — I **saw** him at school.
10. were — There **were** toys in the box.

**WRITING APPLICATION** Have children complete and illustrate the following sentence frames.

I wish I could catch _____.

I saw a _____ that is one inch long.

I saw a bug that is one inch long.

## Objectives

- *To use /ch/ ch, tch and other known letter-sounds to spell and write words*
- *To spell and write known high-frequency words*

### Spelling Words

| | | | |
|---|---|---|---|
| 1. | **chip** | 6. | **match** |
| 2. | **chin** | 7. | **wish** |
| 3. | **inch** | 8. | **shop** |
| 4. | **such** | 9. | **saw** |
| 5. | **catch** | 10. | **were** |

# High-Frequency Words

## Objectives
- *To read high-frequency words*
- *To explore word relationships*

**REVIEW**  Tested

### High-Frequency Words

| air | grow | rain |
|-----|------|------|
| be | need | saw |
| fly | now | too |
| friends | of | was |
| grew | play | watch |

### BELOW-LEVEL

**Reinforce Word Recognition**

If children are having difficulty with a high-frequency word, have them spell it aloud with you while tracing the letters in the air. Then have them write the word on paper.

## Review

**REINFORCE WORD RECOGNITION** Display *Word Cards* for all of the words in a pocket chart. Point to words at random and ask children to read them aloud.

**SORT WORDS** Guide children in sorting the words into two columns by looking at each word and discussing whether it is a noun or is not a noun. Remind children that nouns can be people, places, animals, or things. Then have them read the words in each column aloud.

- Ask: **Which word means the opposite of *work*?** *(play)*

- Ask: **Which words name things that butterflies might do?** *(fly, grow, play)*

- Ask: **Which two words have the same letters but in a different order?** *(saw, was)*

- Ask: **Which words have two letters?** *(be, of)* **Three letters?** *(air, fly, now, saw, too, was)* **Four letters?** *(grew, grow, need, play, rain)*

- Ask: **Which word has the /ch/ sound?** *(watch)*

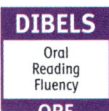

# Fluency
## *Intonation*

### Readers' Theater

▲ **Student Edition, pp. 28–45**

**DIBELS**
Oral Reading Fluency
**ORF**

**PERFORM "A BUTTERFLY GROWS"** To help children improve their fluency, have them perform "A Butterfly Grows" as Readers' Theater. Use the following procedures:

- Read "A Butterfly Grows" aloud, modeling fluent reading with appropriate intonation as children follow along.

- Discuss with children how the storyteller might sound when talking about life as a caterpillar and then as a butterfly.

- Have partners read the selection together. Then have them choose the part of the caterpillar or the butterfly and practice rereading the text with appropriate intonation, making their voices sound as if the animals are really speaking.

- Invite partners to read the selection to classmates.

### ON-LEVEL

**Develop Vocabulary** As you discuss how characters in the story might feel and sound, focus on emotion words, such as *excited* and *surprised*. Act out each word and model how someone feeling that way might sound when speaking.

### Objective
- *To read fluently with appropriate intonation*

### ASSESSMENT

**Monitoring Progress** Periodically, take a timed sample of children's oral reading and measure the number of words read correctly per minute. Children should be accurately reading approximately 60 words per minute by the end of Grade 1.

### Fluency Support Materials

**Fluency Builders, Grade 1,** Lesson 13

**Audiotext** *Student Edition* selections are available on *Audiotext Grade 1,* CD 3.

**Strategic Intervention Teacher Guide,** Lesson 13

# Sequence
## *Comprehension*

## Objective
• *To identify and describe the sequence of a story*

## Skill Trace

 **Sequence**

| Preview | T46 |
|---|---|
| Introduce | T54–T55 |
| Reteach | S6–S7, S26–S27 |
| Review | T78, T90, T100, T230, T238–T239, T262, T274, T284 |
| Test | Bk 1–3 |
| Maintain | Monitor Comprehension Bk 1–4, 1–5 |

### ● ADVANCED

**Independent Practice** Invite children to recall a story they have recently read. Have them write the sequence of story events in their notebook or on a flow chart.

## Review

☐ **REVIEW THE SKILL** Ask children to explain sequence. (the order of events in a story) Draw a three-column chart on the board, or use **Transparency GO2,** and add the titles "Hurry and the Monarch," "A Butterfly Grows," and *Fireflies, Fireflies, Light My Way*. Remind children that these are the read-aloud, the *Student Edition* selection, and the *Big Book* they read this week. Ask children to recall the sequence of events from "Hurry and the Monarch," and record their responses.

## Practice/Apply

**GUIDED PRACTICE** Ask volunteers to tell the sequence of events in "A Butterfly Grows." Write their responses in the second column. Then repeat with *Fireflies, Fireflies, Light My Way*.

| "Hurry and the Monarch" | "A Butterfly Grows" | Fireflies, Fireflies, Light My Way |
|---|---|---|
| First, a butterfly lands on Hurry's back and they get to know each other. | First, the caterpillar hatches out of an egg. | First, the child sees fireflies. They lead him to meet many animals. |
| Next, the butterfly flies away, and Hurry meets a caterpillar. | Next, the caterpillar eats and grows. It becomes a chrysalis. | Next, the child finds alligators that chase him. |
| Last, the caterpillar becomes a butterfly and leaves. | Last, the caterpillar becomes a butterfly. | Last, he gets away from the alligators. |

**INDEPENDENT PRACTICE** Have children page through "Rich Gets Big" in their *Student Edition* to help them recall the selection. Ask children to tell about the sequence of events.

# Build Robust Vocabulary

## Listening/Speaking

### Review

**REINFORCE MEANINGS** Ask children the following questions.

- Would you find it *astonishing* to watch someone *devour* thirty sandwiches for lunch? Why or why not?

- Would you *continue* to *doubt* a friend who told you each day that his cat could talk? Why?

- How could you *examine* a caterpillar that was *transforming* itself into a butterfly?

**MAKE CHOICES** Pose these choices and have children explain their responses:

- If you find a TV program *astonishing,* would you want to watch it or turn off the TV? Why?

- If you *doubt* what someone has told you, would you disagree or agree with that person? Why?

- If you *continue* to talk during a fire drill, are you following the rules or breaking them? Why?

- If you put a cup of water in the freezer, would it be *transformed* or stay the same? Explain.

- If you wanted to *examine* a caterpillar, would you use your eyes or your ears? Why?

- Would you be more likely to *devour* your dinner if you had a snack right after lunch or after school? Why?

**Objective**

- *To review robust vocabulary*

**REVIEW**

**Build Robust Vocabulary**

| | |
|---|---|
| astonishing | doubt |
| continue | examine |
| devour | transform |

 **MONITOR PROGRESS**

**Build Robust Vocabulary**

| **IF** children do not demonstrate understanding of the words and have difficulty using them, | **THEN** model using each word in several sentences. Have children repeat each sentence. |
|---|---|

**Small-Group Instruction, pp. S8–S9:**

- 🔴 **BELOW-LEVEL:** Reteach
- 🔵 **ON-LEVEL:** Reinforce
- 🟢 **ADVANCED:** Extend

# Grammar

## Names of Days and Months

| 5-DAY GRAMMAR | |
| --- | --- |
| DAY 1 | Introduce Names of Days and Months |
| DAY 2 | Dictate Names of Days and Months |
| DAY 3 | Add Days and Months to Sentences |
| DAY 4 | Revise Names of Days and Months |
| DAY 5 | Write Names of Days and Months |

## Objectives

- *To write complete, coherent sentences that contain the names of days and months*
- *To capitalize the names of days and months correctly*

### Daily Proofreading

**saturday is the first day of march.**

(Saturday, March)

### ✓ Language Arts Checkpoint

If children have difficulty with the concepts, see pages S10–S11 to reteach.

▲ Practice Book, p. 8

## Review

**WRITE NAMES OF DAYS AND MONTHS** Display **Transparency LA25** again, and lead children in reciting in order the days of the week and the months of the year. Write on the board a sentence that describes one of the months, such as the one below, and read it with children. Use this sentence to review how to compose a complete, coherent sentence that contains both a telling part and an action part. Have a volunteer point to the month. Ask children to recall how the name of a month or a day always begins. (with a capital letter)

**I like to play in the snow in January.**

## Practice/Apply

**GUIDED PRACTICE** Invite volunteers to share sentences about what they like to do during different months of the year. Write each sentence on the board without capitalizing the name of the month. Work with children to correct the capitalization. Have them check to make sure that each sentence tells a complete thought.

**INDEPENDENT PRACTICE** Have each child choose a month, making sure each month is selected at least once. Tell children to make a page for a class book by writing and illustrating a sentence telling something special that they like to do during this month. Remind them to refer to the list of months for help with spelling. After children have shared their pages, display them in random order. Have the group put the pictures in sequential order to show a year's worth of sentences. Compile the pages into a class book and display for children to read and enjoy.

Day 5

5-DAY WRITING
DAY 1  Modeled Writing
DAY 2  Shared Writing
DAY 3  Shared Writing
DAY 4  Independent Writing
DAY 5  Independent Writing

# Independent Writing
## Sequence Story

## Write a Story

**WRITE**  Have children continue writing their sequence stories from Day 4. Tell them to use their graphic organizers for ideas. Remind them that their writing should tell a story.

**WRITING TRAIT  ORGANIZATION**  Remind children that they should write their sentences in the correct order so that their readers will be able to understand when things happened in the story. Tell them to use words like *first, next,* and *last* to help show the order of events. Encourage them to also try new transition words such as *then, after, before,* and *finally*.

**REVISE**  Have children read their sequence stories to a partner. Read the list of criteria for sequence stories to children. Then have them use the list to improve their writing. Ask them to add sequence words, change words, and fix mistakes until they are pleased with their story. Guide children to use basic capitalization skills, such as capitalizing the first word in a sentence, the pronoun *I,* and proper nouns such as the names of days and months.

> ### Sequence Story
>
> - It tells events in order.
> - It uses words such as first, next, and last.
> - It has a beginning, a middle, and an ending.

## Share

**AUTHOR'S CHAIR**  Have children make a neat copy of their sequence stories, illustrate it, and then take turns sharing. Before children share, have them determine a purpose for listening, such as to get information about things classmates have done. Coach listeners to respond constructively through applause or by telling what they liked about the author's work. Have listeners ask questions to clarify understanding.

### Objective

- *To write a story with the events in a logical sequence*

 **Writing Prompt**

**Self-Selected Writing**  Have children look at pictures to generate ideas about a topic. Then have them write about it.

**WEEKLY LESSON TEST**

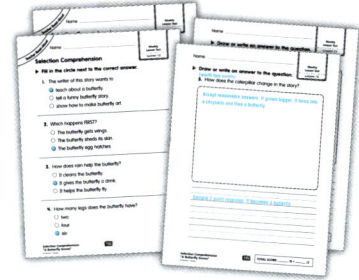

▲ Weekly Lesson Tests, pp. 126–136

- Selection Comprehension with Short Response
- Phonics and Spelling
- High-Frequency Words
- Focus Skill
- Robust Vocabulary
- Grammar
- Fluency

**GO online**  For prescriptions, see p. A2. Also available electronically on *StoryTown* Online Assessment and ExamView®.

  **Podcasting:** Assessing Fluency

# Leveled Readers
## *Reinforcing Skills and Strategies*

Genre: Nonfiction

## From Chick to Hen

**SUMMARY** Readers learn how a chick grows and changes over time—from an egg into a hen.

- **phonics** Digraph /ch/*ch, tch*
- **High-Frequency Words:** *air, fly, friends, grew, need, play, rain, watch*

● **Sequence**

### Before Reading

**BUILD BACKGROUND/SET A PURPOSE** Ask children to share what they know about chicks hatching and how they change as they grow. Guide children to preview the book and set a purpose for reading.

### Reading the Book

**PAGES 2–8 MAIN IDEA** What is this story about? (how a chick hatches, grows, and changes into a hen)

**PAGES 2–8 ● SEQUENCE** What happens first? (A chick hatches from an egg.) **After the chick hatches, how does it change?** (Possible response: It gets much bigger and its color changes as it becomes a hen.)

**REREAD FOR FLUENCY** Have partners read alternate pages of the selection aloud several times with appropriate intonation.

### Think Critically          *(See inside back cover for questions.)*

**①  SEQUENCE** It ate. Then it grew into a big chick that could play with friends. Then the chick grew into a hen that could fly.

**②ᅠ COMPARE AND CONTRAST** Chicks are small, fluffy, and yellow, with little legs and a tiny beak. Hens are much bigger. They are brown, and have large wings, and a crest.

**③ᅠ NOTE DETAILS** The chick needed to eat.

**④ᅠ GRAPHIC AIDS** Possible response: to keep the eggs warm

**⑤ᅠ PERSONAL RESPONSE** Responses will vary.

## LEVELED READER TEACHER GUIDE

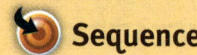

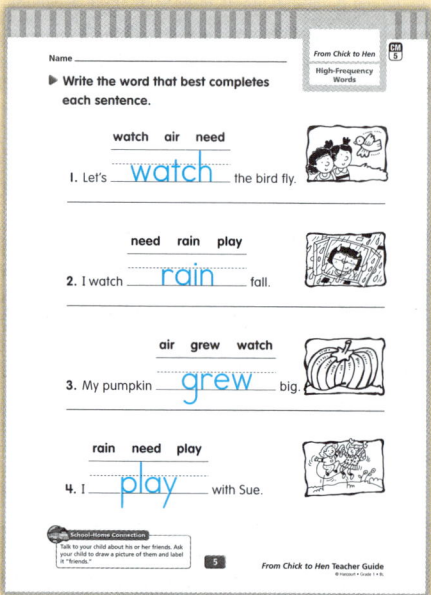

▲ High-Frequency Words, p. 5

▲ Comprehension, p. 6

**Go online**

www.harcourtschool.com/storytown

★ **Leveled Readers, online**
*Searchable by genre, skill, vocabulary, level, or title*
★ **Student Activities and Teacher Resources, online**

**ON-LEVEL**

Genre: Nonfiction

# A Kitten Grows

**SUMMARY** Readers learn how a very young kitten grows and changes over time.

- **phonics** Digraph /ch/*ch, tch*
- **High-Frequency Words:** *air, fly, friends, grew, need, play, rain, watch*
-  **Sequence**

## Before Reading

**BUILD BACKGROUND/SET A PURPOSE** Ask children to raise their hands if they have a cat. Ask: **Was it a kitten when you got it? What was it like?** Invite children to share their experiences and observations. Then guide them to preview the book and set a purpose for reading it.

## Reading the Book

**PAGES 2–8**  **SEQUENCE** **Apart from eating and growing bigger, what happens to the kitten after it is born?** (Possible response: It can see because its eyes open. It can leave the box to play and explore.)

**PAGE 8** **AUTHOR'S PURPOSE** **Why do you think the author wrote this selection?** (to tell facts about how a kitten grows and changes)

**REREAD FOR FLUENCY** Have partners choose the pages they find most interesting to read aloud several times with appropriate intonation.

## Think Critically *(See inside back cover for questions.)*

① **SEQUENCE** When the kitten is born, it can smell but cannot see. It drinks milk to grow. Soon, it grows bigger and can open its eyes.

② **NOTE DETAILS** The kitten goes back to its box.

③ **FICTION/NONFICTION** There are photographs of real kittens. The words tell information about kittens.

④ **NOTE DETAILS** Possible response: The kitten needs milk to grow.

⑤ **PERSONAL RESPONSE** Responses will vary.

**LEVELED READER TEACHER GUIDE**

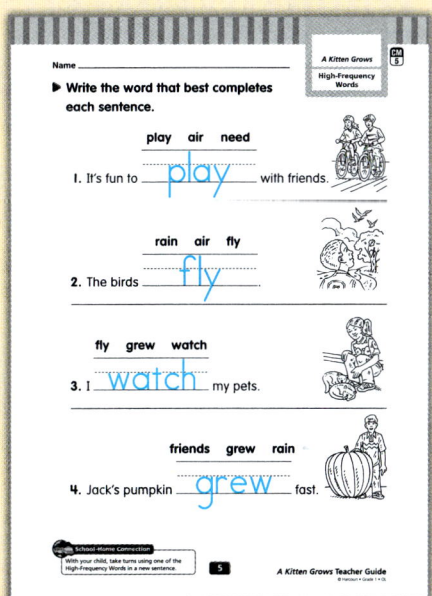

▲ High-Frequency Words, p. 5

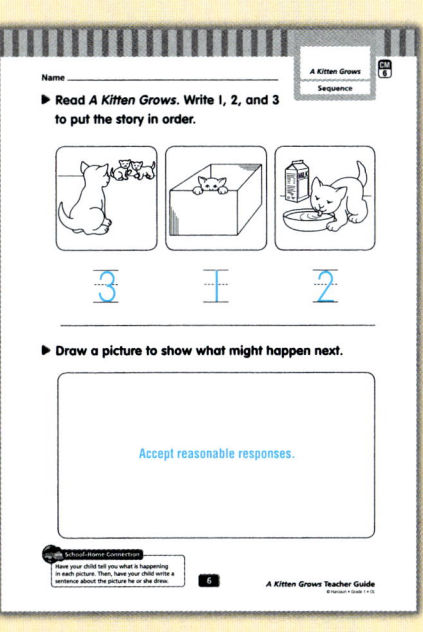

▲ Comprehension, p. 6

# Leveled Readers

*Reinforcing Skills and Strategies*

Genre: Nonfiction

## ADVANCED

## A Frog's Life

**SUMMARY** Once it hatches, a tadpole goes through many changes until it becomes an adult frog.

- **phonics** Digraph /ch/*ch, tch*
- **High-Frequency Words:** *air, fly, friends, grew, need, play, rain, watch*

**Sequence**

### Before Reading

**BUILD BACKGROUND/SET A PURPOSE** Have children tell what they know about frogs and share any experiences they have had. Ask: **Where do frogs live? How do they move? What are baby frogs called? How do they grow and change?** Have children set a purpose for reading the book.

### Reading the Book

**PAGES 2–5** **SEQUENCE** What happens first in the life of a frog? *(It hatches from its egg as a tadpole.)* **What must a tadpole do to live and grow?** *(It must eat and try not to be eaten.)*

**PAGES 6–8** **NOTE DETAILS** What can a tadpole do once it has legs and its tail is gone? *(Possible response: It can leave the pond, jump, and go back in the pond.)*

**REREAD FOR FLUENCY** Have children reread the selection several times with appropriate intonation at a speech-like pace.

### Think Critically *(See inside back cover for questions.)*

1 **SEQUENCE** At first, a tadpole has a long tail and no legs. As it gets older, it grows legs and its tail gets shorter. Then, its legs are long and it has no tail. It is a frog.

2 **COMPARE AND CONTRAST** It can come out of the water and jump.

3 **NOTE DETAILS** Tadpoles need to watch out for ducks and fish.

4 **SETTING** They live in ponds.

5 **PERSONAL RESPONSE** Responses will vary.

**LEVELED READER TEACHER GUIDE**

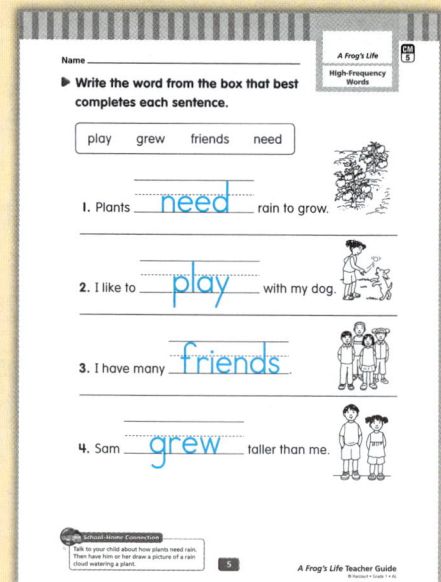

▲ High-Frequency Words, p. 5

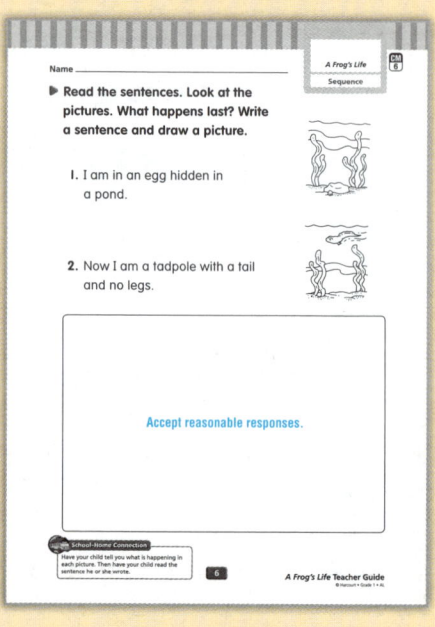

▲ Comprehension, p. 6

**www.harcourtschool.com/storytown**

★ **Leveled Readers, online**
  *Searchable by genre, skill, vocabulary, level, or title*
★ **Student Activities and Teacher Resources, online**

**E L L**

Genre: Nonfiction

# A Child Grows

**SUMMARY** Readers learn how babies grow and change into toddlers.

- **Strong Picture Support**
- **Concept Vocabulary**
- **Scaffolded Language Development**

## Before Reading

**BUILD BACKGROUND/SET A PURPOSE** Have children share experiences they have had with a baby brother or sister or other infant. Ask: **What was he/she like as a newborn? How has he/she changed since then?** Guide children to preview the book and set a purpose for reading it.

## Reading the Book

**PAGES 2–8** **SEQUENCE** **In what ways do the babies in this story change as they get older?** (Possible response: At first, the babies drink milk from a bottle. As they get older, they grow bigger and learn to sit up, to play with other babies, and to walk by themselves.)

**PAGE 8** **USE PRIOR KNOWLEDGE** **On page 8, it says that the little girl can walk. What other things will she soon learn to do?** (Possible responses: run, talk, feed herself)

**REREAD FOR FLUENCY** Read each page aloud and have children echo-read, using the same expression and intonation.

## Scaffolded Language Development

*(See inside back cover for teacher-led activity.)*

Provide additional examples and explanation as needed.

**LEVELED READER TEACHER GUIDE**

▲ Build Background, p. 5

▲ Scaffolded Language Development, p. 6

## THEME WRITING OVERVIEW

**Reading-Writing Connection** ➤ **Respond to a Selection**

| LESSON | FORM | TRAIT |
|--------|------|-------|
| 13 | Sequence Story | Organization |
| 14 | E-mail | Conventions |
| 15 | Personal Narrative | Voice |
| 16 | Invitation | Ideas |
| 17 | Friendly Letter | Voice |
| 18 | Thank-You Letter | Word Choice |

# Shared Writing: Respond to a Selection

## Children will

**Writing Trait** ▶ Ideas

- Learn how to generate ideas for writing.

**Writing Trait** ▶ Word Choice

- Learn how to choose words to reflect ideas.

**Writing Trait** ▶ Organization

- Contribute to the drafting of a shared writing piece.

**Writing Trait** ▶ Word Choice

- Learn how to revise a piece of writing to improve word choice.

**Writing Trait** ▶ Conventions

- Apply appropriate end punctuation to sentences.

# Set the Stage

## *Shared Writing: Respond to a Selection*

## Objectives

- *To understand that sentences are complete thoughts*
- *To understand that you can write sentences to respond to a selection*

### Introduce the Writing Form

**TALK ABOUT READING AND RESPONDING TO A SELECTION**  Tell children that they will be working together throughout this theme to write their thoughts about a selection. Explain that whenever people read, they have thoughts about what they are reading. For example, do they like it? Does it remind them of something else? Do they already know some of the information that's included in what they are reading? Explain that when people *write down* these thoughts, they are responding to the selection.

**Think Aloud**  Think about when we read "Land of Ice" and "All on the Map." These are both nonfiction selections. That means the information in them is true. Do you remember the pictures in those selections? Did the pictures help you to understand what you were reading? Was the writer trying to tell you something? What information did you already know? How did you know that information? What did you learn from these selections? What type of nonfiction books do *you* like to read?

**STAGES OF THE WRITING PROCESS**  Adjust the pacing to meet children's needs. Guide them back and forth between the steps until the final product meets established criteria.

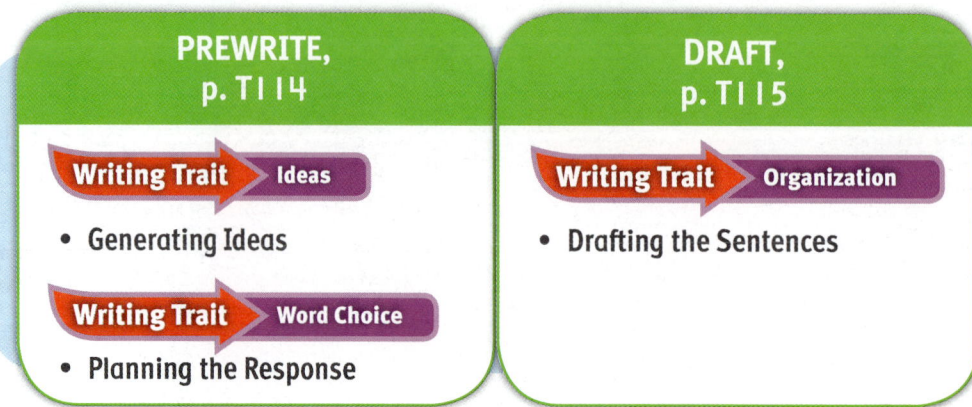

| PREWRITE, p. T114 | DRAFT, p. T115 |
|---|---|
| **Writing Trait** ▶ Ideas | **Writing Trait** ▶ Organization |
| • Generating Ideas | • Drafting the Sentences |
| **Writing Trait** ▶ Word Choice | |
| • Planning the Response | |

## Use Text as a Model

**DISCUSS PARTS OF A STORY RESPONSE** Tell children that you will read to them "Jane Meets David Greybeard" (*Read-Aloud Anthology*, page 96). Ask them to listen carefully to hear how the writer introduces the topic and then gives his thoughts and feelings about it. After reading the selection, explain that a response to the selection can be written in which children give their thoughts and feelings. Display Transparency GO3 and guide children in completing the organizer.

▲ **Read-Aloud Anthology, p. 96**

**E L L**

**Clarify Meaning** Tell children that *to categorize* means to group things that are alike. Provide simple examples such as the following:

**food: pizza, grapes, ham**

**animals: dogs, cats, lions**

**sports: baseball, soccer, tennis**

| What This Selection Is About | What I Know About This | What I Didn't Know | What I Liked |
|---|---|---|---|
| Jane Goodall and her chimps | | Chimps live in small groups. | They can share information. |

| REVISE, p. T116 | PROOFREAD, p. T116 | PUBLISH, p. T117 |
|---|---|---|
| **Writing Trait** ▶ Word Choice<br>• Revising a Draft | **Writing Trait** ▶ Conventions<br>• Checking for End Punctuation | • Creating a Wall Display |

# Student Writing Model

## Objective

*To understand the stages of the writing process*

### Discuss the Model

**READ PAGES 50–51** Have children open their *Student Edition* to page 50. Read the page aloud. Explain that these pages show what the children knew and what information they learned. Tell children that first the class read "A Butterfly Grows." Then the class named things they knew and things that they learned from reading the selection. Finally, they followed along as the teacher read aloud the sentences.

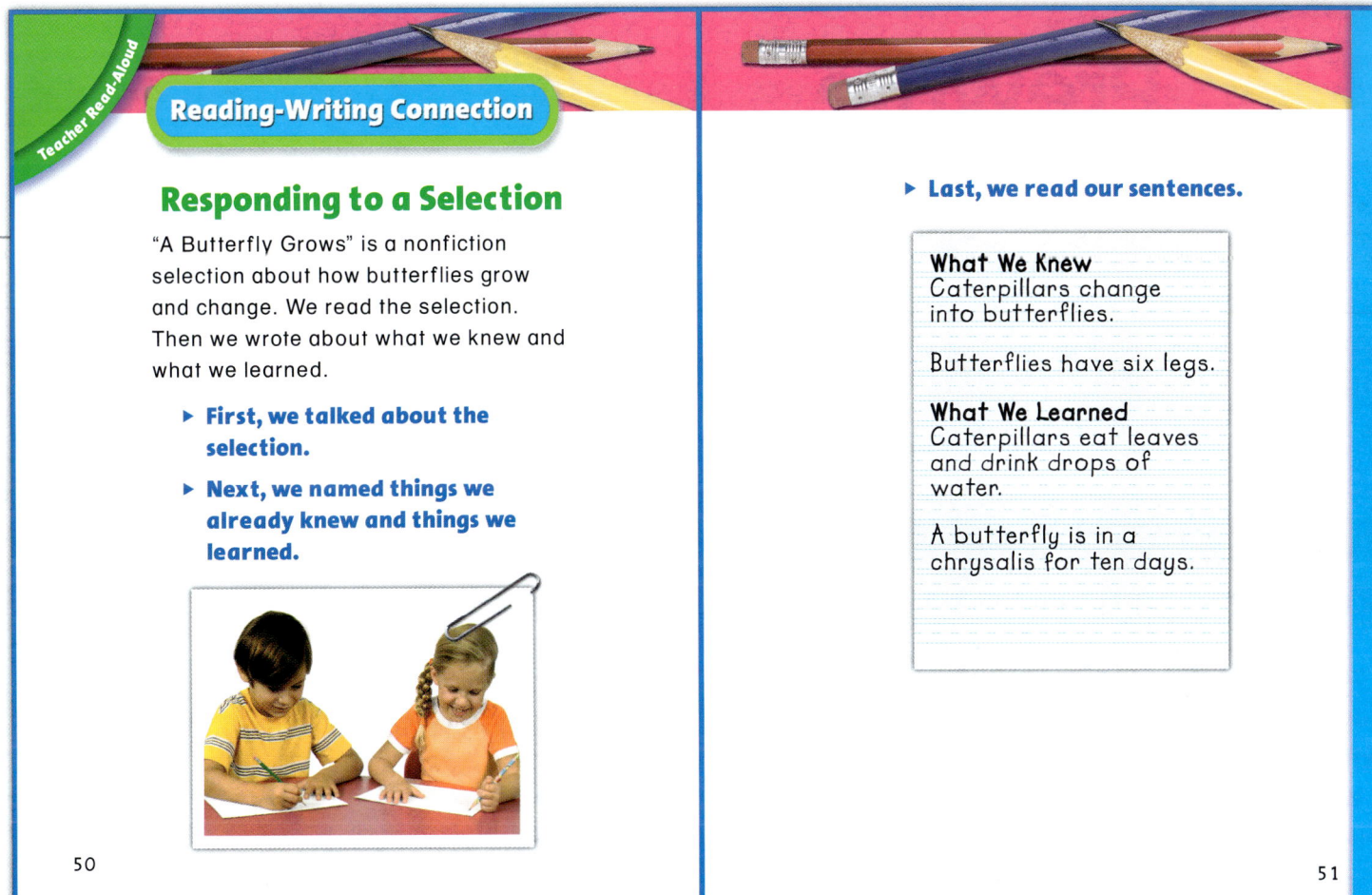

**Teacher Read-Aloud**

**Reading-Writing Connection**

## Responding to a Selection

"A Butterfly Grows" is a nonfiction selection about how butterflies grow and change. We read the selection. Then we wrote about what we knew and what we learned.

▶ **First, we talked about the selection.**

▶ **Next, we named things we already knew and things we learned.**

50

▶ **Last, we read our sentences.**

**What We Knew**
Caterpillars change into butterflies.

Butterflies have six legs.

**What We Learned**
Caterpillars eat leaves and drink drops of water.

A butterfly is in a chrysalis for ten days.

51

**READ STUDENT WRITING MODEL**    Read the chart of sentences on page 51 and point out that these are the sentences that the class wrote about "A Butterfly Grows." Ask children what they enjoyed about the class's lists.

Tell children that they will follow the same process to write their thoughts about a selection they have read. Explain that they first will read a selection. Then they will need to come up with plan.

# Prewrite

## GENERATING IDEAS
### Writing Trait → Ideas

**Objective**
*To learn how to generate ideas for writing*

### Teach/Model

**DISCUSS TOPICS**  Tell children the following:

**We are going to write sentences about a selection. In "Land of Ice," the author used the idea of an icy area to write sentences about animals that live in or near ice. We need to think of ideas or categories for what our lists will be about.**

### Apply to Writing

**BRAINSTORM**  Help children generate ideas before they begin writing. Guide them to make a plan. Have them brainstorm ideas. Record their suggestions on the board.

### Ideas

What we already know

What we learned

What it reminded me of

Interesting facts

What we thought about the pictures

## PLANNING THE RESPONSE
### Writing Trait → Word Choice

**Objective**
*To choose words to reflect ideas*

### Teach/Model

**REVIEW**  Tell children that when writing a response to a story or a piece of nonfiction, a writer uses words such as *best*, *surprised*, *I'm not sure*, *I wonder*, and *I believe*. These words help them tell what they have learned and how they feel about what they learned.

**Think Aloud**  **I might write that I wasn't sure about some of the information, or I might wonder how something or someone does something. All of this is a response.**

### Apply to Writing

**CHOOSE A TOPIC**  Reread "Land of Ice" with children. Then review the Ideas list with children. Help them brainstorm words or phrases that clarify the ideas.

# Draft

## DRAFTING THE SENTENCES
Writing Trait ➤ Organization

### Objective
*To contribute to the drafting of a shared writing piece*

### Teach/Model

 **USE A GRAPHIC ORGANIZER** Guide children to suggest things they learned from the selection "Land of Ice" as well as things they already knew. Use **Transparency GO1** to record their ideas.

| What We Knew | What We Learned |
|---|---|
| Animals can live where there is ice. | A baby seal is called a pup. |
| Penguins flap their wings to swim fast. | Red sea stars live under the ice. |

### Apply to Writing

**CREATE SENTENCES** Lead children to dictate sentences to you, basing their ideas on the transparency. Remind children that as they tell their sentences, they should use words that tell their thoughts about "Land of Ice." Write their sentences on chart paper and read them aloud. Write a title at the top of the page.

## LAND OF ICE

We knew that animals can live where there is ice, but we could not believe there were so many.

We were surprised to learn that seals have lots of fat and thick fur.

We wonder how the red sea stars live under ice.

Some of us already knew that penguins flapped their wings to swim fast. It reminded some of us of swimming in the pool.

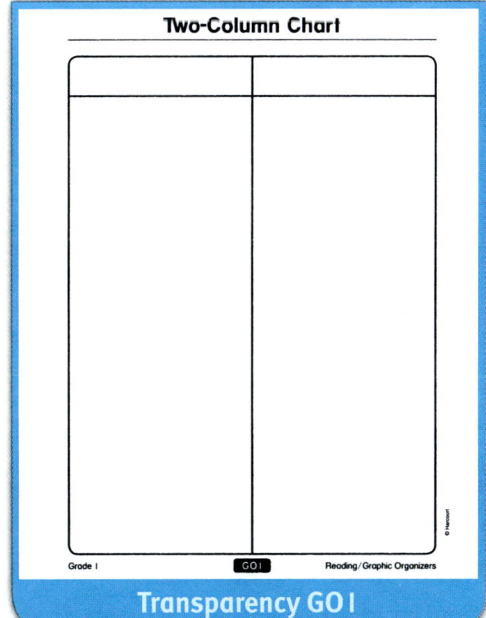

**Transparency GO1**

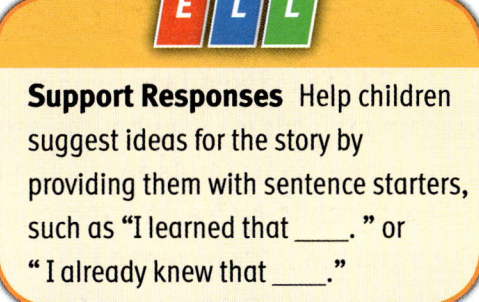

**E L L**

**Support Responses** Help children suggest ideas for the story by providing them with sentence starters, such as "I learned that ____." or "I already knew that ____."

# Revise/Proofread

## REVISING A DRAFT
Writing Trait ➤ Word Choice

### Objective
*To learn how to revise a piece of writing to improve word choice*

### Teach/Model

**MODEL ADDING WORDS TO EXPRESS THOUGHTS**
Remind children that certain words or phrases help to let others know how you feel about a certain piece of writing. Write the following phrases and words on the board.

> I believe
> I wonder
> the best
> surprised
> I'm not sure

Read the list aloud and reinforce that clear, well-chosen words and phrases should be used in their writing.

Then read aloud the first sentence of the draft. Talk through with children whether the sentence clearly tells what they think about "Land of Ice." Demonstrate how to insert a word or phrase to revise the writing.

### Apply to Writing

**REVISE SENTENCES** Reread the remaining sentences. Discuss with children whether the sentence clearly lets others know what they thought about "Land of Ice." If children feel that a change is needed, invite a child to mark a caret on the chart paper to show where the change would occur. Then write their suggested change.

## CHECKING FOR END PUNCTUATION
Writing Trait ➤ Conventions

### Objective
*To apply appropriate end punctuation*

### Teach/Model

**REVIEW** Remind children that they have learned three kinds of end punctuation—periods, question marks, and exclamation points. Guide them to recall that periods end telling sentences, question marks end asking sentences, and exclamation points end sentences said with excitement.

Tell children that good writers reread their writing to be sure that they used correct end punctuation. Point out a sentence in the draft and explain why it has the appropriate end mark.

### Apply to Writing

**CHECK FOR END PUNCTUATION** Tell children that you will now review the class sentences to make sure the correct punctuation has been used. Read the sentences aloud, and have children point out the punctuation at the end of each sentence. Ask children to confirm that each sentence ends with the correct mark. Guide them to change end punctuation as necessary.

# Evaluate/Publish

## Objective
*To publish student-generated text*

### Creating a Wall Display

**COPY SENTENCES** Display the chart of sentences. Assign each child a sentence from the chart. Ask children to copy their sentence onto paper. Remind them to make sure that their sentence starts with a capital letter and ends with the correct punctuation. Have children cut out their sentences and glue them to drawing paper. Have them illustrate their sentences. Display them on a wall or create a bulletin board.

### CONFERENCE

**Copying Sentences** Meet with children to check that they understand that their sentences should begin with a capital letter and end with the correct punctuation.

What We Learned.

A baby seal is called a pup.

What We Knew.

Animals can live where there is ice.

### ✓ ASSESSMENT

**OBSERVATION CHECKLIST** Complete the following checklist to assess children's participation in the development of the class sentences.

---

#### Observation Checklist

☐ Demonstrates awareness of print concepts.

☐ Makes appropriate contributions of ideas, thoughts, and responses.

☐ Contributes phrases or sentences that reflect known oral structures.

☐ Completes or extends formulaic expressions and grammatical patterns.

☐ Demonstrates knowledge of punctuation and capitalization.

---

List the features that you want to see in the completed sentences. Then read the sentences aloud and tell children to evaluate them. Lead children to identify the most effective features:

- complete sentences that tell what children knew or what they learned from reading a selection
- a capital letter at the beginning of the sentence
- correct punctuation at the end of the sentence

# Lesson 14

## WEEK AT A GLANCE

### Phonemic Awareness
Phoneme Blending and Deletion

### ✓ Phonics
*r*-Controlled Vowel /är/*ar*
Inflections *-s, -ed, -ing*

### ✓ Spelling
*far, farm, arm, art, part, park, chin, such, fly, watch*

### ✓ High-Frequency Words
*again, feel, house, know, loud, Mrs., put, say*

### Reading
**"Mark's Big Day"** by Monica Greenfield
REALISTIC FICTION

**"Putting on a Play"** NONFICTION

### ✓ Fluency
Intonation

### ✓ Comprehension
 Author's Purpose/Point of View
 Summarize

### ✓ Robust Vocabulary
*approached, energetic, pace, blunder, reassure, excel*

### ✓ Grammar
Names of Holidays

### Writing
Form: E-mail
Trait: Conventions

### Weekly Lesson Test

 = Focus Skill    = Focus Strategy    = Tested Skill

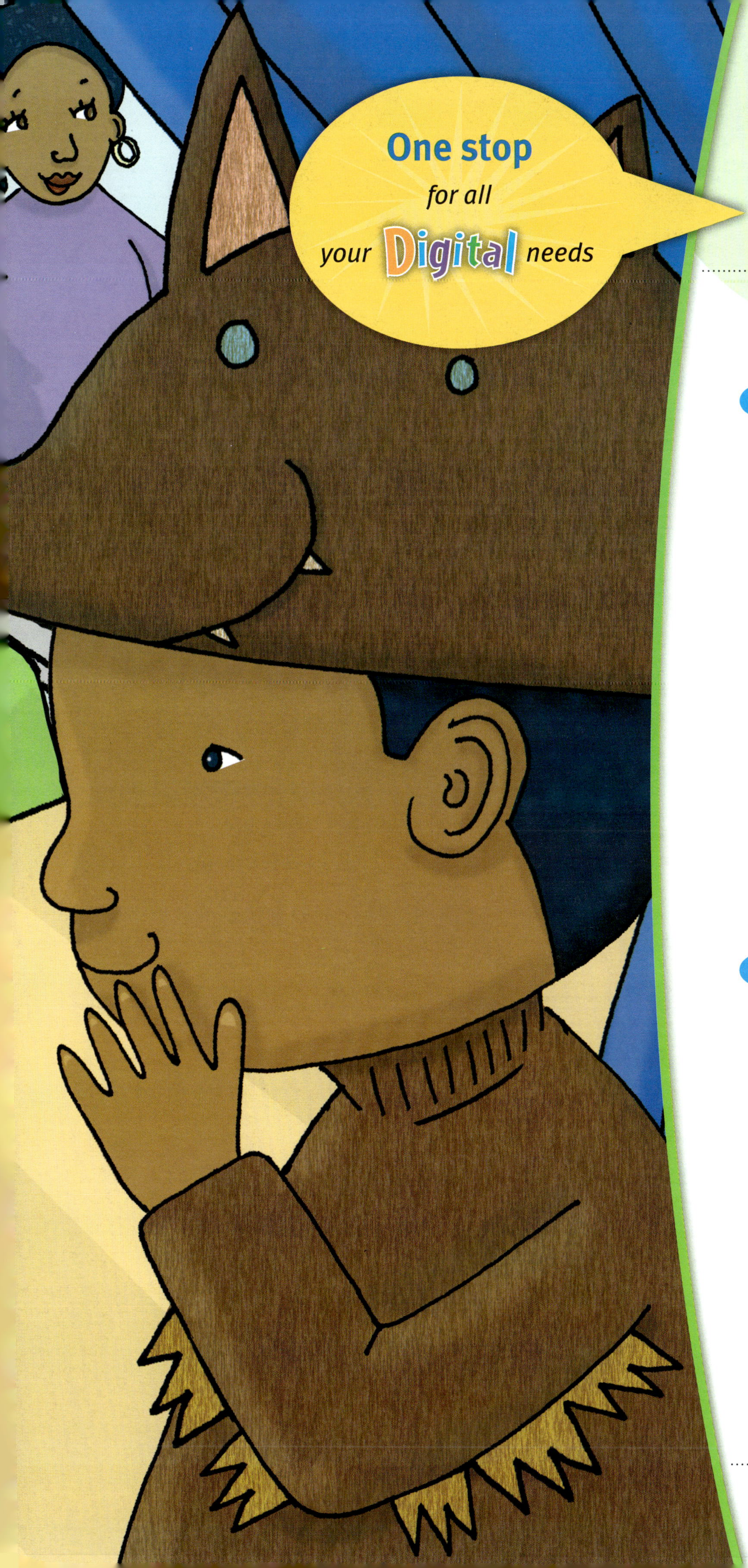

One stop *for all* *your* **Digital** *needs*

# Digital
## CLASSROOM

 www.harcourtschool.com/storytown
*To go along with your print program*

### FOR THE TEACHER

**Prepare**
 **Professional Development**
*in the Online TE*

 *Videos for Podcasting*

**Plan & Organize**
 **Online TE & Planning Resources***

**Teach**
 **Transparencies**
*for electronic projection*

**Assess**
 **Online Assessment***
*with Student Tracking System and Prescriptions*

### FOR THE STUDENT

**Read**
 **Student eBook***

 **Strategic Intervention Interactive Reader**

 **Leveled Readers**

**Practice & Apply**
 **Splash into Phonics CD-ROM**

 *Also available on CD-ROM*

# Literature Resources

## STUDENT EDITION

 **GO online** eBook **STUDENT EDITION**

**Get Started Story**

**Ann's Trip to the Stars, pp. 54–61**

Genre: **Realistic Fiction**

**Mark's Big Day**

by Monica Greenfield
illustrated by Shane Evans

**SOCIAL STUDIES** **Mark's Big Day, pp. 66–87**

*by Monica Greenfield* Mark almost lets his nerves get the best of him before his big performance in the school play.

 **Accelerated Reader™**

*Practice Quizzes for the Selection*

 **Audiotext** *Student Edition selections are available on Audiotext Grade 1, CD 3 and 6.*

**Genre Study**
**Realistic fiction** stories are made-up, but have characters like people we know.

**Comprehension Strategy**
**Summarize** As you read, stop every few pages and think about the important things that have happened so far.

**Paired Selections**

**Putting on a Play**

Genre: **Nonfiction**

◀ **Reading Across Texts**
**Comparing Realistic Fiction and Nonfiction**

## ADDITIONAL READING

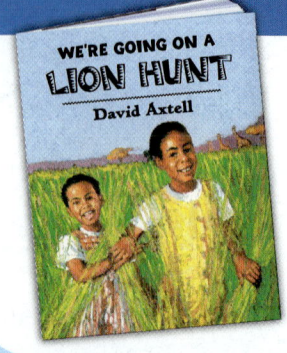

**Big Book**
*We're Going on a Lion Hunt*

**Decodable Book**
"Charming Carmel"
★ Applies *r*-Controlled Vowel /är/*ar*

# Support for Differentiated Instruction

 **GO online** **LEVELED READERS**

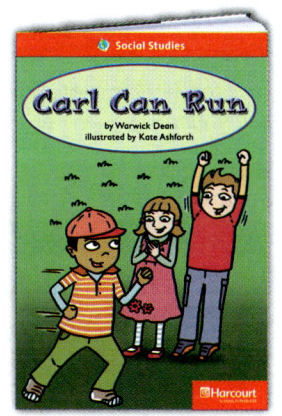

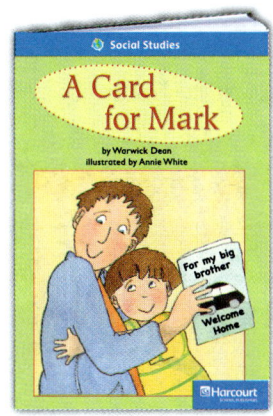

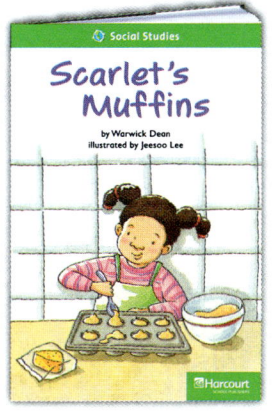

**● BELOW-LEVEL**       **● ON-LEVEL**       **● ADVANCED**

**E L L**

## LEVELED PRACTICE

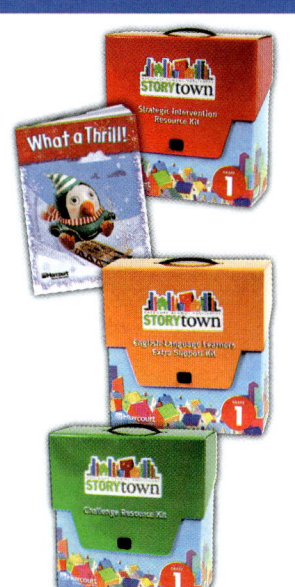

◀ **Strategic Intervention Resource Kit, Lesson 14**

◀ **Strategic Intervention Interactive Reader, Lesson 14**
Strategic Intervention Interactive Reader Online

◀ **ELL Extra Support Kit, Lesson 14**

◀ **Challenge Resource Kit, Lesson 14**

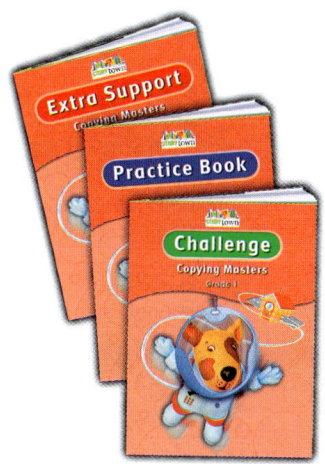

**● BELOW-LEVEL**
Extra Support Copying Masters, pp. 9–14

**● ON-LEVEL**
Practice Book, pp. 9–15

**● ADVANCED**
Challenge Copying Masters, pp. 9–14

## ADDITIONAL RESOURCES

- Spelling Practice Book, pp. 46–48
- Grammar Practice Book, pp. 53–56
- Reading Transparencies R27–R28
- Language Arts Transparencies LA27–LA28
- Test Prep System
◀ **Literacy Center Kit, Cards 66–70**
◀ **Sound/Spelling Card**
- Fluency Builders
◀ **Photo Cards**
- Read-Aloud Anthology, p. 56

##  ASSESSMENT

✓ **Weekly Lesson Tests**

- Comprehension
- Phonics and Spelling
- Focus Skill
- Robust Vocabulary
- High-Frequency Words
- Grammar
- Fluency

 **GO online**
www.harcourtschool.com/storytown
- Online Assessment
*Also available on CD-ROM—ExamView®*

# Suggested Lesson Planner

## Day 1

## Day 2

### Step 1 — Whole Group

## Daily Language
- Oral Language
- High-Frequency Words
- Shared Reading
- Phonemic Awareness

### Day 1

**QUESTION OF THE DAY,** p. T130
*Imagine that you will look for a wild animal. What is it? Where will you look?*

**READ ALOUD,** p. T130
*Big Book: We're Going on a Lion Hunt*

**WORD WALL,** p. T131

**PHONEMIC AWARENESS,** p. T131
Phoneme Blending

▲ Big Book

### Day 2

**QUESTION OF THE DAY,** p. T146
*What are you like today? How might you change as you grow up?*

**SHARED READING,** p. T146
*Big Book of Rhymes and Poems,* "Growing Up"

**WORD WALL,** p. T147

**PHONEMIC AWARENESS,** p. T147
Phoneme Blending

## Word Work

- phonics
- Spelling
- High-Frequency Words

### Day 1

 , p. T132
Introduce: *r*-Controlled Vowel /är/*ar*

**SPELLING,** p. T135
Pretest: *far, farm, arm, art, part, park, chin, such, fly, watch*

**HIGH-FREQUENCY WORDS,** p. T136
Review: *cold, play, says, her*

### Day 2

phonics, p. T148
Review: *r*-Controlled Vowel /är/*ar*

**SPELLING,** p. T148
Word Building

**HIGH-FREQUENCY WORDS**
Words to Know, p. T152
Introduce: *again, feel, house, know, loud, Mrs., put, say*

## Skills and Strategies
- Reading
- Fluency
- Comprehension
- Build Robust Vocabulary

### Day 1

**READING,** p. T136
Get Started Story, "Ann's Trip to the Stars"
Decodable Text
*Options for Reading*

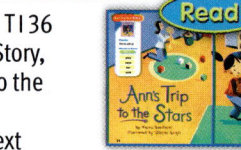
▲ Student Edition

**FLUENCY,** p. T141
Intonation

**COMPREHENSION,** p. T142
Read-Aloud: "The Hare and the Tortoise"
Preview: Author's Purpose/Point of View

**BUILD ROBUST VOCABULARY,** p. T143
Introduce: *approached, energetic, pace*

### Day 2

**READING,** p. T154
"Mark's Big Day"
*Options for Reading*

▲ Student Edition

**COMPREHENSION,** pp. T151, T154
Introduce: Author's Purpose/Point of View
Introduce: Summarize

**RETELLING/FLUENCY,** p. T166
Intonation

**BUILD ROBUST VOCABULARY,** p. T167
Review: *approached, energetic, pace*

### Step 2 — Small Groups

**Suggestions for Differentiated Instruction *(See pp. T124–T125.)***

### Step 3 — Whole Group

## Language Arts
- Grammar
- Writing

### Day 1

**GRAMMAR,** p. T144
Introduce: Names of Holidays

***Daily Proofreading***
does your arm hurt. (Does, hurt?)

 **MODELED WRITING,** p. T145
Introduce: E-mail
Writing Trait: Conventions

**Writing Prompt** *Write and draw about something you have enjoyed doing at school.*

### Day 2

**GRAMMAR,** p. T168
Review: Names of Holidays

***Daily Proofreading***
my friends saw a shark? (My, shark.)

 **SHARED WRITING,** p. T169
Review: E-mail
Writing Trait: Conventions

**Writing Prompt** *Draw and write about a party you attended.*

 = Focus Skill     = Focus Strategy     = Tested Skill

**Skills at a Glance**

• *r*-Controlled Vowel /är/*ar*
• Inflections *–s, –ed, –ing*

**Comprehension**
⊙ **FOCUS SKILL** Author's Purpose/Point of View
⊙ **FOCUS STRATEGY** Summarize

**Phonemic Awareness**
Phoneme Blending and Deletion

**Fluency**
Intonation

**Vocabulary**
**HIGH-FREQUENCY:** *again, feel, house, know, loud, Mrs., put, say*
**ROBUST:** *approached, energetic, pace, blunder, reassure, excel*

# Day 3

**QUESTION OF THE DAY,** p. T170
*What would you like to do or be when you grow up? Tell why.*

**SHARED READING,** p. T170
*Big Book of Rhymes and Poems,* "Growing Up"

**WORD WALL,** p. T171

✓ **PHONEMIC AWARENESS,** p. T171
Phoneme Deletion

✓ **phonics,** p. T172
Review: *r*-Controlled Vowels /är/*ar*, /ôr/*or*

✓ **SPELLING,** p. T173
State the Generalization

✓ **HIGH-FREQUENCY WORDS,** p. T174
Review: *again, feel, house, know, loud, Mrs., put, say*

✓ **FLUENCY,** p. T175
Intonation: "Mark's Big Day"

✓ **COMPREHENSION,** p. T176
⊙ Review: Author's Purpose/Point of View
Paired Selection: "Putting on a Play"

**CONNECTIONS,** p. T178

✓ **BUILD ROBUST VOCABULARY,** p. T179
Introduce: *blunder, reassure, excel*

▲ Student Edition

# Day 4

**QUESTION OF THE DAY,** p. T182
*Do you ever speak in a very loud voice? When is it all right to do this? Why?*

**SHARED READING,** p. T182
*Big Book of Rhymes and Poems,* "At the Top of My Voice"

**WORD WALL,** p. T183

✓ **PHONEMIC AWARENESS,** p. T183
Phoneme Deletion

✓ **phonics,** p. T184
Introduce: Inflections *–s, –ed, –ing*

✓ **SPELLING,** p. T185
Review Spelling Words

✓ **HIGH-FREQUENCY WORDS,** p. T186
Review: *again, feel, house, know, loud, Mrs., put, say*

✓ **FLUENCY,** p. T187
Intonation: "Mark's Big Day"

✓ **COMPREHENSION,** p. T188
⊙ Review: Author's Purpose/Point of View
*Big Book: We're Going on a Lion Hunt*

✓ **BUILD ROBUST VOCABULARY,** p. T189
Review: *blunder, reassure, excel*

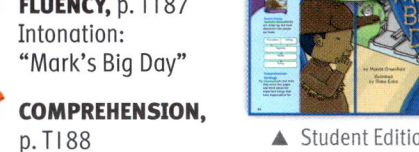
▲ Student Edition

# Day 5

**QUESTION OF THE DAY,** p. T192
*How could you make the ground thunder? How could you make the world ring?*

**SHARED READING,** p. T192
*Big Book of Rhymes and Poems,* "At the Top of My Voice"

**WORD WALL,** p. T193

✓ **PHONEMIC AWARENESS,** p. T193
Phoneme Deletion

✓ **phonics,** p. T194
Review: Inflections *–s, –ed, –ing*

✓ **SPELLING,** p. T195
Posttest

✓ **HIGH-FREQUENCY WORDS,** p. T196
Review: *again, feel, house, know, loud, Mrs., put, say*

✓ **FLUENCY,** p. T197
Intonation: "Mark's Big Day"

✓ **COMPREHENSION,** p. T198
⊙ Review: Author's Purpose/Point of View

✓ **BUILD ROBUST VOCABULARY,** p. T199
Review

▲ Student Edition

🔴 **BELOW-LEVEL**  🔵 **ON-LEVEL**  🟢 **ADVANCED**  **E L L**

✓ **GRAMMAR,** p. T180
Review: Names of Holidays

*Daily Proofreading*
i was born on thanksgiving. (I, Thanksgiving)

✏ **SHARED WRITING,** p. T181
Review: E-mail
Writing Trait: Conventions

**Writing Prompt** *Write a note telling a partner to bring an item to school tomorrow.*

✓ **GRAMMAR,** p. T190
Review: Names of Holidays

*Daily Proofreading*
I play tag last monday. (played, Monday)

✏ **INDEPENDENT WRITING,** p. T191
Review: E-mail
Writing Trait: Conventions

**Writing Prompt** *Draw a picture of a computer, and write about how you like to use it.*

✓ **GRAMMAR,** p. T200
Review: Names of Holidays

*Daily Proofreading*
did Mom park the car. (Did, car?)

✏ **INDEPENDENT WRITING,** p. T201
Review: E-mail
Writing Trait: Conventions

**Writing Prompt** *Write an e-mail message to a friend.*

# Suggested Small Group Planner

  45-60+ Minutes

|  | **Day 1** | **Day 2** |
|---|---|---|
|   15+ Min. each ● **BELOW-LEVEL** | **Teacher-Directed** *Student Edition:* Get Started Story, "Ann's Trip to the Stars," p. T136  ▲ Student Edition  **Independent** ⭐ Listening/Speaking Center, p. T128 Extra Support Copying Masters, p. 9 | **Teacher-Directed** *Student Edition:* "Mark's Big Day," p. T154  ▲ Student Edition  **Independent** ⭐ Reading Center, p. T128 Extra Support Copying Masters, p. 11 |
|  15+ Min. each ● **ON-LEVEL** | **Teacher-Directed** *Student Edition:* Get Started Story, "Ann's Trip to the Stars," p. T136  ▲ Student Edition  **Independent** ⭐ Reading Center, p. T128 Practice Book, p. 9 | **Teacher-Directed** *Student Edition:* "Mark's Big Day," p. T154  ▲ Student Edition  **Independent** ⭐ Letters and Sounds Center, p. T129 Practice Book, p. 11 |
| 15+ Min. each ● **ADVANCED** | **Teacher-Directed** Leveled Reader: "Scarlet's Muffins," p. T204 Before Reading 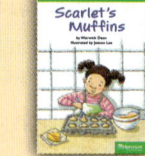 ▲ Leveled Reader  **Independent** ⭐ Letters and Sounds Center, p. T129 Challenge Copying Masters, p. 9 | **Teacher-Directed** Leveled Reader: "Scarlet's Muffins," p. T204 Read the Book 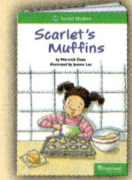 ▲ Leveled Reader  **Independent** ⭐ Word Work Center, p. T129 Challenge Copying Masters, p. 11 |
| E L L **English-Language Learners** *In addition to the small-group suggestions above, use the ELL Extra Support Kit to promote language development.*  | **LANGUAGE DEVELOPMENT SUPPORT** **Teacher-Directed** ELL TG, Day 1  **Independent** ELL Copying Masters, Lesson 14 | **LANGUAGE DEVELOPMENT SUPPORT** **Teacher-Directed** ELL TG, Day 2  **Independent** ELL Copying Masters, Lesson 14 |
| **Intervention**   ▲ Strategic Intervention Resource Kit    ▲ Strategic Intervention Interactive Reader | Strategic Intervention TG, Day 1 Strategic Intervention Practice Book, Lesson 14 | Strategic Intervention TG, Day 2 Strategic Intervention Interactive Reader, Lesson 14  ▲ Strategic Intervention Interactive Reader |

 = **Literacy Center Cards**

## MONITOR PROGRESS
**Small-Group Instruction**

| Phonemic Awareness/ Phonics | High-Frequency Words | Fluency | Comprehension | Robust Vocabulary | Language Arts Checkpoint |
|---|---|---|---|---|---|
| *r*-Controlled Vowel /är/*ar* p. S12 | *again, feel, house, know, loud, Mrs., put, say* p. S13 | Intonation pp. S14–S15 | **Focus Skill** Author's Purpose/Point of View pp. S16–S17 | *approached, energetic, pace, blunder, reassure, excel* pp. S18–S19 | **Grammar:** Names of Holidays **Writing:** E-mail pp. S20–S21 |

# Day 3

**Teacher-Directed**
Leveled Reader:
"Carl Can Run," p. T202
Before Reading; Read the Book

**Independent**
⭐ Word Work Center, p. T129
Extra Support Copying Masters,
p. 12

▲ Leveled Reader

**Teacher-Directed**
Leveled Reader:
"A Card for Mark," p. T203
Before Reading; Read the Book

**Independent**
⭐ Writing Center, p. T129
Practice Book, p. 12

▲ Leveled Reader

**Teacher-Directed**
Leveled Reader:
"Scarlet's Muffins," p. T204
Think Critically

**Independent**
⭐ Listening/Speaking Center,
p. T128
Challenge Copying Masters, p. 12

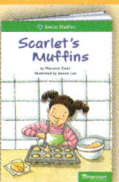
▲ Leveled Reader

**LANGUAGE DEVELOPMENT SUPPORT**
**Teacher-Directed**
Leveled Reader:
"The Play," p. T205
Before Reading; Read the Book
ELL TG, Day 3

**Independent**
ELL Copying Masters, Lesson 14

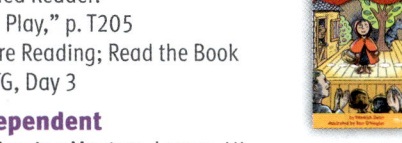
▲ Leveled Reader

Strategic Intervention TG, Day 3
Strategic Intervention
Interactive Reader, Lesson 14
Strategic Intervention
Practice Book, Lesson 14

▲ Strategic Intervention Interactive Reader

# Day 4

**Teacher-Directed**
Leveled Reader:
"Carl Can Run," p. T202
Reread for Fluency

**Independent**
⭐ Letters and Sounds Center,
p. T129
Cut-Out/Fold-Up Book, Practice
Book, pp. 47–48

▲ Leveled Reader

**Teacher-Directed**
Leveled Reader:
"A Card for Mark," p. T203
Reread for Fluency

**Independent**
⭐ Word Work Center, p. T129
Cut-Out/Fold-Up Book: Practice
Book, pp. 47–48

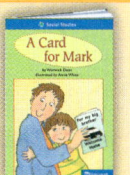
▲ Leveled Reader

**Teacher-Directed**
Leveled Reader:
"Scarlet's Muffins," p. T204
Reread for Fluency
Self-Selected Reading: Classroom
Library Collection

**Independent**
⭐ Writing Center, p. T129
Cut-Out/Fold-Up Book: Practice Book,
pp. 47–48

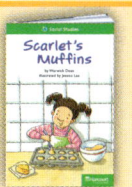
▲ Leveled Reader

**LANGUAGE DEVELOPMENT SUPPORT**
**Teacher-Directed**
Leveled Reader:
"The Play," p. T205
Reread for Fluency
ELL TG, Day 4

**Independent**
ELL Copying Masters, Lesson 14

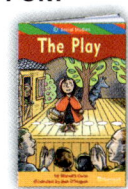
▲ Leveled Reader

Strategic Intervention TG, Day 4
Strategic Intervention
Interactive Reader, Lesson 14

▲ Strategic Intervention Interactive Reader

# Day 5

**Teacher-Directed**
Leveled Reader:
"Carl Can Run," p. T202
Think Critically

**Independent**
⭐ Writing Center, p. T129
Leveled Reader: Reread for Fluency
Extra Support Copying Masters,
p. 14

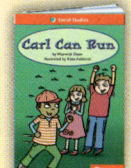
▲ Leveled Reader

**Teacher-Directed**
Leveled Reader:
"A Card for Mark," p. T203
Think Critically

**Independent**
⭐ Listening/Speaking Center,
p. T128
Leveled Reader: Reread for Fluency
Practice Book, p. 14

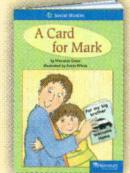
▲ Leveled Reader

**Teacher-Directed**
Leveled Reader:
"Scarlet's Muffins," p. T204
Reread for Fluency
Self-Selected Reading: Classroom
Library Collection

**Independent**
⭐ Reading Center, p. T128
Leveled Reader: Reread for Fluency
Challenge Copying Masters, p. 14

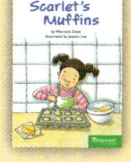
▲ Leveled Reader

**LANGUAGE DEVELOPMENT SUPPORT**
**Teacher-Directed**
Leveled Reader:
"The Play," p. T205
Think Critically
ELL TG, Day 5

**Independent**
Leveled Reader:
Reread for Fluency
ELL Copying Masters, Lesson 14

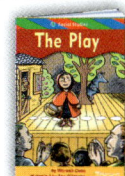
▲ Leveled Reader

Strategic Intervention TG, Day 5
Strategic Intervention
Interactive Reader, Lesson 14

▲ Strategic Intervention Interactive Reader

# Leveled Readers & Leveled Practice
## Reinforcing Skills and Strategies

## LEVELED READERS SYSTEM

- **Leveled Readers**
- **Leveled Readers CD**
- **Leveled Reader Teacher Guides**
  - *Comprehension*
  - *High-Frequency Words*
  - *Oral Reading Fluency Assessment*
- **Response Activities**
- **Leveled Readers Assessment**

See pages T202–T205 for lesson plans.

### BELOW-LEVEL

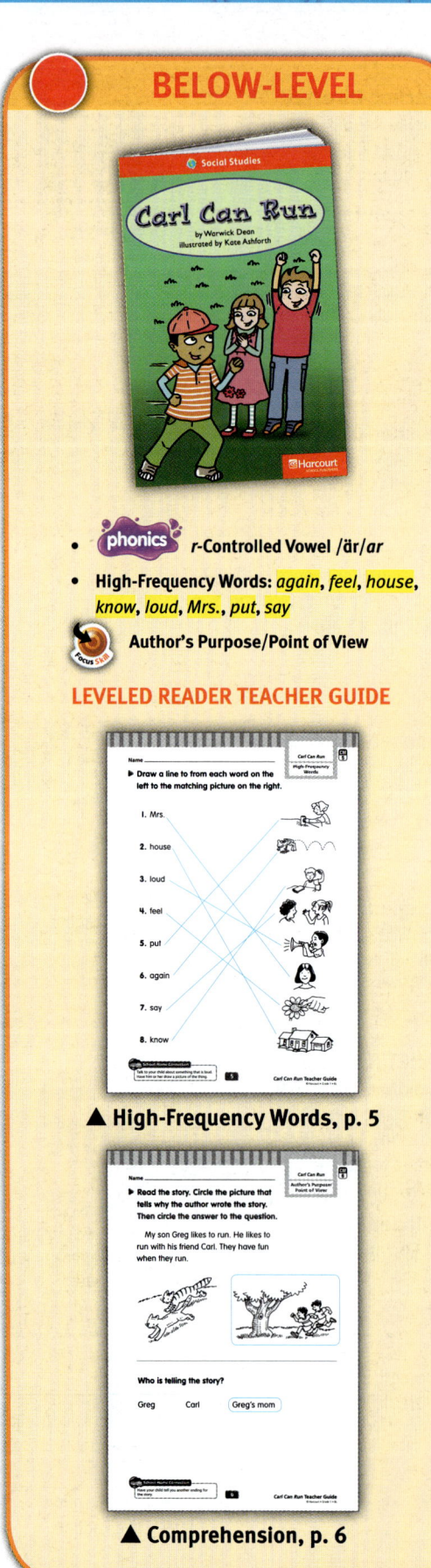

- **phonics** *r*-Controlled Vowel /är/*ar*
- **High-Frequency Words:** *again, feel, house, know, loud, Mrs., put, say*

  **Author's Purpose/Point of View**

**LEVELED READER TEACHER GUIDE**

▲ High-Frequency Words, p. 5

▲ Comprehension, p. 6

### ON-LEVEL

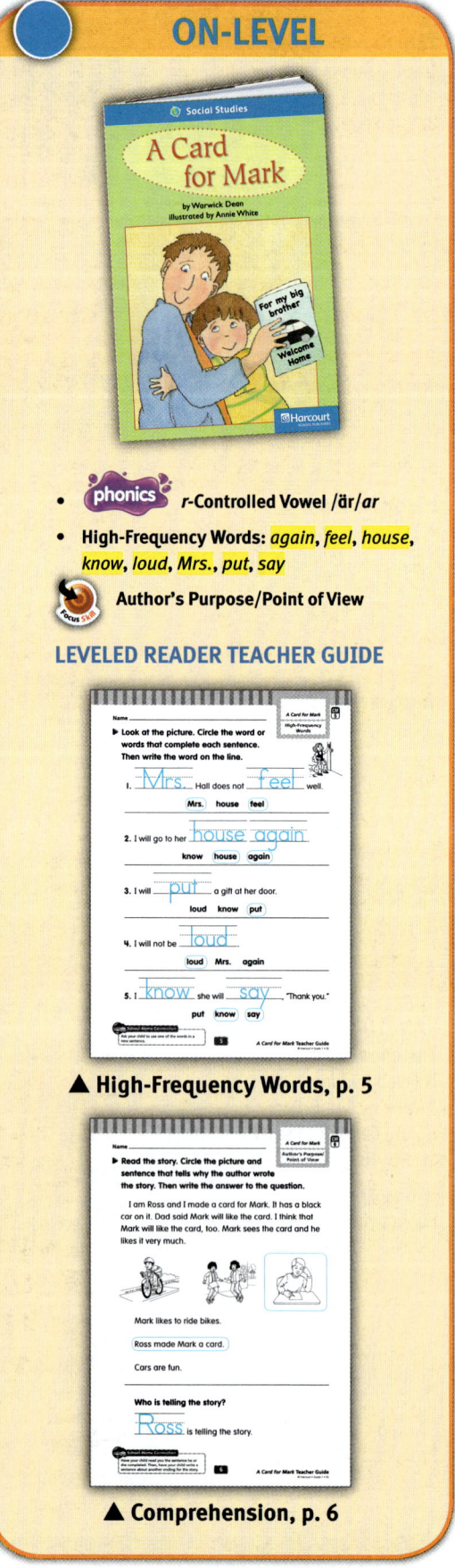

- **phonics** *r*-Controlled Vowel /är/*ar*
- **High-Frequency Words:** *again, feel, house, know, loud, Mrs., put, say*

  **Author's Purpose/Point of View**

**LEVELED READER TEACHER GUIDE**

▲ High-Frequency Words, p. 5

▲ Comprehension, p. 6

**www.harcourtschool.com/storytown**

Go online

★ **Leveled Readers, online**
*Searchable by Genre, Skill, Vocabulary, Level, or Title*
★ **Student Activities and Teacher Resources, online**

## ADVANCED

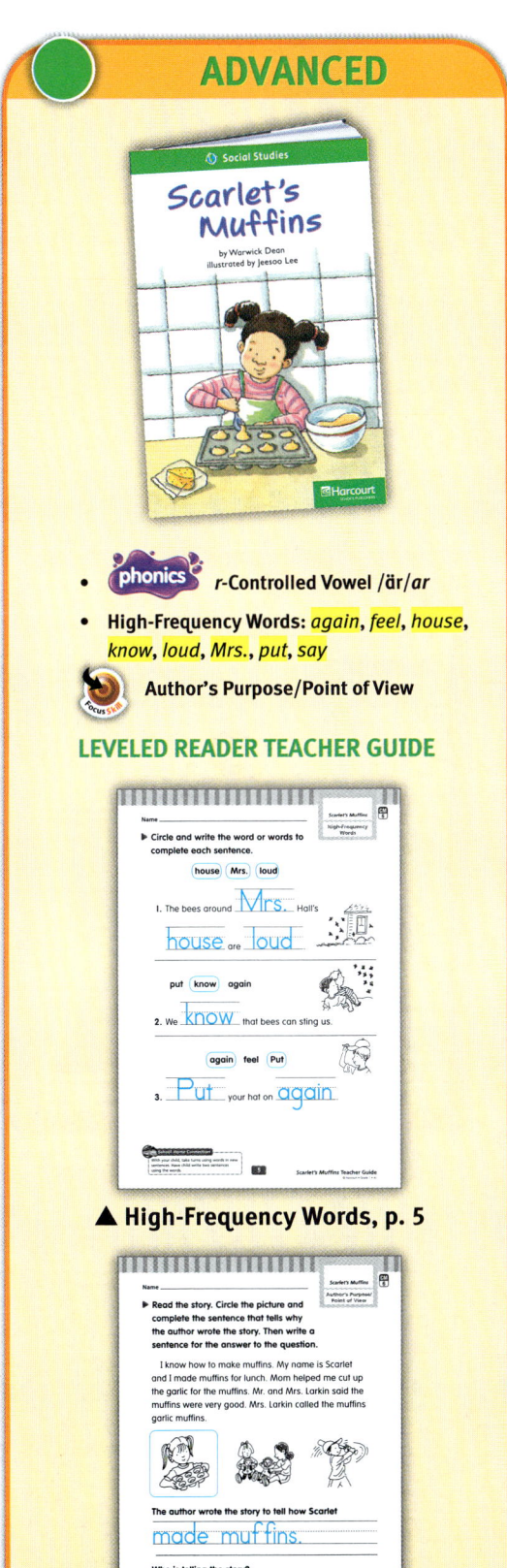

Scarlet's Muffins
by Warwick Dean
illustrated by Jeesoo Lee

- **phonics** *r*-Controlled Vowel /är/*ar*
- **High-Frequency Words:** *again*, *feel*, *house*, *know*, *loud*, *Mrs.*, *put*, *say*
- Author's Purpose/Point of View

### LEVELED READER TEACHER GUIDE

▲ **High-Frequency Words, p. 5**

▲ **Comprehension, p. 6**

## ELL

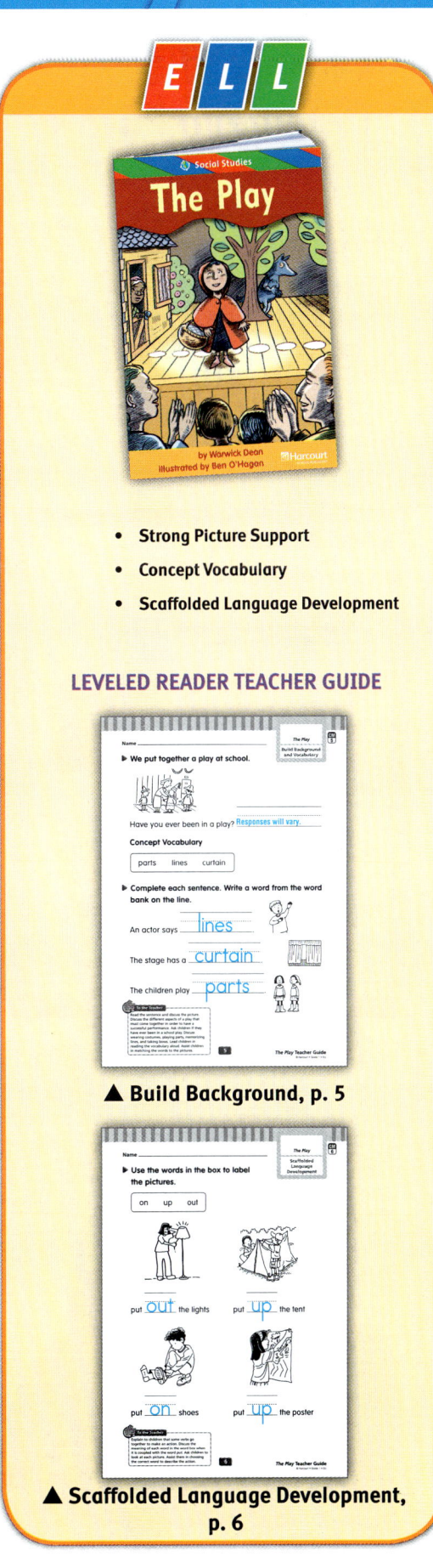

The Play
by Warwick Dean
illustrated by Ben O'Hagan

- **Strong Picture Support**
- **Concept Vocabulary**
- **Scaffolded Language Development**

### LEVELED READER TEACHER GUIDE

▲ **Build Background, p. 5**

▲ **Scaffolded Language Development, p. 6**

## CLASSROOM LIBRARY

### for Self-Selected Reading

**EASY**

▲ *What's Bugging Pamela?* by Michael Dodd. NARRATIVE NONFICTION

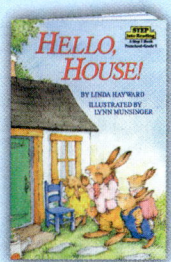

**AVERAGE**

▲ *Hello, House!* by Linda Hayward. FOLKTALE

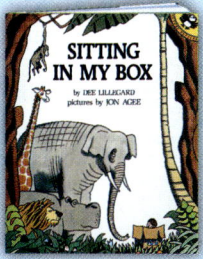

**AVERAGE**

▲ *Sitting in My Box* by Dee Lillegard. FANTASY

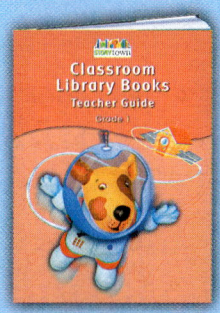

▲ **Classroom Library Books Teacher Guide, pp. 20–23, 40–47**

# Literacy Centers
*15 Min. each*

## Management Support

While you provide direct instruction to individuals or small groups, other children can work on literacy center activities.

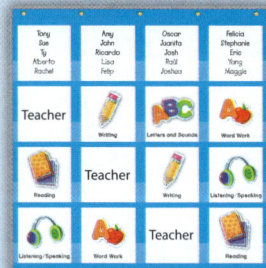

▲ Literacy Centers Pocket Chart

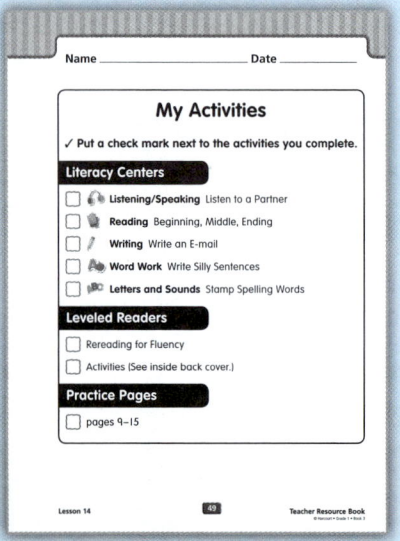

▲ Teacher Resource Book, p. 49

## Homework for the Week

**TEACHER RESOURCE BOOK, PAGE 18**
The *Homework Copying Master* provides activities to complete for each day of the week.

**www.harcourtschool.com/ storytown**

---

### LISTENING/SPEAKING
## Listen to a Partner

**Objectives** *To practice reading in a manner that sounds like natural speech; to practice listening attentively*

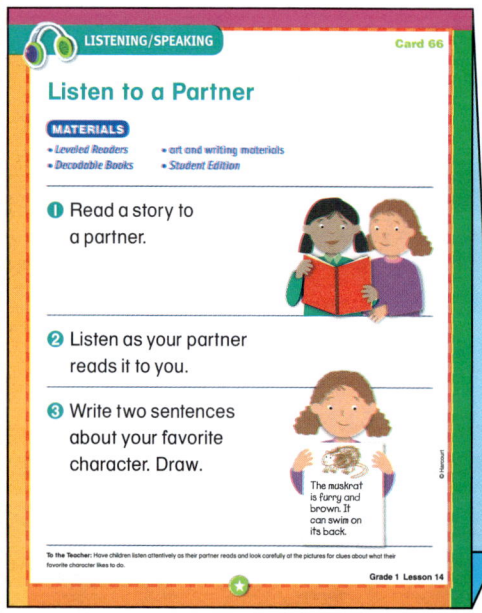

⭐ **Literacy Center Kit • Card 66**

---

### READING
## Beginning, Middle, Ending

**Objective** *To improve comprehension of a story by using a graphic organizer*

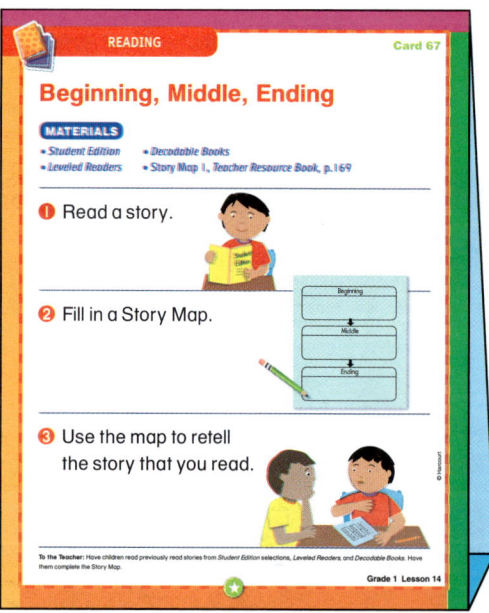

⭐ **Literacy Center Kit • Card 67**

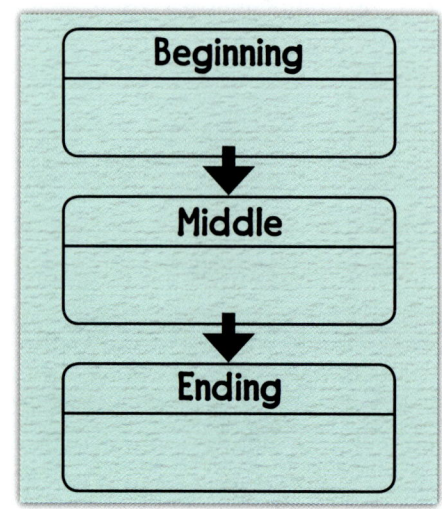

Beginning

↓

Middle

↓

Ending

---

**Go online**

www.harcourtschool.com/storytown

★ Additional Literacy Center Activities
★ Resources for Parents and Teachers

Differentiated
for Your Needs

 **WRITING**

# Write an E-mail

**Objective** *To practice writing a personal response*

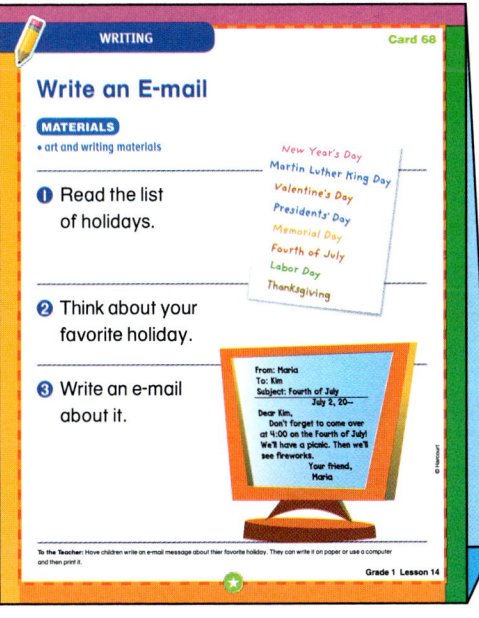

**WRITING** Card 68

## Write an E-mail

**MATERIALS**
• art and writing materials

New Year's Day
Martin Luther King Day
Valentine's Day
Presidents' Day
Memorial Day
Fourth of July
Labor Day
Thanksgiving

❶ Read the list of holidays.

❷ Think about your favorite holiday.

❸ Write an e-mail about it.

From: Maria
To: Kim
Subject: Fourth of July
July 2, 20—

Dear Kim,
Don't forget to come over at 4:00 on the Fourth of July! We'll have a picnic. Then we'll see fireworks.
Your friend,
Maria

To the Teacher: Have children write an e-mail message about their favorite holiday. They can write it on paper or use a computer and then print it.

Grade 1 • Lesson 14

⭐ **Literacy Center Kit • Card 68**

Our Thanksgiving

---

**WORD WORK**

# Write Silly Sentences

**Objective** *To recognize and write high-frequency words*

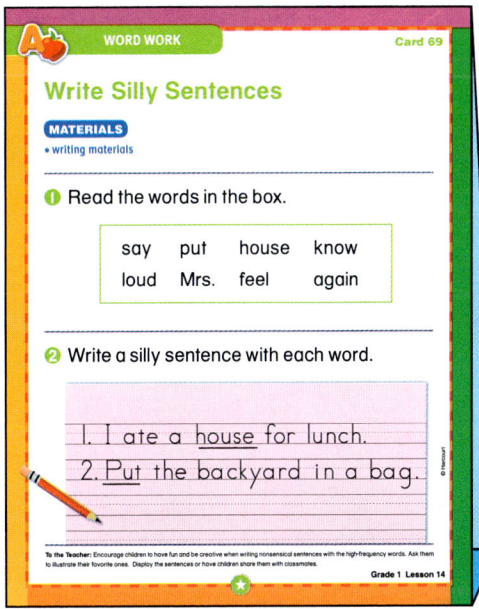

**WORD WORK** Card 69

## Write Silly Sentences

**MATERIALS**
• writing materials

❶ Read the words in the box.

| say | put | house | know |
| loud | Mrs. | feel | again |

❷ Write a silly sentence with each word.

1. I ate a house for lunch.
2. Put the backyard in a bag.

To the Teacher: Encourage children to have fun and be creative when writing nonsensical sentences with the high-frequency words. Ask them to illustrate their favorite ones. Display the sentences or have children share them with classmates.

Grade 1 • Lesson 14

⭐ **Literacy Center Kit • Card 69**

I ate a house for lunch.

---

**LETTERS AND SOUNDS**

# Stamp Spelling Words

**Objective** *To build and read this week's spelling words*

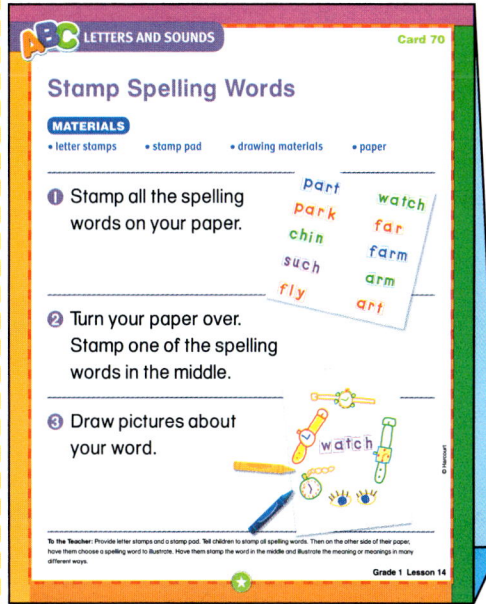

**LETTERS AND SOUNDS** Card 70

## Stamp Spelling Words

**MATERIALS**
• letter stamps  • stamp pad  • drawing materials  • paper

❶ Stamp all the spelling words on your paper.

part    watch
park    far
chin    farm
such    arm
fly     art

❷ Turn your paper over. Stamp one of the spelling words in the middle.

❸ Draw pictures about your word.

watch

To the Teacher: Provide letter stamps and a stamp pad. Tell children to stamp all spelling words. Then on the other side of their paper, have them choose a spelling word to illustrate. Have them stamp the word in the middle and illustrate the meaning or meanings in many different ways.

Grade 1 • Lesson 14

⭐ **Literacy Center Kit • Card 70**

## Day at a Glance

### Day 1

**Phonemic Awareness**
- Phoneme Blending

 **and Spelling**
- Introduce: *r*-Controlled Vowel /är/*ar*
- Pretest

**Reading**
- Get Started Story: "Ann's Trip to the Stars," *Student Edition,* pp. 54–61

 Read!

**Fluency**
- Intonation

**Comprehension**
- *Read-Aloud Anthology:* "The Hare and the Tortoise"
  Preview: Author's Purpose/Point of View

**Robust Vocabulary**
- Introduce: *approached, energetic, pace*

**Grammar**
- Introduce: Names of Holidays

**Modeled Writing**
- E-mail

# Warm-Up Routines

## Oral Language

**Objective** *To listen and respond appropriately to oral communication*

### Question of the Day

Imagine that you will look for a wild animal. What is it? Where will you look?

Have children brainstorm the names of wild animals, and discuss where each animal might live. Have children complete these sentence frames:

**I will look for a _____. I will look in _____.**

## Read Aloud

**Objective** *To listen for a purpose*

**Routine Card 17** **BIG BOOK** Share *We're Going on a Lion Hunt.* Read aloud the author/illustrator's name, and have children describe his role(s).

- **Set a purpose and read.** Tell children to listen to find out where the children go. Invite them to listen responsively as you read this version of a classic story. Create hand gestures for children to do when you say *over, under, around,* and *through.* Have children use the gestures to participate actively when you read this patterned story. Then ask them to identify the most exciting part.

▲ Big Book
*Were Going on a Lion Hunt*

## Word Wall

**Objective** *To read high-frequency words*

**REVIEW HIGH-FREQUENCY WORDS** Review *cold, play, says, her, fly, watch,* and other previously learned high-frequency words. Say each word, ask a volunteer to point to it, and have children read it aloud. Then point to words at random, and have children reread them. Repeat several times to reinforce instant recognition.

| cold | play | says |
|------|------|------|
| her | fly | watch |

## Phonemic Awareness

**Objective** *To blend phonemes into recognizable words*

**Routine Card 1** **PHONEME BLENDING** Tell children that you will say some words very slowly. Model by saying /b/ /e/ /l/ /t/ slowly, and then say the word naturally—*belt*. Say the following phonemes, having children blend the sounds to say the words:

/är/ /m/ (arm)   /d/ /r/ /i/ /l/ (drill)   /g/ /a/ /s/ /p/ (gasp)

/g/ /r/ /i/ /n/ (grin)   /är/ /t/ (art)   /k/ /är/ /d/ (card)

/b/ /a/ /th/ (bath)   /b/ /r/ /u/ /sh/ (brush)   /k/ /ô/ /s/ /t/ (cost)

/b/ /är/ /n/ (barn)   /f/ /är/ /m/ (farm)

 Podcasting: Phoneme Blending

# r-Controlled Vowel /är/ar

 **phonics** *and Spelling*

## Objectives

- *To recognize and generate the sound /är/ar*
- *To build and blend words with /är/ar*
- *To use /är/ar and other known letter-sounds to spell words*
- *To spell known high-frequency words*

## Skill Trace

 **Tested** *r-Controlled Vowel /är/ar*

| Introduce | T132–T135 |
|---|---|
| Reteach | S12 |
| Review | TT148–T150, T172–T173, T185 |
| Test | Bk 1-3 |
| Maintain | Bk 1-5, T348–T349 |

 Refer to *Sounds of Letters CD* Track 13 for pronunciation of /är/.

March

---

### Connecting Letter to Sound

**Routine Card 12** **DEVELOP PHONEMIC AWARENESS OF /är/** Say the word *arch.* Have children say the word. Repeat for the words *armor* and *artist.* Say: **The words *arch, armor,* and *artist* begin with the /är/ sound.** Have children say /är/ several times.

**CONNECT LETTERS AND SOUND** Display *Sound/Spelling Card ar* and say the letter names. Explain that the letters *a* and *r* together stand for the /är/ sound, the sound at the beginning of *arm.* Have children say /är/ several times as you touch the letters.

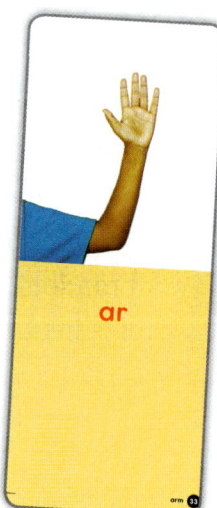

▲ **Sound/Spelling Card**

**DISCRIMINATE /är/** Give each child an *a* and an *r* Word Builder Card. Say: **When I say a word that begins with /är/, hold up your cards and say /är/. When I say a word that does not begin with /är/, hold the cards behind your back.**

arm   army   ripe   arch   camel   awning   arctic

Tell children that some words have the sound /är/ in the middle. Tell children that *park* has /är/ in the middle. Say *park,* elongating the vowel sound—/pärk/. Then say it naturally—*park.* Say the following words, elongating the medial sound, and have children identify the words that have the /är/ sound:

barn   cat   bark   parka   paste   garden

Then repeat the procedure for the final position with these words:

star   far   fork   later   car   for

**5-DAY PHONICS**

| DAY 1 | Introduce *r*-Controlled Vowel /är/*ar* |
| DAY 2 | Word Building with *r*-Controlled Vowel /är/*ar* |
| DAY 3 | Word Building |
| DAY 4 | Inflections -*s*, -*ed*, -*ing* (no spelling change) |
| DAY 5 | Inflections -*s*, -*ed*, -*ing* (no spelling change) |

## Word Blending

**DIBELS**
Nonsense Word Fluency
**NWF**

**WORDS WITH /är/*ar*** Demonstrate each step with *Letter Cards* and a pocket chart. Have children repeat each step after you, using their *Word Builder Cards* and *Word Builders*.

**Routine Card 13**

**BLEND AND READ *CAR*** Hold up the *c* and say /k/. Hold up *a* and *r* together and say /är/.

- Place the letters *c, a, r* in the pocket chart. Make sure the letters *a* and *r* touch. Have children do the same with their letters and *Word Builders*.

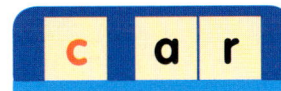

- Point to the letter *c* and say /k/. Point to the *a* and *r* and say /är/. Have children do the same.

- Slide the *a* and *r* next to *c*. Run your hand under the letters as you blend the sounds by elongating them—/kär/. Have children repeat.

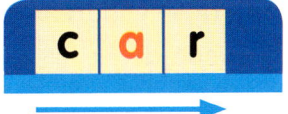

- Read *car* naturally. Repeat, having children read the word with you.

Follow the same procedures for *cart, tar, star, start,* and *smart*.

## Professional Development

 **Podcasting:** Word Blending, Gr. 1

**E L L**

**Blend and Read** Use *Photo Cards* to support word meaning as children blend and read. For example, after children blend *star*, display the *Photo Card 142 (stars)* and have them blend and read *stars*. You can also have children blend and read *Photo Cards 4 (arm), 29 (cart), 56 (farm), 126 (scarf),* and *166 (yard)*.

▲ Photo Cards 142, 166

**ADVANCED**

**Brainstorm Words** Have volunteers brainstorm a list of words with /är/ that they already know. Challenge them to write a sentence with as many /är/ words as possible.

car ▶

# r-Controlled Vowel /är/ar

 **phonics** *and Spelling*

## Professional Development

 **Podcasting:** Word Building, Gr. 1; Spelling and Dictation, Gr. 1

### BELOW-LEVEL

**Build Spelling Words** Have children use *Word Builder Cards a* and *t* to build the word *at* in their *Word Builders*. Then have them add an *r* between the *a* and the *t*. Lead them in reading aloud the word *art* as they track the letters. Repeat with *am* to build *arm* and *pat* to build *part*.

## Word Building

**Routine Card 14**

**BUILD SPELLING WORDS** Use *Letter Cards* and a pocket chart. Have children use their *Word Builder Cards* and *Word Builders*. Place the *Letter Cards f, a,* and *r* in the pocket chart. Have children say the name and sound for the letter *f* and for *a, r* together. Then read *far* naturally.

Have children build and read new words. Write them on the board. Say:

- **Add *m* to the end of *far*. What word did you make?**
- **Take away the *f*. What did you make?**
- **Change *m* to *t*. What did you make?**
- **Add *p* before *a*. What did you make?**

Have children read the words on the board.

| f | a | r |
|---|---|---|

| f | a | r | m |
|---|---|---|---|

| a | r | m |
|---|---|---|

| a | r | t |
|---|---|---|

| p | a | r | t |
|---|---|---|---|

### BELOW-LEVEL · ON-LEVEL · ADVANCED

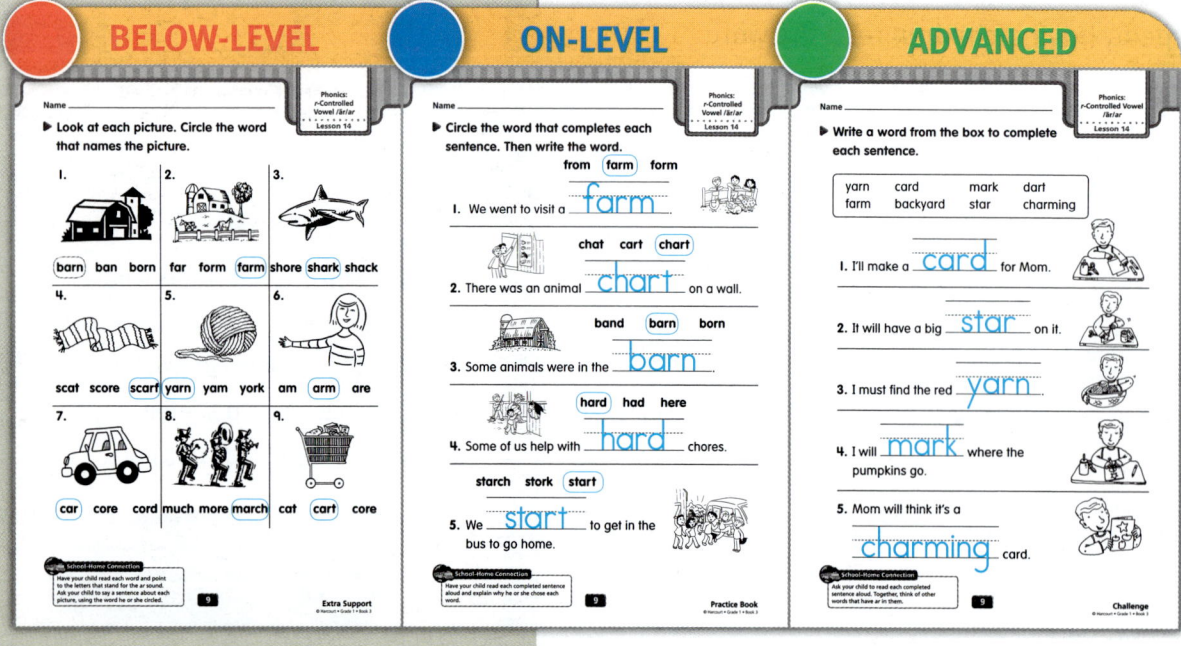

▲ **Extra Support, p. 9**  ▲ **Practice Book, p. 9**  ▲ **Challenge, p. 9**

### ELL

- Group children according to academic levels, and assign one of the pages on the left.
- Clarify any unfamiliar concepts as necessary. See *ELL Teacher Guide,* Lesson 14, for support in scaffolding instruction.

**5-DAY SPELLING**

| DAY 1 | Pretest |
| DAY 2 | Word Building |
| DAY 3 | State the Generalization |
| DAY 4 | Review |
| DAY 5 | Posttest |

## Introduce Spelling Words

**PRETEST** Say the first word and read the dictation sentence. Repeat the word as children write it. Write the word on the board and have children check their spelling. Tell them to circle the word if they spelled it correctly or write it correctly if they did not. Repeat for words 2–10.

### Words with /är/*ar*

| | | |
|---|---|---|
| 1. | far | The ocean is **far** away. |
| 2. | farm | Horses live on that **farm.** |
| 3. | arm | Please raise your right **arm.** |
| 4. | art | We drew pictures in **art** class. |
| 5. | part | I ate **part** of the apple. |
| 6. | park | We play ball in the **park.** |

### Review

| | | |
|---|---|---|
| 7. | chin | The baby had food on her **chin.** |
| 8. | such | There is **such** a lot to do! |

### High-Frequency

| | | |
|---|---|---|
| 9. | fly | We saw the birds **fly** away. |
| 10. | watch | Dad will **watch** the baby. |

### Spelling Words

| | | | |
|---|---|---|---|
| 1. | far | 6. | park |
| 2. | farm | 7. | chin |
| 3. | arm | 8. | such |
| 4. | art | 9. | fly |
| 5. | part | 10. | watch |

---

✓ **MONITOR PROGRESS**

#### Phonics: *r*-Controlled Vowel /är/*ar*

**IF** children have difficulty building and reading words with *r*-controlled vowel /är/,

**THEN** help them blend and read the words *far, farm, arm, art, part,* and *park* individually.

**Small-Group Instruction, p. S12:**

● **BELOW-LEVEL:** Reteach   ● **ON-LEVEL:** Reinforce   ● **ADVANCED:** Extend

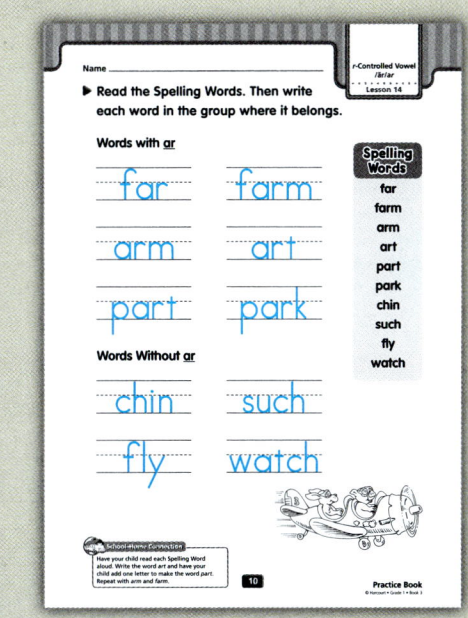

▲ Practice Book, p. 10

# Reading

*Get Started Story:* Ann's Trip to the Stars

## Objectives
- *To use letter-sound knowledge to read decodable text*
- *To review high-frequency words*
- *To develop fluency*

## Professional Development

 **Podcasting:** Reading Decodable Text, Gr. 1

## Options for Reading

 **BELOW-LEVEL**

**Echo-Reading** Have children echo-read each sentence. Pause to discuss it using the Monitor Comprehension questions. Have children frame and read words with /är/*ar*.

 **ON-LEVEL**

**Monitor Comprehension** Have children read the story aloud, page by page. Ask the Monitor Comprehension questions as you go. Then lead them in retelling the story and describing their favorite parts.

 **ADVANCED**

**Independent Reading** Have children read each page silently, looking up each time they finish a page. Ask the Monitor Comprehension questions as you go, and then discuss what things they think are strange in the story.

### Apply *r*-Controlled Vowel /är/*ar*

**READ DECODABLE TEXT** Write the following sentences on the board. Tell children that the sentences are about a girl in a story they will read.

**Ann starts her long trip.**

**It is dark.**

- Have children read the sentences as you track the print.
- Have volunteers frame and read the words with /är/*ar*.
- Tell children that many of the words in the story have the /är/ sound.

**Routine Card 17** **INTRODUCE THE STORY** Have children look at the title page and read aloud the title. Ask them to point to the names of the author and the illustrator as you read them aloud. Discuss the illustration. Tell children they will read the story to find out how the girl uses her imagination to travel into outer space.

**Preview** Preview the story with a picture walk. Use the illustrations to develop meaning for the text. Then guide children through the story, using the Monitor Comprehension questions.

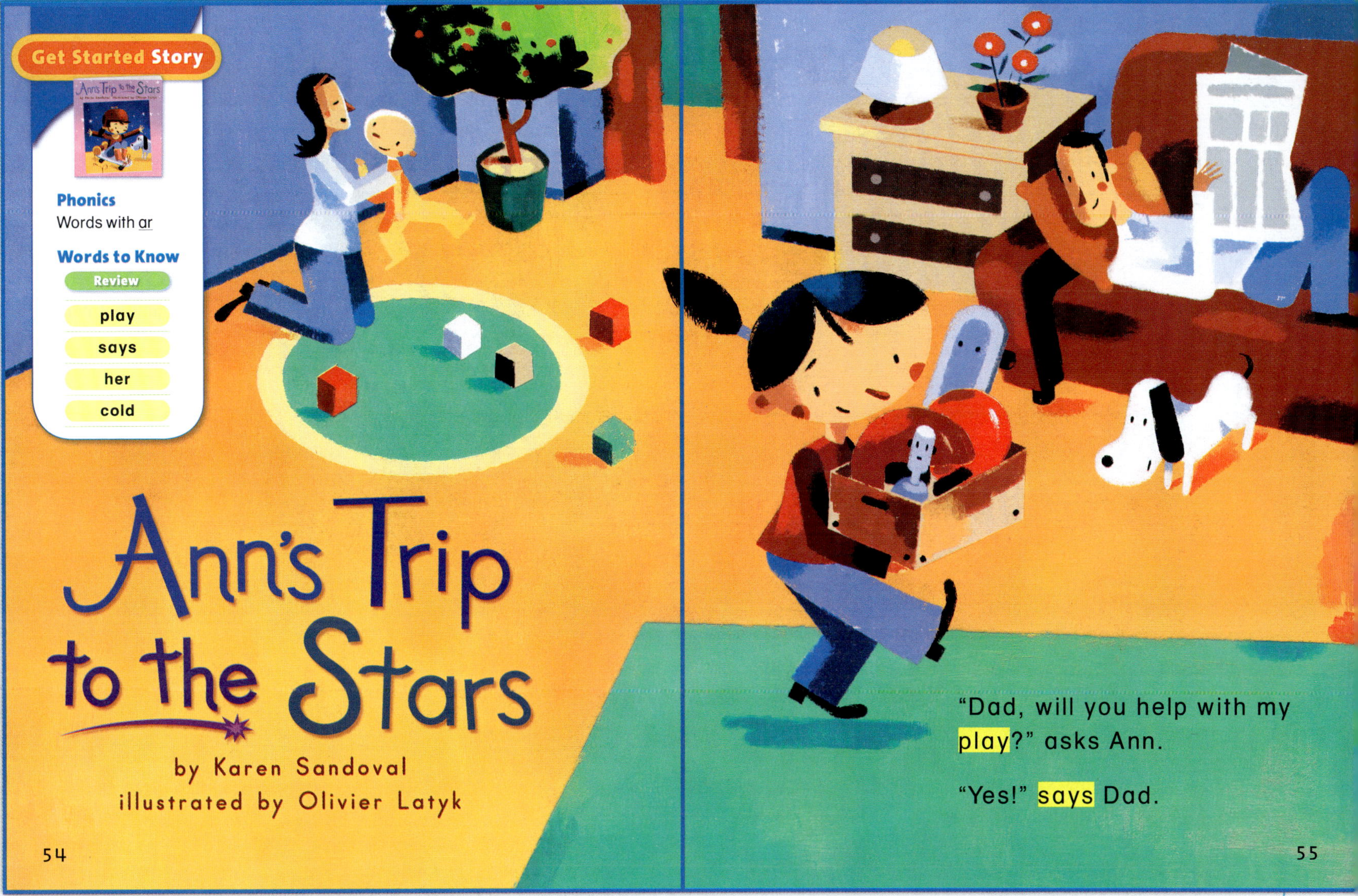

Get Started Story

**Phonics**
Words with <u>ar</u>

**Words to Know**

Review

play

says

her

cold

# Ann's Trip to the Stars

by Karen Sandoval
illustrated by Olivier Latyk

54

"Dad, will you help with my <mark>play</mark>?" asks Ann.

"Yes!" <mark>says</mark> Dad.

55

# Monitor Comprehension

**PAGES 54–55** Say: **It looks like the girl is inside her house. What are some things you see in this room? Let's read on to find out what the girl is going to do.**

1 **NOTE DETAILS** What does the girl need help with? (her play)

2 **NOTE DETAILS** What does Dad say when Ann asks for help? (Yes!)

**Clarify Meaning** Tell children that a play is a story that is acted out. Talk about things that would be needed to perform a play, such as scenery, props, actors, and words for the actors to say.

## TECHNOLOGY

 **eBook** "Ann's Trip to the Stars" is available in an eBook.

 **Audiotext** "Ann's Trip to the Stars" is available on *Audiotext Grade 1*, CD 6.

# Monitor Comprehension

**HIGH-FREQUENCY WORDS**

**Review** Remind children that they have already learned to read the high-frequency words *my, go, says, cold,* and *the.* Have them frame and read those words on these two pages.

**PAGES 56–57** Say: **I wonder why the girl is wearing a helmet and sitting on her skateboard? Let's read to find out.**

1. **CHARACTERS' MOTIVATIONS** **Why do you think the girl wears and uses objects from her house?** (They help her pretend that she is really traveling through space.) **Why is she sitting on a skateboard?** (She is pretending that the skateboard is her spaceship.)

2. **NOTE DETAILS** **What is the mother acting as in this play?** (She is the sun.) **How do you know?** (She is carrying a large yellow ball of yarn.) **What does the large red ball represent?** (Mars) **Why?** (Mars is red.)

"My ship crashes!" Ann yells. "It is dark. Sharp rocks block my path."

"My ship will not start," says Ann.

Bark! Bark!

"Carl has a kit to fix it!"

58

59

# Monitor Comprehension

**PAGES 58–59** Say: It looks like the girl is upset. I wonder what she is doing now. Let's read to find out.

1 **DRAW CONCLUSIONS** What do you think happened to the girl's spaceship? (It crashed.) What do you think she is pretending to do now? (She is pretending it is a big problem.)

2 **DRAW CONCLUSIONS** Who is Carl? (the dog) What part in the play do you think Carl plays? (someone who can fix things) Why? (He is carrying something and Ann says it is a kit for fixing the ship.)

## STRATEGIC READING

**Words with /är/ar** Remind children that this story includes many words with *r*-controlled vowel /är/*ar*. Ask them to count and read the words with /är/*ar* on these two pages.

"I fix my ship and blast off! I am back," says Ann. "The end!"

60

Dad claps. Mom claps. Ben stands and claps, and Carl barks. "Thanks!" says Ann with a big grin.

61

# Monitor Comprehension

**PAGES 60–61** Say: **I see Ann's family watching her and clapping. Let's read to find out why.**

**1** **SEQUENCE** **What happens at the end of Ann's play?** (She pretends to come back from outer space; her family claps.)

**2** 🌋 **AUTHOR'S PURPOSE** **Why do you think the author wrote this story?** (to make us laugh)

**3** **IDENTIFY WITH CHARACTERS** **Would you enjoy putting on a play as Ann does in this story? Why or why not?** (Responses will vary.)

## BUILD VOCABULARY

**Use Imagination** Remind children that Ann uses her imagination to take a trip to the stars. She pretends that things in her house are real things that she would see or take on her trip. Encourage children to tell how the girl uses her imagination to change these things into objects for her trip:

- skateboard: spaceship
- bike helmet: space helmet
- ball of yarn: the sun
- ball: Mars
- socks: rocks

# Check Comprehension
## *Retelling*

## Retell

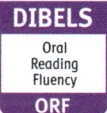

**DIBELS** Oral Reading Fluency **ORF**

**RETELL "ANN'S TRIP TO THE STARS"** Ask children to name the main character of the story and tell where it takes place. Then have volunteers tell about the events in the order in which they happened. Write their responses in a flowchart such as the one below.

| | | |
|---|---|---|
| The girl asks for help with her play about going into space. | → She pretends to visit Mars. She pretends her ship breaks and then gets fixed. | → Her family claps for her at the end of her play. |

## Repeated Reading

**DIBELS** Oral Reading Fluency **ORF**

**READ WITH A PARTNER** Have partners reread "Ann's Trip to the Stars" aloud three or four times. Listen to partners read, and give them feedback about stressing the appropriate words as they read so that their reading sounds like natural speech.

#  Comprehension
## *Read Aloud*

## Objectives
- *To set a purpose for listening*
- *To understand characteristics of fables*

## Daily Comprehension
 **Author's Purpose/ Point of View**

| | |
|---|---|
| **DAY 1:** | Preview Author's Purpose/ Point of View *Read-Aloud Anthology* |
| **DAY 2:** | Introduce Author's Purpose/ Point of View *Teacher Edition* |
| **DAY 3:** | Review Author's Purpose/ Point of View *Paired Selection Teacher Edition* |
| **DAY 4:** | Review Author's Purpose/ Point of View *Big Book* |
| **DAY 5:** | Review Author's Purpose/ Point of View Comparing Texts |

**Connect to Prior Knowledge** Display *Photo Card 114 (rabbit)*. Have children pantomime how a rabbit moves. Explain that a hare is a relative of the rabbit. Then explain that a tortoise is a slow-moving turtle. Have children pantomime the movements of a tortoise. Then have them predict who might win a race between a hare and a tortoise.

### Before Reading

**CONNECT TO PRIOR KNOWLEDGE** Tell children that they will listen to an old story about a hare and a tortoise who have a race. Explain to children that a hare is a relative of the rabbit and that a tortoise is a type of turtle. Ask children which animal they think can run faster, and encourage them to explain their thinking.

▲ *Read-Aloud Anthology,* "The Hare and the Tortoise," p. 56

**GENRE STUDY: FABLE** Explain that "The Hare and the Tortoise" is a fable. Model your thinking by saying:

**Think Aloud** **A fable is a story that teaches a lesson. It may have animals that talk and act like people. Fables often use these animals to teach a lesson about how people should treat each other.**

 **PREVIEW THE SKILL: AUTHOR'S PURPOSE/ POINT OF VIEW** Tell children that an author has a reason for writing a story. Explain that sometimes the author writes a story to entertain the reader and sometimes the author writes a story to give the reader information. Conclude by telling children that they will be discussing why the author wrote "The Hare and the Tortoise" later in the week. Then read the fable to children.

### After Reading

**RESPOND** Invite children to name elements of the story that make it a fable. List their ideas on the board and discuss them.

# Build Robust Vocabulary

## Listening/Speaking: *Words from the Read-Aloud*

### Teach/Model

Routine Card 15

**INTRODUCE ROBUST VOCABULARY** Use *Routine Card 15* to introduce the words.

❶ Put the word in **selection context.**
❷ Provide the **Student-Friendly Explanation** for children.
❸ Have children **say the word** with you.
❹ Use the word in other contexts, and have children **interact with the word's meaning.**
❺ Say the Student-Friendly Explanation again, and ask children to **name the word** that goes with it.

● **Selection Context:** The hare agreed to race and **approached** the starting line.

❹ **Interact with Word Meaning:** If I approached the door, I would move closer to it. If I approached you, I would move closer to where you are sitting.

● **Selection Context:** The hare bragged that a slow, poky tortoise could never beat a fast, **energetic** hare.

❹ **Interact with Word Meaning:** I feel energetic if I sleep well and then eat a healthful breakfast. Do you feel energetic if you do these things, too? Why?

● **Selection Context:** The tortoise kept up a slow, steady **pace** during the race.

❹ **Interact with Word Meaning:** If a race was short, I would run at a fast pace. If a race was long, I would run at a much slower pace.

### Practice/Apply

**GUIDED PRACTICE** Ask children to do the following:
- Imagine that a strange dog approached you on the street. Tell a classmate how you might feel.
- Imagine that you are in bed and your alarm has just gone off. Show how you might get up if you were feeling very energetic.

### Objective
- *To develop robust vocabulary through discussing a literature selection*

INTRODUCE **Tested** ✓

**Student-Friendly Explanations**

**approached** If you approached something, you moved toward it.

**energetic** If you are energetic, you are filled with energy.

**pace** Your pace is how fast you are going.

E L L

**Introduce Vocabulary** Act out the meaning of each word. For example, for *pace,* demonstrate walking at a slow *pace* and then at a fast pace. Have children imitate your actions as they repeat each word.

**pace**

# Grammar
## Names of Holidays

**5-DAY GRAMMAR**

| | |
|---|---|
| **DAY 1** | Introduce Names of Holidays |
| **DAY 2** | Dictate Sentences About Holidays |
| **DAY 3** | Write Sentences About Holidays |
| **DAY 4** | Revise Names of Holidays |
| **DAY 5** | Write Holiday Messages |

## Objectives
- To recognize names of holidays
- To capitalize names of holidays correctly

## Daily Proofreading

**does your arm hurt.**

(Does, hurt?)

### Names of Holidays

Valentine's Day    Fourth of July

Presidents' Day    Thanksgiving Day

Grade 1, Lesson 14    LA27    Grammar: Names of Holidays

**Transparency LA27**

## Teach/Model

**INTRODUCE THE CONCEPT** Display an annual calendar. Recall with children that it shows the names of months and days. Explain that many calendars also show important holidays. Turn to the month of November and have children find the fourth Thursday of the month. Then point to and track the word *Thanksgiving* as you read it aloud. Write the following sentence on the board and track the print as you read it aloud to children and then with children.

**We celebrate Thanksgiving in November.**

Have a volunteer underline the holiday. Ask children how the word begins. (with a capital letter) Explain that the name of a holiday always begins with a capital letter. Explain that when the holiday has two or more words, such as *Mother's Day,* both words are usually capitalized.

## Guided Practice

**NAME HOLIDAYS** Display **Transparency LA27**. Ask: **What holiday do you think of when you look at the first picture? How do we celebrate this holiday?** Model an answer: **On Valentine's Day, we send cards called valentines.** Write the sentence on the board and point out the name of the holiday and its capitalization. Ask other questions about the holidays associated with the pictures, and have children respond.

## Practice/Apply

**CAPITALIZE NAMES OF HOLIDAYS** Write on the board one of the sentences children say, using a lowercase beginning letter when writing the name of the holiday. Read it aloud with them, and have them write it correctly.

# Modeled Writing
### E-mail

**5-DAY WRITING**

| DAY 1 | Modeled Writing |
| --- | --- |
| DAY 2 | Shared Writing |
| DAY 3 | Shared Writing |
| DAY 4 | Independent Writing |
| DAY 5 | Independent Writing |

## Teach/Model

**INTRODUCE E-MAIL** Display **Transparency LA28,** and explain that this is an e-mail that a girl wrote as a reminder to a friend. Read the e-mail to children, and talk about the different parts. Explain that the computer adds the date automatically. Together, develop a list of the characteristics of a well-written e-mail. Remind children to check with an adult before using e-mail.

### E-mail Message

- Use a computer to get and send e-mail.
- From shows your e-mail address.
- To shows the e-mail address of the person the message is going to.
- Subject tells what the e-mail is about.
- The message can begin with a greeting and end with your name.

**CONVENTIONS** Have children identify the capital letters and periods in the e-mail message in the student model.

## Guided Practice

**DRAFT AN E-MAIL** Model the first sentence about an upcoming event, such as: *Remember to bring lunch on Thursday for our trip to the museum.* Talk about the main idea of the message. Have children discuss how to complete the "From," "To," and "Subject" lines.

## Practice/Apply

**SHARE AN E-MAIL** Have children draw pictures of an upcoming event. For example, it might be a family member's birthday, a class project, or a community activity. Ask partners to take turns sharing their pictures and the main idea of a message they might send as an e-mail reminder. Save children's pictures to use on Days 2–5.

## Objectives

- *To understand the form of e-mail messages*
- *To develop a list of criteria for effective e-mail*
- *To generate ideas for writing*

### Writing Prompt

**Write About School** Have children write about and draw something they have enjoyed doing at school recently.

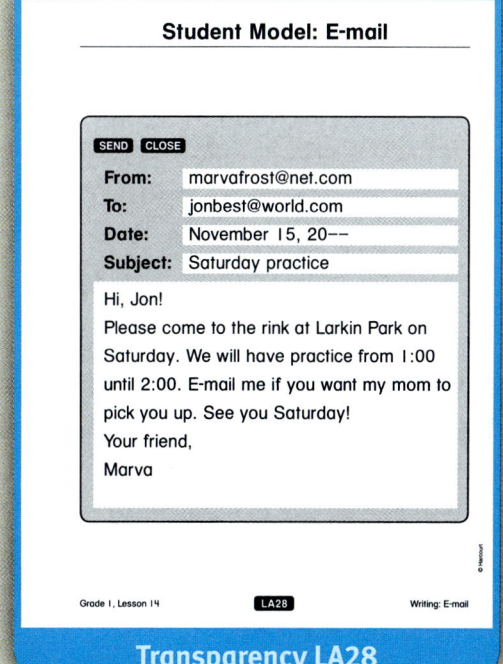

**Student Model: E-mail**

SEND CLOSE

| From: | marvafrost@net.com |
| --- | --- |
| To: | jonbest@world.com |
| Date: | November 15, 20–– |
| Subject: | Saturday practice |

Hi, Jon!
Please come to the rink at Larkin Park on Saturday. We will have practice from 1:00 until 2:00. E-mail me if you want my mom to pick you up. See you Saturday!
Your friend,
Marva

Grade 1, Lesson 14          LA28          Writing: E-mail

**Transparency LA28**

## Day at a Glance

### Day 2

**Phonemic Awareness**
- Phoneme Blending

 **phonics** and Spelling
- Review: *r*-Controlled Vowel /är/*ar*
- Build Words

**Comprehension**

 Introduce: Author's Purpose and Point of View

**High-Frequency Words**
- Introduce: *again*, *feel*, *house*, *know*, *loud*, *Mrs.*, *put*, *say*

**Reading**
- "Mark's Big Day," *Student Edition*, pp. 66–87

**Read!**

**Fluency**
- Intonation

**Robust Vocabulary**
- Review: *approached*, *energetic*, *pace*

**Grammar**
- Review: Names of Holidays

**Shared Writing**
- E-mail

# Warm-Up Routines

## Oral Language

**Objective** *To listen and respond appropriately to oral communication*

### Question of the Day

What are you like today? How might you change as you grow up?

Write these frames. Initiate discussion; have children complete them.

**Today, I am _____. When I grow up, I might be _____.**

## Read Aloud

**Objective** *To listen for a purpose*

**BIG BOOK OF RHYMES AND POEMS** Display the poem and read the title and the poet's name. Ask children to describe the poet's role. Guide children to determine a purpose for listening. Suggest that they listen to find out what the poet wonders about growing up. After you read, ask children to identify the question the poet asks about growing up. Guide children to understand that the phrase *the Me I was* refers to the child that every adult once was. Encourage children to answer the question by telling what parts of themselves will stay the same and what parts will probably change as they grow up.

▲ Big Book of Rhymes and Poems, p. 27

## Word Wall

**Objective** *To read high-frequency words*

**REVIEW HIGH-FREQUENCY WORDS** Review *air, fly, friends, grew, need, play, rain, watch* and other previously learned high-frequency words. Say each word, ask a volunteer to point to it, and have children read it aloud. Then point to words at random, and have children reread them.

| | | | |
|---|---|---|---|
| air | fly | friends | grew |
| need | play | rain | watch |

## Phonemic Awareness

**Objective** *To blend phonemes into recognizable words*

**Routine Card 1**

**PHONEME BLENDING** Tell children they will sing a song and blend the sounds they hear in each word. Model the first word for them. Have children count the sounds in each word.

*(Sung to the tune of "If You're Happy and You Know It.")*

**If you're happy and you know it, say this word: /j/ /u/ /m/ /p/.**
**If you're happy and you know it, say this word: /j/ /u/ /m/ /p/.**
**If you're happy and you know it, then you really want to show it.**
**If you're happy and you know it, say this word.** (jump)

| | | |
|---|---|---|
| /p/ /i/ /n/ (pin) | /j/ /är/ (jar) | /h/ /u/ /g/ /z/ (hugs) |
| /s/ /a/ /t/ (sat) | /f/ /är/ (far) | /t/ /o/ /p/ (top) |
| /m/ /e/ /t/ (met) | /s/ /k/ /är/ (scar) | /h/ /u/ /n/ /t/ (hunt) |
| /l/ /i/ /p/ /s/ (lips) | /h/ /är/ /d/ (hard) | /är/ /m/ (arm) |

 **Podcasting: Phoneme Blending**

# r-Controlled Vowel /är/ ar

 **phonics** *and Spelling*

## Objectives

- *To blend sounds into words*
- *To spell three- and four-letter /är/ar words and high-frequency words*

## Skill Trace

**Tested** *r-Controlled Vowel /är/ ar*

| | |
|---|---|
| Introduce | T132–T135 |
| Reteach | S12 |
| Review | T148–T150, T172–T173, T185 |
| Test | Bk 1-3 |
| Maintain | Bk 1-5, T348–T349 |

## Spelling Words

| | |
|---|---|
| 1. **far** | 6. **park** |
| 2. **farm** | 7. **chin** |
| 3. **arm** | 8. **such** |
| 4. **art** | 9. **fly** |
| 5. **part** | 10. **watch** |

## Word Building

**DIBELS** Nonsense Word Fluency **NWF**

**Routine Card 14**

**BUILD AND READ A SPELLING WORD** Place the *Letter Cards f, a,* and *r* in the pocket chart. Arrange the cards so that *a* and *r* are touching. Remind children that the letters *ar* together stand for one sound—/är/. Ask children to say the sound of *f* and then *ar* together. Then read the word naturally—*far*.

**BUILD SPELLING WORDS** Ask children which letter you should add to make *far* become *farm*. (Add *m*.) Ask them which letter you should take away to make *farm* become *arm*. (Take away *f*.) Continue building spelling words 4–6 in this manner. Have children repeat each step after you and then read the words.

---

🔴 **BELOW-LEVEL**

**Build Spelling Words** Some children may benefit from a hands-on experience during this activity. In this case, have them use *Word Building Cards* and *Word Builders* to follow your lead in constructing each spelling word and reading it aloud.

 **E L L**

**Discriminate** Children may be confused, because the letter name *r* sounds like /är/. Explain that /är/ is the sound of the letters *a* and *r* together and that /r/ is the sound of the letter *r* when it is not combined with other letters. Have them say the words *arm* and *rip* and listen for the difference in the beginning sounds.

**5-DAY** PHONICS/SPELLING

| DAY 1 | Pretest |
| DAY 2 | Word Building |
| DAY 3 | State the Generalization |
| DAY 4 | Review |
| DAY 5 | Posttest |

## Read Words in Context

**APPLY PHONICS** Write the following sentences on the board or on chart paper. Have children read each sentence silently. Then track the print as children read the sentence aloud.

> How <u>far</u> is it to the <u>farm</u>?
>
> I bumped my <u>arm</u> on the desk.
>
> <u>Art</u> class is the best <u>part</u> of the day!
>
> Mom said we could go to the <u>park</u>.
>
> I had a small cut on my <u>chin</u>.
>
> We had <u>such</u> a good time!
>
> Let's <u>watch</u> the robins!

**WRITE** Dictate several /är/ar words from the pocket chart. Have children write the words on a dry-erase board or in their notebook.

phonics **Resources**

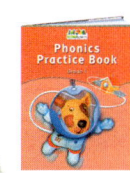

**Phonics Practice Book,** pp. 73–76

**BELOW-LEVEL**    **ON-LEVEL**    **ADVANCED**

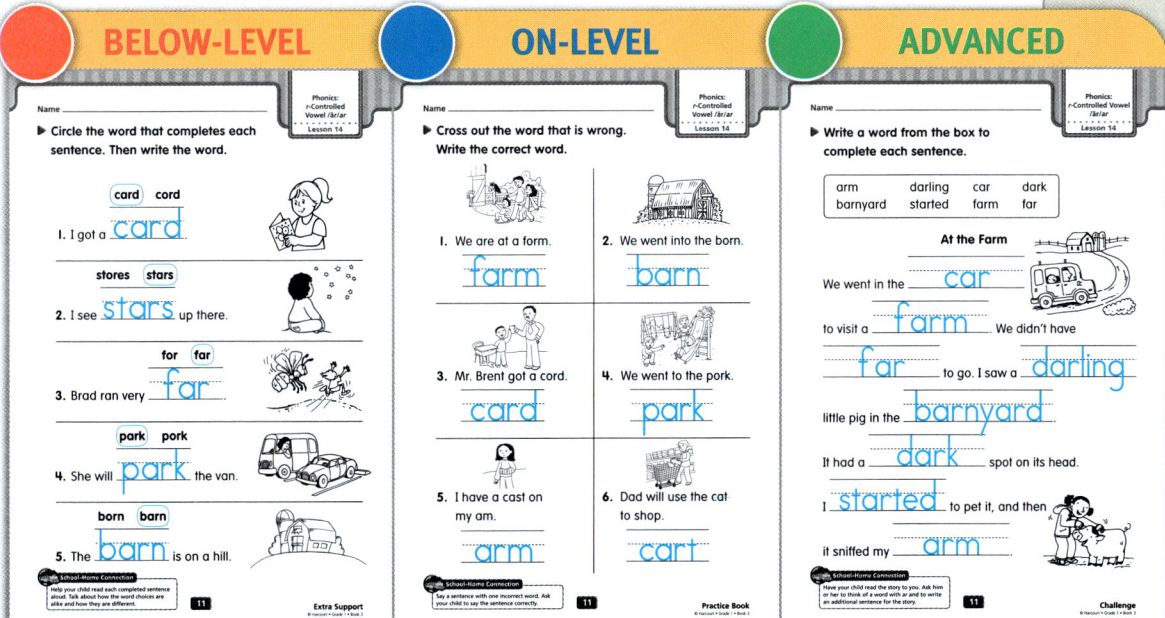

▲ Extra Support, p. 11     ▲ Practice Book, p. 11     ▲ Challenge, p. 11

**E L L**

- Group children according to academic levels, and assign one of the pages on the left.

- Clarify any unfamiliar concepts as necessary. See *ELL Teacher Guide,* Lesson 14, for support in scaffolding instruction.

Teacher Read-Aloud

# Phonics Skill

## Words with ar

The letters **ar** can stand for the sound at the beginning of the words **art** and **arm**.

art

arm

The letters **ar** can stand for the same sound in the middle of **yarn** and at the end of **star**.

yarn

star

62

**Look at each picture. Read the words. Tell which word names the picture.**

card
cart
cord

scar
scout
scarf

GO online www.harcourtschool.com/storytown

**Try This!**

**Read the story.**

We went to a farm in the car. It was very far. We saw animals at the barn. We went on a cart. At night, we saw some stars.

63

## Practice/Apply

**GUIDED PRACTICE** Have children turn to pages 62–63 in the *Student Edition*. Provide a model by reading to them the information about words with *r*-controlled vowel /är/*ar* on page 62. Lead them through the activity at the top of page 63 for guided practice.

**Try This!** **INDEPENDENT PRACTICE** Tell children that they will read this short story. Explain that they should use what they know about the *r*-controlled vowel sound /är/ to help them read the words. Have children read the story silently and then aloud. Discuss the story, and ask volunteers to identify the *r*-controlled vowel words.

## E L L

**Try This!** Help children with the Try This! Display *Photo Cards* for *arm, farm, garden,* and *stars*. Read the words with children. Have volunteers point to the letters that stand for the /är/ sound.

arm    farm

▲ Photo Cards 4, 56, 61, 142

# Author's Purpose/Point of View *Comprehension*

## Teach/Model

**INTRODUCE THE SKILL** Explain that when authors write, they have a reason for writing. They think about this reason when they decide how to tell the story. Read aloud this excerpt from "The Hare and the Tortoise."

> **Being the most talented doesn't always mean that you'll come out on top. Hard work is more important. Slow and steady wins the race.**

Then model how to recognize the author's purpose and point of view.

**Think Aloud** In this story, the author shows that the hare likes to brag and laugh at others, while the tortoise works hard and keeps trying his best. At the end of the story, the author tells readers the lesson that the story teaches. I think the author's purpose is to teach us that working hard at something can make good things happen.

## Practice/Apply

**GUIDED PRACTICE** Recall with children "Ann's Trip to the Stars" from the *Student Edition*. Tell them that good readers ask themselves questions to figure out an author's purpose. A reader can ask: **Why did the author write this story?** Lead children to understand that the author wrote this story to entertain the reader. Point out that the author made the girl character be the one who is telling the story. It is told from her point of view. Ask: **How can you tell that Ann is telling the story?** (The author uses the word *I*. This is what Ann would say if she were telling the story.)

**INDEPENDENT PRACTICE** Recall with children other stories they have read recently. Guide them to determine the author's purpose and the point of view of each one.

### Objective
• *To identify an author's purpose and point of view*

### Skill Trace
 **Tested** **Author's Purpose/ Point of View**

| | |
|---|---|
| Preview | T142 |
| Introduce | T151 |
| Reteach | S16–S17, S56–S57 |
| Review | T176, T188, T198, T490, T499, T524, T538, T548 |
| Test | Bk 1-3 |
| Maintain | Monitor Comprehension, Bk 1-4 to 1-5 |

# High-Frequency Words
**Words to Know**

## Objective
- *To read high-frequency words*

### INTRODUCE
**High-Frequency Words**

| | |
|---|---|
| again | loud |
| feel | Mrs. |
| house | put |
| know | say |

### MONITOR PROGRESS

**High-Frequency Words**

| **IF** children have difficulty reading and spelling the words, | **THEN** display two sets of word cards, and have them read and match the words. |
|---|---|

**Small-Group Instruction, p. S13:**

🔴 **BELOW-LEVEL:** Reteach
🔵 **ON-LEVEL:** Reinforce
🟢 **ADVANCED:** Extend

## Teach/Model

 **Routine Card 16**

**INTRODUCE WORDS** Write the words *again, feel, house, know, loud, Mrs., put,* and *say* on the board.

- Point to and read *again.* Repeat it, having children say it with you.
- Say **I like that game. Let's play it** *again.*
- Point to each letter as you spell the word. Have children spell the word with you.
- Have children reread the word.

Repeat for the remaining words. Use the following sentences:

> They **feel** sad that they are selling their **house.**
>
> I don't **know** what to **say** about that.
>
> **Mrs.** Frank heard a **loud** noise.
>
> I **put** the books into a box.

## Guided Practice

**STUDENT EDITION PAGES 64–65** Ask children to turn to *Student Edition* pages 64–65. Have children point to and read aloud each of the highlighted words. Talk about the artwork. Then ask volunteers to read aloud the sentences.

**STORY WORDS** List the following words on the board and read the words aloud: *blow, mistake, shy,* and *wolf.* Repeat, having children read the words with you. Mention that in the story "Mark's Big Day," the children are putting on a play in which a wolf tries to blow a house in. Explain that one of the children is shy and is worried about making a mistake in playing the part of a wolf. Point to the words again, and have children read them aloud.

## Words to Know

**High-Frequency Words**

feel

put

house

Mrs.

say

loud

again

know

"I **feel** a chill in the air," said Mark. He **put** on a hat. He left the **house** and went to school.

At school, **Mrs.** Parks said, "**Say** your part, Mark. Be **loud**." Mark said his part.

"Now say it **again**. I **know** you can do a good job!" she said.

www.harcourtschool.com/storytown

64

65

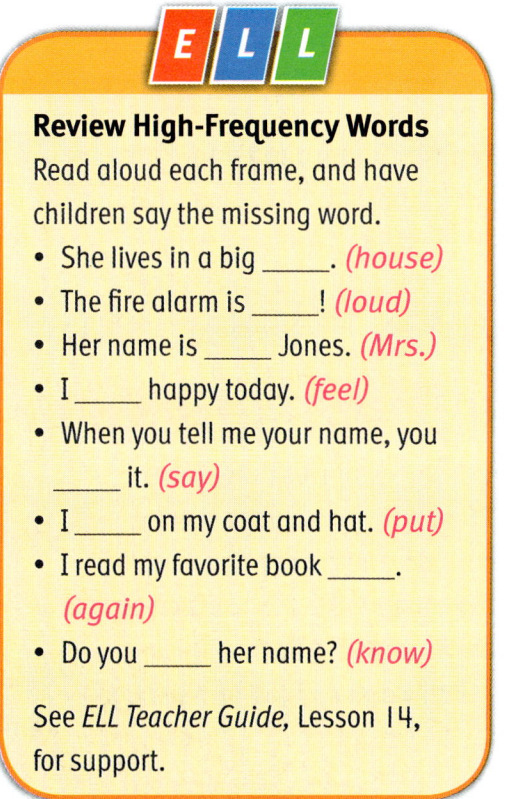

**E L L**

**Review High-Frequency Words**

Read aloud each frame, and have children say the missing word.

- She lives in a big _____. (house)
- The fire alarm is _____! (loud)
- Her name is _____ Jones. (Mrs.)
- I _____ happy today. (feel)
- When you tell me your name, you _____ it. (say)
- I _____ on my coat and hat. (put)
- I read my favorite book _____. (again)
- Do you _____ her name? (know)

See *ELL Teacher Guide*, Lesson 14, for support.

#  Reading

*Student Edition:* **Mark's Big Day**

## Objectives

- *To understand the characteristics of realistic fiction*
- *To summarize as a strategy for comprehension*
- *To apply word knowledge to the reading of a text*

 **Podcasting:** Use Story Structures, Gr. I

## Options for Reading

 **BELOW-LEVEL**

**Preview** Have children preview the story by looking at the illustrations. Guide them to predict what will happen. Read each page, and have children echo-read. Discuss with the Monitor Comprehension questions.

 **ON-LEVEL**

**Monitor Comprehension** Have children read the story aloud. Ask the Monitor Comprehension questions after each page. Then lead them in retelling the events.

 **ADVANCED**

**Independent Reading** Have children read each page silently, looking up each time they finish a page. Ask the Monitor Comprehension questions after they finish. Discuss how Mark changes throughout the story.

### Genre Study

**DISCUSS REALISTIC FICTION** Point to the genre label on *Student Edition* page 66 and tell children that this selection is realistic fiction. Remind them that realistic fiction stories tell about things that could really happen. Point out that realistic fiction has people as characters and tells about things that readers could have done themselves. Then use **Transparency GO13** or copy the story map onto the board. Tell children that they can fill it in for any fiction story they read.

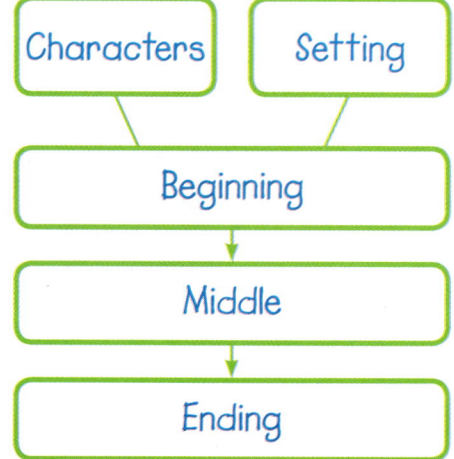

### Comprehension Strategies

 **SUMMARIZE** Remind children that when they summarize, they tell just the most important things that happen in a story.

**Think Aloud** In "The Hare and the Tortoise," the hare brags about how fast he can run. The tortoise challenges him to a race. The hare quickly takes the lead and decides he has enough time to take a nap and still win the race. The tortoise crosses the finish line while the hare is still sleeping.

Then read aloud the sentence under Comprehension Strategy on page 66. Point out that thinking about these ideas can help them understand a story better.

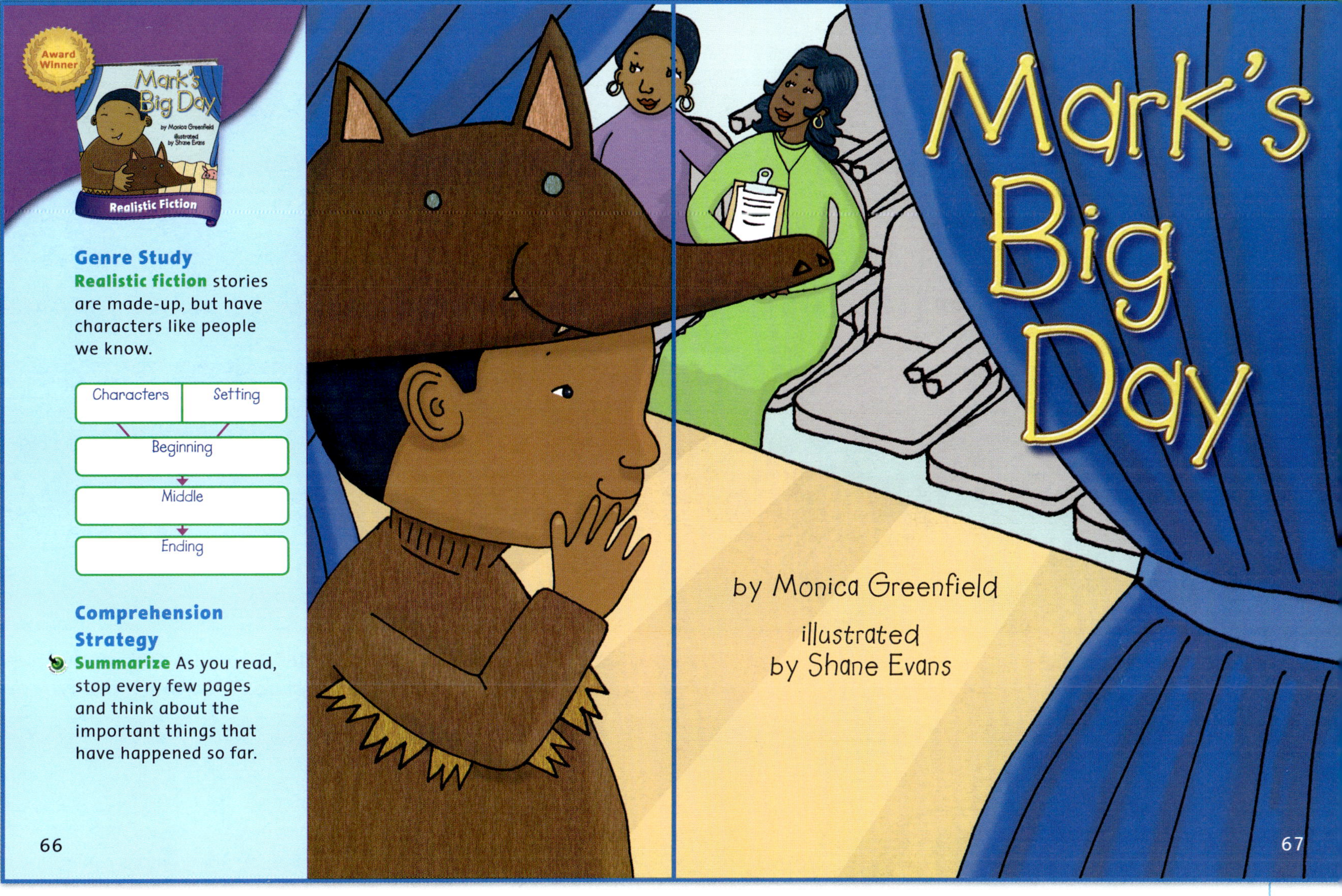

## Genre Study

**Realistic fiction** stories are made-up, but have characters like people we know.

| Characters | Setting |
|---|---|

Beginning

Middle

Ending

## Comprehension Strategy

**Summarize** As you read, stop every few pages and think about the important things that have happened so far.

66

# Mark's Big Day

by Monica Greenfield

illustrated
by Shane Evans

67

## Build Background

**DISCUSS BEING IN A PLAY** Say: **This is a story about a boy who is playing a part in a class play. Tell about a time that you went to or acted in a play.**

 Routine Card **17** **SET A PURPOSE AND PREDICT** Tell children that this is a story they will read to enjoy.

- Read the title to children.

- Identify the boy as Mark. Have children page through the selection and make predictions based on the illustrations.

- List the predictions on the board.

- Invite children to read the story to find out what happens when Mark performs in the class play.

## TECHNOLOGY

 **eBook** "Mark's Big Day" is available in an eBook.

 **Audiotext** "Mark's Big Day" is available on *Audiotext Grade 1*, CD 3 for subsequent readings.

Mark's clock went <u>bing</u>, <u>bing</u>, <u>bing</u>.
He did not want to get up.

Bing!
Bing! Bing!

Toys

Toys

Exit

Mom called, "Mark, get up and
get dressed. It's your big day!"

68

69

# Monitor Comprehension

**PAGES 68–69** Say: I see a ringing alarm clock. Where and when do you think this story takes place? Let's read to find out if our predictions are correct.

**1** **SETTING** Do you think this story begins early in the morning or at bedtime? How do you know? (It begins early in the morning in Mark's bedroom; Mark's alarm clock is going off, and his mother tells him to get up.)

**2** **CHARACTERS' EMOTIONS** How does Mark feel? Find and read the sentence that tells. (He does not feel happy; *He did not want to get up.*)

**3** **FIGURATIVE LANGUAGE** What does Mom mean when she says this is Mark's "big day"? (Possible response: She means that something important is going to happen.)

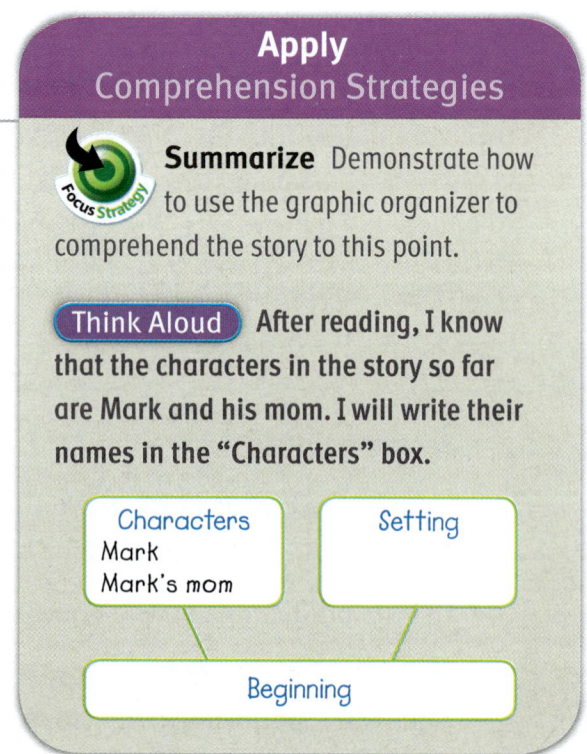

## Apply
## Comprehension Strategies

**Focus Strategy**

**Summarize** Demonstrate how to use the graphic organizer to comprehend the story to this point.

**Think Aloud** After reading, I know that the characters in the story so far are Mark and his mom. I will write their names in the "Characters" box.

| Characters | Setting |
|---|---|
| Mark | |
| Mark's *mom* | |

| Beginning |
|---|

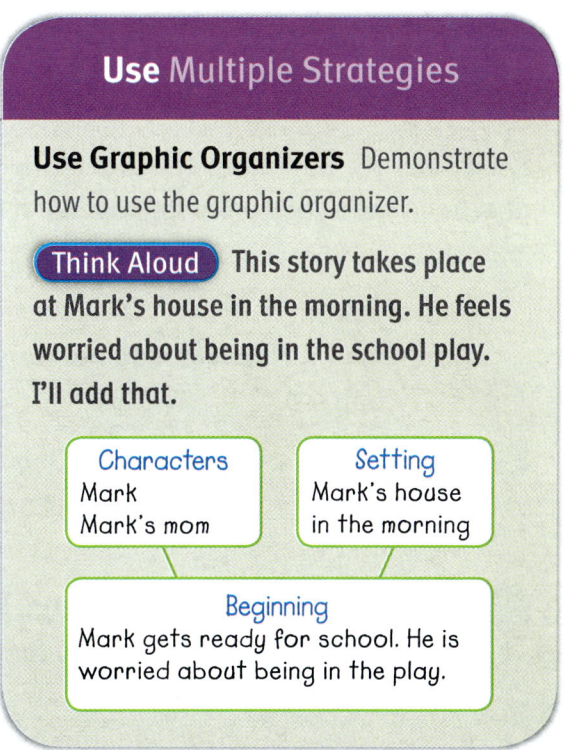

Mark was thinking of the school play. His part was hard for him. He felt shy. Mark **put** on his jacket, hat, and scarf.

70

71

# Monitor Comprehension

**PAGES 70–71** Say: **Mark looks worried. Let's read to find out why.**

**①** **NOTE DETAILS/APPLY PHONICS** **What piece of clothing does Mark put around his neck? Find and read the word that tells.** *(scarf)*

**②** **CHARACTERS' EMOTIONS** **What word describes how Mark feels about performing in the play?** *(shy)*

**③** **DRAW CONCLUSIONS** **What reason explains why Mark is worried?** (He is thinking of how hard his part in the school play is.)

**④** **MAKE PREDICTIONS** **Where do you think Mark is going? Why do you think this?** (Possible response: He is getting ready to go to school because he has eaten breakfast and is now putting on his jacket, hat, and scarf.)

## Use Multiple Strategies

**Use Graphic Organizers** Demonstrate how to use the graphic organizer.

**Think Aloud** This story takes place at Mark's house in the morning. He feels worried about being in the school play. I'll add that.

| Characters | Setting |
|---|---|
| Mark<br>Mark's mom | Mark's house in the morning |

| Beginning |
|---|
| Mark gets ready for school. He is worried about being in the play. |

"Wish me luck," Mark said. He got a big hug from Mom. His dog barked. "Thanks, Mom. Thanks, Champ," Mark said with a grin.

72

At school, Mrs. Parks asked the children to say their parts.

73

# Monitor Comprehension

**PAGES 72–73** Say: **I can see that Mark is at his home and then he's at school. Let's read on to find out what Mark is doing at school.**

**1** **NOTE DETAILS/APPLY PHONICS** **How do Mom and Champ wish Mark luck?** (Mom gives Mark a big hug, and Champ gives a happy bark.) **Find and read the word that tells what Champ did.** (barked)

**2** **SETTING** **What is the story setting on page 73? How can you tell?** (Mark is now at school; the picture shows a stage and Mark's teacher and classmates.)

**3** **DRAW CONCLUSIONS** **Who is Mrs. Parks? Why do you think Mrs. Parks wants the children to say their parts?** (Mrs. Parks is a teacher at Mark's school; she wants to have the children practice saying their parts before they perform the play.)

**E L L**

**Word Meanings** Write the word *part* on the board and help children blend the sounds to read the word. Explain that *part* has several meanings. Point out that *part* can mean "a piece" and it can also mean "the lines an actor speaks in a play." Help children build concept vocabulary by using the illustrations to help explain other terms associated with a play, such as *stage, scenery, costumes, director, rehearsal,* and *cast.*

"I'll huff and I'll puff and I'll blow your house in," Mark said. It was too soft.

"Say it again, Mark," Mrs. Parks called. "I'll blow your house in," Mark said. It was soft again.

# Monitor Comprehension

**PAGES 74–75** Say: **Look at the way Mark is dressed. Let's read on to find out what character he is playing.**

**1** **NOTE DETAILS** **How do the pictures and the words go together?** (The pictures show Mark with a wolf mask and scenery that looks like the little pigs' house. Mark is saying the part of the wolf.)

**2** **DRAW CONCLUSIONS** **What do you think is the name of the school play? What makes you think this?** ("The Three Little Pigs"; the scenery, costumes, and words are from that story.)

**3** **DRAW CONCLUSIONS** **Why does Mrs. Parks want Mark to say his part again?** (Mark's voice is too soft when he says his part and he needs more practice.)

**BELOW-LEVEL**

**Build Background** If children are unfamiliar with the traditional tale of "The Three Little Pigs," you may wish to share a summary of the story with them. As you do so, point out that the words that Mark speaks are taken directly from the story.

"You are the wolf. This wolf is not shy," said Mrs. Parks.

"This is hard, but I <mark>know</mark> you can do it, Mark. Just act like a big wolf."

76

77

# Monitor Comprehension

**PAGES 76–77** Say: I see that Mrs. Parks is talking to Mark. What do you think she is saying? Let's read to find out.

**①** **NOTE DETAILS** What does Mrs. Parks say about the wolf? (She says that this wolf is not shy.)

**②** **CHARACTERS' EMOTIONS** How does Mark probably feel? (He probably feels very shy and nervous about performing.)

**③** **DRAW CONCLUSIONS** What does Mrs. Parks tell Mark about his part? (She says it is hard, but she knows he can do it.) Why do you think she says this? (to make Mark feel better; to help him know that he can do well)

**SCIENCE**

## SUPPORTING STANDARDS

**Wolf Facts** Share facts about wolves. Wolves live in groups called packs. Packs of gray or timber wolves are found in Alaska and Canada; in western states such as Idaho, Montana, and Wyoming; and in Great Lakes states. Adult wolves average 5 to 6 feet in length and weigh about 70 to 100 pounds. They are usually gray in color but can also be black or white. Wolf pups are born in the spring, and all members of the pack help care for the young.

The play started. Soon it was time for Mark to say his part.

"I'll huff and I'll puff and I'll blow your house OUT!" he called.

Three Pigs' House

78

79

# Monitor Comprehension

**PAGES 78–79** Say: **It looks like the children are performing their play. Let's read to find out how Mark does.**

**1** **NOTE DETAILS** **What does Mark say when it's time for him to say his part?** (He says, "I'll huff and I'll puff and I'll blow your house OUT!")

**2** **MAKE COMPARISONS** **What do you notice when you compare what Mark says on this page with what Mark says on page 75?** (In practice, he says he'll blow the house IN. During the play, he says he'll blow the house OUT.)

**3** **DRAW CONCLUSIONS** **Why do you think Mark changed the words?** (Possible response: He was probably feeling very nervous and so he forgot what he was supposed to say.)

## Use Multiple Strategies

**Adjust Reading Rate** Remind children that good readers adjust their reading speed to help them understand a part of the story that is unclear. Suggest that children reread pages that were unclear to them the first time they read them.

**Summarize** Help children summarize what has happened in the story so far. Some children may benefit from looking back at the illustrations to help them recall the important story events.

Focus Strategy

The children looked at Mark.
He had made a mistake.

**Three Pigs' House**

"Oh! I'll huff and I'll puff and
I'll blow your house IN!" Mark said
with a big wolf snarl.

80

81

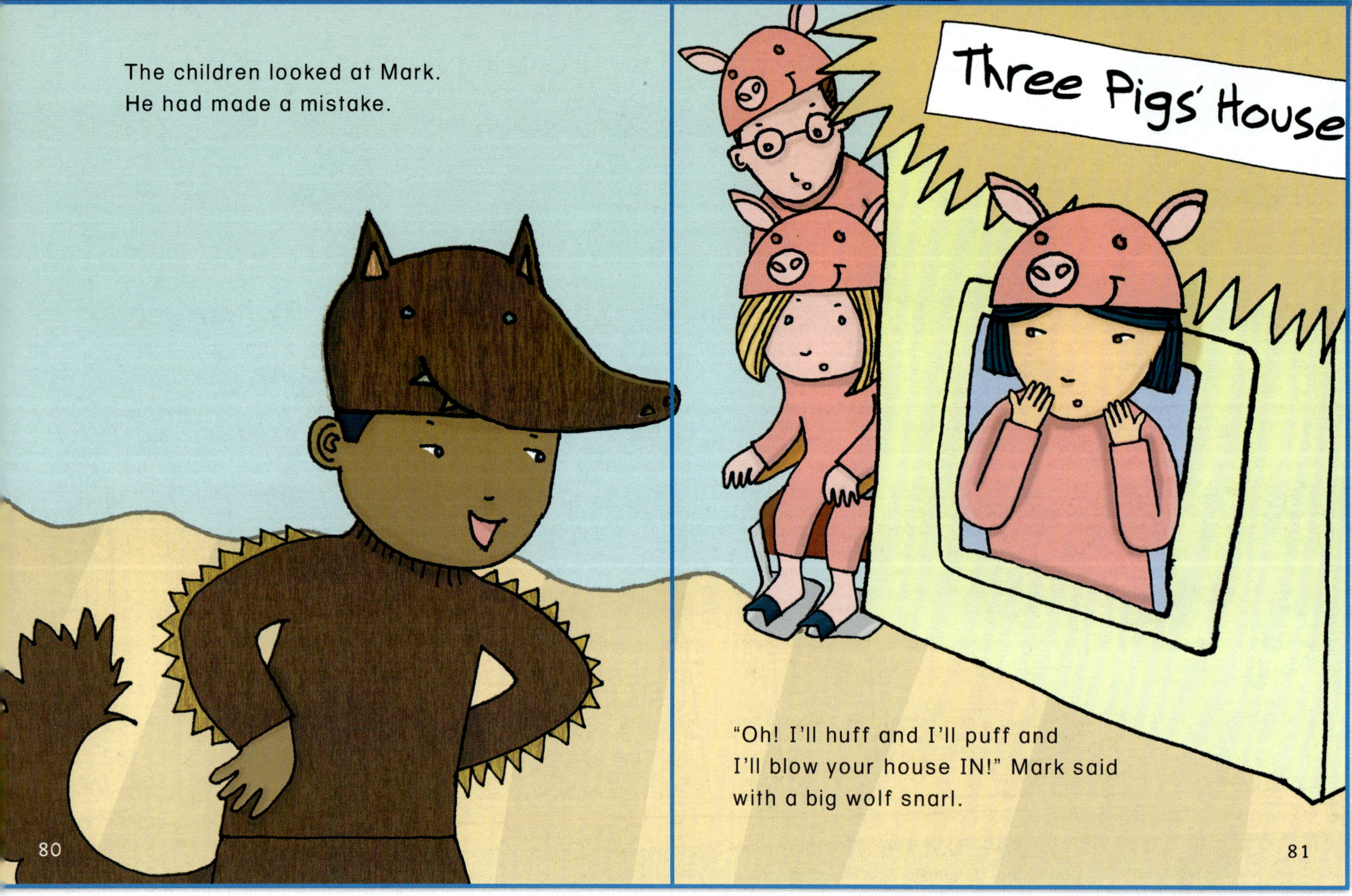

# Monitor Comprehension

**PAGES 80–81** Say: **I see that the children look surprised. I wonder what Mark will do next. Let's read on to find out.**

**1 CAUSE AND EFFECT** **What do the other children do after Mark says his part?** (They stop and look at him.) **Why do they do this?** (because Mark made a mistake and he was loud; they are surprised)

**2 NOTE DETAILS** **What does Mark do next?** (He says his part again, and this time it's right.)

**3 CONTEXT CLUES** Focus children's attention on the word *snarl*. Point out the letters *ar*. Have children identify the vowel sound and then blend the sounds to read the word. Have children use other sentences on the pages, the illustrations, and what they know about wolves to help them figure out the meaning of *snarl*. **What is a *snarl*?** (a fierce sound that an angry wolf makes)

## Apply
### Comprehension Strategies

**Summarize** Demonstrate how to use the graphic organizer.

**Think Aloud** To help me remember and better understand what I've read, I'm going to write down the most important things that have happened in the middle of the story.

### Middle
Mark tries and tries to say his part loudly. His teacher helps. Finally, he says his line loudly, but it's wrong!

"Don't feel bad, Mark," Mrs. Parks said.

"I don't," Mark said. "I feel good."
"You do?" asked Mrs. Parks.

82

83

# Monitor Comprehension

**PAGES 82–84** Say: **Mrs. Parks and Mark are talking. Let's read to find out what they are saying to each other.**

1 **CHARACTERS' MOTIVATIONS** Mrs. Parks says, "Don't feel bad, Mark." What does this tell you about Mrs. Parks? (She is worried that Mark might feel upset because of his mistake; she's trying to help Mark.)

2 **CHARACTERS' EMOTIONS** How is Mark feeling? (He says he feels good.) **Why does he feel this way?** (He doesn't feel shy anymore and was loud like the wolf should be.)

3 **SPECULATE** How do you think Mark will feel the next time he is asked to be in a school play? Why? (Possible response: He'll like being in the play because he won't feel too shy to say his part.)

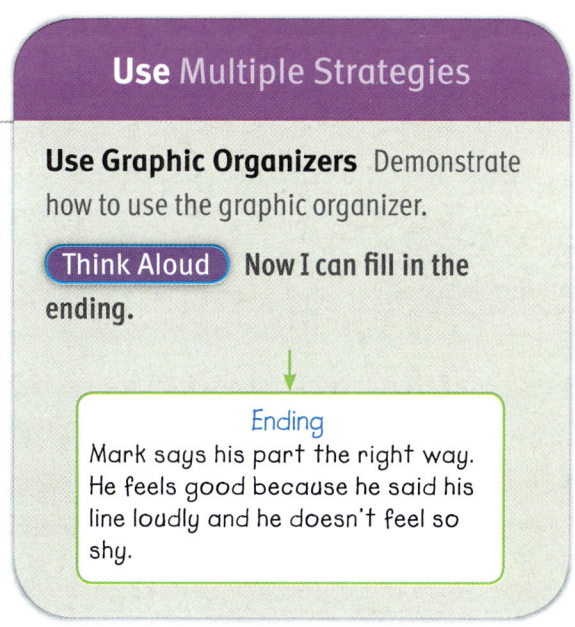

## Use Multiple Strategies

**Use Graphic Organizers** Demonstrate how to use the graphic organizer.

**Think Aloud** Now I can fill in the ending.

↓

**Ending**
Mark says his part the right way. He feels good because he said his line loudly and he doesn't feel so shy.

"Yes! I wasn't shy. I was **LOUD**!"
Mark said with a big grin.

## Think Critically

Teacher Read-Aloud

1. What do you think the author wanted you to learn from the story?
   AUTHOR'S PURPOSE/POINT OF VIEW

2. Who helps Mark at home? Who helps Mark at school? DETAILS

3. Why do you think Mark says his part softly at first? MAKE INFERENCES

4. Why is Mark able to say his part loudly during the play? DRAW CONCLUSIONS

5. **WRITE** Write about how you would act as the wolf in a play. What kind of costume would you wear? WRITING RESPONSE

84

85

# Think Critically

## Respond to the Literature

1. Focus Skill — Possible response: If you make a mistake, it is important to keep going and do your best. **AUTHOR'S PURPOSE/POINT OF VIEW**

2. Mark's mom helps him at home. Mrs. Parks helps him at school. **NOTE DETAILS**

3. Possible response: Mark is a little shy and doesn't want other people to hear him. **MAKE INFERENCES**

4. Mark isn't afraid of saying his part in the play anymore. **DRAW CONCLUSIONS**

5. **WRITE** Possible response: I would be a sneaky wolf. I would have a long tail and scruffy ears. **WRITING RESPONSE**

## LISTENING/SPEAKING

**Conversation** Guide children to:
- participate in a conversation
- speak clearly and use appropriate volume
- use speaking vocabulary
- listen attentively to others
- ask questions for clarification and understanding

After the discussion, guide children to recognize how the words and language they used to discuss the story are different from the less-formal language they use at home.

## Meet the Author
## Monica Greenfield

Monica Greenfield comes from a family of writers. Her mother writes stories and poems, and so did her grandmother. Her daughter loves to write, also.

"Words can be very powerful. I can use words to make children laugh, give them something to think about, or let them know how strong they are."

## Meet the Illustrator
## Shane Evans

Shane Evans has illustrated many children's books. He has created art for people all over the world. His art has been shown in Africa, Paris, New York, and Chicago. Mr. Evans also likes to speak at schools. He encourages children to use their own special talents.

www.harcourtschool.com/storytown

86

87

# Meet the Author and the Illustrator

**PAGES 86–87**  Explain that these pages tell about the people who wrote and illustrated the story "Mark's Big Day." Identify Monica Greenfield and Shane Evans in the photographs. Remind children that an author writes a story and that an illustrator creates pictures to go with the writing. Read aloud pages 86–87. Encourage children to follow along as you read.

 # Check Comprehension
### *Retelling*

## Objectives
- *To practice retelling a story*
- *To read with proper intonation in a manner that sounds like natural speech*

### RETELLING RUBRIC

| | |
|---|---|
| 4 | Uses details to clearly retell the story |
| 3 | Uses some details to retell the story |
| 2 | Retells the story with some inaccuracies |
| 1 | Is unable to retell the story |

### Retell

  **AUTHOR'S PURPOSE AND POINT OF VIEW** Ask children to tell the author's purpose and identify who tells the story. (Possible response: to tell how a child felt good even after making a mistake; the author)

**REVISIT THE GRAPHIC ORGANIZER** Display completed **Transparency GO13**. Have a volunteer use the story map to retell the story.

**STORY RETELLING CARDS** The cards for "Mark's Big Day" can be used for a retelling or as an aid to completing the story map.

▲ Story Retelling Cards, 1–6, "Mark's Big Day"

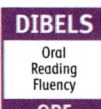 # Fluency

### Teach/Model

 **INTONATION** Remind children that good readers emphasize some words more than others—usually the most important words. Read aloud from page 77 of "Mark's Big Day": **Just act like a *big* wolf,** and then **Just act like a big *wolf*.** Point out how the first reading fits better with the story in which Mark is trying to be a *loud* wolf.

### Practice/Apply

**ECHO-READ** Read aloud the story, one page at a time, modeling appropriate intonation and having children echo-read.

# Build Robust Vocabulary

## Listening/Speaking: *Words from the Read-Aloud*

### Review Robust Vocabulary

**USE VOCABULARY IN DIFFERENT CONTEXTS** Remind children of the Student-Friendly Explanations of *approached, energetic,* and *pace.* Then discuss each Vocabulary Word with them in a context different from that in which it was used in "The Hare and the Tortoise." Use the following examples:

**approached**

- **What would you do if a bug approached you?**

- **What would you do if we were playing a game and I asked you to approach your partner?**

- **Tell about something that you would NOT approach.**

**energetic**

- **Would you be surprised if someone told you he or she felt energetic after a long bike ride? Why or why not?**

- **If you are tired, what are some things that you can do to make yourself feel more energetic?**

- **How could you help a family member if you are feeling energetic?**

**pace**

- **Would you be more likely to read a hard story at a fast pace or at a slow pace? Why?**

- **If I told you that we were going to walk down the hall at a fast pace, how would we move?**

- **How would you compare your pace to the pace of a racehorse? How would you compare your pace to the pace of a caterpillar?**

## Objective

- *To develop robust vocabulary to describe ideas*

### Student-Friendly Explanations

**approached** If you approached something, you moved toward it.

**energetic** If you are energetic, you are filled with energy.

**pace** Your pace is how fast you are going.

### "RESEARCH SAYS"

"Because rich instruction outcomes were greater than traditional instruction outcomes on the tasks that presented words in context, it appears that richness of instruction provides an advantage for integrating words and context."

—McKeown, Beck, Omanson, & Pople (1985), p. 533

**Use Vocabulary in Different Contexts** Act out doing a chore like sweeping in an *energetic* way and in a way that looks the opposite of *energetic.* Ask children to identify the action that looked *energetic.*

# Grammar
## Names of Holidays

**5-DAY GRAMMAR**

| DAY 1 | Introduce Names of Holidays |
| DAY 2 | Dictate Sentences About Holidays |
| DAY 3 | Write Sentences About Holidays |
| DAY 4 | Revise Names of Holidays |
| DAY 5 | Write Holiday Messages |

### Objectives
- *To dictate sentences with names of holidays*
- *To use basic capitalization skills to capitalize proper nouns*

### Daily Proofreading

**my friends saw a shark?**

(My, shark.)

**Display Pictures** Tell children that the United States celebrates its independence—the country's birthday—on the Fourth of July. Show pictures of typical celebrations on this day that include fireworks and flags. Invite volunteers to share their experiences.

▲ **Grammar Practice Book, p. 53**

## Review

**USE A LITERATURE MODEL** Tell children that today they will listen to a rhyme that tells about a holiday. Read the rhyme, emphasizing the rhythm and rhyme. Reread it a few times for children's enjoyment, and invite children to pretend to march in the parade as they chant it along with you.

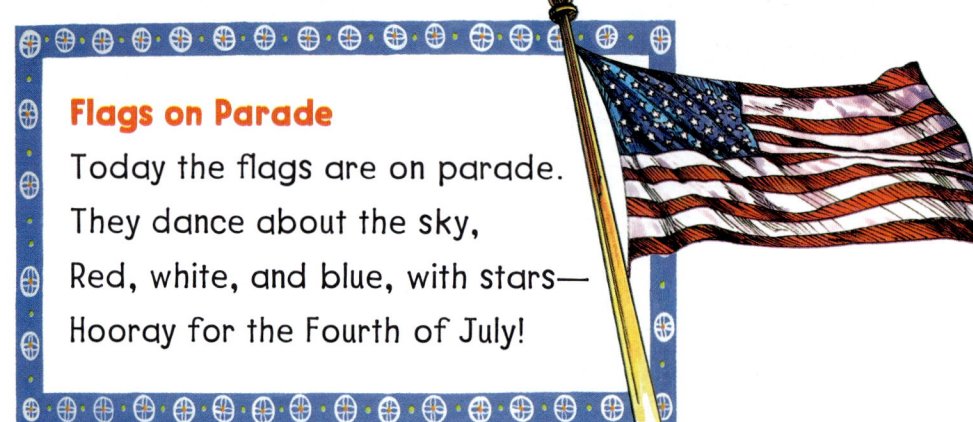

**Flags on Parade**

Today the flags are on parade.
They dance about the sky,
Red, white, and blue, with stars—
Hooray for the Fourth of July!

Write the last two lines of the rhyme on the board. Track the print and read the sentence to children. Have volunteers identify the name of the holiday and tell what kind of letter is used to begin each important word. *(Fourth of July; a capital letter)*

## Practice/Apply

**GUIDED PRACTICE** Have volunteers dictate sentences about holidays. Write them on the board and read them with children, tracking the print. Have children identify the names of holidays.

> **Fourth of July is fun, because we see fireworks.**
> **On Valentine's Day, we make and send valentines.**
> **We visit my grandparents on Thanksgiving.**
> **On Memorial Day, we have a picnic.**

**INDEPENDENT PRACTICE** Ask children to copy one of the sentences. Have them read aloud the sentence to a partner, identify the holiday, and identify the words that are capitalized.

# Shared Writing

*E-mail*

| 5-DAY WRITING | |
|---|---|
| DAY 1 | Modeled Writing |
| DAY 2 | Shared Writing |
| DAY 3 | Shared Writing |
| DAY 4 | Independent Writing |
| DAY 5 | Independent Writing |

## Write Together

**REVIEW E-MAIL** Remind children that an e-mail is a message sent or received on a computer. Point out that an e-mail has e-mail addresses, a subject line, and a message. Review the parts of an e-mail.

**GENERATE IDEAS** Have children look again at the picture they drew on Day 1. Choose an idea, and ask children to think of an e-mail message that they could send as a reminder about this event.

**MODEL WRITING** Have volunteers expand on the contents of the message as you record their ideas in an e-mail on chart paper, using the Step-by-Step Writing Instruction as a guide. Save it for Day 3.

### Step-by-Step Writing Instruction

| | | |
|---|---|---|
| **1** | Make up an e-mail address. We'll write it on the "From" line. |  lenfox@net.com |
| **2** | Make up an e-mail address for the person getting the message. It goes on the "To" line. | tedhouse@sky.com |
| **3** | Tell the main idea of the message. We'll write this on the "Subject" line. | Jan's Surprise Party |
| **4** WRITING TRAIT | How do we write the greeting? What kind of letter begins a person's name? <br><br> What is the message? We will indent the first word like this. | Dear Ted,<br><br> Don't forget to come to Jan's surprise party this Saturday. It starts at 2:00. Write to me if you have questions. |
| **5** | How do we write the closing? Remember to sign your name. | Your friend,<br>Len |
| **6** | Let's read Len's e-mail to Ted together. | |

## Objectives

- *To generate ideas before writing on assigned tasks*
- *To contribute to an e-mail message*

## Writing Prompt

**Write About a Party** Have children draw a picture of and write about a party they have attended.

▲ **Writer's Companion, Lesson 14**

● **ADVANCED**

**Discuss E-mail** Help children compare e-mail to letters sent by regular mail. Discuss how the addresses used differ. Then talk about how the "Subject" line helps the reader know what the e-mail is about. Point out that e-mail is often shorter than letters sent in the mail. Invite children to write "e-mails" to one another.

## Day at a Glance

### Day 3

**Phonemic Awareness**
- Phoneme Deletion

 **phonics** **and Spelling**
- Review: *r*-Controlled Vowel /är/*ar*
- Maintain: *r*-Controlled, *ore* /ôr/*or*
- State the Generalization

**High-Frequency Words**
- Review: *again*, *feel*, *house*, *know*, *loud*, *Mrs.*, *put*, *say*

**Fluency**
- Intonation

**Comprehension**
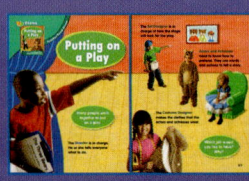 Review: Author's Purpose/Point of View

**Reading**
- "Putting on a Play," *Student Edition,* pp. 88–89

**Robust Vocabulary**
- Introduce: *blunder, reassure, excel*

**Grammar**
- Review: Names of Holidays

**Shared Writing** ✏
- E-mail

# Warm-Up Routines

## Oral Language

**Objective** *To listen attentively and respond appropriately to oral communication*

> ### Question of the Day
> What would you like to do or be when you grow up? Tell why.

Help children brainstorm different jobs. Invite them to tell why each appeals to them. Have children help you complete the following sentence frame:

**When I grow up, I would like to _____ because _____.**

## Read Aloud

**Objectives** *To understand concepts of print; to recite a poem*

**BIG BOOK OF RHYMES AND POEMS** Ask children to tell what they remember about the poem. As you read, use your hand to emphasize that text moves from left to right and from top to bottom on the page. Read the poem several times inviting children to chime in. Then call on individuals, partners, or small groups to take turns reciting the poem as they become familiar with the words. After reading, invite children to ask questions about the poem and discuss the answers.

▲ Big Book of Rhymes and Poems, p. 27

## Word Wall

**Objective** *To read high-frequency words*

**REVIEW HIGH-FREQUENCY WORDS** Review *again, feel, house, know, loud, Mrs., put, say,* and other previously-learned high-frequency words. Say each word, ask a volunteer to point to it, and have children read it aloud. Then point to words at random, and have children reread them.

| again | feel | house | know |
|-------|------|-------|------|
| loud | Mrs. | put | say |

## Phonemic Awareness

**Objective** *To delete initial phonemes from words*

**Routine Card 9**

**PHONEME DELETION** Tell children that you will say some words and ask them to remove the beginning sound in each word. Model by saying: *part* **without the /p/ is** *art.* Say the following words and beginning sounds. Then have children delete the beginning sound to form a new word.

*cash* **without /k/** (ash)   *tin* **without /t/** (in)   *brim* **without /b/** (rim)

*pat* **without /p/** (at)   *drag* **without /d/** (rag)   *can* **without /k/** (an)

*harm* **without /h/** (arm)   *band* **without /b/** (and)   *plot* **without /p/** (lot)

*snip* **without /s/** (nip)   *trim* **without /t/** (rim)   *slip* **without /s/** (lip)

# Build Words
 phonics *and Spelling*

| 5-DAY PHONICS | |
|---|---|
| **DAY 1** | Introduce *r*-Controlled Vowel /är/*ar* |
| **DAY 2** | Word Building with *r*-Controlled Vowel /är/*ar* |
| **DAY 3** | Word Building |
| **DAY 4** | Inflections -*s*, -*ed*, -*ing* (no spelling change) |
| **DAY 5** | Inflections -*s*, -*ed*, -*ing* (no spelling change) |

## Objectives

- *To discriminate between the letter-sound associations /är/ar and /ôr/or, ore*
- *To use /är/ar and other known letter-sounds to decode words*
- *To read and write common word families*

## Skill Trace

 Tested *r*-Controlled Vowels

| | /är/*ar* | /ôr/*or, ore* |
|---|---|---|
| Introduce | T132–T135 | Bk 1-2, T394–T397 |
| Reteach | S12 | Bk 1-2, S42–S43 |
| Review | T148–T150, T172–T173 | Bk 1-2, T410–T412, T434–T435 |
| Test | Bk 1-3 | Bk 1-2 |
| Maintain | Bk 1-5, T348–T349 | T172 |

---

*r*-Controlled Vowel /är/*ar*

Carl was visiting the farm.
He wanted to go to the art store for a card.
He went out to the barn to get his car,
but the car did not start.
"The store is not far," said Carl.
"If I cannot go in a car,
I'll go in a cart!"

Grade 1, Lesson 14    R27    Phonics: *r*-Controlled Vowels /ä/*ar*; /ôr/*or, ore*

**Transparency R27**

---

## Word Building

**DIBELS** Nonsense Word Fluency **NWF** | Routine Card **14**

**BUILD AND READ WORDS** Use a pocket chart and *Letter Cards*. Have children repeat each step with their *Word Builders* and *Word Builder Cards*.

Build the word *far*. Have children say the word naturally—*far*. Lead children in building words that contain the *r*-controlled vowels /ar/ and /ôr/ by saying:

- **Change the *a* to *o*. Read the word.**
- **Add an *m* after *r*. Read the word.**
- **Change *o* to *a*. Read the word.**

Continue in a similar manner to have children build and read these words: *art, cart, part, port; core, cord, card, cart.*

## Read Words in Context

**READ SENTENCES** Display **Transparency R27** or write the sentences on the board or on chart paper. Have children choral-read the sentences as you track the print. Then ask volunteers to read each sentence aloud. Call on volunteers to underline or frame words that have the sound /är/ or /ôr/.

**5-DAY SPELLING**
DAY 1 Pretest
DAY 2 Word Building
**DAY 3 State the Generalization**
DAY 4 Review
DAY 5 Posttest

## Review Spelling Words

**STATE THE GENERALIZATION** List spelling words 1–6 on chart paper or the board, and have children read them. Ask: **What is the same in each word?** (Each word has the /är/ sound; they all have *a* and *r*.) Have volunteers read each word and underline the letters that stand for the /är/ sound.

**REVIEW WORDS** List spelling words 7–8. Talk about what is the same in both words. (Both words have the /ch/ sound spelled with the letters *ch*.) Have children read and spell the words.

**HIGH-FREQUENCY WORDS** List spelling words 9–10. Remind children that they have seen and read these words many times. Run your hand under *fly* as you read it, and ask children to look carefully at the letters. Ask them to close their eyes, picture the word in their mind, and spell it with you. Repeat for *watch*.

**WRITE** Have children write the spelling words in their notebook. Remind them to use their best handwriting and to use the list to check their spelling.

## Handwriting
**LETTER SPACING** Remind children to make sure their letters are not too close together or too far apart.

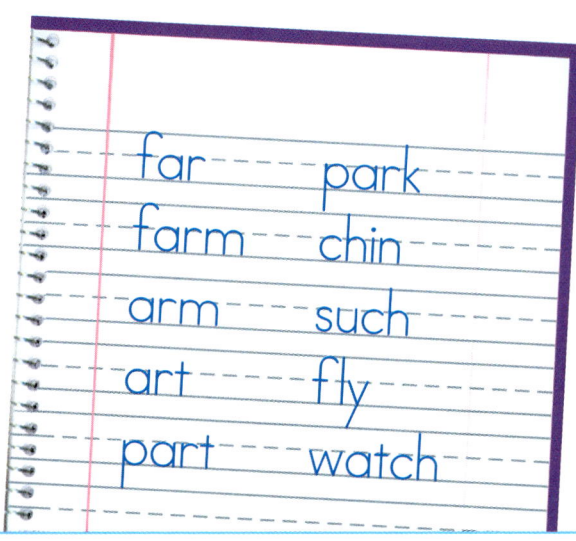

### Spelling Words
1. far
2. farm
3. arm
4. art
5. part
6. park
7. chin
8. such
9. fly
10. watch

### Decodable Book
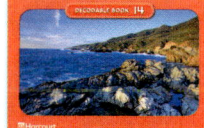

- **Phonics**
  *r*-Controlled Vowel /är/ *ar*
- **Decodable Words**
  See the list on page R11.

Decodable Book 14 ▲
"Charming Carmel"

Have children who need additional decoding practice read "Charming Carmel" in *Decodable Book 14*. See also Decodable Books, online (Take-Home Version).

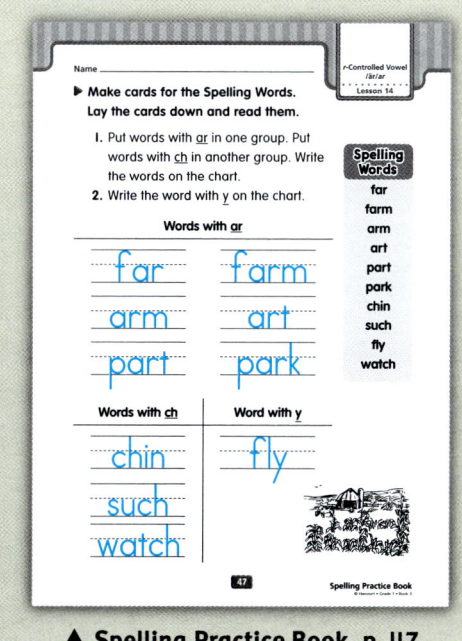

▲ Spelling Practice Book, p. 47

# High-Frequency Words

## Objective
• To read high-frequency words

**REVIEW** | Tested ✓

### High-Frequency Words

| | |
|---|---|
| again | loud |
| feel | Mrs. |
| house | put |
| know | say |

**Model Usage** Tell children that the word *Mrs.* is used to address a woman who is married. Together list names of women who work at your school who are addressed with *Mrs.* before their last names.

### Review

**DISPLAY THE WORDS** Write the word *again.* Have a volunteer read it. Erase the word and ask children to spell it. Repeat this routine for *feel, house, know, loud, Mrs., put,* and *say.*

### Practice/Apply

**GUIDED PRACTICE** Give each child a set of word cards (*Teacher Resource Book,* p.138), and have children arrange them in order by the number of letters in each word. Then ask: **Which words have three letters?** *(Mrs., put, say)* Read the three-letter words together. Continue with the four- and five-letter words.

**INDEPENDENT PRACTICE** Have children work with a partner, and have each of them turn his or her word cards face down. Direct them to take turns turning over a word card and saying the word. The partner then uses the word in a sentence. Have children continue until all of their words have been turned over. Finally, have them practice writing the words in their notebook.

**BELOW-LEVEL**    **ON-LEVEL**    **ADVANCED**

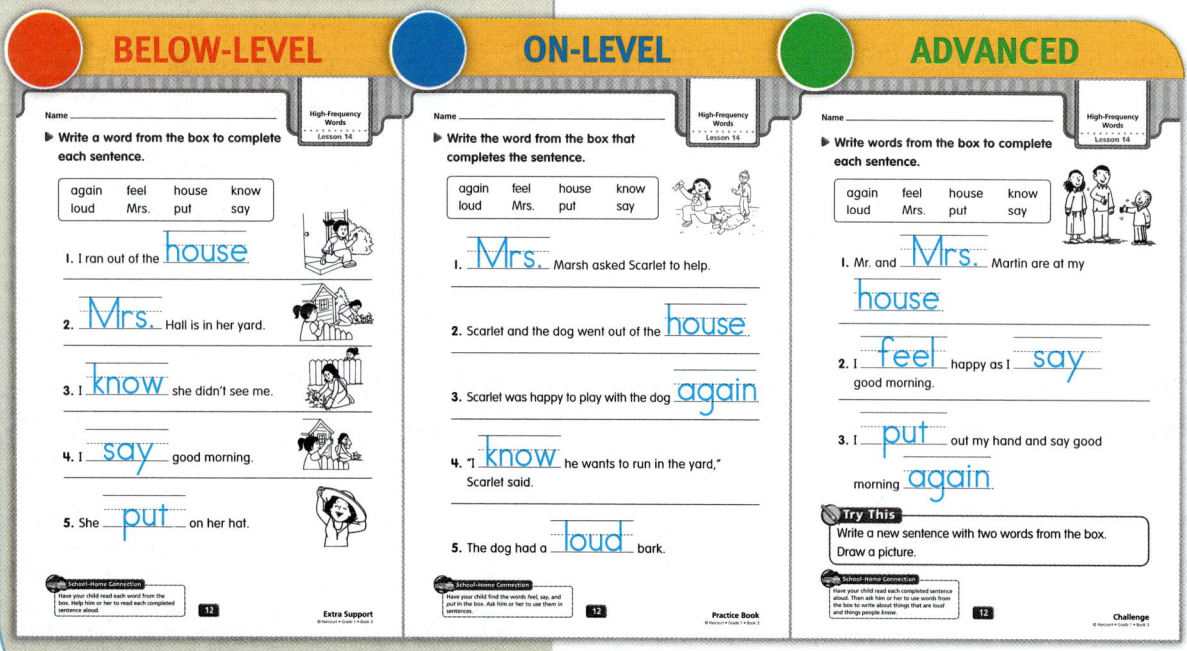

• Group children according to academic levels, and assign one of the pages on the left.

• Clarify any unfamiliar concepts as necessary. See *ELL Teacher Guide,* Lesson 14, for support in scaffolding instruction.

▲ Extra Support, p. 12    ▲ Practice Book, p. 12    ▲ Challenge, p. 12

# Fluency

*Intonation*

## Objective
- *To read with fluency in a manner that sounds like natural speech*

## Review

**DIBELS** Oral Reading Fluency **ORF**

**REVIEW USING APPROPRIATE INTONATION** Remind children that punctuation in sentences gives them clues about how loudly or softly to read the words. Have children open their *Student Edition* to page 79. Explain that capital letters such as in the word *out* and the exclamation point are often signals for readers to read strongly and a little louder. Model reading this page and have children repeat it. Then remind them that a sentence ending in a period is read in a calmer, softer voice while an exclamation point means to read words in a stronger way.

**Listen for Intonation** Encourage children to close their eyes and listen as you read each sentence in "Mark's Big Day." After each sentence, have them tell you which word(s) you stressed.

## Practice/Apply

**GUIDED PRACTICE** Distribute rhythm sticks to the class. If none are available, have children clap instead. Teach this jump rope rhyme:

Charlie over the water,
Charlie over the sea,
Charlie caught a blackbird,
But he can't catch me!

As a class, discuss the chant's rhythm. Have children beat their rhythm sticks together in a steady beat and say the rhyme again. Point out that parts of some words are said more loudly. Ask: **Which is right—** _Char_lie _o_ver the _wa_ter or Char_lie_ o_ver_ _the_ _wa_ter. (the first) Explain that sometimes only the first part of a word is stressed.

**INDEPENDENT PRACTICE** Have each child select a page from the story and practice reading it aloud with appropriate intonation in a manner that sounds like natural speech. Then invite volunteers to read their chosen sections.

 **MONITOR PROGRESS**

### Fluency

| **IF** children have difficulty reading in a manner that sounds like natural speech, | **THEN** model raising and lowering your voice as you have children echo-read with you. |
|---|---|

**Small-Group Instruction, pp. S14–S15:**

- **BELOW-LEVEL:** Reteach
- **ON-LEVEL:** Reinforce
- **ADVANCED:** Extend

# Author's Purpose/Point of View *Comprehension*

## Objectives

- *To understand the author's purpose for writing a selection*
- *To apply word knowledge to the reading of a text*

## Skill Trace

**Tested** **Objective Subhead**

| | |
|---|---|
| Preview | T142 |
| Introduce | T151 |
| Reteach | S16–S17, S56–S57 |
| **Review** | **T176, T188, T198, T490, T499, T524, T538, T548** |
| Test | Bk 1-3 |
| Maintain | Monitor Comprehension, Bks 1-4 to 1-5 |

## Review

**REVIEW AUTHOR'S PURPOSE/POINT OF VIEW** Remind children that authors have reasons for writing stories and articles. Help them recall why the author wrote "The Hare and the Tortoise" from the *Read-Aloud Anthology*.

## Practice/Apply

**GUIDED PRACTICE** Ask children to tell why they think the author wrote "Mark's Big Day" in the *Student Edition*. Ask them how they can tell that the author is the one telling the story, and not a character, like Mark.

**INDEPENDENT PRACTICE** Have children apply their knowledge of author's purpose/point of view by completing *Practice Book* page 13. Children will also apply their knowledge of these concepts when they listen and respond to "Putting on a Play."

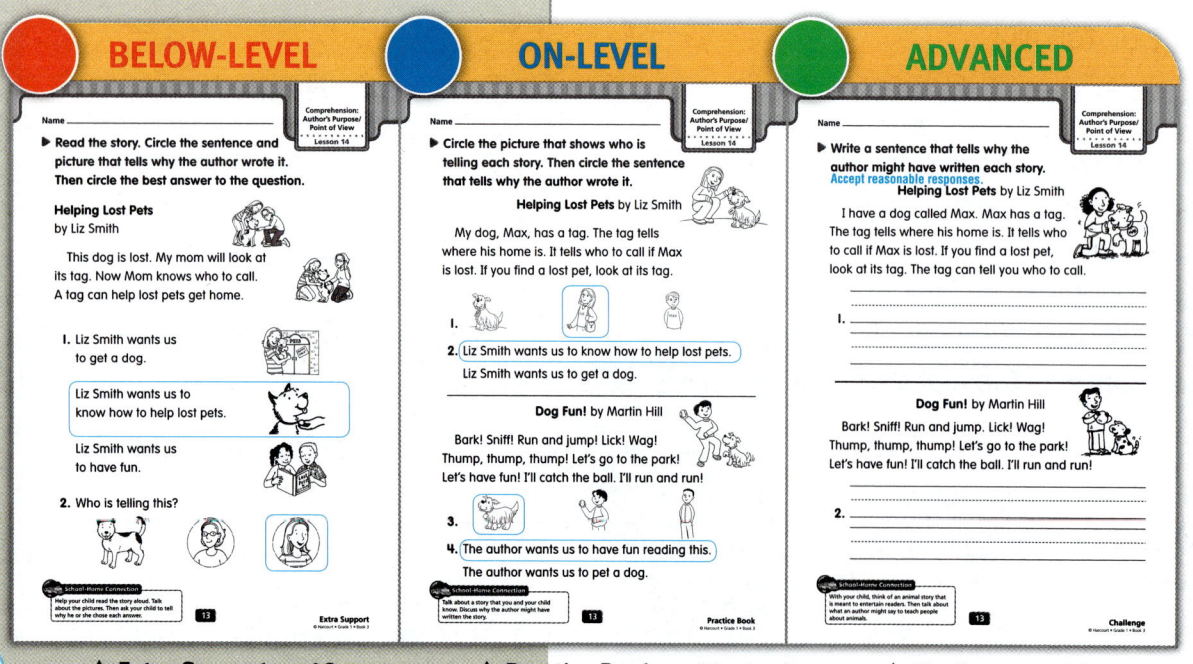

▲ Extra Support, p. 13    ▲ Practice Book, p. 13    ▲ Challenge, p. 13

- Group children according to academic levels, and assign one of the pages on the left.

- Clarify any unfamiliar concepts as necessary. See *ELL Teacher Guide*, Lesson 14, for support in scaffolding instruction.

## Drama

### Putting on a Play

Nonfiction

*Teacher Read-Aloud*

# Putting on a Play

Many people work together to put on a play.

The **Director** is in charge. He or she tells everyone what to do.

The **Set Designer** is in charge of how the stage will look for the play.

**Actors and Actresses** need to know how to pretend. They use words and actions to tell a story.

The **Costume Designer** makes the clothes that the actors and actresses wear.

Which job would you like to have? Why?

*The Three Bears: Putting on a Play*

88

89

---

# Reading

## *Student Edition: Paired Selection*

### Read Aloud

**MONITOR LISTENING COMPREHENSION** As you read, point out the captions. Help children use the captions to gather information. Monitor listening comprehension by using the following:

- **NOTE DETAILS** **What job does the director of a play have?** (The director is in charge and tells everyone what to do.)

- **AUTHOR'S PURPOSE/POINT OF VIEW** **Why do you think the author wrote "Putting on a Play"?** (to give the reader information)

- **GENRE** **Is "Putting on a Play" nonfiction or make-believe?** (non-fiction) **How can you tell?** (It has photographs. It tells about real jobs.)

**E L L**

**Build Background** Bring in parts of costumes or props that might be used in a play. Discuss what types of characters might wear or use each piece. Ask children to describe other costume pieces or props each character might need.

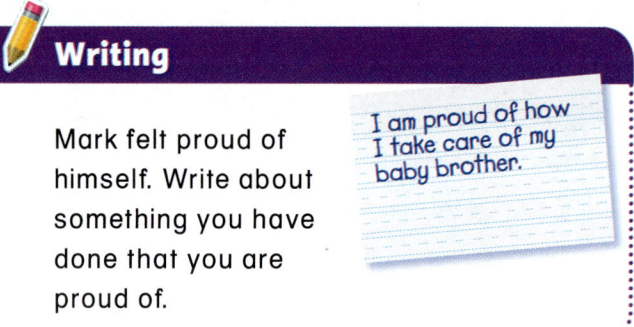

## Connections

### Comparing Texts

❶ What job from "Putting on a Play" do you think Mark would like? Why?
(I think he would like being the actor since he learned to speak loudly.)

❷ Tell what you liked about Mark's play or about a play you have seen.
(Accept reasonable responses.)

❸ What would you tell a friend who felt shy or afraid?
(Accept reasonable responses.)

 **Writing**

Mark felt proud of himself. Write about something you have done that you are proud of.

> I am proud of how I take care of my baby brother.

### Phonics

Make and read new words.

Start with **far**.

Add **m** to the end.

Take away the **f**.

Change **m** to **t**.

Add **p** to the beginning.

### Fluency Practice

Read the story aloud with a partner. Read softly where Mark speaks softly. Read like the Big Bad Wolf where Mark does!

> I'll huff and I'll puff . . .

90

91

# Connections

 **WRITING**

 **Write About Being Proud**
Guide children to write for a familiar occasion, audience, and purpose. Have them write about something they have done that makes them feel proud. Children can illustrate their writing and share it in small groups.

> I am proud of helping to paint Grandma's house.

**PHONICS**

**Word Building** Distribute to children Word Builder Cards f, a, r, m, t, and p. Have children practice manipulating the cards to build and read far, farm, arm, art, and part.

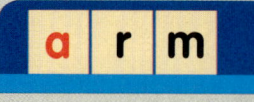

**FLUENCY**

**Partner Reading** Ask partners to take turns reading pages of the story. Remind children to make their voice sound as if someone is really speaking as they read, saying some words louder than others.

> Just act like a big wolf.
>
> Oh! I'll huff and I'll puff and I'll blow your house IN!

# Build Robust Vocabulary

**Listening/Speaking:** *Words About the Selection*

## Teach/Model

**Routine Card 15**

**INTRODUCE ROBUST VOCABULARY** Use *Routine Card 15* to introduce the words.

❶ Put the word in **selection context.**
❷ Provide the **Student-Friendly Explanation** for children.
❸ Have children **say the word** with you.
❹ Use the word in other contexts, and have children **interact with the word's meaning.**
❺ Say the Student-Friendly Explanation again, and ask children to **name the word** that goes with it.

❶ **Selection Context:** When Mark made a **blunder** during the play, all the children looked at him.
❹ **Interact with Word Meaning:** I made a *blunder* when I was singing a song because I forgot the words. Have you ever made a *blunder* like that?

❶ **Selection Context:** Mrs. Parks tried to **reassure** Mark by telling him not to feel bad about forgetting his part.
❹ **Interact with Word Meaning:** If we do a class play, I would *reassure* you by telling you that you can do a good job.

❶ **Selection Context:** Mark wanted to **excel** by saying his part in a loud voice.
❹ **Interact with Word Meaning:** I want to *excel* at playing the piano, so I practice each day.

## Practice/Apply

**GUIDED PRACTICE** Ask children to do the following:
- Tell what you would do if you made a *blunder* during a class play.
- Imagine that your friend is afraid to ride a bike. Tell what you would say to *reassure* your friend about learning to ride.
- Name two things at which you *excel.*

### Objective
- *To develop vocabulary to describe ideas*

**INTRODUCE** Tested ✓

## Student-Friendly Explanations

**blunder** If you make a blunder, you make a bad or silly mistake.

**reassure** If you reassure someone, you tell him or her that everything will be all right.

**excel** If you excel at something, you are very good at it.

**E L L**

**Introduce Vocabulary** Pantomime how you would feel if you made a blunder, if you wanted to reassure someone, and if you felt you had excelled at something. Guide children to do the same.

# Grammar
## Names of Holidays

**5-DAY GRAMMAR**

| | |
|---|---|
| **DAY 1** | Introduce Names of Holidays |
| **DAY 2** | Dictate Sentences About Holidays |
| **DAY 3** | Write Sentences About Holidays |
| **DAY 4** | Revise Names of Holidays |
| **DAY 5** | Write Holiday Messages |

### Objective
- *To apply knowledge of the basic rules of capitalization when writing the names of holidays*

### Daily Proofreading

**i was born on thanksgiving**
(I, Thanksgiving.)

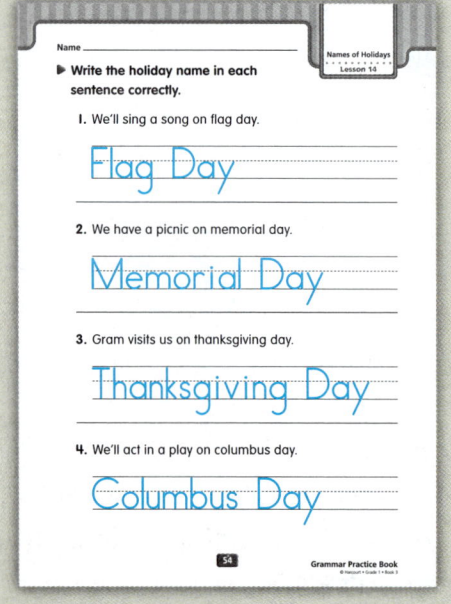

▲ **Grammar Practice Book, p. 54**

## Review

**DICTATE SENTENCES ABOUT HOLIDAYS** Talk with children about class celebrations of various holidays. Model a sentence about one of these holidays, such as: **On Valentine's Day, we make valentines to give one another.** Ask children to dictate other sentences that include the name of a holiday. Record their sentences without capitalizing these proper nouns. Then read the sentences to children. Have them identify the names of holidays.

**How Our Class Celebrates Holidays**

On presidents' day, we learned a song to sing.

On april fools' day, we had fun playing silly tricks.

We made cards to take home for mother's day.

For thanksgiving, we made turkeys from pinecones.

## Practice/Apply

**GUIDED PRACTICE** Reread the first sentence to children, tracking the print. Model how to correct it by capitalizing the first letter in each important word in the name of the holiday. Explain: **The words** *Presidents' Day* **name a holiday. We always capitalize the first letter of all important words in a holiday.** Follow a similar procedure for the other sentences. Then track the print and read aloud the finished sentences with children. Ask them if the names of holidays are written correctly.

**INDEPENDENT PRACTICE** Have children write another sentence that could be added to the sentences about holidays. Suggest that they write another sentence about their favorite holiday. Ask partners to read their sentences to one another. Remind them to check that the name of the holiday is written correctly.

| 5-DAY WRITING | |
| --- | --- |
| DAY 1 | Modeled Writing |
| DAY 2 | Shared Writing |
| DAY 3 | Shared Writing |
| DAY 4 | Independent Writing |
| DAY 5 | Independent Writing |

# Shared Writing

*E-mail*

## Write Together

**REVIEW WITH A LITERATURE MODEL** Write the e-mail below on the board or display it using a computer. Explain that the day before the play, Mrs. Parks might have sent this e-mail to Mark.

After reading, ask children to determine the main idea of the message. Have them use this information to tell what Mrs. Parks might have written in the subject line. (Possible response: Remember Your Costume)

 **PRACTICE WRITING** Choose another picture from among those that children drew on Day 1. Continue helping them write, modeling how to compose an e-mail about the event in the picture.

> Dear Mark,
>
> Tomorrow is the play. Please remember to bring your wolf costume.
> See you in the morning.
> Your teacher,
> Mrs. Parks

**WRITING TRAIT** **CONVENTIONS** Stop occasionally to read the e-mail with children. Have them tell how the sentences begin and end. Have them point out use of capital letters in the names of people, places, days, months, or holidays.

## Share

**DISCUSS E-MAIL** Read the finished e-mail message with children, tracking the print. Then ask them to

- Identify each part of the e-mail, explain its purpose, and tell what information it contains.
- Identify capital letters and end marks and tell why they are used.

Display the finished e-mail. Explain that children can use this message as a model when they write their own e-mails on Days 4 and 5.

## Objective
- *To compose coherent sentences in an e-mail*

 ### Writing Prompt

**Write a Note** Have children write a brief note to a partner to remind him or her to bring something to school the next day. Allow time for children to share their messages with each other.

### ADVANCED

**Compose an E-mail** Ask children to suppose that Mark's dad was out of town. Have them compose an e-mail message in which Mark tells his dad about his performance in the school play.

## Day at a Glance
### Day 4

**Phonemic Awareness**
- Phoneme Deletion

 **and Spelling**
- Introduce: Inflections *-s, -ed, -ing*

**High-Frequency Words**
- Review: again, feel, house, know, loud, Mrs., put, say

**Fluency**
- Intonation
- "Mark's Big Day," *Student Edition*, pp. 66–87

**Comprehension**
- Review: Author's Purpose/ Point of View

- Big Book: *We're Going on a Lion Hunt*

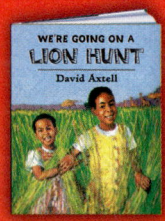

**Robust Vocabulary**
- Review: *blunder, reassure, excel*

**Grammar**
- Review: Names of Holidays

**Independent Writing**
- E-mail

# Warm-Up Routines

## Oral Language

**Objective** *To listen attentively and respond appropriately to oral communication*

### Question of the Day

Do you ever speak in a very loud voice?

When is it all right to do this? Why?

Help children identify when it is important to speak in a loud voice, and discuss why. Have children help you complete these sentence frames:

**I speak in a loud voice when _____. I do this so _____.**

## Read Aloud

**Objective** *To explore figurative language*

**BIG BOOK OF RHYMES AND POEMS** Display the poem and read the title and the poet's name. Explore the meaning of the title by having children discuss what it means to say something at the top of their voice. Read the poem, and have children listen for words that name loud sounds. Read the poem again and have children respond through movement by stamping their feet each time they hear a reference to a loud sound in the poem.

▲ **Big Book of Rhymes and Poems, p. 28**

## Word Wall

**Objective** *To read high-frequency words*

**REVIEW HIGH-FREQUENCY WORDS** Review *cold, play, says, her, again, feel, house, know,* and previously learned high-frequency words. Say each word, ask a volunteer to point to it, and have children read it aloud. Then point to words at random, and have children reread them. Repeat several times to reinforce instant recognition.

| | | | |
|---|---|---|---|
| cold | play | says | her |
| again | feel | house | know |

## Phonemic Awareness

**Objective** *To delete final phonemes from words*

**Routine Card 9** **PHONEME DELETION** Tell children that you will say some words and ask them to remove the final sound in each word. Model by saying: *Ant* **without /t/ is** *an.* Say the following and have children delete the ending sound to form a new word:

*farm* **without /m/** (far)  *inch* **without /ch/** (in)  *gasp* **without /p/** (gas)

*start* **without /t/** (star)  *bust* **without /t/** (bus)  *jars* **without /z/** (jar)

*hump* **without /p/** (hum)  *stilt* **without /t/** (still)  *past* **without /t/** (pass)

*goat* **without /t/** (go)  *worn* **without /n/** (wore)  *stark* **without /k/** (star)

*stark* **without /k/** (star)

# Inflections -s, -ed, -ing
phonics

**5-DAY PHONICS**

| | |
|---|---|
| DAY 1 | Introduce *r*-Controlled Vowel /är/*ar* |
| DAY 2 | Word Building with *r*-Controlled Vowel /är/*ar* |
| DAY 3 | Word Building |
| DAY 4 | Inflections -s, -ed, -ing (no spelling change) |
| DAY 5 | Inflections -s, -ed, -ing (no spelling change) |

## Objectives
- *To recognize root words*
- *To read inflected forms with -s, -ed, and -ing with no spelling changes*

## Skill Trace

**Tested** **Inflections** (no spelling change)

| | -s, | -ed, -ing |
|---|---|---|
| Introduce | Bk 1-1, T84 | Bk 1-1, T458 |
| Review | Bk 1-1, T94–T95 Bk 1-3, T184, T194 | Bk 1-1, T468–T469; Bk 1-3, T184, T194 |
| Maintain | Bk 1-4, T374 | |

### phonics Resources

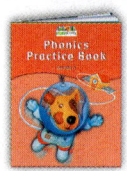

Phonics Practice Book, pp. 77–78

**Inflections -s, -ed, -ing**

Ron was looking at his plant box.
He planted some plants.
Then he watered them.
Every day, he looked at his plants.
Soon the little plants started to grow.
One day, Ron picked the plants.
Now Ron feels good.
He is eating his plants.

Grade 1, Lesson 14    R28    Phonics: Inflections -s, -ed, -ing

**Transparency R28**

## Teach/Model

**INTRODUCE -s, -ed, -ing** Write the following words on the board and have children read them:

**park    parks    parked    parking**

Review with children how the words are alike and different. (They all have the same root word; the last three words have different endings.) Have volunteers underline the root words and circle the endings.

## Guided Practice

**ADD ENDINGS** Make a chart as shown. Model reading the words: Cover -s in *plants* and read the root word. Uncover and point to -s and say /s/. Then say the word naturally—*plants*. Repeat for the other words. As children read the words, have them identify two sounds that *s* can stand for: /s/ in *plants* and /z/ in *waters*. Then have them identify the three sounds that -ed can stand for: /əd/ in *planted,* /t/ in *looked,* and /d/ in *watered.* Save the chart for Day 5.

| Root Word | Add -s | Add -ed | Add -ing |
|---|---|---|---|
| plant | plants | planted | planting |
| look | looks | looked | looking |
| pick | picks | picked | picking |
| water | waters | watered | watering |

## Practice/Apply

**READ WORDS IN CONTEXT** Display **Transparency R28**. Have children read each sentence silently. Then have volunteers read the sentences aloud. Point to the words with inflections and have children identify the root words and the endings. Track the print as you lead children in choral-reading the sentences.

# r-Controlled Vowel /är/ ar  phonics and Spelling

**5-DAY SPELLING**
DAY 1 Pretest
DAY 2 Word Building
DAY 3 State the Generalization
DAY 4 Review
DAY 5 Posttest

## Build Words

**MAP LETTERS TO SOUNDS** Use *Letter Cards* and a pocket chart to form words. Have children listen to your directions and change one letter in each word to spell a spelling word. Then have a volunteer change the *Letter Card* in the pocket chart.

- Form *far* in the pocket chart and have children read it. Ask: **Which spelling word can you make by adding a letter?** (farm)

- Leave *farm* in the pocket chart. Ask: **Which spelling word can you make by removing the first letter?** (arm)

- Leave *arm* in the pocket chart. Ask: **Which spelling word can you make by changing the last letter?** (art)

Follow a similar procedure with the following words: *art* (part), *part* (park), *chip* (chin), and *much* (such).

**HIGH-FREQUENCY WORDS** Remind children that there are some other words they have to remember how to spell. Tell them that *fly* is one such word. Tell children to picture the word and then write it. Repeat with *watch*.

### Objectives
- *To use /är/ar and other known letter-sounds to spell and write words*
- *To spell and write known high-frequency words*

### Spelling Words

| | |
|---|---|
| 1. far | 6. park |
| 2. farm | 7. chin |
| 3. arm | 8. such |
| 4. art | 9. fly |
| 5. part | 10. watch |

**ADVANCED**

**Build Words with /är/ar** Have partners place *Word Builder Cards* *a* and *r* in a *Word Builder*. Ask them to use other *Word Builder Cards* to make more words containing this vowel sound. Have them list each word on paper. Have children share their words with classmates.

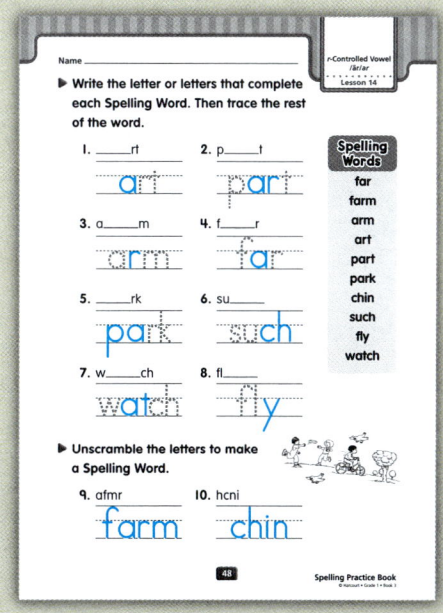

▲ Spelling Practice Book, p. 48

# High-Frequency Words

## Objective
- *To read high-frequency words*

### REVIEW

### High-Frequency Words

| | |
|---|---|
| again | loud |
| feel | Mrs. |
| house | put |
| know | say |

### BELOW-LEVEL

**Use Word Cards** To simplify slotting high-frequency words in the story strips, display several word cards as choices for each blank. Have children make their selection from these words by trying out each word in the context of the sentence to see if it makes sense.

**Reinforce Words** Before children slot the high-frequency words in the story strips, review the pronunciation and meaning of each one. When possible, act out the word, such as modeling how to *put* on a jacket, or draw a picture of a word, such as *house*.

### Review

**READ AND WRITE WORDS** Duplicate and distribute an uncut story strip page *(Teacher Resource Book,* p. 224) for each child. Then do the following:

- Have children read the story title in the first strip. Explain that the sentences tell the story, but some have missing words.

- Display *Word Cards* for the high-frequency words, or list the words on the board. Have children read each word.

| | | | |
|---|---|---|---|
| again | feel | house | know |
| loud | Mrs. | put | say |

### Practice/Apply

**GUIDED PRACTICE** Direct children to read all the story strip sentences and to write the missing words in the blanks.

> "I'll blow your _____ in," Mark said.

**INDEPENDENT PRACTICE** After children complete the story strip page, have them cut apart the strips. Have partners work together to read and match their story strips and then to arrange the events in the order in which they happen in the story. Have children take the story strips home to share with family members.

Children read the words in context in the Cut-Out/Fold-Up Book "Stars by Carla."

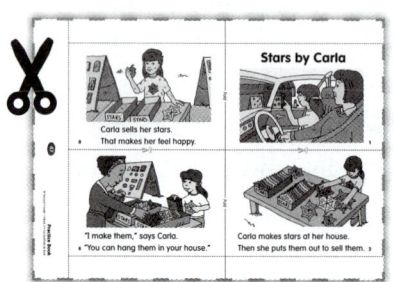

◄ "Stars by Carla"
Practice Book, pp. 47–48

# Fluency
## Intonation

## Review

**DIBELS**
Oral Reading Fluency
**ORF**

**MODEL READING WITH APPROPRIATE INTONATION** Remind children that when good readers read, they say some words louder than others. Show children how to

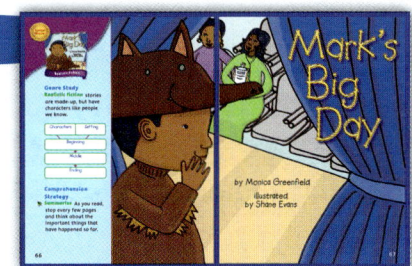

▲ Student Edition, pp. 66–87

- stress a word in a sentence to show that it is important.

- change the meaning of a sentence by stressing a different word.

**Think Aloud** **I'm going to read some pages from "Mark's Big Day." As I read, I'm going to watch for the important words in a sentence, like *huff, puff,* and *blow.* I will say those words a little more strongly. Read each page after me, just the way I read it.**

## Practice/Apply

**GUIDED PRACTICE** Have partners read "Mark's Big Day" aloud three or four times. Have children read aloud with appropriate intonation in a manner that sounds like natural speech. Remind them to stress the words that are written with all capital letters. Listen to partners read, giving them feedback about their intonation and offering them guidance for improving their fluency.

**INDEPENDENT PRACTICE** Have children make a tape-recording of themselves reading a section of "Mark's Big Day" aloud. Guide them to self-select by choosing the part they liked best. Remind them to pay attention to their intonation as they read. After making their recording, have them listen to the recording and critique their own reading for fluency and intonation.

## Objectives

- *To build fluency through rereading a story*

- *To read in a manner that sounds like natural speech*

## Additional Related Reading

Guide children to self-select related books, such as these:

- *The Feelings Book* by Todd Parr. Megan Tingley, 2005. **EASY**

- *Going to School (My World)* by Tammy J. Schlepp. Copper Beech, 2001. **AVERAGE**

- *The School Play* by Rosemary Wells. Hyperion, 2001. **CHALLENGE**

### BELOW-LEVEL

**Fluency Practice** Have children reread for fluency, using "Star" in the *Strategic Intervention Interactive Reader, Decodable Book 14,* or the appropriate *Leveled Reader.* (See pages T202–T205.) Guide them to select a small portion of a story and practice reading it several times.

# Author's Purpose/Point of View *Comprehension*

## Objective

- *To determine the author's purpose/point of view while listening to a story*

## Skill Trace

 **Tested** Author's Purpose/ Point of View

| | |
|---|---|
| Preview | T142 |
| Introduce | T151 |
| Reteach | S16–S17, S56–S57 |
| Review | T176, T188, T198, T490, T499, T524, T538, T548 |
| Test | Bk 1-3 |
| Maintain | Monitor Comprehension, Bks 1-4 to 1-5 |

### ✓ MONITOR PROGRESS

**Comprehension: Author's Purpose/Point of View**

| **IF** children have difficulty determining the author's purpose, | **THEN** have them suggest a favorite story and help them identify the author's purpose. |
|---|---|

**Small-Group Instruction, pp. S16–S17:**

🔴 **BELOW-LEVEL:** Reteach
🔵 **ON-LEVEL:** Reinforce
🟢 **ADVANCED:** Extend

---

### Review

**TALK ABOUT AUTHOR'S PURPOSE/POINT OF VIEW** Ask children to identify purposes that authors have when writing a story. (to inform, to give directions, to entertain, to teach a lesson) Remind them that authors may tell the story themselves or have a character tell the story.

**USE PRIOR KNOWLEDGE/SET A PURPOSE** Invite children to think about what the author's purpose is and who is telling the story as they listen to you read the story.

**EXAMINE CONCEPTS OF PRINT** As you read aloud, point out the use of boldface, italics, and large type for emphasis. Model appropriate intonation. Also call attention to the words *swish, swash, splish, splash, squish, squash,* and *crash.* Tell children that these words sound like the sounds they represent. Then have children respond through music in a way that reflects understanding and interpretation by chanting the story's repetitive text in a song-like manner.

▲ **Big Book**

### Practice/Apply

**GUIDED PRACTICE** Monitor listening comprehension as you read, using the following:

- **MAIN IDEA** What is this story mostly about? (Two girls are looking for a lion.)

- 🌀 **AUTHOR'S PURPOSE/POINT OF VIEW** What is the author's purpose? (to entertain) Who tells this story? (the girls) How do you know? (the word *We*)

- **RECOGNIZE TEXT STRUCTURE** What pattern does this story follow? (The girls go through obstacles to get to the cave; then they go back through the same obstacles to get home.)

**INDEPENDENT PRACTICE** Have small groups draw a simple map of the journey. Have them use the girls' point of view to retell the story, telling it as if they were on the lion hunt, too.

# Build Robust Vocabulary

## Listening/Speaking: *Words About the Selection*

### Review Robust Vocabulary

**USE VOCABULARY IN DIFFERENT CONTEXTS** Remind children of the Student-Friendly Explanations of *blunder, reassure,* and *excel.* Then discuss each word, using the following examples:

**blunder** Tell children that you will name some things. If they think that something is a *blunder,* they should say, "Oops!" If not, they should say nothing.

| | |
|---|---|
| misspelling a word | doing a hard problem |
| sharpening a pencil | spilling a glass of milk |
| mispronouncing a word | leaving lunch on the bus |

**reassure** Tell children that you will say some things. If they might say these things to *reassure* someone, they should show "thumbs up." If not, they should do nothing.

| | |
|---|---|
| You can do it! | I believe in you! |
| Don't even try! | Give it your best! |
| You'll do just fine! | Forget it! |
| Don't give up! | You'll be terrific! |

**excel** Tell children that you will name some things. If they would like to *excel* at these things, they should say, "Yes!" If not, they should say nothing.

riding a bike
putting on a jacket
walking a dog
eating a sandwich
reading a hard book
scoring a goal

### Objective
- *To develop robust vocabulary*

**Tested**

**REVIEW** ✓

### Student-Friendly Explanations

**blunder** If you make a blunder, you make a bad or silly mistake.

**reassure** If you reassure someone, you tell him or her that everything will be all right.

**excel** If you excel at something, you are very good at it.

### BELOW-LEVEL

**Use Vocabulary in Different Contexts** Provide children with a very specific context, such as playing in a T-ball game. Ask them to describe a blunder someone might make, how they might reassure someone on the team, and how they might excel at the game.

# Grammar
## Names of Holidays

**5-DAY GRAMMAR**

| | |
|---|---|
| **DAY 1** | Introduce Names of Holidays |
| **DAY 2** | Dictate Sentences About Holidays |
| **DAY 3** | Write Sentences About Holidays |
| **DAY 4** | **Revise Names of Holidays** |
| **DAY 5** | Write Holiday Messages |

### Objective
• *To apply knowledge of the basic rules of capitalization when writing the name of a holiday*

### Daily Proofreading

**I play tag last monday.**

(played, Monday)

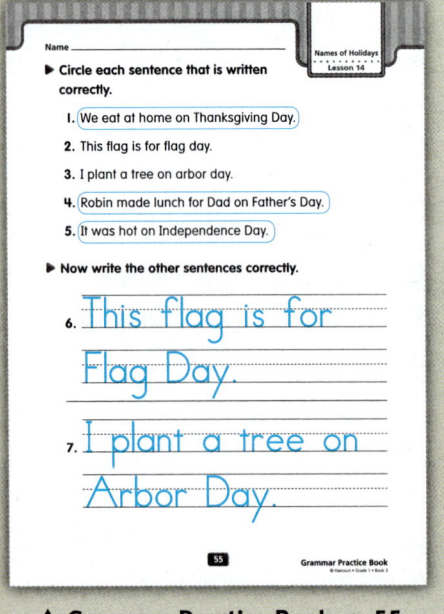

▲ Grammar Practice Book, p. 55

## Review

**IDENTIFY NAMES OF HOLIDAYS** Flip through a calendar with children and identify holidays that are observed by your school. Say: **With what holiday do we begin the very first day of the year?** (New Year's Day) **What do we need to remember to do when we write the holiday** *New Year's Day*? (to capitalize the first letter of each important word) Write *New Year's Day* on the board. Continue in the same manner to elicit and then list other holidays as children dictate them.

## Practice/Apply

**GUIDED PRACTICE** Write the following sentence frames on the board and read them aloud to children.

In January we celebrate _____ and_____.
We celebrate Valentine's Day and _____ in February.
The first day of April is called _____.
At the end of May, we celebrate _____.
Our country's birthday is called the _____.

Work with children to add names of holidays to complete the sentences. As they dictate, write their responses. Ask volunteers to help spell words and to tell how to capitalize them.

**INDEPENDENT PRACTICE** Write these sentences on the board and read them aloud to children. Explain that the names of holidays are not written correctly. Have children choose two sentences and write them correctly by adding capital letters.

I sent valentines on valentine's day.
We give thanks on thanksgiving.
We went to the park on the fourth of july.
The third Monday in February is presidents' day.

Day **4**

| 5-DAY WRITING | |
|---|---|
| DAY 1 | Modeled Writing |
| DAY 2 | Shared Writing |
| DAY 3 | Shared Writing |
| **DAY 4** | **Independent Writing** |
| DAY 5 | Independent Writing |

# Independent Writing *E-mail*

## Write an E-mail

**GENERATE IDEAS** Have children view an e-mail message, and read it aloud to them. Have them listen closely to determine the main idea and suggest a subject line for the e-mail. Then, tell children they will write their own e-mail message to a friend or relative. Have them look again at the pictures showing a special event from Day 1. On a separate sheet of paper, have them list words related to the event.

**REVIEW CHARACTERISTICS** Display the list of characteristics of a well-written e-mail message from Day 1, and read it with children.

**WRITING TRAIT** **CONVENTIONS** Have volunteers dictate sentences from an e-mail message. Record the sentences, and have children tell where to use capital letters and periods. Remind them to write their own messages in the same way.

**WRITE** Guide children to write for a familiar occasion, audience, and purpose. For example, the occasion might be a family party. You may wish to provide children with the format of an e-mail with spaces labeled *From, To, Subject,* and *Message.* Tell children that they will follow this form to draft an e-mail. Help children write messages that move from left to right on the page. Teach them to begin at the top of the page and move down the page as they write. Remind children to spell correctly words ending in *-s, -ed,* and *-ing* and known high-frequency words. You may want children to draft their e-mails on a computer, using an e-mail program. Tell children not to click on the SEND button. Instead, show them how to save their e-mail as a draft so it can be revised on Day 5.

### Objective
• *To draft an e-mail message*

### Writing Prompt

**Write Sentences** Have children draw a picture and write several sentences telling what they like to do using a computer.

### E-mail Message

• Use a computer to get and send e-mail.
• <u>From</u> shows your e-mail address.
• <u>To</u> shows the e-mail address of the person the message is going to.
• <u>Subject</u> tells what the e-mail is about.
• The message can begin with a greeting and end with your name.

### E L L

**Support Writing** Provide children with these sentence frames to help them write their e-mail message:

Date

Dear _____,
Don't forget to come to _____.
See you on _____ at _____.

Your friend,

_____

## Day at a Glance

**Day 5**

### Phonemic Awareness
- Phoneme Deletion

 **and Spelling**
- Review: Inflections *-s, -ed, -ing*
- Posttest: *r*-Controlled Vowel /är/*ar*

### High-Frequency Words
- Review

### Fluency
- Intonation
- "Mark's Big Day," *Student Edition*, pp. 66–87

 **Read!**

### Comprehension
Review: Author's Purpose/Point of View

### Robust Vocabulary
- Review

### Grammar
- Review: Names of Holidays

### Independent Writing
- E-mail

---

# Warm-Up Routines

## Oral Language

**Objectives** *To listen attentively and respond appropriately to oral communication; to explore figurative language*

### Question of the Day

How could you make the ground thunder? How could you make the world ring?

Have children discuss the meaning of "the ground thunders" or "the world rings." Write these frames and help children complete them.

**I could _____ to make the ground thunder.**

**I could _____ to make the world ring.**

## Read Aloud

**Objective** *To understand concepts of print*

**BIG BOOK OF RHYMES AND POEMS** Ask children to tell what they remember about the poem. Then read it, modeling reading from left to right and top to bottom. Point out to children that in many poems, the first word in each line is often written with a capital letter even if it is not the first word in the sentence. Read the poem again, and have children identify the rhyming words. Then read the poem and have children join in.

▲ Big Book of Rhymes and Poems, p. 28

## Word Wall

**Objective**  *To read high-frequency words*

**REVIEW HIGH-FREQUENCY WORDS**  Review *loud, Mrs., put, say, fly, watch,* and other previously learned high-frequency words. Say each word, ask a volunteer to point to it, and have children read it aloud. Then point to words at random, and have children reread them. Repeat several times to reinforce instant recognition.

| | | |
|---|---|---|
| loud | Mrs. | put |
| say | fly | watch |

## Phonemic Awareness

**Objective**  *To delete medial phonemes from words*

**Routine Card 9**

**PHONEME DELETION**  Tell children they will sing a song and delete the middle sound they hear in a given word. Model an example. *(Sing to the tune of "The Farmer in the Dell.")*

*Nest* without /s/ is *net*. *Nest* without /s/ is *net*.
**Hi-ho, the derrio.** *Nest* without /s/ is *net*.

Continue singing the song, using the words below. Have children participate while singing the song by clapping as they sing each new word.

| | | |
|---|---|---|
| *silk* without /l/ (sick) | *melt* without /l/ (met) | *clasp* without /s/ (clap) |
| *fact* without /k/ (fat) | *hint* without /n/ (hit) | *pest* without /s/ (pet) |
| *mast* without /s/ (mat) | *trunk* without /n/ (truck) | *past* without /s/ (pat) |
| *west* without /s/ (wet) | *fast* without /s/ (fat) | *can't* without /n/ (cat) |

# Inflections -s, -ed, -ing

phonics

| 5-DAY PHONICS | |
|---|---|
| DAY 1 | Introduce *r*-Controlled Vowel /är/*ar* |
| DAY 2 | Word Building with *r*-Controlled Vowel /är/*ar* |
| DAY 3 | Word Building |
| DAY 4 | Inflections -s, -ed, -ing (no spelling change) |
| DAY 5 | Inflections -s, -ed, -ing (no spelling change) |

## Objectives

- To recognize root words
- To read inflectional forms with no spelling changes

## Skill Trace

**Tested** **Inflections (no spelling change)**

| | -s, | -ed, -ing |
|---|---|---|
| Introduce | Bk 1-1, T84 | Bk 1-1, T458 |
| Review | Bk 1-1, T94–T95; Bk 1-3 T184, T194 | Bk 1-1, T468–T469; Bk 1-3 T184, T194 |
| Maintain | Bk 1-4, T374 | BK 1-4 T374 |

## Review

**ROOT WORDS AND ENDINGS** Remind children that endings can be added to root words to make new words.

- Write *jump*. Say: **The word *jumps* is made by adding *-s* to the root word *jump*.** Write *jumps and have children read it.*

- Follow the same procedure to review the formation of the words *jumped* and *jumping*.

## Work with Patterns

**ADDING ENDINGS** Display the chart from Day 4. Ask children to read the words, and have volunteers underline the root words.

| Root Word | Add -s | Add -ed | Add -ing |
|---|---|---|---|
| plant | plants | planted | planting |
| look | looks | looked | looking |
| pick | picks | picked | picking |
| water | waters | watered | watering |

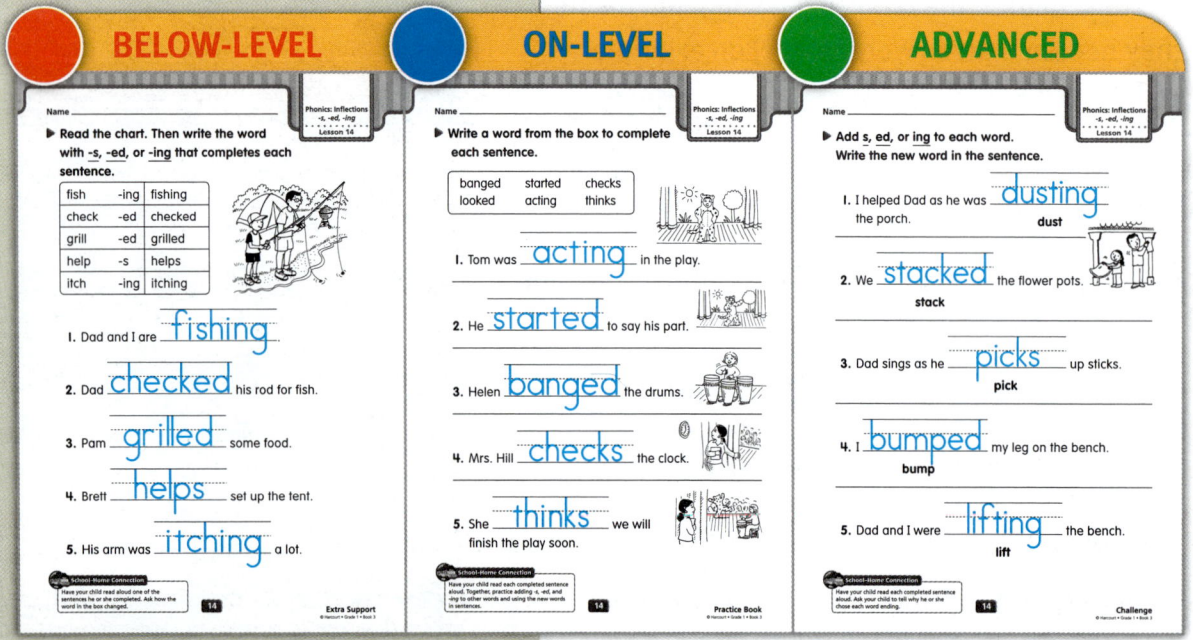

▲ Extra Support, p. 14　　▲ Practice Book, p. 14　　▲ Challenge, p. 14

**E L L**

- Group children according to academic levels, and assign one of the pages on the left.

- Clarify any unfamiliar concepts as necessary. See *ELL Teacher Guide*, Lesson 14, for scaffolding instruction.

5-DAY SPELLING

| | |
|---|---|
| DAY 1 | Pretest |
| DAY 2 | Word Building |
| DAY 3 | State the Generalization |
| DAY 4 | Review |
| DAY 5 | Posttest |

# r-Controlled Vowel /är/ar phonics and Spelling

## Assess

**POSTTEST** Assess children's progress. Use the dictation sentences from Day 1.

### Words with /är/ar

1. far     The ocean is **far** away.
2. farm     Horses live on that **farm.**
3. arm     Please raise your right **arm.**
4. art     We drew pictures in **art** class.
5. part     I ate **part** of the apple.
6. park     We play ball in the **park.**

### Review

7. chin     The baby had food on her **chin.**
8. such     There is **such** a lot to do!

### High-Frequency

9. fly     We saw the birds **fly** away.
10. watch     Dad will **watch** the baby.

**WRITING APPLICATION** Have children complete and illustrate the following sentence frames.

**The best part of art is _____.**

**We can go to the park to watch _____.**

We can go to the park to watch the swan.

## Objectives

- *To use /är/ar and other known letter-sounds to spell and write words*
- *To spell and write known high-frequency words*

### Spelling Words

| | | | |
|---|---|---|---|
| 1. | **far** | 6. | **park** |
| 2. | **farm** | 7. | **chin** |
| 3. | **arm** | 8. | **such** |
| 4. | **art** | 9. | **fly** |
| 5. | **part** | 10. | **watch** |

### ● ADVANCED

**Multiple-Meaning Words**
Remind children that *park*, *fly*, and *watch* have more than one meaning. Have children write sentences that show each meaning. Have children share their work with the class.

# High-Frequency Words

## Objectives
• *To read high-frequency words*
• *To explore word relationships*

**REVIEW**

### High-Frequency Words

| | | |
|---|---|---|
| again | house | put |
| came | know | say |
| does | loud | use |
| feel | Mrs. | your |

**Reinforce Word Recognition**
Have children respond to simple commands that include the high-frequency words. First, display one high-frequency *Word Card,* such as *put.* Then give a simple command using the word, and ask children to carry it out; for example, say: **Put your hand on your arm.** Repeat with the other high-frequency words.

---

**Review**

**REINFORCE WORD RECOGNITION** Display *Word Cards* for all the words in a pocket chart. Point to words at random and ask volunteers to read them.

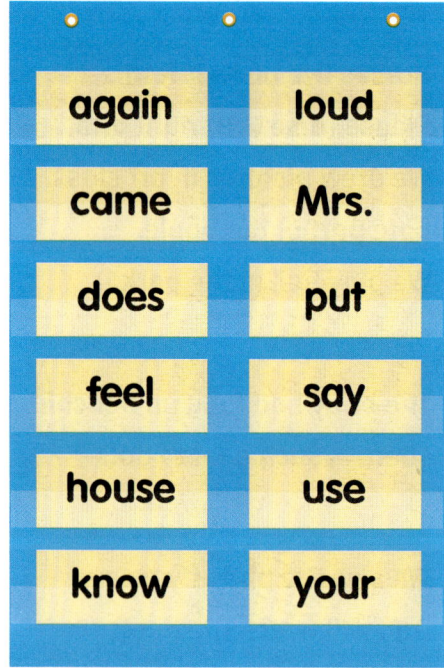

**SORT WORDS** Guide children as they sort the words into columns according to the number of letters. Then point to each column, and have children read the words in the column aloud.

• Ask: **Which word rhymes with *mouse*?** *(house)*
• Ask: **Which word begins with a silent letter?** *(know)*
• Ask: **Which word begins with the last sound you hear in *loud*?** *(does)*
• Ask: **Which word rhymes with *may*?** *(say)*
• Ask: **Which word means the opposite of *soft*?** *(loud)*

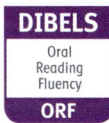

# Fluency

## Intonation

## Readers' Theater

**DIBELS**
Oral
Reading
Fluency
**ORF**

**PERFORM "MARK'S BIG DAY"** To help children improve their fluency, have them perform "Mark's Big Day" as Readers' Theater. Use the following procedures:

- Read "Mark's Big Day" aloud, modeling fluent reading with appropriate intonation as children follow along.

- Discuss with children how characters might feel and sound throughout the story.

- Have groups of three read the story together. Then have them choose the parts of Mark, Mom, or Mrs. Parks and practice re-reading the story with appropriate intonation.

- Listen to small groups read. Provide feedback and support.

- Invite small groups to read the story to classmates. Have children read aloud with fluency in a manner that sounds like natural speech.

### ELL

**Develop Vocabulary** As you discuss how characters in the story might feel, use emotion words, such as *shy, nervous, confident, encouraging,* and *helpful.* Help children understand the meanings of the words.

### Objective

- *To read fluently with appropriate intonation*

### ASSESSMENT

**Monitoring Progress** Periodically, take a timed sample of children's oral reading and measure the number of words read correctly per minute. Children should be accurately reading approximately 60 words per minute by the end of Grade 1.

### Fluency Support Materials

**Fluency Builders, Grade 1,** Lesson 14
● ● ●

**Audiotext** *Student Edition* selections are available on *Audiotext Grade 1,* CD 3.

**Strategic Intervention Teacher Guide,** Lesson 14

# Author's Purpose/
# Point of View *Comprehension*

## Objective
- *To identify and describe the author's purpose/point of view*

## Skill Trace

 **Tested** Author's Purpose/
Point of View

| | |
|---|---|
| Preview | T142 |
| Introduce | T151 |
| Reteach | S16–S17, S56–S57 |
| Review | T176, T188, T198, T490, T499, T524, T538, T548 |
| Test | Bk 1-3 |
| Maintain | Monitor Comprehension, Bks 1-4 to 1-5 |

### ADVANCED

**Independent Practice** Invite children to describe the author's purpose and point of view of other stories they have read.

## Review

**REVIEW THE SKILL** Ask children to explain different reasons that authors write stories and articles. (to entertain, to inform, to give instructions) Then remind them that authors may tell the story themselves or have one of the characters tell the story. Draw a three-column chart on the board with the titles "The Hare and the Tortoise," "Mark's Big Day," and *We're Going on a Lion Hunt* at the top. Remind children that these are the read-aloud, the *Student Edition* selection, and the *Big Book* that they read this week. Draw two rows, one for "Author's Purpose" and one for "Point of View." Write the author's purpose for "The Hare and the Tortoise" in the first column. Identify who is telling the story in "The Hare and the Tortoise," and write it in the next row.

## Practice/Apply

**GUIDED PRACTICE** Have children brainstorm and discuss why the author wrote "Mark's Big Day" and identify who is telling the story. Write their responses in the second column of the chart. Then have them repeat the process for *We're Going on a Lion Hunt,* and write their responses in the last column.

| | "The Hare and the Tortoise" | "Mark's Big Day" | We're Going on a Lion Hunt |
|---|---|---|---|
| **Author's Purpose** | to entertain to teach a lesson | to entertain to encourage | to entertain |
| **Point of View** | the author | the author | the girls |

**INDEPENDENT PRACTICE** Have children page through their *Student Edition* to help them recall selections they have already read. Ask each one to name one of the selections, tell why he or she thinks the author wrote it, and identify who is telling the story.

# Build Robust Vocabulary

## Listening/Speaking

### Review

**REINFORCE MEANINGS** Ask children the following questions:

- If you were *approached* by a bear in the woods, would you move at a slow *pace* or a fast *pace?*

- If you felt *energetic*, would you be likely to *excel* in a race? Why?

- If a classmate was worried about making a *blunder* during a class play, what could you say to *reassure* this person?

**MAKE WORD WEBS** Guide children to complete graphic organizers to enrich their understanding of *energetic and excel*. For *excel*, ask children to name indoor and outdoor activities at which they excel.

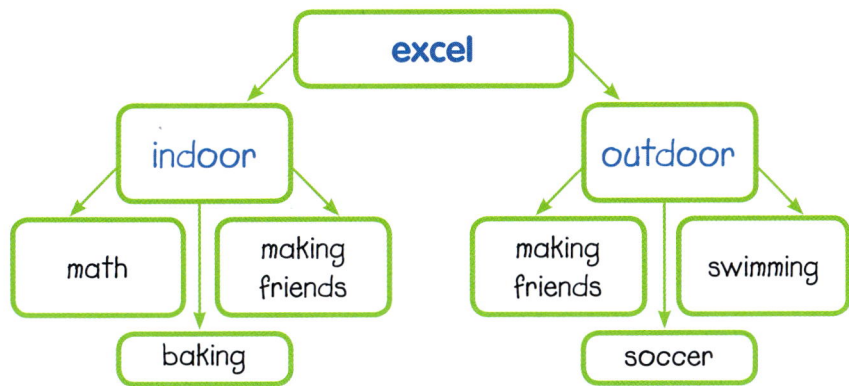

Make another graphic organizer for *energetic*. Have children tell what makes them feel energetic and what does not.

# Grammar
## Names of Holidays

**5-DAY GRAMMAR**

| | |
|---|---|
| DAY 1 | Introduce Names of Holidays |
| DAY 2 | Dictate Sentences About Holidays |
| DAY 3 | Write Sentences About Holidays |
| DAY 4 | Revise Names of Holidays |
| DAY 5 | Write Holiday Messages |

## Objective
- *To write complete, coherent sentences that contain the names of holidays*

### Daily Proofreading

**did Mom park the car.**
(Did, car?)

### ✓ Language Arts Checkpoint

If children have difficulty with the concepts, see page S20–S21 to reteach.

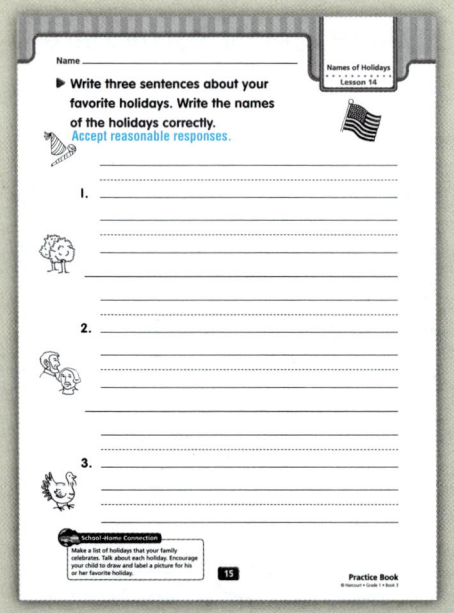

▲ Practice Book, p. 15

---

### Review

**COMPOSE SENTENCES ABOUT HOLIDAYS** Tell children that in March, they can make cards to send to friends to wish them a happy St. Patrick's Day. Guide children to write for a familiar occasion, audience, and purpose. Model for children a message that you might include on the card, such as the one below. After you write the message on the board, read it aloud with children. Have them identify the holiday in the message and tell what is special about the way you have written it. (The important words in the name of the holiday are capitalized.)

**Be sure to wear green on St. Patrick's Day!**

### Practice/Apply

**GUIDED PRACTICE** Have volunteers share other holiday greetings. Write them on chart paper, but do not capitalize the names of the holidays. Then work with children to help them correct the capitalization. Display this list and encourage children to refer to it as they create cards.

**INDEPENDENT PRACTICE** Distribute colored construction paper and crayons. Then have children work independently to create their own card with a greeting that includes the name of a holiday. Remind them to check to make sure that they have capitalized all the important words in each holiday name. Invite children to share their finished cards with classmates. Then have children work as a group to sort them by holiday. Have children use these cards to help create a bulletin board display that features the names of days, months, and holidays.

# Independent Writing *E-mail*

| **5-DAY** WRITING | |
| --- | --- |
| **DAY I** | Modeled Writing |
| **DAY 2** | Shared Writing |
| **DAY 3** | Shared Writing |
| **DAY 4** | Independent Writing |
| **DAY 5** | Independent Writing |

## Write an E-mail

**WRITE** Have children view an e-mail message, and read it aloud to them. Have them listen closely to determine the main idea of the message. Then have them brainstorm appropriate Subject headings for the piece, and ask them to continue writing their own e-mail. Suggest that before completing the Subject line, they compose the message first.

**CONVENTIONS** Remind children that their e-mail message should be written correctly so the person receiving the message can understand it. Have children check to make sure that special names of people, places, dates, and the first word in each sentence are capitalized.

**REVISE** Have children read their e-mail message to a partner and check to make sure that their message makes sense. Read to children the list of criteria for e-mail messages, and have them use the list to improve their writing. If computers are available, have them input and spell-check their messages. Remind them to make sure that the e-mail addresses they are using are accurate. Point out that if the address is incorrect, their e-mail will not be delivered.

### E-mail Message

- Use a computer to get and send e-mail.

- <u>From</u> shows your e-mail address.

- <u>To</u> shows the e-mail address of the person the message is going to.

- <u>Subject</u> tells what the e-mail is about.

- The message can begin with a greeting and end with your name.

## Share

**AUTHOR'S CHAIR** After children make a final copy of their e-mail messages, invite them to share their e-mail with the group. Guide children to listen to the e-mail message to determine the subject. Then, after reading the message, the presenter can read the Subject line.

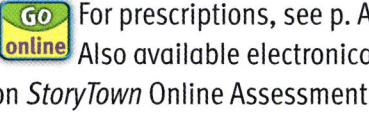

## Objectives

- *To write, edit, publish, and share an e-mail message*

- *To use correct punctuation and capitalization*

## Writing Prompt

**Write an E-mail** Have children write an e-mail message to a friend.

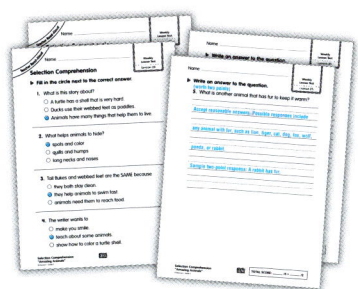

**Tested**

### WEEKLY LESSON TEST

▲ **Weekly Lesson Tests, pp. 137–147**

- Selection Comprehension with Short Response
- Phonics and Spelling
- High-Frequency Words
- Focus Skill
- Robust Vocabulary
- Grammar
- Fluency

**GO online** For prescriptions, see p. A3. Also available electronically on *StoryTown* Online Assessment and ExamView®.

 **Podcasting:** Assessing Fluency

# Leveled Readers

*Reinforcing Skills and Strategies*

## BELOW-LEVEL

## Carl Can Run

**SUMMARY** Carl falls down during a race, but he gets up, puts his cap back on, and continues running anyway.

- **phonics** *r*-Controlled /är/*ar*
- **High-Frequency Words:** *again, feel, house, know, loud, Mrs., put, say*

**Author's Purpose/Point of View**

**LEVELED READER TEACHER GUIDE**

▲ High-Frequency Words, p. 5

### Before Reading

**BUILD BACKGROUND/SET A PURPOSE** Have children tell about a race they knew they wouldn't win. Ask: **Did you give up, or keep going? How did you feel?** Then guide children to set a purpose for reading the story.

### Reading the Book

**PAGES 6–8 SEQUENCE What happens after the race begins?** (First, the children start running. Next, Carl falls and drops his hat. Then, Mrs. Archer gives Carl his hat and Carl finishes the race.)

**PAGE 8 AUTHOR'S PURPOSE/POINT OF VIEW Why do you think the author wrote this story?** (Possible response: To show that you shouldn't give up on something, even if you can't always win.)

**REREAD FOR FLUENCY** Have partners read alternate pages of the story several times with appropriate intonation and expression.

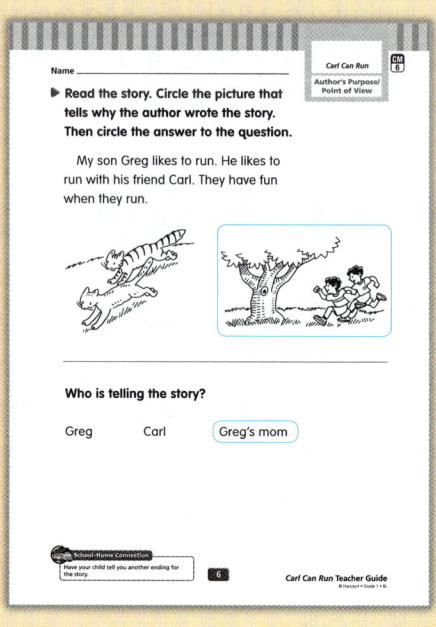

▲ Comprehension, p. 6

### Think Critically  *(See inside back cover for questions.)*

**1** **NOTE DETAILS** The children had a race at Greg's house.

**2** **CHARACTERS' EMOTIONS** Possible responses: sad, upset

**3** **CHARACTERS' TRAITS** Possible response: She picked up Carl's hat and helped Carl when he fell down.

**4** **AUTHOR'S PURPOSE/POINT OF VIEW** Carl is not telling the story because the author uses the words "said Carl," not "I said."

**5** **PERSONAL RESPONSE** Responses will vary.

## ON-LEVEL

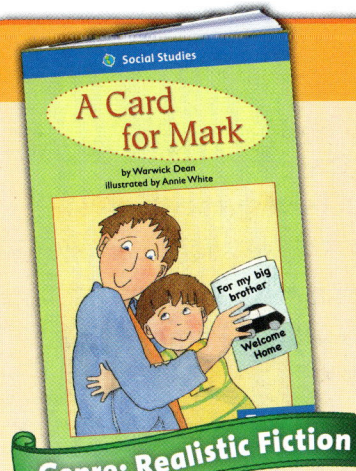

Genre: **Realistic Fiction**

# A Card for Mark

**SUMMARY** After realizing that he has made a mistake, Ross wants to make a new card for his brother Mark. Mark, however, is happy with the card just as it is.

- **phonics** *r*-Controlled /är/*ar*
- **High-Frequency Words:** *again, feel, house, know, loud, Mrs., put, say*

  **Author's Purpose/Point of View**

### Before Reading

**BUILD BACKGROUND/SET A PURPOSE** Have children share their card-making experiences. Ask: **Did you make a card for someone special? Who? Was it for a special occasion? How did you decorate the card? What did you write? Did the person like it?** Then guide children to preview the story and set a purpose for reading it.

### Reading the Book

**PAGE 2** **NOTE DETAILS** **What color is the car Ross draws?** (black)

**PAGE 8** **AUTHOR'S PURPOSE/POINT OF VIEW** **Why does Mark tell Ross not to change the card?** (Mark says he likes black cars.) **Why do you think the author told this story?** (Possible response: To show that you can appreciate a kind thought or action from someone.)

**REREAD FOR FLUENCY** Have children reread the story several times, using different voices for Ross, Dad, and Mark.

### Think Critically     *(See inside back cover for questions.)*

① **NOTE DETAILS** Ross made a card for Mark.

② **CHARACTERS' EMOTIONS** Possible responses: sad, bad, upset

③ **CHARACTERS' TRAITS** Mark was kind because he told Ross he liked black cars and gave Ross a hug.

④ **AUTHOR'S PURPOSE/POINT OF VIEW** No, because the author uses the words "Ross" and "said Ross."

⑤ **PERSONAL RESPONSE** Responses will vary.

**LEVELED READER TEACHER GUIDE**

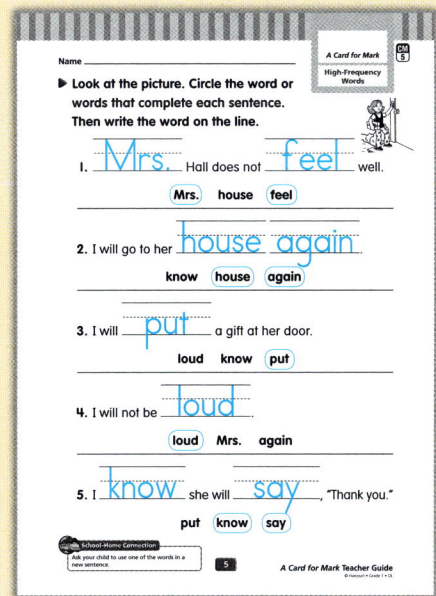

▲ **High-Frequency Words, p. 5**

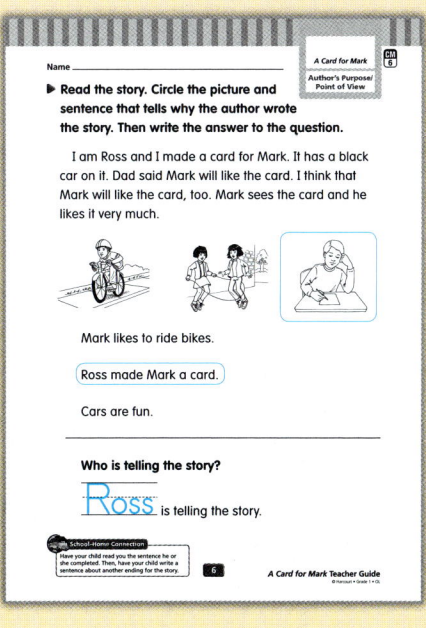

▲ **Comprehension, p. 6**

# Leveled Readers

*Reinforcing Skills and Strategies*

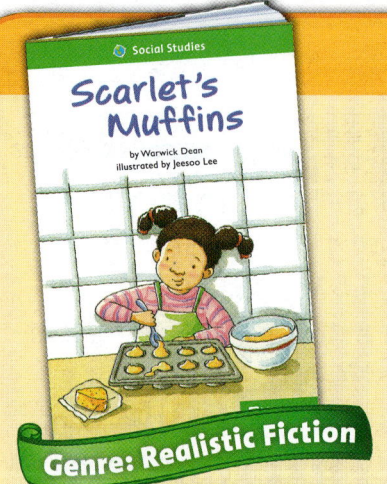

ADVANCED

## Scarlet's Muffins

**SUMMARY** Scarlet bakes cheese muffins and forgets the cheese, but the garlic she adds makes up for the missing ingredient.

**Genre: Realistic Fiction**

 **phonics** *r*-Controlled /är/*ar*

- **High-Frequency Words:** *again, feel, house, know, loud, Mrs., put, say*

 **Author's Purpose/Point of View**

### Before Reading

**BUILD BACKGROUND/SET A PURPOSE** Ask: **Have you ever forgotten an ingredient when baking or cooking? What were you making? What happened?** Then have children set a purpose for reading the story.

### Reading the Book

**PAGES 2–8 PLOT** **What does Scarlet make?** (muffins) **What ingredient does she forget?** (cheese) **What do Scarlet's guests think of these muffins without the cheese?** (They are good garlic muffins.)

**PAGES 2–8 AUTHOR'S PURPOSE/POINT OF VIEW** **Why do you think the author had Scarlet forget the cheese?** (Possible response: To show that sometimes mistakes can make something good.)

**REREAD FOR FLUENCY** Have children use different voices for the characters as they reread the story several times with appropriate intonation.

### Think Critically

*(See inside back cover for questions.)*

1. **NOTE DETAILS** Scarlet forgot to put cheese in the muffins.

2. **CHARACTERS' EMOTIONS** Possible responses: worried, upset

3. **BEGINNING, MIDDLE, ENDING** Mr. Larkin said he was going to come to lunch again. Scarlet felt happy.

4. **AUTHOR'S PURPOSE/POINT OF VIEW** Scarlet is not telling the story, because the author uses the words "she" and "Scarlet."

5. **PERSONAL RESPONSE** Responses will vary.

**LEVELED READER TEACHER GUIDE**

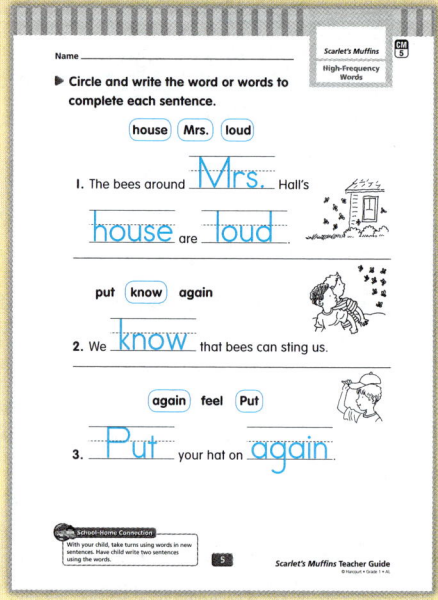

▲ High-Frequency Words, p. 5

▲ Comprehension, p. 6

**Go online**

★ **Leveled Readers, online**
*Searchable by genre, skill, vocabulary, level, or title*
★ **Student Activities and Teacher Resources, online**

**Genre: Realistic Fiction**

# The Play

**SUMMARY** A group of children work hard to put on a play, and when the curtain goes up, they are ready!

- **Strong Picture Support**
- **Concept Vocabulary**
- **Scaffolded Language Development**

## Before Reading

**BUILD BACKGROUND/SET A PURPOSE** Ask children to recall a time when they were in a play. Have them tell about the things they had to do to get ready for "opening night"—such as learning their parts, gathering props, and making costumes and scenery. Have them tell about the performance. Then guide children to preview the story and set a purpose for reading it.

## Reading the Book

**PAGES 2–7 NOTE DETAILS, GRAPHIC AIDS, SEQUENCE What play are the children putting on?** (Little Red Riding Hood) **Tell everything they do before the curtain goes up.** (They learn their lines, they put on costumes, and they go on the stage.)

**PAGES 2–8 AUTHOR'S PURPOSE/POINT OF VIEW What do you think the author wants readers to know?** (Possible response: If you want a play to be good, everyone has to work together.)

**REREAD FOR FLUENCY** Model reading each page with expression and intonation as children follow along and then echo-read.

## Scaffolded Language Development

*(See inside back cover for teacher-led activity.)*

Provide additional examples and explanation as needed.

**LEVELED READER TEACHER GUIDE**

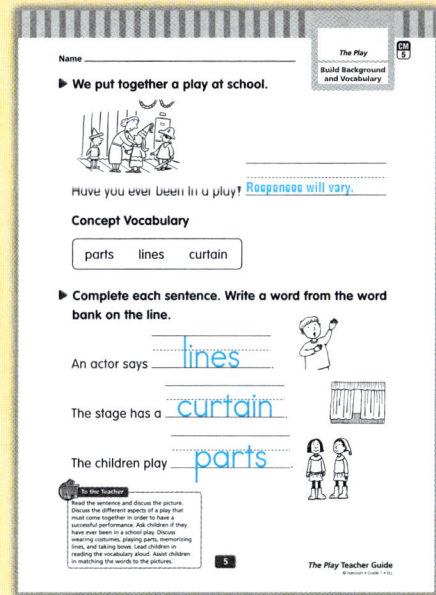

▲ Build Background, p. 5

▲ Scaffolded Language Development, p. 6

# Lesson 15

### Phonemic Awareness
Phoneme Segmentation and Deletion

### ✓ Phonics
Digraphs /kw/*qu*, /hw/*wh*
Inflections *-ed*, *-ing*

### ✓ Spelling
*quit, quick, quiz, whiz, which, when, arm, part, house, put*

### ✓ High-Frequency Words
*about*, *books*, *family*, *name*, *people*, *read*, *work*, *writing*

### Reading
**"Tomás Rivera"** by Jane Medina
BIOGRAPHY

**"I Can"** POETRY

### ✓ Fluency
Reading Rate

### ✓ Comprehension
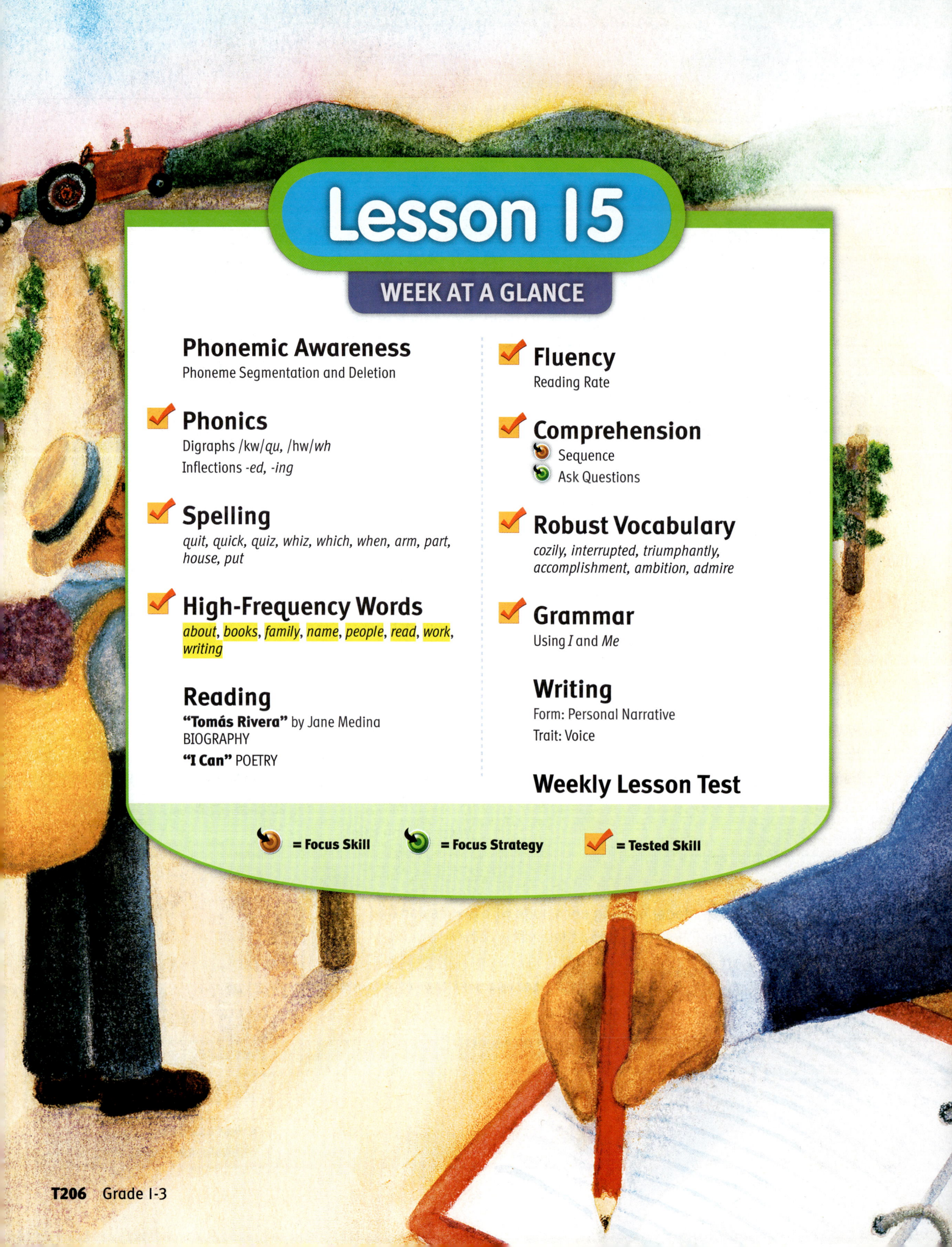 Sequence
Ask Questions

### ✓ Robust Vocabulary
*cozily, interrupted, triumphantly, accomplishment, ambition, admire*

### ✓ Grammar
Using *I* and *Me*

### Writing
Form: Personal Narrative
Trait: Voice

### Weekly Lesson Test

= Focus Skill  = Focus Strategy  ✓ = Tested Skill

**One stop** *for all your* Digital *needs*

# Digital
## CLASSROOM

 www.harcourtschool.com/storytown
*To go along with your print program*

---

### FOR THE TEACHER

**Prepare**  Professional Development
in the Online TE

 *Videos for Podcasting*

**Plan & Organize**  Online TE & Planning Resources*

**Teach**  Transparencies
for electronic projection

**Assess**  Online Assessment*
with Student Tracking System and Prescriptions

---

### FOR THE STUDENT

**Read**  Student eBook*

 Strategic Intervention Interactive Reader

 Leveled Readers

**Practice & Apply**  Splash into Phonics CD-ROM

 *Also available on CD-ROM*

# Literature Resources

## STUDENT EDITION

 **Go online** eBook STUDENT EDITION

 **Get Started Story**

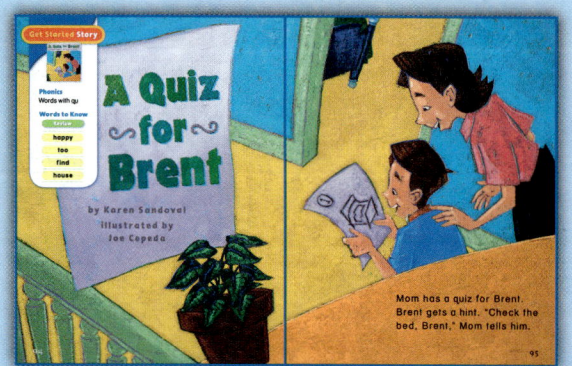

**A Quiz for Brent, pp. 94–101**

## Genre: Biography

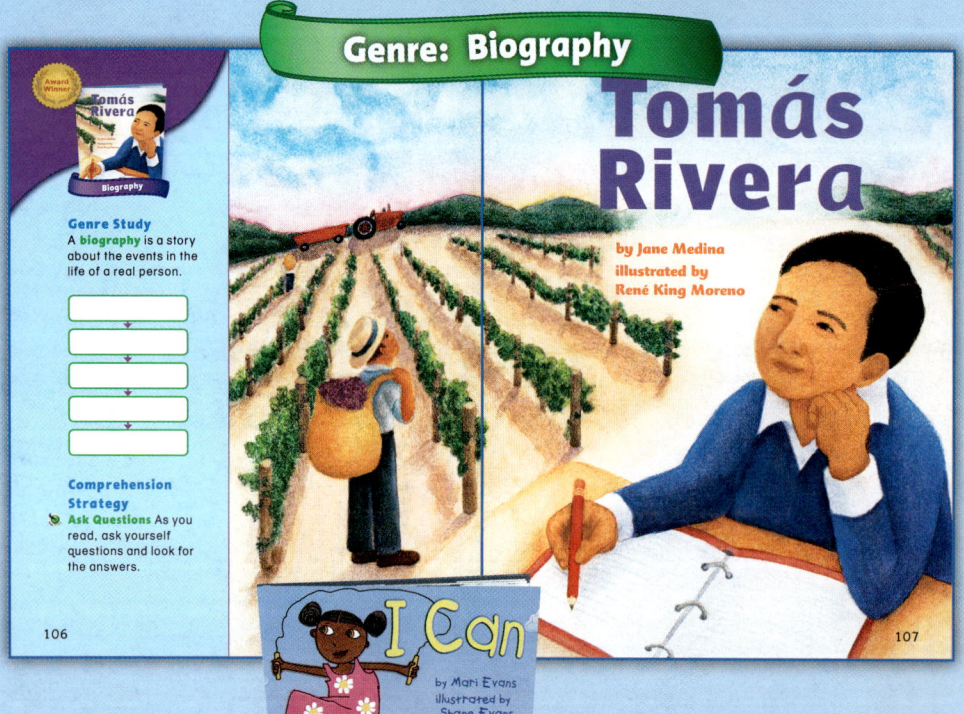

 **SOCIAL STUDIES** **Tomás Rivera, pp. 106–123**

*by Jane Medina, illustrated by René King Moreno* Tomás Rivera works hard with his family. When his grandfather introduces him to books, it changes his life.

**Accelerated Reader**

*Practice Quizzes for the Selection*

 **Audiotext** *Student Edition selections are available on Audiotext Grade 1, CD 3 and 6.*

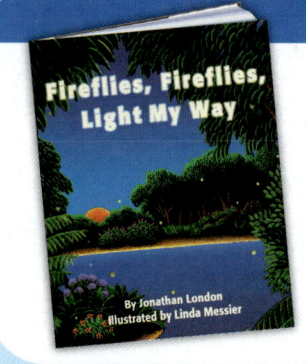

◄ **Reading Across Texts**
**Comparing a Biography and Poetry**

## Genre: Poetry

**Paired Selections**

## ADDITIONAL READING

**Big Book**
*Fireflies, Fireflies, Light My Way*

**Decodable Book**
"Quint and the Squids"
★ Applies Digraph /kw/ *qu*
"Which Animal Is It?",
"Whack! Wham!"
★ Applies Digraph /hw/ *wh*

# Support for Differentiated Instruction

 **LEVELED READERS**

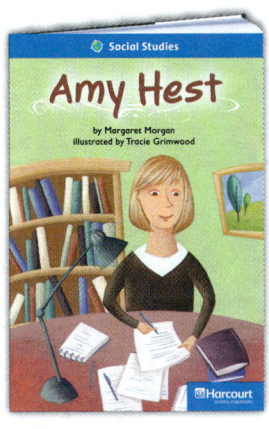

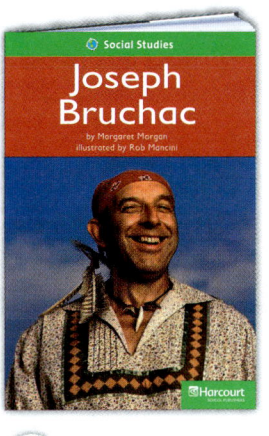

 **BELOW-LEVEL**      **ON-LEVEL**     ● **ADVANCED**

**E L L**

## LEVELED PRACTICE

◄ **Strategic Intervention Resource Kit, Lesson 15**

◄ **Strategic Intervention Interactive Reader, Lesson 15**
Strategic Intervention Interactive Reader Online

◄ **ELL Extra Support Kit, Lesson 15**

◄ **Challenge Resource Kit, Lesson 15**

● **BELOW-LEVEL**
Extra Support Copying Masters, pp. 16–21

● **ON-LEVEL**
Practice Book, pp. 16–22

● **ADVANCED**
Challenge Copying Masters, pp. 16–21

## ADDITIONAL RESOURCES

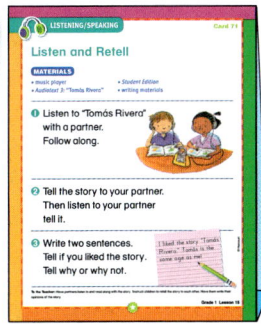

- Spelling Practice Book, pp. 49–51
- Grammar Practice Book, pp. 57–60
- Reading Transparencies R29–R30
- Language Arts Transparencies LA29–LA30
- Test Prep System
◄ **Literacy Center Kit, Cards 71–75**
◄ **Sound/Spelling Card**
- Fluency Builders
◄ **Photo Cards**
- Read-Aloud Anthology, p. 58

## ASSESSMENT

✔ **Weekly Lesson Tests**
- Comprehension
- Phonics and Spelling
- Focus Skill
- Robust Vocabulary
- High-Frequency Words
- Grammar
- Fluency

 **www.harcourtschool.com/storytown**
- Online Assessment
*Also available on CD-ROM—ExamView®*

# Suggested Lesson Planner

## Day 1

## Day 2

**Step 1** **Whole Group**

### Daily Language
- Oral Language
- High-Frequency Words
- Shared Reading
- Phonemic Awareness

**QUESTION OF THE DAY,** p. T218
*Imagine walking through the woods. What animals do you see? What are they doing?*

**READ ALOUD,** p. T218
*Big Book: Fireflies, Fireflies, Light My Way*

**WORD WALL,** p. T219

✓ **PHONEMIC AWARENESS,** p. T219
Phoneme Segmentation

▲ Big Book

**QUESTION OF THE DAY,** p. T234
*What kinds of books do you like to read?*

**SHARED READING,** p. T234
*Big Book of Rhymes and Poems,* "Books to the Ceiling"

**WORD WALL,** p. T235

✓ **PHONEMIC AWARENESS,** p. T235
Phoneme Segmentation

### Word Work
-  phonics
- Spelling
- High-Frequency Words

✓ 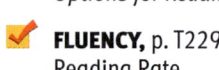 **phonics**, p. T220
Introduce: Digraphs /kw/*qu*, /hw/*wh*

✓ **SPELLING,** p. T223
Pretest: *quit, quick, quiz, whiz, which, when, arm, part, house, put*

✓ **HIGH-FREQUENCY WORDS,** p. T225
Review: *find, too, happy, house*

✓  **phonics**, p. T236
Review: Digraphs /kw/*qu*, /hw/*wh*

✓ **SPELLING,** p. T236
Word Building

✓ **HIGH-FREQUENCY WORDS**
Words to Know, p. T240
Introduce: *about, books, family, name, people, read, work, writing*

### Skills and Strategies
- Reading
- Fluency
- Comprehension
- Build Robust Vocabulary

**READING,** p. T224
Get Started Story, "A Quiz for Brent"
Decodable Text
*Options for Reading*

▲ Student Edition

✓ **FLUENCY,** p. T229
Reading Rate

✓ **COMPREHENSION,** p. T230
Read-Aloud: "The Best Apple Crisp in the World"
Preview: Sequence

✓ **BUILD ROBUST VOCABULARY,** p. T231
Introduce: *cozily, interrupted, triumphantly*

**READING,** p. T242
"Tomás Rivera"
*Options for Reading*

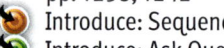
▲ Student Edition

✓ **COMPREHENSION,** pp. T238, T242
Introduce: Sequence
Introduce: Ask Questions

✓ **RETELLING/FLUENCY,** p. T252
Reading Rate

✓ **BUILD ROBUST VOCABULARY,** p. T253
Review: *cozily, interrupted, triumphantly*

**Step 2** **Small Groups**

### Suggestions for Differentiated Instruction *(See pp. T212–T213.)*

**Step 3** **Whole Group**

### Language Arts
- Grammar
- Writing

✓ **GRAMMAR,** p. T232
Introduce: Using *I* and *Me*

**Daily Proofreading**
i like to eat apples (I, apples.)

 **MODELED WRITING,** p. T233
Introduce: Personal Narrative
Writing Trait: Voice

**Writing Prompt** *Write and draw about an important event in the life of a family member.*

✓ **GRAMMAR,** p. T254
Review: Using *I* and *Me*

**Daily Proofreading**
That quilt is for Me (me.)

 **SHARED WRITING,** p. T255
Review: Personal Narrative
Writing Trait: Voice

**Writing Prompt** *Draw and write about something you did today.*

 = Focus Skill    = Focus Strategy    = Tested Skill

### Skills at a Glance

 **phonics**
- Digraphs /kw/*qu*, /hw/*wh*
- Inflections –*ed*, –*ing*

**Comprehension**
 FOCUS SKILL  Sequence

FOCUS STRATEGY
Ask Questions

**Phonemic Awareness**
Phoneme Segmentation and Deletion

**Fluency**
Reading Rate

**Vocabulary**
HIGH-FREQUENCY: *about, books, family, name, people, read, work, writing*

ROBUST: *cozily, interrupted, triumphantly, accomplishment, ambition, admire*

## Day 3

**QUESTION OF THE DAY,** p. T256
*Do you like to read books? Why?*

**SHARED READING,** p. T256
*Big Book of Rhymes and Poems,* "Books to the Ceiling"

**WORD WALL,** p. T257

**PHONEMIC AWARENESS,** p. T257
Phoneme Deletion

**phonics**, p. T258
Review: Digraphs /kw/*qu*, /hw/*wh*, /th/*th*

**SPELLING,** p. T259
State the Generalization

**HIGH-FREQUENCY WORDS,** p. T260
Review: *about, books, family, name, people, read, work, writing*

**FLUENCY,** p. T261
Reading Rate:
"Tomás Rivera"

**COMPREHENSION,** p. T262
Review: Sequence
Paired Selection:
"I Can"

▲ Student Edition

**CONNECTIONS,** p. T264

**BUILD ROBUST VOCABULARY,** p. T265
Introduce: *accomplishment, ambition, admire*

## Day 4

**QUESTION OF THE DAY,** p. T268
*Where do you like to go to think? What is the place like?*

**SHARED READING,** p. T268
*Big Book of Rhymes and Poems,* "And There"

**WORD WALL,** p. T269

**PHONEMIC AWARENESS,** p. T269
Phoneme Deletion

**phonics**, p. T270
Introduce: Inflections –*ed*, –*ing*

**SPELLING,** p. T271
Review Spelling Words

**HIGH-FREQUENCY WORDS,** p. T272
Review: *about, books, family, name, people, read, work, writing*

**FLUENCY,** p. T273
Reading Rate:
"Tomás Rivera"

**COMPREHENSION,** p. T274
Review: Sequence
*Big Book: Fireflies, Fireflies, Light My Way*

▲ Student Edition

**BUILD ROBUST VOCABULARY,** p. T275
Review: *accomplishment, ambition, admire*

## Day 5

**QUESTION OF THE DAY,** p. T278
*If you could create your own secret place, what would it look like?*

**SHARED READING,** p. T278
*Big Book of Rhymes and Poems,* "And There"

**WORD WALL,** p. T279

**PHONEMIC AWARENESS,** p. T279
Phoneme Segmentation and Deletion

**phonics**, p. T280
Review: Inflections –*ed*, –*ing*

**SPELLING,** p. T281
Posttest

**HIGH-FREQUENCY WORDS,** p. T282
Review: *about, books, family, name, people, read, work, writing*

**FLUENCY,** p. T283
Reading Rate:
"Tomás Rivera"

**COMPREHENSION,** p. T284
Review: Sequence

▲ Student Edition

**BUILD ROBUST VOCABULARY,** p. T285
Review

---

 **BELOW-LEVEL**    ON-LEVEL    ADVANCED    E L L

---

**GRAMMAR,** p. T266
Review: Using *I* and *Me*

***Daily Proofreading***
me went to the parc. (I, park)

**SHARED WRITING,** p. T267
Review: Personal Narrative
Writing Trait: Voice

**Writing Prompt**  *Write about what you would like to do or be when you grow up.*

**GRAMMAR,** p. T276
Review: Using *I* and *Me*

***Daily Proofreading***
Jim and me are runing to school. (I, running)

**INDEPENDENT WRITING,** p. T277
Review: Personal Narrative
Writing Trait: Voice

**Writing Prompt**  *Tell a few things you have done today in the order that you did them.*

**GRAMMAR,** p. T286
Review: Using *I* and *Me*

***Daily Proofreading***
dad plays basketball with I. (Dad, me)

**INDEPENDENT WRITING,** p. T287
Review: Personal Narrative
Writing Trait: Voice

**Writing Prompt**  *Draw and write about something you hope to learn this year.*

# Suggested Small Group Planner

45–60+ Minutes

| | Day 1 | Day 2 |
|---|---|---|
| **BELOW-LEVEL**<br>15+ Min. each | **Teacher-Directed**<br>*Student Edition:*<br>Get Started Story,<br>"A Quiz for Brent,"<br>p. T224<br><br>**Independent**<br>⭐ Listening/Speaking Center, p. T216<br>Extra Support Copying Masters, p. 16<br><br> ▲ Student Edition | **Teacher-Directed**<br>*Student Edition:*<br>"Tomás Rivera," p. T242<br><br>**Independent**<br>⭐ Reading Center, p. T216<br>Extra Support Copying Masters, p. 18<br><br>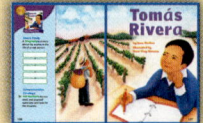 ▲ Student Edition |
| **ON-LEVEL**<br>15+ Min. each | **Teacher-Directed**<br>*Student Edition:*<br>Get Started Story,<br>"A Quiz for Brent," p. T224<br><br>**Independent**<br>⭐ Reading Center, p. T216<br>Practice Book, p. 16<br><br> ▲ Student Edition | **Teacher-Directed**<br>*Student Edition:*<br>"Tomás Rivera," p. T242<br><br>**Independent**<br>⭐ Letters and Sounds Center, p. T217<br>Practice Book, p. 18<br><br>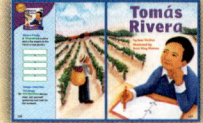 ▲ Student Edition |
| **ADVANCED**<br>15+ Min. each | **Teacher-Directed**<br>Leveled Reader:<br>"Joseph Bruchac," p. T290<br>Before Reading<br><br>**Independent**<br>⭐ Letters and Sounds Center, p. T217<br>Challenge Copying Masters, p. 16<br><br>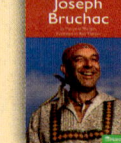 ▲ Leveled Reader | **Teacher-Directed**<br>Leveled Reader:<br>"Joseph Bruchac," p. T290<br>Read the Book<br><br>**Independent**<br>⭐ Word Work Center, p. T217<br>Challenge Copying Masters, p. 18<br><br> ▲ Leveled Reader |
| **E L L**<br>**English-Language Learners**<br><br>*In addition to the small-group suggestions above, use the ELL Extra Support Kit to promote language development.*<br><br> | **LANGUAGE DEVELOPMENT SUPPORT**<br>**Teacher-Directed**<br>ELL TG, Day 1<br>**Independent**<br>ELL Copying Masters, Lesson 15 | **LANGUAGE DEVELOPMENT SUPPORT**<br>**Teacher-Directed**<br>ELL TG, Day 2<br>**Independent**<br>ELL Copying Masters, Lesson 15 |
| **Intervention**<br><br> <br>▲ Strategic Intervention Resource Kit  ▲ Strategic Intervention Interactive Reader | Strategic Intervention TG, Day 1<br>Strategic Intervention Practice Book, Lesson 15 | Strategic Intervention TG, Day 2<br>Strategic Intervention Interactive Reader, Lesson 15<br><br> ▲ Strategic Intervention Interactive Reader |

 **= Literacy Center Cards**

| **Phonemic Awareness/ Phonics** | **High-Frequency Words** | **Fluency** | **Comprehension** | **Robust Vocabulary** | **Language Arts Checkpoint** |
|---|---|---|---|---|---|
| Digraphs /kw/*qu*, /hw/*wh* p. S22 | *about*, *books*, *family*, *name*, *people*, *read*, *work*, *writing* p. S23 | Reading Rate pp. S24–S25 | Focus Skill Sequence pp. S26–S27 | *cozily*, *interrupted*, *triumphantly*, *accomplishment*, *ambition*, *admire* pp. S28–S29 | **Grammar:** Using *I* and *Me* **Writing:** Personal Narrative pp. S30–S31 |

# Day 3

**Teacher-Directed**
Leveled Reader: "Susan L. Roth," p. T288
Before Reading; Read the Book

**Independent**
Word Work Center, p. T217
Extra Support Copying Masters, p. 19

▲ Leveled Reader

**Teacher-Directed**
Leveled Reader: "Amy Hest," p. T289
Before Reading; Read the Book

**Independent**
Writing Center, p. T217
Practice Book, p. 19

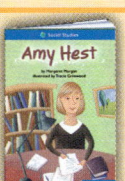
▲ Leveled Reader

**Teacher-Directed**
Leveled Reader: "Joseph Bruchac," p. T290
Think Critically

**Independent**
Listening/Speaking Center, p. T216
Challenge Copying Masters, p. 19

▲ Leveled Reader

**LANGUAGE DEVELOPMENT SUPPORT**
**Teacher-Directed**
Leveled Reader: "Grandparents," p. T291
Before Reading; Read the Book
ELL TG, Day 3

**Independent**
ELL Copying Masters, Lesson 15

▲ Leveled Reader

Strategic Intervention TG, Day 3
Strategic Intervention Interactive Reader, Lesson 15
Strategic Intervention Practice Book, Lesson 15

▲ Strategic Intervention Interactive Reader

# Day 4

**Teacher-Directed**
Leveled Reader: "Susan L. Roth," p. T288
Reread for Fluency

**Independent**
Letters and Sounds Center, p. T217
Cut-Out/Fold-Up Book, Practice Book, pp. 49–50

▲ Leveled Reader

**Teacher-Directed**
Leveled Reader: "Amy Hest," p. T289
Reread for Fluency

**Independent**
Word Work Center, p. T217
Cut-Out/Fold-Up Book: Practice Book, pp. 49–50

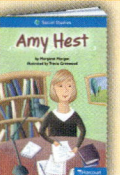
▲ Leveled Reader

**Teacher-Directed**
Leveled Reader: "Joseph Bruchac," p. T290
Reread for Fluency
Self-Selected Reading: Classroom Library Collection

**Independent**
Writing Center, p. T217
Cut-Out/Fold-Up Book: Practice Book, pp. 49–50

▲ Leveled Reader

**LANGUAGE DEVELOPMENT SUPPORT**
**Teacher-Directed**
Leveled Reader: "Grandparents," p. T291
Reread for Fluency
ELL TG, Day 4

**Independent**
ELL Copying Masters, Lesson 15

▲ Leveled Reader

Strategic Intervention TG, Day 4
Strategic Intervention Interactive Reader, Lesson 15

▲ Strategic Intervention Interactive Reader

# Day 5

**Teacher-Directed**
Leveled Reader: "Susan L. Roth," p. T288
Think Critically

**Independent**
Writing Center, p. T217
Leveled Reader: Reread for Fluency
Extra Support Copying Masters, p. 21

▲ Leveled Reader

**Teacher-Directed**
Leveled Reader: "Amy Hest," p. T289
Think Critically

**Independent**
Listening/Speaking Center, p. T216
Leveled Reader: Reread for Fluency
Practice Book, p. 21

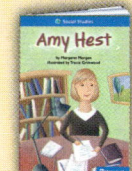
▲ Leveled Reader

**Teacher-Directed**
Leveled Reader: "Joseph Bruchac," p. T290
Reread for Fluency
Self-Selected Reading: Classroom Library Collection

**Independent**
Reading Center, p. T216
Leveled Reader: Reread for Fluency
Challenge Copying Masters, p. 21

▲ Leveled Reader

**LANGUAGE DEVELOPMENT SUPPORT**
**Teacher-Directed**
Leveled Reader: "Grandparents," p. T291
Think Critically
ELL TG, Day 5

**Independent**
Leveled Reader: Reread for Fluency
ELL Copying Masters, Lesson 15

▲ Leveled Reader

Strategic Intervention TG, Day 5
Strategic Intervention Interactive Reader, Lesson 15

▲ Strategic Intervention Interactive Reader

# Leveled Readers & Leveled Practice
## Reinforcing Skills and Strategies

## LEVELED READERS SYSTEM

- **Leveled Readers**
- **Leveled Readers CD**
- **Leveled Reader Teacher Guides**
  - *Comprehension*
  - *High-Frequency Words*
  - *Oral Reading Fluency Assessment*
- **Response Activities**
- **Leveled Readers Assessment**

See pages T288–T291 for lesson plans.

### BELOW-LEVEL

- **phonics** Digraphs /kw/*qu*, /hw/*wh*
- **High-Frequency Words:** *about*, *books*, *family*, *name*, *people*, *read*, *work*, *writing*
- Sequence

**LEVELED READER TEACHER GUIDE**

▲ High-Frequency Words, p. 5

▲ Comprehension, p. 6

### ON-LEVEL

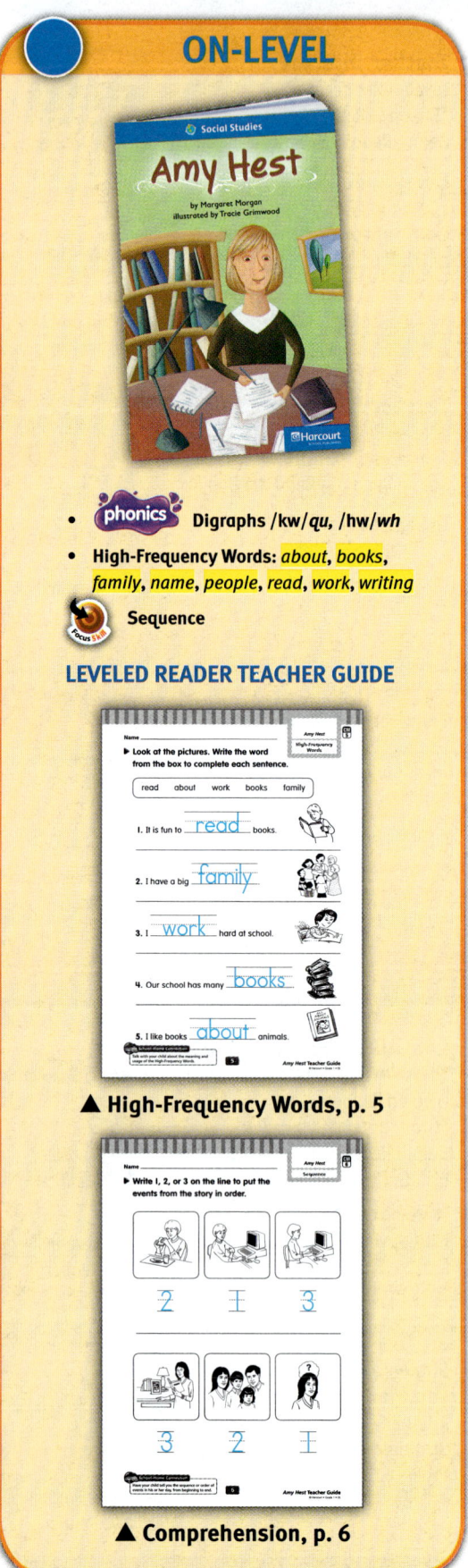

- **phonics** Digraphs /kw/*qu*, /hw/*wh*
- **High-Frequency Words:** *about*, *books*, *family*, *name*, *people*, *read*, *work*, *writing*
- Sequence

**LEVELED READER TEACHER GUIDE**

▲ High-Frequency Words, p. 5

▲ Comprehension, p. 6

**www.harcourtschool.com/storytown**

**Go online**

★ Leveled Readers, online
*Searchable by Genre, Skill, Vocabulary, Level, or Title*
★ Student Activities and Teacher Resources, online

## ADVANCED

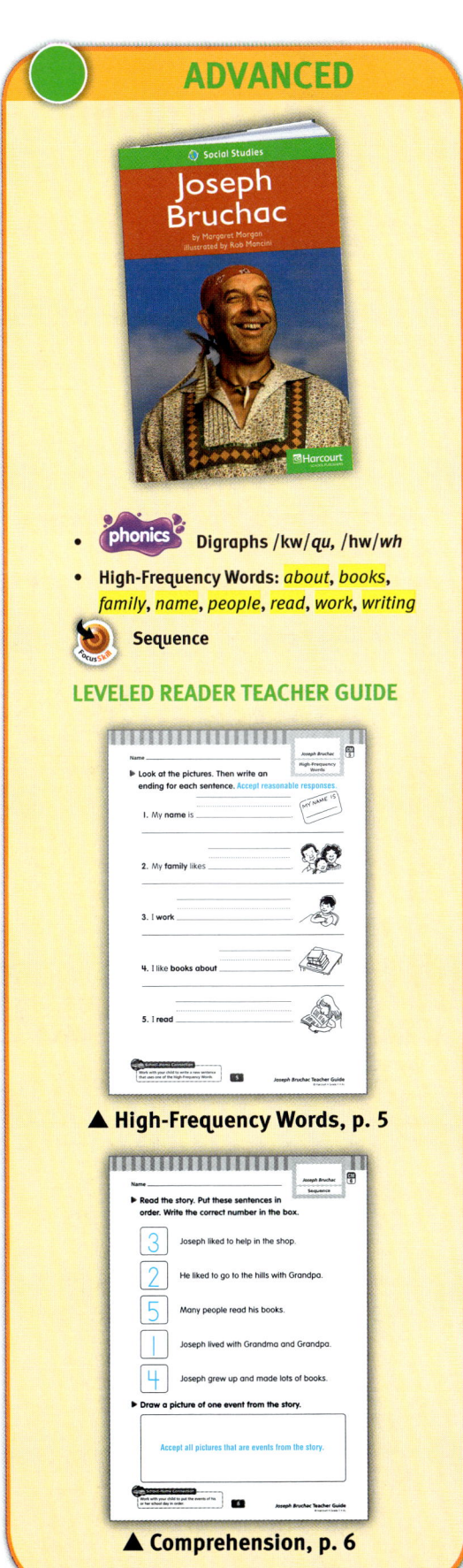

- **phonics** Digraphs /kw/*qu*, /hw/*wh*
- **High-Frequency Words:** *about*, *books*, *family*, *name*, *people*, *read*, *work*, *writing*
- **Focus Skill** Sequence

### LEVELED READER TEACHER GUIDE

▲ High-Frequency Words, p. 5

▲ Comprehension, p. 6

## E L L

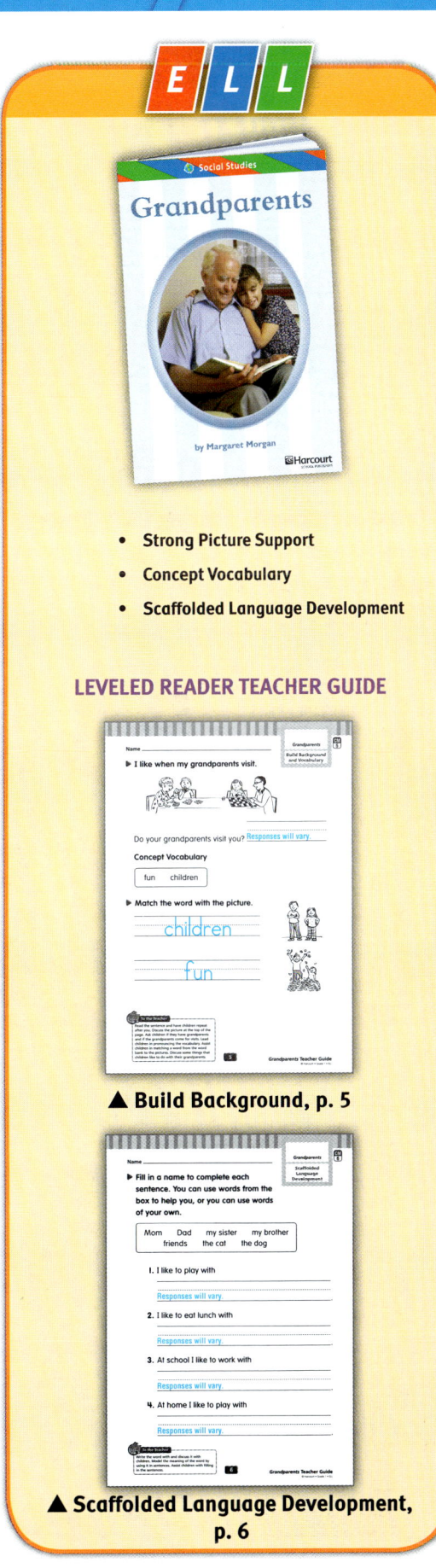

- **Strong Picture Support**
- **Concept Vocabulary**
- **Scaffolded Language Development**

### LEVELED READER TEACHER GUIDE

▲ Build Background, p. 5

▲ Scaffolded Language Development, p. 6

## CLASSROOM LIBRARY

## for Self-Selected Reading

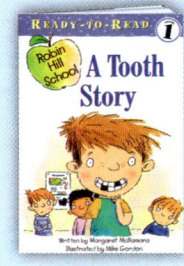

**AVERAGE**

▲ *A Tooth Story* by Margaret McNamara.
**REALISTIC FICTION**

**AVERAGE**

▲ *Hello, House!* by Linda Hayward.
**FOLKTALE**

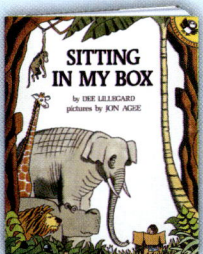

**AVERAGE**

▲ *Sitting in My Box* by Dee Lillegard.
**FANTASY**

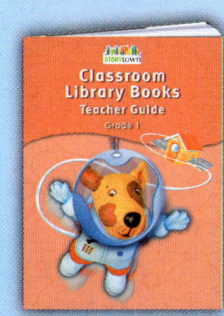

▲ Classroom Library Books Teacher Guide, pp. 36–39, 40–47

# Literacy Centers

*15 Min. each*

## Management Support

While you provide direct instruction to individuals or small groups, other children can work on literacy center activities.

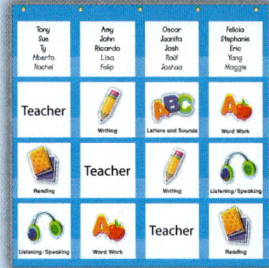

▲ Literacy Centers Pocket Chart

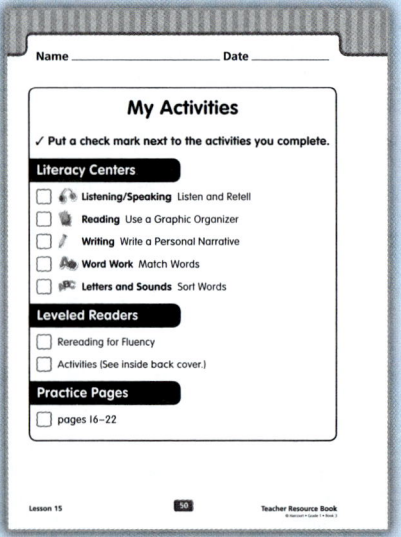

▲ Teacher Resource Book, p. 50

## Homework for the Week

**TEACHER RESOURCE BOOK, PAGE 19**

The *Homework Copying Master* provides activities to complete for each day of the week.

**Go online**
www.harcourtschool.com/
storytown

---

### LISTENING/SPEAKING
## Listen and Retell

**Objective** To listen to, read, and retell a story

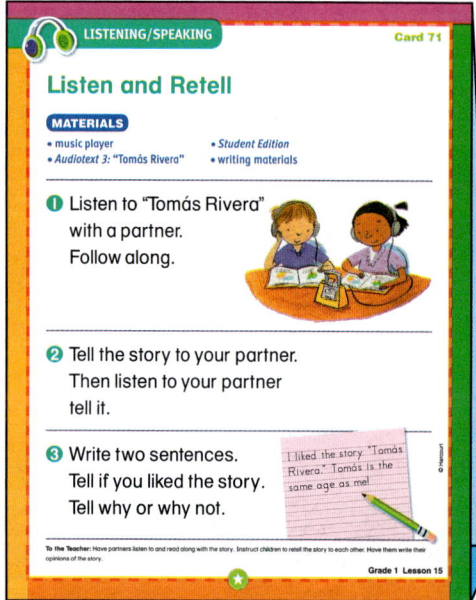

**Listen and Retell** — Card 71

**MATERIALS**
- music player
- Audiotext 3: "Tomás Rivera"
- Student Edition
- writing materials

1. Listen to "Tomás Rivera" with a partner. Follow along.

2. Tell the story to your partner. Then listen to your partner tell it.

3. Write two sentences. Tell if you liked the story. Tell why or why not.

*I liked the story "Tomás Rivera." Tomás is the same age as me!*

To the Teacher: Have partners listen to and read along with the story. Instruct children to retell the story to each other. Have them write their opinions of the story.

Grade 1 Lesson 15

⭐ **Literacy Center Kit • Card 71**

---

### READING
## Use a Graphic Organizer

**Objective** To reread a familiar story and use a graphic organizer to record sequence

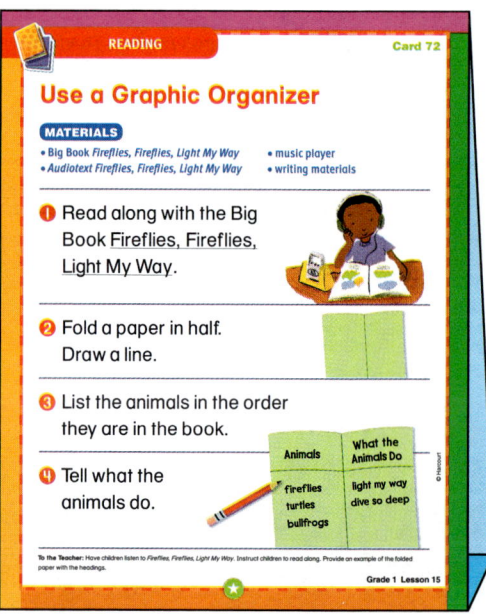

**Use a Graphic Organizer** — Card 72

**MATERIALS**
- Big Book *Fireflies, Fireflies, Light My Way*
- Audiotext *Fireflies, Fireflies, Light My Way*
- music player
- writing materials

1. Read along with the Big Book *Fireflies, Fireflies, Light My Way.*

2. Fold a paper in half. Draw a line.

3. List the animals in the order they are in the book.

4. Tell what the animals do.

| Animals | What the Animals Do |
|---|---|
| fireflies turtles bullfrogs | light my way dive so deep |

To the Teacher: Have children listen to *Fireflies, Fireflies, Light My Way.* Instruct children to read along. Provide an example of the folded paper with the headings.

Grade 1 Lesson 15

⭐ **Literacy Center Kit • Card 72**

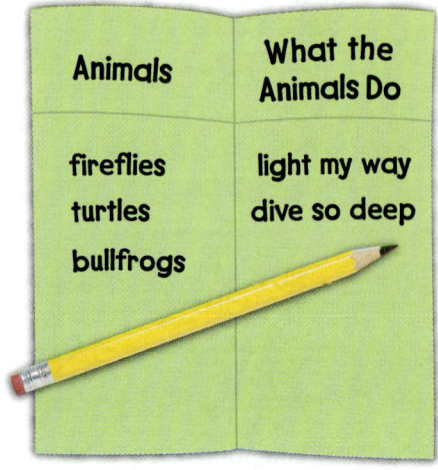

| Animals | What the Animals Do |
|---|---|
| fireflies turtles bullfrogs | light my way dive so deep |

---

 **WRITING**

# Write a Personal Narrative

*Objective* To use a web to aid in planning a personal narrative

 **WORD WORK**

# Match Words

*Objective* To read and write high-frequency words

**ABC** **LETTERS AND SOUNDS**

# Sort Words

*Objective* To identify, sort, and write words spelled with qu and wh

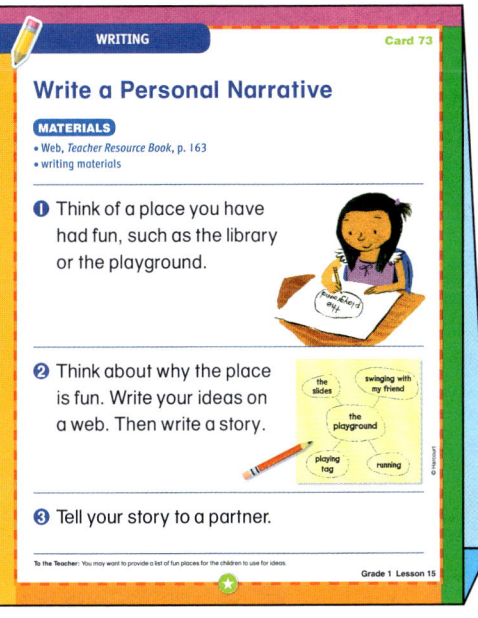

**Literacy Center Kit • Card 73**

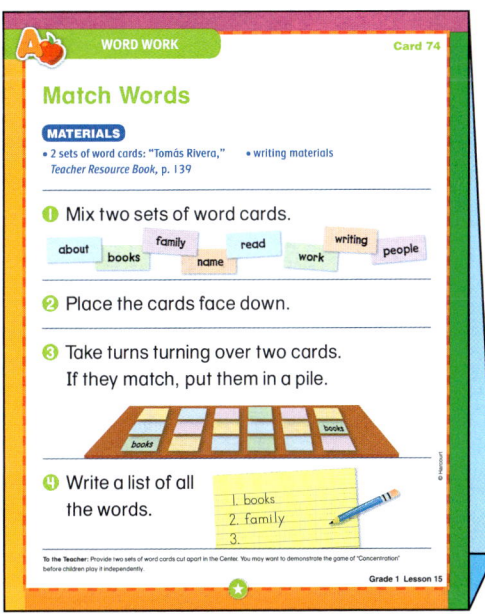

**Literacy Center Kit • Card 74**

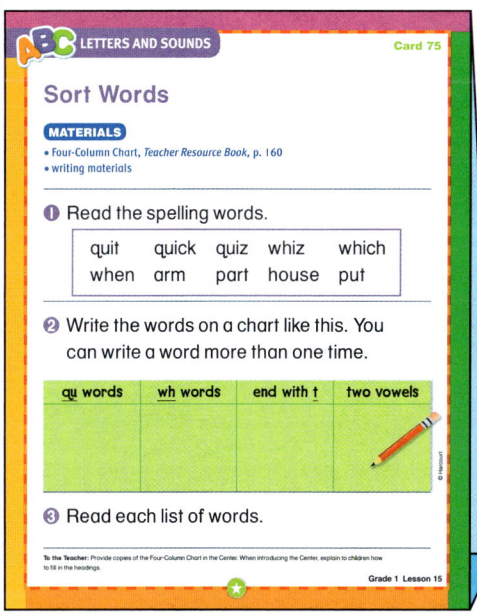

**Literacy Center Kit • Card 75**

family

family

Day at a Glance

## Day at a Glance

### Day 1

### Phonemic Awareness
- Phoneme Segmentation

 **and Spelling**
- Introduce: Digraphs /kw/*qu*, /hw/*wh*
- Pretest

### Reading
- *Get Started Story:* "A Quiz for Brent," *Student Edition,* pp.94–101

**Read!**

### Fluency
- Reading Rate

### Comprehension
- *Read-Aloud Anthology:* "The Best Apple Crisp in the World" Review: Sequence

### Robust Vocabulary
- Introduce: *cozily, interrupted, triumphantly*

### Grammar
- Introduce: Using *I* and *Me*

### Modeled Writing
- Personal Narrative

---

# Warm-Up Routines

## Oral Language

**Objective** *To listen attentively and respond appropriately to oral communication*

### Question of the Day

Imagine walking through the woods.

What animals do you see?

What are they doing?

Lead children in brainstorming a list of woodland animals and their actions. Then help children complete these sentence frames.

**I see _____ and _____. They are _____.**

## Read Aloud

**Objectives** *To set a purpose for listening; to listen to a selection read aloud*

**BIG BOOK** Read the information on the cover. Ask children to describe the roles of the author and the illustrator. Then discuss what they remember about the book, and help them set a purpose for listening to the book again. Tell children to look at the illustrations as you read and to listen for action words that tell how the animals move. Encourage children to join in on the repeated phrases. Then invite volunteers to act out words such as *leap,* *paddle,* and *scuttle.*

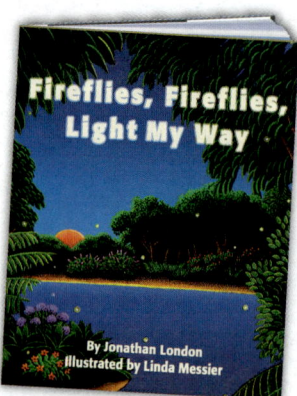

▲ Big Book
*Fireflies, Fireflies, Light My Way*

## Word Wall

**Objective** *To read high-frequency words*

**REVIEW HIGH-FREQUENCY WORDS** Review *happy, too, house, find, put, what, where, he, see, my,* and other previously learned high-frequency words. Say a word, ask a volunteer to point to it, and have children read it aloud. Repeat several times to reinforce recognition.

**happy**    **too**    **house**    **find**

## Phonemic Awareness

**Objective** *To segment words into phonemes*

**PHONEME SEGMENTATION** Tell children that you are going to say a word and that they will then say each sound they hear in the word. Model by saying: *swim.* **I hear four sounds in** *swim*—/s/ /w/ /i/ /m/**.** Have children segment the following words into phonemes:

**best** (/b/ /e/ /s/ /t/)    **cheese** (/ch/ /ē/ /z/)    **nest** (/n/ /e/ /s/ /t/)

**shack** (/sh/ /a/ /k/)    **and** (/a/ /n/ /d/)    **play** (/p/ /l/ /ā/)

**when** (/hw/ /e/ /n/)    **whip** (/hw/ /i/ /p/)    **run** (/r/ /u/ /n/)

**sniff** (/s/ /n/ /i/ /f/)    **fish** (/f/ /i/ /sh/)    **frog** (/f/ /r/ /o/ /g/)

### frog
### (/f/ /r/ /o/ /g/)

 Podcasting: Phoneme Segmentation

# Digraphs /kw/ *qu,* /hw/ *wh*

 **phonics** *and Spelling*

## Objectives

- *To recognize and generate the sounds for the digraphs* qu *and* wh
- *To build and blend words with /kw/qu and /hw/wh and other known letter-sounds*
- *To use /kw/qu, /hw/wh, and other known letter-sounds to spell words*
- *To spell known high-frequency words*

## Skill Trace

**Tested** **Digraphs /kw/** *qu,* **/hw/** *wh*

| | |
|---|---|
| Introduce | T220–T223 |
| Reteach | S22 |
| Review | T236–T237, T258–T259, T271 |
| Test | Bk 1-3 |
| Maintain | Bk 1-4, T352–T353 |

 Refer to *Sounds of Letters CD* Track 14 for pronunciation of /kw/, /w/, and /hw/.

### Connecting Letter to Sound

**Routine Card 12** **DEVELOP PHONEMIC AWARENESS OF /kw/ AND /hw/** Say the word *queen.* Have children say the word. Repeat for the words *quiet* and *quilt.* Say: **The words *queen, quiet,* and *quilt* begin with the /kw/ sound.** Have children say /kw/ several times. Repeat this procedure for the sound /hw/. Use the words *whale, wheel,* and *whistle.*

**CONNECT LETTER AND SOUND** Display *Sound/Spelling Card Qq* and say the letter name. Point out the *qu.* Explain that the letters *q* and *u* together stand for the /kw/ sound, the sound at the beginning of *queen.* Have children say /kw/ several times as you touch the letters. Then hold up the *Sound/Spelling Card wh* and say the letter names. Explain that these letters together stand for the /hw/ sound, the sound at the beginning of *whale.* Have children repeat the sound several times as you touch both letters at the same time.

▲ **Sound/Spelling Card**

**DISCRIMINATE /kw/ AND /hw/** Give each child a *q* and a *u* Word Builder Card. Say: **When I say a word that begins with /kw/, hold up your cards and say /kw/. When I say a word that does not begin with /kw/, keep the cards in your lap.** Say these words:

quiet  pink  quit  quart  grill  quite  king

Then distribute *Word Builder Cards w* and *h.* Tell children to display these cards when they hear a word that begins with /hw/. Otherwise, they should keep the cards in their laps. Say:

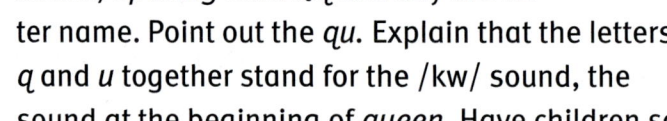

wheel  whale  help  while  what  let  white

whale

| **5-DAY PHONICS** | |
|---|---|
| **DAY 1** | Introduce /kw/*qu*, /hw/*wh* |
| **DAY 2** | Word Building with /kw/*qu*, /hw/*wh* |
| **DAY 3** | Build Words |
| **DAY 4** | Inflections *-ed*, *-ing* (CVC) |
| **DAY 5** | Inflections *-ed*, *-ing* (CVC) |

## Word Blending

**DIBELS**
Nonsense Word Fluency
**NWF**

**WORDS WITH /kw/*qu* AND /hw/*wh*** Demonstrate each step with *Letter Cards* and a pocket chart. Have children repeat each step after you, using their *Word Builder Cards* and *Word Builders*.

**Routine Card 13**

**BLEND AND READ *QUILT*** Hold up *qu* and say /kww/. Hold up *i* and say /ii/. Hold up *l* and say /ll/. Hold up *t* and say /t/.

- Place *q, u, i, l, t* in the pocket chart. Have children do the same with their letters and *Word Builders*.

- Point to *qu* and say /kww/. Point to *i* and say /ii/. Prompt children to repeat after you.

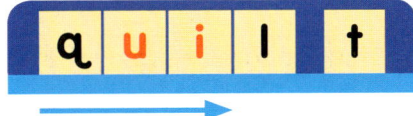

- Slide *i* next to *qu*. Run your hand under the letters as you blend the sounds, elongating them—/kwwii/. Have children repeat.

- Point to *l* and say /ll/. Have children do the same.

- Slide *l* next to *qui*. Slide your hand under *quil* as you blend the sounds by elongating them—/kwwiill/. Have children repeat.

- Point to *t* and say /t/. Have children do the same.

- Slide *t* next to *quil*. Slide your hand under *quilt* as you blend the sounds by elongating them—/kwwiillt/. Have children repeat.

- Read *quilt* naturally. Have children read the word with you.

Follow the same procedure for *quit, quick,* and *quack.* Then lead children in blending words with /hw/*wh*: *whip, whiz, when.*

## Professional Development

 **Podcasting:** Word Blending, Gr. 1

 **E L L**

**Extra Support for /kw/** If children have difficulty recalling that *qu* stands for /kw/ instead of /k/, have them place a finger in front of their lips to feel the expelled air when they say the sound.

▲ **Photo Card 113**

**● ADVANCED**

**Word Meanings** Have children blend the word *quip.* Explain that a quip is a funny response to something said by someone else. Example: **If a friend asked why your dog likes going to the beach, you might reply with the quip, "because he likes being a hot dog."**

# Digraphs /kw/ qu, /hw/ wh

 **phonics** *and Spelling*

---

## Professional Development

 **Podcasting:** Word Building, Gr. 1; Spelling and Dictation, Gr. 1

---

## Word Building

**Routine Card 14**

**BUILD SPELLING WORDS** Use *Letter Cards* and a pocket chart. Have children use their *Word Builder Cards* and *Word Builders*.

Place the *Letter Cards q, u, i,* and *t* in the pocket chart. Slide your hands under the letters as you slowly read the word—/kwwiit/. Then read *quit* naturally.

Have children build and read new words. As they build each word, write it on the board. Say:

- **Change *t* to *ck*. What did you make?**
- **Change *ck* to *z*. What did you make?**

- **Change *qu* to *wh*. What did you make?**
- **Change *z* to *ch*. What did you make?**

- **Take away *ich*. Add *en* after *wh*. What did you make?**

Have children read all the words.

---

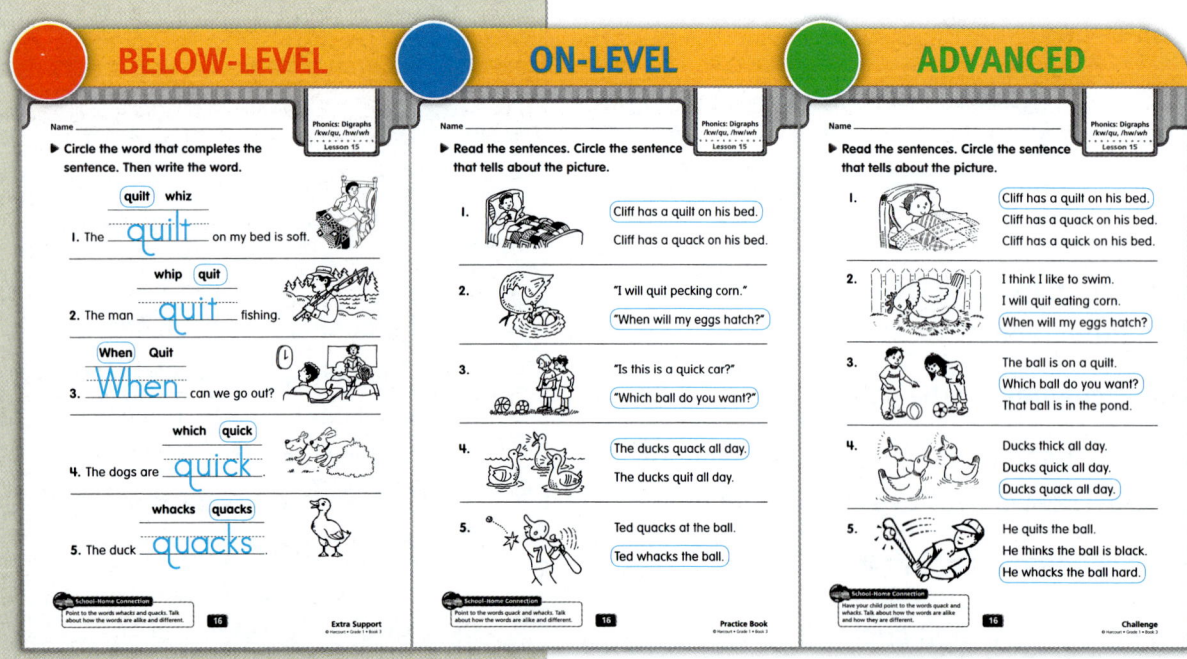

BELOW-LEVEL ▲ Extra Support, p. 16

ON-LEVEL ▲ Practice Book, p. 16

ADVANCED ▲ Challenge, p. 16

---

**ELL**

- Group children according to academic levels, and assign one of the pages on the left.

- Clarify any unfamiliar concepts as necessary. See *ELL Teacher Guide,* Lesson 15, for support in scaffolding instruction.

**5-DAY SPELLING**

| | |
|---|---|
| **DAY 1** | Pretest |
| **DAY 2** | Word Building |
| **DAY 3** | State the Generalization |
| **DAY 4** | Review |
| **DAY 5** | Posttest |

## Introduce Spelling Words

**PRETEST** Say the first word and read the dictation sentence. Repeat the word as children write it. Write the word on the board and have children check their spelling. Tell them to circle the word if they spelled it correctly or write it correctly if they did not. Repeat for words 2–10.

### Words with /kw/*qu* and /hw/*wh*

1. quit     We won't **quit** until we are done.
2. quick    You have to be **quick** to win this race.
3. quiz     I want to get the answers right on the **quiz.**
4. whiz     Sam is a **whiz** at math.
5. which   Kate wondered **which** hat was hers.
6. when    I'll let you know **when** we're ready to go.

### Review

7. arm      Ann fell and hurt her **arm.**
8. part     Jerome's bike needs a new **part.**

### High-Frequency

9. house   My **house** is made of bricks.
10. put      Carla **put** a poster on her wall.

**Spelling Words**

| | |
|---|---|
| 1. **quit** | 6. **when** |
| 2. **quick** | 7. **arm** |
| 3. **quiz** | 8. **part** |
| 4. **whiz** | 9. **house** |
| 5. **which** | 10. **put** |

### MONITOR PROGRESS ✓

#### Phonics: Digraphs /kw/*qu*, /hw/*wh*

| **IF** children have difficulty spelling words with digraphs /kw/*qu* and /hw/*wh*, | **THEN** have them slide a finger under each word, reading and spelling it aloud. |
|---|---|

**Small-Group Instruction, p. S22:**

 **BELOW-LEVEL:** Reteach     **ON-LEVEL:** Reinforce     **ADVANCED:** Extend

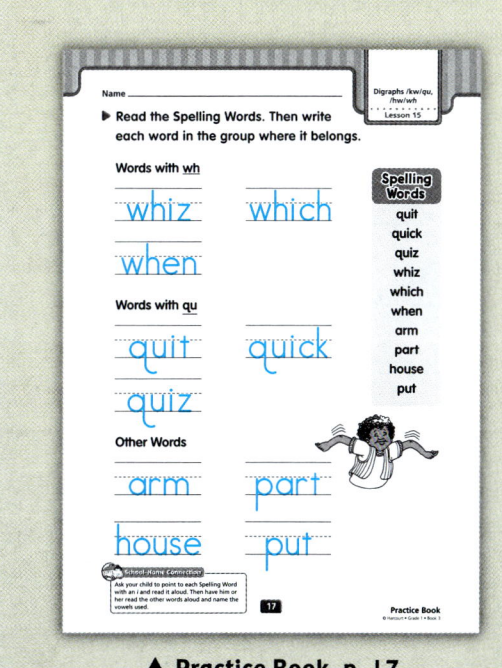

▲ Practice Book, p. 17

# Reading

*Get Started Story:* **A Quiz for Brent**

## Objectives

- *To use letter-sound knowledge to read decodable text*
- *To develop fluency*
- *To review high-frequency words*

 **Podcasting:** Reading Decodable Text, Gr. 1

## Options for Reading

 **BELOW-LEVEL**

**Echo-Reading** Have children echo-read each sentence. Pause to discuss it, using the Monitor Comprehension questions. Have children frame and read words with the digraphs /kw/*qu* and /hw/*wh*.

 **ON-LEVEL**

**Monitor Comprehension** Have children read the story aloud, page by page. Ask the Monitor Comprehension questions as you go. Then lead children in retelling the story and describing their favorite parts.

 **ADVANCED**

**Independent Reading** Have children read each page silently, looking up each time they finish a page. Ask the Monitor Comprehension questions as you go. Discuss what other clues Granddad could have given Brent.

## Apply Digraphs /kw/*qu* and /hw/*wh*

**READ DECODABLE TEXT** Write the following sentences on the board. Tell children that the sentences are about a boy in a story they will read.

**Brent has a quiz.**

**When will he quit?**

- Have children read each sentence as you track the print.
- Have children frame and read words with the digraph /kw/*qu* or /hw/*wh*.
- Tell them that many of the words in the story have the /kw/ and /hw/ sounds.

**Routine Card 17** **INTRODUCE THE STORY** Have the children look at the title page and read aloud the title. Ask them to point to the names of the author and the illustrator as you read them aloud. Have them look at the first page of the story. Discuss the illustration. Ask children to use what they know from the title and the illustration to make predictions about the story. Tell children they will read the story to find out what Brent finds.

**Preview** Preview the story with a picture walk. Use the illustrations to develop meaning for the text. Then guide children through the story, using the Monitor Comprehension questions.

Get Started Story

**Phonics**
Words with qu

**Words to Know**

| Review |
| happy |
| too |
| find |
| house |

# A Quiz for Brent

by Karen Sandoval
illustrated by
Joe Cepeda

94

Mom has a quiz for Brent.
Brent gets a hint. "Check the
bed, Brent," Mom tells him.

95

# Monitor Comprehension

**PAGES 94–95** Have children look at the title page and the first page of the story. Say: **I see Brent in the picture. I wonder what the drawing is for. Let's read to find out.**

**APPLY PHONICS** **What is Brent doing in this story?** (Brent has a quiz.) **Read the word that tells.**

**Clarify Meaning** Tell children that a *quiz* is a kind of questioning game. Invite children to share a time they had a quiz.

## TECHNOLOGY

 **eBook** "A Quiz for Brent" is available in an eBook.

 **Audiotext** "A Quiz for Brent" is available on *Audiotext Grade 1*, CD 6 for subsequent readings.

# Monitor Comprehension

**PAGES 96–97** Say: **In the picture, I see a red bucket. I wonder what Brent is going to do with the bucket. Let's read more to find out.**

1 **NOTE DETAILS/APPLY PHONICS** **What is the red bucket on?** (a quilt) **Read the word that tells.**

2 **PERSONAL RESPONSE** **Do you have a quilt on your bed? What does it look like?** (Responses will vary.)

3 **MAKE PREDICTIONS** **What do you think Brent will do next?** (Possible response: I think he will go where the drawing shows him to go.)

Think, Brent, think!
A big, tan cloth is on the
desk. Brent is happy he got
that hint, too.

98

What will Brent find? Is it Mom?
Is it Dad? Brent will finish his
quiz out of the house.

99

# Monitor Comprehension

**PAGES 98–99** Say: **Brent is happy to get his hints. He is enjoying this quiz. Let's read to find out where the search will end.**

**1** **APPLY PHONICS** The question *What will Brent find?* includes a word with the /hw/ sound. What word is it? *(what)* **Find and read the word.**

**2** **DETERMINE CHARACTERS' TRAITS** Do you think Brent's mom and dad know what is at the end of Brent's quiz? (Possible response: Yes, because they helped him with the hints throughout the story.)

**STRATEGIC READING**

**Words with /kw/ *qu* and /hw/ *wh***
Remind children that the story includes many words with the /kw/ and the /hw/ sounds. Ask them to point to and read the words that begin with /kw/ or /hw/ on these pages.

Brent will not quit.
He runs to the yard!
Quick, Brent, quick!

100

It's Granddad! Brent is
glad he did not quit!

101

# Monitor Comprehension

**PAGES 100–101** Say: **On page 100, we see Brent in the driveway.
He is carrying a bucket and a towel. I wonder what he is going to do.
Let's read to find out.**

**1** APPLY PHONICS   **Brent does not give up on his quiz. What word
does the author use instead of saying "give up"?** (quit)

**2** DRAW CONCLUSIONS   **What do you think Brent will do? How do
you know?** (He will help Granddad wash the car. He has a bucket
and towel to use. Granddad has a hose.)

**3** MAKE JUDGMENTS   **Do you think Brent had fun with his quiz?**
(Possible response: Yes, he was excited and did not want to quit
during his quiz.) **Would you enjoy this type of quiz?** (Possible
response: Yes, I love surprises.)

# Check Comprehension
*Retelling*

## Retell

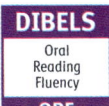

**DIBELS** Oral Reading Fluency **ORF**

**RETELL "A QUIZ FOR BRENT"** Ask children to name the main character of "A Quiz for Brent." Have volunteers tell what happened at the beginning, in the middle, and at the end of the story. Write their responses in a story map like the one shown. Guide children to use the information in the graphic organizer to retell what happened at the beginning, in the middle, and at the end of "A Quiz for Brent."

> **Beginning**
> Brent gets his first hint. He finds a bucket.

> **Middle**
> Brent follows more hints in his quiz. He finds a cloth and then goes outside.

> **Ending**
> Brent finds Granddad. They will wash the car.

### Objectives
- *To practice retelling a story*
- *To read fluently in a manner that sounds like natural speech*

### RETELLING RUBRIC

| 4 | Uses details to clearly retell the story |
|---|---|
| 3 | Uses some details to retell the story |
| 2 | Retells the story with some inaccuracies |
| 1 | Is unable to retell the story |

### Professional Development

 **Podcasting:** Auditory Modeling

 # Fluency

## Repeated Reading

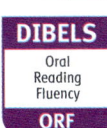

**DIBELS** Oral Reading Fluency **ORF**

**READ WITH A PARTNER** Have children work with a partner to reread "A Quiz for Brent" three or four times. Listen to partners read, and give them feedback about speeding up or slowing down as needed when they read. For example, have children read more slowly the sentences that tell what Brent finds so that they can understand the sentences better. Have them read repeated lines, such as *Think, Brent, think!,* more quickly since that sentence is familiar. Circulate, and give children guidance for improving their fluency.

# Comprehension
## *Read Aloud*

## Daily Comprehension

### Sequence

| DAY 1: | Review Sequence *Read-Aloud Anthology* |
|---|---|
| DAY 2: | Review Sequence *Student Edition* |
| DAY 3: | Review Sequence *Paired Selection Student Edition* |
| DAY 4: | Review Sequence *Big Book* |
| DAY 5: | Review Sequence *Comparing Texts* |

### ON-LEVEL

**Fiction and Nonfiction** Discuss the difference between fiction and nonfiction stories. Ask children to recall nonfiction stories they have read recently in school. Have them share the facts, real events, and real people they read about. Then discuss realistic fiction stories they have read, describing what makes the made-up characters and events seem real.

### Before Reading

**CONNECT TO PRIOR KNOWLEDGE** Tell children they will be listening to a selection about a grandmother who makes a dessert from apples. Ask children if they have ever eaten an apple dessert. Discuss other foods they have eaten that contain apples.

▲ Read-Aloud Anthology, "The Best Apple Crisp in the World," p. 58

**GENRE STUDY: REALISTIC FICTION**
Explain that "The Best Apple Crisp in the World" is a made-up story, but the characters do things that could happen in real life. Model your thinking by saying:

**Think Aloud** **The characters are made-up, but they seem like people I know. You could follow the recipe in the story to really make the apple dessert, just like the characters did.**

 **REVIEW THE SKILL: SEQUENCE** Tell children that authors give information in an order that makes sense. They tell what happens first, next, and last. Explain that knowing the order of the events, or the **sequence,** can help readers better understand the information. Model the skill by discussing the steps in making a simple snack, such as Bugs on a Log. Say: **First, get a clean piece of celery. Next, spread some peanut butter in the middle of the celery. Then, put some raisins on top of the peanut butter.** Conclude by telling children that they will be discussing the sequence of "The Best Apple Crisp in the World" later in the week. Then read the story to them.

### After Reading

**RESPOND** Discuss what children like about the story. Ask volunteers to tell about a meal or dessert that is special to their cultural heritage.

# Build Robust Vocabulary

## Listening/Speaking: *Words from the Read-Aloud*

### Teach/Model

**Routine Card 15**   **INTRODUCE ROBUST VOCABULARY**   Use *Routine Card 15* to introduce the words from "The Best Apple Crisp in the World."

❶ Put the word in **selection context.**
❷ Provide the **Student-Friendly Explanation** for children.
❸ Have children **say the word** with you.
❹ Use the word in other contexts, and have children **interact with the word's meaning.**
❺ Say the Student-Friendly Explanation again, and ask children to **name the word** that goes with it.

❶ **Selection Context:** They sat **cozily** around the kitchen table.
❹ **Interact with Word Meaning:** My mom sits cozily in her chair when she reads. She sits in a way that makes her feel comfortable. How do you get cozy when you read at home?

❶ **Selection Context:** This time Jake **interrupted**. "How many apples?"
❹ **Interact with Word Meaning:** It is not polite to interrupt people when they are speaking. If you needed to interrupt someone, how could you do so politely?

❶ **Selection Context:** "Exactly one cup!" Jake said **triumphantly**.
❹ **Interact with Word Meaning:** I might shout triumphantly after I won my soccer game. What might make you feel triumphant?

### Practice/Apply

**GUIDED PRACTICE**   Ask children to do the following:
- Sit cozily—in a way that feels cozy—at their desks.
- Interrupt you when you start talking.
- Say "I did it!" triumphantly.

### Objective
- *To develop robust vocabulary through discussing a literature selection*

**INTRODUCE**   Tested ✓
### Student-Friendly Explanations

**cozily**   If you lie cozily in bed, you are warm, comfortable, and relaxed.

**interrupted**   If you interrupted something, you stopped it in the middle.

**triumphantly**   If you say something triumphantly, you say it in an excited way that shows you are proud of what you have done.

**E L L**

**Introduce Vocabulary**   Role-play with children a variety of situations where *cozily, interrupted,* and *triumphantly* are used.

cozily

# Grammar

### Using I and Me

**5-DAY GRAMMAR**

| | |
|---|---|
| **DAY 1** | Introduce Using *I* and *Me* |
| **DAY 2** | Dictate Sentences Using *I* and *Me* |
| **DAY 3** | Add *I* and *Me* to Sentences |
| **DAY 4** | Revise Sentences Using *I* and *Me* |
| **DAY 5** | Write Sentences Using *I* and *Me* |

## Objectives

- *To understand that the words* I *and* me *take the place of some naming words*
- *To use* I *in the subject of the sentence and* me *in the predicate*

## Daily Proofreading

**i like to eat apples**

(I, apples.)

### Using *I* and *Me*

1. I lost my ball in the park.
2. Mom helped me look for it.
3. I tossed the ball to Mom.
4. Mom tossed the ball to me.

Grade 1, Lesson 15    LA29    Grammar: Using *I* and *Me*

**Transparency LA29**

## Teach/Model

**INTRODUCE THE CONCEPT** Read aloud some sentences from "The Best Apple Crisp in the World" (*Read-Aloud Anthology,* pages 58-61). Ask children to listen for the words *I* and *me.*

- **Well, I always use this pan.**

- **That's half an hour—just long enough for me to beat you at Go Fish while the apple crisp cooks!**

Point out that Grandma is speaking in both sentences and uses *I* and *me* instead of her name. Write on the board simple sentences using the pronouns *I* and *me.*

**I like stories.**

**Grandma tells me lots of stories.**

Underline *I* and *me* as you read the sentences. Explain that *I* is used in the naming part of the sentence, and *me* is used in the telling—or action—part of the sentence. Ask children to identify the naming part of the first sentence. (I) Remind children that *I* is always written with a capital letter. Then have them identify the telling part of this sentence. (like stories) Repeat with the second sentence.

## Guided Practice

**SAY SENTENCES USING *I* AND *ME*** Display **Transparency LA29.** Ask a volunteer to read aloud the first two sentences and circle the words *I* and *me.* Ask: **In what part of the sentence is each word found?** Repeat with the second pair of sentences.

## Practice/Apply

**SAY SENTENCES USING *I* AND *ME*** Say: **I like to read. Books make me happy.** Ask children to share sentences about things they like, using *I* and *me.* Write several on the board. Have children tell how to punctuate the sentences. Talk about in what part of the sentence *I* or *me* appears and whether the word is capitalized.

# Modeled Writing
## *Personal Narrative*

**5-DAY WRITING**

| | |
|---|---|
| **DAY 1** | Modeled Writing |
| **DAY 2** | Shared Writing |
| **DAY 3** | Shared Writing |
| **DAY 4** | Independent Writing |
| **DAY 5** | Independent Writing |

## Teach/Model

**INTRODUCE PERSONAL NARRATIVE** Display **Transparency LA30,** and explain that this is a story written by a child about an event in the child's life. This kind of story is called a **personal narrative.** Read it to children, and talk about what they learn about the child. Together, develop a list of the characteristics of a well-written personal narrative.

### Personal Narrative

- A personal narrative tells about something that has happened in a person's life.
- It has a beginning, a middle, and an ending.
- It has words like I and me.

**WRITING TRAIT** **VOICE** Explain that writers use words in their own special way to show how they feel. They use words to show that what they are writing about is important. Ask children to identify words in the student model that show how the child feels.

## Guided Practice

**DRAFT A PERSONAL NARRATIVE** Model saying sentences that might begin a personal narrative: **I got a puppy at last! I named him Sam. I love him so much, but he is such a scamp! One day, Sam . . .** Point out how *I* is used to show that this happened to the writer. Talk about words that show how the writer feels about the puppy. Have volunteers suggest a few sentences to add to the narrative.

## Practice/Apply

**SHARE A PERSONAL NARRATIVE** Have children draw a picture showing an interesting event in their lives. These events might include a holiday memory or a favorite school event. Save children's pictures to use on Days 4 and 5.

## Objectives
- *To understand that a personal narrative tells about someone's experiences*
- *To develop a list of criteria for effective personal narratives*

## Writing Prompt

**Family Member** Have children write and draw about an important event in the life of a family member.

---

**Student Model: Personal Narrative**

I moved to Texas when I was five. We packed boxes and put them in a big truck. I felt so sad. We drove for many hours. Then we saw our new house. It looked nice. My new room was just right for me. I decided that day that I liked Texas!

Grade 1, Lesson 15    LA30    Writing: Personal Narrative

**Transparency LA30**

## Day at a Glance

### Day 2

**Phonemic Awareness**
- Phoneme Segmentation

 **and Spelling**
- Review: Digraphs /kw/*qu,* /hw/*wh*
- Build Words

**Comprehension**

Review: Sequence

**High-Frequency Words**
- Introduce: *about, books, family, name, people, read, work, writing*

**Reading**
- "Tomás Rivera," *Student Edition,* pp. 106–123

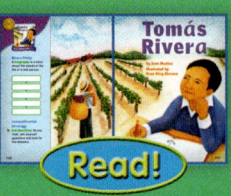

**Fluency**
- Reading Rate

**Robust Vocabulary**
- Review: *cozily, interrupted, triumphantly*

**Grammar**
- Review: Using *I* and *Me*

**Shared Writing** ✏️
- Personal Narrative

# Warm-Up Routines

## Oral Language

**Objective** *To listen attentively and respond appropriately to oral communication*

### Question of the Day
**What kinds of books do you like to read?**

Encourage children to use the terms *fiction* and *nonfiction* when describing their books. Then have children complete the following sentence frame.

**My favorite book is _____ because _____.**

## Read Aloud

**Objectives** *To listen for a purpose; to listen for enjoyment*

**BIG BOOK OF RHYMES AND POEMS** Read the title and the name of the poet. Discuss the poet's role. Tell children to listen to find out if they agree with the poet. Read the poem aloud. Invite children to share their thoughts about it. Ask them how the poet feels about books and how they know. Ask if they feel the same way.

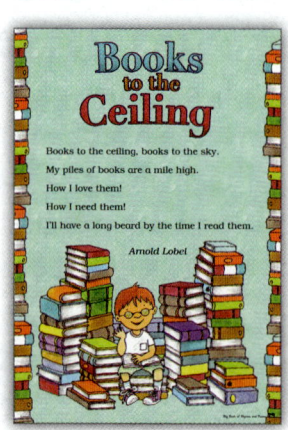

▲ Big Book of Rhymes and Poems, p. 29

# Word Wall

**Objective** *To read high-frequency words*

**REVIEW HIGH-FREQUENCY WORDS** Review *again, feel, house, know, loud, Mrs., put, say,* and other previously learned high-frequency words. Say a word, have a volunteer point to it, and have the group read the word aloud. Then point to words at random and have children read them.

| again | feel | house | know |
|---|---|---|---|

# Phonemic Awareness

**Objective** *To segment words into phonemes*

**DIBELS** Phoneme Segmentation Fluency **PSF**

**Routine Card 8**

**PHONEME SEGMENTATION** Tell children they will sing a song and say words one sound at a time. Model by singing the first line below to the tune of "Bingo." Then say the next line and segment the sounds in *bugs*. Repeat the routine for the other words, having children repeat the word you say and then segment the sounds.

Sing: **There are some kids who like to sing**
　　　**and say the sounds in words -o.**
Say: **The word is *bugs—bugs,* /b/ /u/ /g/ /z/.**

**filled** (/f/ /i/ /l/ /d/)　　　**rush** (/r/ /u/ /sh/)

**queen** (/kw/ /ē/ /n/)　　　**bump** (/b/ /u/ /m/ /p/)

**champ** (/ch/ /a/ /m/ /p/)　　**blink** (/b/ /l/ /i/ /n/ /k/)

**king** (/k/ /i/ /ng/)　　　**whiz** (/hw/ /i/ /z/)

 Podcasting: Phoneme Segmentation

# Digraphs /kw/ *qu*, /hw/ *wh*

 **phonics** *and Spelling*

## Objectives

- *To blend sounds into words*
- *To spell four- and five-letter short vowel words and high-frequency words*

## Skill Trace

 **Tested** **Digraphs /kw/ *qu*, /hw/ *wh***

| | |
|---|---|
| Introduce | T220–T223 |
| Reteach | S22 |
| **Review** | **T236–T237, T258–T259** |
| Test | Bk 1-3 |
| Maintain | Bk 1-4, T352–T353 |

### Spelling Words

1. quit
2. quick
3. quiz
4. whiz
5. which
6. when
7. arm
8. part
9. house
10. put

## Word Building

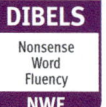 **DIBELS** Nonsense Word Fluency **NWF**

 **Routine Card 14**

**BUILD AND READ A SPELLING WORD** Place the *Letter Cards q, u, i,* and *t* in the pocket chart. Arrange the cards so that *q* and *u* are touching. Remind children that the letters *qu* stand for /kw/. Then read the word with children.

**BUILD SPELLING WORDS** Ask children which letter you should change to make *quit* become *quick*. (Change *t* to *ck*.) Ask them which letters to change to make *quick* become *quiz*. (Change *ck* to *z*.) Continue building spelling words 4–6 in this manner. Have children repeat each step after you and then read the words.

---

**BELOW-LEVEL**

**Build Spelling Words** Write the words on the board. Point to each word and read it aloud. Have children repeat the word. For auditory and kinesthetic reinforcement, ask children to use their finger to trace the word on their desktop. Have children say each letter as they form the word.

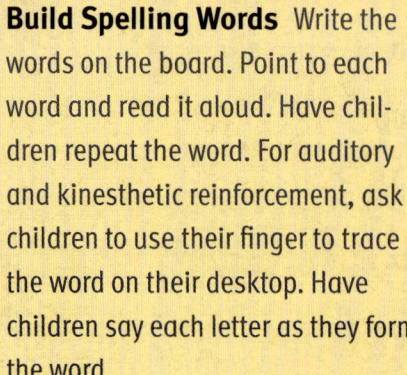 **ELL**

**Build Spelling Words** Some children may have difficulty differentiating the final sound /z/ from /s/. Write the words *quits* and *quiz* on the board. Track the print and read both words with children, elongating the /z/ sound in *quiz*. Then have children identify which word ends with the sound /z/.

**5-DAY PHONICS/SPELLING**

| DAY 1 | Pretest |
| --- | --- |
| DAY 2 | Word Building |
| DAY 3 | State the Generalization |
| DAY 4 | Review |
| DAY 5 | Posttest |

## Read Words in Context

**APPLY PHONICS** Write the following sentences on the board or on chart paper. Have children read each sentence silently. Then track the print as children read the sentence aloud.

> We had a <u>quick</u> <u>quiz</u> in class.
>
> <u>Which</u> <u>part</u> goes here?
>
> <u>When</u> is the <u>quiz</u>?
>
> Beth is a <u>whiz</u> at math.
>
> <u>Quit</u> pinching my <u>arm</u>!

**WRITE** Dictate several underlined words from the sentences. Have children write the words on a dry-erase board or in their notebook.

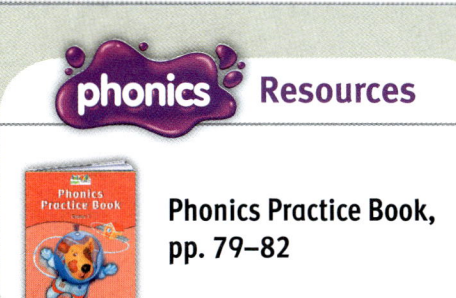

**phonics Resources**

**Phonics Practice Book, pp. 79–82**

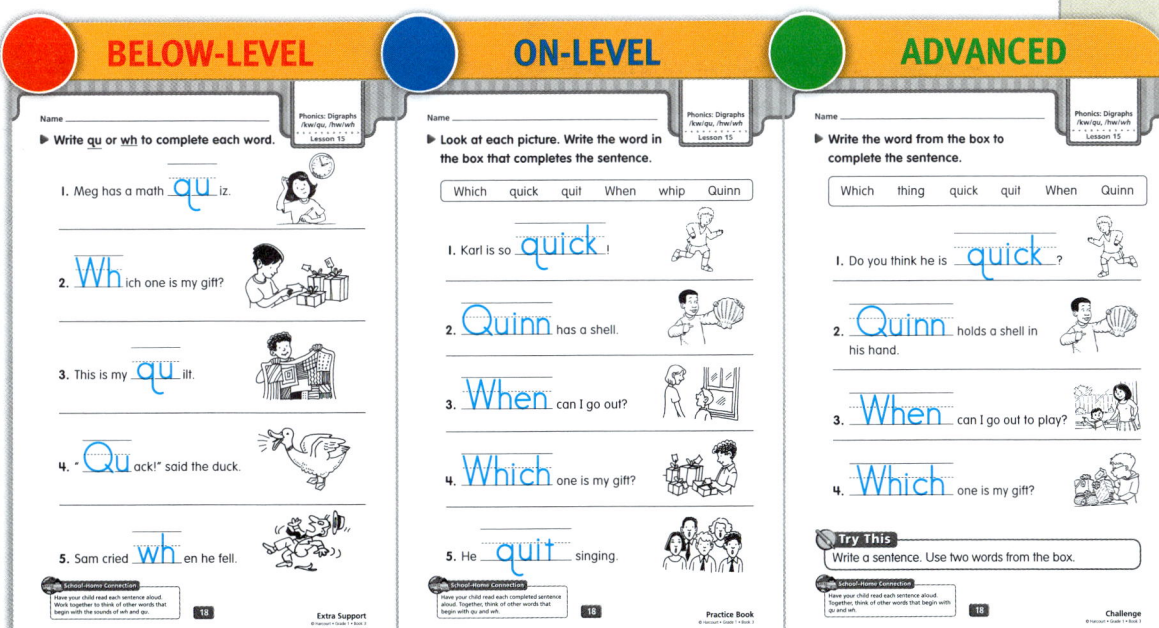

▲ Extra Support, p. 18    ▲ Practice Book, p. 18    ▲ Challenge, p. 18

**ELL**

- Group children according to academic levels, and assign one of the pages on the left.

- Clarify any unfamiliar concepts as necessary. See *ELL Teacher Guide*, Lesson 15, for support in scaffolding instruction.

# Sequence
*Comprehension*

## Objective

• *To understand the order of events in a selection*

## Skill Trace

 **Sequence**

| | |
|---|---|
| Preview | T46 |
| Introduce | T54–T55 |
| Reteach | S6–S7, S26–S27 |
| Review | **T78, T90, T100, T230, T238–T239, T262, T274, T284** |
| Test | Bk 1-3 |
| Maintain | Monitor Comprehension, Bks 1-4, 1-5 |

## "RESEARCH SAYS"

"In general, then, the results of this study suggest that direct instruction of a conventional text structure can facilitate formation of a macrostructure for that type of text."

—Armbruster, Anderson, & Ostertag
(1987, p. 345)

## Teach/Model

**REVIEW THE SKILL** Remind children that the sequence of a piece of writing is the order in which events happen. Read aloud the following excerpt from "The Best Apple Crisp in the World" (*Read-Aloud Anthology*, p. 58).

> **"One stick of butter is a quarter pound—and that's how much we need! Jake—wash your hands. You can do this part." Grandma showed Jake how to mush the butter right into the flour and sugar and cinnamon until it was all crumbly.**

Then model for children how to recognize sequence.

**Think Aloud** I know the order of the events in this story is important because Grandma is baking something. When I bake, I need to do things in a certain order to make the food come out right. I read that first, Jake washes his hands. Next, he mashes the butter into the other ingredients. And last, it all makes a crumbly mixture. Jake washes his hands before he mashes in the butter. If the sequence of the story is changed so that Jake washes his hands after mashing in the butter, the story would not make as much sense.

## Practice/Apply

**GUIDED PRACTICE** Read *Student Edition* page 102 to children and ask them to recall what *sequence* means. Then have children look at the pictures at the top of page 103 and follow along as you read aloud the text. Ask children to think about the sequence and tell what happens first, next, and last. (First, there is an egg. Next, it grows into a tadpole. Last, it grows into a frog with legs.) Talk with children about why it is important that these events happen in a certain order.

# Focus Skill

## Sequence

Authors tell about things in the order in which they happen. The order makes sense. This order is called the **sequence**.

Look at the pictures.

They show a sequence of first, next, and last.

Look at the pictures. Do they show a sequence? What happens first, next, and last?

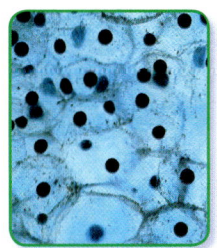  

**Try This!**

Look at these pictures. Put them in order. Tell what happens first, next, and last.

Go online www.harcourtschool.com/storytown

102

103

---

**Try This!** **INDEPENDENT PRACTICE** Discuss the pictures, and then have children read along as you read aloud the directions. Ask children to use words that help listeners follow the correct sequence as they tell what the pictures are about. *(first, next, last)*

**BELOW-LEVEL**

**Try This!** Help children with the Try This! activity by guiding them to arrange *Photo Cards* into a meaningful sequence and talking about it. You can use *Photo Cards 72* (hen), *50* (egg); *32* (caterpillar), *24* (butterfly); *129* (seed), *108* (plant), *58* (flower).

**Photo Card 50** ▶

egg

# High-Frequency Words

**Words to Know**

## Objective
• *To read high-frequency words*

**INTRODUCE**

### High-Frequency Words

| | |
|---|---|
| about | people |
| books | read |
| family | work |
| name | writing |

---

### MONITOR PROGRESS

#### High-Frequency Words

| **IF** children have difficulty reading and spelling the words, | **THEN** display two sets of word cards, and have them read and match the words. |
|---|---|

Small-Group Instruction, p. S23:

🔴 **BELOW-LEVEL:** Reteach
🔵 **ON-LEVEL:** Reinforce
🟢 **ADVANCED:** Extend

---

## Teach/Model

**Routine Card 16**

**INTRODUCE WORDS** Write *about, books, family, name, people, read, work,* and *writing* on the board.

• Point to and read *about.* Repeat, having children say it with you.

• Say: **We will read a story *about* a real person.**

• Point to each letter as you spell the word. Have children spell the word with you.

• Have children reread the word.

Repeat for the remaining words. Use the following sentences:

These ***books*** are ***about*** bugs.

There are four ***people*** in my ***family***.

Please ***read*** the ***name*** on this paper.

Weeding a garden is hard ***work***.

Keep ***writing*** until your story is finished.

## Guided Practice

**STUDENT EDITION PAGES 104–105** Have children point to and read aloud each of the highlighted words on page 104. Talk about the artwork. Then ask volunteers to read aloud the sentences on page 105.

**STORY WORDS** List *library, stories, teacher, Texas,* and *Tomás Rivera* on the board. Read the words aloud. Repeat, having children read the words with you. Point to each story word as it is mentioned in this explanation: **Tomás Rivera is one of the characters in the story. The setting for this story is Texas. Tomás's grandpa takes him to the library so that he can read many stories. When Tomás grows up, he wants to be a teacher.** Point to the words again, and have children read them aloud.

## Words to Know

**High-Frequency Words**

books

about

read

work

writing

people

family

name

I have **books about** cars and trucks. It is fun to **read** lots of books.

I like to **work** on stories, too. I am **writing** one to tell **people** about my **family**. It is hard work, but I like it! I will put my **name** on it.

GO online www.harcourtschool.com/storytown

104

105

**E L L**

**Review High-Frequency Words**
Hold up *Photo Card 91* (moon) and say: **Lia will read books about the moon.** Have children practice using *read, books,* and *about* in the sentence frame with other *Photo Cards*. See *ELL Teacher Guide,* Lesson 15, for support in scaffolding instruction.

**Photo Card 91 ▶**

moon

# Reading

*Student Edition:* **Tomás Rivera**

## Objectives

- *To understand genre: biography*
- *To ask questions as a strategy for comprehension*

 **Podcasting:** Graphic Organizers, Gr. K–1

## Options for Reading

 **BELOW-LEVEL**

**Preview** Have children preview the selection by looking at the illustrations. Read each page of the selection to children, and have them read it after you. Use the Monitor Comprehension questions for discussion.

 **ON-LEVEL**

**Monitor Comprehension** Have children read the selection aloud, page by page. Ask the Monitor Comprehension questions as you go. Then lead children in retelling the important events in Tomás's life.

 **ADVANCED**

**Independent Reading** Have children read each page silently, looking up each time they finish a page. Ask the Monitor Comprehension questions as you go. Discuss what Tomás does to make his dreams come true.

## Genre Study

**DISCUSS BIOGRAPHY: PAGE 106** Point to and read the genre label. Explain that a **biography** is a story written about a real person. Point out that the events in the story really happened to the person. Then use **Transparency GO7** or copy the graphic organizer on the board. Tell children that they can fill in this sequence chart to help them better understand the order of the events in many nonfiction and fiction selections they read.

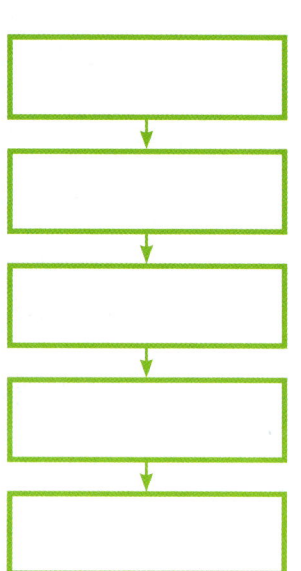

## Comprehension Strategies

**ASK QUESTIONS: PAGE 106** Tell children that asking questions before, during, and after reading will help them understand the selection. Provide this example:

**Think Aloud** In "The Best Apple Crisp in the World," the events in the story happen in a certain order, or sequence. If I ask questions, I can understand it better. Why do Jake and Grandma pour in sugar before they bake the crisp? I think that if they don't, the food will not taste sweet enough. Now I know why the story happens in this sequence.

Then read aloud the text under Comprehension Strategy. Point out to children that thinking about these ideas can help them to understand a story better. Explain that they will work together to use the sequence chart as they read "Tomás Rivera."

## Genre Study

A **biography** is a story about the events in the life of a real person.

## Comprehension Strategy

**Ask Questions** As you read, ask yourself questions and look for the answers.

Biography

106

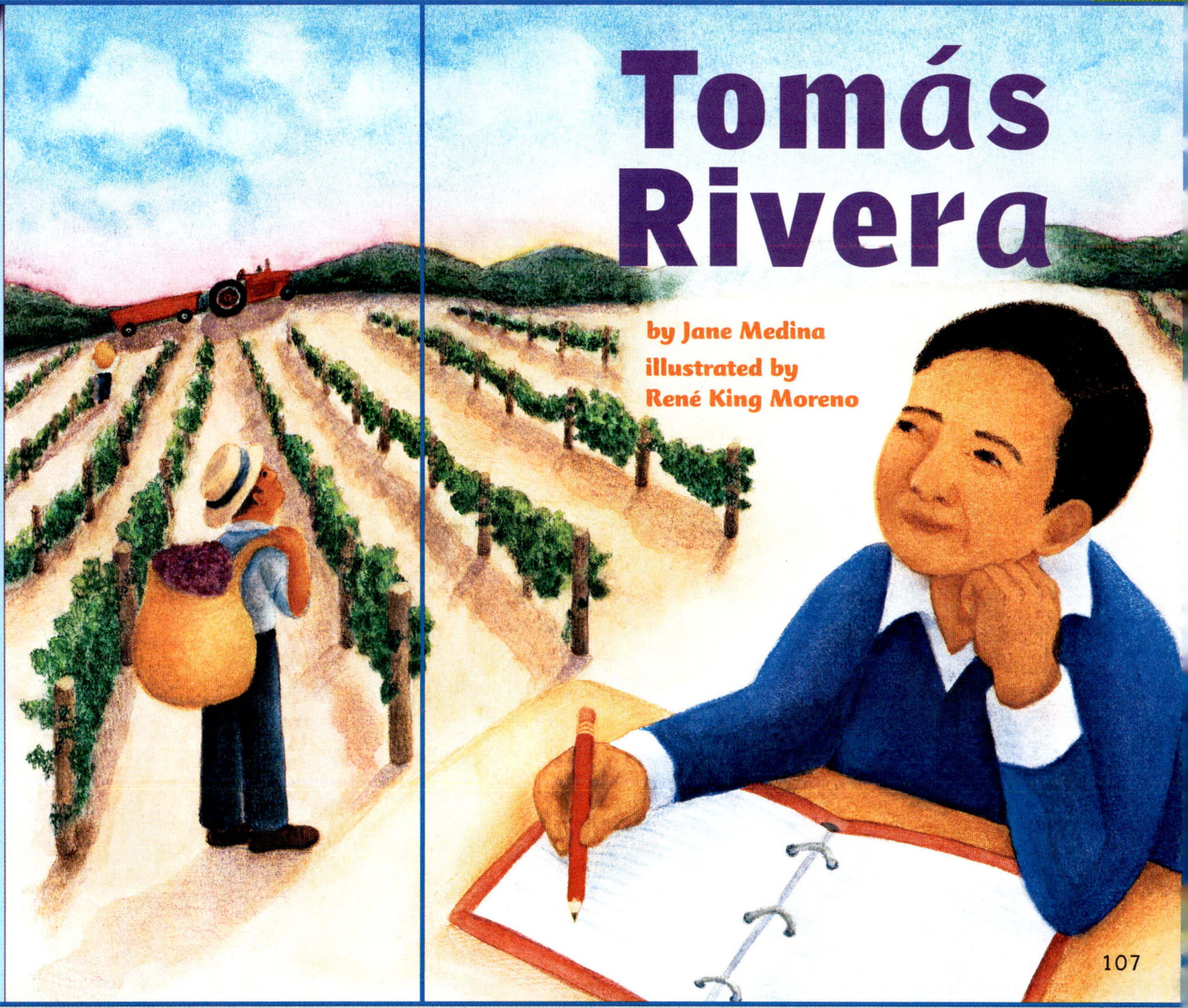

# Tomás Rivera

by Jane Medina

illustrated by
René King Moreno

107

## Build Background

**DISCUSS HOPES AND DREAMS** Tell children that this is a story about a boy who had hopes for his future and who then worked hard to make them come true. Ask volunteers to tell about some of their hopes and dreams for the future.

 **Routine Card 17**

**SET A PURPOSE AND PREDICT** Read aloud the title. Tell children that they will read to become informed about Tomás Rivera's life.

- Identify the boy as Tomás, and ask children to share questions they have about his life. List the questions on the board.

- Invite children to read the selection to find out more about Tomás's life. Guide them to compare and contrast the region where Tomás lives and the things he does with their own region and lives.

## TECHNOLOGY

 **eBook** "Tomás Rivera" is available in an eBook.

 **Audiotext** "Tomás Rivera" is available on *Audiotext Grade 1*, CD 3 for subsequent readings.

Tomás Rivera was born in Texas. Tomás and his **family** went from farm to farm picking crops.

108

Tomás helped pick crops all day. It was hard **work**. At night he had fun with his Grandpa.

109

# Monitor Comprehension

**PAGES 108–109** Say: **Look at the illustrations, and tell where Tomás might be. Why do you think so? Let's read to find out what Tomás is doing here.**

**①** **SEQUENCE** **Where does Tomás's life begin? How do you know?** (It begins in Texas; the story says that he was born in Texas.)

**②** **NOTE DETAILS** **What does Tomás do all day? What does he do in the evening?** (He helps his family pick crops; he has fun with Grandpa.)

**③** **DETERMINE CHARACTERS' TRAITS** **Do you think Tomás is a hard worker? What makes you think this?** (Yes, Tomás is a hard worker; he works all day picking crops, which is a hard job.)

## Apply
### Comprehension Strategies

**Ask Questions** Demonstrate how to ask questions to help comprehend the selection.

**Think Aloud** After reading these pages, I have some questions. *Who is in Tomás's family? How does Tomás feel about picking crops? I wonder what Tomás does for fun.* I think about these questions as I go on to the next page. I read on to see if the answers are in the words or the pictures. As I read, I wonder about things and have many more questions.

"Come quick, children!" Grandpa called. "It's time for stories!"

110

"You tell the best stories!" Tomás said. "I want to tell good stories, too."

111

# Monitor Comprehension

**PAGES 110–111** Say: **Let's discuss the illustrations. Who do you think the characters are in the pictures? Let's read to find out what they are doing.**

**1** **NOTE DETAILS** **Why does Grandpa gather the children around him?** (He tells them stories.)

**2** **DETERMINE CHARACTERS' EMOTIONS** **How do you think the children feel about Grandpa's stories? What makes you think this?** (They like his stories. The pictures show them listening and smiling; Tomás says that Grandpa tells the best stories.)

**SOCIAL STUDIES**

### TOMÁS RIVERA (1935–1984)

Dr. Rivera grew up in Texas and graduated from college there. He was a poet, educator, writer, college administrator, and dedicated community leader. The library in the illustration on page 120 is located at the University of California, Riverside, where Dr. Rivera served as chancellor from 1979 until he died. He was the first Mexican American to serve as chancellor in the University of California system.

"We can get lots of stories
for you, Tomás," said Grandpa.
"When?" asked Tomás.

112

"Let's go now!" Grandpa said
with a wink. "Quick, hop in!"

113

# Monitor Comprehension

**PAGES 112–113** Say: **Look at the illustration and compare that truck to trucks you see today. Why do you think the illustrator shows a truck from long ago? Now let's read to find out what Tomás is doing.**

**1** **NOTE DETAILS** **How is Grandpa going to help Tomás?** (He will help Tomás find many stories.)

**2** **UNDERSTAND CHARACTERS' ACTIONS** **Why do you think Grandpa offers to take Tomás right away?** (Possible responses: Grandpa is kind; he knows how much Tomás wants to learn to tell stories.)

**3** **MAKE PREDICTIONS** **Where do you think Tomás and Grandpa will go? Why do you think so?** (Possible response: They probably will go to a library, because that's a place where you can find lots of stories.)

## SOCIAL STUDIES

### SUPPORTING STANDARDS

**Discuss Language and Culture** Guide children to compare language that reflects customs, regions, and cultures by asking them to tell what names they call their grandparents and what special things their grandparents do. Also, help children to connect their own experiences with the language and customs of others by talking about how the things Tomás has done in the selection are the same as and different from the things they do in their daily lives.

"This is a library," said Grandpa. "Look at all the books!" gasped Tomás as he clapped his hands.

114

"Read all you can, Tomás. It will help you think of lots of stories," said Grandpa.

115

# Monitor Comprehension

**PAGES 114–115** Say: **I see a lot of books on these pages. Where are Tomás and Grandpa? Let's read to find out.**

**①** **CONFIRM PREDICTIONS** **Where do Tomás and Grandpa go?** (to the library)

**②** **DETERMINE CHARACTERS' EMOTIONS** **How do you think Tomás feels when he and Grandpa go inside the library? What makes you think this?** (He's excited; he says things in an excited way and he claps his hands.)

**③** **SEQUENCE EVENTS/SUMMARIZE** **What have you learned about Tomás Rivera's life so far?** (He was born in Texas; he and his family travel from farm to farm picking crops; he loves to listen to Grandpa's stories and wants to learn to tell stories; Grandpa takes him to a library.)

---

**Use Multiple Strategies**

**Ask Questions** Say: Asking myself questions as I read helps me understand the story better. I ask myself, "What kinds of books will Tomás read from the library?" I will read on to see if I can find out.

**Use Decoding/Phonics** Say: When I came to the word *clapped* on page 114, I realized that I know the smaller word *clap* that could help me read this long word. I also noticed the ending *-ed*. By putting the *-ed* ending on the root word *clap*, I could read the word—*clapped*.

Tomás read lots and lots of books.
He read **about** bugs, stars, and cars.
Tomás started thinking of stories.

116

Tomás started telling his stories.
Then he started **writing** them.

117

# Monitor Comprehension

**PAGES 116–117** Say: **Tomás looks like he is enjoying himself. Let's read to find out what happens as Tomás reads books.**

1. **NOTE DETAILS    What does Tomás read about?** (bugs, stars, and cars)

2. **DETERMINE CHARACTERS' TRAITS    What do Tomás's book choices tell about him?** (He is interested in many different kinds of things.)

3. **MAKE INFERENCES    How do you think reading a lot of books might help Tomás tell and write his own stories?** (Possible responses: Reading books could give him ideas and information for his own stories; seeing how others write could show him how to write well.)

## Map the Selection

**Fill in the Sequence Chart** Work with children to list the main events from Tomás's life. Add information throughout the selection.

> Tomás was born in Texas. He and his family go from farm to farm picking crops.

> Tomás loves to listen to Grandpa's stories. He wants to learn to tell stories. Grandpa takes him to a library to get books.

When he grew up, Tomás got a job as a teacher. He still kept writing stories.

118

Tomás Rivera's stories tell about **people** picking crops, just as his family did. Lots of people read his books.

119

# Monitor Comprehension

**PAGES 118–120** Say: **In these pictures, we see Tomás grown up. He looks happy. Let's read to the end of the selection to find out what Tomás does.**

**1** **NOTE DETAILS** **What jobs does Tomás have as a grown-up?** (He is a teacher and a writer.)

**2** **DRAW CONCLUSIONS** **Why do you think Tomás Rivera's name is on a library?** (Possible response: He became famous; people knew he loved books and they wanted to remember his good work as a teacher and a writer.)

**3** **RECOGNIZE AUTHOR'S PURPOSE** **Why do you think the author wrote about Tomás Rivera's life?** (Possible response: She might have wanted to show children that hard work can help you fulfill your dreams and do great things in your life.)

**ON-LEVEL**

**Changes in Setting and Characters** Remind children that a story's setting is *where* and *when* it takes place. Point out that in a story about someone's life, a **biography,** the story often begins with the person's life as a child and then tells the important events that happen in the correct order as the child grows up. Have children look through the selection and estimate how old Tomás is in each picture. Discuss the changes in Tomás and in the setting.

Now his name is on a big library.
Many people visit the library.
They get books, just as Tomás did.

120

## Think Critically

**Teacher Read-Aloud**

1. How does Tomás feel about books after he goes to the library with Grandpa? **SEQUENCE**

2. Why does Grandpa want Tomás to read lots of books? **MAKE INFERENCES**

3. How does Tomás learn to tell stories? **PLOT**

4. Why do you think Tomás Rivera wrote stories about people picking crops? **DRAW CONCLUSIONS**

5. **WRITE** Write about a job you would like to have someday. **WRITING RESPONSE**

121

# Think Critically

## Respond to the Literature

1. Tomás is excited and reads many books. **SEQUENCE**

2. Grandpa wants Tomás to read so that Tomás can get ideas to tell his own stories. **MAKE INFERENCES**

3. Tomás reads about many things and gets ideas for his own stories. **PLOT**

4. Possible response: Tomás knew a lot about the life of people who pick crops since that's what he did. He wanted others to know about this life. **DRAW CONCLUSIONS**

5. **WRITE** Responses will vary. **WRITING RESPONSE**

### Listening/Speaking

**Discussion** Guide children to:
- express their ideas in a discussion
- use speaking vocabulary
- listen attentively to others
- ask questions for clarification and understanding

Teacher Read-Aloud

**Meet the Author**
# Jane Medina

Jane Medina read a lot about Tomás Rivera so that she could tell this story about his life. She hopes the story will help children think as Tomás Rivera did.

❝If you work hard and do well in school, you can do anything you want to do!❞

**Meet the Illustrator**
# René King Moreno

When René King Moreno was young, she loved to spend her spare time drawing and painting. She studied art in school, and now she illustrates children's books.

GO online  www.harcourtschool.com/storytown

122                                                                          123

# Meet the Author and the Illustrator

**PAGES 122–123** Explain that these pages tell about the people who created the story "Tomás Rivera." Identify the author, Jane Medina, in the photograph on page 122 and the illustrator, René King Moreno, in the photograph on page 123. Remind children that an **author** writes a story and an **illustrator** creates pictures to go with the writing. Read aloud pages 122–123. Encourage children to follow along as you read.

# Check Comprehension
## Summarizing

### Objectives
- *To practice summarizing a selection*
- *To read at a rate appropriate for the text*

### SUMMARIZING RUBRIC

| | |
|---|---|
| 4 | Uses details to clearly summarize the selection |
| 3 | Uses some details to summarize the selection |
| 2 | Summarizes the selection with some inaccuracies |
| 1 | Is unable to summarize the selection |

### Summarize

**DIBELS** Oral Reading Fluency **ORF**

**SEQUENCE** Remind children that the sequence of a selection is the order of the events in the selection.

**REVISIT THE GRAPHIC ORGANIZER** Display completed **Transparency GO7.** Guide children to tell in the correct sequence the important events in Tomás Rivera's life.

**STORY RETELLING CARDS** The cards for "Tomás Rivera" can be used for retelling events or as an aid to completing the Sequence Chart. Lead children to respond to the selection by talking about it in a way that reflects understanding and interpretation.

▲ Story Retelling Cards 1–6, "Tomás Rivera"

# Fluency

### Teach/Model

**DIBELS** Oral Reading Fluency **ORF**

**ADJUSTING READING RATE** Tell children that good readers read at a speed that helps them understand a story. Model for children how to adjust reading rate as you read pages from "Tomás Rivera" that have dialogue or important facts.

### Practice/Apply

**ECHO-READ** Read aloud more pages from the story, modeling how to adjust reading rate. Have children follow along and echo-read.

### BELOW-LEVEL

**Fluency Practice** For fluency practice, have children read *Decodable Book 15*, the appropriate *Leveled Reader* (pp. T288–T291), or "Tom's Books" in the *Book 1-3 Strategic Intervention Interactive Reader.*

# Build Robust Vocabulary

## Listening/Speaking: *Words from the Read-Aloud*

### Review Robust Vocabulary

**USE VOCABULARY IN DIFFERENT CONTEXTS** Remind children of the Student-Friendly Explanations of *cozily, interrupted,* and *triumphant-ly.* Then discuss each Vocabulary Word with them in a context different from that in which it was used in "The Best Apple Crisp in the World." Use the following examples:

**cozily**
- **If you are lying cozily on the couch, how do you feel?**
- **Would you sit cozily in a cold room with broken chairs?**
- **Do you sleep cozily at night?**

**interrupted**
- **Have you ever interrupted your parents?**
- **Do you think it is polite to interrupt people who are talking?**
- **How do you feel when others interrupt you?**

**triumphantly**
- **Have you ever triumphantly won a game?**
- **Do you think you would see a smile or a frown on a person who has triumphantly done something?**
- **Name times you have felt triumphant.**

### Objective
- *To review robust vocabulary through discussing ideas*

**REVIEW**

#### Student-Friendly Explanations

**cozily** If you lie cozily in bed, you are warm, comfortable, and relaxed.

**interrupted** If you interrupted something, you stopped it in the middle.

**triumphantly** If you say something triumphantly, you say it in an excited way that shows you are proud of what you have done.

**Use Vocabulary** Guide children to act out situations where *cozily, interrupted,* and *triumphantly* are used. Some examples: a child is napping cozily; two children are talking and a third child interrupts, announcing something triumphantly. Then allow partners or small groups to create their own skits, incorporating the Vocabulary Words.

# Grammar

## *Using* I *and* Me

**5-DAY** GRAMMAR

|  | |
|---|---|
| **DAY 1** | Introduce Using *I* and *Me* |
| **DAY 2** | Dictate Sentences Using *I* and *Me* |
| **DAY 3** | Add *I* and *Me* to Sentences |
| **DAY 4** | Revise Sentences Using *I* and *Me* |
| **DAY 5** | Write Sentences Using *I* and *Me* |

## Objectives

- *To use* I *in the subject of the sentence and* me *in the predicate*
- *To use knowledge of the basic rules of capitalization*

## Daily Proofreading

**That quilt is for Me**

(me.)

▲ **Grammar Practice Book, p. 57**

## Review

**USE A LITERATURE MODEL** Tell children that they will listen to a rhyme that has the words *I* and *me*. Read the rhyme several times, encouraging children to act it out.

> I tap my feet. 1, 2, 3.
>
> Now tap *your* feet. You're just like me!
>
> I clap my hands. 1, 2, 3.
>
> Now clap *your* hands. You're just like me!

Write the first two lines on the board. Track the print and have children choral-read the lines. Ask them which sentence has *I* and which one has *me*. Ask: **In which part of the sentence is *I* used?** (the naming part) **In which part of the sentence is *me* used?** (the telling part) Substitute *me* for *I* in the first sentence so that children can hear an incorrect example. Then say the sentence correctly. Repeat for *You're just like me!*, substituting *I* for *me*.

## Practice/Apply

**GUIDED PRACTICE** Write the following sentence frames on the board and have children read them silently:

_____ like snacks.     A duck quacked at _____.

Ask volunteers to write *I* and *me* in the correct blanks. Read the sentences with children. Then have children dictate more sentences, using similar frames. List these sentences and read them with the group.

**INDEPENDENT PRACTICE** Ask children to copy a sentence with *I* and one with *me* from the board. Remind them that the word *I* is always a capital letter. Have partners check each other's sentences.

# Shared Writing
*Personal Narrative*

**5-DAY WRITING**

| | |
|---|---|
| **DAY 1** | Modeled Writing |
| **DAY 2** | Shared Writing |
| **DAY 3** | Shared Writing |
| **DAY 4** | Independent Writing |
| **DAY 5** | Independent Writing |

## Write Together

**REVIEW PERSONAL NARRATIVE** Remind children that a personal narrative tells about a person's life. Write the following on the board: *My first day of school was scary. I felt so shy. Then I met Sam. Sam was my very first friend.* As you write, have children identify what makes this a personal narrative.

**GENERATE IDEAS** Guide children to select a focus for a personal narrative they will write as a group. Have them think about recent classroom events and choose one to write about. Work together to fill in a story map with their ideas.

 **MODEL WRITING** Have volunteers dictate sentences as you write them on chart paper, using the Step-by-Step Writing Instruction as a guide. Then track the print and read the sentences with children. Save the sentences for Day 3.

### Objectives

- *To compose coherent sentences in a personal narrative*
- *To generate ideas before writing on assigned tasks*
- *To select a focus for writing*

### Writing Prompt

**Writing About Today** Have children draw and write about something they have done today.

## Step-by-Step Writing Instruction

| | | |
|---|---|---|
| **1** | Say a sentence that begins our story. | One day, I went on a trip to the post office. |
| **2** | Remember that each sentence begins with a capital letter. How do I write the first word? | One |
| **3** | Say your sentence again. Let's write the rest of it. How do I write the word *I*? | One day, I went on a trip to the post office |
| **4** WRITING TRAIT | This sentence tells about something you did. What mark comes at the end of a telling sentence? | One day, I went on a trip to the post office. |
| **5** | Say a sentence that tells what happens next. Tell me how to write it. Notice how we used the word *me* correctly. | My friend Sam sat with me on the bus. |

▲ Writer's Companion, Lesson 15

Day at a Glance

## Day 3

### Phonemic Awareness
- Phoneme Deletion

### phonics and Spelling
- Digraphs /kw/*qu*, /hw/*wh*, /th/*th*
- State the Generalization

### High-Frequency Words
- Review: *about, books, family, name, people, read, work, writing*

### Fluency
- Reading Rate
- "Tomás Rivera," *Student Edition,* pp. 106–120

### Comprehension

**Review: Sequence**

### Reading
- "I Can," *Student Edition,* pp. 124–125

### Robust Vocabulary
- Introduce: *accomplishment, admire, ambition*

### Grammar
- Review: Using *I* and *Me*

### Shared Writing
- Personal Narrative

# Warm-Up Routines

## Oral Language

**Objective** *To listen attentively and respond appropriately to oral communication*

### Question of the Day
**Do you like to read books? Why?**

Discuss why children enjoy reading. Encourage them to explain their responses. Have children complete the following sentence frame:

**I like reading books because _____.**

## Read Aloud

**Objectives** *To identify vocabulary words in familiar text; to participate in reciting a contemporary poem*

**BIG BOOK OF RHYMES AND POEMS**
Reread this contemporary poem and encourage children to join in reciting it, especially on the repeated words. Then discuss the meanings of *ceiling, piles, miles,* and *beard.* Ask children why they think the poet said *I'll have a long beard by the time I read them.* (Possible response: He will be very old by the time he reads such a big pile of books.)

▲ **Big Book of Rhymes and Poems, p. 29**

## Word Wall

**Objective** *To read high-frequency words*

**REVIEW HIGH-FREQUENCY WORDS** Review *about, books, family, name, people, read, work, writing.* Say a word, have a volunteer point to it, and have the group read the word aloud. Then point to words at random and have children reread them. Repeat several times to reinforce instant recognition.

| about | books | family | name |
|-------|-------|--------|------|
| people | read | work | writing |

## Phonemic Awareness

**Objective** *To delete ending phonemes from words*

**Routine Card 9** **PHONEME DELETION** Tell children you will say some words and ask them to remove the ending sound in each word. Model by saying: **Listen. What sound do you hear at the end of *fork*?** (/k/) Now let's say *fork* without /k/ at the end—*for*. Say the following words, and have children delete the last sound to form a new word.

*card* without /d/ (car)    *road* without /d/ (row)    *belt* without /t/ (bell)

*seal* without /l/ (sea)    *goat* without /t/ (go)    *plant* without /t/ (plan)

*dent* without /t/ (den)    *meat* without /t/ (me)    *fern* without /n/ (fur)

**card without /d/**
**car**

# Build Words

## phonics and Spelling

**5-DAY PHONICS**

| | |
|---|---|
| **DAY 1** | Introduce /kw/*qu*, /hw/*wh* |
| **DAY 2** | Word Building with /kw/*qu*, /hw/*wh* |
| **DAY 3** | Build Words |
| **DAY 4** | Inflections -ed, -ing (CVC) |
| **DAY 5** | Inflections -ed, -ing (CVC) |

### Objectives

- *To use /kw/qu, /hw/wh, and /th/th and other known letter-sounds to decode words*
- *To recognize spelling patterns*

### Skill Trace

| Tested ✓ | /kw/*qu*, /hw/*wh* | /th/*th* |
|---|---|---|
| Introduce | T220–T223 | Bk 1-2, T132–T135 |
| Reteach | S22 | Bk 1-2, S12 |
| Review | T236–T237, T258–T259, T271 | Bk 1-2 T148–T149, T172,–T173, T522 |
| Test | Bk 1-3 | Bk 1-2 |
| Maintain | T352–T353 | T258–T259 |

---

**Digraphs /kw/*qu*, /hw/*wh*, /th/*th***

Quinn is my cat.
He is as quick as a wink!
He kicks his legs. Bump! Thud!
What upset the bucket?
Quinn did it!
Whiz! Which way did Quinn go?
There he is on my thick quilt.

Grade 1, Lesson 15    R29    Phonics: Digraphs /kw/qu, /hw/wh, /th/th

**Transparency R29**

---

## Word Building

**DIBELS** Nonsense Word Fluency **NWF**

**Routine Card 14**

**BUILD AND READ WORDS** Use a pocket chart and *Letter Cards.* Have children repeat each step with their *Word Builders* and *Word Builder Cards.*

Build the word *whiz.* Frame the letters *wh* and ask children what sound these letters stand for. (/hw/) Then read the word with children.

Lead children in building and reading new words. Say:

- **Change *wh* to *qu*. Read the word.**
- **Change *z* to *ck*. Read the word.**
- **Change *qu* to *th*. Read the word.**

Continue in a similar manner to have children build and read these word pairs: *then-when; quack-whack; whip-quip.*

| w | h | i | z |
|---|---|---|---|
| q | u | i | z |
| q | u | i | c | k |
| t | h | i | c | k |

## Read Words in Context

**READ SENTENCES** Display **Transparency R29** or write the sentences on the board or on chart paper. Have children read the story silently, and then choral-read the story as you track the print. Then ask volunteers to read each sentence aloud. Call on other volunteers to underline or frame words that have /kw/*qu*, /hw/*wh*, or /th/*th*.

**5-DAY SPELLING**

| DAY 1 | Pretest |
| DAY 2 | Word Building |
| DAY 3 | **State the Generalization** |
| DAY 4 | Review |
| DAY 5 | Posttest |

## Review Spelling Words

**STATE THE GENERALIZATION** List spelling words 1–6 on chart paper or the board and have children read them. Ask: **What is the same about words 1–3?** (Each word has the /kw/ sound; they all begin with *qu*.) Then discuss what is the same about words 4–6. (Each word has the /hw/ sound; they all begin with *wh*.) Have volunteers read each word and underline the letters that stand for /kw/ or /hw/ in each word. Tell children that the letters *qu* are used to spell the /kw/ sound and that the letters *wh* are used to spell the /hw/ sound.

**REVIEW WORDS** List spelling words 7 and 8. Talk about what is the same in both words. (Both words have the sound /är/ spelled by the letters *ar*.) Have children read and spell the words.

**HIGH-FREQUENCY WORDS** List spelling words 9–10. Remind children that they have seen and read these words many times. Run your hand under *house* as you read it, and ask children to look carefully at the letters. Ask them to close their eyes, picture the word in their minds, and spell it with you. Repeat for *put*.

# Handwriting

**LETTER SPACING** Have children write the spelling words in their notebook. Remind children to use proper letter spacing to make their words more readable. Model how to write words so that the letters are neither too close together nor too far apart. Have children check their words for correct letter spacing.

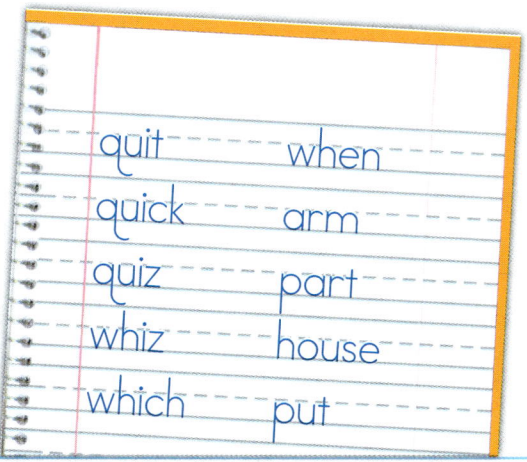

### Spelling Words

| | | | |
|---|---|---|---|
| 1. | quit | 6. | when |
| 2. | quick | 7. | arm |
| 3. | quiz | 8. | part |
| 4. | whiz | 9. | house |
| 5. | which | 10. | put |

### Decodable Book

- **Phonics**
  Digraphs *qu*, *wh*
- **Decodable Words**
  See the lists on page R11.

Decodable Book 15 ▲

Have children who need additional decoding practice read stories in *Decodable Book 15*. See also *Decodable Books* online (Take-Home Version).

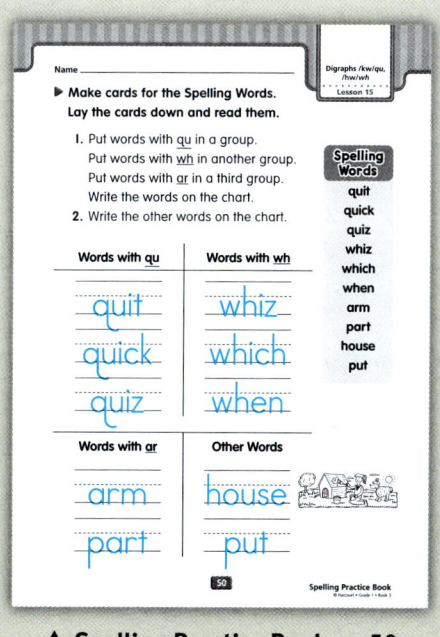

▲ **Spelling Practice Book, p. 50**

# High-Frequency Words

## Objective

- *To read high-frequency words*

REVIEW   Tested

### High-Frequency Words

| | |
|---|---|
| about | people |
| books | read |
| family | work |
| name | writing |

**Review Vocabulary** Use pictures, actions, and objects to aid in explaining word meanings. For example, display books and a card with the label *books*.

## Review

**PANTOMIME THE WORDS** Display *Word Cards about, books, family, name, people, read, work,* and *writing* or write the words on the board. Have a volunteer act out one of the words. Some words, such as *family* and *people*, may require several volunteers. When the group guesses the word, have children say and spell it together. Continue with the rest of the words.

## Practice/Apply

**GUIDED PRACTICE** Give each child a set of word cards (*Teacher Resource Book,* p 139). Ask children to spread the cards out in front of them. Then randomly call out one of the words, and have children hold up the matching card, repeating the word aloud. Continue until children respond quickly and accurately.

**INDEPENDENT PRACTICE** Have children work in pairs. One child holds up a word card and the other child reads the word. If the word is read correctly, the reader gets to keep the card. Continue until the reader has all the word cards. Then partners should switch roles. After the game, have children write the words in their notebook.

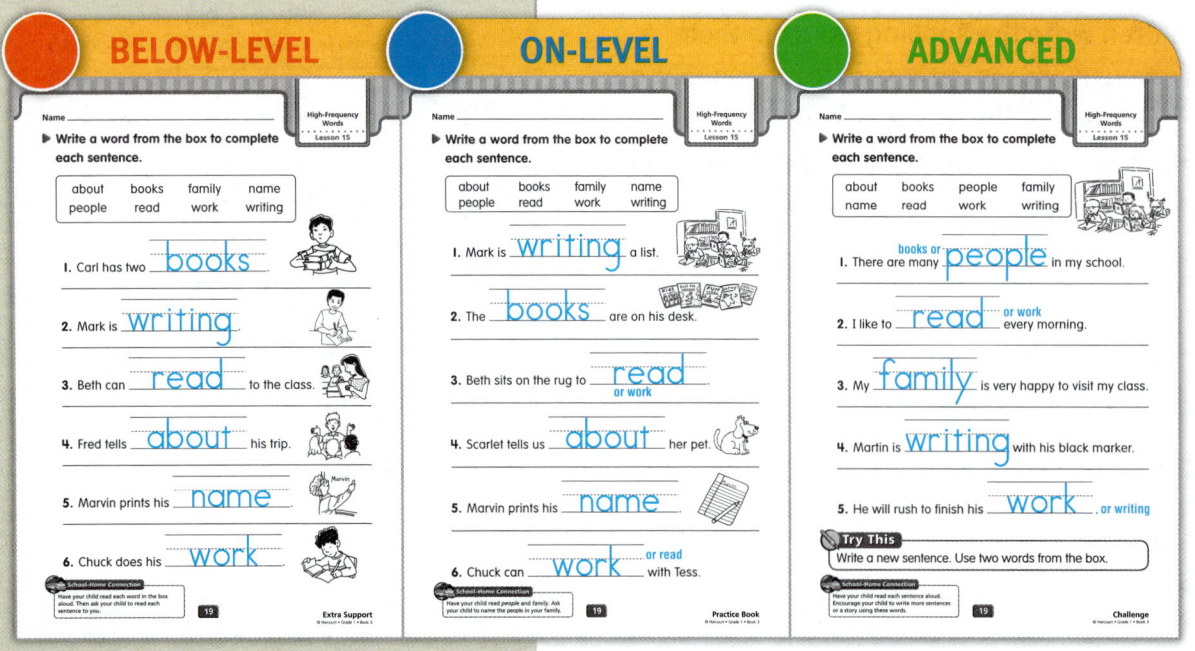

**BELOW-LEVEL**   **ON-LEVEL**   **ADVANCED**

▲ Extra Support, p. 19    ▲ Practice Book, p. 19    ▲ Challenge, p. 19

- Group children according to academic levels, and assign one of the pages on the left.

- Clarify any unfamiliar concepts as necessary. See *ELL Teacher Guide,* Lesson 15, for support in scaffolding instruction.

# Fluency
## *Reading Rate*

## Review

**DIBELS** Oral Reading Fluency **ORF**

**REVIEW READING RATE** Have children open their *Student Edition* to pages 110–111, and invite a pair of volunteers to read the parts of Grandpa and Tomás. Tell children to read the dialogue so that it sounds as if the characters are really speaking to one another. Explain that the characters are having a lively, quick conversation, so their words are probably said quickly.

Then have other volunteers read pages 116–117. Tell children to read this part more slowly to help everyone understand the important information. After volunteers have finished, help children understand the importance of changing the speed at which they read depending on what they are reading, to help them understand the text.

## Practice/Apply

**GUIDED PRACTICE** Read the selection aloud, adjusting the reading rate as needed, depending on the difficulty of the sentences. Have children echo-read each page. Discuss times it was appropriate for the reading rate to speed up and times it was good to slow down.

**INDEPENDENT PRACTICE** Ask children to choose a page from the selection and practice reading it at a rate that is appropriate for the text. Have children form small groups and read their pages to the group. Encourage group members to offer positive encouragement to the readers. Circulate and provide feedback for adjusting reading rate and improving fluency.

### Objective
- *To read at a rate appropriate for the text*

**ADVANCED**

**Read Longer Passages** Invite children who do well using appropriate reading rates to read longer passages in the selection or other nonfiction texts. Allow them an opportunity to practice and present their reading to a group.

✓ **MONITOR PROGRESS**

### Fluency

| **IF** the children have difficulty reading at a rate that is appropriate for the text, | **THEN** model the appropriate rate for them and have them echo-read. |
| --- | --- |

**Small-Group Instruction, pp. S24–S25:**

🔴 **BELOW-LEVEL:** Reteach
🔵 **ON-LEVEL:** Reinforce
🟢 **ADVANCED:** Extend

# Sequence
## *Comprehension*

## Objectives
- *To recognize that events in stories happen in a sequence that makes sense*
- *To listen attentively and respond appropriately to contemporary poetry*
- *To recognize characteristics of poetry*

### Skill Trace

 **Tested**  **Sequence**

| | |
|---|---|
| Preview | T46 |
| Introduce | T54–T55 |
| Reteach | S6–S7, S26–S27 |
| Review | **T78, T90, T100, T230, T238–T239, T262, T274, T284** |
| Test | Bk 1-3 |
| Maintain | Monitor Comprehension, Bks 1-4, 1-5 |

## Review

**REVIEW SEQUENCE** Remind children that events in a story happen in a sequence that makes sense. Ask children to think about the order of events in "The Best Apple Crisp in the World" (*Read-Aloud Anthology*, p. 58). Ask: **Can you eat apple crisp before you make it?** Lead children to conclude that the sequence in the story matches the order in which things happen in real life.

## Practice/Apply

**GUIDED PRACTICE** Ask children to listen to some directions and tell whether they are in a sequence that makes sense. Have children repeat and pantomime the directions in the correct sequence. Say:
- **Put on your shoes, put on your socks, go outside.**
- **Put cereal in a bowl, eat, pour in some milk.**

**INDEPENDENT PRACTICE** Have children apply their knowledge of sequence by completing *Practice Book* page 20.

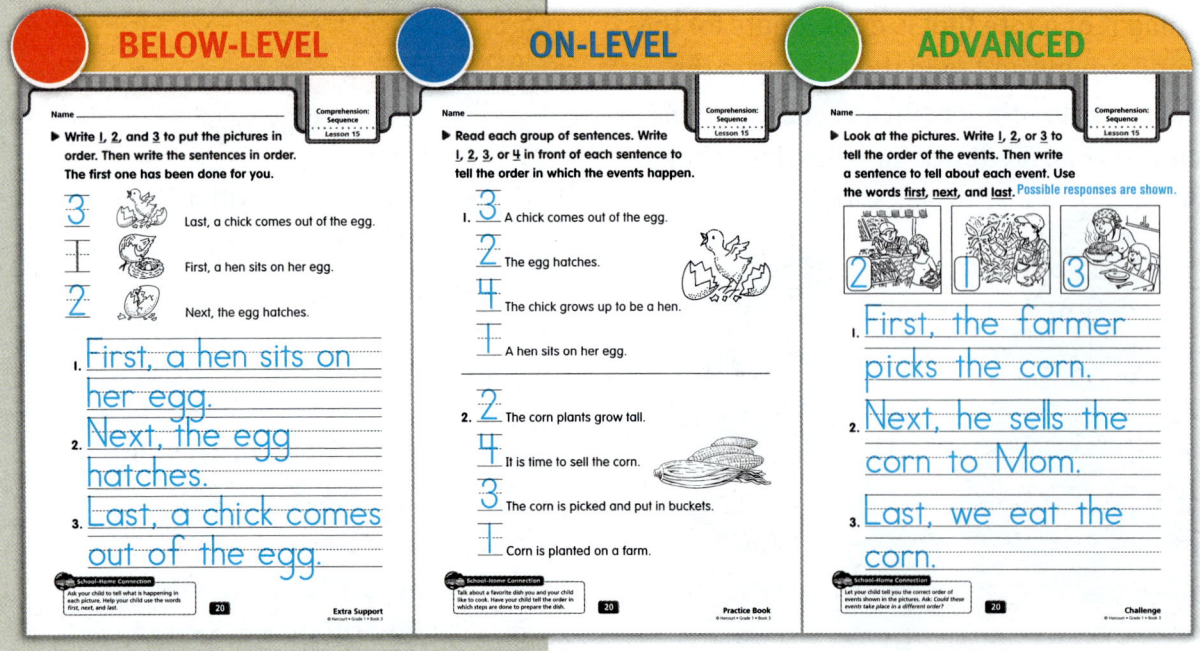

▲ Extra Support, p. 20      ▲ Practice Book, p. 20      ▲ Challenge, p. 20

- Group children according to academic levels, and assign one of the pages on the left.
- Clarify any unfamiliar concepts as necessary. See *ELL Teacher Guide,* Lesson 15, for support in scaffolding instruction.

Social Studies

Teacher Read-Aloud

Poetry

# I Can

by Mari Evans
illustrated by Shane Evans

I can
be anything
I can
do anything
I can
think
anything
big
or tall
OR
high or low
W I D E
or narrow
fast or slow
because I
CAN
and
I
WANT
TO!

124    125

---

# Reading

## Student Edition: Paired Selection

### Read Aloud

**MONITOR LISTENING COMPREHENSION** Read aloud the poem at least twice. Use the following to discuss it:

- **MAIN IDEA** **What is the poem "I Can" about?** ("I Can" is about how someone can be, do, and think anything.)

- **PERSONAL RESPONSE** **What are some things you can do?** (Possible response: I can ride a bike and read.)

- **GENRE** Tell children that poems use words in creative ways and that some poems rhyme and some do not. Ask: **Does this poem rhyme?** (No.) **How are words used in creative ways?** (Possible response: Words like *tall* and *wide* are used to tell how someone can think.)

**E L L**

**Pantomime Concepts** Remind children that the child in the poem can think anything. Work with children to create hand movements to show big, tall, high, low, wide, narrow, fast, and slow. Then read the poem again, and have children make the hand movements and join in on the words.

**W I D E**
**narrow**

## Connections

### Comparing Texts

❶ How is Tomás like the girl in the poem "I Can"?
Possible response: They both believe they can do great things.

❷ Why is it important to believe you can do the things you want to do?
Possible response: If you do, then you will try hard to learn new things.

❸ What things did Tomás do that you also like to do?
Accept reasonable responses.

### Writing

Write about something special you did with a family member or friend. Tell what happened first, next, and last.

> One day, my dad and I went to the park. We played basketball together. I won! Then we ate ice cream cones. It was fun!

126

### Phonics

Make and read new words.

Start with **quick**.

Change  i  to  a .

Change  q  u  to  w  h .

Change  c  k  to  t .

Change  a  t  to  e  n .

### Fluency Practice

Read "Tomás Rivera" with a classmate. Take turns reading the pages. Read the easy parts quickly. Read the harder parts more slowly.

127

# Connections

## ⏱ WRITING

 **Writing** Encourage children to fill out a graphic organizer to plan their writing. Remind children to tell what happens first, next, and last.

First
↓
Next
↓
Last

## ⏱ PHONICS

**Word Building** Distribute to children *Word Builder Cards q, u, i, c, k, a, w, h, t, e,* and *n.* Have children practice manipulating the cards to build and read the words *quick, quack, whack, what,* and *when.*

## ⏱ FLUENCY

**Partner Reading** Have partners take turns reading pages of "Tomás Rivera." Remind children to speed up or slow down their reading, depending on how hard the sentences are. Encourage them to read the dialogue in a lively, quick way to make it sound like natural speech.

When?

Let's go now! Quick, hop in!

# Build Robust Vocabulary

## Listening/Speaking: *Words About the Selection*

### Teach/Model

 **INTRODUCE ROBUST VOCABULARY** Use *Routine Card 15* to introduce the words.

Routine Card **15**

❶ Put the word in **selection context.**

❷ Provide the **Student-Friendly Explanation** for children.

❸ Have children **say the word** with you.

❹ Use the word in other contexts, and have children **interact with the word's meaning.**

❺ Say the Student-Friendly Explanation again, and ask children to **name the word** that goes with it.

❶ **Selection Context:** A great **accomplishment** for Tomás Rivera was writing his first book.

❹ **Interact with Word Meaning:** Running a mile was an accomplishment for me. Tell about one of your accomplishments.

❶ **Selection Context:** When Tomás grew up, many people began to **admire** his books.

❹ **Interact with Word Meaning:** I admire Dr. Seuss because he wrote funny, clever rhymes. Name a person you admire. Tell why.

❶ **Selection Context:** Tomás's **ambition** was to tell stories like Grandpa.

❹ **Interact with Word Meaning:** My ambition is to learn to play a musical instrument. Do you have this ambition, too?

### Practice/Apply

**GUIDED PRACTICE** Ask children to do the following:
* Tell about an accomplishment they worked hard for.
* Name things that would make them admire someone.
* Name an ambition they have about learning something new.

### Objective
* *To develop robust vocabulary to describe ideas*

**INTRODUCE** Tested ✓

**Student-Friendly Explanations**

**accomplishment** If you have had an accomplishment, you have worked hard to get something done.

**admire** If you admire someone, you think that person is very special because of the things he or she does.

**ambition** If you have an ambition, you want to do something very much.

**Support for Concepts** Provide drawing paper and crayons. Then give simple directions using the Vocabulary Words, such as: **Draw a picture of a family member you admire, because you think he or she is kind. Draw yourself doing something great—a great accomplishment. Draw yourself learning to do something you have the ambition to do.**

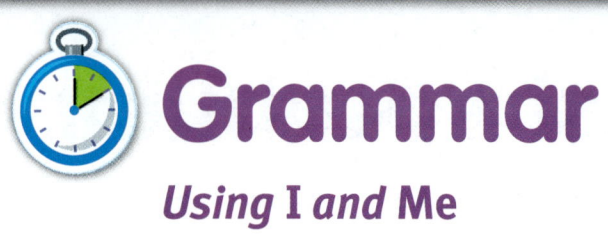

# Grammar
*Using* I *and* Me

**5-DAY GRAMMAR**

**DAY 1** Introduce Using *I* and *Me*
**DAY 2** Dictate Sentences Using *I* and *Me*
**DAY 3** Add *I* and *Me* to Sentences
**DAY 4** Revise Sentences Using *I* and *Me*
**DAY 5** Write Sentences Using *I* and *Me*

## Objective

• *To apply knowledge of rules for using* I *and* me *correctly in sentences*

## Daily Proofreading

me went to the parc.
(I, park)

---

## Review

**DICTATE SENTENCES USING *I* AND *ME*** Provide model sentences like these to show children how to use *I* and *me* in sentences that are about more than one person:

> **Sam and I saw a squirrel.**
>
> **It was looking at Sam and me.**

Remind children that *I* is used in the naming part of the sentence and *me* is used in the telling part. Then have children dictate sentences about something that they did or saw recently with a friend. Record their sentences, and read them with children. Ask volunteers to underline *I* and *me*.

> **Anna and <u>I</u> saw a dog.**
> **The dog barked at Anna and <u>me</u>.**
> **Rick and <u>I</u> saw the crossing guard.**
> **She waved at Rick and <u>me</u>.**

## Practice/Apply

**GUIDED PRACTICE** Write sentences like the following, have children read them, and have volunteers tell where to write *I* and *me*:

> **Todd and _____ went to the park.** (I)
> **My dad went with Todd and _____.** (me)

Have children read the corrected sentences as you track the print. Then replace *I* with *me* in the first sentence and read it to children. Talk about how *me* doesn't sound correct. Restore the word *I* and read the corrected sentence. Repeat with the second sentence.

**INDEPENDENT PRACTICE** Have children write a pair of sentences like those above, using *I* and *me*. Then ask children to read aloud their sentences to one another in small groups. Have them check to make sure that each sentence uses the word *I* or *me* correctly.

▲ **Grammar Practice Book, p. 58**

# Shared Writing
*Personal Narrative*

**5-DAY** WRITING
| | |
|---|---|
| **DAY 1** | Modeled Writing |
| **DAY 2** | Shared Writing |
| **DAY 3** | Shared Writing |
| **DAY 4** | Independent Writing |
| **DAY 5** | Independent Writing |

## Write Together

**REVIEW WITH A LITERATURE MODEL** Write the following passage on the board. Tell children that if Tomás had written "Tomás Rivera" as a personal narrative, it may have begun like this. Have children read the passage silently and then aloud. Point out how *I* is used in the passage.

> I was born in Texas. My family and I went from farm to farm picking crops. I helped pick crops all day. It was hard work. At night, I had fun with my grandpa and his stories.

**PRACTICE WRITING** Have children look again at the story map from Day 2 for ideas. Continue to help children, modeling how to write a personal narrative. Add sentences to those written on Day 2.

**WRITING TRAIT**  **VOICE** Remind children that writers often include words that help show their feelings. Ask children which words in the passage above help show how Tomás feels.

### Personal Narrative

- A personal narrative tells about something that has happened in a person's life.
- It has a beginning, a middle, and an ending.
- It has words like <u>I</u> and <u>me</u>.

## Share

**DISCUSS THE SENTENCES** Read the finished personal narrative with children, tracking the print. Then ask children to:

- check to see if the sentences describe a personal experience.
- identify words that show what is important to the writer.
- identify personal words, such as *I* and *me,* and check that they are used correctly.

Display the personal narrative. Children can use it as a writing model for Days 4 and 5.

## Objective
- *To compose a coherent personal narrative*

## Writing Prompt

**Ambitions** Have children write about one of their ambitions by telling what they would like to do or be when they grow up.

Day at a Glance

## Day 4

### Phonemic Awareness
• Phoneme Deletion

### phonics and Spelling
• Introduce: Inflections *-ed, -ing* (double final consonant)
• Review: Digraphs /kw/*qu*, /hw/*wh*

### High-Frequency Words
• Review: *about, books, family, name, people, read, work, writing*

### Fluency
• Reading Rate
• "Tomás Rivera," *Student Edition*, pp. 106–120

### Comprehension

Review: Sequence

• Big Book: *Fireflies, Fireflies, Light My Way*

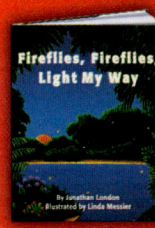

### Robust Vocabulary
• Review: *accomplishment, admire, ambition*

### Grammar
• Review: Using *I* and *Me*

### Independent Writing
• Personal Narrative

# Warm-Up Routines

## Oral Language

**Objectives** *To listen attentively and respond appropriately to oral communication; to express personal preferences*

> ### Question of the Day
> Where do you like to go to think?
> What is the place like?

Have children complete the following sentence frame:

**I like to think in _____ because _____.**

## Read Aloud

**Objectives** *To appreciate the rhythm and rhyme of a poem; to relate the poem to one's life*

**BIG BOOK OF RHYMES AND POEMS** Point to and read aloud the title of the poem and the name of the poet. Ask children to listen to the rhythm and rhyme as you read the poem. Then reread the poem, and ask children to listen to find out why someone wants a secret place. After reading, ask: *What does the person do in the secret place? What do you think the secret place looks like? How does this poem make you feel?*

▲ Big Book of Rhymes and Poems, p. 30

# Word Wall

**Objectives** *To read high-frequency words*

**REVIEW HIGH-FREQUENCY WORDS** Review *about, books, family, name, some,* and other previously learned high-frequency words. Say a word, ask a volunteer to point to it, and have children read it aloud. Then point to words at random and have children reread them. Repeat several times to reinforce instant recognition.

about  books  family  name  some

# Phonemic Awareness

**Objective** *To delete the beginning phoneme from a word*

Routine Card **9** **PHONEME DELETION** Tell children you will say a word and ask them to repeat it without the beginning sound. Model by saying: **The word is *harm*. Now say *harm* without /h/. The new word is *arm*.** Say the following and have children delete the first sound to form a new word.

*pin* without /p/ (in)

*cup* without /k/ (up)

*bend* without /b/ (end)

*where* without /hw/ (air)

*part* without /p/ (art)

*wheel* without /hw/ (eel)

*block* without /b/ (lock)

*thunder* without /th/ (under)

*for* without /f/ (or)

*that* without /th/ (at)

**wheel without /hw/ (eel)**

# Inflections -ed, -ing

**phonics**

**5-DAY PHONICS**

|  | |
|---|---|
| DAY 1 | Introduce /kw/*qu,* /hw/*wh* |
| DAY 2 | Word Building with /kw/*qu,* /hw/*wh* |
| DAY 3 | Build Words |
| **Day 4** | **Inflections -ed, -ing (CVC)** |
| DAY 5 | Inflections -ed, -ing (CVC) |

## Objectives

- *To recognize root words*
- *To read inflectional forms with -ed and -ing with a doubled final consonant*

## Skill Trace

**Tested** **Inflections -ed, -ing (double final consonant)**

| | |
|---|---|
| **Introduce** | T270–T271 |
| Review | T280, T444, T454 |
| Maintain | Bk 1-5, T98 |
| Test | Bk 1-3 |

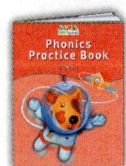
**phonics** **Resources**

**Phonics Practice Book, pp. 83–84**

---

**Inflections -ed, -ing (double final consonant)**

Pam <u>hopped</u> up and down.
She was looking for Grandma.
Pam <u>spotted</u> Grandma and <u>hugged</u> her.
Pam <u>grinned</u> and began <u>clapping</u> her hands.
She said, "Let's go <u>shopping</u>!"
"Yes! <u>Shopping</u> and <u>chatting</u> are fun!"
    said Grandma.

Grade 1, Lesson 15    R30    Phonics: Inflections -ed, -ing
(double final consonant)

**Transparency R30**

---

## Teach/Model

**INTRODUCE DOUBLING FINAL CONSONANTS** Write these words on the board:

**stop        stopped        stopping**

After you read the words, ask children to identify the root word and the endings added to it. *(stop; -ed, -ing)* Point out that the root word changed when each ending was added. Explain that when the root word has a short vowel followed by one consonant, the final consonant is doubled before the ending is added. Remind children that the ending -ed can stand for the sound /t/ in *stopped,* /d/ in *jogged,* and /əd/ in *skidded.*

## Guided Practice

**ADD ENDINGS** Make a chart as shown. Model reading the words by doing the following: Cover -ped in *stepped* and read the root word. Uncover, point to -ed, and say /t/. Blend the root word with the ending—*stepped.* Repeat for the other words, having children tell how to write the words in each row. Have them read the words aloud.

| Root Word | Double the consonant. Add -ed. | Double the consonant. Add -ing. |
|---|---|---|
| step | stepped | stepping |
| drag | dragged | dragging |
| hop | hopped | hopping |
| bat | batted | batting |

## Practice/Apply

**READ WORDS IN CONTEXT** Display **Transparency R30.** Have children read the sentences aloud. Then point to each underlined word, and have children tell how the root word changed when the ending was added.

# Digraphs /kw/ *qu,* /hw/ *wh* phonics *and Spelling*

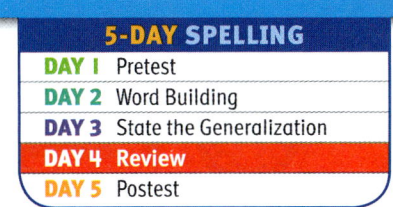

**5-DAY** SPELLING

| DAY 1 | Pretest |
| --- | --- |
| DAY 2 | Word Building |
| DAY 3 | State the Generalization |
| **DAY 4** | **Review** |
| DAY 5 | Postest |

## Build Words

**MAP LETTERS TO SOUNDS** Use *Letter Cards* and a pocket chart to form words. Have children listen to your directions and change one letter in each word to form a spelling word. Have them write the word on a sheet of paper or in their notebook. Then have a volunteer change the *Letter Card* in the pocket chart.

- Form *quilt* and have children read it. Ask: **Which spelling word can you make by taking out *l*?** (quit)

- Form *whip* and have children read it. Ask: **Which spelling word can you make by changing the last letter?** (whiz)

- Leave *whiz* in the pocket chart. Ask: **Which spelling word can you make by changing the first two letters?** (quiz)

Follow a similar procedure with the following words: *quiz* (quick), *then* (when), *art* (part), *part* (arm), and *rich* (which).

**HIGH-FREQUENCY WORDS** Remind children that there are some other words they have to remember how to spell. Tell them that *house* is one such word. Tell children to picture the word in their minds and then write it. Continue with *put*.

### Objectives

- *To use /kw/qu, /hw/wh, and other known letter-sounds to spell and write words*
- *To spell and write known high-frequency words*

### Spelling Words

| | | | |
| --- | --- | --- | --- |
| 1. | quit | 6. | when |
| 2. | quick | 7. | arm |
| 3. | quiz | 8. | part |
| 4. | whiz | 9. | house |
| 5. | which | 10. | put |

**E L L**

**Map Letters to Sounds** Some children may have difficulty differentiating /hw/ in *whiz* from /h/ in *his*. Provide additional practice by having children say /hw/*wh* words.

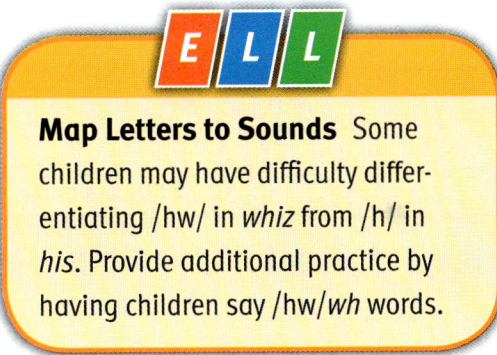

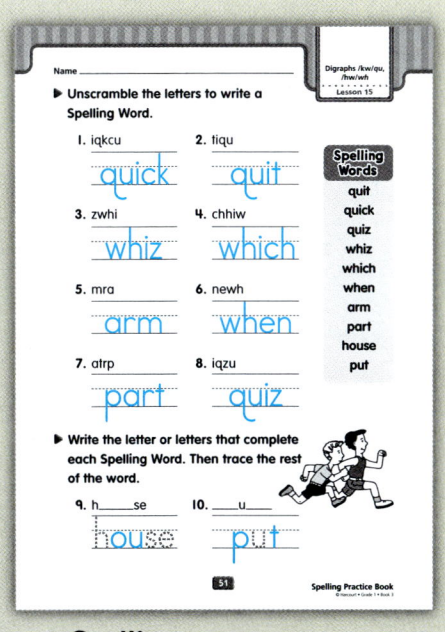

▲ **Spelling Practice Book, p. 51**

# High-Frequency Words

## Objective
- *To read high-frequency words*

REVIEW — Tested

### High-Frequency Words

| | |
|---|---|
| about | people |
| books | read |
| family | work |
| name | writing |

### ● ADVANCED

**Expand Sentences** Have children select several of the story strips to elaborate upon. For example, if children chose the sentence *He read lots of books,* they might expand it by writing: *He read lots of books about bugs, stars, and cars.*

### E L L

**Review Story Events** Use the *Student Edition* illustrations for support as you read each sentence aloud. Point out picture details to help clarify the text for children.

## Review

**READ AND WRITE WORDS** Duplicate and distribute to each child an uncut story strip page (*Teacher Resource Book,* p. 225). Then do the following:

- Have children read the story title on the first strip. Explain that the sentences tell the story, but some have missing words.

- Display *Word Cards* for the high-frequency words, or list the words on the board. Have children read each word.

## Practice/ Apply

**GUIDED PRACTICE** Direct children to read all the story strip sentences and to write the missing words in the blanks.

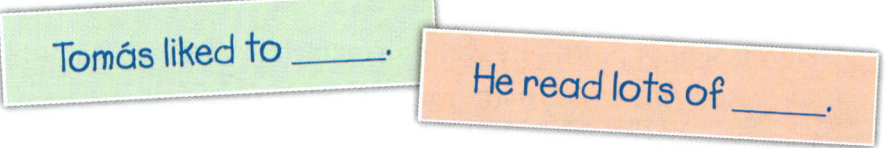

**INDEPENDENT PRACTICE** After children complete the story strip page, have them cut apart the strips, mix them up, and then arrange them back in the sequence of the selection. Have partners check each other to make sure the strips are in the correct order. Children can take the story strips home to share with family members.

Children read the words in context in the Cut-Out/Fold-Up Book "Ducks in the Night."

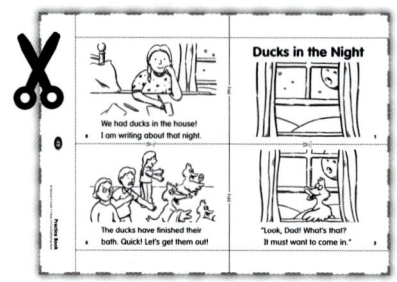

◄ **"Ducks in the Night"** *Practice Book,* pp. 49–50

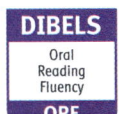

# Fluency
## *Reading Rate*

### Review

**MODEL READING AT AN APPROPRIATE RATE** Remind children that good readers are careful to read at the right speed so that they can understand the words. Show children how to:

▲ Student Edition, pp. 106–123

- choose the correct reading rate for the difficulty of the text.
- change the reading rate in response to the text.

**Think Aloud** **I'm going to read "Tomás Rivera" one page at a time. As I read, I'm going to make sure that I am reading at the right speed so that I can understand all the words and ideas. At times, I may read a little faster if the characters are speaking or a little slower if there is a lot of important information. Read each page after me, just the way I read it.**

### Practice/Apply

**GUIDED PRACTICE** Have partners reread "Tomás Rivera" aloud three or four times. Listen to partners read, giving them feedback about their reading rate and guidance for improving their fluency.

**INDEPENDENT PRACTICE** Have small groups take the parts of Tomás, Grandpa, and a narrator and practice reading "Tomás Rivera" fluently, adjusting their reading rate as needed. Then have each group make stick puppets with the character cutouts (*Teacher Resource Book,* page 194) and use them to act out the selection as they read it aloud for classmates. Have the audience listen carefully and politely to the performance.

### Objectives
- *To build fluency through rereading a selection*
- *To read at a rate appropriate for the text*

### BELOW-LEVEL

**Fluency Practice** Have children reread for fluency, using "Tom's Books" in the *Book 1-3 Strategic Intervention Interactive Reader, Decodable Book 15,* or the appropriate *Leveled Reader.* (See pages T288–T291.) Guide children to select a small portion of a story and practice reading it several times.

### Additional Related Reading

Guide children to self-select related books, such as these:

- ***Reading Makes You Feel Good*** by Todd Parr. Little, Brown, 2005. **EASY**
- ***I Can Be Anything*** by Ena Keo. Steck-Vaughn, 1997. **AVERAGE**
- ***All Kinds of Farms*** by Daniel Shepard. Capstone, 2004. **CHALLENGE**

# Sequence
*Comprehension*

## Objectives

- *To determine the sequence of events while listening to a selection*
- *To identify the selection as a text that has a sequenced text structure*

## Skill Trace

 **Sequence**

| | |
|---|---|
| Preview | T46 |
| Introduce | T54–T55 |
| Reteach | S6–S7, S26–S27 |
| **Review** | **T78, T90, T100, T230, T238–T239, T262, T274, T284** |
| Test | Bk 1-3 |
| Maintain | Monitor Comprehension, Bks 1-4, 1-5 |

 **MONITOR PROGRESS**

**Comprehension: Sequence**

| | |
|---|---|
| **IF** children have difficulty identifying the sequence of events, | **THEN** have them tell about a favorite story. Help them identify the order of events. |

**Small-Group Instruction, pp. S26–S27:**

- ● **BELOW-LEVEL:** Reteach
- ● **ON-LEVEL:** Reinforce
- ● **ADVANCED:** Extend

---

### Review

**TALK ABOUT SEQUENCE** Review how to recognize the sequence of events in a selection. Ask children what sequence is. (the order of events) Explain that in the *Big Book Fireflies, Fireflies, Light My Way,* there is an order in which the storyteller sees the animals. This order is repeated at the end of the book when all the animals are listed.

▲ **Big Book**

**USE PRIOR KNOWLEDGE/SET A PURPOSE** Guide children to use prior knowledge to set a purpose for listening to the book again.

**EXAMINE CONCEPTS OF PRINT** Guide children to look for repeated words. Ask volunteers to frame the words and read them with children. Point out the space between the words. Encourage children to participate actively when you read this patterned selection by inviting them to join in, especially on the repeated words and phrases.

### Practice/Apply

**GUIDED PRACTICE** Monitor listening comprehension as you read, using the following questions:

- **SETTING** **Where and when does this story take place? How do you know?** (It takes place at night in the woods near a pond. I know it's night because of the dark sky and because fireflies are seen at night.)

- **Page 30** **SEQUENCE** **How does this page help you remember the sequence of the story?** (The list shows the animals in the same order that the storyteller sees them; it shows the sequence of the story.)

**INDEPENDENT PRACTICE** Have children draw a simple map showing the storyteller's walk through the woods to the pond. Have them label the path with the animals the storyteller saw along the way. Then have them use this map to summarize the story sequence and retell the story.

# Build Robust Vocabulary

## Listening/Speaking: *Words About the Selection*

### Review Robust Vocabulary

**USE VOCABULARY IN DIFFERENT CONTEXTS** Remind children of the Student-Friendly Explanations of *accomplishment, admire, ambition.* Discuss each Vocabulary Word with them in a context different from the context of "Tomás Rivera." Use these examples:

**accomplishment** Tell children you will name some things. If they think it is an accomplishment they would want to achieve, they should say, "What an accomplishment!" If not, they should say nothing.

| | |
|---|---|
| becoming the President | writing a song |
| writing your name | fighting a fire |
| making a bed | taking a nap |

**admire** Tell children you will name some people. If they admire the person, they should clap. If not, they should do nothing.

| | |
|---|---|
| a sports star | a crying baby |
| a good student | a champion runner |
| a bank robber | the mayor of a big city |

**ambition** Tell children that you will name some activities. If they think that the activity names an ambition that most children have, they should signal "thumbs up." If not, they should do nothing.

| | |
|---|---|
| winning a race | hitting a home run |
| eating an apple | starring in a play |
| meeting a famous person | going to sleep |

## Objective

• *To review robust vocabulary*

### REVIEW

### Student-Friendly Explanations

**accomplishment** If you have had an accomplishment, you have worked hard to get something done.

**admire** If you admire someone, you think that person is very special because of the things he or she does.

**ambition** If you have an ambition, you want to do something very much.

 **ADVANCED**

**Using Words in Context** Have children share oral sentences in which they name one of their ambitions. Ask them to identify a person they admire for a similar accomplishment.

# Grammar

*Using I and Me*

**5-DAY GRAMMAR**

| | |
|---|---|
| **DAY 1** | Introduce Using *I* and *Me* |
| **DAY 2** | Dictate Sentences Using *I* and *Me* |
| **DAY 3** | Add *I* and *Me* to Sentences |
| **DAY 4** | Revise Sentences Using *I* and *Me* |
| **DAY 5** | Write Sentences Using *I* and *Me* |

## Objective

• *To use knowledge of the appropriate use of I and me in sentences*

## Daily Proofreading

**Jim and me are runing to school.**

(I, running)

---

### Review

**REVIEW USAGE OF *I* AND *ME*** Review that the word *I* is used in the naming part of a sentence and *me* is used in the telling part. Write on the board *Ann and me,* and have children read the words aloud. Ask: **Does this group of words belong in the naming part of a sentence or the telling part? These words belong in the telling part, because I see the word *me*. If I added words to make a sentence, I might say:** *Mom fixed a snack for Ann and me.* Add these words to complete the sentence, and have children read it aloud.

### Practice/Apply

**GUIDED PRACTICE** Write the following word groups on the board:

| | |
|---|---|
| Mark and I | Pam and me |
| Mom and I | Dad and me |
| you and I | you and me |

Tell children that some of these word groups belong in the naming part of a sentence, and others belong in the telling part. Ask children to identify in which part each word group belongs. Have children dictate words to complete each sentence.

**INDEPENDENT PRACTICE** Have children choose one of the word groups and write a new sentence using it. Have children work with partners to check that their sentences are written correctly.

Mark and I like to read about rockets.

---

**Name** _____

Using *I* and me
Lesson 15

▶ Circle each word group that belongs in the naming part of a sentence.

1. Cal and I
2. Ellen and me
3. Mom and me
4. you and I
5. you and me

▶ Choose three of the word groups and add words to them to make sentences. Write the sentences correctly.
Possible responses are shown.

6. Cal and I like pets.
7. Dad hugs Ellen and me.
8. You and I are pals.

59

Grammar Practice Book

▲ Grammar Practice Book, p. 59

# Independent Writing
## Personal Narrative

## Write Narratives

**GENERATE IDEAS** Tell children that they will write their own personal narrative about something that has happened in their life. Have them look again at the pictures they drew on Day 1. Then have them complete a story map about this event or another important time in their lives. Ask them to fill in the story map with pictures or words to tell about the beginning, middle, and ending of their story.

Beginning
↓
Middle
↓
Ending

**REVIEW CHARACTERISTICS** Display the list of characteristics of a well-written personal narrative from Day 1, and read it to children.

**WRITING TRAIT** **VOICE** Ask children to share sentences about how they feel about an event or experience in their life. Write the sentences on the board. Work with children to circle the words that describe feelings and that tell the reader that an idea is important.

**Personal Narrative**

- A personal narrative tells about something that has happened in a person's life.
- It has a beginning, a middle, and an ending.
- It has words like <u>I</u> and <u>me</u>.

 **WRITE** Tell children to write a draft of their personal narrative. Guide them to select a focus for their writing by telling them to look at their pictures and story maps for ideas. Have children use an organizational structure in their writing, referring to their story maps to help them write a beginning, a middle, and an ending.

## Objectives

- *To select a focus when writing*
- *To write a coherent personal narrative*

## Writing Prompt

**Sequence** Have children write several sentences in time-order telling what they have done during school today.

### BELOW-LEVEL

**Discuss the Sentences** If children have difficulty composing sentences for their personal narrative, allow them to share their story orally with you. Guide them in understanding that each part of their story can be written down to describe their personal experience.

### ADVANCED

**Elaborate on Ideas** Encourage children to elaborate on the events in their personal narratives by adding details. Ask them also to add unique words that will help to show their "voice" in their writing.

# Warm-Up Routines

## Day at a Glance

### Day 5

**Phonemic Awareness**
- Phoneme Segmentation and Deletion

 **phonics and Spelling**
- Review: Inflections -ed, -ing (double final consonant)
- Posttest: Digraphs /kw/*qu*, /hw/*wh*

**High-Frequency Words**
- Review

**Fluency**
- Reading Rate
- "Tomás Rivera," *Student Edition*, pp. 106–120

**Comprehension**
- Review: Sequence

**Robust Vocabulary**
- Review

**Grammar**
- Review: *Using* I *and* Me

**Independent Writing**
- Personal Narrative

---

## Oral Language

**Objective** *To listen attentively and respond appropriately to oral communication*

### Question of the Day

If you could create your own secret place, what would it look like?

Have children complete the following sentence frame.

**My secret place would look like _____ .**

---

## Read Aloud

**Objective** *To visualize and imagine the meaning of the text*

**BIG BOOK OF RHYMES AND POEMS**
Reread "And There" to children and have them describe what they think the poet's secret place looks like. Explain that many poems have a mood, such as happy, sad, or peaceful. Ask children what mood they feel from the poem, and why. Have children choral-read "And There" for enjoyment and to practice fluency.

▲ Big Book of Rhymes and Poems, p. 30

---

# Word Wall

**Objective** *To read high-frequency words*

**REVIEW HIGH-FREQUENCY WORDS** Review *people, read, work, writing, house, put,* and any other previously learned high-frequency words. Say a word, ask a volunteer to point to it, and have children read it aloud. Then point to words at random and have children reread them.

| people | read | writing |
|--------|------|---------|
| house | work | put |

# Phonemic Awareness

**Objectives** *To segment words into phonemes; to delete medial phonemes from words*

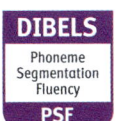
**DIBELS**
Phoneme Segmentation Fluency
**PSF**

**Routine Card 8**

**Routine Card 9**

**PHONEME SEGMENTATION AND DELETION** Tell children you will say a word and they will separate it into sounds. Then they will say the word without the middle consonant sound. Model by saying: **Say the sounds in *pats*—/p/ /a/ /t/ /s/. Say *pats* without the /t/—*pass*.** Use the following, having children segment the sounds and then delete the middle consonant sound:

**Say the sounds in *cast*.** (/k/ /a/ /s/ /t/)  **Say *cast* without /s/.** (cat)

**Say the sounds in *fact*.** (/f/ /a/ /k/ /t/)  **Say *fact* without /k/.** (fat)

**Say the sounds in *vest*.** (/v/ /e/ /s/ /t/)  **Say *vest* without /s/.** (vet)

**Say the sounds in *nest*.** (/n/ /e/ /s/ /t/)  **Say *nest* without /s/.** (net)

 Podcasting: Phoneme Segmentation

# Inflections -ed, -ing
## phonics

**5-DAY PHONICS**

| | |
|---|---|
| **DAY 1** | Introduce /kw/*qu*, /hw/*wh* |
| **DAY 2** | Word Building with /kw/*qu*, /hw/*wh* |
| **DAY 3** | Build Words |
| **DAY 4** | Inflections -*ed*, -*ing* (CVC) |
| **DAY 5** | Inflections -*ed*, -*ing* (CVC) |

## Objectives

- To recognize root words
- To read inflectional forms with spelling changes

## Skill Trace

 **Tested** Inflections -*ed*, -*ing* (double final consonant)

| | |
|---|---|
| Introduce | T270–T271 |
| Review | T280, T444, T454 |
| Maintain | Bk 1-5, T98 |
| Test | Bk 1-3 |

## Review

**ROOT WORDS AND ENDINGS** Remind children that if the root word has a short vowel followed by one consonant, the final consonant is doubled before an ending is added. Write *rip*. Say, **The word *ripping* is made by doubling the final consonant of *rip* and adding -*ing*: r-i-p-p-i-n-g.** Repeat for *ripped*.

## Work with Patterns

**ADD ENDINGS** Make a chart like the one below. Have children read each root word. Ask volunteers to underline the root word, circle the doubled consonant, and draw two lines under the ending.

| Root Word | Double the consonant. Add -*ed*. | Double the consonant. Add -*ing*. |
|---|---|---|
| quiz | quizzed | quizzing |
| whiz | whizzed | whizzing |
| bat | batted | batting |
| hop | hopped | hopping |

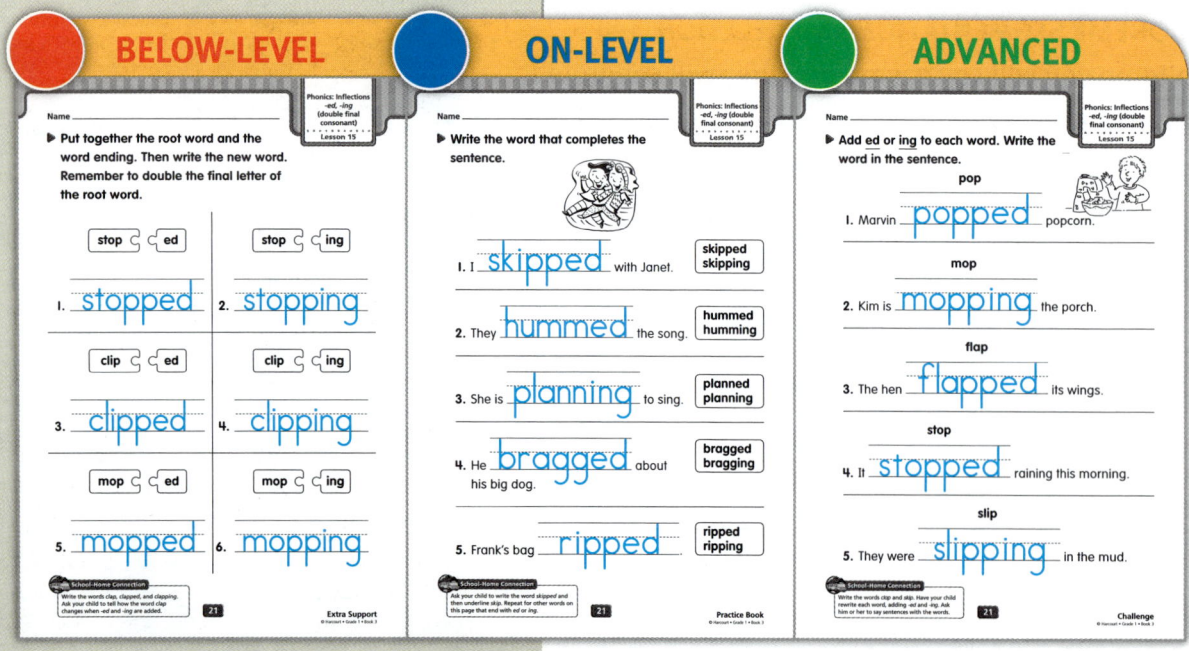

**BELOW-LEVEL**

Name ____

▶ Put together the root word and the word ending. Then write the new word. Remember to double the final letter of the root word.

stop ⊂ ⊃ ed       stop ⊂ ⊃ ing
1. stopped       2. stopping

clip ⊂ ⊃ ed       clip ⊂ ⊃ ing
3. clipped       4. clipping

mop ⊂ ⊃ ed       mop ⊂ ⊃ ing
5. mopped       6. mopping

**Extra Support**   21

**ON-LEVEL**

Name ____

▶ Write the word that completes the sentence.

1. I skipped with Janet.    [skipped / skipping]
2. They hummed the song.    [hummed / humming]
3. She is planning to sing.    [planned / planning]
4. He bragged about his big dog.    [bragged / bragging]
5. Frank's bag ripped    [ripped / ripping]

**Practice Book**   21

**ADVANCED**

Name ____

▶ Add ed or ing to each word. Write the word in the sentence.

pop
1. Marvin popped popcorn.

mop
2. Kim is mopping the porch.

flap
3. The hen flapped its wings.

stop
4. It stopped raining this morning.

slip
5. They were slipping in the mud.

**Challenge**   21

▲ Extra Support, p. 21    ▲ Practice Book, p. 21    ▲ Challenge, p. 21

## E L L

- Group children according to academic levels, and assign one of the pages on the left.

- Clarify any unfamiliar concepts as necessary. See *ELL Teacher Guide*, Lesson 15, for support in scaffolding instruction.

**5-DAY SPELLING**

| DAY 1 | Pretest |
|---|---|
| DAY 2 | Word Building |
| DAY 3 | State the Generalization |
| DAY 4 | Review |
| **DAY 5** | **Posttest** |

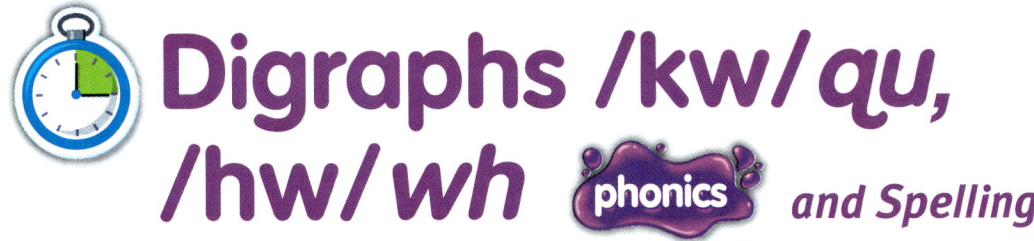

# Digraphs /kw/ *qu,* /hw/ *wh* phonics *and Spelling*

## Assess

**POSTTEST** Assess children's progress. Use the dictation sentences from Day 1.

**Words with /kw/ *qu,* /hw/ *wh***

1. quit — We won't **quit** until we are done.
2. quick — You have to be **quick** to win this race.
3. quiz — I want to get the answers right on the **quiz.**
4. whiz — Sam is a **whiz** at math.
5. which — Kate wondered **which** hat was hers.
6. when — I'll let you know **when** we're ready to go.

**Review**

7. arm — Ann fell and hurt her **arm.**
8. part — Jerome's bike needs a new **part.**

**High-Frequency**

9. house — My **house** is made of bricks.
10. put — Carla **put** a poster on her wall.

**WRITING APPLICATION** Have children complete and illustrate the following sentence frames.

> **I am a whiz at _____.**
>
> **We had a quick quiz on _____.**

I am a whiz at skating.

## Objectives

- *To use /kw/qu, /hw/wh, and other known letter-sounds to spell words*
- *To spell known high-frequency words*

### Spelling Words

| 1. **quit** | 6. **when** |
|---|---|
| 2. **quick** | 7. **arm** |
| 3 **quiz** | 8. **part** |
| 4. **whiz** | 9. **house** |
| 5. **which** | 10. **put** |

### BELOW-LEVEL

**Posttest** If children have difficulty spelling the decodable words, pronounce the words so that each phoneme can be distinctly heard—for example, /kw/ /i/ /t/. Have children repeat the segmented word as they write the letter or letters that stand for each phoneme.

#  High-Frequency Words

## Objectives
- *To read high-frequency words*
- *To explore word relationships*

**REVIEW** Tested ✓

### High-Frequency Words

| | |
|---|---|
| about | put |
| books | read |
| family | some |
| house | work |
| name | writing |
| people | |

---

**BELOW-LEVEL**

**Kinesthetic Support for Syllables** Review with children that a syllable is a word part that can be heard when they say the word. Have children hold a hand under their chin, touching it, and say each word to feel the number of syllables. Then have them sort the words according to the number of syllables, using *Word Cards* in a pocket chart.

---

## Review

**REINFORCE WORD RECOGNITION** Display *Word Cards* in a pocket chart. Point to words at random and have children read them.

**SORT WORDS** Lead children in reading each word aloud and clapping out the syllables. For example, the word *family* has three syllables. Then help children sort the words into three groups based on the number of syllables. Have them read the words in each column aloud.

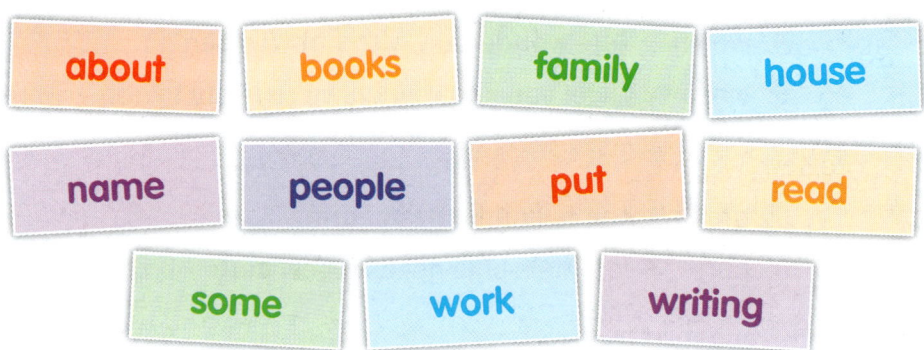

- Direct children to the words with one syllable. Ask: **Which of these words names more than one thing? How do you know?** (*books; an -s has been added to the root word.*)

- Point to the word *read*. Ask: **What are two ways to say this word?** (*/rēd/ and /red/*) Have volunteers use the words in sentences.

- Ask: **Which words name things you might see at home?** (*books, family, house, people*)

- Ask: **Which words name things you might do at home?** (*read, work, writing*)

- Ask: **Which words end with the /t/ sound?** (*about, put*)

- Ask: **Which words end with the /m/ sound?** (*name, some*)

# Fluency
## *Reading Rate*

**DIBELS**
Oral Reading Fluency
**ORF**

**PERFORM "TOMÁS RIVERA"** To help children improve their fluency, have them perform "Tomás Rivera" as a Readers' Theater. Use the following procedures:

- Read "Tomás Rivera" aloud, modeling fluent reading at a rate appropriate for the text. Have children follow along.

- Discuss how your rate of reading changes depending on whether the characters are speaking about everyday things or there are a lot of facts and important information in the text.

- Assign children to groups of three and have them read the story together. One child can choose the part of the narrator while the other two read the parts of Grandpa and Tomás. Have them practice reading the story fluently, adjusting their reading rate as needed.

- Listen to the groups read. Provide feedback and support.

- Invite each group to read the selection to classmates. Remind children to focus on reading at an appropriate reading rate.

### Objective
- *To read fluently with an appropriate reading rate*

**✓ ASSESSMENT**

**Monitor Progress** Periodically, take a timed sample of children's oral reading and measure the number of words read correctly per minute. Children should be accurately reading approximately 60 words per minute by the end of Grade 1.

**ELL**

**Develop Vocabulary** Discuss words related to Tomás Rivera, such as *library, stories, teacher, Texas,* and *Grandpa.* Read with children the sentences in the selection that contain these words, and discuss the words' meanings. Encourage children to reread these sentences at an appropriate reading rate.

### Fluency Support Materials

**Fluency Builders, Grade 1,** Lesson 15
● ● ●

**Audiotext** *Student Edition* selections are available on *Audiotext Grade 1,* CD 3.

**Strategic Intervention Teacher Guide,** Lesson 15

# Sequence
## *Comprehension*

## Objective
- *To identify and describe the sequence of a selection*

## Skill Trace

 **Sequence**

| | |
|---|---|
| Preview | T46 |
| Introduce | T54–T55 |
| Reteach | S6–S7, S26–S27 |
| **Review** | **T78, T90, T100, T230, T238–T239, T262, T274, T284** |
| Test | Bk 1-3 |
| Maintain | Monitor Comprehension, Bks 1-4, 1-5 |

---

## ADVANCED

**Independent Practice** Invite children to retell in the correct sequence the important events of other stories they have read. Ask them to tell how they were able to determine the sequence.

---

### Review

**REVIEW THE SKILL** Ask children to explain what the sequence of a story is. (It is the order in which events happen in a story.) Draw a three-column chart on the board with the titles "The Best Apple Crisp in the World," "Tomás Rivera," and *Fireflies, Fireflies, Light My Way.* Write the sequence of events for "The Best Apple Crisp in the World" in the first column. Read the sequence aloud to children. Guide children to retell the spoken message by summarizing it.

### Practice/Apply

**GUIDED PRACTICE** Ask volunteers to name the sequence of events in "Tomás Rivera." Write their responses in the second column of the chart. Then have them tell the sequence of events in *Fireflies, Fireflies, Light My Way,* and write them in the last column.

| "The Best Apple Crisp in the World" | "Tomás Rivera" | Fireflies, Fireflies, Light My Way |
|---|---|---|
| First, | First, | First, |
| Next, | Next, | Next, |
| Last, | Last, | Last, |

**INDEPENDENT PRACTICE** Have children page through their *Student Edition* to help them recall selections they have already read. Ask each of them to name one of the selections and tell about the sequence of events in the story. You may want to have children do this activity with the Get Started Story "A Quiz for Brent."

# Build Robust Vocabulary

*Listening/Speaking*

---

### Review

**REINFORCE MEANINGS** Ask children the following questions:

- If someone has made an *accomplishment,* do you think he or she had an *ambition?* Why?

- Do you think you would *admire* someone who *triumphantly* won the Olympics?

- How would you feel if you were *interrupted* while *cozily* reading in your bed?

**MAKE WORD WEBS** Guide children to complete word webs to enrich their understanding of *accomplishment* and *ambition,* using **Transparency GO6**. Write *accomplishment* in the center of a word web and have children name people and tell about their major accomplishments. Write their responses around the wheel.

the Olympic athlete who won the marathon

My grandma knits blankets for people in the hospital.

**accomplishment**

Mr. Park— teacher of the year

My dad taught me how to swim.

Begin another word web for *ambition.* Have children share some of their ambitions and record their responses.

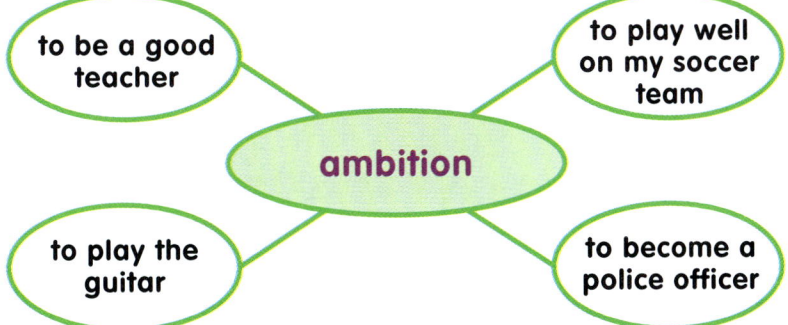

to be a good teacher

to play well on my soccer team

**ambition**

to play the guitar

to become a police officer

---

### Objective

- *To review robust vocabulary*

REVIEW Tested

**Build Robust Vocabulary**

| | |
|---|---|
| cozily | accomplishment |
| interrupted | admire |
| triumphantly | ambition |

---

✓ **MONITOR PROGRESS**

**Build Robust Vocabulary**

**IF** children do not demonstrate understanding of the words and have difficulty using them,

**THEN** model using each word in several sentences, and have children repeat each sentence.

**Small-Group Instruction, pp. S28–S29:**

🔴 **BELOW-LEVEL:** Reteach
🔵 **ON-LEVEL:** Reinforce
🟢 **ADVANCED:** Extend

---

# Grammar
## Using *I* and *Me*

| 5-DAY GRAMMAR | |
| --- | --- |
| DAY 1 | Introduce Using *I* and *Me* |
| DAY 2 | Dictate Sentences Using *I* and *Me* |
| DAY 3 | Add *I* and *Me* to Sentences |
| DAY 4 | Revise Sentences Using *I* and *Me* |
| DAY 5 | Write Sentences Using *I* and *Me* |

## Objective

- *To write sentences correctly using* I *and* me

## Daily Proofreading

**dad plays basketball with I.**

(Dad, me)

 ## Language Arts Checkpoint

If children have difficulty with the concepts, see page S30–S31 to reteach.

▲ **Practice Book, p. 22**

## Review

**COMPOSE SENTENCES USING *I* AND *ME*** Model sentences using *I* and *me* that are related to the *Big Book Fireflies, Fireflies, Light My Way.* Write the sentences on the board, and have children read them silently and then aloud. Ask children to tell why the words *I* and *me* are used correctly. (*I* is used in the naming part of a sentence and *me* is used in the telling part.)

| | |
| --- | --- |
| **I am at the pond.** | **Come run with me!** |
| **Tim and I see a frog.** | **Come jump with Tim and me!** |

## Practice/Apply

**GUIDED PRACTICE** Have volunteers say sentences using *I* and *me* about other animals that make the woods or a pond their home. Write each one on the board, occasionally making errors in the way the pronouns are used. Work with children to correct the errors. Have them identify in which part of the sentence *I* or *me* appears.

**INDEPENDENT PRACTICE** Have partners choose one animal that they might see in a nearby woods or pond. Have each pair work together to write two sentences about the animal, using the words *I* and *me*. Have them illustrate their sentences with a large picture of their animal on the same paper.

Then have children attach their work to a long piece of mural paper or display it along a hallway. Have pairs take turns leading a "nature walk" through the woods by reading their sentences and pointing out their animals to others in the group.

Carla and I see a fox in his den. The fox runs by Carla and me.

# Independent Writing

*Personal Narrative*

| 5-DAY WRITING | |
|---|---|
| **DAY 1** | Modeled Writing |
| **DAY 2** | Shared Writing |
| **DAY 3** | Shared Writing |
| **DAY 4** | Independent Writing |
| **DAY 5** | **Independent Writing** |

## Write Independently

**WRITE** Have children continue writing their personal narratives from Day 4. Remind them that their story should tell about something that has happened in their lives.

**WRITING TRAIT** **VOICE** Remind children that good writers use words to let their readers know what things are important. They use words to show how they feel. Encourage children to do these things in their writing.

> ### Personal Narrative
> • A personal narrative tells about something that has happened in a person's life.
>
> • It has a beginning, a middle, and an ending.
>
> • It has words like I and me.

**REVISE** Have children read their personal narratives to a partner and check to see that the story tells about things that really happened. Read the list of criteria for a Personal Narrative to children, and have them use the list to improve their writing. Challenge children to use in their writing some of the high-frequency words they have learned. Have them add words and fix mistakes until they are satisfied with their personal narrative. Encourage children to write their story on several pages and illustrate it. Children can make a binding, creating a book version.

## Share

**AUTHOR'S CHAIR** After children make a final copy of their stories, invite them to take turns in the Author's Chair. You may want to make a video-tape for family members to view. Encourage children to read at an appropriate rate so that listeners can understand their story. Remind the audience to listen attentively and to applaud at the end of a story. End the presentation by asking children to summarize the important events in the correct order for each story.

## Objectives

• *To write, edit, publish, and share a coherent personal narrative*

• *To use voice in writing*

### Writing Prompt

**Learning** Have children write about something they hope to learn this year.

## WEEKLY LESSON TEST

▲ **Weekly Lesson Tests, pp. 148–159**

• Selection Comprehension with Short Response
• Phonics and Spelling
• High-Frequency Words
• Focus Skill
• Robust Vocabulary
• Grammar
• Fluency

**GO online** For prescriptions, see p. A4. Also available electronically on *StoryTown* Online Assessment and ExamView®.

 **Podcasting:** Assessing Fluency

# Leveled Readers

*Reinforcing Skills and Strategies*

**Genre: Biography**

## BELOW-LEVEL

## Susan L. Roth

**SUMMARY** Readers meet author and illustrator Susan L. Roth and learn about her life and some of her books about animals.

- **phonics** Digraphs /kw/*qu*, /hw/*wh*
- **High-Frequency Words:** *about, books, family, name, people, read, work, writing*
- Sequence

### LEVELED READER TEACHER GUIDE

▲ **High-Frequency Words, p. 5**

### Before Reading

**BUILD BACKGROUND/SET A PURPOSE** Have children tell the title of their favorite book about animals and explain why it is their favorite. Talk about the roles of authors and illustrators. Ask children if writing and illustrating books would be something they might like to do one day. Guide children to preview the book and set a purpose for reading it.

### Reading the Book

**PAGES 2–3 SEQUENCE** After Susan L. Roth made animals, what did her parents like to do? (hang up her work)

**PAGES 2–5 GRAPHIC AIDS** What materials does Susan use to make her animals? (Possible responses: fabric, yarn, paper)

**REREAD FOR FLUENCY** Have partners read alternate pages of the selection several times with expression and at an appropriate rate.

### Think Critically    *(See inside back cover for questions.)*

1. **SEQUENCE** She made animals. She writes and makes animals.

2. **MAKE INFERENCES** Possible response: Yes, because they were quick to hang her work.

3. **GENRE** Possible response: It is nonfiction because the book has pictures of a real person and is about real events.

4. **NOTE DETAILS** *It's a Dog's New York.*

5. **PERSONAL RESPONSE** Reponses will vary.

▲ **Comprehension, p. 6**

www.harcourtschool.com/storytown

**Go online**

★ **Leveled Readers, online**
*Searchable by genre, skill, vocabulary, level, or title*
★ **Student Activities and Teacher Resources, online**

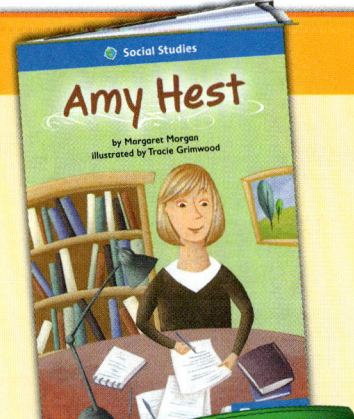

Social Studies

**Amy Hest**
by Margaret Morgan
illustrated by Tracie Grimwood

**Genre: Biography**

## ON-LEVEL

# Amy Hest

**SUMMARY** Readers meet author Amy Hest, who enjoyed reading books as a child and now enjoys writing them, especially about families.

- **phonics** **Digraphs /kw/** *qu*, **/hw/** *wh*
- **High-Frequency Words:** *about, books, family, name, people, read, work, writing*
- **Sequence**

### Before Reading

**BUILD BACKGROUND/SET A PURPOSE** Invite children to pretend they are a famous author who is writing a book about his or her family. Say: **Name some characters for your book. What title would you use?** Then guide children to preview *Amy Hest* and set a purpose for reading this book.

### Reading the Book

**PAGES 4–8** **CLASSIFY/CATEGORIZE** **Name some kinds of things Amy likes to write about.** (Possible responses: families, animals, things people say)

**PAGE 8** **SEQUENCE** **When Amy finds it hard to think, what does she do?** (She eats something good.) **Then what is she able to do?** (more writing)

**REREAD FOR FLUENCY** Have partners choose the pages they found most interesting about Amy Hest and read them aloud several times at an appropriate speed and with expression.

### Think Critically
*(See inside back cover for questions.)*

1 **GENRE** Possible response: It gives true information and has photographs.

2 **SEQUENCE** She read books. She writes books.

3 **SPECULATE** Possible responses: food gives you energy; it's hard to think when you are hungry.

4 **NOTE DETAILS** Things people say help Amy.

5 **PERSONAL RESPONSE** Reponses will vary.

**LEVELED READER TEACHER GUIDE**

▲ **High-Frequency Words, p. 5**

▲ **Comprehension, p. 6**

# Leveled Readers
*Reinforcing Skills and Strategies*

**ADVANCED**

## Joseph Bruchac

**SUMMARY** Readers meet Joseph Bruchac, an author who likes writing and telling tales. They learn about his childhood and how it influenced him.

**Genre: Biography**

 **phonics** Digraphs /kw/*qu*, /hw/*wh*
- **High-Frequency Words:** *about, books, family, name, people, read, work, writing*
- **Sequence**

### Before Reading

**BUILD BACKGROUND/SET A PURPOSE** Ask: **Have you ever listened to someone tell a story or tale? What was it about?** Have children preview the book and set a purpose for reading it.

### Reading the Book

**PAGES 2–8** **SEQUENCE** **What did Joseph like to do with his grandma when he was young?** (read) **What did he hear in the shop?** (tales) **When he is grown, what does Joseph tell?** (his own tales) **Where might you find one of his tales?** (in a book he has written)

**PAGE 7 GRAPHIC AIDS** Looking at Joseph Bruchac's book covers on page 7, what do you think these stories are about? (Possible responses: a chipmunk, a runner, a turtle)

**REREAD FOR FLUENCY** Have children reread the selection aloud several times at a speech-like pace.

### Think Critically *(See inside back cover for questions.)*

1. **SEQUENCE** He read them with his grandma. He writes books.

2. **NOTE DETAILS** his grandma and grandpa

3. **GENRE** Possible response: It gives true information and has photographs.

4. **SPECULATE** Possible responses: He gets them from the tales he heard growing up and from his walks in the hills with his grandpa.

5. **PERSONAL RESPONSE** Reponses will vary.

**LEVELED READER TEACHER GUIDE**

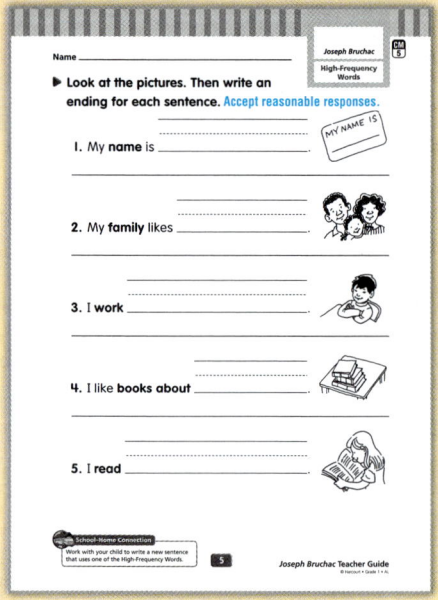

▲ High-Frequency Words, p. 5

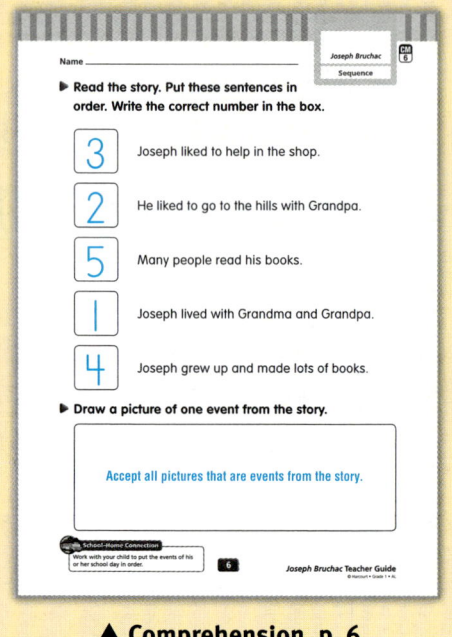

▲ Comprehension, p. 6

## www.harcourtschool.com/storytown

**Go online**

★ **Leveled Readers, online**
*Searchable by genre, skill, vocabulary, level, or title*
★ **Student Activities and Teacher Resources, online**

*by Margaret Morgan*

**Genre: Nonfiction**

# Grandparents

**SUMMARY** Readers discover some of the fun things that children and grandparents can do together.

- **Strong Picture Support**
- **Concept Vocabulary**
- **Scaffolded Language Development**

## Before Reading

**BUILD BACKGROUND/SET A PURPOSE** Have children tell about things they enjoy doing with their grandparents. Make a list. Then guide children to preview the book and set a purpose for reading it. Afterward, review the list with children and check off the fun things that were mentioned in the book.

## Reading the Book

**PAGES 2–8**  **SEQUENCE, AUTHOR'S PURPOSE/POINT OF VIEW** What does the author want readers to know? (Children can have fun with their grandparents.) **What is the first thing the author says children and grandparents can do together?** (go for walks) **Next?** (read books) **Then?** (play games) **Last?** (shop)

**PAGES 7–8 PERSONAL RESPONSE** Do your grandparents live near or far away? What do you like to do most with your grandparents when they visit? (Responses will vary.)

**REREAD FOR FLUENCY** Have children choral-read with you, using the same expression, intonation, and rate.

## Scaffolded Language Development

*(See inside back cover for teacher-led activity.)*

Provide additional examples and explanation as needed.

**LEVELED READER TEACHER GUIDE**

▲ **Build Background, p. 5**

▲ **Scaffolded Language Development, p. 6**

# Lesson 16

## WEEK AT A GLANCE

### Phonemic Awareness
Phoneme Blending, Segmentation, and Deletion

### ✓ Phonics
*r*-Controlled Vowels /ûr/*er, ir, ur*
Inflections *-er, -est*

### ✓ Spelling
*her, fur, turn, bird, girl, first, quit, when, name, work*

### ✓ High-Frequency Words
*always, by, Cow's, join, nice, please, room*

### Reading
**"One More Friend"** by Alma Flor Ada
FANTASY

**"Good Friends"** NONFICTION

### ✓ Fluency
Reading Rate

### ✓ Comprehension
 Main Idea
 Summarize

### ✓ Robust Vocabulary
*captured, mercy, struggling, compatible, amiable, relax*

### ✓ Grammar
Using *He, She, It,* and *They*

### Writing
Form: Invitation
Trait: Ideas

### Weekly Lesson Test

 = Focus Skill      = Focus Strategy      = Tested Skill

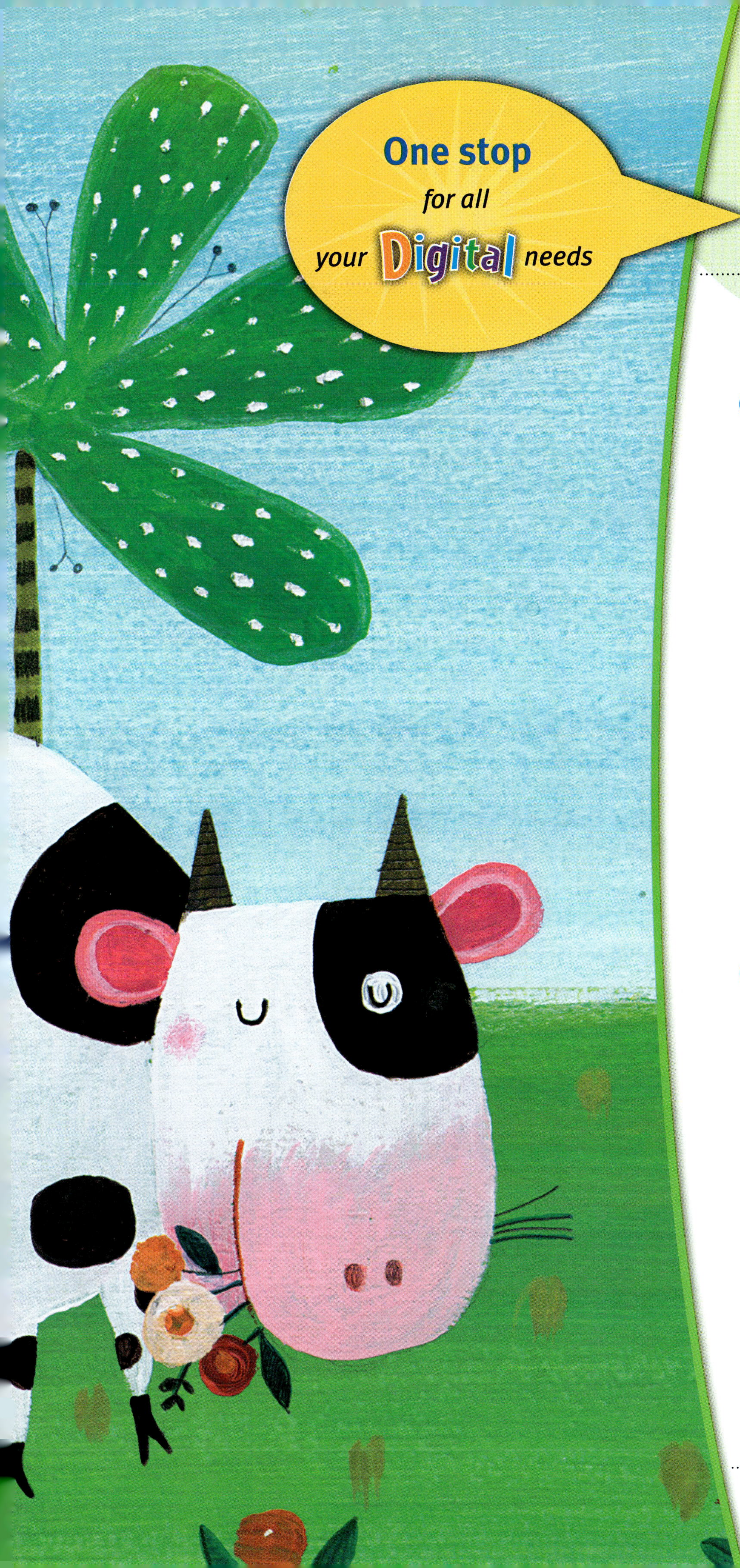

One stop *for all* your **Digital** needs

# Digital
## CLASSROOM

 www.harcourtschool.com/storytown
*To go along with your print program*

## FOR THE TEACHER

**Prepare**
 Professional Development
*in the Online TE*

 **Videos for Podcasting**

**Plan & Organize**
 Online TE & Planning Resources*

**Teach**
 Transparencies
*for electronic projection*

**Assess**
 Online Assessment*
*with Student Tracking System and Prescriptions*

## FOR THE STUDENT

**Read**
 Student eBook*

 Strategic Intervention Interactive Reader

 Leveled Readers

**Practice & Apply**
 Splash into Phonics CD-ROM

 *Also available on CD-ROM

# Literature Resources

## STUDENT EDITION

 Go online eBook STUDENT EDITION

 Get Started Story

**A Perfect Lunch, pp. 130–137**

**Genre: Fantasy**

**Genre Study**
A **fantasy** is a story that has make-believe characters and events.

**Comprehension Strategy**
**Summarize** As you read, stop every few pages and think about the important things that have happened so far.

142

143

 **SOCIAL STUDIES** **One More Friend, pp. 142–159**

*retold by Alma Flor Ada, illustrated by Sophie Fatus* One by one, friends are invited to climb in to share the hammock. When a huge elephant arrives, it finds its own way to join in.

 Accelerated Reader™

*Practice Quizzes for the Selection*

**Audiotext** *Student Edition selections are available on Audiotext Grade 1, CD 3 and 6.*

Paired Selections

**Genre: Nonfiction**

◀ **Reading Across Texts** **Comparing a Fantasy and Nonfiction**

## ADDITIONAL READING

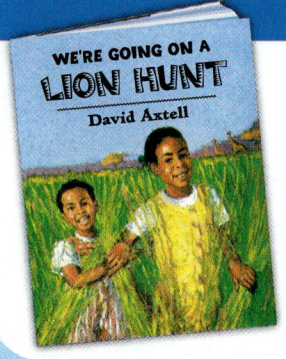

**Big Book** *We're Going on a Lion Hunt*

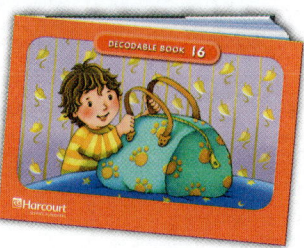

**Decodable Book** "Helping a Bird," "King Curtis and Shirl," "Burt's Bag"

★ Applies *r*-Controlled Vowels /ûr/er, ir, ur

# Support for Differentiated Instruction

 **LEVELED READERS**

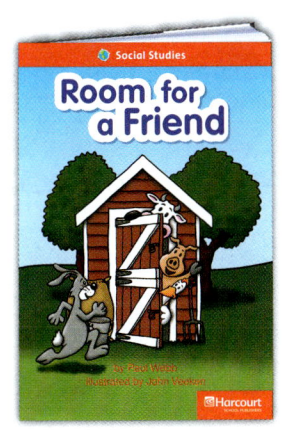

● **BELOW-LEVEL**

● **ON-LEVEL**

● **ADVANCED**

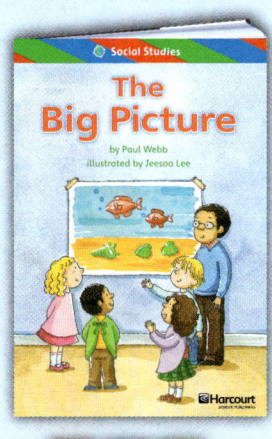

**E L L**

## LEVELED PRACTICE

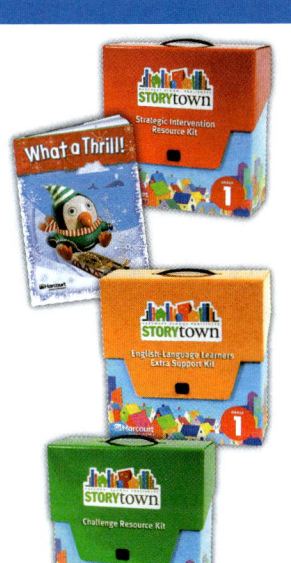

◄ **Strategic Intervention Resource Kit, Lesson 16**

◄ **Strategic Intervention Interactive Reader, Lesson 16**
Strategic Intervention Interactive Reader Online

◄ **ELL Extra Support Kit, Lesson 16**

◄ **Challenge Resource Kit, Lesson 16**

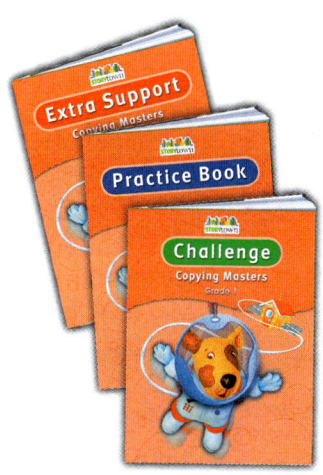

● **BELOW-LEVEL**
Extra Support Copying Masters, pp. 23–28

● **ON-LEVEL**
Practice Book, pp. 23–29

● **ADVANCED**
Challenge Copying Masters, pp. 23–28

## ADDITIONAL RESOURCES

• Spelling Practice Book, pp. 52–54
• Grammar Practice Book, pp. 61–64
• Reading Transparencies R31–R32
• Language Arts Transparencies LA31–LA32
• Test Prep System
◄ Literacy Center Kit, Cards 76–80
◄ Sound/Spelling Card
• Fluency Builders
◄ Photo Cards
• Read-Aloud Anthology, p. 62

## ASSESSMENT

✓ **Weekly Lesson Tests**
• Comprehension
• Phonics and Spelling
• Focus Skill
• Robust Vocabulary
• High-Frequency Words
• Grammar
• Fluency

 **www.harcourtschool.com/storytown**
• Online Assessment
*Also available on CD-ROM—ExamView®*

| | **Day 1** | **Day 2** |
|---|---|---|
| **Step 1 Whole Group** | | |

### Daily Language
- Oral Language
- High-Frequency Words
- Shared Reading
- Phonemic Awareness

**Day 1**

**QUESTION OF THE DAY,** p. T304
*Think about a lion you have seen. Where did you see it, what did it look like, and what was it doing?*

**READ ALOUD,** p. T304
*Big Book: We're Going on a Lion Hunt*

**WORD WALL,** p. T305

✓ **PHONEMIC AWARENESS,** p. T305
Phoneme Blending

▲ Big Book

**Day 2**

**QUESTION OF THE DAY,** p. T320
*How might a new child in our class feel? Why?*

**SHARED READING,** p. T320
*Big Book of Rhymes and Poems,* "The New Girl"

**WORD WALL,** p. T321

✓ **PHONEMIC AWARENESS,** p. T321
Phoneme Segmentation

### Word Work

- phonics
- Spelling
- High-Frequency Words

**Day 1**

✓ phonics, p. T306
Introduce: *r*-Controlled Vowel /ûr/*er, ir, ur*

✓ **SPELLING,** p. T309
Pretest: *her, fur, turn, bird, girl, first, quit, when, name, work*

✓ **HIGH-FREQUENCY WORDS,** p. T311
Review: *no, now, oh, out, friends*

**Day 2**

✓ phonics, p. T322
Review: *r*-Controlled Vowel /ûr/*er, ir, ur*

✓ **SPELLING,** p. T322
Word Building

✓ **HIGH-FREQUENCY WORDS**
Words to Know, p. T326
Introduce: *always, by, Cow's, join, nice, please, room*

### Skills and Strategies
- Reading
- Fluency
- Comprehension
- Build Robust Vocabulary

**Day 1**

**READING,** p. T310
Get Started Story, "A Perfect Lunch"
Decodable Text
*Options for Reading*

 Read!

▲ Student Edition

✓ **FLUENCY,** p. T315
Reading Rate

✓ **COMPREHENSION,** p. T316
Read-Aloud: "The Lion and the Mouse"
🌀 Preview: Main Idea

✓ **BUILD ROBUST VOCABULARY,** p. T317
Introduce: *captured, mercy, struggling*

**Day 2**

**READING,** p. T328
"One More Friend"
*Options for Reading*

 Read!

▲ Student Edition

✓ **COMPREHENSION,** pp. T324, T328
🌀 Introduce: Main Idea
🌀 Introduce: Summarize

✓ **RETELLING/FLUENCY,** p. T338
Reading Rate

✓ **BUILD ROBUST VOCABULARY,** p. T339
Review: *captured, mercy, struggling*

**Step 2 Small Groups**

**Suggestions for Differentiated Instruction** *(See pp. 298–T299.)*

**Step 3 Whole Group**

### Language Arts
- Grammar
- Writing

**Day 1**

✓ **GRAMMAR,** p. T318
Introduce: Using *He, She, It,* and *They*

*Daily Proofreading*
The lion naps in hs den *(his, den.)*

 **MODELED WRITING,** p. T319
Introduce: Invitation
Writing Trait: Ideas

**Writing Prompt** *Draw and write about a time when you were invited to do something fun.*

**Day 2**

✓ **GRAMMAR,** p. T340
Review: Using *He, She, It,* and *They*

*Daily Proofreading*
she is my friend *(She, friend.)*

 **SHARED WRITING,** p. T341
Review: Invitation
Writing Trait: Ideas

**Writing Prompt** *List people you would invite and things you would need for a party.*

 **= Focus Skill**     **= Focus Strategy**     **= Tested Skill**

**Skills at a Glance**

 **phonics**
• *r*-Controlled Vowel /ûr/*er, ir, ur*
• Inflections *–er, –est*

**Comprehension**
FOCUS SKILL Main Idea
FOCUS STRATEGY Summarize

**Phonemic Awareness**
Phoneme Blending, Segmentation, and Deletion
**Fluency**
Reading Rate

**Vocabulary**
HIGH-FREQUENCY: *always, by, Cow's, join, nice, please, room*
ROBUST: *captured, mercy, struggling, compatible, amiable, relax*

# Day 3

**QUESTION OF THE DAY,** p. T342
*Think about your friends. How would you describe what a friend is?*

**SHARED READING,** p. T342
*Big Book of Rhymes and Poems,* "The New Girl"

**WORD WALL,** p. T343

✓ **PHONEMIC AWARENESS,** p. T343
Phoneme Deletion

✓  , p. T344
Review: *r*-Controlled Vowel /ûr/*er, ir, ur*; Short Vowels /i/*i*, /e/*e*, /u/*u*

✓ **SPELLING,** p. T345
State the Generalization

✓ **HIGH-FREQUENCY WORDS,** p. T346
Review: *always, by, Cow's, join, nice, please, room*

✓ **FLUENCY,** p. T347
Reading Rate:
"One More Friend"

✓ **COMPREHENSION,** p. T348
Review: Main Idea
Paired Selection:
"Good Friends"

▲ Student Edition

**CONNECTIONS,** p. T350

✓ **BUILD ROBUST VOCABULARY,** p. T351
Introduce: *compatible, amiable, relax*

# Day 4

**QUESTION OF THE DAY,** p. T354
*What animal do you think makes the best pet? Tell why you think so.*

**SHARED READING,** p. T354
*Big Book of Rhymes and Poems,* "Notice"

**WORD WALL,** p. T355

✓ **PHONEMIC AWARENESS,** p. T355
Phoneme Deletion

✓  , p. T356
Introduce: Inflections *–er, –est*

✓ **SPELLING,** p. T357
Review Spelling Words

✓ **HIGH-FREQUENCY WORDS,** p. T358
Review: *always, by, Cow's, join, nice, please, room*

✓ **FLUENCY,** p. T359
Reading Rate:
"One More Friend"

✓ **COMPREHENSION,** p. T360
Review: Main Idea
*Big Book: We're Going on a Lion Hunt*

▲ Student Edition

✓ **BUILD ROBUST VOCABULARY,** p. T361
Review: *compatible, amiable, relax*

# Day 5

**QUESTION OF THE DAY,** p. T364
*What kind of pet do you have or would like to have?*

**SHARED READING,** p. T364
*Big Book of Rhymes and Poems,* "Notice"

**WORD WALL,** p. T365

✓ **PHONEMIC AWARENESS,** p. T365
Phoneme Blending and Segmentation

✓ 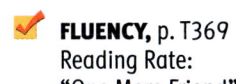 , p. T366
Review: Inflections *–er, –est*

✓ **SPELLING,** p. T367
Posttest

✓ **HIGH-FREQUENCY WORDS,** p. T368
Review: *always, by, Cow's, join, nice, please, room*

✓ **FLUENCY,** p. T369
Reading Rate:
"One More Friend"

✓ **COMPREHENSION,** p. T370
Review: Main Idea

▲ Student Edition

✓ **BUILD ROBUST VOCABULARY,** p. T371
Review

---

● **BELOW-LEVEL** ● **ON-LEVEL** ● **ADVANCED** **E L L**

---

✓ **GRAMMAR,** p. T352
Review: Using *He, She, It,* and *They*

***Daily Proofreading***
she and I like to swim (She, swim.)

✏ **SHARED WRITING,** p. T353
Review: Invitation
Writing Trait: Ideas

**Writing Prompt** *Describe how the invitations your class wrote are alike and different.*

✓ **GRAMMAR,** p. T362
Review: Using *He, She, It,* and *They*

***Daily Proofreading***
they had fun at the zoo (They, zoo.)

✏ **INDEPENDENT WRITING,** p. T363
Review: Invitation
Writing Trait: Ideas

**Writing Prompt** *Write about a favorite occasion or holiday that your family celebrates.*

✓ **GRAMMAR,** p. T372
Review: Using *He, She, It,* and *They*

***Daily Proofreading***
it feels nice in the shade (It, shade.)

✏ **INDEPENDENT WRITING,** p. T373
Review: Invitation
Writing Trait: Ideas

**Writing Prompt** *Write about a party, picnic, or other event to which you were invited.*

# Suggested Small Group Planner

45-60+ Minutes

| | Day 1 | Day 2 |
|---|---|---|
|   15+ Min. each ● **BELOW-LEVEL** | **Teacher-Directed** *Student Edition:* Get Started Story, "A Perfect Lunch," p. T310  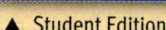 ▲ Student Edition **Independent** ⭐ Listening/Speaking Center, p. T302 Extra Support Copying Masters, p. 23 | **Teacher-Directed** *Student Edition:* "One More Friend," p. T328  ▲ Student Edition **Independent** ⭐ Reading Center, p. T302 Extra Support Copying Masters, p. 25 |
|   15+ Min. each ● **ON-LEVEL** | **Teacher-Directed** *Student Edition:* Get Started Story, "A Perfect Lunch," p. T310   ▲ Student Edition **Independent** ⭐ Reading Center, p. T302 Practice Book, p. 23 | **Teacher-Directed** *Student Edition:* "One More Friend," p. T328  ▲ Student Edition **Independent** ⭐ Letters and Sounds Center, p. T303 Practice Book, p. 25 |
|   15+ Min. each ● **ADVANCED** | **Teacher-Directed** Leveled Reader: "A New Friend," p. T376 Before Reading  ▲ Leveled Reader **Independent** ⭐ Letters and Sounds Center, p. T303 Challenge Copying Masters, p. 23 | **Teacher-Directed** Leveled Reader: "A New Friend," p. T376 Read the Book  ▲ Leveled Reader **Independent** ⭐ Word Work Center, p. T303 Challenge Copying Masters, p. 25 |
|  **English-Language Learners** *In addition to the small-group suggestions above, use the ELL Extra Support Kit to promote language development.*  | **LANGUAGE DEVELOPMENT SUPPORT** **Teacher-Directed** ELL TG, Day 1 **Independent** ELL Copying Masters, Lesson 16 | **LANGUAGE DEVELOPMENT SUPPORT** **Teacher-Directed** ELL TG, Day 2 **Independent** ELL Copying Masters, Lesson 16 |
| **Intervention** 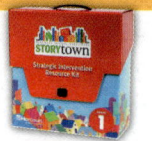 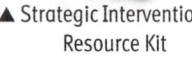  ▲ Strategic Intervention Resource Kit ▲ Strategic Intervention Interactive Reader | Strategic Intervention TG, Day 1 Strategic Intervention Practice Book, Lesson 16 | Strategic Intervention TG, Day 2 Strategic Intervention Interactive Reader, Lesson 16  ▲ Strategic Intervention Interactive Reader |

 = **Literacy Center Cards**

| MONITOR PROGRESS Small-Group Instruction | Phonemic Awareness/ Phonics | High-Frequency Words | Fluency | Comprehension | Robust Vocabulary | Language Arts Checkpoint |
|---|---|---|---|---|---|---|
| | *r*-Controlled Vowel /ûr/*er, ir, ur* p. S32 | *always, by, Cow's, join, nice, please, room* p. S33 | Reading Rate pp. S34–S35 | Focus Skill Main Idea pp. S36–S37 | *captured, mercy, struggling, compatible, amiable, relax* pp. S38–S39 | Grammar: Using *He, She, It,* and *They* Writing: Invitation pp. S40–S41 |

## Day 3

**Teacher-Directed**
Leveled Reader:
"Room for a Friend,"
p. T374
Before Reading; Read the Book

**Independent**
⭐ Word Work Center, p. T303
Extra Support Copying Masters, p. 26

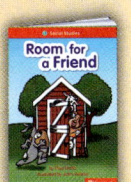
▲ Leveled Reader

**Teacher-Directed**
Leveled Reader:
"Always Room for More," p. T375
Before Reading; Read the Book

**Independent**
⭐ Writing Center, p. T303
Practice Book, p. 26

▲ Leveled Reader

**Teacher-Directed**
Leveled Reader:
"A New Friend," p. T376
Think Critically

**Independent**
⭐ Listening/Speaking Center, p. T302
Challenge Copying Masters, p. 26

▲ Leveled Reader

**LANGUAGE DEVELOPMENT SUPPORT**
**Teacher-Directed**
Leveled Reader:
"The Big Picture," p. T377
Before Reading; Read the Book
ELL TG, Day 3

**Independent**
ELL Copying Masters, Lesson 16

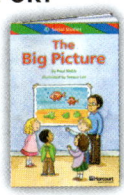
▲ Leveled Reader

Strategic Intervention TG, Day 3
Strategic Intervention
Interactive Reader, Lesson 16
Strategic Intervention
Practice Book, Lesson 16

▲ Strategic Intervention Interactive Reader

## Day 4

**Teacher-Directed**
Leveled Reader:
"Room for a Friend,"
p. T374
Reread for Fluency

**Independent**
⭐ Letters and Sounds Center, p. T303
Cut-Out/Fold-Up Book, Practice Book, pp. 51–52

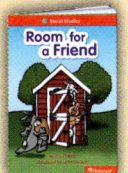
▲ Leveled Reader

**Teacher-Directed**
Leveled Reader:
"Always Room for More," p. T375
Reread for Fluency

**Independent**
⭐ Word Work Center, p. T303
Cut-Out/Fold-Up Book: Practice Book, pp. 51–52

▲ Leveled Reader

**Teacher-Directed**
Leveled Reader:
"A New Friend," p. T376
Reread for Fluency
Self-Selected Reading: Classroom Library Collection

**Independent**
⭐ Writing Center, p. T303
Cut-Out/Fold-Up Book: Practice Book, pp. 51–52

▲ Leveled Reader

**LANGUAGE DEVELOPMENT SUPPORT**
**Teacher-Directed**
Leveled Reader:
"The Big Picture," p. T377
Reread for Fluency
ELL TG, Day 4

**Independent**
ELL Copying Masters, Lesson 16

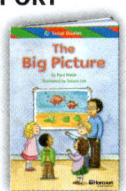
▲ Leveled Reader

Strategic Intervention TG, Day 4
Strategic Intervention
Interactive Reader, Lesson 16

▲ Strategic Intervention Interactive Reader

## Day 5

**Teacher-Directed**
Leveled Reader:
"Room for a Friend,"
p. T374
Think Critically

**Independent**
⭐ Writing Center, p. T303
Leveled Reader: Reread for Fluency
Extra Support Copying Masters, p. 28

▲ Leveled Reader

**Teacher-Directed**
Leveled Reader:
"Always Room for More," p. T375
Think Critically

**Independent**
⭐ Listening/Speaking Center, p. T302
Leveled Reader: Reread for Fluency
Practice Book, p. 28

▲ Leveled Reader

**Teacher-Directed**
Leveled Reader:
"A New Friend," p. T376
Reread for Fluency
Self-Selected Reading: Classroom Library Collection

**Independent**
⭐ Reading Center, p. T302
Leveled Reader: Reread for Fluency
Challenge Copying Masters, p. 28

▲ Leveled Reader

**LANGUAGE DEVELOPMENT SUPPORT**
**Teacher-Directed**
Leveled Reader:
"The Big Picture," p. T377
Think Critically
ELL TG, Day 5

**Independent**
Leveled Reader:
Reread for Fluency
ELL Copying Masters, Lesson 16

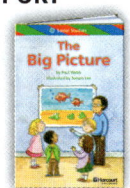
▲ Leveled Reader

Strategic Intervention TG, Day 5
Strategic Intervention
Interactive Reader, Lesson 16

▲ Strategic Intervention Interactive Reader

# Leveled Readers & Leveled Practice
## *Reinforcing Skills and Strategies*

## LEVELED READERS SYSTEM

- **Leveled Readers**
- **Leveled Readers CD**
- **Leveled Reader Teacher Guides**
  - *Comprehension*
  - *High-Frequency Words*
  - *Oral Reading Fluency Assessment*
- **Response Activities**
- **Leveled Readers Assessment**

See pages T374–T377 for lesson plans.

---

### BELOW-LEVEL

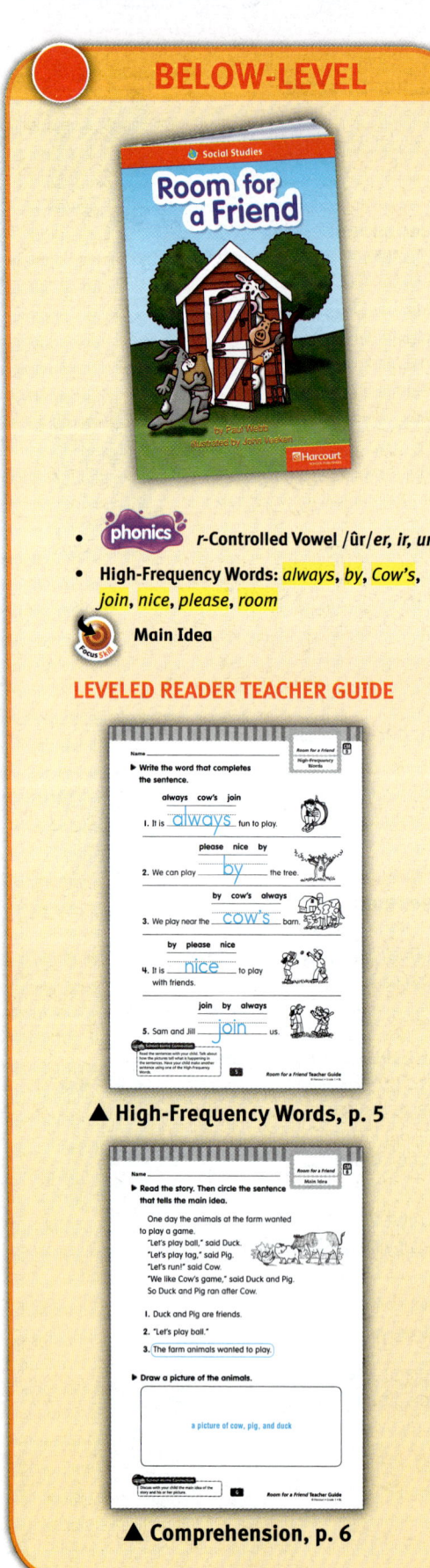

- **phonics** *r-Controlled Vowel /ûr/er, ir, ur*
- **High-Frequency Words:** *always*, *by*, *Cow's*, *join*, *nice*, *please*, *room*
- **Main Idea**

**LEVELED READER TEACHER GUIDE**

▲ High-Frequency Words, p. 5

▲ Comprehension, p. 6

---

### ON-LEVEL

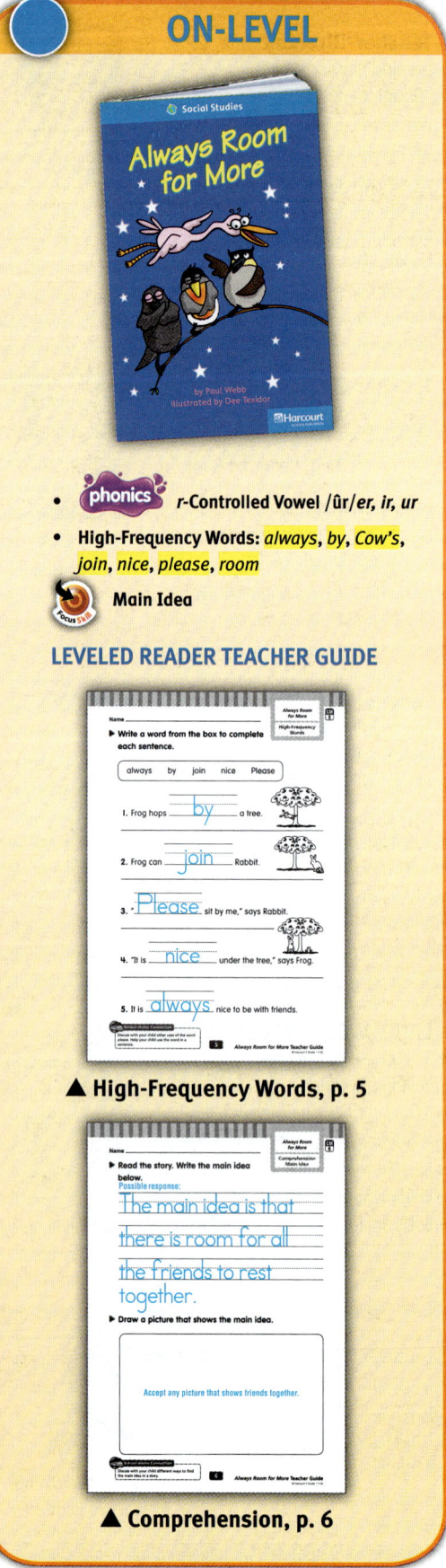

- **phonics** *r-Controlled Vowel /ûr/er, ir, ur*
- **High-Frequency Words:** *always*, *by*, *Cow's*, *join*, *nice*, *please*, *room*
- **Main Idea**

**LEVELED READER TEACHER GUIDE**

▲ High-Frequency Words, p. 5

▲ Comprehension, p. 6

---

**www.harcourtschool.com/storytown**

★ **Leveled Readers, online**
*Searchable by Genre, Skill, Vocabulary, Level, or Title*
★ **Student Activities and Teacher Resources, online**

## ADVANCED

-  *r*-Controlled Vowel /ûr/*er, ir, ur*
- **High-Frequency Words:** *always, by, Cow's, join, nice, please, room*
- **Main Idea**

### LEVELED READER TEACHER GUIDE

▲ **High-Frequency Words, p. 5**

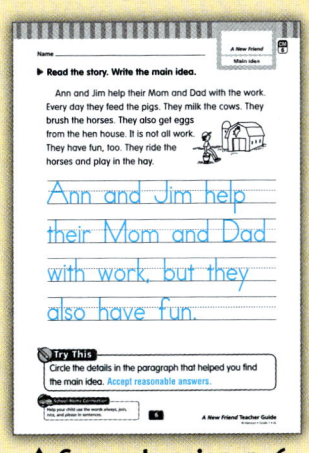

▲ **Comprehension, p. 6**

## ELL

- **Strong Picture Support**
- **Concept Vocabulary**
- **Scaffolded Language Development**

### LEVELED READER TEACHER GUIDE

▲ **Build Background, p. 5**

▲ **Scaffolded Language Development, p. 6**

## CLASSROOM LIBRARY
## for Self-Selected Reading

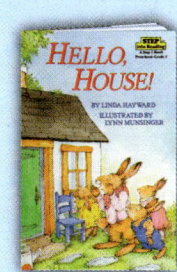

**AVERAGE**

▲ *Hello, House!* by Linda Hayward.
**FOLKTALE**

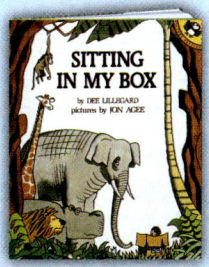

**AVERAGE**

▲ *Sitting in My Box* by Dee Lillegard.
**FANTASY**

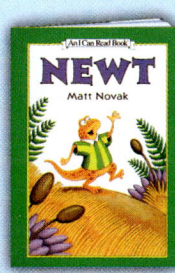

**CHALLENGE**

▲ *Newt* by Matt Novak.
**FANTASY**

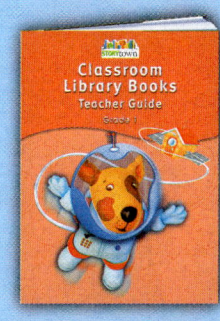

▲ **Classroom Library Books Teacher Guide, pp. 40–47, 56–59**

# Literacy Centers

*15 Min. each*

## Management Support

While you provide direct instruction to individuals or small groups, other children can work on literacy center activities.

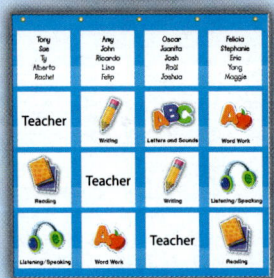

▲ **Literacy Centers Pocket Chart**

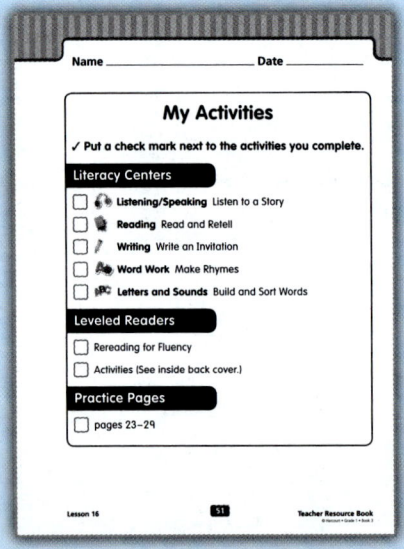

▲ **Teacher Resource Book, p. 51**

## Homework for the Week

**TEACHER RESOURCE BOOK, PAGE 20**

The *Homework Copying Master* provides activities to complete for each day of the week.

www.harcourtschool.com/storytown

---

### LISTENING/SPEAKING

## Listen to a Story

**Objective** To listen to a story for information and enjoyment

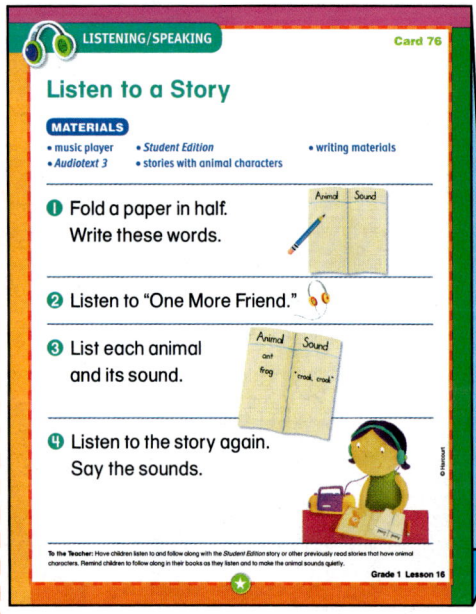

⭐ **Literacy Center Kit • Card 76**

---

### READING

## Read and Retell

**Objective** To identify the main idea and supporting details in a story

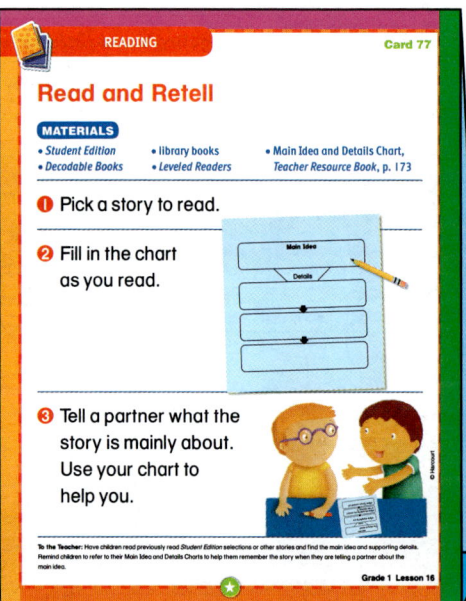

⭐ **Literacy Center Kit • Card 77**

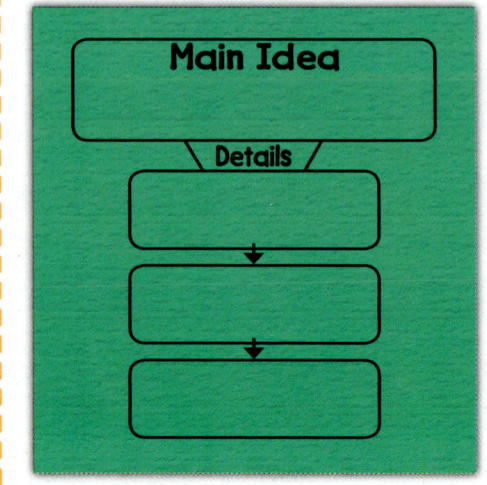

## ✏️ WRITING

# Write an Invitation

**Objective** To create an invitation for a familiar occasion

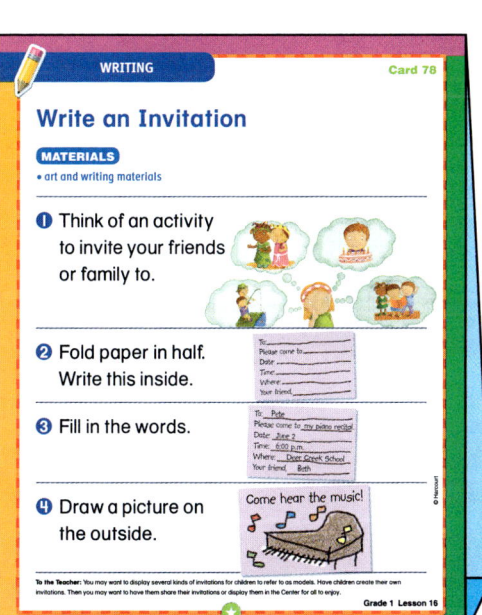

**Literacy Center Kit • Card 78**

## 🍎 WORD WORK

# Make Rhymes

**Objective** To write high-frequency words and use them in a different context

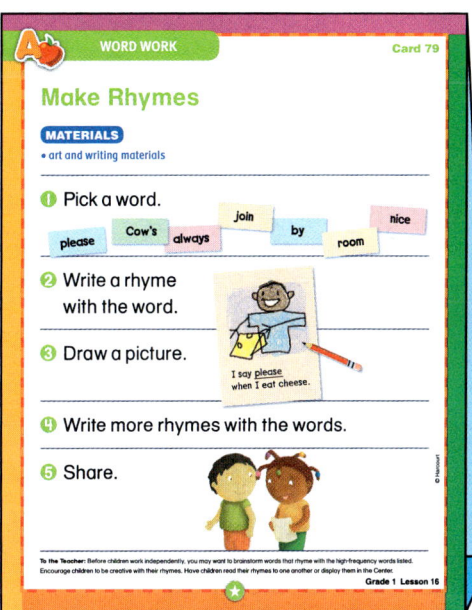

**Literacy Center Kit • Card 79**

## ABC LETTERS AND SOUNDS

# Build and Sort Words

**Objective** To build and sort words with r-controlled vowels spelled er, ir, ur

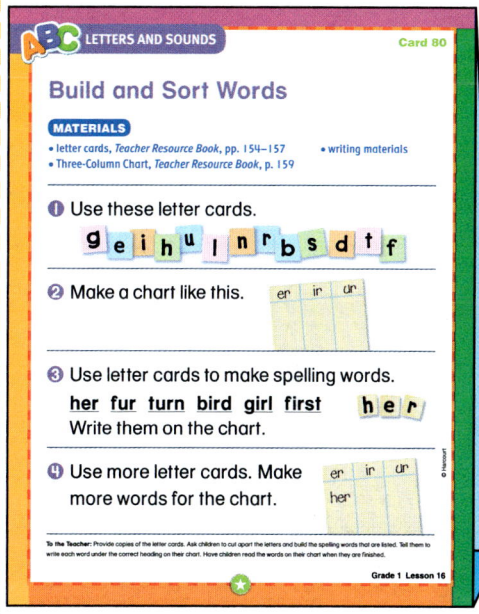

**Literacy Center Kit • Card 80**

## Day at a Glance

### Day 1

### Phonemic Awareness
- Phoneme Blending

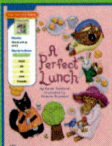  **phonics and Spelling**
- Introduce: *r*-Controlled Vowels /ûr/*er, ir, ur*
- Pretest

### Reading
- Get Started Story: "A Perfect Lunch," *Student Edition,* pp. 130–137

**Read!**

### Comprehension
- *Read Aloud Anthology:* "The Lion and the Mouse"
  Preview: Main Idea

 *Focus Skill*

### Fluency
- Reading Rate

### Robust Vocabulary
- Introduce: *captured, mercy, struggling*

### Grammar
- Introduce: Using *He, She, It, They*

### Modeled Writing ✏️
- Invitation

---

# Warm-Up Routines

## Oral Language

**Objective** *To listen and respond appropriately to oral communication*

### Question of the Day

Think about a lion you have seen. Where did you see it, what did it look like, and what was it doing?

Write the following sentence frames and initiate discussion by helping children complete them.

**I saw a lion _____. The lion had _____. It was _____.**

## Read Aloud

**Objectives** *To listen for a purpose; to identify sound and direction words*

**Routine Card 17** **BIG BOOK** Share *We're Going on a Lion Hunt* with children. Read aloud the title. Then read the name of the author and discuss his role as author *and* illustrator.

- **Set a purpose and read.** Tell children to listen to find out if the girls find a lion. Then reread the story, and have children chime in.

- **Respond.** Review words such as *swish, swash, over,* and *under.* Help children name categories, such as *sound words* and *direction words.* Have them verbally classify words from the story into appropriate categories.

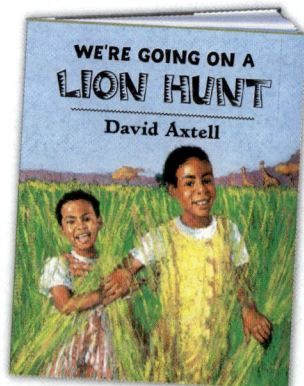

▲ Big Book *We're Going on a Lion Hunt*

# Word Wall

**Objective** *To read high-frequency words*

**REVIEW HIGH-FREQUENCY WORDS** Review *friends, no, now, oh, says,* and other previously learned high-frequency words. Say each word, ask a volunteer to point to it, and have children read it aloud. Then point to words at random, and have children reread them.

friends

no

now

oh

says

# Phonemic Awareness

**Objective** *To blend phonemes into recognizable words*

**Routine Card 1** **PHONEME BLENDING** Tell children that you are going to say some words from *We're Going on a Lion Hunt.* Explain that you will say each word very slowly. Model by saying /h/ /u /n/ /t/; then say the word naturally—*hunt.* Say the following phonemes, having children blend the sounds to say the words:

/l/ /ī/ /ə/ /n/ (lion)

/k/ /a/ /ch/ (catch)

/g/ /r/ /a/ /s/ (grass)

/l/ /ā/ /k/ (lake)

/b/ /i/ /g/ (big)

/s/ /p/ /l/ /a/ /sh/ (splash)

/s/ /w/ /ä/ /m/ /p/ (swamp)

/b/ /e/ /t/ /ûr/ (better)

/n/ /ō/ /z/ (nose)

/m/ /ā/ /n/ (mane)

/p/ /ô/ /z/ (paws)

/k /r/ /a/ /sh/ (crash)

**/m/ /ā/ /n/**
**mane**

 **Podcasting: Phoneme Blending**

# r-Controlled Vowels /ûr/er, ir, ur

 **phonics** *and Spelling*

## Objectives

- *To recognize and generate r-controlled vowel sound /ûr/er, ir, ur*
- *To build and blend words with r-controlled vowel sound /ûr/er, ir, ur and other known letter-sounds*
- *To use r-controlled /ûr/er, ir, ur and other known letter-sounds to spell words*
- *To spell known high-frequency words*

## Skill Trace

**Tested** ✓ *r-Controlled Vowels /ûr/er, ir, ur*

| Introduce | T306–T309 |
|---|---|
| Reteach | S32 |
| Review | T322–T323, T344–T345 |
| Test | Bk 1-3 |
| Maintain | Bk 1-5, T348–T349 |

## Connecting Letter to Sound

**Routine Card 12** **DEVELOP PHONEMIC AWARENESS OF /ûr/** Say the word *bird*. Have children say the word. Repeat for the words *her* and *turn*. Say: **The words *bird, her,* and *turn* have the /ûr/ sound.** Have children say /ûr/ several times.

**CONNECT LETTER AND SOUND** Display *Sound/Spelling Card ir, er, ur*. Say the letter names. Explain that each pair of letters can stand for the /ûr/ sound, as in *bird*.

**DISCRIMINATE /ûr/** Say: **When I say a word that ends with /ûr/, snap your fingers. When I say a word that does not end with /ûr/, put your hands on your lap.** Say these words:

fur    car    her    dear    stir    purr

Tell children that some words have the /ûr/ sound in the middle. Say *first,* elongating the /ûr/ sound. Tell children that *first* has /ûr/ in the middle. Then have children snap their fingers when they hear /ûr/ in the medial position in the following words:

burn    fort    bird    cart    third    perch

Then have children discriminate between medial and final sounds. Have them say each of the following words and tell if they hear the /ûr/ sound in the middle or at the end.

twirl    burr    sir    first    fur    curve

▲ Sound/Spelling Card

## Word Blending

**DIBELS**
Nonsense
Word
Fluency
**NWF**

**WORDS WITH /ûr/***er, ir, ur* Demonstrate each step with *Letter Cards* and a pocket chart. Have children repeat each step after you, using their *Word Builder Cards* and *Word Builders*.

**Routine Card 13**

**BLEND AND READ** *fern* Hold up *f* and say /ff/. Hold up *e* and *r* together and say /ûrr/. Hold up *n* and say /nn/.

- Place the letters *f, e, r, n* in the pocket chart. Have children do the same with their letters and *Word Builders*.

- Point to *f* and say /ff/. Point to *er* together and say /ûrr/. Prompt children to repeat after you.

- Slide *er* next to *f.* Run your hand under the letters as you blend the sounds, elongating them—/ffûrr/. Have children repeat.

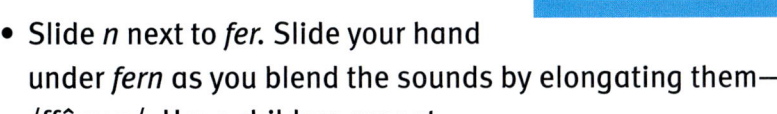

- Point to *n* and say /nn/. Have children do the same.

- Slide *n* next to *fer.* Slide your hand under *fern* as you blend the sounds by elongating them—/ffûrrnn/. Have children repeat.

- Read *fern* naturally. Repeat, having children read the word with you.

Follow the same procedure for *hurt, stir,* and *herd.*

## Professional Development

 **Podcasting:** Word Blending, Gr. 1

### ● ADVANCED

**Blend Sounds** Tell children you will give them directions. Explain that they must listen carefully and blend a word to know what to do.

- Stand up and /t/ /ûr/ /n/ around three times.

- Flap your arms like a /b/ /ûr/ /d/.

- Spell your /f/ /ûr/ /s/ /t/ name.

- Pretend to /s/ /t/ /ûr/ something in a pot.

### ● BELOW-LEVEL

**Reinforce /ûr/***er, ir, ur* To reinforce that *er, ir,* and *ur* stand for the /ûr/ sound, have children copy the words *fern, hurt, stir,* and *term* in their nootbooks using a colored pencil or crayon to write the letters *er, ir,* and *ur.* Then have children say the words, pointing to the letters that stand for the *r*-controlled vowel sound /ûr/ in each word.

# r-Controlled Vowels /ûr/er, ir, ur

 **and Spelling**

## Professional Development

 **Podcasting:** Word Building, Gr. 1; Spelling and Dictation, Gr. 1

### ● ADVANCED

**Make Words** Rather than telling children which letters to change, have them figure it out independently. Challenge them to change one word to another in the fewest number of steps. Model the procedure using the words *her* and *fur*. Think aloud as you show children the steps: **I compare the words *her* and *fur* to see how they are different. I start with *her*. I change *h* to *f*. Then I change *e* to *u*. Now I have *fur*.**

## Word Building

 **BUILD SPELLING WORDS** Use *Letter Cards* and a pocket chart. Have children use their *Word Builder Cards* and *Word Builders*.

Place the *Letter Cards h, e,* and *r* in the pocket chart. Slide your hand under the letters as you slowly read the word—/hhûrr/. Then read it naturally—*her*.

Have children build and read new words. As they build each word, write it on the board. Say:

• **Change *h* to *f*. Change *e* to *u*. What word did you make?**

• **Change *f* to *t*. Add *n* at the end. What word did you make?**

Continue with the words *bird* and *girl*. Then have children read the words on the board.

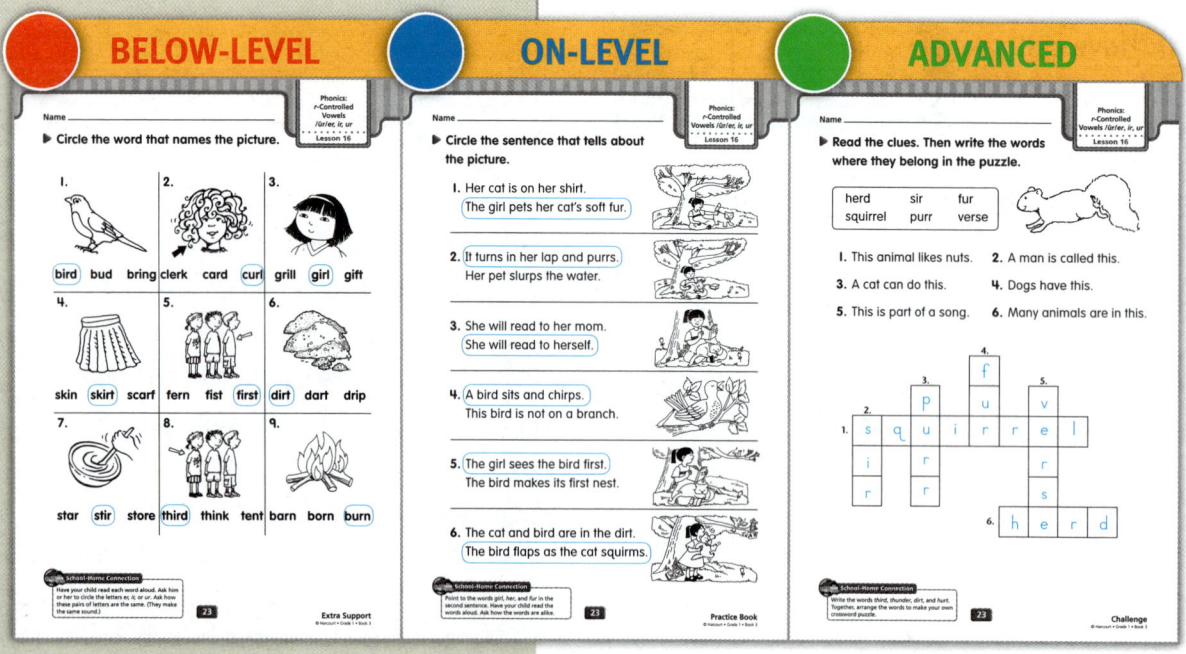

▲ Extra Support, p. 23  ▲ Practice Book, p. 23  ▲ Challenge, p. 23

**ELL**
• Group children according to academic levels, and assign one of the pages on the left.

• Clarify any unfamiliar concepts as necessary. See *ELL Teacher Guide*, Lesson 16, for scaffolding instruction.

**5-DAY SPELLING**

| DAY 1 | Pretest |
| DAY 2 | Word Building |
| DAY 3 | State the Generalization |
| DAY 4 | Review |
| DAY 5 | Posttest |

## Introduce Spelling Words

**PRETEST** Say the first word and read the dictation sentence. Repeat the word as children write it. Write the word on the board and have children check their spelling. Tell them to circle the word if they spelled it correctly, or write it correctly if they did not. Repeat for words 2-10.

### Words with /ûr/*er, ir, ur*

| 1. | her | Where did Sara put **her** new mittens? |
| 2. | fur | Our cat has soft **fur** on its body. |
| 3. | turn | It's your **turn** to play the game. |
| 4. | bird | A young **bird** flew to its nest. |
| 5. | girl | Ann is the new **girl** in our class. |
| 6. | first | I am the **first** one in line. |

### Review

| 7. | quit | The workers have **quit** for the day. |
| 8. | when | Please line up **when** the bell rings. |

### High-Frequency

| 9. | name | The boy's **name** is Jacob. |
| 10. | work | Do you **work** hard in school? |

---

### Spelling Words

| 1. her | 6. first |
| 2. fur | 7. quit |
| 3. turn | 8. when |
| 4. bird | 9. name |
| 5. girl | 10. work |

---

## ✓ MONITOR PROGRESS

### Phonics: *r*-Controlled Vowels /ur/*er, ir, ur*

| **IF** children have difficulty building and reading words with *r*-controlled vowel sound /ûr/, | **THEN** help them blend and read the words *her, fur, turn, bird, girl,* and *first*. |

**Small Group Instruction, p. S32:**

● **BELOW-LEVEL:** Reteach  ● **ON-LEVEL:** Reinforce  ● **ADVANCED:** Extend

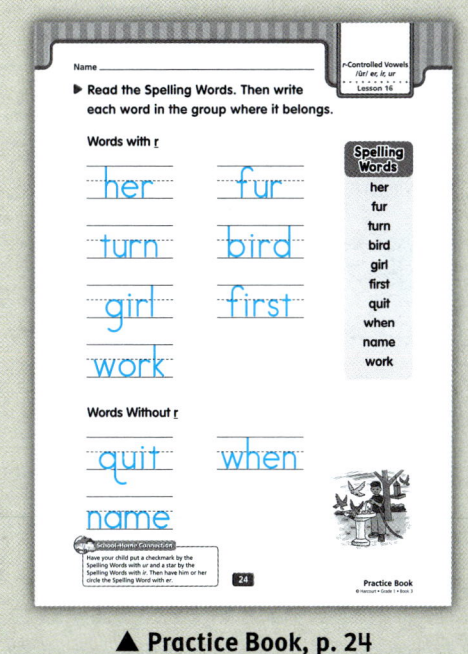

▲ Practice Book, p. 24

# Reading

## Get Started Story: A Perfect Lunch

### Objectives
- *To use letter-sound knowledge to read decodable text*
- *To review high-frequency words*
- *To develop fluency*

 **Podcasting:** Reading Decodable, Gr. 1

## Options for Reading

 **BELOW-LEVEL**

**Echo-Reading** Have children echo-read each sentence. Pause to discuss it, using the Monitor Comprehension questions. Have children frame and read /ûr/ words.

 **ON-LEVEL**

**Monitor Comprehension** Guide children through the story, page by page. Ask the Monitor Comprehension questions as you go. Then lead children in retelling the story and describing their favorite parts.

 **ADVANCED**

**Independent Reading** Have children read each page silently, looking up each time they finish a page. Ask the Monitor Comprehension questions as you go. Then lead children in a discussion about how Meg fits all of the unexpected guests.

### Apply *r*-Controlled Vowels

**READ DECODABLE TEXT** Write the following sentences on the board. Tell children that the sentences are about animal characters in a story they will read.

**Ben comes first.**

**Kit is third.**

- Have children read the sentences as you track the print.
- Ask volunteers to frame and read the words with /ûr/.
- Tell children that many words in the story have the /ûr/ sound.

**Routine Card 17** **INTRODUCE THE STORY** Have children look at the title page and read aloud the title. Ask children to point to the names of the author and the illustrator as you read them aloud. Discuss the illustration. Tell children they will read the story to find out how the cow makes room for her barnyard friends as they join her for lunch.

**Preview** Preview the story with a picture walk. Use the illustrations to develop meaning for the text. Then guide children through the story, using the Monitor Comprehension questions.

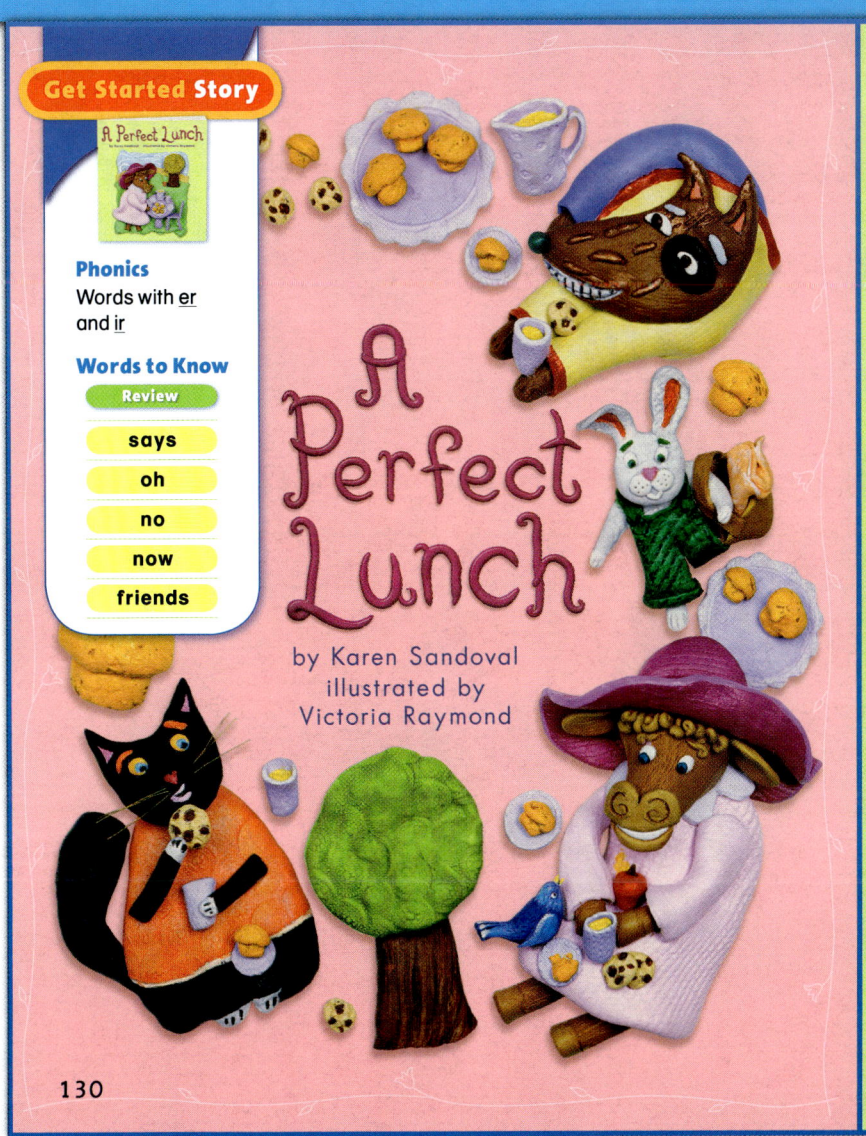

**Get Started Story**

**Phonics**
Words with <u>er</u> and <u>ir</u>

**Words to Know**

Review

says
oh
no
now
friends

**A Perfect Lunch**

by Karen Sandoval
illustrated by
Victoria Raymond

130

"Come for lunch," says Meg.
She is serving corn muffins.
Meg sets out her best dishes.
"How charming!" she grins.

131

# Monitor Comprehension

**PAGES 130–131** Say: **The cow looks busy. Let's read to find out what she is doing.**

1. **NOTE DETAILS/APPLY PHONICS** **What is Meg setting out?** (her best dishes and cups) **Why?** (She is serving muffins and something to drink.) **Find and read the words** *serving* **and** *her*. **What sound do you hear in both words that is the same?** (/ûr/)

2. **DRAW CONCLUSIONS** **How many friends do you think Meg is expecting?** (one) **What clues can you find in the picture to show why you may be right?** (The picture shows that she has set the table for two, herself and one guest.)

**E L L**

**Clarify Meaning** Tell children that *perfect* means "very good" or "excellent." Talk with them about what a perfect lunch might be like.

## TECHNOLOGY

 **eBook** "A Perfect Lunch" is available in an eBook.

 **Audiotext** "A Perfect Lunch" is available on *Audiotext Grade 1*, CD 6 for subsequent readings.

Ben comes first. He sits
with Meg. Ben fills his glass.
**Squirt!** He squirts Meg.
"**Oh, no!**" yells Ben.

132

Liz is next. She sits with Ben.
Liz picks up her muffin, and her
skirt bumps Ben.

133

# Monitor Comprehension

**PAGES 132–133** Say: **I see Meg and Ben seated at the table. Then Liz joins them. Let's read to find out if Meg can fit another at her table.**

**1** **NOTE DETAILS/APPLY PHONICS** **What does Ben do to Meg?** (He squirts her.) **What does Liz do to Ben?** (Her skirt bumps him.) **Point to and read the words that have the /ûr/ sound.** (squirts, skirt)

**2** **RELATE PICTURES TO TEXT** **What does the picture on page 132 help you to understand about how Meg feels about Ben squirting her?** (She looks surprised. She doesn't look mad.)

**3** **EXPRESS PERSONAL OPINIONS** **Would you rather be squirted by Ben or bumped with Liz's skirt? Why?** (Possible response: I'd rather be bumped with Liz's skirt because it wouldn't be as messy.)

Kit is third. She sits with Liz. Kit sips her drink and drops her muffin in the dirt. Meg's big hat brim hits Ben.

134

Here is Jen. Where can this bird sit? Perhaps this twig will do the trick. Liz looks up and bumps Meg's hat.

135

# Monitor Comprehension

**PAGES 134–135** Say: **Meg makes room for two more friends. Let's read to find out more about them.**

**1** **NOTE DETAILS** **Who joins Meg next?** (Kit and Jen) **How has Meg made room for them?** (Meg turned over a flowerpot for Kit and she sees a tree branch Jen can perch on.) **So far, how many friends have joined Meg in all?** (four)

**2** **NOTE DETAILS/APPLY PHONICS** **Where is Kit's muffin?** (in the dirt) **What vowel sound do you hear in the word** *dirt*? (/ûr/) **Who perches in the tree?** (Jen, the bird)

### STRATEGIC READING

**Words with /ûr/** Remind children that this story includes many words with *r*-controlled vowels /ûr/*er, ir, ur*. Ask them to count and read the /ûr/ words they find on these two pages.

Tap, tap, tap! It's Bert!

"Oh, no! Where will Bert sit?"
they all ask.

136

"Let's have a picnic!" says Bert.

"It's a perfect day now with all my
friends," Meg says. Meg and all
her friends have a perfect lunch!

137

# Monitor Comprehension

**PAGES 136–137** Say: **It looks crowded around Meg's table. Let's read
to see if any more friends join Meg for lunch.**

**1** **NOTE DETAILS/APPLY PHONICS** Who joins Meg next? (Bert)
Where does Bert sit? (on a blanket) What sound do the words
*Bert* and *perfect* share? (/ûr/) Find the words and read them.

**2** **DETERMINE CHARACTERS' EMOTIONS** How do you think Meg
and her friends feel as they have lunch? Why? (Possible response: They feel happy and relaxed because they have plenty
of room on the blanket.)

**3** **DRAW CONCLUSIONS** What kind of friend is Meg? Why do you
think so? (Meg is a good friend because she makes room for all
her friends.)

## HIGH-FREQUENCY WORDS

**Review** Remind children that they
have already learned to read the high-
frequency words *have*, *where*, *friends*,
*says*, and *my*. Have them frame and read
these words on pages 136–137.

# Check Comprehension

*Retelling*

## Retell

**DIBELS**
Oral Reading Fluency
**ORF**

**RETELL "A PERFECT LUNCH"** Ask children to name the characters in "A Perfect Lunch" and tell where the story takes place. Then have volunteers tell what happens at the beginning, middle, and end of the story. Write their responses in a chart such as the one shown below.

| Beginning | Middle | Ending |
|---|---|---|
| Meg gets ready for lunch. | Ben, Liz, Kit, and Jen come by. Meg serves muffins and something to drink. | Bert comes last. Then everyone sits on a blanket and has a picnic lunch. |

# Fluency

## Repeated Reading

**DIBELS**
Oral Reading Fluency
**ORF**

**READ WITH A PARTNER** Have partners reread "A Perfect Lunch" three or four times. Suggest that they read one page at a time. Readers should pay attention to their reading rate. Listeners should follow along and make sure the reader does not read too fast or too slowly. Listen to partners read, and give them feedback about their reading rate and guidance for improving their fluency.

## Objectives

- *To practice retelling a story*
- *To read with fluency at an appropriate rate*

### RETELLING RUBRIC

| | |
|---|---|
| 4 | Uses details to retell the story clearly |
| 3 | Uses some details to retell the story |
| 2 | Retells the story with some inaccuracies |
| 1 | Is unable to retell the story |

## Professional Development

 **Podcasting:** Auditory Modeling

# Comprehension
## *Read Aloud*

## Objectives

- *To set a purpose for listening*
- *To understand characteristics of fable*

## Daily Comprehension
### Main Idea

| | |
|---|---|
| **DAY 1:** | Preview Main Idea *Read-Aloud Anthology* |
| **DAY 2:** | Introduce Main Idea *Student Edition* |
| **DAY 3:** | Review Main Idea *Paired Selection Student Edition* |
| **DAY 4:** | Review Main Idea *Big Book* |
| **DAY 5:** | Review Main Idea *Comparing Texts* |

### E L L

**Connect to Prior Knowledge**

If possible, display pictures of a real lion and mouse for children to refer to as they share their knowledge of the two animals.

---

### Before Reading

▲ Read-Aloud Anthology, "The Lion and the Mouse," p. 62

**CONNECT TO PRIOR KNOWLEDGE** Tell children that they will be listening to the story "The Lion and the Mouse." Explain that a lion and a mouse are the only characters in the story and that the mouse unexpectedly helps the lion. Tell children to listen for how the mouse helps the lion. Ask children to share what they know about real lions and mice.

**GENRE STUDY: FABLE** Explain that "The Lion and the Mouse" is a fable, originally written down by a Greek man named Aesop who lived hundreds of years ago.

**Think Aloud** This is a story whose characters are animals that talk and act like people. The story also teaches a lesson or a moral about how to treat other people. Those characteristics help me understand that this story is a fable.

**PREVIEW THE SKILL: MAIN IDEA** Tell children that the main idea is the most important idea in a story or a part of a story. The main idea is what that part of the selection is mostly about. Conclude by telling children that they will be discussing the main idea of "The Lion and the Mouse" later in the week. Then read the fable to them.

### After Reading

**RESPOND** Remind children of the definition of a fable. Then ask them to name aspects of the story that tell them it is a fable. List their ideas on the board and discuss them.

# Build Robust Vocabulary

## Listening/Speaking: *Words from the Read-Aloud*

### Teach/Model

Routine Card 15

**INTRODUCE ROBUST VOCABULARY** Use *Routine Card 15* to introduce the words.

❶ Put the word in **selection context.**
❷ Provide for children the **Student-Friendly Explanation.**
❸ Have children **say the word** with you.
❹ Use the word in other contexts, and have children **interact with the word's meaning.**
❺ Say the Student-Friendly Explanation again, and ask children to **name the word** that goes with it.

❶ **Selection Context:** The lion <mark>captured</mark> the tiny mouse with its huge paw.
❹ **Interact with Word Meaning:** I once captured a butterfly and then let it go after looking at it. Would you want to capture and observe a spider or a turtle? Why?

❶ **Selection Context:** The terrified mouse begged the lion for <mark>mercy</mark>.
❹ **Interact with Word Meaning:** If you had been the lion, would you have shown mercy, or would you have eaten the mouse?

❶ **Selection Context:** The mouse found the King of Beasts <mark>struggling</mark> to free himself from the hunters' tangled net.
❹ **Interact with Word Meaning:** I'd be struggling if I had to tie my shoes with one hand. Would you struggle more to write your name with your eyes closed or to make your bed using only one hand?

### Practice/Apply

**GUIDED PRACTICE** Ask children to do the following:
• Imagine that the zipper on your jacket is stuck. Show how you'd look while struggling to take off your jacket.
• Imagine that you are Jack in "Jack and the Beanstalk." The giant has just captured you. Show how you would ask for mercy.

### Objective
• *To develop robust vocabulary through discussing a literature selection*

### INTRODUCE
**Student-Friendly Explanations**

<mark>captured</mark> If you have captured something, you have caught it and are not letting it go.

<mark>mercy</mark> If you show kindness or forgiveness to someone who has done something wrong, you show mercy.

<mark>struggling</mark> If you are struggling, you are making a great effort with your body or mind to do something.

**Introduce Vocabulary** Illustrate word meanings with actions and facial expressions. For the word *mercy*, for example, put your hand over your heart, exhale, and show an expression of relief on your face to demonstrate how someone who has just been shown mercy might react.

#  Grammar

## Using He, She, It, and They

**5-DAY GRAMMAR**

| | |
|---|---|
| **DAY 1** | Introduce Using *He, She, It,* and *They* |
| **DAY 2** | Rewrite Sentences |
| **DAY 3** | Revise Sentences |
| **DAY 4** | Complete Sentences |
| **DAY 5** | Write Sentences |

## Objectives

- *To recognize that* he, she, it, *and* they *can take the place of names of people, animals, places, and things*
- *To use* he, she, it, *and* they *correctly*

## Daily Proofreading

**The lion naps in hs den**

(his, den.)

Using *He, She, It,* and *They*

Grade 1, Lesson 16　　LA31　　Grammar: Using *He, She, It, and They*

**Transparency LA31**

## Teach/Model

**INTRODUCE THE CONCEPT** Read aloud this pair of sentences about "The Lion and the Mouse" (*Read-Aloud Anthology,* pages 62–63):

**The lion decided to take a short nap one day.**

**He stretched out and soon fell asleep.**

Explain that both sentences tell about the lion, but the second sentence begins with *He* instead of *The lion.* Say: **He can take the place of the name of an animal, boy, or man.** Write this sentence on the board:

**Greg has a red car.**

Ask what word can take the place of *Greg.* *(He)* Write *He has a red car.* Continue with these sentences: *Ann has a truck. The truck is black. The children have fun.* Elicit that *She* can replace *Ann, It* can replace *The truck,* and *They* can replace *The children.*

## Guided Practice

**USE *HE, SHE, IT,* AND *THEY* TO ANSWER QUESTIONS** Display **Transparency LA31.** Have children describe the scene. Ask: **Where is the boy?** Model an answer: **He is on the swing.** Write the sentence on the board, pointing out that *He* replaces *the boy.* Ask other questions about the scene. Have children respond using a pronoun.

## Practice/Apply

**WRITE *HE, SHE, IT,* AND *THEY*** List the following on the board:

| | | | |
|---|---|---|---|
| Mr. Mott | Ann | the cat | the boys |
| my sister | the friends | the pond | Ben |

Have children read the words with you. Then say a pronoun, such as *he.* Ask a volunteer to write *he* beside a word on the board that it might replace, such as *Mr. Mott.*

# Modeled Writing

*Invitation*

**5-DAY WRITING**

| DAY 1 | Modeled Writing |
| DAY 2 | Shared Writing |
| DAY 3 | Shared Writing |
| DAY 4 | Independent Writing |
| DAY 5 | Independent Writing |

## Teach/Model

**INTRODUCE AN INVITATION** Ask children to tell about a time when they were invited to do something that was fun. Have them tell how they were invited—in person, by telephone, by written invitation. Then display **Transparency LA32,** and explain that it is an invitation made by a child. Read the invitation to children and point out the parts. Together, develop a list of characteristics of a well-written invitation.

### An Invitation Tells

* **who** is invited
* **what** the event is
* **when** the event is
* **where** the event is
* **who** is sending the invitation

**WRITING TRAIT** **IDEAS** Have children tell the main idea of the student model invitation. Point out how the rest of the invitation gives important information about that event to help the person being invited understand.

## Guided Practice

**MODEL AN INVITATION** Model saying the parts of an invitation, such as: **You and your family are invited to a Class Picnic. We'll celebrate the end of the year with games and great food. Date: Saturday, June 19. Time: 11:00–5:00. Where: Hill Park. From: Your teacher.** Point out that you told who is invited, what the event is, when and where to come, and who sent the invitation.

## Practice/Apply

**BRAINSTORM IDEAS FOR INVITATIONS** Ask children to think of a special classroom occasion or event for which they would want to send an invitation. Record their ideas on the board or use the web on **Tranparency G06.** Save the ideas for Day 2.

## Objectives

* *To understand the purpose of an invitation*
* *To develop a list of criteria for an invitation*
* *To generate ideas for writing*

### Writing Prompt

**Write About an Event** Have children draw and write about a time when they were invited to do something that was fun. What were they invited to do? Who invited them? Did they have fun?

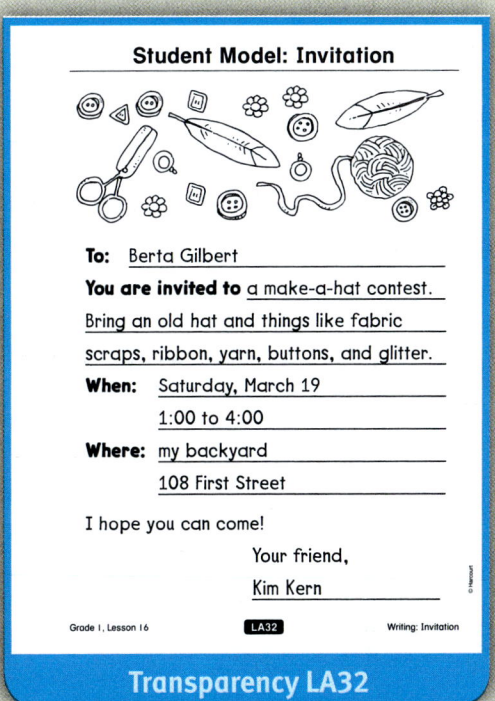

**Student Model: Invitation**

**To:** Berta Gilbert

**You are invited to** a make-a-hat contest. Bring an old hat and things like fabric scraps, ribbon, yarn, buttons, and glitter.

**When:** Saturday, March 19
1:00 to 4:00

**Where:** my backyard
108 First Street

I hope you can come!

Your friend,
Kim Kern

Grade 1, Lesson 16    LA32    Writing: Invitation

**Transparency LA32**

## Day at a Glance
### Day 2

**Phonemic Awareness**
- Phoneme Segmentation

 **phonics and Spelling**
- Review: *r*-Controlled Vowels /ûr/ *er, ir, ur*
- Word Building

**Comprehension**
 Introduce: Main Idea

**High-Frequency Words**
- Introduce: *always, by, Cow's, join, nice, please, room*

**Reading**
- "One More Friend," *Student Edition*, pp. 142–159
**Read!**

**Fluency**
- Reading Rate

**Robust Vocabulary**
- Review: *captured, mercy, struggling*

**Grammar**
- Review: Using *He, She, It, They*

**Shared Writing**
- Invitation

# Warm-Up Routines

## Oral Language

**Objective** *To listen attentively and respond appropriately to oral communication*

### Question of the Day
How might a new child in our class feel?
Why?

Help brainstorm possible feelings and emotions. Then discuss why a new classmate might feel that way. Have children help you complete the following sentence frame:

**Someone new might feel _____ because _____.**

## Read Aloud

**Objective** *To listen for a purpose*

**BIG BOOK OF RHYMES AND POEMS** Display the poem and read the title and the poet's name. Have children describe the poet's role. Then ask them to listen to find out what the poem's narrator (a child) thinks about a new girl. After you read, ask children to tell what the child thinks. Then ask how they would try to make a new boy or girl feel welcome. Reread the poem, tracking the print, and encourage children to chime in.

▲ Big Book of Rhymes and Poems, p. 31

## Word Wall

**Objective** *To read high-frequency words*

**REVIEW HIGH-FREQUENCY WORDS** Review *about, books, family, name, read, work, writing, people,* and other previously learned high-frequency words. Say each word, ask a volunteer to point to it, and have children read it aloud. Then point to words at random, and have children reread them.

| | | | |
|---|---|---|---|
| about | books | family | name |
| read | work | writing | people |

## Phonemic Awareness

**Objective** *To segment words into phonemes*

**DIBELS** Phoneme Segmentation Fluency **PSF**

**Routine Card 8**

**PHONEME SEGMENTATION** Remind children of the lion in *We're Going on a Lion Hunt.* Say *lion* slowly, emphasizing each sound. Ask children what sounds they hear in *lion.* (/l/ /ī/ /ə/ /n/) As they say each sound, have them snap their fingers. Repeat, using the names for animals, places, things, sounds, and other words they heard in *We're Going on a Lion Hunt.*

**grass** (/g/ /r/ /a/ /s/)     **hunt** (/h/ /u/ /n/ /t/)

**nose** (/n/ /ō/ /z/)     **swamp** (/s/ /w/ /o/ /m/ /p/)

**mane** (/m/ /ā/ /n/)     **lake** (/l/ /ā/ /k/)

**home** (/h/ /ō/ /m/)     **cave** (/k/ /ā/ /v/)

**door** (/d/ /ôr/)     **crash** (/k/ /r/ /a/ /sh/)

 Podcasting: Phoneme Segmentation

# r-Controlled Vowels /ûr/er, ir, ur

 **and Spelling**

## Objectives

- *To blend sounds into words*
- *To spell r-controlled /ûr/er, ir, ur words*

## Skill Trace

 **r-Controlled Vowels /ûr/er, ir, ur**

| | |
|---|---|
| Introduce | T306–T309 |
| Reteach | S32 |
| **Review** | **T322–T323, T344–T345, T357** |
| Test | Bk 1-3 |
| Maintain | Bk 1-5, T348–T349 |

### Spelling Words

| | | | |
|---|---|---|---|
| 1. | her | 6. | first |
| 2. | fur | 7. | quit |
| 3. | turn | 8. | when |
| 4. | bird | 9. | name |
| 5. | girl | 10. | work |

## Word Building

**DIBELS**
Nonsense Word Fluency
**NWF**

**Routine Card 14**

**BUILD AND READ A SPELLING WORD** Place the *Letter Cards h, e, r* in the pocket chart. Ask children to say the name and sound of each letter, combining *er* to say the sound /ûr/. Say the word naturally—*her*. Ask children to do the same.

**BUILD SPELLING WORDS** Ask children which letters you should change to make *her* become *fur*. (Change *h* to *f* and *e* to *u*.) Then ask what letter you should change and what letter you should add to make *fur* become *turn*. (Change *f* to *t* and add *n* at the end.) Continue building spelling words 4–6 in this manner, asking children to name the letters that should be added, changed, or taken away to become a spelling word. Have children repeat each step after you and then read the words.

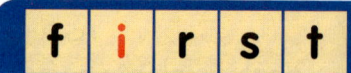

---

### BELOW-LEVEL

**Build Spelling Words** Write the words on the board. Point to each word, one at a time, and read it aloud. Have children repeat it and trace it with a finger for kinesthetic reinforcement.

### ADVANCED

**Build New Words** Beginning with *sir*, have children build and read *dirt, bird, burn, fern,* and *fur*. Then have children use the words in sentences.

**sir   dirt   bird**

## Read Words in Context

**APPLY PHONICS** Write the following sentences on the board or on chart paper. Have children read each sentence silently. Then track the print as children read the sentence aloud.

The girl had her turn after me.

Does a bird have fur?

Who is first in line?

When do you quit playing for the day?

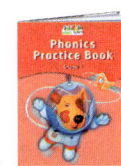

**WRITE** Dictate several /ûr/ words from the pocket chart. Have children write the words on a dry-erase board or in their notebook.

 **phonics** **Resources**

**Phonics Practice Book, pp. 85–88**

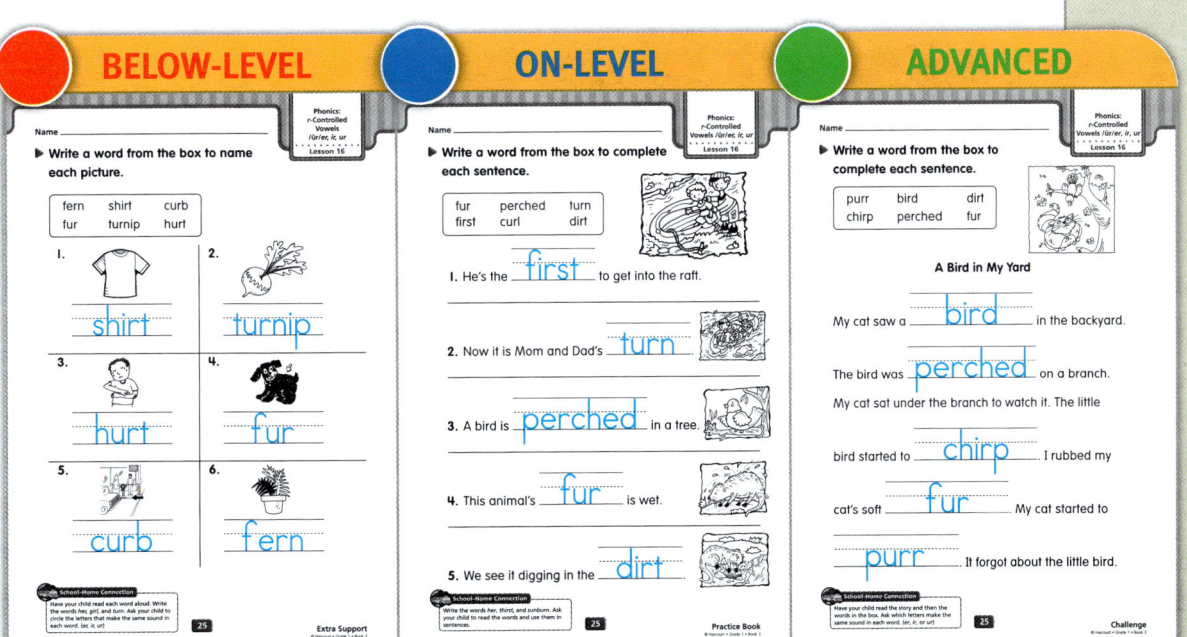

▲ Extra Support, p. 25          ▲ Practice Book, p. 25          ▲ Challenge, p. 25

**ELL**

- Group children according to academic levels, and assign one of the pages on the left.

- Clarify any unfamiliar concepts as necessary. See *ELL Teacher Guide*, Lesson 16, for support in scaffolding instructions.

# Main Idea

*Comprehension*

## Objective

- *To recognize the main idea*

## Skill Trace

 **Main Idea**

## Teach/Model

**INTRODUCE THE SKILL** Tell children that the main idea of a story is what it is mostly about. Help children recall the main events in "The Lion and the Mouse," *Read-Aloud Anthology,* p. 62. Then read aloud the last paragraph of the story.

> After the lion was free, he remembered what the little mouse had once said to him: *"You never know when you may need the help of someone like me."* The lion smiled because those words had come true. The little mouse had saved the life of the King of Beasts.

Then model for children how to recognize the main idea.

**Think Aloud** The main idea of a story is what it is mostly about. I remembered the most important events in "The Lion and the Mouse." The lion caught the mouse but let him go. Later, when the lion was caught in a net, the tiny mouse returned the kindness and helped the mighty lion escape. I know this story teaches a lesson. It is the main idea of the story. The last paragraph helps me know that this story is about helping others—that when you help others, others are likely to help you in return.

## Practice/Apply

**GUIDED PRACTICE** Read *Student Edition* page 138 to children, and remind them how to recognize the main idea. Then have children look at the picture at the top of page 139 and follow along as you read aloud the sentence and questions. Ask children what important things they see in the picture. (trees, a sidewalk, a girl, and a dog on a leash) Elicit from children that the main idea of the picture is that a girl is walking her dog.

Teacher Read-Aloud

# Focus Skill

## Main Idea

What a story is mostly about is the **main idea**.

Look at the picture.

The main idea is that a family is having dinner.

138

**Look at the picture. What is the main idea? How do you know?**

### Try This!

Look at this picture. Tell what you think the main idea is.

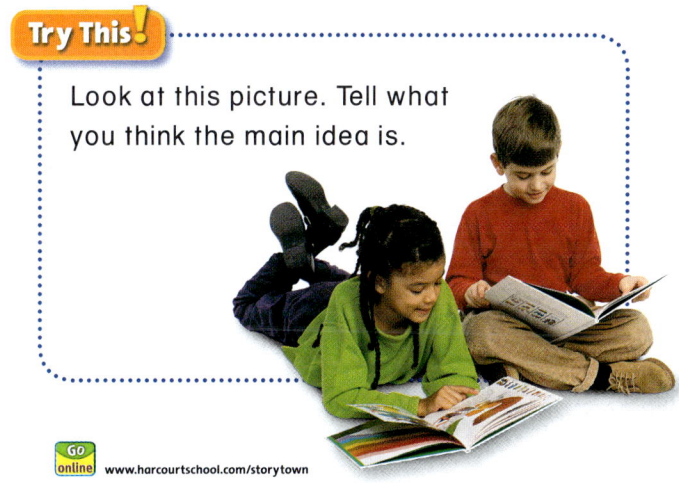

GO online  www.harcourtschool.com/storytown

139

---

**Try This!** **INDEPENDENT PRACTICE** Discuss the picture, and then have children follow along as you read aloud the sentences. As children identify the main idea, ask them to tell how they know. (The main idea is that a girl and a boy are reading books. I see a boy sitting, looking at a book in his lap, and a girl lying down, looking at a book.)

### ADVANCED

**Try This!** Have children write a main idea sentence that tells about the picture and then write several sentences with details to tell more about the main idea.

**The children are reading books.**

# High-Frequency Words
## Words to Know

## Objectives
• To read high-frequency words

### High-Frequency Words

| | |
|---|---|
| always | nice |
| by | please |
| Cow's | room |
| join | |

 **MONITOR PROGRESS**

### High-Frequency Words

| **IF** children have difficulty reading and spelling the words, | **THEN** display a second set of word cards, and have them read and match the words. |
|---|---|

**Small-Group Instruction, p. S33:**

🔴 **BELOW-LEVEL:** Reteach
🔵 **ON-LEVEL:** Reinforce
🟢 **ADVANCED:** Extend

## Teach/Model

**Routine Card 16** **INTRODUCE WORDS** Write the words *always, by, Cow's, join, nice, please,* and *room* on the board.

• Point to and read *always.* Repeat. Have children say it with you.

• Say: **I *always* brush my teeth at bedtime.**

• Point to each letter as you spell the word. Have children spell it with you.

• Have children reread the word.

Repeat for the remaining words. Use the following sentences:

• **Jack came *by* last night.**

• **That calf is *Cow's* baby.**

• **I am going to *join* the soccer team.**

• **It is *nice* to be here.**

• ***Please* go to your *room*.**

## Guided Practice

**REVIEW WITH STUDENT EDITION PAGES 140–141** Ask children to turn to *Student Edition* pages 140–141. Have children point to and read aloud each of the highlighted words. Talk about the illustration. Then ask volunteers to read aloud the sentences.

**STORY WORDS** List *elephant, hammock, kindness, lamb,* and *shade* on the board. Read the words aloud. Repeat, having children read the words with you. Mention that an elephant and a lamb are two animal characters in the story "One More Friend." Discuss the meanings of *kindness, hammock,* and *shade.* Then point to all the words again, and have children read them aloud.

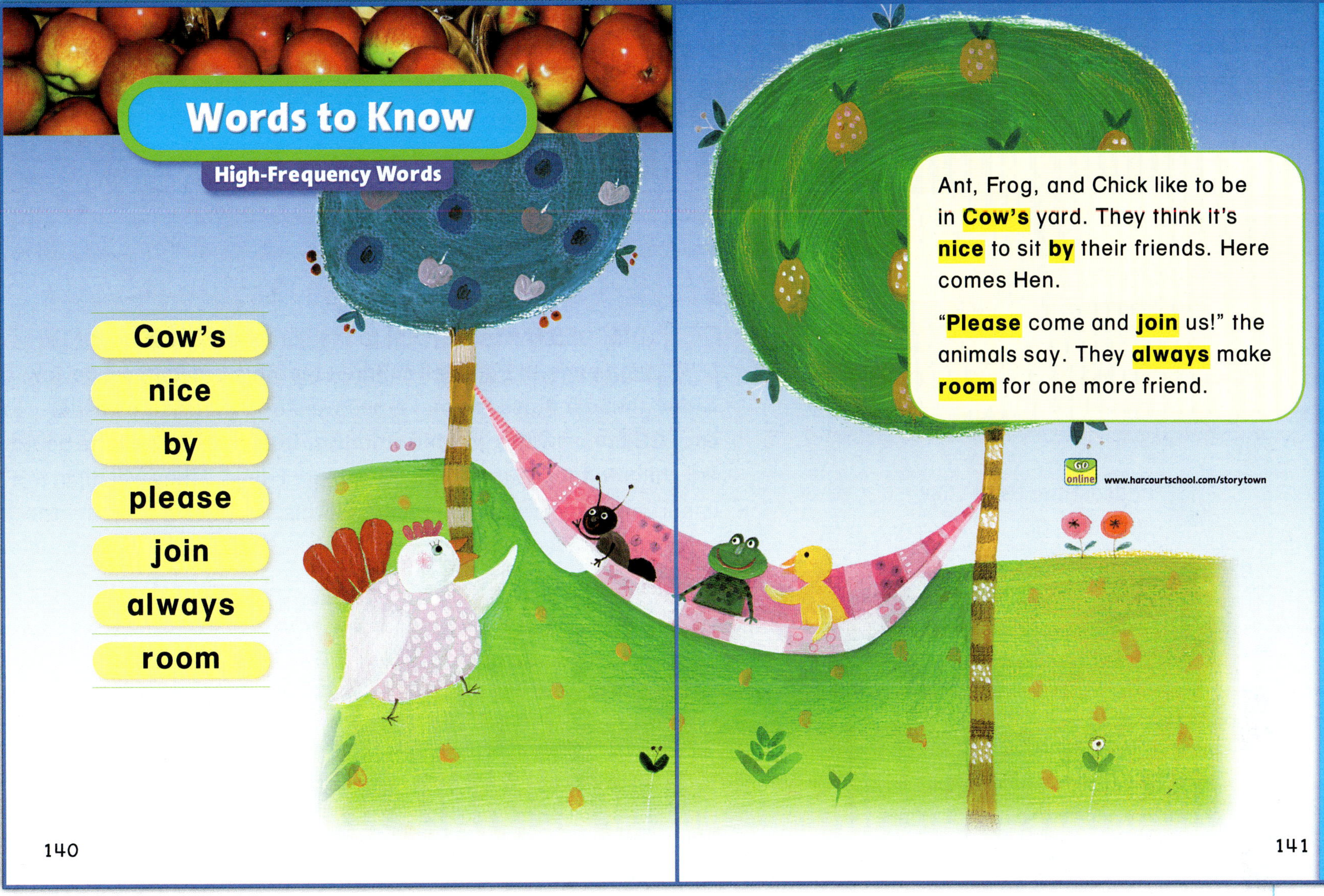

## Words to Know

**High-Frequency Words**

Cow's

nice

by

please

join

always

room

Ant, Frog, and Chick like to be in **Cow's** yard. They think it's **nice** to sit **by** their friends. Here comes Hen.

"**Please** come and **join** us!" the animals say. They **always** make **room** for one more friend.

www.harcourtschool.com/storytown

140

141

---

### E L L

**Reinforce High-Frequency Words**
After children read the sentences on page 141, ask questions that require them to respond with a short answer, *yes* or *no,* or to point to something in the illustration. Use questions such as the following, incorporating the highlighted words in the discussion:

- Where are the animals?
- Do they think it's nice to sit by each other?
- What is Ant saying?

#  Reading

## *Student Edition:* One More Friend

## Objectives

- *To understand genre: fantasy*
- *To use summarizing as a strategy for comprehension*

 **Podcasting:** Using Story Structures, Gr. 1

## Options for Reading

 **BELOW-LEVEL**

**Preview** Have children preview the story by looking at the illustrations. Guide them to identify the characters and setting and tell what is happening. Read each page to children, and have them read it after you. Use the Monitor Comprehension questions to discuss it.

 **ON-LEVEL**

**Monitor Comprehension** Have children read aloud, page by page. Ask the Monitor Comprehension questions as you go. Then lead them in retelling the important events.

 **ADVANCED**

**Independent Reading** Have children read each page silently, looking up each time they finish a page. Ask the Monitor Comprehension questions as you go. Then lead a discussion about how Ant is kind.

## Genre Study

**DISCUSS FANTASY** Point to the genre label on *Student Edition* page 142 and tell children that this is a *fantasy*. Review that a fantasy is a make-believe story. Then use **Transparency GO7** or copy the graphic organizer from page 142 on the board. Tell children that as they read "One More Friend," they will fill in the important story events. Tell them that this story has a pattern—the same kind of event repeats.

```
┌──────────────────────────┐
└──────────────────────────┘
            ↓
┌──────────────────────────┐
└──────────────────────────┘
            ↓
┌──────────────────────────┐
└──────────────────────────┘
            ↓
┌──────────────────────────┐
└──────────────────────────┘
            ↓
┌──────────────────────────┐
└──────────────────────────┘
```

## Comprehension Strategies

 **SUMMARIZE** Tell children that as they read, they can summarize by telling just the most important events:

**Think Aloud** In "The Lion and the Mouse," a mouse wakes a sleeping lion, and the lion catches the mouse. The mouse begs for mercy, and the lion lets him go. Then one day, the lion gets caught in a net. The mouse finds the lion and chews through the net to free him.

Then read aloud the sentence under Comprehension Strategy on page 142. Point out that summarizing can help readers understand a story better. Explain that children will work together to use a sequence chart as they read "One More Friend" to help them summarize the story.

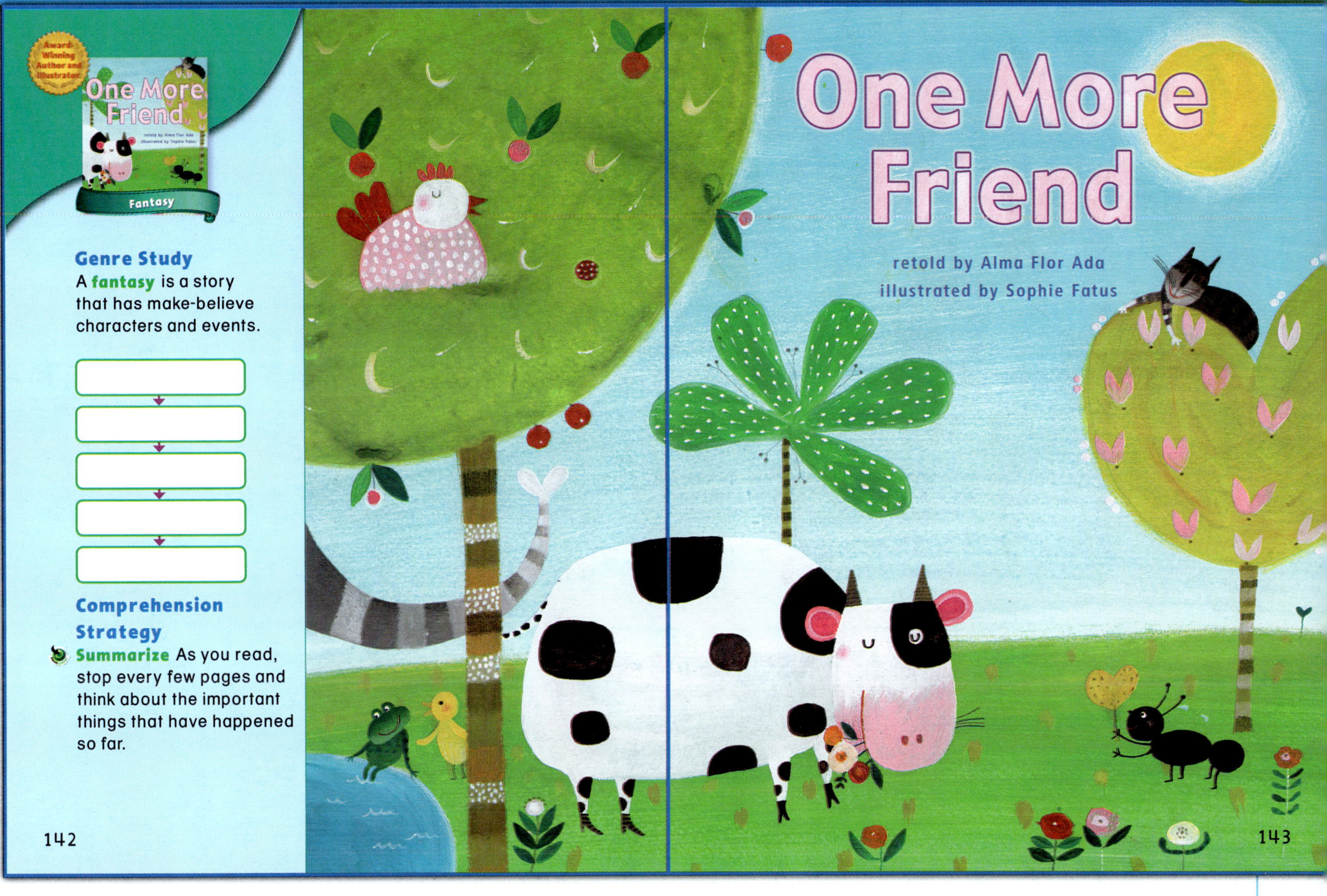

## Genre Study

A **fantasy** is a story that has make-believe characters and events.

[ ]
↓
[ ]
↓
[ ]
↓
[ ]
↓
[ ]

## Comprehension Strategy

**Summarize** As you read, stop every few pages and think about the important things that have happened so far.

Award-Winning Author and Illustration

One More Friend

Fantasy

# One More Friend

retold by Alma Flor Ada
illustrated by Sophie Fatus

142

143

## Build Background

**DISCUSS KINDNESS** Say: **This story is a fantasy that teaches a lesson about kindness. Tell how you show each other kindness.**

**Routine Card 17**

**SET A PURPOSE AND PREDICT** Tell children that this is a story they will read to enjoy and to learn the lesson it teaches.

- Read the title and the names of the author and illustrator.

- In the illustration, identify Ant and Cow as story characters and talk about the hammock. Ask children to tell what the setting is. Ask them what lesson they think the story might teach.

- List predictions on the board.

- Invite children to read to discover the lesson of the story.

## TECHNOLOGY

 **eBook** "One More Friend" is available in an eBook.

 **Audiotext** "One More Friend" is available on *Audiotext Grade 1*, CD 3 for subsequent readings.

"My, it's nice to rest in the shade!"
Ant is happy in the hammock in Cow's
backyard.

144

145

# Monitor Comprehension

**PAGES 144–145** Say: **We can see that Cow is not in the hammock. Ant is. How do you think Ant feels? Let's read to find out.**

**1** **NOTE DETAILS** **How does Ant feel?** (happy)

**2** **MAKE INFERENCES** **Why do you think Ant is happy?** (Possible response: It gets hot in the sun. The hammock is in the shade, so it's cooler. This makes Ant feel happy.)

**3** **RELATE PICTURES TO TEXT** **How does the picture help you understand the meaning of the words *hammock* and *shade*?** (Possible response: I see Ant in a hammock in the shade. This shows me that a *hammock* is a hanging bed and *shade* is a place that's not in the sun.)

Frog hops up. "Ribbit ribbit!"
"Jump up, Frog! Be the first!" calls Ant.
"There's always room for one more.
Please don't say you can't!"

146

Chick skips by. "Chirp chirp!"
"Come join us, little bird!" calls Ant.
"There's always room for one more.
Please don't say you can't!"

147

# Monitor Comprehension

**PAGES 146–147** Say: **I think Ant is talking to the frog and then I see the frog in the hammock. I wonder what Ant says to the frog. Let's read to find out.**

**①** **NOTE DETAILS** **Who says "Ribbit ribbit"?** (Frog) **Who says "Chirp chirp"?** (Chick) **Who says "Come jump up! Be the first!"** (Ant) **Who jumps up first?** (Frog) **What does Ant say to both Frog and Chick? Find and read the sentences.** ("There's always room for one more. Please don't say you can't!")

**②** **MAKE PREDICTIONS** **What do you think will happen when the next animal passes by?** (Possible response: The next animal will say the sound it makes. Ant will invite it into the hammock.)

**E L L**

**Words for Animal Sounds**
Animals make the same sounds worldwide, but languages express them in different ways. In Spanish, for example, a chick says *pío-pío* and a frog says *cruá-cruá*. As children read the story, help them to associate the animals with the sounds they make. Ask either **Who says *ribbit ribbit*?** or **What does a frog say?**

Hen steps up. "Cluck cluck!"
"Come join us! Be the third!" calls Ant.
"There's always room for one more.
Please don't say you can't!"

148

Duck flaps his wings. "Quack quack!"
"Come join us, good sir!" calls Ant.
"There's always room for one more.
Please don't say you can't!"

149

# Monitor Comprehension

**PAGES 148–149** Say: **I see two new characters. Let's see if your predictions about what will happen are right.**

**1** **CONFIRM PREDICTIONS** **What happens when the animals come to the hammock?** (Ant invites Hen and Duck into the hammock, saying, "There's always room for one more. Please don't say you can't!")

**2** **VOCABULARY/APPLY PHONICS** **Frog was first, and Chick was next. What is the word for being "number 2" in order?** *(second)* **Hen is next. Find and read the word that tells what Hen is.** *(third)* **What vowel sound does** *third* **have in the middle?** (/ûr/)

**3** **NOTE DETAILS** **What does Hen say?** (Cluck cluck) **Who joins Ant next?** (Duck) **What does Duck say?** (Quack quack) **How many animals are there in the hammock now?** (five)

## Use Multiple Strategies

**Ask Questions** Say: As I read, I can ask myself, "Why is Ant asking the animals to come into the hammock? How many animals will go into the hammock? What might happen if too many animals get in the hammock?" I will read to find out.

**Reread** Say: Sometimes I reread a part of a story that was confusing at first. This helps me to understand it better.

"My, it's nice to rest in the shade!"
Ant, Frog, Chick, Hen, and Duck are
all happy in the hammock in Cow's
backyard.

150

Cat slinks by in the grass. "Purr purr!"
"Come join us and curl up!" calls Ant.
"There's always room for one more.
Please don't say you can't!"

151

# Monitor Comprehension

**PAGES 150–151** Say: **It looks a bit crowded in the hammock. Let's read to find out who else joins Ant.**

**1**  **SUMMARIZE** **What has happened in the story so far?** (Possible response: Ant has invited Frog, Chick, Hen, Duck, and Cat, in that order, to come into the hammock.)

**2** **EXPRESS PERSONAL OPINIONS** **What words would you choose to describe what Ant is like? Why?** (Possible responses: friendly and kind, because Ant invites each animal into the hammock)

**3** **AUTHOR'S CRAFT** **What is the pattern in the story?** (An animal comes by, makes its noise, and Ant invites him or her into the hammock.)

## SCIENCE

### SUPPORTING STANDARDS

**Shadows** Demonstrate for children, using light and classroom objects, that light cannot pass through opaque objects. Help children relate this to the trees supporting the hammock in the story. When objects block light from the sun, they cast shadows on the ground, and this is called *shade*.

Lesson 16 (*Student Edition*, pp. 150–151) **T333**

Dog and Lamb run up. "Bark bark! Baaa baaa!"
"Come join us! It's your turn!" calls Ant.
"There's always room for one more.
Please don't say you can't!"

152

"My, it's nice to rest in the shade!"
Ant, Frog, Chick, Hen, Duck, Cat, Dog,
and Lamb are all happy in the hammock
in Cow's backyard.

153

# Monitor Comprehension

**PAGES 152–153** Say: **There are a lot of animals in the hammock. Do you think they're enjoying the hammock? Let's read to find out.**

1. **DETERMINE CHARACTERS' EMOTIONS** Are the animals comfortable in the hammock? How can you tell? (Possible response: Yes; they look happy even though it is crowded.)

2. **MAKE JUDGMENTS** Do you think Dog and Lamb should get into the hammock? Why or why not? (Possible response: Yes; even though the hammock is crowded, it is pretty big, and Ant says, "There's always room for one more.")

3. **NOTE DETAILS** How many animals are there in the hammock? (eight)

## Apply
### Comprehension Strategies

**Summarize** Fill in the sequence chart with children as they read. Then guide them to summarize the story so far.

**Think Aloud** Ant invites each animal that passes by to come into the hammock because there's always room for more.

> Ant is happy in the hammock in the shade.

↓

> Ant invites Frog. Frog gets into the hammock.

↓

> Chick gets into the hammock.

↓

Then up jumps Cow.
Who is this now?
It's a big elephant!
What will Ant say?
Oh, no! She can't. . .

But Ant calls out,
"Come join us!"

154

155

# Monitor Comprehension

**PAGES 154–156** Say: **I see an elephant! Do you think Ant will invite the elephant to join them? What will happen? Let's read to find out.**

**①** **EXPRESS PERSONAL OPINIONS** **Were you surprised when Ant asked the elephant to join them? Tell why or why not.** (Possible response: Yes; an elephant is too big for a hammock.)

**②** **CONFIRM PREDICTIONS** **Did the story end the way you thought it would end?** (Accept reasonable responses.)

**③** **MAIN IDEA** **Sometimes the main idea of a story is a lesson about how to treat others. What do you think the main idea of this story is?** (There's always a way to include all your friends when you are kind and caring.)

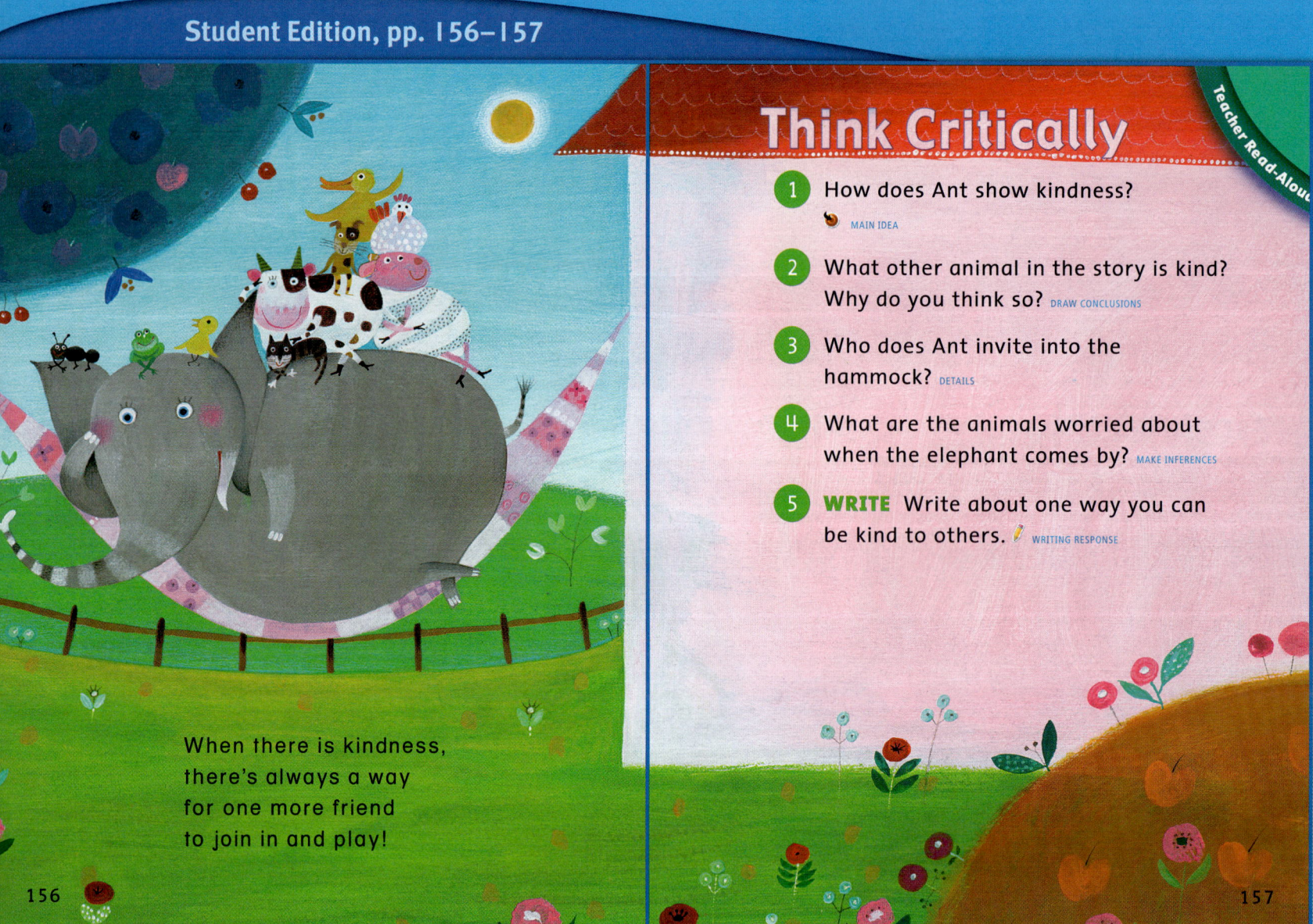

When there is kindness, there's always a way for one more friend to join in and play!

156

## Think Critically

1. How does Ant show kindness? MAIN IDEA

2. What other animal in the story is kind? Why do you think so? DRAW CONCLUSIONS

3. Who does Ant invite into the hammock? DETAILS

4. What are the animals worried about when the elephant comes by? MAKE INFERENCES

5. **WRITE** Write about one way you can be kind to others. WRITING RESPONSE

157

Teacher Read-Aloud

# Think Critically

### Respond to the Literature

1. Ant invites each animal that passes by to join the other animals in the hammock in the shade. **MAIN IDEA**

2. Cow is kind to let Ant and the other animals use the hammock. **DRAW CONCLUSIONS**

3. Ant invites Frog, Chick, Hen, Duck, Cat, Dog, Lamb, and the elephant. **DETAILS**

4. The animals are worried that there is no room in the hammock for the big elephant. **MAKE INFERENCES**

5. **WRITE** Possible response: You can be kind to others in lots of ways. One way is to invite a new boy or girl to join you and your friends when you play on the playground. **WRITING RESPONSE**

### LISTENING/SPEAKING: Conversation

Guide children to:

- participate in a conversation
- speak clearly and use appropriate volume
- use speaking vocabulary
- listen attentively to others
- ask questions for clarification and understanding

After the discussion, guide children to recognize how the language they used to discuss the story is different from the less-formal language they use at home.

### Meet the Author
### Alma Flor Ada

The ideas for "One More Friend" come from Alma Flor Ada's childhood. She loved hammocks as a child in Cuba, and slept on them many times. Also, at her house they were always making room at the table for a relative or visitor. Her cousin would often say, "There's always room for one more!"

### Meet the Illustrator
### Sophie Fatus

Sophie Fatus is an artist who grew up in France and now lives in Italy. She loves animals and enjoys painting them very much, like the ones in this story. She hopes that her artwork will help children remember to like each other and be kind to one another.

www.harcourtschool.com/storytown

158

159

# Meet the Author and the Illustrator

**PAGES 158–159** Explain that these pages tell about the person who wrote "One More Friend" and the person who illustrated it. Identify Alma Flor Ada in the photograph on page 158 as the author and Sophie Fatus in the photograph on page 159 as the illustrator. Ask children to describe the roles of the **author** and the **illustrator**. Read aloud pages 158–159. Encourage children to follow along as you read.

# Check Comprehension
## Retelling

## Retell

**DIBELS** Oral Reading Fluency ORF

**MAIN IDEA** Remind children that the main idea is what a story is mostly about. Ask them to tell the main idea of "One More Friend."

**REVISIT THE GRAPHIC ORGANIZER** Display completed **Transparency GO7.** Guide children to use it to summarize, telling the main idea and the sequence of important events.

**STORY RETELLING CARDS** The cards for "One More Friend" can be used for a retelling or as an aid to completing the sequence chart.

▲ Story Retelling Cards 1–6, "One More Friend"

## Fluency

### Teach/Model

**DIBELS** Oral Reading Fluency ORF

**READING RATE** Have children open to pages 146–147 of "One More Friend." Remind them to read silently at a rate that allows them to understand what they read and to read aloud at a rate that allows listeners to understand and stay interested in the story. Model reading aloud at an appropriate rate.

### Practice/Apply

**PAIRED READING** Have children select several pages and practice reading aloud. Have partners take turns sharing their oral reading.

# Build Robust Vocabulary

## Listening/Speaking: *Words from the Read-Aloud*

### Review Robust Vocabulary

**USE VOCABULARY IN DIFFERENT CONTEXTS** Remind children of the Student-Friendly Explanations for *captured, mercy,* and *struggling.* Then discuss each word using the following examples:

**captured**
- Tell about a story you have read or listened to in which a character was captured.
- Pretend you are trying to capture a big bug. Show how you would do it.
- Has anything ever captured your attention so that you didn't want to do anything else? Tell about it.

**mercy**
- Think about a time when someone showed you mercy after you did something you shouldn't have. What did that person say to you? How did you feel afterward?
- Tell about a time that you would show another person mercy.
- Pretend you are an actor on stage, playing the role of the lion in "The Lion and the Mouse." In this version, the hunters get to you before the mouse can chew through the net. What do you say to convince the hunters to show you mercy?

**struggling**
- If you saw a friend struggling to open a box, what would you do?
- How might you look and act if you were struggling to carry a very heavy box across the room?
- What is the best thing to do if you are struggling with your homework?

## Objective
- *To review robust vocabulary through discussing ideas*

**REVIEW** | Tested ✓

### Student-Friendly Explanations

**captured** If you have captured something, you have caught it and are not letting it go.

**mercy** If you show kindness or forgiveness to someone who has done something wrong, you show mercy.

**struggling** If you are struggling, you are making a great effort with your body or mind to do something.

### ADVANCED

**Use Vocabulary in Different Contexts** Write the Vocabulary Words on index cards. Children take turns choosing a card. Read the word to the child, and ask him or her to use the word in an original sentence.

# Grammar

## Using He, She, It, and They

| 5-DAY GRAMMAR | |
|---|---|
| DAY 1 | Introduce Using *He, She, It,* and *They* |
| DAY 2 | **Rewrite Sentences** |
| DAY 3 | Revise Sentences |
| DAY 4 | Complete Sentences |
| DAY 5 | Write Sentences |

## Objectives

- *To recognize pronouns* he, she, it, *and* they *and the names they replace*
- *To rewrite sentences using* he, she, it, *and* they

### Daily Proofreading

**she is my friend**

(She, friend.)

**Pronouns** Subject pronouns in children's home language may be omitted because the verb ending indicates whether the subject is *I, you, he/she/it, we,* or *they.* Model and reinforce the use of subject pronouns in English.

▲ Grammar Practice Book, p. 61

## Review

**USE A LITERATURE MODEL** Tell children they will listen to a poem that uses words to replace the names of people, animals, or things. Read the poem several times, having children join in.

I patted my dog; he licked me.
I stroked my cat; she licked me, too.
I tickled my hamster; she bit me.
If I hug my sisters, what will *they* do?

Reread the poem line by line and have children identify the pronouns *(he, she, she, they)* and the word each pronoun replaces. *(dog, cat, hamster, sisters)*

## Practice/Apply

**GUIDED PRACTICE** Hand a girl a book and say: **[Child's name] has a book.** Write the sentence on the board. Ask which words can be used in place of the girl's name and a book. *(she, it)* Write the new sentence on the board below the first one, and have children read it with you. Repeat for *he* and *they.*

**INDEPENDENT PRACTICE** Draw a sandwich on the board, and write the following sentences, underlining the words as shown:

<u>The children</u> made a sandwich.  <u>The sandwich</u> is big.
<u>Ann</u> cuts the sandwich.  <u>Ben</u> gets the milk.

Have children read the sentences. Then ask them to write each sentence using *he, she, it,* or *they* in place of the underlined words. Then call on volunteers to read the sentences to the group and tell why they used *he, she, it,* or *they.*

| **5-DAY** WRITING | |
| --- | --- |
| **DAY 1** | Modeled Writing |
| **DAY 2** | Shared Writing |
| **DAY 3** | Shared Writing |
| **DAY 4** | Independent Writing |
| **DAY 5** | Independent Writing |

# Shared Writing

*Invitation*

## Write Together

**REVIEW INVITATIONS** Display the model invitation from Day 1 and ask volunteers to recall the parts of an invitation. Ask children to share reasons to send an invitation.

**GENERATE IDEAS** Guide children to write for a familiar occasion, audience, and purpose. Work with them to choose an event from the web created on Day 1 to write a group invitation about.

**MODEL WRITING** Have volunteers dictate the invitation as you record it, using the Step-by-Step Writing Instruction as a guide. Track the print and read it with children. Save and complete the invitation for Day 3.

### Step-by-Step Writing Instruction

| | | |
| --- | --- | --- |
| **1** | How do I write *To?* The mark that follow it is called a colon. How do I write the name of who is being invited? | To: Mr. Burns's Class |
| **2** | What is the event? How do I write that sentence? What mark belongs at the end? | You are invited to our art show. |
|  **3** | Let's add an interesting idea to help our readers understand more about the event. How do I write it? What are some interesting words to use? | We will snack on yummy fruit and veggies, too! |
| **4** | How do I write the word *When?* We need to tell the date and time. How do I begin the name of the day of the week? The month? How do I write the time? | When: Friday, May 21 at 2:00 |
| **5** | How do I write *Where?* What comes next? | Where: Room 6 |
| **6** | Who is the invitation from? How do I write those words? Now let's read the whole invitation. | Your friends, Mrs. Clark's Class |

## Objectives

- *To identify the parts of an invitation*
- *To generate ideas for an invitation*
- *To compose an invitation*

### Writing Prompt

**Lists** Have children imagine they are planning a party, and have them make a list of people to invite and of things they will need for the party.

▲ **Writer's Companion, Lesson 16**

**Writing the Date** The order of the month and day in a date can vary. For example, in Spanish, May 21 would be written as *21 de mayo.* Unlike in English, the name of the month does not begin with a capital letter. Provide opportunities for children to read and write dates in English.

Day at a Glance

## Day 3

### Phonemic Awareness
- Phoneme Deletion

###  phonics and Spelling
- Review: *r*-Controlled /ûr/*er, ir, ur*
- Maintain: Short /i/*i*, /e/*e*, /u/*u*
- State the Generalization

### High-Frequency Words
- Review: *always, by, Cow's, join, nice, please, room*

### Fluency
- Reading Rate
- "One More Friend," *Student Edition*, pp. 142–159

### Comprehension
FocusSkill  Review: Main Idea

### Reading

- "Good Friends," *Student Edition*, pp. 160–161

### Robust Vocabulary
- *compatible, amiable, relax*

### Grammar
- Review: Using *He, She, It, They*

### Shared Writing ✏
- Invitation

# Warm-Up Routines

## Oral Language

**Objective** To listen attentively and respond appropriately to oral communication

### Question of the Day
Think about your friends. How would you describe what a friend is?

Have children share their ideas about what it means to be a friend. Then have children help you complete the following sentence frame:

**A friend is _____.**

## Read Aloud

**Objective** *To identify rhyming words in a poem*

**BIG BOOK OF RHYMES AND POEMS** Ask children to tell what they recall about "The New Girl." As you reread the poem, pause to have children say the rhyming words. (same/name, be/me) Afterward, invite volunteers to role-play two children, one a new child like the girl in the poem, as they introduce themselves and get to know one another. Then reread the poem, modeling fluent reading, and have children join in. Continue until they can recite the poem with you.

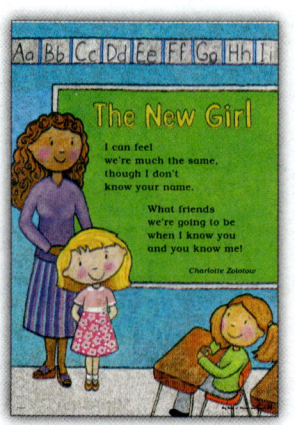

▲ Big Book of Rhymes and Poems, p. 31

# Word Wall

**Objective** *To read high-frequency words*

**REVIEW HIGH FREQUENCY WORDS** Review *always, by, Cow's, join, nice, please, room,* and other previously learned high-frequency words. Say each word, ask a vounteer to point to it, and have children read it aloud. Then point to words at random, and have children reread them. Repeat several times to reinforce instant recognition.

| always | by | Cow's | join |
|--------|-----|-------|------|

| nice | please | room |
|------|--------|------|

# Phonemic Awareness

**Objective** *To delete phonemes to make new words*

**Routine Card 9**

**PHONEME DELETION** Tell children that you are going to ask them to make new words by taking away a sound. Model with the word *her.* Say: **If I say the word *herd* without /d/, I get *her*.**

*same* without /m/ (say)      *that* without /th/ (at)

*chart* without /ch/ (art)     *quiz* without /kw/ (is)

*drip* without /r/ (dip)     *skip* without /k/ (sip)

*nice* without /n/ (ice)     *inch* without /ch/ (in)

*farmer* without /ûr/ (farm)     *runner* without /ûr/ (run)

**Shape without /sh/ is ape.**

# Build Words

 **phonics** and Spelling

| 5-DAY PHONICS | |
| --- | --- |
| DAY 1 | Introduce *r*-Controlled Vowels /ûr/*er, ir, ur* |
| DAY 2 | Word Building with *r*-Controlled Vowels /ûr/*er, ir, ur* |
| DAY 3 | Build Words |
| DAY 4 | Introduce Inflections *-er, -est* |
| DAY 5 | Review Inflections *-er, -est* |

## Objectives

- *To discriminate between the letter-sound associations /ûr/er, ir, ur, /i/i, /e/e, and /u/u*

- *To use /ûr/er, ir, ur, and known letter-sounds to decode words*

- *To read and write words with /ûr/er, ir, ur, /i/i, /e/e, and /u/u*

- *To read and write spelling words*

## Skill Trace

**Tested** ✓

| | /ûr/*er, ir, ur* | /u/u |
| --- | --- | --- |
| Introduce | T306–T309 | Bk 1-2, T220–T223 |
| Reteach | S32 | Bk 1-2, S22 |
| **Review** | **T322–T323, T344–T345, T357** | Bk 1-2, T236–T237 T260–T261 |
| Test | Bk 1-3 | Bk 1-2 |
| Maintain | Bk 1-5, T348–T349 | T344–T345 |

*r*-Controlled Vowels /ûr/ *er, ir, ur*

Look at that girl in the pink shirt.
She has dots on her red skirt.
Her name is Fern Burns.
Look at her curls.
Fern has fun when she twirls.
Watch her turn and spin!

Grade 1, Lesson 16    R31    Phonics: *r*-Controlled Vowels /ûr/*er, ir, ur*; Short Vowels /e/e, /i/i, /u/u

**Transparency R31**

## Word Building

**DIBELS**
Nonsense Word Fluency
**NWF**

**Routine Card 14**

**BUILD AND READ WORDS** Use a pocket chart and *Letter Cards*. Have children repeat each step with their *Word Builders* and *Word Builder Cards*.

Build the word *bun*. Then have them say the word naturally—*bun*. Lead children in building and reading a new word by saying:

- **Add *r* after *u*. Read the word.** *(burn)*

- **Build *fist* and have children read it.**

- **Add *r* after *i*. Read the word.** *(first)*

Continue in a similar matter with these words: *bet/Bert, cub/curb, hut/hurt, fist/first,* and *bid/bird*.

## Read Words in Context

**READ SENTENCES** Display **Transparency R31** or write the sentences on the board or on chart paper. Then, have children choral-read the sentences as you track the print. Tell children to use context clues to construct meaning for any unfamiliar words. For example, if children are unfamiliar with *skirt,* have them use the letter-sounds to sound out the word and then look for something in the illustration that has dots on it. Help children use the illustration for clues to confirm other unknown words. Then, ask volunteers to read each sentence aloud. Call on volunteers to underline or frame words with the /ûr/ sound.

**5-DAY SPELLING**

| | |
|---|---|
| **DAY 1** | Pretest |
| **DAY 2** | Word Building |
| **DAY 3** | State the Generalization |
| **DAY 4** | Review |
| **DAY 5** | Posttest |

## Review Spelling Words

**STATE THE GENERALIZATION** List spelling words 1–6 on the board and have children read them. Ask: **How are all the words alike?** (Each word has the /ûr/ sound.) Have volunteers read each word and underline the letters that stand for the /ûr/ sound. Tell children that *er, ir,* and *ur* are used to spell the /ûr/ sound.

**REVIEW WORDS** List spelling words 7–8. Ask what letters stand for the /kw/ sound in *quit (qu)* and the /hw/ sound in *when (wh)*. Have children read and spell the words.

**HIGH-FREQUENCY WORDS** List spelling words 9–10. Remind children that they have seen and read these words many times. Run your hand under *name* as you read it, and ask children to look carefully at the letters. Ask them to close their eyes, picture the word, and spell it with you. Repeat for *work*.

**WRITE** Have children write the spelling words in their notebook. Remind them to use their best handwriting and to use the list to check their spelling.

# Handwriting

**LETTER FORMATION** Remind children to cross the letters *t* and *f* when they write the words *fur, turn, first,* and *quit*. Guide them to use correct letter formation, using the Handwriting Models, page R4.

---

### Spelling Words

| | |
|---|---|
| 1. her | 6. first |
| 2. fur | 7. quit |
| 3. turn | 8. when |
| 4. bird | 9. name |
| 5. girl | 10. work |

### Decodable Book

- **Phonics**
  *r*-Controlled Vowels /ûr/*er, ir, ur*
- **Decodable Words** See the list on page R11.

Decodable Book 16 ▲

Have children who need additional decoding practice read *Decodable Book 16*. See also *Decodable Books* online (Take-Home version).

▲ **Spelling Practice Book, p. 53**

# High-Frequency Words

## Objective
- *To read high-frequency words*

**REVIEW**  Tested

### High-Frequency Words

| always | nice |
|--------|------|
| by | please |
| Cow's | room |
| join | |

## Review

**DISPLAY THE WORDS** Write the word *always*. Have a volunteer read it. Erase the word, and ask children to spell it. Repeat this routine for *by, Cow's, join, nice, please,* and *room.* Point out that *cows* (more than one) and *Cow's* (possessive) sound the same.

## PRACTICE/APPLY

**GUIDED PRACTICE** Provide each child with a set of word cards (*Teacher Resource Book,* p. 140). Have children spread out the cards in front of them. As you randomly call out a word, have children hold up the matching card. Repeat until they can respond quickly and accurately.

**INDEPENDENT PRACTICE** Have partners take turns holding up a card for the other partner to read. Children should read the cards several times and then write the words in their notebook.

always

Cow's

please

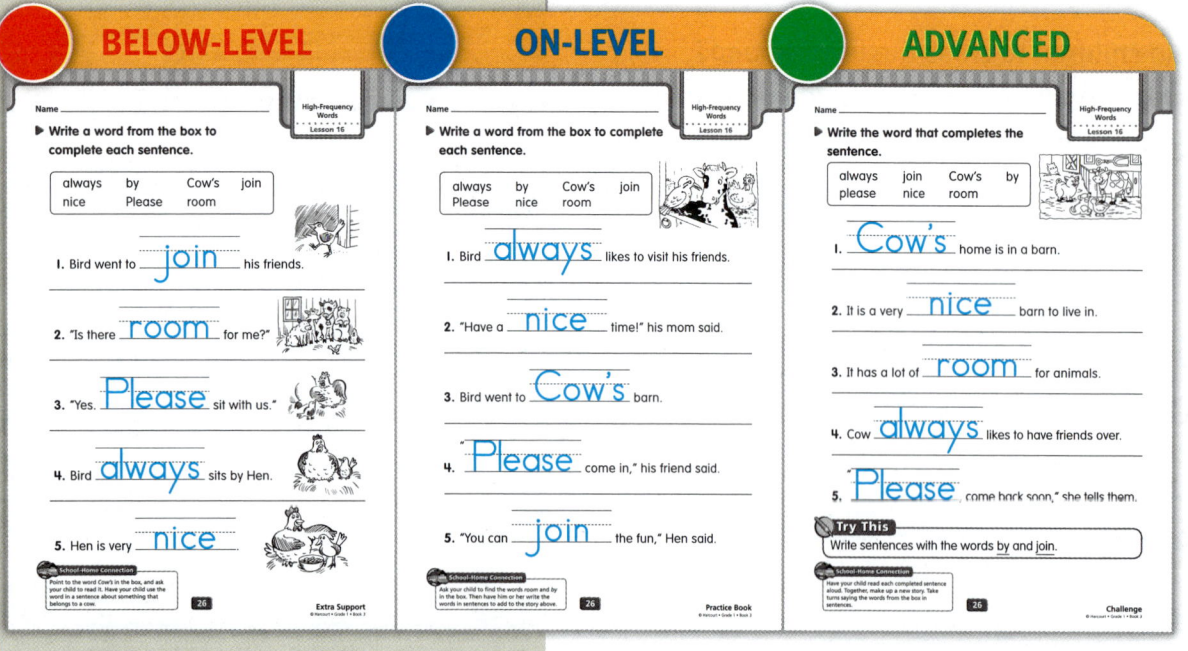

▲ Extra Support, p. 26    ▲ Practice Book, p. 26    ▲ Challenge, p. 26

### E L L

- Group children according to academic levels, and assign one of the pages on the left.

- Clarify any unfamiliar concepts as necessary. See *ELL Teacher Guide,* Lesson 16, for support in scaffolding instruction.

# Fluency
*Reading Rate*

## Review

**DIBELS** Oral Reading Fluency **ORF**

**REVIEW PUNCTUATION** Have children open their *Student Edition* to pages 146–147, and invite a volunteer to name the punctuation in each sentence, including quotation marks, commas, and end punctuation. Discuss the importance of punctuation and how it affects reading rate. For example, remind children to pause briefly at each end punctuation mark before continuing to read. Have children follow along as you model:

- reading spoken words in a way that sounds natural.

- add meaning by changing the rate of your reading.

## Practice/Apply

**GUIDED PRACTICE** Invite volunteers to choose a sentence on page 148, 149, 150, or 151. Have classmates suggest a reading rate that might be a typical way one of the characters in the story might speak, for example, quickly like an excited hen or more slowly for the part about the cat. Then have volunteers read their chosen sentences with a reading rate that helps portray a character. After children read, provide encouragement and feedback. Ask them to comment on their reading rate. Discuss when it was appropriate to read quickly and when they should have slowed down.

**INDEPENDENT PRACTICE** Have each child draw on his or her personal interests to select a page from the story and practice reading it aloud at a rate that is appropriate for the text and for the audience. Have children form small groups and take turns reading aloud their page to the group. Ask group members to provide positive encouragement to each reader.

## Objectives

- *To read with fluency in a manner that sounds like natural speech*
- *To read at a rate appropriate for the text*

 **ADVANCED**

**Expression and Intonation**
Challenge children who have mastered an appropriate reading rate for the text to add dramatic expression and intonation as they read. Invite them to present a short reading to the class.

 **MONITOR PROGRESS**

**Fluency**

| **IF** children have difficulty reading at a rate that is appropriate for the text, | **THEN** model the appropriate rate for them and invite them to echo-read the story with you. |
|---|---|

**Small-Group Instruction, pp. S34–S35:**

🔴 **BELOW-LEVEL:** Reteach
🔵 **ON-LEVEL:** Reinforce
🟢 **ADVANCED:** Extend

# Main Idea
## Comprehension

### Objectives
- *To identify main idea*
- *To listen attentively to a nonfiction article read aloud*
- *To distinguish nonfiction from fiction*

### Skill Trace
 **Main Idea**

| | |
|---|---|
| Preview | T316 |
| Introduce | T324–T325 |
| Reteach | S36–S37, S46–S47 |
| Review | **T348, T360, T370, T402, T410, T436, T448, T458** |
| Test | Bk 1-3 |
| Maintain | Monitor Comprehension, Bks 1-4, 1-5 |

## Review

**REVIEW MAIN IDEA** Remind children that the main idea of a story or selection is what it is mostly about. Have children recall the story "The Lion and the Mouse" from the *Read-Aloud Anthology,* and guide them to determine the main idea. If children need help, read these sentences and have them choose which tells the main idea best:

- Lions like to sleep.
- Be nice to others and they will be nice to you.
- The mouse helped the lion get free.

## Practice/Apply

**GUIDED PRACTICE** Ask children to state the main idea of "One More Friend" from the *Student Edition*.

**INDEPENDENT PRACTICE** Have children apply their knowledge of main idea by completing *Practice Book* page 27. Children will also apply their knowledge of main idea when they listen and respond to the nonfiction selection about friends, which follows.

▲ Extra Support, p. 27     ▲ Practice Book, p. 27     ▲ Challenge, p. 27

- Group children according to academic levels, and assign one of the pages on the left.
- Clarify any unfamiliar concepts as necessary. See *ELL Teacher Guide,* Lesson 16, for scaffolding instruction.

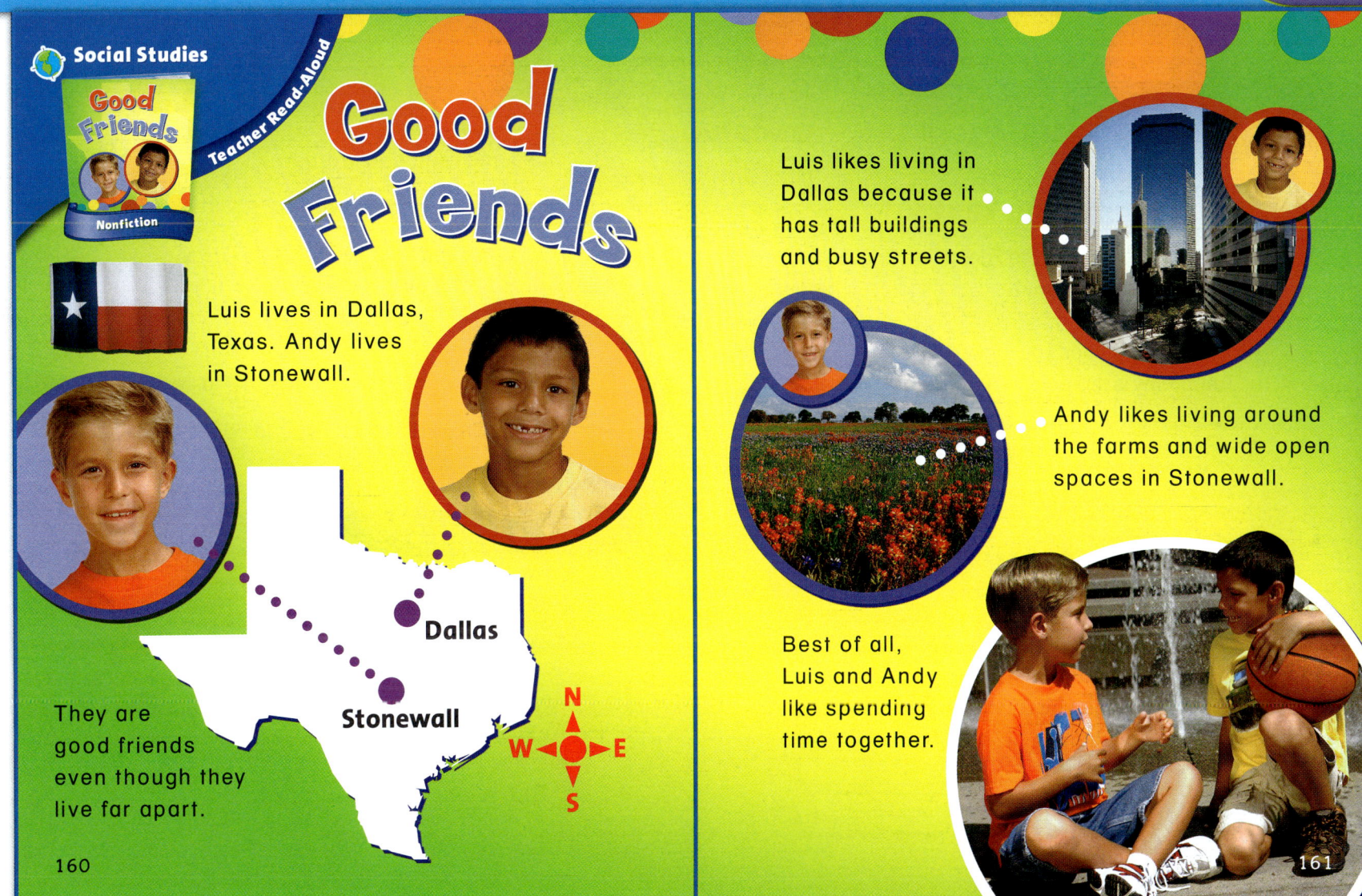

Social Studies

**Good Friends**

Nonfiction

Teacher Read-Aloud

# Good Friends

Luis lives in Dallas, Texas. Andy lives in Stonewall.

They are good friends even though they live far apart.

Dallas

Stonewall

N W E S

160

Luis likes living in Dallas because it has tall buildings and busy streets.

Andy likes living around the farms and wide open spaces in Stonewall.

Best of all, Luis and Andy like spending time together.

161

# Reading

## *Student Edition: Paired Selection*

### Read Aloud

**USE PRIOR KNOWLEDGE/SET A PURPOSE** Guide children to use prior knowledge and set a purpose for listening.

**MONITOR LISTENING COMPREHENSION** As you read, monitor listening comprehension by using these questions:

- **NOTE DETAILS** **Where does Luis live?** (Dallas, Texas) **Where does Andy live?** (Stonewall) **How are the places alike?** (They are places in Texas.) **How are they different?** (Dallas has many tall buildings; Stonewall has open spaces and farms.)

- **MAIN IDEA** **What is the main idea of this selection?** (You can be friends even if you live far apart.)

**ON-LEVEL**

**Build Background** Display a map of the United States and a map of the world or a globe. As children name the towns or cities, states, or countries where their friends live, point out each location on the map or globe. Invite children to share what they know about the places where their friends live.

## Connections

### Comparing Texts

1. Did you like "One More Friend" or "Good Friends" better? Why?
(Responses will vary. Children should support their answers.)

2. Think of a person you know who is like Ant. How is this person like Ant?
(Possible response: My big brother's job is to sweep the floor. He likes cleaning up.)

3. How would you be kind to someone?
(Responses will vary.)

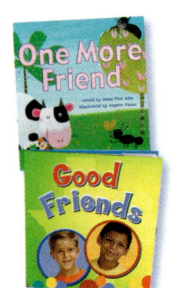

### Writing

Write a note to invite a friend to your house. List the things you plan to do when he or she visits.

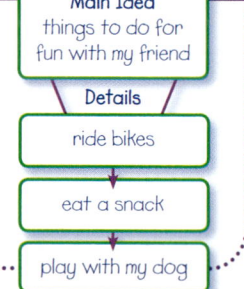

Main Idea
things to do for fun with my friend

Details

ride bikes

eat a snack

play with my dog

### Phonics

Make and read new words.

Start with the word **sir**.

Change **s** to **b**. Add **d** to the end.

Change **b** to **t h**.

Take off **t**. Change **i** to **e**.

Change **e** to **u** and **d** to **t**.

### Fluency Practice

Read "One More Friend" with a classmate. Read each sentence together. Read at a steady pace. Try to keep the rhythm of the words.

There's always room for one more.

Please don't say you can't!

162

163

# Connections

## Connections

### WRITING

**Write a Note** Guide children to list fun activities to do with a friend during a visit. Have them use the lists to write a note inviting a friend.

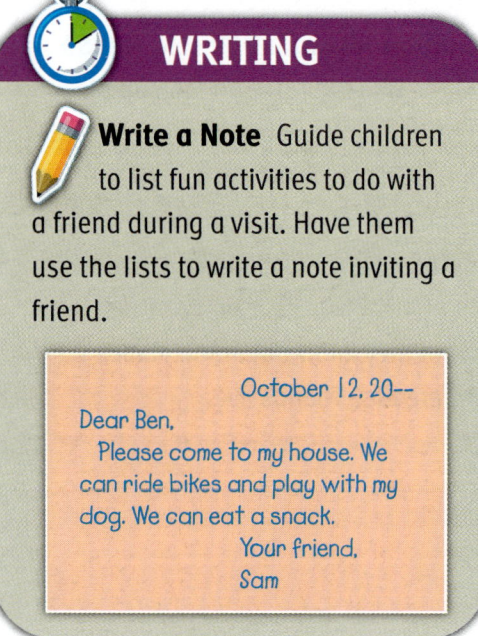

October 12, 20--
Dear Ben,
    Please come to my house. We can ride bikes and play with my dog. We can eat a snack.
                Your friend,
                Sam

### PHONICS

**Word Building** Distribute to children *Word Builder Cards b, d, e, h, i, r, s, t,* and *u*. Have children practice manipulating the cards to build and read *sir, bird, third, herd,* and *hurt*.

s i r

### FLUENCY

**Partner Reading** Explain to partners that they will read sentences from "One More Friend" together. Remind them to read at a rate that is steady and that keeps the rhythm of the words so that listeners are able to understand and enjoy the story.

"There's always room for one more."

"Please don't say you can't!"

# Build Robust Vocabulary

### Listening/Speaking: *Words About the Selection*

## Teach/Model

**INTRODUCE ROBUST VOCABULARY** Use *Routine Card 15* to introduce the words.

❶ Put the word in **selection context**.
❷ Provide for children the **Student-Friendly Explanation**.
❸ Have children **say the word** with you.
❹ Use the word in other contexts, and have children **interact with the word's meaning.**
❺ Say the Student-Friendly Explanation again, and ask children to **name the word** that goes with it.

❶ **Selection Context:** Ant, Frog, Chick, Hen, Duck, Cat, Dog, and Lamb were happy and <mark>compatible</mark> in the hammock.

❹ **Interact with Word Meaning:** My friends and I are compatible and do many things together. Are you more compatible with children your own age or with adults?

❶ **Selection Context:** Ant is an <mark>amiable</mark> character who happily invites all the animals passing by to join her in the hammock.

❹ **Interact with Word Meaning:** Is it more fun to be around someone who is amiable or someone who is not? Why?

❶ **Selection Context:** All the animals were able to <mark>relax</mark> in the hammock in Cow's backyard.

❹ **Interact with Word Meaning:** I like to relax by sitting on my porch swing. Would you rather relax on my porch or at the beach?

## Practice/Apply

**GUIDED PRACTICE** Ask children to do the following:

- Tell whether cats and birds are compatible.
- Tell something an amiable person might say or do.
- Name something you like to do when you relax.

### Objective
- *To develop robust vocabulary to describe ideas*

**Tested**

**INTRODUCE** ✓

### Student-Friendly Explanations

**compatible** When people or animals are compatible, they are able to be together or get along with each other.

**amiable** Someone who is amiable is good-natured and friendly.

**relax** When you relax, you are not uneasy or upset about anything; you spend time resting or doing things for fun.

🟢 **ADVANCED**

**Apply Words to Other Stories**
Have children choose a favorite story or book. Ask them to identify a character who is amiable, characters who are compatible, and those who are not.

# Grammar

*Using* He, She, It, *and* They

**5-DAY GRAMMAR**

| DAY 1 | Introduce Using *He*, *She*, *It*, and *They* |
| DAY 2 | Rewrite Sentences |
| DAY 3 | Revise Sentences |
| DAY 4 | Complete Sentences |
| DAY 5 | Write Sentences |

## Objective
- *To use* he, she, it, *and* they *correctly*

## Daily Proofreading

**she and I like to swim**

(She, swim.)

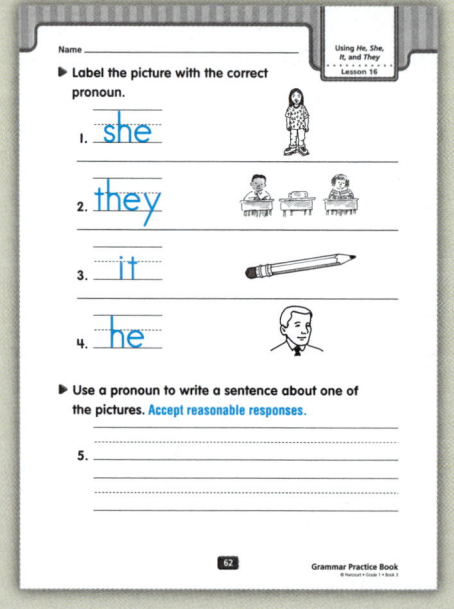

▲ Grammar Practice Book, p. 62

### Review

**DICTATE SENTENCES** Model and write a sentence on the board about a child, such as *Dan wore a red shirt today.* Ask volunteers to dictate more sentences with the name or names of other children and things. Read aloud each sentence, underlining the name or names of children and things. Ask children what words they can use to take the place of the underlined words in the naming part of each sentence. (*he, she, it,* or *they*) Then rewrite each sentence below the original sentence, using an *incorrect* pronoun.

Dan wore a red shirt today.
They wore a red shirt today.

The bell rang.
She rang.

Ann sits next to me.
It sits next to me.

Ben and Bob read a story.
He and he read a story.

### Practice/Apply

**GUIDED PRACTICE** Read aloud the first pair of sentences. Model how to rewrite the second sentence correctly, replacing *They* with *He.* Explain: **Dan is a boy.** *He* **is the word that takes the place of the name of one boy.** Have children help you correct the remaining sentences, telling which word to use and why. Then reread each pair of sentences with children, tracking the print.

**INDEPENDENT PRACTICE** Ask each child to write a sentence naming one or more person, animal, or thing. Have children trade sentences with a partner and rewrite the sentence, using *he, she, it,* or *they.* Have partners read their sentences to each other, making sure they used *he, she, it,* or *they* correctly.

Day **3**

5-DAY **WRITING**
DAY 1 Modeled Writing
DAY 2 Shared Writing
**DAY 3 Shared Writing**
DAY 4 Independent Writing
DAY 5 Independent Writing

# Shared Writing
*Invitation*

## Write Together

**REVIEW WITH A LITERATURE MODEL** Have children recall what the story "One More Friend" is mainly about. Then copy on chart paper and read aloud the following imaginary invitation from Ant.

> To: Frog, Chick, Hen, Duck, Cat, Dog, Lamb
>
> You are invited to a picnic. You may get to ride on an elephant, too!
>
> When: Saturday, July 14, 12:00–5:00
>
> Where: Cow's backyard
>
> Please come!
>
> Your friend,
>
> Ant

Point out that the invitiation tells who is invited, what the event is, when and where the event is, and who sent the invitation.

**PRACTICE WRITING** Choose another idea from the web from Day 1 to compose a group invitation about. Model how to write the invitation as children dictate the information.

**IDEAS** As you write the invitation, have children tell why each idea is important. Then point out the detail about riding an elephant in the invitation above, and encourage children to add unique ideas like this to the group's invitation.

## Share

**DISCUSS THE INVITATION** Read with children the completed invitations from Day 2 and from this lesson. Then ask children to:

- identify the main idea or purpose of each invitation.
- identify who is sending and who is receiving the invitation.
- identify what the event is and when and where it will happen.

Display the invitations for children to use as writing models.

### Objectives
- *To understand the parts of an invitation*
- *To understand how to write an invitation correctly*

 **Writing Prompt**

**List Characteristics of Invitations**
Display several commercial invitations for children to examine. Have them list the ways that all the invitations are the same and what they like about various invitations.

### BELOW-LEVEL

**Practice Writing** Display a blank invitation form on chart paper or on the board. Randomly provide the following information, and ask volunteers to tell where to write it:

- 1:00 to 3:00
- Hen and Chick
- birthday party
- Friday, May 1
- Frog, Ant, Cat, Dog, Lamb, Duck, Elephant
- Cow's backyard

## Day at a Glance

### Day 4

## Phonemic Awareness
• Phoneme Deletion

 **and Spelling**
• Introduce: Inflections *-er, -est*
• Review: *r*-Controlled Vowels /ûr/ *er, ir, ur*

## High-Frequency Words
• Review: *always*, *by*, *Cow's*, *join*, *nice*, *please*, *room*

## Fluency
• Reading Rate
• "One More Friend," *Student Edition*, pp. 142–159

## Comprehension
 Review: Main Idea

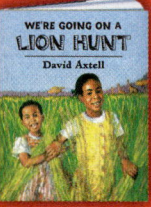
• Big Book: *We're Going on a Lion Hunt*

## Robust Vocabulary
• Review: *compatible, amiable, relax*

## Grammar
• Review: Using *He, She, It, They*

## Independent Writing ✏
• Invitation

# Warm-Up Routines

## Oral Language

**Objective** *To listen and respond appropriately to oral communication*

### Question of the Day
What animal do you think makes the best pet? Tell why you think so.

Have children brainstorm animals they think make the best pets. Then discuss why. Have children help you complete the following sentence frame:

**A _____ is the best pet because _____.**

## Read Aloud

**Objectives** *To appreciate the rhythm and rhyme of a poem; to read classic poetry*

**BIG BOOK OF RHYMES AND POEMS** Display the poem and read the title and the poet's name. Ask children to describe the poet's role. As you read the rhyme, have children participate by barking once when you say *dog*, meowing once when you say *cat*, and croaking once when you say *frog*. Then read the poem again. Have children identify the musical elements of the rhyme, such as its rhyming words. Then track the print and have children read aloud the poem several times. Ask them what they like about it.

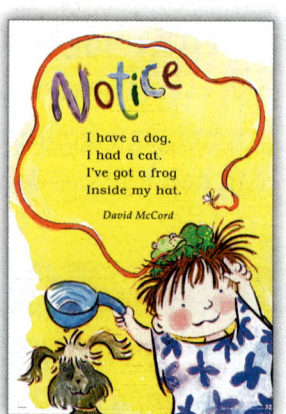
▲ Big Book of Rhymes and Poems, p. 32

## Word Wall

**Objective** *To read high-frequency words*

**REVIEW HIGH-FREQUENCY WORDS** Review *friends, join, nice, please, room,* and other previously learned high-frequency words. Say each word, ask a volunteer to point to it, and have children read it aloud. Then point to words at random, and have children reread them.

friends  join  nice  please  room

## Phonemic Awareness

**Objective** *To delete phonemes in words*

**Routine Card 9**

**PHONEME DELETION** Tell children they will sing a song and take away a sound in a word and guess the new word. Model the first one for children, singing to the tune of "London Bridge Is Falling Down."

**Take away the /ch/ in *chart*, /ch/ in *chart*, /ch/ in *chart*,**
**Take away the /ch/ in *chart*, and say the new word.** (art)

Continue singing the song, using these words:

| | |
|---|---|
| /hw/ in *where* (air) | /ch/ in *perch* (purr) |
| /ch/ in *beach* (bee) | /sh/ in *shown* (own) |
| /th/ in *think* (ink) | /th/ in *tenth* (ten) |
| /t/ in *trash* (rash) | /t/ in *hurt* (her) |
| /t/ in *quilt* (quill) | /r/ in *trap* (tap) |

think − /th/ = ink

# Inflections -er, -est phonics

| 5-DAY PHONICS | |
|---|---|
| DAY 1 | Introduce *r*-Controlled Vowels /ûr/*er, ir, ur* |
| DAY 2 | Word Building with *r*-Controlled Vowels /ûr/*er, ir, ur* |
| DAY 3 | Word Building |
| Day 4 | Introduce Inflections *-er, -est* |
| DAY 5 | Review Inflections *-er, -est* |

## Objectives

- *To recognize inflections* -er, -est
- *To read words with inflections* -er, -est

## Skill Trace

**Inflections *-er, -est***

| | |
|---|---|
| Introduce | T356 |
| Review | T366 |

**Resources**

Phonics Practice Book, pp. 89–90

Inflections *-er, -est*

Burt    Kirk    Fern

Burt has the biggest car.
Kirk's car is bigger than Fern's car.
It is darker than Fern's car, too.
Burt has the darkest car.
Kirk's car is smaller than Burt's car.
Fern has the smallest car.
Her car is the fastest one.

Grade 1, Lesson 16    R32    Phonics: Inflections *-er, -est*

**Transparency R32**

## Teach/Model

**INTRODUCE INFLECTIONS *-ER, -EST*** Cut three strands of string, each one longer than the next. Write the following words as column headings in a chart on chart paper:

**long**          **longer**          **longest**

Display the long and longer strands and describe them as follows: **The string is long. This string is longer.** Repeat the words *long* and *longer,* pointing to each one on the board and to the strand it describes. Then display the longest strand, and describe all three as follows: **The string is long. This string is longer. That string is the longest.** Repeat the words *long, longer,* and *longest,* pointing to each one on the chart and to the strand it describes. Have children read each word. Underline the inflections.

## Guided Practice

**WRITE WORDS WITH INFLECTIONS *-ER, -EST*** Ask a volunteer to stand. Say, for example, **Ann is tall.** Write the word *tall* on the chart. Ask a taller child to stand next to the first child. Ask what word can be used to describe the second child. *(taller)* Then say, for example, **Jack is taller.** Ask a volunteer to write *taller* on the chart. Stand next to the two children. Ask what word can be used to compare you to the two children. *(tallest)* Say: **I am the tallest.** Ask a volunteer to write *tallest* on the chart. Continue in a similar way to illustrate and have children read words such as *thick/thicker/thickest* and *short/shorter/shortest.*

## Practice/Apply

**READ WORDS IN CONTEXT** Display **Transparency R32.** Have children read each sentence silently. Then call on a volunteer to read aloud the first sentence and underline or frame the word that ends with *-er* or *-est.* Continue with the other sentences. Then reread the sentences together. Write the underlined words on the chart, and ask volunteers to identify and write each root word. Save the chart for use on Day 5.

# r-Controlled Vowels /ûr/ *er, ir, ur*

**phonics** *and Spelling*

**5-DAY SPELLING**

**DAY 1** Pretest
**DAY 2** Word Building
**DAY 3** State the Generalization
**DAY 4** Review
**DAY 5** Posttest

## Build Words

**MAP LETTERS TO SOUNDS** Use *Letter Cards* and a pocket chart to form words. Have children listen to your directions and change letters in each word to spell a spelling word. Then have a volunteer change the *Letter Card(s)* in the pocket chart.

- Form *hen* in the pocket chart and have children read it. Ask: **Which spelling word can you make by changing the last letter?** *(her)*

- Form *her* and have children read it. **Which spelling word can you make by changing the first and second letters?** *(fur)*

- Leave *fur* in the pocket chart. Ask: **Which spelling word can you make by changing the first letter and adding a letter to the end?** *(turn)*

Follow a similar procedure with the following words: *bid (bird)*, *gill (girl)*, *fist (first)*, *sit (quit)*, *hen (when)*.

**HIGH-FREQUENCY WORDS** Remind children that there are some other words they have to remember how to spell. Tell them that *name* is one such word. Tell children to picture the word and then write it. Have a volunteer build the word. Continue with *work*.

### Objectives

- *To use /ûr/er, ir, ur and other known letter-sounds to spell and write words*

- *To spell and write known high-frequency words*

### Spelling Words

| | |
|---|---|
| 1. her | 6. first |
| 2. fur | 7. quit |
| 3. turn | 8. when |
| 4. bird | 9. name |
| 5. girl | 10. work |

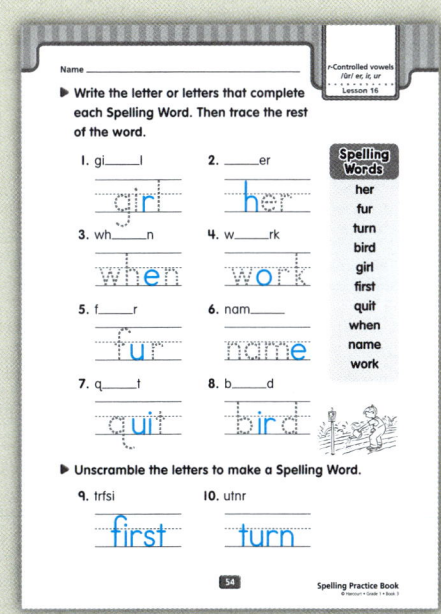

▲ Spelling Practice Book, p. 54

---

**BELOW-LEVEL**

**Map Letters to Sounds** Display *Letter Cards* for each word in random order. For each word, help children make a connection between a sound and its letter or letters by having them arrange the letters to spell the word. Then have them write the word.

# High-Frequency Words

## Objective
- *To read high-frequency words*

**REVIEW** Tested ✓

### High-Frequency Words

| | | |
|---|---|---|
| always | nice | join |
| by | please | |
| Cow's | room | |

### ● ADVANCED

**Write Sentences** Have children choose three high-frequency words and write a sentence for each, underlining the word. Then have partners take turns reading their sentences aloud to each other, saying "Chirp chirp," "Cluck cluck," or "Quack quack" when they come to an underlined high-frequency word. The listener responds by telling which word makes sense.

### E L L

**Story Events** Display the high-frequency *Word Cards*. Have each child in turn pick a card and read the word. Help the child find the word in the story in the *Student Edition* and then read the sentence with you.

## Review

**READ AND WRITE WORDS** Duplicate and distribute an uncut story strip page (*Teacher Resource Book,* p. 226) for each child. Then do the following:

- Have children read the story title in the first strip. Explain that the sentences tell the story, but some have missing words.

- Display *Word Cards* for the high-frequency words, or list the words on the board. Have children read each word.

| Cow's | nice | join | always |
|---|---|---|---|

## Practice/Apply

**GUIDED PRACTICE** Direct children to read all the story strip sentences and to write the missing words in the blanks.

> "Come _____ us! Be the third!" calls Ant.

> "_____ don't say you can't."

**INDEPENDENT PRACTICE** After children complete the story strip page, have them cut apart the strips. Have partners work together to read and match their story strips and then arrange the strips in story order. Have children take the story strips home to share.

Children read the words in context in the Cut-Out/Fold-Up Book "Jump, Twirl, and Play."

◀ "Jump, Twirl, and Play"

*Practice Book,* pp. 51–52

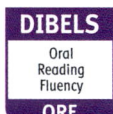

# Fluency
## *Reading Rate*

---

### Objectives

- *To read at an appropriate rate*
- *To build fluency through rereading a story*

### Review

**DIBELS**
Oral Reading Fluency
**ORF**

**MODEL READING AT AN APPROPRIATE RATE** Remind children that good readers read at a steady pace so that listeners can understand and stay interested in what is being read. Show children how to read at an appropriate rate.

▲ Student Edition, pp. 142–159

**Think Aloud** I'm going to read "One More Friend," one page at a time. I will read at just the right speed—not too fast and not too slowly—so that you can understand what I'm reading. Read each page after me, just the way I read it.

### Practice/Apply

**GUIDED PRACTICE** Have partners reread "One More Friend" aloud three or four times. Remind them to read at a steady pace so that they and their listeners will understand and stay interested in the story. Listen to partners read, giving them feedback about their reading rate and guidance for improving their fluency.

**INDEPENDENT PRACTICE** Have partners take turns as a storyteller and practice reading pages from "One More Friend." Remind children to read at a steady rate. Children can then make stick puppets with the character cutouts on *Teacher Resource Book* page 195 and use them to show which character is speaking as they read aloud the story to a small group. Remind the audience to listen carefully and quietly.

---

**BELOW-LEVEL**

**Fluency Practice** Have children reread for fluency, using "Please Get In!" in the *Strategic Intervention Interactive Reader, Decodable Book 16,* or the appropriate *Leveled Reader.* (See pages T374–T377.) Guide them to select a small portion of a story and practice reading it several times.

---

### Additional Related Reading

Guide children to self-select related books, such as these:

- ***In My World*** by Lois Ehlert. Harcourt, 2006   **EASY**
- ***Who Sank the Boat?*** by Pamela Allen. Putnam, 1996.   **AVERAGE**
- ***The Napping House*** by Audrey Wood. Harcourt, 2004.   **CHALLENGE**

# Main Idea
## Comprehension

▲Big Book

### Objective
- *To recognize main idea while listening to a story*

### Skill Trace

 **Main Idea**

| | |
|---|---|
| Preview | T316 |
| Introduce | T324–T325 |
| Reteach | S36–S37, S46–S47 |
| Review | T348, T360, T370, T402, T410, T436, T448, T458 |
| Test | Bk 1-3 |
| Maintain | Monitor Comprehension, Bks 1-4, 1-5 |

### ✓ MONITOR PROGRESS

 **Comprehension: Main Idea**

| | |
|---|---|
| **IF** children have difficulty recognizing a story's main idea, | **THEN** recall a story with them and help them identify the main idea. |

**Small-Group Instruction, pp. S36–S37:**

- 🔴 **BELOW-LEVEL:** Reteach
- 🔵 **ON-LEVEL:** Reinforce
- 🟢 **ADVANCED:** Extend

## Review

**TALK ABOUT MAIN IDEA** Review with children the concept of main idea. Ask them to tell what a main idea is. (what a story is mostly about)

**USE PRIOR KNOWLEDGE/SET A PURPOSE** Display *Big Book We're Going on a Lion Hunt.* Tell children that this is a story they will listen to for enjoyment.

**EXAMINE CONCEPTS OF PRINT** Display a page of text. Review with children that the print is read left to right, top to bottom on the page. Frame a sentence between your hands. Recall with children how to identify the group of words as a sentence. Point out the space before and after the sentence and between the lines of text. Remind them how letters placed together make up words. Have children note the difference between an individual letter, a word, and a sentence.

## Practice/Apply

**GUIDED PRACTICE** Monitor listening comprehension as you read, using questions such as the following:

- **Pages 6–7: MAKE INFERENCES** What details in the text and illustration help you understand how the girls feel? (Possible response: They look as though they are walking slowly. Maybe they are nervous. Then they look excited.)

- **Page 12:** 🟢 **SUMMARIZE** What has happened so far? (Two girls on a lion hunt have gone through tall grass, a lake, and a swamp, and they have just come to a big dark cave.)

- 🔴 **MAIN IDEA** What are the girls doing? (They are on a lion hunt.)

**INDEPENDENT PRACTICE** Remind children that they know the main idea of the story—two girls going on a lion hunt. Ask children to tell how they know. List responses on the board.

# Build Robust Vocabulary

## Listening/Speaking: *Words About the Selection*

### Review Robust Vocabulary

**USE VOCABULARY IN DIFFERENT CONTEXTS** Remind children that they were introduced to the words *compatible, amiable,* and *relax* after reading "One More Friend." Guide children to develop their vocabulary by discussing the Student-Friendly Explanations of these words. Ask these questions:

**compatible**

- Suppose a new family with a child your age moves in next door. How can you learn if the two of you are compatible?

- How might a group of children behave if they are NOT compatible?

- In what ways are you and your best friend compatible?

**amiable**

- Name a storybook character who is amiable and one who is not. Give a reason for each choice.

- Is it more fun to be around someone who is amiable than someone who is not? Why?

- What is a good way to show that you are an amiable person?

**relax**

- Is it easy for you to relax during a thunderstorm? Why or why not?

- Where do you like to be when you relax? Why?

- How do you feel after you relax? Why?

## Objective

- *To review robust vocabulary*

### Student-Friendly Explanations

**compatible** When people or animals are compatible, they are able to be together or get along with each other.

**amiable** Someone who is amiable is good-natured and friendly.

**relax** When you relax, you are not uneasy or upset about anything; you spend time resting or doing things for fun.

### ADVANCED

**Words that Mean the Same**
Have children form pairs or small groups and each choose one of the Vocabulary Words. Challenge children to brainstorm and list as many words as they can think of that have the same or almost the same meaning. Have partners and groups share and compare their word lists.

# Grammar

## Using He, She, It, and They

**5-DAY GRAMMAR**

| DAY 1 | Introduce Using *He, She, It,* and *They* |
| DAY 2 | Rewrite Sentences |
| DAY 3 | Revise Sentences |
| **DAY 4** | **Complete Sentences** |
| DAY 5 | Write Sentences |

### Objective

• *To use* he, she, it, *and* they *correctly*

### Daily Proofreading

**they had fun at the zoo**
(They, zoo.)

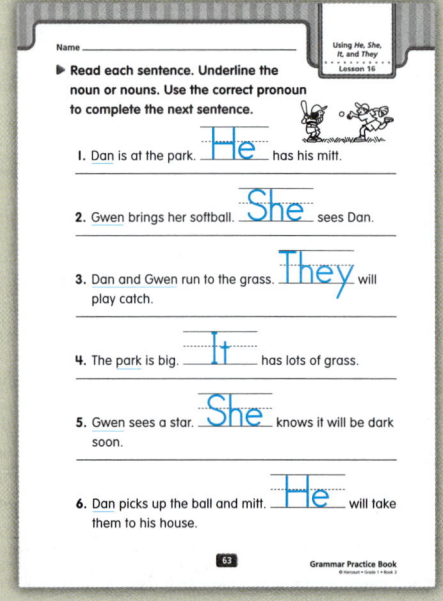

▲ **Grammar Practice Book, p. 63**

## Review

**IDENTIFY *HE, SHE, IT,* AND *THEY*** Review with children that *he, she, it,* and *they* can take the place of naming words in sentences. Say: **Jack has a new pet. He has a kitten.** Ask: **What word did I use in place of *Jack* in the second sentence?** *(He)* Remind children that *he* can take the place of a word that names a boy or man. Follow a similar procedure with these sentences:

• **The kitten has gray fur. *It* is ten weeks old.**

• **Jack and Jill play with the kitten. *They* have fun.**

• **Jill fed the kitten. *She* gave it water, too.**

## Practice/Apply

**GUIDED PRACTICE** Write the following on the board:

he     she     it     they

<u>The contest</u> is over. _____ was fun.

<u>Fern</u> finished first. _____ won!

<u>Kirk</u> was next. ___ ran fast.

<u>Burt and Bart</u> were third.
_____ didn't run as fast.

As you read each pair of sentences, ask children to tell which word to use in the second sentence in place of the underlined word or words in the first sentence—*he, she, it,* or *they*—and to tell why. Call on a volunteer to write *He, She, It,* or *They* in the space. Then, tracking the print, read aloud the sentences together.

**INDEPENDENT PRACTICE** Have children work in small groups to write pairs of sentences, using the sentences on the board as models. Tell children to include a naming word or two in the first sentence and then to complete the second sentence with *he, she, it,* or *they*. Have the groups share and compare their sentences.

| 5-DAY WRITING | |
| --- | --- |
| DAY 1 | Modeled Writing |
| DAY 2 | Shared Writing |
| DAY 3 | Shared Writing |
| **DAY 4** | **Independent Writing** |
| DAY 5 | Independent Writing |

# Independent Writing

## *Invitation*

## Write Invitations

**GENERATE IDEAS** Guide children to write for a familiar occasion, audience, and purpose. Explain that they will design and write their own invitation for a real or made-up special event. Ask children to jot down notes answering questions about the event to plan the invitation.

Who? Zack, Ben, Greg, Mike

What? swim party

When? Saturday, May 30

       3:00

Where? my house

Who? Justin

### An Invitation Tells

- <u>who</u> is invited
- <u>what</u> the event is
- <u>when</u> the event is
- <u>where</u> the event is
- <u>who</u> is sending the invitation

**REVIEW CHARACTERISTICS** Display the list of characteristics of a well-written invitation from Day 1, and read it with children.

**IDEAS** Have several volunteers dictate parts of their invitations. As you record them on the board, ask children to tell why each detail is important and what might happen if they forgot to include it.

**WRITE** Display the invitations children helped write on Days 2 and 3 to use as models. Have children use their notes to draft their own invitations. Save the drafts to have children revise on Day 5.

To: Zack

You are invited to a swim party! Bring a towel and a big appetite.

When: Saturday, May 30, 3:00
Where: my house

## Objective

- *To draft an invitation*

## Writing Prompt

**Write About a Celebration** Have children write about a favorite occasion or holiday that their families celebrate. They may want to draw a picture to show the celebration.

### BELOW-LEVEL

**Use a Form** Provide children with an invitation form to fill in as they work on their drafts if they need help remembering the information to include.

# Warm-Up Routines

**Day at a Glance**

**Day 5**

## Phonemic Awareness
- Phoneme Blending
- Phoneme Segmentation

## phonics and Spelling
- Review: Inflections *-er, -est*
- Posttest: *r*-Controlled Vowels /ûr/*er, ir, ur*

## High-Frequency Words
- Review

## Fluency
- Reading Rate
- "One More Friend," *Student Edition*, pp. 142–159

## Comprehension

Review: Main Idea

## Robust Vocabulary
- Review

## Grammar
- Review: Using *He, She, It, They*

## Independent Writing
- Invitation

---

## Oral Language

**Objective**  *To listen and respond appropriately to oral communication*

### Question of the Day
What kind of pet do you have or would like to have?

Guide children to name the kinds of pets they like and describe them. Then write the following sentence frames and help children complete them. Have children practice reading them aloud with fluency.

**My pet is a _____ named _____.  My pet is _____.**

---

## Read Aloud

**Objectives**  *To read classic poetry; to innovate on a poem*

**BIG BOOK OF RHYMES AND POEMS**  Track the print, and have children read aloud the poem. Then ask them to reread it, clapping for rhyming words in lines 1 and 3 and stomping in lines 2 and 4.

**Create new verses.** Cover *dog* and *frog* with large self-stick notes. Ask children to think of other animals or objects that could be in the hat and write them on the papers. Read the new version with children. Continue with more words, encouraging children to think of pairs of rhyming words.

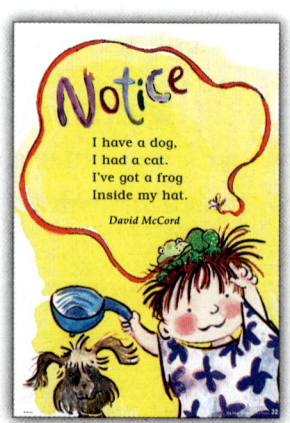

▲ Big Book of Rhymes and Poems, p. 32

# Word Wall

**Objective** *To read high-frequency words*

**REVIEW HIGH-FREQUENCY WORDS** Review *always, by, join, quit, when,* and other previously learned high-frequency words. Say a word, ask a volunteer to point to it, and have children read it aloud. Then point to words at random and have children reread them.

| always | by | join | quit | when |
|---|---|---|---|---|

# Phonemic Awareness

**Objectives** *To blend phonemes into words; to segment words into phonemes*

**Routine Card 1** **PHONEME BLENDING** Children will blend sounds to say words. Model by saying /d/ /o/ /g/. Then say the word naturally—*dog.* Say the following phonemes, having children blend the sounds to say the words:

/f/ /r/ /e/ /n/ /d/ (friend)    /k/ /r/ /ō/ /k/ (croak)    /ch/ /ûr/ /p/ (chirp)

/j/ /u/ /m/ /p/ (jump)    /f/ /ûr/ /s/ /t/ (first)    /p/ /l/ /ē/ /z/ (please)

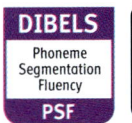

**DIBELS** Phoneme Segmentation Fluency **PSF** **Routine Card 8** **PHONEME SEGMENTATION** Tell children they will now say the sounds they hear in words. Model by saying *frog*—/f/ /r/ /o/ /g/.

**third** (/th/ /ûr/ /d/)    **lamb** (/l/ /a/ /m/)    **cluck** (/k/ /l/ /u/ /k/)

**room** (/r/ /o͞o/ /m/)    **curl** (/k/ /ûr/ /l/)    **friend** (/f/ /r/ /e/ /n/ /d/)

**shade** (/sh/ /ā/ /d/)    **chick** (/ch/ /i/ /k/)    **please** (/p/ /l/ /ē/ /z/)

 Podcasting: Phoneme Blending, Segmentation

# Inflections -er, -est  phonics

**5-DAY PHONICS**

| DAY 1 | Introduce *r*-Controlled Vowels /ûr/*er, ir, ur* |
|---|---|
| DAY 2 | Word Building with *r*-Controlled Vowels /ûr/*er, ir, ur* |
| DAY 3 | Build Words |
| DAY 4 | Introduce Inflections *-er, -est* |
| DAY 5 | Review Inflections *-er, -est* |

## Objectives

• *To recognize inflections* -er, -est
• *To build words with inflection* -er

## Skill Trace

### Inflections *-er, -est*

| Introduce | T356 |
|---|---|
| **Review** | **T366** |

## Review

**INFLECTIONS -ER , -EST** Remind children that *-er* and *-est* can be added to describing words such as *long* and *tall* to describe two and more than two people, animals, places, or things. Say, for example: **(Name of a child) is tall. (Name of a child) is taller. I am the tallest.**

Display the chart created on Day 4 (p. T356). Ask volunteers to read the words, underline the root words, and circle the endings.

## Work with Patterns

**BUILD WORDS WITH -ER** Write the word *farm* on the board, and have children read the word with you. Then write *+ er = farmer*. Point out that by adding *-er* to *farm* you have made a naming word. Have children read the word *farmer*. Follow a similar procedure with *truck, help, sing,* and *hunt*. Then invite children to suggest other words.

**farm + er = farmer**

truck + er = \_\_\_\_\_          help + er = \_\_\_\_\_
sing + er = \_\_\_\_\_           hunt + er = \_\_\_\_\_

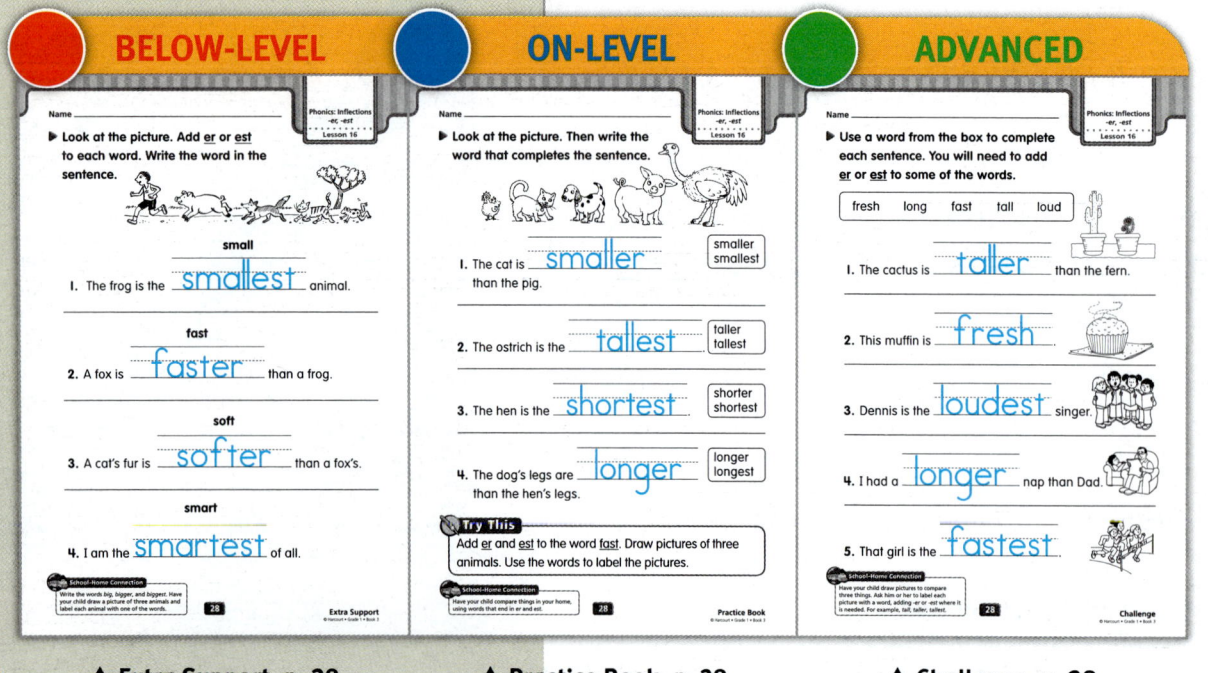

| BELOW-LEVEL | ON-LEVEL | ADVANCED |
|---|---|---|
| ▲ Extra Support, p. 28 | ▲ Practice Book, p. 28 | ▲ Challenge, p. 28 |

**ELL**

• Group children according to academic levels, and assign one of the pages on the left.

• Clarify any unfamiliar concepts as necessary. See *ELL Teacher Guide*, Lesson 16, for scaffolding support.

# r-Controlled Vowels
## /ûr/ er, ir, ur  phonics and Spelling

**5-DAY SPELLING**

| | |
|---|---|
| **DAY 1** | Pretest |
| **DAY 2** | Word Building |
| **DAY 3** | State the Generalization |
| **DAY 4** | Review |
| **DAY 5** | Posttest |

## Assess

**POSTTEST** Assess children's progress. Use the dictation sentences from Day 1.

1. her     Where did Sara put **her** new mittens?
2. fur     Our cat has soft **fur** on its body.
3. turn    It's your **turn** to play the game.
4. bird    A young **bird** flew to its nest.
5. girl    Ann is the new **girl** in our class.
6. first   I am the **first** one in line.

### Review

7. quit    The workers have **quit** for the day.
8. when    Please line up **when** the bell rings.

### High-Frequency

9. name    The boy's **name** is Jacob.
10. work   Do you **work** hard in school?

**WRITING APPLICATION** Have children complete and illustrate the following sentence frames:

If I had a girl bird, I'd name her _____.

When it's my turn to be first in line, I feel _____.

If I had a girl bird, I'd name her Sasha.

### Objectives

- *To use* r-controlled /ûr/ er, ir, ur *and other known letter-sounds to spell and write words*
- *To spell and write known high-frequency words*

### Spelling Words

| | | | |
|---|---|---|---|
| 1. | **her** | 6. | **first** |
| 2. | **fur** | 7. | **quit** |
| 3. | **turn** | 8. | **when** |
| 4. | **bird** | 9. | **name** |
| 5. | **girl** | 10. | **work** |

### ● ADVANCED

**Write Sentences** Ask children to write and illustrate a story about a girl who has a pet bird with fur instead of feathers, using as many of the spelling words as they can.

 # High-Frequency Words

## Objectives
- *To read high-frequency words*
- *To explore word relationships*

 **REVIEW** **Tested** ✓

### High-Frequency Words

| | | |
|---|---|---|
| always | every | nice |
| by | happy | please |
| Cow's | head | room |
| does | join | said |

 **ADVANCED**

**Words That Rhyme** Invite children to choose one of the words, such as *does*. Write the word on the board. Then ask children to think of other words that rhyme with *does*, such as *buzz*, *fuzz*, and *was*. List each word on the board.

**Review**

**REINFORCE WORD RECOGNITION** Display *Word Cards* for all the words in a pocket chart. Point to words at random and ask volunteers to read them.

**SORT WORDS** Guide children in sorting the words into columns according to the number of letters. Then have them read the words in each column aloud.

- Have children say the four-letter words—*Cow's, does, head, join, nice, room, said*. Ask: **Do any of these words rhyme? Which ones?** *(head, said)*

- Have children say the six-letter words—*please, always*. Ask: **What sound do you hear at the end of both words?** */z/* **Which four-letter words end with the same sound?** *(Cow's, does)*

- Have children say the five-letter words. *(happy, every)* Ask: **How are they alike?** *(They end in y; they end with the same sound, /ē/.)*

- Have children look at all the words. Ask: **Which word begins like *baby* and ends like *cry*?** *(by)*

 # Fluency
*Reading Rate*

## Readers' Theater

**DIBELS**
Oral Reading Fluency
**ORF**

**PERFORM "ONE MORE FRIEND"** To help children improve their fluency, have them perform "One More Friend." Use the following procedure.

▲ Student Edition, pp. 142–159

- Read aloud "One More Friend," modeling fluent reading at an appropriate rate to make it easy for listeners to understand.

- Point out the sentences that Ant speaks. Discuss with children how some phrases and sentences might be read more quickly or more slowly for emphasis and to keep listeners interested.

- Have partners read the story together. Then have them choose the part of Ant or the narrator, who reads all the other lines, and practice rereading the story fluently and at an appropriate rate.

- Listen to sets of partners read. Provide feedback and support.

- Invite partners to read the story to classmates. Remind them to focus on reading at an appropriate rate.

### E L L

**Reinforce Fluency** Point out the quotation marks around the words that Ant speaks. Remind children that Ant is happy to be in the hammock in the shade and eager to share it with all the other animals, so that when Ant says, for example, "Come jump up! Be the first!" children might read Ant's words more quickly.

## Objective
- *To read fluently at an appropriate rate*

 ## ASSESSMENT

**Monitoring Progress** Periodically, take a timed sample of children's oral reading and measure the number of words read correctly per minute. Children should be accurately reading approximately 60 words per minute by the end of Grade 1.

## Fluency Support Materials

 **Fluency Builders,** Grade 1, Lesson 16
● ● ●

 **Audiotext** *Student Edition* selections are available on *Audiotext Grade 1,* CD 3.

 **Strategic Intervention Teacher Guide,** Lesson 16

# Main Idea
*Comprehension*

## Objective
• *To identify the main idea of a story*

## Skill Trace

**Tested** **Main Idea**

| | |
|---|---|
| Preview | T316 |
| Introduce | T324–T325 |
| Reteach | S36–S37, S46–S47 |
| Review | **T348, T360, T370, T402, T410, T436, T448, T458** |
| Test | Bk 1-3 |
| Maintain | Monitor Comprehension, Bks 1-4, 1-5 |

### ADVANCED

**Independent Practice** Invite children to name the main idea of other stories or nonfiction selections they have read and tell how they were able to identify the main idea.

## Review

**REVIEW THE SKILL** Ask children to give the definition of *main idea*. (what a story is mostly about) Draw a three-column chart on the board or use **Transparency GO2**. Add the titles "The Lion and the Mouse," "One More Friend," and *We're Going on a Lion Hunt* at the top of each column. Remind children that these are the read-aloud, the *Student Edition* selection, and the *Big Book* that they read this week. Discuss the main idea of "The Lion and the Mouse," and write it in the first column.

**GUIDED PRACTICE** Ask volunteers to identify the main idea of "One More Friend." Write responses in the second column of the chart. Then have children identify the main idea of *We're Going on a Lion Hunt*, and write it in the last column.

| "The Lion and the Mouse" | "One More Friend" | We're Going on a Lion Hunt |
|---|---|---|
| A lion shows kindness to a mouse, who saves the lion's life in return one day. | An ant shows kindness by making room for all her friends. | Two girls have a hard journey, but also have fun, on a lion hunt. |

**INDEPENDENT READING** Have children page through their *Student Edition* to help them recall selections they have already read. Ask each child to name a selection and tell the main idea.

# Build Robust Vocabulary
## *Listening/Speaking*

### Review

**REINFORCE MEANINGS** Ask children the following questions:

- Do you think someone who is *amiable* would be more *compatible* than someone who is not? Why?

- If you are *struggling* to ride your bike up a steep hill, does your body *relax?*

- Suppose the lion *captured* the mouse again. Should it ask for *mercy* again? Why or why not?

**USE VOCABULARY IN DIFFERENT CONTEXTS** Review each word, using the following examples.

**amiable** Tell children that you will name some familiar characters and if they think a character is amiable, they should say, "Very nice!"

| | |
|---|---|
| Ant in "One More Friend" | Cinderella's stepsisters |
| The Wolf in "The Three Pigs" | Mark in "Mark's Big Day" |

**relax** Tell children that you will describe some situations, and if children think they would be able to relax, they should say, "Ahhhh."

| | |
|---|---|
| riding a roller coaster | reading a book |
| floating on a raft in a pool | listening to music |

**struggling** Tell children that you will name some things that people do. If children think they would struggle to do that activity, they should say "I'm struggling!"

| | |
|---|---|
| row a boat across a lake | carry a lunchbox |
| walk a mile | make pancakes |

## Objective
- *To review robust vocabulary*

**REVIEW**

### Build Robust Vocabulary

| | |
|---|---|
| amiable | mercy |
| compatible | relax |
| captured | struggling |

 **MONITOR PROGRESS**

**Build Robust Vocabulary**

| **IF** children do not demonstrate understanding of the words and have difficulty using them, | **THEN** model using each word in several sentences, and talk about the meanings. |
|---|---|

**Small-Group Instruction, pp. S38–S39:**

- ● **BELOW-LEVEL:** Reteach
- ● **ON-LEVEL:** Reinforce
- ● **ADVANCED:** Extend

# Grammar

### Using He, She, It, *and* They

**5-DAY GRAMMAR**

| | |
|---|---|
| **DAY 1** | Introduce Using *He, She, It, and They* |
| **DAY 2** | Rewrite Sentences |
| **DAY 3** | Revise Sentences |
| **DAY 4** | Complete Sentences |
| **DAY 5** | **Write Sentences** |

## Objectives

- *To use* he, she, it, *and* they *correctly*
- *To dictate and write sentences using* he, she, it, *and* they

## Daily Proofreading

**it feels nice in the shade**

(It, shade.)

## Language Arts Checkpoint

If children have difficulty with the concepts, see pages S40–S41 to reteach.

▲ Practice Book, p. 29

## Review

**USE *HE, SHE, IT,* AND *THEY*** Have each child write each word: *He, She, It, They.* Display the *Big Book We're Going on a Lion Hunt.* Ask children to listen as you say some sentences about the book. Children should then hold up the card for the word that can take the place of the word or words you emphasize. Say:

- ***David Axtell*** wrote this book. *(He)*
- ***Two girls*** hunt for a lion. *(They)*
- ***One little girl*** brings along her bunny. *(She)*
- ***The lion*** follows the girls. *(It)*

## Practice/Apply

**GUIDED PRACTICE** List the following words related to "One More Friend" on the board. Ask volunteers to compose sentences using *he, she, it,* or *they* in place of the words. Record them on the board.

- **a hammock** (*It* is in Cow's backyard.)
- **Ant** (*She* is happy in the hammock.)
- **Frog, Chick, Hen, Cat, Dog, Lamb** (*They* get in the hammock.)

As you read the sentences with children, work with them to correct any errors in usage, reviewing when to use *he, she, it,* and *they.*

**INDEPENDENT PRACTICE** Have small groups choose a familiar story in the *Student Edition* and write sentences to tell about the characters, things, and places in the story. Have group members trade sentences and rewrite them using *he, she, it,* or *they.* Then invite each group to read aloud an original sentence. Have classmates hold up the card for the word that can take the place of the naming word or words at the beginning of the sentence.

| | |
|---|---|
| Ant is in the hammock. | She is in the hammock. |

Day **5**

| 5-DAY WRITING | |
|---|---|
| **DAY 1** | Modeled Writing |
| **DAY 2** | Shared Writing |
| **DAY 3** | Shared Writing |
| **DAY 4** | Independent Writing |
| **DAY 5** | Independent Writing |

# Independent Writing

## *Invitation*

### Write Invitations

 **WRITE** Have children continue to work on the invitation drafts they began on Day 4. Remind them to refer to the model invitations for help.

 **IDEAS** Remind children that the purpose of an invitation is to invite someone to a special event. The invitation must include all the important details, such as the time, place, and date of the event, and who the invitation is from. An invitation may also tell interesting information about the event.

**REVISE** Have children read their invitation to a partner. Reread to children the list of criteria for an invitation, and have them use the list to improve their writing. Ask children to add information that is needed and fix any mistakes. Show them how to use the caret (^) editor's mark to add information.

### An Invitation Tells

- <u>who</u> is invited
- <u>what</u> the event is
- <u>when</u> the event is
- <u>where</u> the event is
- <u>who</u> is sending the invitation

### Share

**AUTHOR'S CHAIR** Have children make a clean copy of their invitations. Invite children to decorate them. They can draw and color, cut and paste, or add decorative stickers or clip-art related to the event. Then invite children to take turns sharing their completed invitations. Afterward, ask children to tell how all the invitations are similar. Then gather and display all the invitations for children to read.

**Author's Chair**

### Objective

- *To draft, revise, and publish an invitation*

### Writing Prompt

**Write and Draw** Have children draw a picture and write about a party, picnic, or other event to which they were invited.

**Tested**

## WEEKLY LESSON TEST

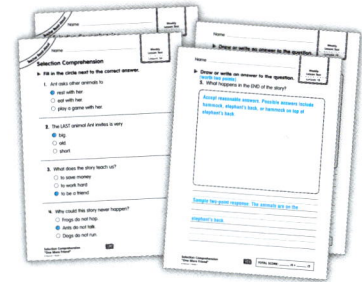

▲ Weekly Lesson Tests pp. 160–170

- Selection Comprehension with Short Response
- Phonics and Spelling
- High-Frequency Words
- Focus Skill
- Robust Vocabulary
- Grammar
- Fluency

 **GO online** For prescriptions, see p. A25. Also available electronically on *StoryTown* Online Assessment and ExamView®.

**Podcasting:** Assessing Fluency

# Leveled Readers
## *Reinforcing Skills and Strategies*

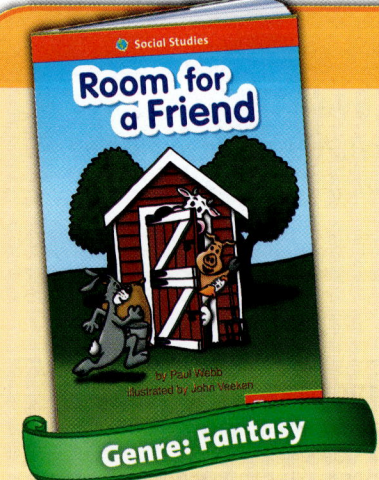

**BELOW-LEVEL**

## Room for a Friend

**SUMMARY** In a game of hide and seek, Cow makes room for some friends, but the shed is too small, and Duck soon finds them.

**Genre: Fantasy**

-  *r*-Controlled Vowels /ûr/ *er, ir, ur*
- **High-Frequency Words:** *always, by, Cow's, join, nice, please, room*
-  **Main Idea**

### Before Reading

**BUILD BACKGROUND/SET A PURPOSE** Ask children if they ever play hide and seek. Encourage them to explain how to play the game and to tell about some of their best hiding spots. Then guide children to preview the story and set a purpose for reading it.

### Reading the Book

**PAGES 2–8**  **MAIN IDEA** What is this story mostly about? (Possible response: a group of animal friends playing hide and seek)

**PAGES 6–8 CHARACTERS' EMOTIONS** How do you think Duck feels when she sees Rabbit's back and then looks in the shed? Why? (Possible response: excited because she had found her friends all in one place)

**REREAD FOR FLUENCY** Have partners read alternate pages of the story several times with expression, especially when reading the words that the characters speak.

### Think Critically
(See inside back cover for questions.)

**1**  **MAIN IDEA** Possible responses: It's fun playing with friends. Friends are good to have. It's nice to include friends in play.

**2 SEQUENCE** Cow hid first. Rabbit was the last to hide.

**3 BEGINNING, MIDDLE, ENDING** It's Rabbit's turn to find everyone.

**4 DRAW CONCLUSIONS** It was easy for Duck to find her friends because she could see Rabbit's back in the doorway of the shed.

**5 PERSONAL RESPONSE** Responses will vary.

**LEVELED READER TEACHER GUIDE**

▲ High-Frequency Words, p. 5

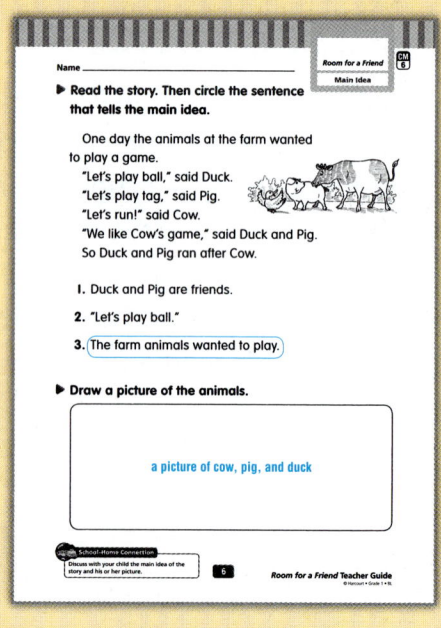

▲ Comprehension, p. 6

**www.harcourtschool.com/storytown**

★ **Leveled Readers, online**
*Searchable by genre, skill, vocabulary, level, or title*
★ **Student Activities and Teacher Resources, online**

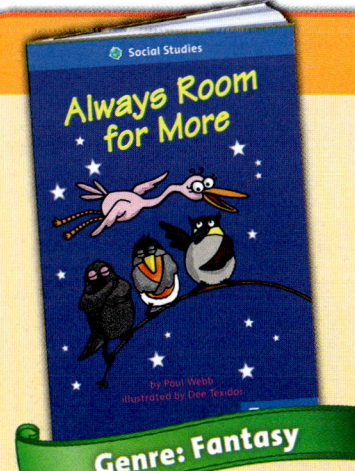
Genre: Fantasy

## ON-LEVEL

# Always Room for More

**SUMMARY** Cow makes room in the barn for Starling, Robin, Lark, and Stork after the flimsy branch they are on gives way.

 **phonics** *r*-Controlled Vowels /ûr/*er, ir, ur*

- **High-Frequency Words:** *always, by, Cow's, join, nice, please, room*

 **Main Idea**

### Before Reading

**BUILD BACKGROUND/SET A PURPOSE** Make a circle on the floor that is large enough for you and several children. Stand in the circle, and ask: **Is there room for more?** Have children respond. Then ask a volunteer to join you in the circle. Repeat until there is room for only one more. Guide children to preview the story and set a purpose for reading it.

### Reading the Book

**PAGES 2–8 SETTING, CHARACTERS** Where and when does this story take place? (on a branch in a barn at night) Who joins Starling on the branch? (Robin, Lark, and then Stork) Who asks Starling, Robin, Lark, and Stork to join her after the branch breaks? (Cow)

**PAGES 2–8**  **MAIN IDEA** How do the friends show each other that they care? (Possible response: They make room for each other.)

**REREAD FOR FLUENCY** Have partners read alternate pages of the story aloud several times with expression and at an appropriate rate.

### Think Critically
*(See inside back cover for questions.)*

1. **NOTE DETAILS** They slept in the barn.
2. **MAIN IDEA** It's important to share. Friends are kind to each other.
3. **PROBLEM/SOLUTION** The branch that they were sitting on snapped and they fell to the ground. Cow asked them to rest with her.
4. **CONTEXT CLUES** The birds say, "There is always room for more."
5. **PERSONAL RESPONSE** Responses will vary.

**LEVELED READER TEACHER GUIDE**

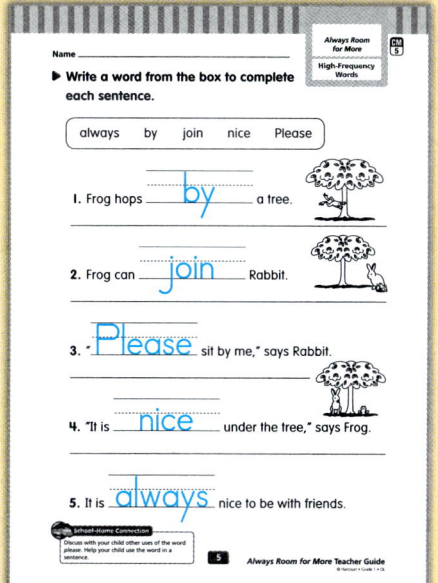
▲ High-Frequency Words, p. 5

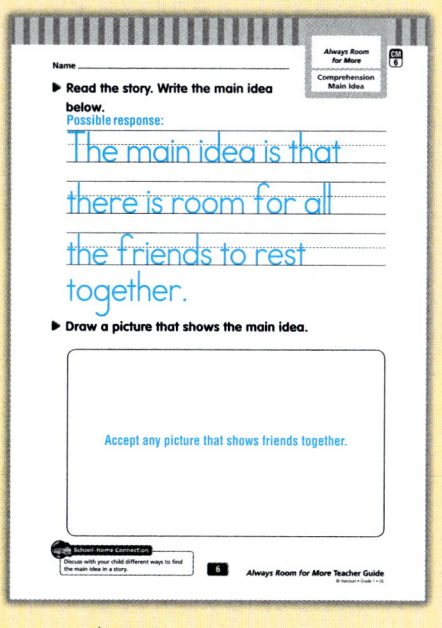
▲ Comprehension, p. 6

# Leveled Readers
*Reinforcing Skills and Strategies*

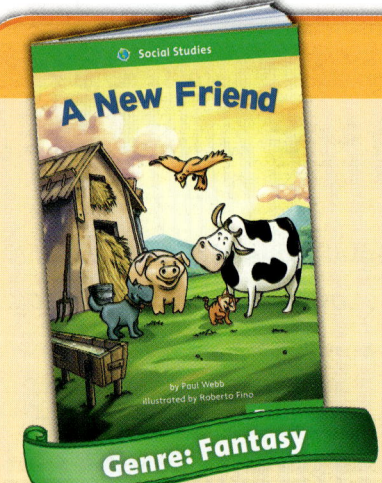

 Social Studies

**A New Friend**

by Paul Webb
Illustrated by Roberto Fino

**Genre: Fantasy**

**ADVANCED**

## A New Friend

**SUMMARY** When Cow enlists the help of Pig, Dog, and Bird to find out what is making the noise on top of the barn, they discover a kitten.

 **phonics** *r*-Controlled Vowels /ûr/*er, ir, ur*

- **High-Frequency Words:** *always, by, Cow's, join, nice, please, room*

 **Main Idea**

### Before Reading

**BUILD BACKGROUND/SET A PURPOSE** Have children tell what they might do if they heard a strange noise coming from the roof of their home. Ask: **Would you try to find out what is making the noise? How?** After sharing their ideas, have children set a purpose for reading the story.

### Reading the Book

**PAGES 2–6 CAUSE AND EFFECT** Cow asks Pig to stand on its back. Pig asks Dog to stand on its back. Dog asks Bird to fly to the top of the barn. **Why?** (They want to know what is making the noise on top of the barn.) **What is it?** (a kitten)

**PAGES 2–8 MAIN IDEA** After reading this story, explain what a friend is. (Possible response: someone kind, caring, and helpful to others)

**REREAD FOR FLUENCY** Have children use different voices for Cow, Pig, Dog, Bird, and Kitten as they reread the story several times.

### Think Critically *(See inside back cover for questions.)*

1. **SETTING** The story took place outside a barn on a farm.

2. **MAIN IDEA** Possible responses: It is important to help each other. It is important to work together.

3. **PROBLEM/SOLUTION** Kitten was stuck on top of the barn. The animals piled high enough for Kitten to reach Dog's back and join them.

4. **CHARACTERS' TRAITS** Kitten thanked the animals for being so nice.

5. **PERSONAL RESPONSE** Responses will vary.

**LEVELED READER TEACHER GUIDE**

▲ High-Frequency Words, p. 5

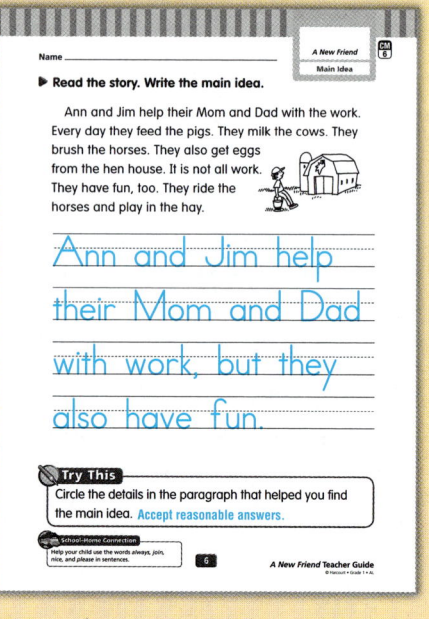

▲ Comprehension, p. 6

**www.harcourtschool.com/storytown**

★ **Leveled Readers, online**
*Searchable by genre, skill, vocabulary, level, or title*
★ **Student Activities and Teacher Resources, online**

**E L L**

# The Big Picture

**SUMMARY** A group of children work together to paint and hang a mural.

- **Strong Picture Support**
- **Concept Vocabulary**
- **Scaffolded Language Development**

## Before Reading

**BUILD BACKGROUND/SET A PURPOSE** Have children tell about a time when they worked together with friends to make something. Ask: **What did you make? How did everyone help? How do you like working together with a group of friends?** Then guide children to preview the story and set a purpose for reading it.

## Reading the Book

**PAGES 2–8 SETTING, CHARACTERS, PLOT Where do you think this story takes place?** (in a classroom) **Who are Bert, Dora, Bess, and Mitch?** (They are a group of children who work together.) **What happens in the story?** (They paint a big picture.)

**PAGE 8 MAIN IDEA What did you learn from the children in this story?** (Possible response: When you and your friends work together on a project, you can make something nice.)

**REREAD FOR FLUENCY** Model reading each page at an appropriate speed. Have children echo-read.

## Scaffolded Language Development

*(See inside back cover for teacher-led activity.)*

Provide additional examples and explanation as needed.

**LEVELED READER TEACHER GUIDE**

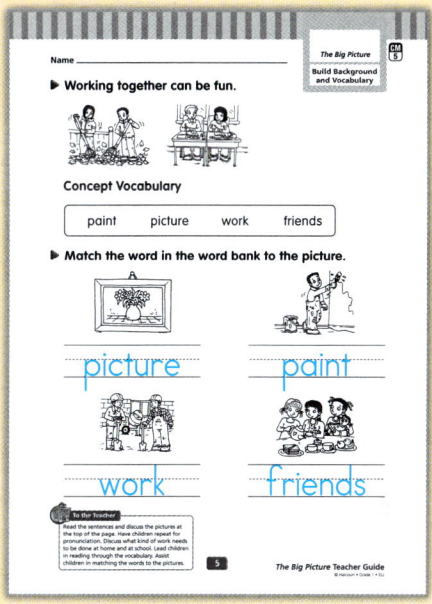

▲ Build Background, p. 5

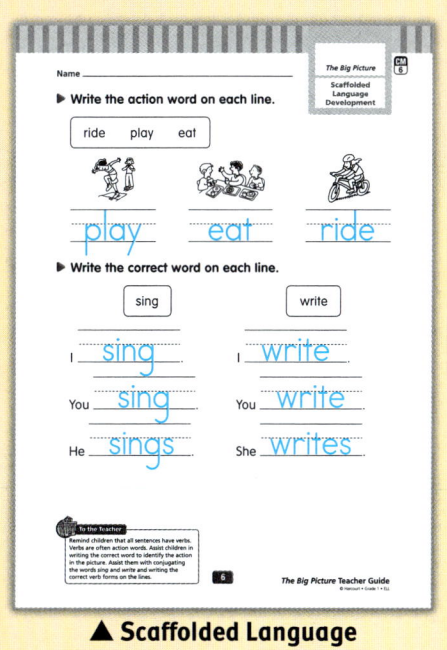

▲ Scaffolded Language Development, p. 6

# Lesson 17

## WEEK AT A GLANCE

### Phonemic Awareness
Phoneme Substitution

### ✓ Phonics
Syllable /əl/-*le*
Inflections *-ed, -ing*

### ✓ Spelling
*hand, handle, wig, wiggle, single, little, turn, girl, by, room*

### ✓ High-Frequency Words
*buy, carry, money, other, paint, paper, would*

### Reading
**"Can Elephants Paint?"** by Katya Arnold
NONFICTION

**"An Elephant's Three T's"** NONFICTION
ARTICLE

### ✓ Fluency
Intonation

### ✓ Comprehension
 Main Idea
 Monitor Comprehension: Reread

### ✓ Robust Vocabulary
*agreement, unnoticed, unthinkable, rejoice, predicament, extraordinary*

### ✓ Grammar
Possessives ('s and pronouns)

### Writing
Form: Friendly Letter
Trait: Voice

### Weekly Lesson Test

 = Focus Skill     = Focus Strategy     = Tested Skill

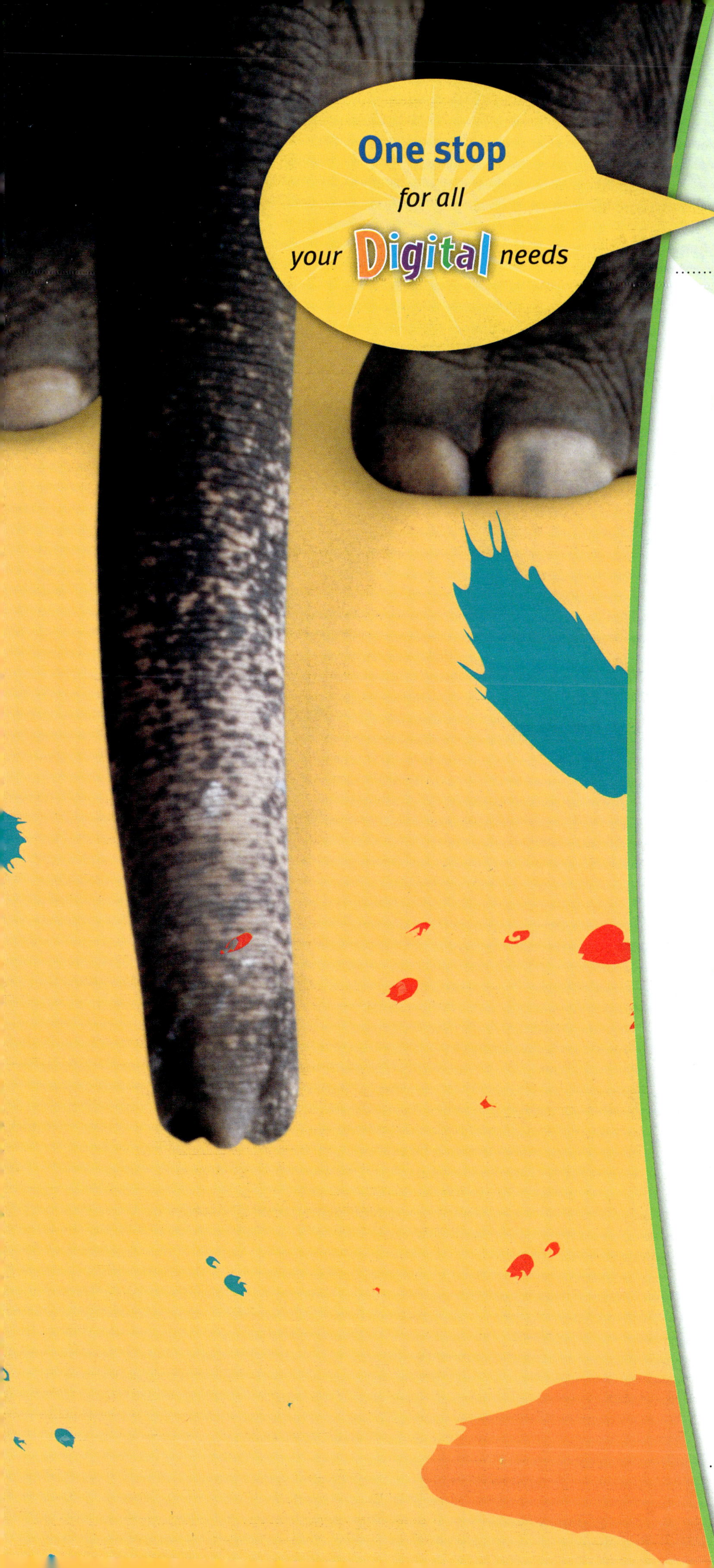

## One stop
*for all*
*your* **Digital** *needs*

# Digital
## CLASSROOM

 www.harcourtschool.com/storytown
*To go along with your print program*

### FOR THE TEACHER

**Prepare**
 **Professional Development**
*in the Online TE*

 **Videos for Podcasting**

**Plan & Organize**
 **Online TE & Planning Resources***

**Teach**
 **Transparencies**
*for electronic projection*

**Assess**
 **Online Assessment***
*with Student Tracking System and Prescriptions*

### FOR THE STUDENT

**Read**
 **Student eBook***

 **Strategic Intervention Interactive Reader**

 **Leveled Readers**

**Practice & Apply**
 **Splash into Phonics CD-ROM**

 **Also available on CD-ROM*

# LESSON 17

# Literature Resources

## STUDENT EDITION

**Jungle Fun, pp. 166–173**

**Genre: Nonfiction**

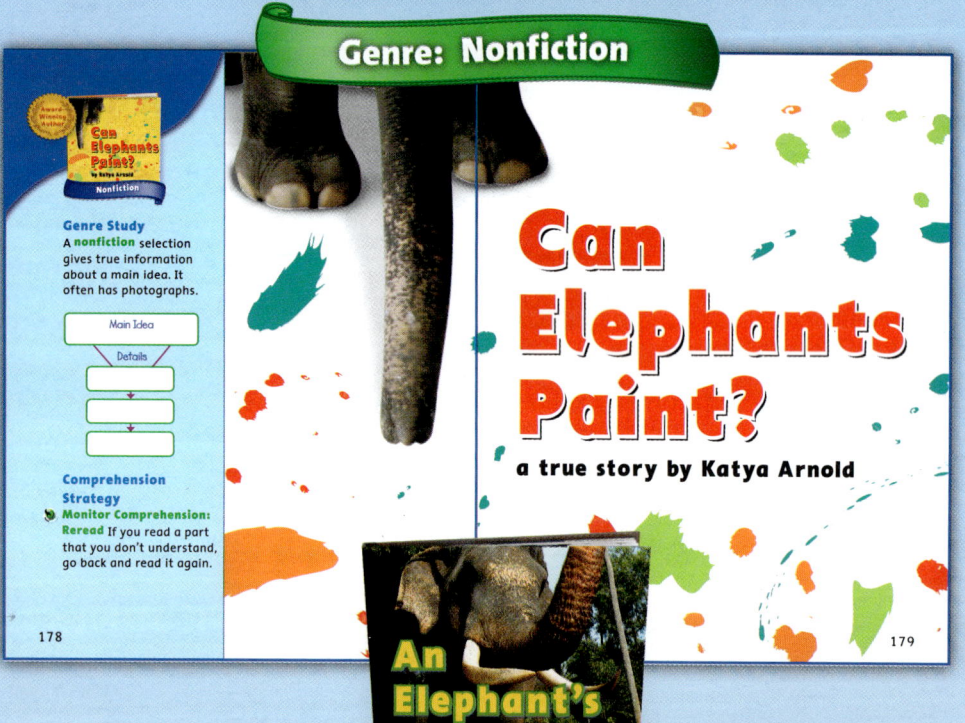

 **Can Elephants Paint? pp. 178–199**

*a true story by Katya Arnold* Lucky the elephant learns to paint. She and other elephants can now earn money for their village.

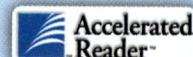

*Practice Quizzes for the Selection*

 **Audiotext** *Student Edition selections are available on Audiotext Grade 1, CD 3 and 6.*

**Paired Selections**

**Genre: Nonfiction Article**

◀ **Reading Across Texts**
**Comparing Two Nonfiction Pieces**

## ADDITIONAL READING

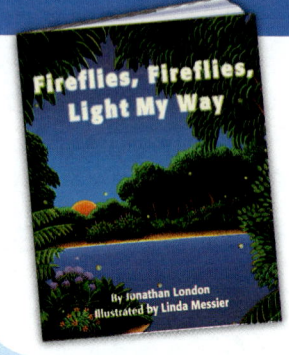

**Big Book**
*Fireflies, Fireflies, Light My Way*

**Decodable Book**
"Little Ann's Nap"
★ Applies Syllable /əl/-*le*

# Support for Differentiated Instruction

 LEVELED READERS

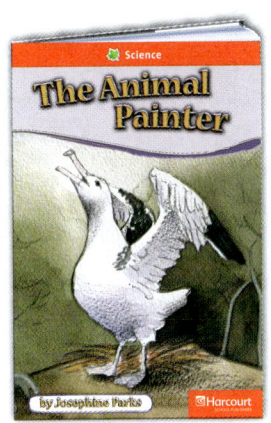

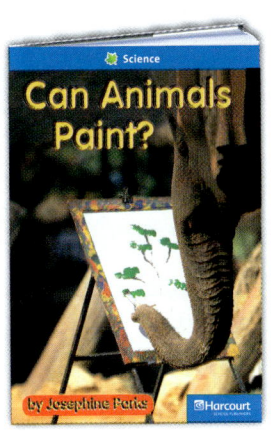

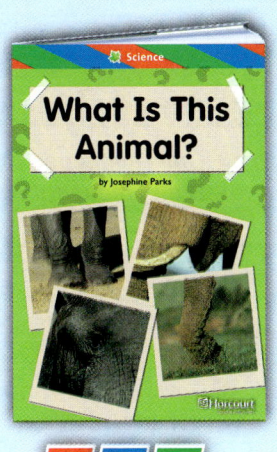

● **BELOW-LEVEL**    ● **ON-LEVEL**    ● **ADVANCED**    **E L L**

## LEVELED PRACTICE

◀ **Strategic Intervention Resource Kit,** Lesson 17

◀ **Strategic Intervention Interactive Reader,** Lesson 17
Strategic Intervention Interactive Reader Online

◀ **ELL Extra Support Kit,** Lesson 17

◀ **Challenge Resource Kit,** Lesson 17

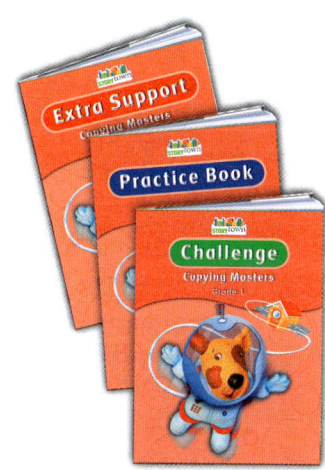

● **BELOW-LEVEL**
Extra Support Copying Masters, pp. 30–35

● **ON-LEVEL**
Practice Book, pp. 30–36

● **ADVANCED**
Challenge Copying Masters, pp. 30–35

## ADDITIONAL RESOURCES

- Spelling Practice Book, pp. 55–57
- Grammar Practice Book, pp. 65–68
- Reading Transparencies R33–R34
- Language Arts Transparencies LA33–LA34
- Test Prep System
◀ **Literacy Center Kit,** Cards 81–85
◀ **Sound/Spelling Card**
- Fluency Builders
◀ **Photo Cards**
- Read-Aloud Anthology, p. 64

## ✓ ASSESSMENT

✓ **Weekly Lesson Tests**
- Comprehension
- Phonics and Spelling
- Focus Skill
- Robust Vocabulary
- High-Frequency Words
- Grammar
- Fluency

 **www.harcourtschool.com/storytown**
- Online Assessment
*Also available on CD-ROM—ExamView®*

 Go online ePlanner

 90+ Minutes

# Suggested Lesson Planner

| | Day 1 | Day 2 |
|---|---|---|
|  **Step 1** Whole Group — 20-60+ Minutes | | |

## Day 1

**QUESTION OF THE DAY,** p. T390
*What helps you fall asleep? Why?*

**READ ALOUD,** p. T390
*Big Book: Fireflies, Fireflies, Light My Way*

**WORD WALL,** p. T391

✓ **PHONEMIC AWARENESS,** p. T391
Phoneme Substitution

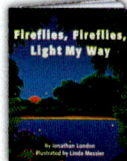
▲ Big Book

 phonics, p. T392
Introduce: Syllable /əl/–*le*

✓ **SPELLING,** p. T395
Pretest: *hand, handle, wig, wiggle, single, little, turn, girl, by, room*

✓ **HIGH-FREQUENCY WORDS,** p. T397
Review: *soon, make, family, join, animals*

**READING,** p. T396
Get Started Story, "Jungle Fun"
Decodable Text
*Options for Reading*

 Read!
▲ Student Edition

✓ **FLUENCY,** p. T401
Intonation

✓ **COMPREHENSION,** p. T402
Read-Aloud: "How the Rainbow Came to Be"
🔴 Preview: Main Idea

✓ **BUILD ROBUST VOCABULARY,** p. T403
Introduce: *agreement, unnoticed, unthinkable*

## Day 2

**QUESTION OF THE DAY,** p. T406
*What do you think elephants do to have fun? Tell why.*

**SHARED READING,** p. T406
*Big Book of Rhymes and Poems,* "Elephant Song"

**WORD WALL,** p. T407

✓ **PHONEMIC AWARENESS,** p. T407
Phoneme Substitution

 phonics, p. T408
Review: Syllable /əl/–*le*

✓ **SPELLING,** p. T408
Word Building

✓ **HIGH-FREQUENCY WORDS**
Words to Know, p. T412
Introduce: *buy, carry, money, other, paint, paper, would*

**READING,** p. T414
"Can Elephants Paint?"
*Options for Reading*

Read!
Can Elephants Paint?
▲ Student Edition

✓ **COMPREHENSION,** pp. T410, T414
🔴 Introduce: Main Idea
🟢 Introduce: Reread

✓ **RETELLING/FLUENCY,** p. T426
Intonation

✓ **BUILD ROBUST VOCABULARY,** p. T427
Review: *agreement, unnoticed, unthinkable*

---

## Step 1 Whole Group
### Daily Language
- Oral Language
- High-Frequency Words
- Shared Reading
- Phonemic Awareness

### Word Work
-  phonics
- Spelling
- High-Frequency Words

### Skills and Strategies
- Reading
- Fluency
- Comprehension
- Build Robust Vocabulary

 **Step 2** Small Groups — 45+ Minutes

## Suggestions for Differentiated Instruction *(See pp. T384–T385.)*

 **Step 3** Whole Group — 15-20+ Minutes

### Language Arts
- Grammar
- Writing

✓ **GRAMMAR,** p. T404
Introduce: Possessives

*Daily Proofreading*
His dogg is black (dog, black.)

 **MODELED WRITING,** p. T405
Introduce: Friendly Letter
Writing Trait: Voice

**Writing Prompt** *Draw and write about something new you have done recently.*

✓ **GRAMMAR,** p. T428
Review: Possessives

Daily Proofreading
her name is jan. (Her, Jan)

 **SHARED WRITING,** p. T429
Review: Friendly Letter
Writing Trait: Voice

**Writing Prompt** *Tell how you would feel if a good friend moved away.*

---

 = Focus Skill      = Focus Strategy      = Tested Skill

 **phonics**
- Syllable /əl/–*le*
- Inflections –*ed*, –*ing*

**Comprehension**
 FOCUS SKILL  Main Idea

FOCUS STRATEGY  Reread

**Phonemic Awareness**
Phoneme Substitution

**Fluency**
Intonation

**Vocabulary**
HIGH-FREQUENCY: *buy*, *carry*, *money*, *other*, *paint*, *paper*, *would*

ROBUST: *agreement*, *unnoticed*, *unthinkable*, *rejoice*, *predicament*, *extraordinary*

## Day 3

**QUESTION OF THE DAY,** p. T430
*Where would you play with an elephant? What would you do?*

**SHARED READING,** p. T430
*Big Book of Rhymes and Poems,* "Elephant Song"

**WORD WALL,** p. T431

☑ **PHONEMIC AWARENESS,** p. T431
Phoneme Substitution

☑  **phonics**, p. T432
Review: Syllable /əl/–*le*

☑ **SPELLING,** p. T433
State the Generalization

☑ **HIGH-FREQUENCY WORDS,** p. T434
Review: *buy*, *carry*, *money*, *other*, *paint*, *paper*, *would*

☑ **FLUENCY,** p. T435
Intonation: "Can Elephants Paint?"

☑ **COMPREHENSION,** p. T436
Review: Main Idea
Paired Selection: "An Elephant's Three T's"

**CONNECTIONS,** p. T438

☑ **BUILD ROBUST VOCABULARY,** p. T439
Introduce: *rejoice*, *predicament*, *extraordinary*

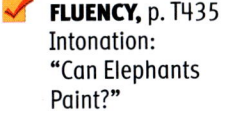 Read!

▲ Student Edition

☑ **GRAMMAR,** p. T440
Review: Possessives

***Daily Proofreading***
this is Todds money. (This, Todd's)

 **SHARED WRITING,** p. T441
Review: Friendly Letter
Writing Trait: Voice

 **Writing Prompt**  *Draw and write about the kind of art you like to make or look at.*

## Day 4

**QUESTION OF THE DAY,** p. T442
*What does an elephant look like? Describe it.*

**SHARED READING,** p. T442
*Big Book of Rhymes and Poems,* "Elephant"

**WORD WALL,** p. T443

☑ **PHONEMIC AWARENESS,** p. T443
Phoneme Substitution

☑  **phonics**, p. T444
Introduce: Inflections –*ed*, –*ing*

☑ **SPELLING,** p. T445
Review Spelling Words

☑ **HIGH-FREQUENCY WORDS,** p. T446
Review: *buy*, *carry*, *money*, *other*, *paint*, *paper*, *would*

☑ **FLUENCY,** p. T447
Intonation: "Can Elephants Paint?"

☑ **COMPREHENSION,** p. T448
Review: Main Idea
*Big Book: Fireflies, Fireflies*

☑ **BUILD ROBUST VOCABULARY,** p. T449
Review: *rejoice*, *predicament*, *extraordinary*

 Read!

▲ Student Edition

☑ **GRAMMAR,** p. T450
Review: Possessives

***Daily Proofreading***
is that book her (Is, hers?)

 **INDEPENDENT WRITING,** p. T451
Review: Friendly Letter
Writing Trait: Voice

 **Writing Prompt**  *Write a note to a friend or relative about a favorite place.*

## Day 5

**QUESTION OF THE DAY,** p. T452
*What can elephants do with their trunks? Why is that amazing?*

**SHARED READING,** p. T452
*Big Book of Rhymes and Poems,* "Elephant"

**WORD WALL,** p. T453

☑ **PHONEMIC AWARENESS,** p. T453
Phoneme Substitution

☑ **phonics**, p. T454
Review: Inflections –*ed*, –*ing*

☑ **SPELLING,** p. T455
Posttest

☑ **HIGH-FREQUENCY WORDS,** p. T456
Review: *buy*, *carry*, *money*, *other*, *paint*, *paper*, *would*

☑ **FLUENCY,** p. T457
Intonation: "Can Elephants Paint?"

☑ **COMPREHENSION,** p. T458
Review: Main Idea

☑ **BUILD ROBUST VOCABULARY,** p. T459
Review

 Read!

▲ Student Edition

☑ **GRAMMAR,** p. T460
Review: Possessives

***Daily Proofreading***
is their plant as big as you (Is, yours?)

 **INDEPENDENT WRITING,** p. T461
Review: Friendly Letter
Writing Trait: Voice

 **Writing Prompt**  *Draw and write about a topic of your choice.*

● **BELOW-LEVEL**  ● **ON-LEVEL**  ● **ADVANCED**   ELL

# Suggested Small Group Planner

  45-60+ Minutes

| | **Day 1** | **Day 2** |
|---|---|---|
|  **● BELOW-LEVEL** 15+ Min. each | **Teacher-Directed** *Student Edition:* Get Started Story, "Jungle Fun," p. T396 <br><br> **Independent** 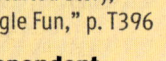 Listening/Speaking Center, p. T388 <br> Extra Support Copying Masters, p. 30 <br>  ▲ Student Edition | **Teacher-Directed** *Student Edition:* "Can Elephants Paint?" p. T414 <br><br> **Independent** 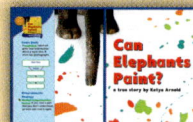 Reading Center, p. T388 <br> Extra Support Copying Masters, p. 32 <br> ▲ Student Edition |
|  **● ON-LEVEL** 15+ Min. each | **Teacher-Directed** *Student Edition:* Get Started Story, "Jungle Fun," p. T396 <br><br> **Independent** Reading Center, p. T388 <br> Practice Book, p. 30 <br> ▲ Student Edition | **Teacher-Directed** *Student Edition:* "Can Elephants Paint?" p. T414 <br><br> **Independent** Letters and Sounds Center, p. T389 <br> Practice Book, p. 32 <br> ▲ Student Edition |
| **● ADVANCED** 15+ Min. each | **Teacher-Directed** Leveled Reader: "Congo the Painter," p. T464 <br> Before Reading <br><br> **Independent** Letters and Sounds Center, p. T389 <br> Challenge Copying Masters, p. 30 <br>  ▲ Leveled Reader | **Teacher-Directed** Leveled Reader: "Congo the Painter," p. T464 <br> Read the Book <br><br> **Independent** Word Work Center, p. T389 <br> Challenge Copying Masters, p. 32 <br>  ▲ Leveled Reader |

 **E L L**

### English-Language Learners

*In addition to the small-group suggestions above, use the ELL Extra Support Kit to promote language development.*

| | |
|---|---|
| **LANGUAGE DEVELOPMENT SUPPORT** <br> **Teacher-Directed** <br> ELL TG, Day 1 <br> **Independent** <br> ELL Copying Masters, Lesson 17 | **LANGUAGE DEVELOPMENT SUPPORT** <br> **Teacher-Directed** <br> ELL TG, Day 2 <br> **Independent** <br> ELL Copying Masters, Lesson 17 |

### Intervention

▲ Strategic Intervention Resource Kit    ▲ Strategic Intervention Interactive Reader

| | |
|---|---|
| Strategic Intervention TG, Day 1 <br> Strategic Intervention Practice Book, Lesson 17 | Strategic Intervention TG, Day 2 <br> Strategic Intervention Interactive Reader, Lesson 17 <br>  ▲ Strategic Intervention Interactive Reader |

 **= Literacy Center Cards**

**MONITOR PROGRESS**

**Small-Group Instruction**

| Phonemic Awareness/ Phonics | High-Frequency Words | Fluency | Comprehension | Robust Vocabulary | Language Arts Checkpoint |
|---|---|---|---|---|---|
| Syllable /əl/–*le* p. S42 | *buy, carry, money, other, paint, paper, would* p. S43 | Intonation pp. S44–S45 | Focus Skill Main Idea pp. S46–S47 | *agreement, unnoticed, unthinkable, rejoice, predicament, extraordinary* pp. S48–S49 | **Grammar:** Possessives **Writing:** Friendly Letter pp. S50–S51 |

## Day 3

**Teacher-Directed**
Leveled Reader:
"The Animal Painter,"
p. T462
Before Reading; Read the Book

**Independent**
Word Work Center, p. T389
Extra Support Copying Masters,
p. 33

▲ Leveled Reader

**Teacher-Directed**
Leveled Reader:
"Can Animals Paint?"
p. T463
Before Reading; Read the Book

**Independent**
Writing Center, p. T389
Practice Book, p. 33

▲ Leveled Reader

**Teacher-Directed**
Leveled Reader:
"Congo the Painter," p. T464
Think Critically

**Independent**
Listening/Speaking Center,
p. T388
Challenge Copying Masters, p. 33

▲ Leveled Reader

**LANGUAGE DEVELOPMENT SUPPORT**
**Teacher-Directed**
Leveled Reader:
"What Is This Animal?" p. T465
Before Reading; Read the Book
ELL TG, Day 3

**Independent**
ELL Copying Masters, Lesson 17

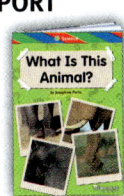
▲ Leveled Reader

Strategic Intervention TG, Day 3
Strategic Intervention
Interactive Reader, Lesson 17
Strategic Intervention
Practice Book, Lesson 17

▲ Strategic Intervention Interactive Reader

## Day 4

**Teacher-Directed**
Leveled Reader:
"The Animal Painter," p. T462
Reread for Fluency

**Independent**
Letters and Sounds Center,
p. T389
Cut-Out/Fold-Up Book, Practice Book, pp. 53–54

▲ Leveled Reader

**Teacher-Directed**
Leveled Reader:
"Can Animals Paint?" p. T463
Reread for Fluency

**Independent**
Word Work Center, p. T389
Cut-Out/Fold-Up Book: Practice Book, pp. 53–54

▲ Leveled Reader

**Teacher-Directed**
Leveled Reader:
"Congo the Painter," p. T464
Reread for Fluency
Self-Selected Reading: Classroom Library Collection

**Independent**
Writing Center, p. T389
Cut-Out/Fold-Up Book: Practice Book, pp. 53–54

▲ Leveled Reader

**LANGUAGE DEVELOPMENT SUPPORT**
**Teacher-Directed**
Leveled Reader:
"What Is This Animal?" p. T465
Reread for Fluency
ELL TG, Day 4

**Independent**
ELL Copying Masters, Lesson 17

▲ Leveled Reader

Strategic Intervention TG, Day 4
Strategic Intervention
Interactive Reader, Lesson 17

▲ Strategic Intervention Interactive Reader

## Day 5

**Teacher-Directed**
Leveled Reader:
"The Animal Painter," p. T462
Think Critically

**Independent**
Writing Center, p. T389
Leveled Reader: Reread for Fluency
Extra Support Copying Masters, p. 35

▲ Leveled Reader

**Teacher-Directed**
Leveled Reader:
"Can Animals Paint?" p. T463
Think Critically

**Independent**
Listening/Speaking Center,
p. T388
Leveled Reader: Reread for Fluency
Practice Book, p. 35

▲ Leveled Reader

**Teacher-Directed**
Leveled Reader:
"Congo the Painter," p. T464
Reread for Fluency
Self-Selected Reading: Classroom Library Collection

**Independent**
Reading Center, p. T388
Leveled Reader: Reread for Fluency
Challenge Copying Masters, p. 35

▲ Leveled Reader

**LANGUAGE DEVELOPMENT SUPPORT**
**Teacher-Directed**
Leveled Reader:
"What Is This Animal?" p. T465
Think Critically
ELL TG, Day 5

**Independent**
Leveled Reader:
Reread for Fluency
ELL Copying Masters, Lesson 17

▲ Leveled Reader

Strategic Intervention TG, Day 5
Strategic Intervention
Interactive Reader, Lesson 17

▲ Strategic Intervention Interactive Reader

# Leveled Readers & Leveled Practice
## Reinforcing Skills and Strategies

## LEVELED READERS SYSTEM

- **Leveled Readers**
- **Leveled Readers CD**
- **Leveled Reader Teacher Guides**
  - *Comprehension*
  - *High-Frequency Words*
  - *Oral Reading Fluency Assessment*
- **Response Activities**
- **Leveled Readers Assessment**

See pages T462–T465 for lesson plans.

### BELOW-LEVEL

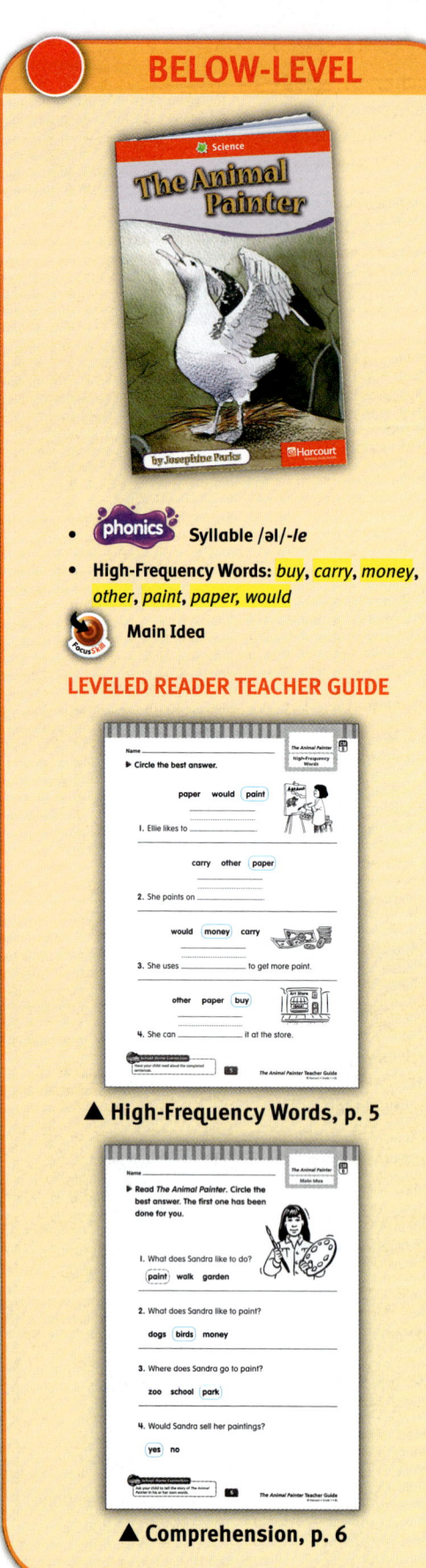

- **phonics** Syllable /əl/-*le*
- **High-Frequency Words:** *buy*, *carry*, *money*, *other*, *paint*, *paper*, *would*
- **Main Idea**

**LEVELED READER TEACHER GUIDE**

▲ High-Frequency Words, p. 5

▲ Comprehension, p. 6

### ON-LEVEL

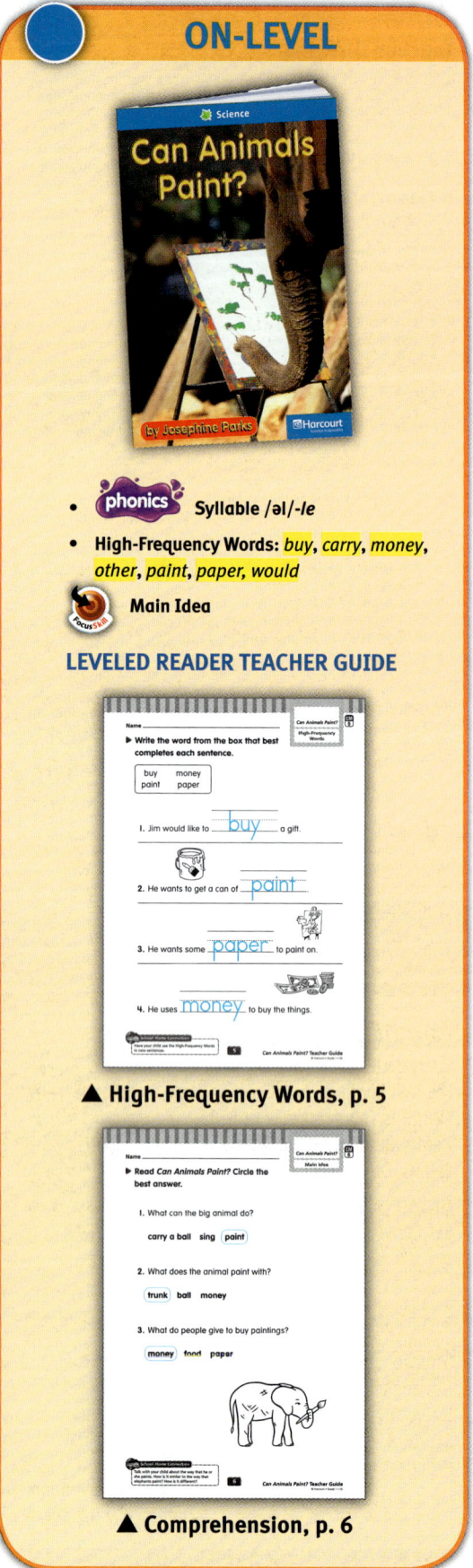

- **phonics** Syllable /əl/-*le*
- **High-Frequency Words:** *buy*, *carry*, *money*, *other*, *paint*, *paper*, *would*
- **Main Idea**

**LEVELED READER TEACHER GUIDE**

▲ High-Frequency Words, p. 5

▲ Comprehension, p. 6

**www.harcourtschool.com/storytown**

★ **Leveled Readers, online**
*Searchable by Genre, Skill, Vocabulary, Level, or Title*
★ **Student Activities and Teacher Resources, online**

## ADVANCED

- phonics  Syllable /əl/-*le*
- **High-Frequency Words:** *buy, carry, money, other, paint, paper, would*

 **Main Idea**

### LEVELED READER TEACHER GUIDE

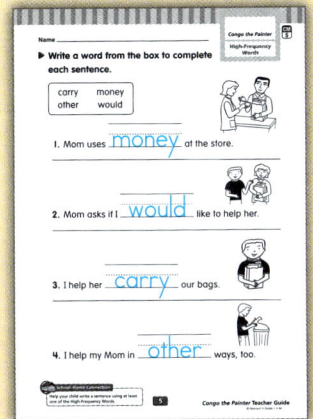

▲ **High-Frequency Words, p. 5**

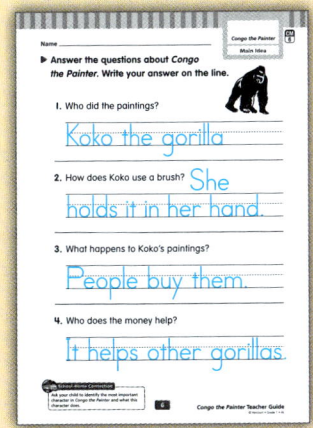

▲ **Comprehension, p. 6**

## E L L

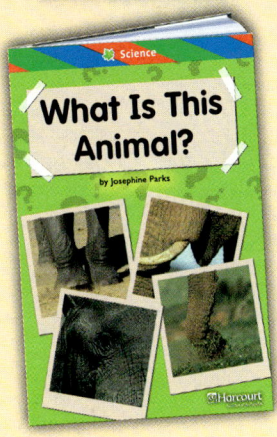

- **Strong Picture Support**
- **Concept Vocabulary**
- **Scaffolded Language Development**

### LEVELED READER TEACHER GUIDE

▲ **Build Background, p. 5**

▲ **Scaffolded Language Development, p. 6**

## CLASSROOM LIBRARY

### for Self-Selected Reading

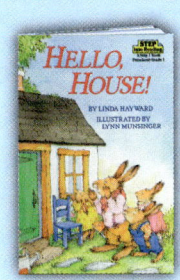

**AVERAGE**

▲ *Hello, House!* by Linda Hayward. **FOLKTALE**

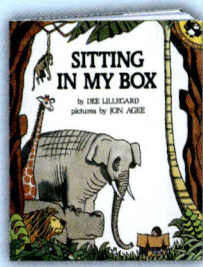

**AVERAGE**

▲ *Sitting In My Box* by Dee Lillegard. **FANTASY**

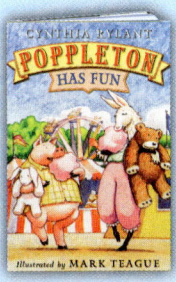

**AVERAGE**

▲ *Poppleton Has Fun* by Cynthia Rylant. **FANTASY**

▲ **Classroom Library Books Teacher Guide, pp. 40–47, 52–55**

# Literacy Centers

15 Min. each

## Management Support

While you provide direct instruction to individuals or small groups, other children can work on literacy center activities.

▲ Literacy Centers Pocket Chart

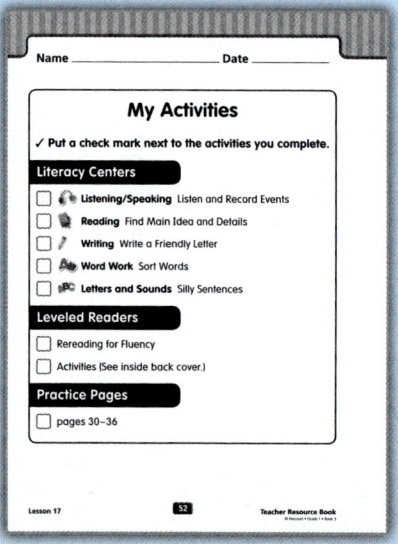

**My Activities**

✓ Put a check mark next to the activities you complete.

**Literacy Centers**

☐ Listening/Speaking  Listen and Record Events
☐ Reading  Find Main Idea and Details
☐ Writing  Write a Friendly Letter
☐ Word Work  Sort Words
☐ Letters and Sounds  Silly Sentences

**Leveled Readers**

☐ Rereading for Fluency
☐ Activities (See inside back cover.)

**Practice Pages**

☐ pages 30–36

Lesson 17 · 52 · Teacher Resource Book

▲ Teacher Resource Book, p. 52

## Homework for the Week

**TEACHER RESOURCE BOOK, PAGE 21**

The *Homework Copying Master* provides activities to complete for each day of the week.

**www.harcourtschool.com/ storytown**

---

### LISTENING/SPEAKING

## Listen and Record Events

*Objective* To develop listening skills by listening to familiar stories

**LISTENING/SPEAKING**  Card 81

**Listen and Record Events**

**MATERIALS**
- Audiotext 3
- art and writing materials
- music player
- library books on tape

❶ Listen to a story. Follow along.

❷ Fold a paper two times. Write 1, 2, 3, 4.

❸ Draw what happens in the story. Write.

To the Teacher: Have children read previously read *Student Edition* selections or library books that have a clear sequence of events. Have them fold paper to create four boxes and then draw and write about the main events from the story in the correct order. Afterward, you may want to have partners retell the main events of their favorite stories to one another.

Grade 1 · Lesson 17

⭐ **Literacy Center Kit • Card 81**

---

### READING

## Find Main Idea and Details

*Objectives* To determine the main idea and to identify supporting details in a story

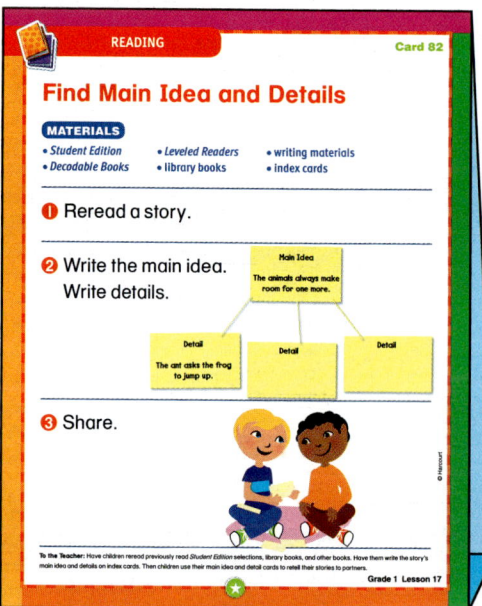

**READING**  Card 82

**Find Main Idea and Details**

**MATERIALS**
- Student Edition
- Decodable Books
- Leveled Readers
- library books
- writing materials
- index cards

❶ Reread a story.

❷ Write the main idea. Write details.

Main Idea
The animals always make room for one more.

Detail — The ant asks the frog to jump up.  Detail  Detail

❸ Share.

To the Teacher: Have children reread previously read *Student Edition* selections, library books, and other books. Have them write the story's main idea and details on index cards. Then children use their main idea and detail cards to retell their stories to partners.

Grade 1 · Lesson 17

⭐ **Literacy Center Kit • Card 82**

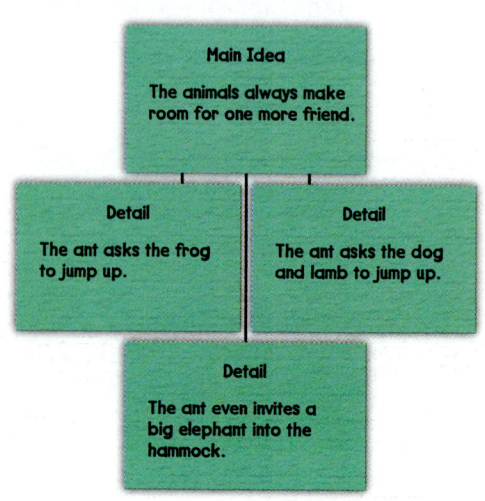

Main Idea
The animals always make room for one more friend.

Detail
The ant asks the frog to jump up.

Detail
The ant asks the dog and lamb to jump up.

Detail
The ant even invites a big elephant into the hammock.

---

**www.harcourtschool.com/storytown**

GO online

★ Additional Literacy Center Activities
★ Resources for Parents and Teachers

**Differentiated** *for Your Needs*

---

## WRITING

### Write a Friendly Letter

*Objective* To write about a familiar event in the form of a friendly letter

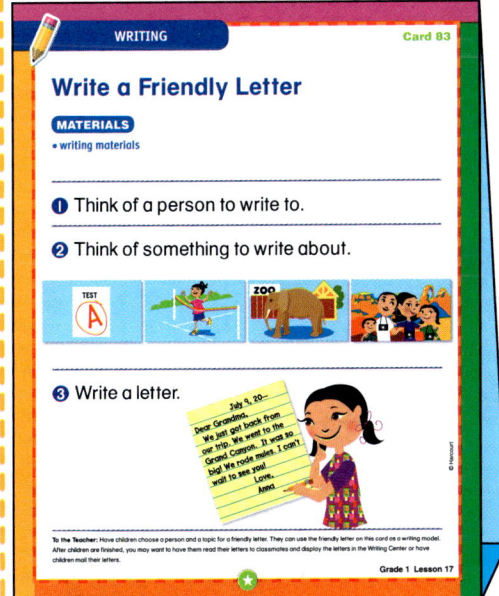

**Literacy Center Kit • Card 83**

---

 ## WORD WORK

### Sort Words

*Objective* To read and sort high-frequency words

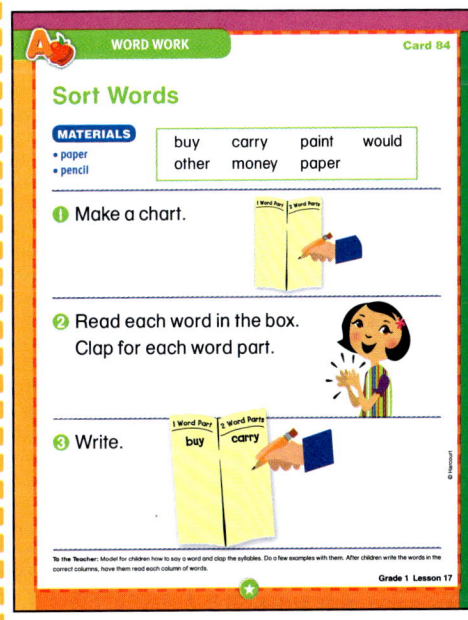

**Literacy Center Kit • Card 84**

| 1 Word Part | 2 Word Parts |
|---|---|
| buy | carry |
| paint | money |
| would | other |
| | paper |

---

## LETTERS AND SOUNDS

### Silly Sentences

*Objective* To identify words with syllable -le and use them in context

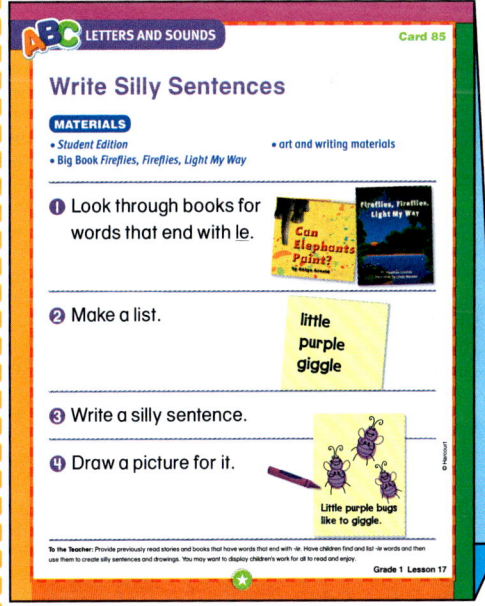

**Literacy Center Kit • Card 85**

purple  wiggle
giggle  pickle
chuckle
sparkle

---

**Day at a Glance**

# Day 1

## Phonemic Awareness
- Phoneme Substitution

 **and Spelling**
- Introduce: Syllable /əl/-*le*
- Pretest

## Reading
- Get Started Story: "Jungle Fun," *Student Edition*, pp. 166–173

## Fluency
- Intonation

## Comprehension
- *Read-Aloud Anthology:* "How the Rainbow Came to Be" Review: Main Idea

## Robust Vocabulary
- Introduce: *agreement, unnoticed, unthinkable*

## Grammar
- Introduce: Possessives

## Modeled Writing
- Friendly Letter

# Warm-Up Routines

## Oral Language

**Objective** *To listen attentively and respond appropriately to oral communication*

### Question of the Day
**What helps you fall asleep? Why?**

Discuss the questions above with children. Write the following sentence frame on the board and help them complete it.

**I like to _____ before I go to bed.**

## Read Aloud

**Objective** *To respond to a story through music*

**BIG BOOK** Reread *Fireflies, Fireflies, Light My Way.* Use the following steps:

- Remind children that the title comes from an old Native American lullaby. Review that a lullaby is a song sung before bedtime. As children listen, ask them to think about why this story might help someone fall asleep.

▲ Big Book
*Fireflies, Fireflies, Light My Way*

- Lead children to respond through music to the story in a way that reflects understanding and interpretation. Lead them in singing some of the words as a bedtime lullaby. Possible traditional tunes to use include "Rock-a-bye Baby," "Hush Little Baby," or "Sleep, My Child."

# Word Wall

**Objective** *To read high-frequency words*

**REVIEW HIGH-FREQUENCY WORDS** Review *by, room, animals, make, family, join,* and other previously learned high-frequency words. Say each word, ask a volunteer to point to it, and have children read it aloud. Then point to words at random, and have children reread them. Repeat several times to reinforce instant recognition.

| | | |
|---|---|---|
| by | room | animals |
| make | family | join |

# Phonemic Awareness

**Objective** *To substitute initial phonemes to make new words*

**Routine Card 10** **PHONEME SUBSTITUTION: INITIAL** Tell children that you will say some words, and they will change the first sound to make a new word. Model by saying: **The word is** *park.* **I will change /p/ to /b/. The new word is** *bark.* Model with another word and sound, and have children name the new word. Say: **The word is** *look.* **Change /l/ to /t/. What is the new word?** (took) Continue with these words:

**gate, /g/ to /l/** (late)

**cable, /k/ to /t/** (table)

**nurse, /n/ to /p/** (purse)

**handle, /h/ to /k/** (candle)

**tickle, /t/ to /p/** (pickle)

**barn, /b/ to /y/** (yarn)

**quiz, /kw/ to /wh/** (whiz)

**when, /wh/ to /th/** (then)

## nurse, /n/ to /p/ (purse)

# Syllable /əl/-le

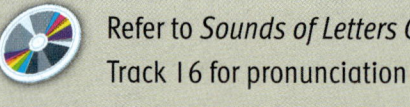 **phonics** *and Spelling*

## Objectives

- *To recognize and generate the sounds for the syllable -le*
- *To build and blend words with /əl/-le and other known letter-sounds*
- *To use /əl/-le and other known letter-sounds to spell words*
- *To spell known high-frequency words*

## Skill Trace
**Syllable /əl/-le**

| | |
|---|---|
| Introduce | T392–T395 |
| Reteach | S42 |
| Review | T408–T409, T432–T433, T445 |

Refer to *Sounds of Letters CD* Track 16 for pronunciation of /əl/.

turtle

## Connecting Letter to Sound

**Routine Card 12**

**DEVELOP PHONEMIC AWARENESS OF /əl/** Remind children that a syllable is a word part. Lead them in clapping out the syllables as they say these words: *tick, tickle; jug, juggle; start, startle.* Point out that *tickle, juggle,* and *startle* have two syllables, and they end with the same syllable. Repeat each word, slightly elongating the sounds in the last syllable: /əəll/. Then say the following words and have children add /əl/ to make new words: *buck (buckle), sniff (sniffle), pad (paddle).*

**CONNECT LETTERS AND SOUNDS** Display the *Sound/Spelling Card* for -le. Say the picture name and explain that the letters -le stand for the sounds at the end of *table*—/əl/. Have children repeat these words as you touch the letters: *buckle, sniffle, paddle.*

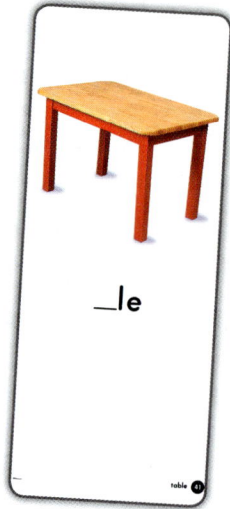

_le

▲ Sound/Spelling Card

**DISCRIMINATE /əl/** Give each child a blank card. Have children write -le. Say: **When I say a word that ends with /əl/, hold up your card and say /əl/. When I say a word that does not end with /əl/, hold your card behind your back.** Say these words:

**tingle    saddle    garden    apple    olive    turtle**

**5-DAY PHONICS**

| DAY 1 | Introduce Syllable /əl/-*le* |
|---|---|
| DAY 2 | Word Building with Syllable /əl/-*le* |
| DAY 3 | Build Words |
| DAY 4 | Inflections -*ed*, -*ing* (double final consonant) |
| DAY 5 | Inflections -*ed*, -*ing* (double final consonant) |

## Word Blending

 **DIBELS** Nonsense Word Fluency **NWF**

**WORDS WITH /əl/-*le*** Demonstrate each step with *Letter Cards* and a pocket chart. Have children repeat each step after you, using their *Word Builder Cards* and *Word Builders*.

 Routine Card **13**

**BLEND AND READ *pickle*** Hold up *p* and say /p/. Hold up *i* and say /ii/. Hold up *ck* and say /k/. Hold up *l* and *e* together and say /əl/.

• Place the letters *p, i, c, k, l, e* in the pocket chart. Have children do the same with their letters and *Word Builders*.

• Slide the letters *p, i, c, k* together. Run your hand under the letters as you read the word *pick*. Have children repeat.

• Slide *le* next to *pick*. Slide your hand under *pickle* as you blend the sounds in the second syllable—pick /əll/. Have children repeat.

• Read *pickle* naturally. Repeat, having children read the word with you.

Follow a similar procedure with the words below. Lead children to recognize word parts by framing or running your hand under the two word parts in each word.

    **jingle**        **jungle**        **pebble**        **middle**

## Professional Development

 **Podcasting:** Word Blending, Gr. 1

**E L L**

**Support Word Meaning** Use *Photo Cards* to support word meaning. For example, as children blend *jungle*, display the card for *jungle*.

jungle

▲ Photo Card 78

**ADVANCED**

**Multimeaning Word** Point out that the word *jingle* has two meanings—"a tinkling sound" and also "a short tune that is easy to remember." Point out that jingles are often sung in ads. Invite children to hum some of their favorite jingles for the group to identify.

# Syllable /əl/-*le*

 **phonics** *and Spelling*

## Professional Development

 **Podcasting:** Word Building, Gr. 1; Spelling and Dictation, Gr. 1

## Word Building

**Routine Card 14**

**BUILD SPELLING WORDS**
Use *Letter Cards* and a pocket chart. Have children use *Word Builder Cards* and *Word Builders*. As children build words, list them on the board.

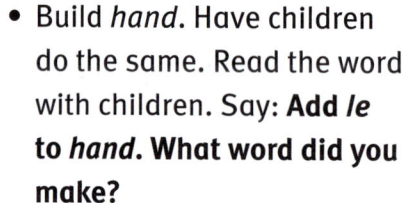

- Build *hand*. Have children do the same. Read the word with children. Say: **Add *le* to *hand*. What word did you make?**

- Remove *handle*. Build *wig* and read it with children. Say: **Add *gle* to *wig*. What word did you make?**

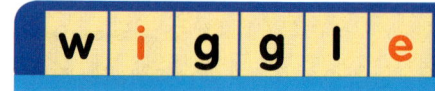

Continue, leading children to build and read *single* and *little*. Then have children read all the words on the board.

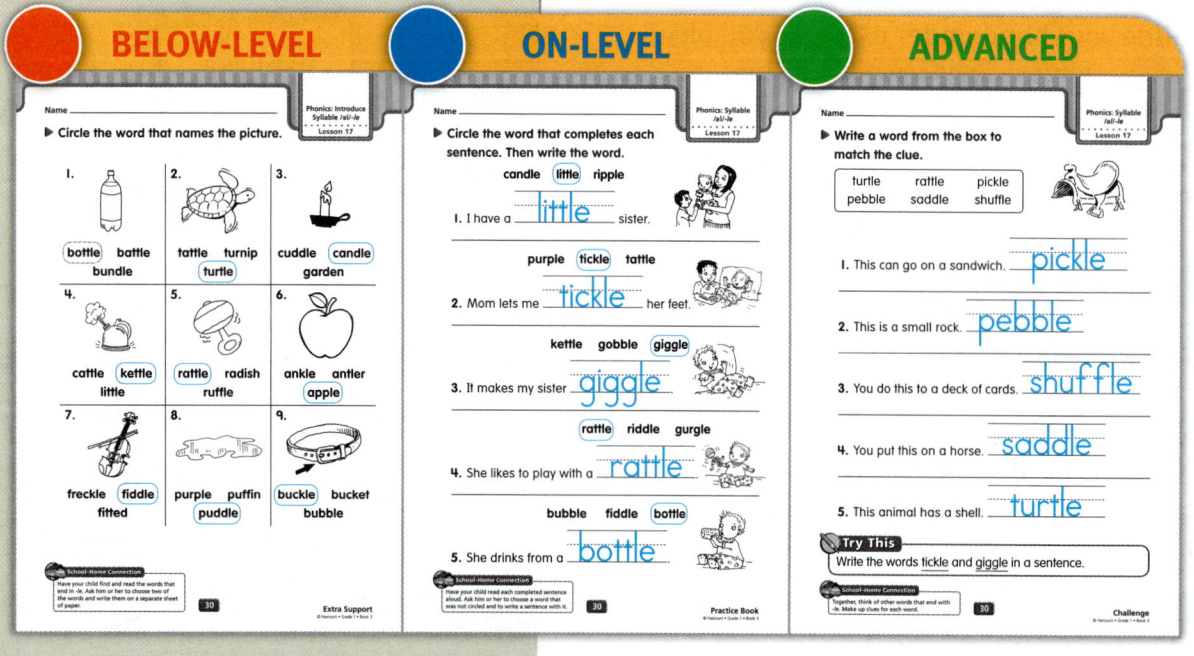

▲ Extra Support, p. 30    ▲ Practice Book, p. 30    ▲ Challenge, p. 30

## ELL

- Group children according to academic levels, and assign one of the pages on the left.

- Clarify any unfamiliar concepts as necessary. See *ELL Teacher Guide*, Lesson 17, for scaffolding instruction.

**5-DAY SPELLING**

| DAY 1 | Pretest |
| DAY 2 | Word Building |
| DAY 3 | State the Generalization |
| DAY 4 | Review |
| DAY 5 | Posttest |

## Introduce Spelling Words

**PRETEST** Say the first word and read the dictation sentence. Repeat the word as children write it. Write the word on the board and have children check their spelling. Tell them to circle the word if they spelled it correctly or write it correctly if they did not. Repeat for words 2–10.

### Words with /əl/-*le*

1. hand    Raise your **hand** before you speak.
2. handle    Carry the basket by the **handle**.
3. wig    The clown wore a curly red **wig**.
4. wiggle    We watched the worm **wiggle**.
5. single    There isn't a **single** cracker left.
6. little    A new puppy is very **little**.

### Review

7. turn    Please **turn** off the television.
8. girl    Is that **girl** your sister?

### High-Frequency

9. by    Please sit **by** me.
10. room    Bob cleaned his messy **room**.

**Spelling Words**

| | | | |
|---|---|---|---|
| 1. | hand | 6. | little |
| 2. | handle | 7. | turn |
| 3. | wig | 8. | girl |
| 4. | wiggle | 9. | by |
| 5. | single | 10. | room |

---

### ✓ MONITOR PROGRESS

#### Phonics: Syllable /əl/-*le*

| **IF** children have difficulty building and reading words with the syllable /əl/-*le*, | **THEN** repeat the words in this manner: *hand—handle, wig—wiggle, sing—single, lit—little.* |
|---|---|

**Small-Group Instruction, p. S42:**

● **BELOW-LEVEL:** Reteach
● **ON-LEVEL:** Reinforce
● **ADVANCED:** Extend

▲ Practice Book, p. 31

#  Reading

## *Get Started Story:* Jungle Fun

### Objectives

- *To use letter-sound knowledge to read decodable text*
- *To review high-frequency words*
- *To develop fluency*

### Professional Development

 **Podcasting:** Reading Decodable Text, Gr. 1

## Options for Reading

 **BELOW-LEVEL**

**Echo-Reading** Have children echo-read each sentence. Pause to discuss it, using the Monitor Comprehension questions. Have children frame and read *-le* words.

 **ON-LEVEL**

**Monitor Comprehension** Have children read the story aloud, page by page. Ask the Monitor Comprehension questions as you go. Then lead them in retelling the story.

 **ADVANCED**

**Independent Reading** Have children read each page silently, looking up each time they finish a page. Ask the Monitor Comprehension questions as you go. Discuss who should win the contest.

### Apply Syllable /əl/-*le*

**READ DECODABLE TEXT** Write the following sentences on the board. Tell children that the sentences are about a story they will read.

**Some animals jump and tumble.**
**Some animals make bells jingle.**

- Have children read the sentences as you track the print.
- Have volunteers frame and read the words with *-le*.
- Tell children that many words in the story have two syllables and end with the /əl/ sounds.

**Routine Card 17** **INTRODUCE THE STORY** Have children look at page 166 and read aloud the title. Ask them to point to the names of the author and the illustrator as you read them aloud. Discuss the illustration. Tell children they will read the story to find out how the animals have fun in the jungle.

 **E L L**

**Preview** Preview the story with a picture walk. Use the illustrations to develop meaning for the text. Then guide children through the story, using the Monitor Comprehension questions.

**Get Started Story**

**Phonics**
Words with le

**Words to Know**
Review

soon

animals

make

family

join

# Jungle Fun

by Nancy Furstinger
illustrated by
Michelle Angers

166

A contest will start **soon**. The contest is in the jungle. The **animals** will do fun tricks. Who will win?

167

# Monitor Comprehension

**PAGE 167** Say: **I see many different animals and some interesting objects. What do you suppose they are up to? Let's read to find out.**

**1** **PLOT** What are the animals getting ready for? (a contest)

**2** **APPLY PHONICS** Where will the contest be held? (in the jungle) Find and read the word that tells.

**Build Vocabulary** Explain that in a talent contest, people use their special skills or abilities. The winner of the contest wins a prize. Invite children to tell about things they do well.

## TECHNOLOGY

**eBook** "Jungle Fun" is available in an eBook.

**Audiotext** "Jungle Fun" is available on *Audiotext Grade 1*, CD 6 for subsequent readings.

Big cats run and jump and tumble.
Little cats giggle and chuckle.

168

Big red foxes juggle balls and pins.
Little red foxes cannot catch the
balls and pins.

169

# Monitor Comprehension

**PAGES 168–169**  Say: **It looks like the contest has started. Let's
read to find out what these animals are doing.**

**1** **NOTE DETAILS/APPLY PHONICS**  **What do the big cats do?** (run,
jump, tumble) **What do the little cats do?** (giggle, chuckle)

**2** **NOTE DETAILS/APPLY PHONICS**  **What do the big foxes do?**
(juggle)

## STRATEGIC READING

**Words with /əl/-*le***  Remind children
that this story includes many two-
syllable words that end with -*le*. Ask
them to count and read these words on
these pages.

An elephant family will join in the fun. They have purple hats that glitter and sparkle.

Big birds ring bells that jingle jangle. Little birds chirp and make bubbles.

170

171

# Monitor Comprehension

**PAGES 170–171**   Say: **Look at the birds and elephants. Let's read to find out what they are doing.**

1. **NOTE DETAILS**   What do the big birds do? (ring bells)

2. **APPLY PHONICS**   What sounds do the bells make? Point to and read the words. (jingle, jangle)

3. **APPLY PHONICS**   What color are the elephants' hats? Point to and read the word that tells. (purple)

**HIGH-FREQUENCY WORDS**

**Review**   Remind children that they have already learned to read the high-frequency words *make*, *family*, and *join*. Ask them to frame and read those words on these pages.

Big elephants stomp and kick.
Little elephants wiggle and turn
and spin.

172

Big animals and little animals all
have fun! Who can do the best
tricks?

You pick!

173

# Monitor Comprehension

**PAGES 172–173**   Say: **Let's read to see who wins the contest.**

**1** **NOTE DETAILS/APPLY PHONICS**   **What do the big elephants do?**
(stomp and kick) **What do the little elephants do?** (wiggle, turn,
spin)

**2** **PLOT**   **How does the story end?** (Readers are asked to pick who
wins the contest.)

**3** **EXPRESS OPINIONS**   **Who would you pick?** (Encourage children
to explain their choices.)

## MAKE A GRAPH

**Vote**   Suggest that children vote to
choose the winners. Guide them to make
a graph to show how many votes each
act receives.

# Check Comprehension
## *Retelling*

## Retell

**DIBELS**
Oral Reading Fluency
**ORF**

**RETELL "JUNGLE FUN"**    Use a graphic organizer such as the chart below. Have children retell the story by naming the characters and telling about their actions.

| Characters | Actions |
|---|---|
| big cats | tumble |
| little cats | giggle, chuckle |
| big foxes | juggle |

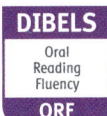 
# Fluency

## Repeated Reading

**DIBELS**
Oral Reading Fluency
**ORF**

**READ WITH A PARTNER**    Organize children into pairs and have them reread "Jungle Fun" three or four times. Listen to partners read, and provide feedback about reading with proper intonation and give guidance for improving fluency.

### Objectives
- *To practice retelling a story*
- *To read fluently in a manner that sounds like natural speech*

### RETELLING RUBRIC

| | |
|---|---|
| **4** | Uses details to clearly retell the story |
| **3** | Uses some details to retell the story |
| **2** | Retells the story with some inaccuracies |
| **1** | Is unable to retell the story |

### Professional Development

 **Podcasting:** Auditory Modeling

# Comprehension
## *Read Aloud*

### Objectives
- *To set a purpose for listening*
- *To understand characteristics of a folktale*

### Daily Comprehension

**Main Idea**

| | |
|---|---|
| **DAY 1:** | **Review Main Idea** **Read-Aloud Anthology** |
| **DAY 2:** | Review Main Idea *Student Edition* |
| **DAY 3:** | Review Main Idea *Paired Selection Student Edition* |
| **DAY 4:** | Review Main Idea *Big Book* |
| **DAY 5:** | Review Main Idea *Comparing Texts* |

**Connect to Prior Knowledge**
Display a chart with colors and color words. Review the colors with children before meeting with the whole group. Encourage children to use the color words to tell about their clothes or physical features such as hair and eyes.

---

### Before Reading

**CONNECT TO PRIOR KNOWLEDGE**    Tell children that they will be listening to a story about how Earth got its colors and how rainbows were created. Ask them to name their favorite color and tell about something that is that color.

**GENRE STUDY: FOLKTALE**    Explain that "How the Rainbow Came to Be" is a folktale.

▲ **Read-Aloud Anthology, "How the Rainbow Came to Be," p. 64**

**Think Aloud**    **A folktale is a story that has been told and retold over many years. Many folktales try to explain the creation of something in the world around us, such as mountains or stars.**

**REVIEW THE SKILL: MAIN IDEA**    Tell children that most stories have a main idea. Remind them that the main idea is what the story is mostly about. Model the skill by describing the main idea of a familiar story. For example, briefly retell "The Tortoise and the Hare," and explain that the main idea is that sometimes it is better to go at a slow and steady pace rather than to go too fast. Tell children that they will discuss the main idea of "How the Rainbow Came to Be" later in the week. Then read the story to them.

### After Reading

**RESPOND**    Ask children to name specific aspects of the story that tell them it is a folktale. List their ideas on the board and discuss them.

# Build Robust Vocabulary

## Listening/Speaking: *Words from the Read-Aloud*

### Teach/Model

**Routine Card 15**

**INTRODUCE ROBUST VOCABULARY** Use *Routine Card 15* to introduce the words.

❶ Put the word in **selection context**.
❷ Provide for children the **Student-Friendly Explanation**.
❸ Have children **say the word** with you.
❹ Use the word in other contexts, and have children **interact with the word's meaning**.
❺ Say the Student-Friendly Explanation again, and ask children to **name the word** that goes with it.

❶ **Selection Context:** Red, Blue, and Yellow are in **agreement** that Earth must have color.
❹ **Interact with Word Meaning:** What agreements do you have with friends about games you play at recess?

❶ **Selection Context:** At first, the butterflies were **unnoticed** because they were the same color as everything else on Earth.
❹ **Interact with Word Meaning:** Would you be unnoticed if you wore all white clothing as you walked through the snow?

❶ **Selection Context:** A planet without color was **unthinkable** to Red, Blue, and Yellow, so they added color to Earth.
❹ **Interact with Word Meaning:** Would a day at school without lunch be unthinkable to you?

### Practice/Apply

**GUIDED PRACTICE** Ask children to do the following:
- A friend broke an agreement. Show or tell how you might feel.
- You want to surprise your friend. Show how you would go up to him or her unnoticed.
- Imagine something unthinkable just happened. Use the expression on your face to show how you feel.

### Objective
- *To develop robust vocabulary through discussing a literature selection*

**INTRODUCE**

### Student-Friendly Explanations

**agreement** When you are in agreement with others, you all think the same thing.

**unnoticed** If you go unnoticed, no one sees you.

**unthinkable** An unthinkable event is something you never thought could or would happen.

**E L L**

**Introduce Vocabulary** Act out the meaning of each word. For example, make an expression of disbelief to show how you might react to an unthinkable event.

**unthinkable**

# Grammar
## Possessives

**5-DAY GRAMMAR**

| DAY 1 | Introduce Possessive Proper Nouns |
| DAY 2 | Introduce Possessive Common Nouns |
| DAY 3 | Introduce Possessive Pronouns *his, her, hers* |
| DAY 4 | Introduce Pronouns *its, their, your, yours* |
| DAY 5 | Review Possessives |

## Objective
• *To recognize possessive proper nouns*

## Daily Proofreading

### His dogg is black
(dog, black.)

**Possessives**

We like Kim's painting.  Juan's lunch is good.

Mark's dog is big.  This is Ann's ball.

Grade 1, Lesson 17    LA33    Grammar: Possessives

**Transparency LA33**

## Teach/Model

**INTRODUCE THE CONCEPT**   Read aloud some sentences containing possessives that tell about "How the Rainbow Came to Be" (*Read-Aloud Anthology,* pages 64–67):

• **Blue's oceans and rivers were beautiful.**

• **Red's bird was bright red.**

Explain that in these sentences, the words *Blue's* and *Red's* show ownership. They show that the oceans and rivers belonged to Blue and the bird belonged to Red. Ask a girl to hold up a book and a boy to hold up a pencil. Write these phrases on the board, read them aloud, and then read them with children.

**Pam's book**

**Hector's pencil**

Underline the word *Pam's,* circle the apostrophe, and identify it for children. Explain that adding *'s* to *Pam* shows that the book belongs to Pam. Using the second example, ask children who owns the pencil, and have them tell how they know. (Hector; the word *Hector's* shows ownership.)

## Guided Practice

**SAY POSSESSIVES**   Display **Transparency LA33.** Identify the boy in the first picture as Mark. Ask: **What belongs to Mark?** Write the phrase *Mark's dog* on the board and have a volunteer point out the possessive. Track the print, and have children read the sentence. Then use a similar pocedure with the other items.

## Practice/Apply

**WRITE POSSESSIVES**   Write on the board some of the phrases that children offer, omitting the *'s* when writing the possessive. Read each phrase aloud, and have children write it correctly.

# Modeled Writing
*Friendly Letter*

**5-DAY WRITING**

| | |
|---|---|
| **DAY 1** | Modeled Writing |
| **DAY 2** | Shared Writing |
| **DAY 3** | Shared Writing |
| **DAY 4** | Independent Writing |
| **DAY 5** | Independent Writing |

## Teach/Model

**INTRODUCE "FRIENDLY LETTER"** Display **Transparency LA34.** Explain that a boy wrote this letter to a friend. Read the letter and talk about the parts. Together, develop a list of characteristics of a well-written friendly letter.

### Friendly Letter

- The <u>heading</u> gives the date.
- The <u>greeting</u> tells who gets the letter.
- The <u>body</u> is the message.
- The <u>closing</u> says good-bye.
- The <u>signature</u> is the writer's name.

**WRITING TRAIT**  **VOICE** Point out that as Todd writes, he thinks about the person to whom he is writing and about his purpose for writing the letter. Discuss how Todd feels about Russ and encourage children to tell why they think this.

## Guided Practice

**DRAFT A MESSAGE** Remind children that the body of a friendly letter is the message. Share several sentences from the body of a letter you might write to a friend, such as **My class's Open House is next week. We are all busy making decorations.** Talk about the news it gives. Have children share news that they might put in a letter to a friend.

## Practice/Apply

**TELL A MESSAGE** Have children draw a picture showing a friend or relative who lives in another place. Have children also draw a picture of something interesting that has happened that they would like to tell that person. Have them add words and phrases that they might include in the letter. Save children's captioned pictures for writing their own letters on Days 4–5.

## Objectives
- *To understand the purpose of each part of a friendly letter*
- *To develop a list of criteria for effective friendly letters*

### Writing Prompt

**Write and Draw** Have children write and draw about something new or interesting they did recently.

**Student Model: Friendly Letter**

April 10, 20—

Dear Russ,

I miss you! How do you like your new house? How is your new school? I have a new dog. His name is Gus. He likes to run and play all the time. Please send me a card or call me.

Your friend,
Todd

Grade 1, Lesson 17    LA34    Writing: Friendly Letter

**Transparency LA34**

## Day at a Glance

### Day 2

**Phonemic Awareness**
• Phoneme Substitution

 **and Spelling**
• Review: Syllable /əl/-*le*
• Word Building

**Comprehension**
 Review: Main Idea

**High-Frequency Words**
• Introduce: *buy, carry, money, other, paint, paper, would*

**Reading**
• "Can Elephants Paint?"
*Student Edition,* pp. 178–199

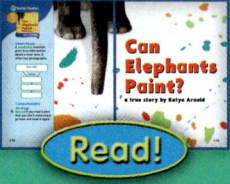

**Fluency**
• Intonation

**Robust Vocabulary**
• Review: *agreement, unnoticed, unthinkable*

**Grammar**
• Review: Possessives

**Shared Writing** 🖊
• Friendly Letter

# Warm-Up Routines

## Oral Language

**Objective** *To listen attentively and respond appropriately to oral communication*

### Question of the Day

**What do you think elephants do to have fun? Tell why.**

Invite children to describe things elephants could do to have fun. Have children help you complete the following sentence frame:

**To have fun, elephants _____ because _____.**

## Read Aloud

**Objectives** *To listen for a purpose; to recognize the pattern of a rhyme*

**BIG BOOK OF RHYMES AND POEMS** Display the poem and explain that it is an old Spanish children's song that was sung as a counting game. Ask children to listen to find out what happens when an elephant goes out to play. After reading, ask where the elephant goes to play and why he asks another elephant to join him. Help children make up additional verses and recite them, telling what happens when two and three elephants go out to play.

▲ **Big Book of Rhymes and Poems, p. 33**

## Word Wall

**Objective** *To read high-frequency words*

**REVIEW HIGH-FREQUENCY WORDS** Review *always, by, Cow's, join, nice, please, room* and other previously learned high-frequency words. Say each word, ask a volunteer to point to it, and have children read it aloud. Then point to words at random, and have children reread them.

| always | by | Cow's | join |

## Phonemic Awareness

**Objective** *To substitute the beginning phoneme in words*

**Routine Card 10**

**PHONEME SUBSTITUTION: INITIAL** Tell children that you will say a word and then make a new word by changing the beginning sound. Say: **The word is** *hop.* **I change /h/ to /m/. The new word is** *mop.* Teach children the song. Model the first example for them.

*(Sung to the tune of "A-Hunting We Will Go.")*

**A-changing we will go; a-changing we will go.
Change /m/ to /d/ in** *mark,* **my friend.
The new word now is** *dark!*

Have children participate by making the following substitutions while singing the song:

**tingle, /t/ to /s/** (single)  **heart, /h/ to /k/** (cart)

**link, /l/ to /p/** (pink)  **quick, /kw/ to /l/** (lick)

**fur, /f/ to /s/** (sir)  **candle, /k/ to /h/** (handle)

**pump, /p/ to /b/** (bump)  **milk, /m/ to /s/** (silk)

# Syllable /əl/ -le

 **phonics** *and Spelling*

## Objectives

- *To blend sounds into words*
- *To spell one- and two-syllable short vowel words and high-frequency words*

## Skill Trace

**Syllable /əl/ -le**

| | |
|---|---|
| Introduce | T392–T395 |
| Reteach | S42 |
| Review | T408–T409, T432–T433 |

### Spelling Words

| | | | |
|---|---|---|---|
| 1. | **hand** | 6. | **little** |
| 2. | **handle** | 7. | **turn** |
| 3. | **wig** | 8. | **girl** |
| 4. | **wiggle** | 9. | **by** |
| 5. | **single** | 10. | **room** |

## Word Building

**DIBELS** Nonsense Word Fluency **NWF**

**Routine Card 14**

**BUILD AND READ A SPELLING WORD** Place the *Letter Cards h, a, n, d* in the pocket chart. Read the word with children.

**BUILD SPELLING WORDS** Ask children what letters should be added to make *hand* become *handle*. After children read *handle*, replace the cards with *w, i, g* and have children read the word. Lead children in building *wiggle*. Use a similar procedure to build spelling words 5–6.

---

| 🔴 **BELOW-LEVEL** | 🟢 **ADVANCED** |
|---|---|
| **Build Spelling Words** Write the words on the board. Point to each word, one at a time, and read it aloud. Have children repeat it and finger trace it in the air as they spell the word aloud. | **Rhyming Words** Write the words *single* and *wiggle* on the board. Have children work with a partner to list all the words they can think of that rhyme with each word. Have pairs compare lists. |
| | **single**  **wiggle** |

**5-DAY** PHONICS/SPELLING

| DAY I | Pretest |
|---|---|
| **DAY 2** | **Word Building** |
| DAY 3 | State the Generalization |
| DAY 4 | Review |
| DAY 5 | Posttest |

## Read Words in Context

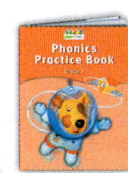

**APPLY PHONICS**   Write the following sentences on the board or on chart paper. Have children read each sentence silently. Then track the print as children read the sentence aloud.

Please do not <u>turn</u> the red <u>handle</u>!

The <u>little</u> <u>girl</u> put a black <u>wig</u> on her head.

It is so dark that I cannot see a <u>single</u> thing.

Stand still and do not <u>wiggle</u>.

Please raise your <u>hand</u> before you speak.

 **WRITE**   Dictate several words from the pocket chart. Have children write the words on a dry-erase board or in their notebooks.

### phonics   Resources

**Phonics Practice Book, pp. 91–94**

### "RESEARCH SAYS"

"Poor decoding skill leads to little reading and little opportunity to increase one's basic vocabulary and knowledge through reading, leaving a shaky foundation for later reading comprehension."

—Juel
(1988), p. 446

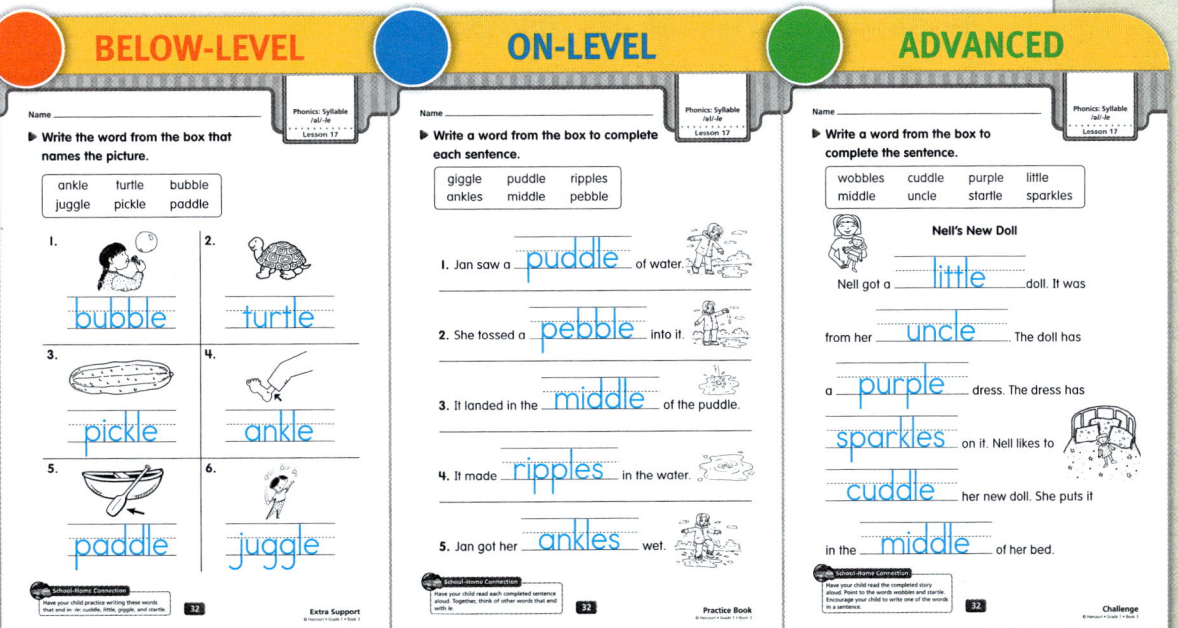

▲ **Extra Support, p. 32**      ▲ **Practice Book, p. 32**      ▲ **Challenge, p. 32**

- Group students according to academic levels, and assign one of the pages on the left.

- Clarify any unfamiliar concepts as necessary. See *ELL Teacher Guide*, Lesson 17, for support in scaffolding instruction.

# Main Idea
### *Comprehension*

## Objective
- *To identify and describe the main idea of a picture*

## Skill Trace
 **Main Idea**

| | |
|---|---|
| Preview | T316 |
| Introduce | T324–T325 |
| Reteach | S36–S37, S46–S47 |
| Review | T348, T360, T370, T402, T410–T411, T436, T448, T458 |
| Test | Bk 1-3 |
| Maintain | Monitor Comprehension, Bks 1-4, 1-5 |

## Teach/Model

**REVIEW MAIN IDEA**  Review main idea with children. Guide them to determine the main idea of a familiar story and identify supporting details. Read aloud the following sentences about "How the Rainbow Came to Be" (*Read-Aloud Anthology*, p. 64–67).

- **At first, Earth was all black and white.**

- **Blue painted the oceans, rivers, and sky.**

- **Red, Blue, and Yellow painted Earth and made many new colors that formed a rainbow.**

Then model how to identify which one tells the main idea.

**Think Aloud**  **The main idea is the most important idea. The first sentence tells me what Earth was like before it had any colors, but this is only one part of the story. It is a detail, not the main idea. The next sentence tells me what Blue did, but this is also only a detail, not the main idea. The last sentence tells me what the colors did together and what they created. This is the main idea or most important idea of the story.**

## Practice/Apply

**GUIDED PRACTICE**  Read *Student Edition* page 174 to children and read the definition of main idea. Talk about the picture and the main idea it illustrates. Then have children look at the picture at the top of page 175 and follow along as you read aloud the sentence and questions. Ask children what the most important idea is in this picture. (The girls are playing a clapping game.) Ask how they know this is the main idea. (The girls are the largest and most important thing in the picture.)

## Focus Skill

### Main Idea

The **main idea** of a story is the most important idea.

Look at the picture.

The main idea is that a boy is learning to tie his shoes.

174

---

Look at the picture. What is the main idea? How do you know?

Look at the picture. Choose the words that name the main idea.

- working on a farm
- working at school
- working at home

GO online www.harcourtschool.com/storytown

175

---

**Try This!** INDEPENDENT PRACTICE   Discuss the picture and then have children follow along as you read aloud the sentences and the three answer choices. Ask children to choose the words that tell the main idea and to tell how they know. (working at school; I know it's a classroom at a school because I see desks and children working.)

---

**E L L**

**Try This!** Help children with the Try This! activity by sharing images of a farm, a classroom, and a family at home. Help children name each location and tell the main idea.

# High-Frequency Words
## Words to Know

### Objective
• *To read high-frequency words*

INTRODUCE Tested

**High-Frequency Words**

| | |
|---|---|
| buy | paint |
| carry | paper |
| money | would |
| other | |

 **MONITOR PROGRESS**

**High-Frequency Words**

| | |
|---|---|
| **IF** children have difficulty reading and spelling the words, | **THEN** display a second set of word cards, and have them match the words. |

**Small-Group Instruction, p. S43:**

 **BELOW-LEVEL:** Reteach

 **ON-LEVEL:** Reinforce

 **ADVANCED:** Extend

---

## Teach/Model

**Routine Card 16**

**INTRODUCE WORDS**  Write the words *buy, carry, money, other, paint, paper,* and *would* on the board.

• Point to and read *buy.* Repeat it, having children say it with you.

• Say: **I *buy* books at the store.**

• Point to each letter as you spell the word. Have children spell the word with you.

• Have children read the word.

Repeat for the remaining words. Use the following sentences:

• Will you *carry* this bag for me?
• I keep my *money* in a piggy bank.
• The *other* books are in that bag.
• We will *paint* the fence tomorrow.
• You may draw on this *paper*.
• I think they *would* like to go with us.

## Guided Practice

**REVIEW WITH STUDENT EDITION PAGES 176–177**  Ask children to turn to *Student Edition* pages 176–177. Have children point to and read aloud each of the highlighted words on page 176. Talk about the artwork. Then ask volunteers to read aloud the sentences.

**STORY WORDS**  Write *idea* and *Lucky* on the board, and read the words aloud. Repeat, having children read the words with you. Mention that in the story "Can Elephants Paint?" one of the characters has a good idea for helping elephants. Explain that one of the elephants in the story is named Lucky. Point to the words again, and have children read them aloud.

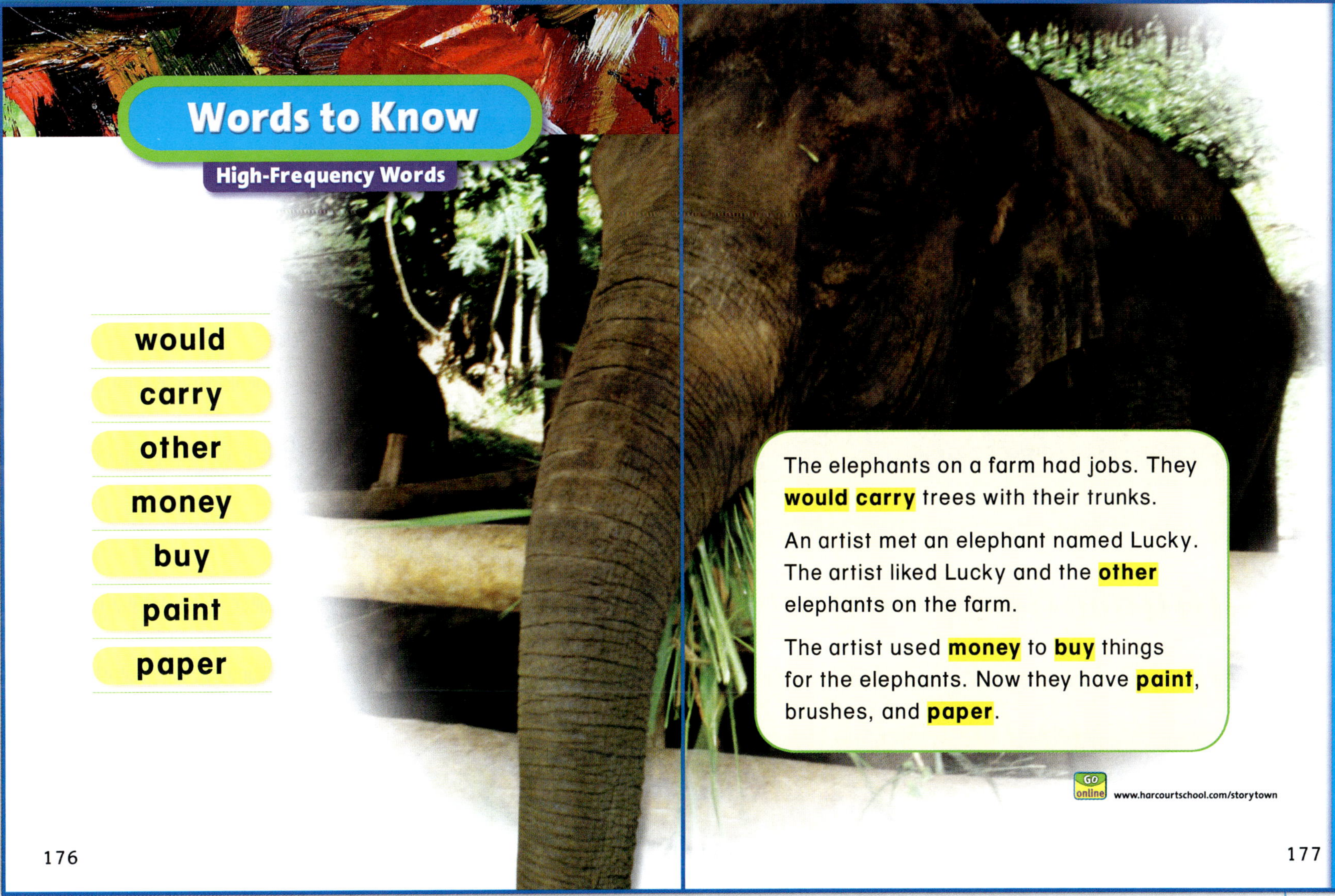

# Words to Know

## High-Frequency Words

- would
- carry
- other
- money
- buy
- paint
- paper

The elephants on a farm had jobs. They **would** **carry** trees with their trunks.

An artist met an elephant named Lucky. The artist liked Lucky and the **other** elephants on the farm.

The artist used **money** to **buy** things for the elephants. Now they have **paint**, brushes, and **paper**.

GO online www.harcourtschool.com/storytown

176 177

## ELL

**Review High-Frequency Words** Hold up *Photo Card 92* (*mop*) and say: **I can carry a mop.** Have children practice using the word *carry* in this sentence. Then invite children to name other objects they can carry and to use them to replace *mop* in new sentences.

See *ELL Teacher Guide,* Lesson 17, for support in scaffolding instruction.

**Photo Card 92** ▶

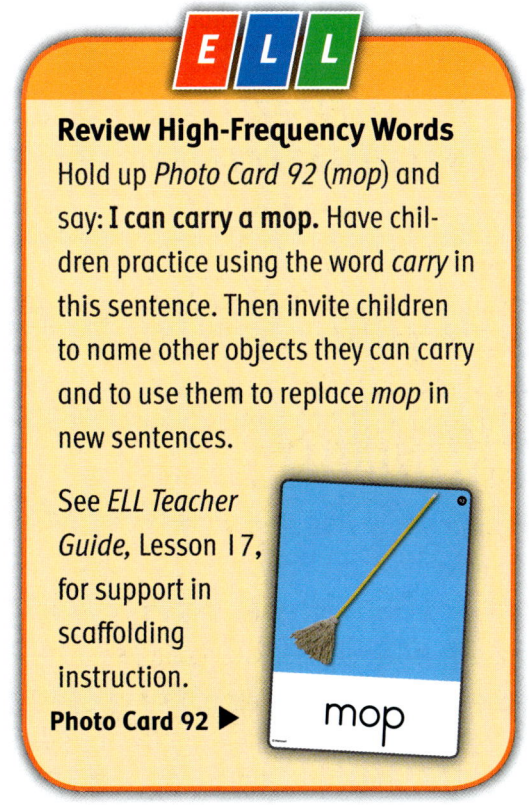

# Reading

*Student Edition:* **"Can Elephants Paint?"**

## Objectives

- *To understand the characteristics of nonfiction*
- *To reread as a strategy for monitoring comprehension*
- *To apply word knowledge to the reading of a text*

 **Podcasting:** Use Graphic Organizers

## Options for Reading

 **BELOW-LEVEL**

**Preview** Have children preview the selection by looking at the photographs. Guide them to predict what it will be about. Read each page to children, and have them echo read.

 **ON-LEVEL**

**Monitor Comprehension** Have children read the selection aloud, page by page. Ask the Monitor Comprehension questions as you go. Then lead them in retelling the selection.

 **ADVANCED**

**Independent Reading** Have children read each page silently, looking up each time they finish a page. Ask them the Monitor Comprehension questions as you go. Then discuss Lucky's new skills.

## Genre Study

**DISCUSS NONFICTION** Point to the genre label on *Student Edition* page 178 and tell children that this is *nonfiction*. Remind children that nonfiction selections tell about things that are true. They include facts about real people, places, things, or events, and often have photographs. Then use **Transparency GO16** or copy the graphic organizer onto the board. Tell children that they can fill it in for any nonfiction selection they read.

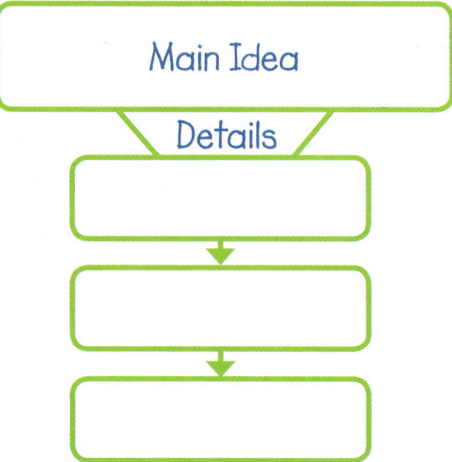

## Comprehension Strategies

**MONITOR COMPREHENSION: REREAD** Tell children that as they read, it is important to think about whether what they are reading makes sense. Point out that if any section of the text seems difficult or confusing, they should go back and reread that part.

**Think Aloud** In "How the Rainbow Came to Be," the author tells about the different sections of Earth that each color painted. I remember that the colors also joined together to create new colors. I can reread the story to help me recall what the new colors were and which parts they colored.

Then read aloud the text under Comprehension Strategy on page 178. Point out that thinking about these ideas can help readers understand a selection better. Explain to children that they will work together to use a Main Idea and Details Chart as they read "Can Elephants Paint?"

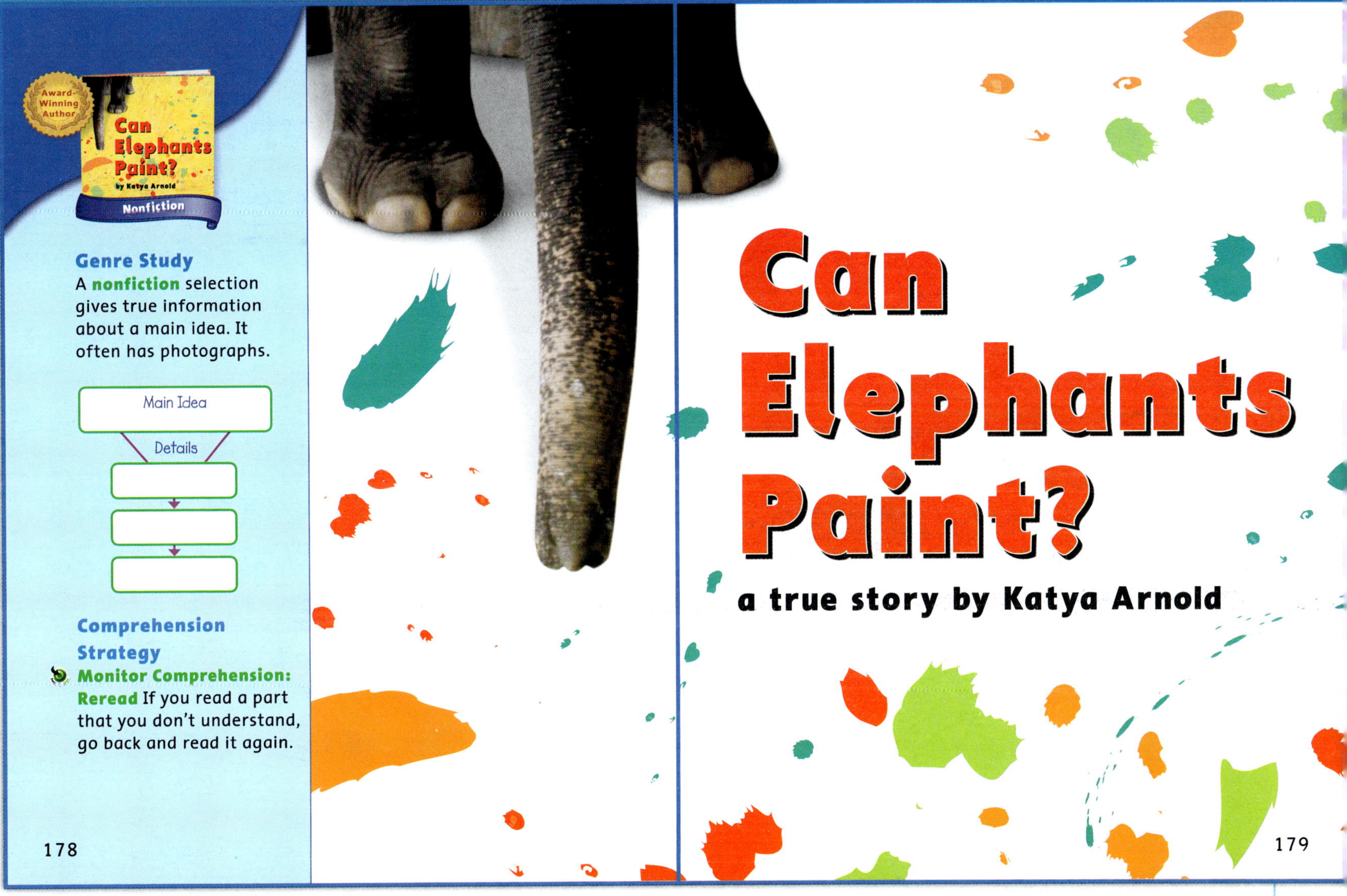
Award-Winning Author
Can Elephants Paint?
by Katya Arnold
Nonfiction
Genre Study
A nonfiction selection gives true information about a main idea. It often has photographs.
Main Idea
Details
Comprehension Strategy
Monitor Comprehension: Reread If you read a part that you don't understand, go back and read it again.
178
Can Elephants Paint?
a true story by Katya Arnold
179

## Build Background

**DISCUSS ELEPHANTS** Say: **This is a story about some elephants that live in the country of Thailand. What do you know about elephants?** After discussion, say: **These elephants learn to do something amazing with their trunks.**

Routine Card 17

**SET A PURPOSE AND PREDICT** Help children set a purpose for reading this contemporary nonfiction piece. Tell them to read it both for pleasure and for information.

- Read the title to children.
- Identify the elephant as Lucky, and ask children to predict what Lucky learns to do. List predictions on the board.
- Invite children to read the selection to find out if Lucky and some other elephants can learn to paint.

## TECHNOLOGY

Go online

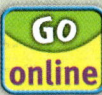

**eBook** "Can Elephants Paint?" is available in an eBook.

**Audiotext** "Can Elephants Paint?" is available on *Audiotext Grade 1*, CD 3 for subsequent readings.

All the elephants on that farm had jobs. They worked in the jungle.

Lucky lived on a farm. She was big and strong.

180

181

# Monitor Comprehension

**PAGES 180–181** Say: **I see an elephant in this photograph. Let's read to find out what the elephant is doing and where it is.**

**1 NOTE DETAILS** **Where do these elephants live and work?** (They live on a farm. They work in the jungle.)

**2 MAKE CONNECTIONS/COMPARE AND CONTRAST** **How is Lucky the same as other elephants you have seen at a zoo or circus? How is Lucky different?** (Possible responses: Same: She is gray and has wrinkly skin; she is big and strong. Different: She has a job in the jungle.)

## Apply
### Comprehension Strategies

**Monitor Comprehension: Reread** Demonstrate how to use the graphic organizer to comprehend the selection to this point.

**Think Aloud** After reading, I am not sure where Lucky works. Since this is an important detail, I go back and reread the words to find out. I learn that the elephants work in the jungle. I will write this in a "Detail" box.

> Main Idea
>
> Detail
>
> Lucky works in the jungle.

Ning worked with Lucky. Ning cut trees. Then Lucky **would carry** them off with her trunk.

182

Ning and Lucky worked hard to get **money**.

On days off, they would swim.

183

# Monitor Comprehension

**PAGES 182–183**   Say: **Look at these photographs. I see a man with the elephant. Let's read to find out who he is.**

**1**  **NOTE DETAILS**   **Who is Ning, and how do Ning and Lucky work together?** (Ning works with Lucky. Ning cuts down trees, and Lucky carries them off with her trunk.)

**2**  **DRAW CONCLUSIONS**   **Do Ning and Lucky have a good partnership? What makes you think this?** (Yes; each does different things; by working together, they can do the job.)

**3**  **FIGURATIVE LANGUAGE**   **Reread the last sentence on page 183. What does the expression *on days off* mean?** (It means "on the days Ning and Lucky are not working.")

**Word Meaning**  Discuss the meaning of the word *hard* on page 183. Point out that when someone works hard, it means that the person puts a lot of effort into a job to do it the right way. Have children share sentences telling about a time when they worked hard to do a job.

One day, all the big trees were cut. There were no more jobs. "What will we do?" asked Ning.

An artist had a good idea. "I think I can help them," she said. The artist went to the farm.

184

185

# Monitor Comprehension

**PAGES 184–185** Say: **Look at these photographs. I see a woman. Who might she be? Let's read to find out.**

**1** **CAUSE AND EFFECT** **What problem do Ning and Lucky have? What causes this problem?** (They are out of a job. There are no more trees for them to cut down and haul away.)

**2** **MAKE INFERENCES** **How do you think Ning probably feels? Why do you think he feels this way?** (Possible response: He probably feels worried and upset because, without a job, he cannot earn the money he needs to live.)

**3** **IMPORTANT DETAILS** **Why does the artist go to the farm?** (She goes to the farm because she thinks she can help Ning and Lucky.)

## SOCIAL STUDIES

### SUPPORTING STANDARDS

**Asian Elephant Art and Conservation Project** Vitaly Komar and Alex Melamid, two Russian artists, founded the first elephant art academy in Thailand in 1998. Since then, the Asian Elephant Art and Conservation Project has expanded to a number of Asian countries. The author of this selection taught in one of these elephant training programs.

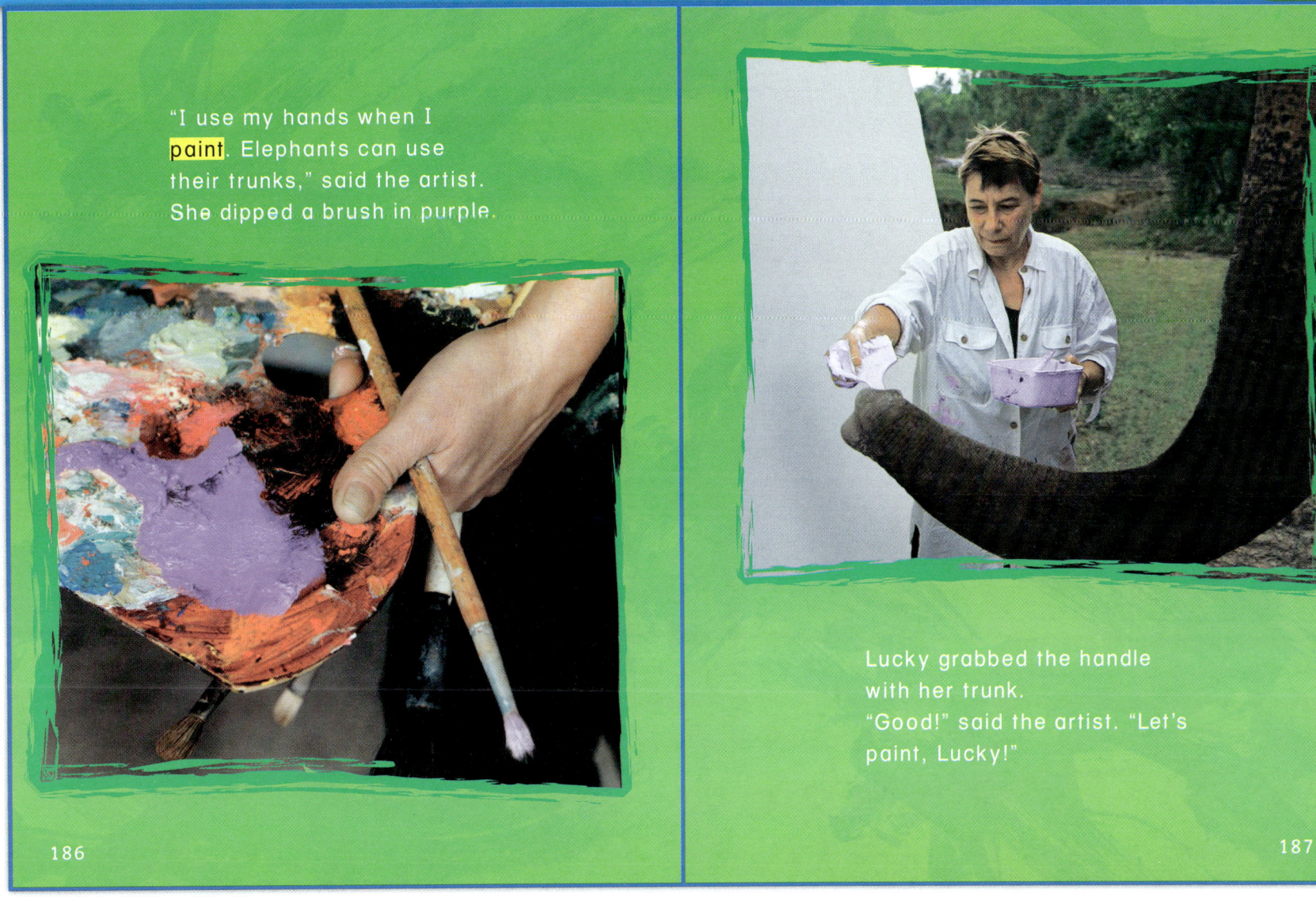

"I use my hands when I paint. Elephants can use their trunks," said the artist. She dipped a brush in purple.

186

Lucky grabbed the handle with her trunk. "Good!" said the artist. "Let's paint, Lucky!"

187

# Monitor Comprehension

**PAGES 186–187**  Say: **I see a paintbrush and paint in these photographs. What do you think the artist is doing? Let's read to find out.**

**①  DRAW CONCLUSIONS   Why does the artist believe that elephants can learn to paint?** (She knows that people use their hands to paint. She thinks that elephants can use their trunks.)

**②  MAKE INFERENCES   Why do you think the artist starts by dipping her brush in paint?** (She wants to show Lucky how to hold and use a brush.)

**③  MAKE PREDICTIONS   Do you think Lucky will be able to learn to paint? Why or why not?** (Possible response: Yes, because she seems interested in what the artist is doing and she can hold the brush with her trunk.)

## Use Multiple Strategies

**Ask Questions**   Say: Asking questions about what I read helps me better understand the selection. When I read this page, I ask myself, "What will Lucky do with the paintbrush? Will she understand how to use it to paint?" As I read more, I will look for answers to my questions.

Lesson 17 (*Student Edition*, pp. 186–187)   **T419**

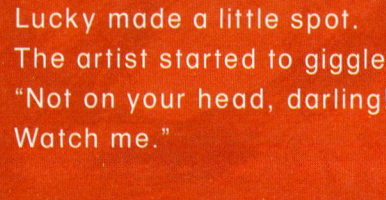

Lucky made a little spot.
The artist started to giggle.
"Not on your head, darling!
Watch me."

188

The artist dragged the brush on the
paper. Then she handed it back to
Lucky. Lucky blinked.
"You can do it!" said the artist.

189

# Monitor Comprehension

**PAGES 188–189**   Say: **I see Lucky touching her head in the first photograph. I see the artist with Lucky in the next photograph. What do you think she is saying to Lucky? Let's read to find out.**

①  **NOTE DETAILS**   **What happens when Lucky tries to paint?** (She puts paint on her head rather than on the paper.) **Find and read the sentence that helps you figure this out.** (You can tell this when the artist says, "Not on your head, darling!")

②  **DRAW CONCLUSIONS**   **How do you think the artist feels when Lucky first tries to paint? What words help you figure this out?** (The artist thinks Lucky is very funny. The text says that she giggles. People giggle when they think something is funny.)

**Word Meaning**   Frame the word *handed* and read it aloud. Demonstrate the word by handing a child a pencil. After a brief pause say: **I handed [Rosa] the pencil.** Pair children and have one partner hand something to the other child. Then direct the partner to hand it back. Have children complete this sentence frame: *I handed ___ a ____, and ____ handed it back to me.*

Lucky made a little purple
dot in the middle.
"You are an artist, Lucky!"

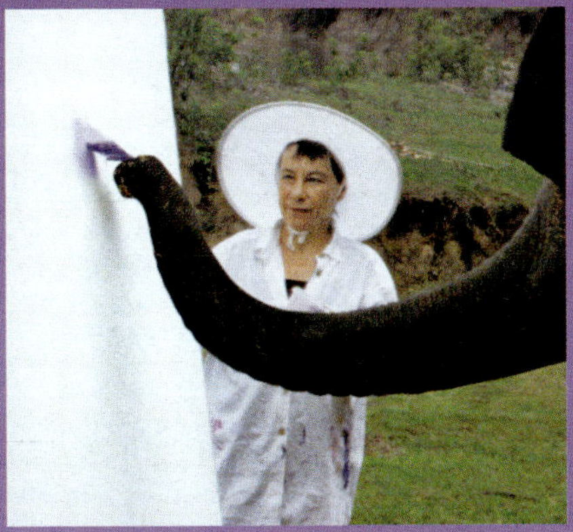

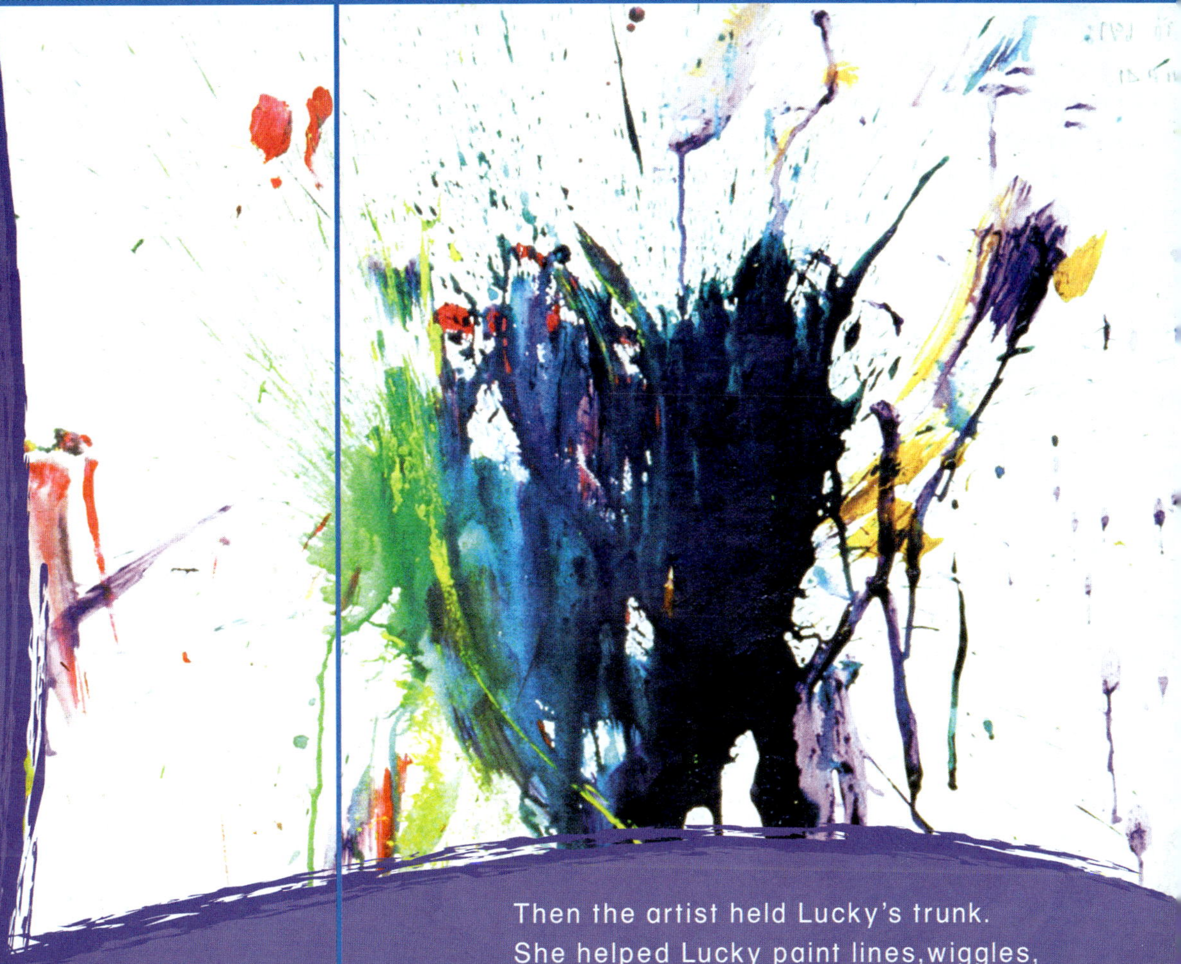

190

Then the artist held Lucky's trunk.
She helped Lucky paint lines, wiggles,
splashes, and little dots.

191

# Monitor Comprehension

**PAGES 190–191**    Say: **Let's look at the photographs. What do you see the artist and Lucky doing? What do you think is happening? Let's read to find out.**

**①**    **CAUSE AND EFFECT    Why does the artist hold Lucky's trunk?** (She wants to show Lucky how to make different movements with the brush.)

**②**    **REREAD    Lucky and the artist paint many shapes. Reread to find words that are used to describe some of these shapes.** (dot, lines, wiggles, splashes) Help children to learn shape words. Draw a circle, triangle, rectangle, and square on the board. Help children name each shape and use words such as *dot, lines, straight,* and *curved* to describe each shape.

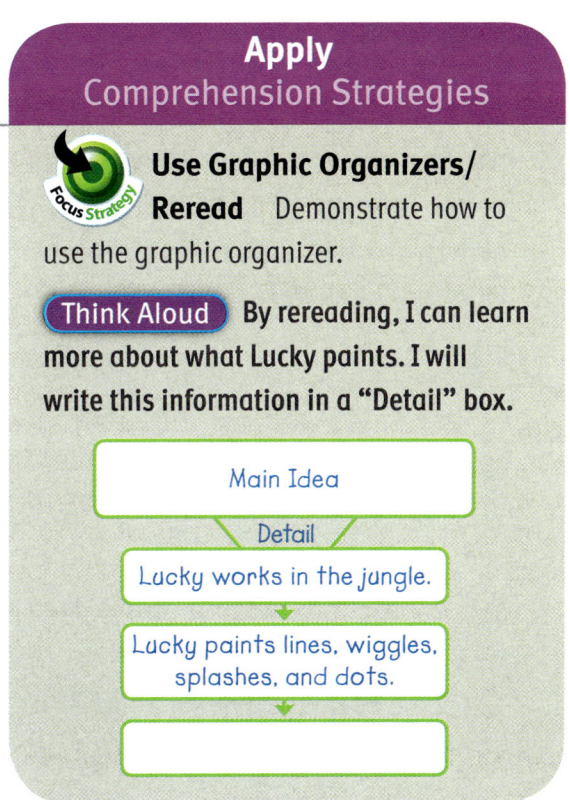

**Apply
Comprehension Strategies**

**Use Graphic Organizers/
Reread**    Demonstrate how to use the graphic organizer.

**Think Aloud**    By rereading, I can learn more about what Lucky paints. I will write this information in a "Detail" box.

Main Idea

Detail

Lucky works in the jungle.

Lucky paints lines, wiggles, splashes, and dots.

Other elephants came by. The artist handed them all brushes.

"How can this help us get money?" Ning was thinking.

This elephant painted lots of marks with her brush.

192

193

# Monitor Comprehension

**PAGES 192–193**   Say: **Let's think about what has happened so far in the story. What work did Lucky do? Why did she need something else to do? What did the artist teach Lucky? Let's read to find out what happens next.**

**1** **NOTE DETAILS**   **What happens when the other elephants come by?** (the artist hands them brushes. They paint, too.)

**2** **MAKE INFERENCES**   **Why does the artist give brushes to the other elephants?** (Possible response: She wants them to paint, too.)

**3** **MAKE INFERENCES**   **What does Ning think about what the artist is doing?** (He can't figure out how it will help them get money.) **How do you think he feels? Why?** (Possible response: worried)

**E L L**

**Figurative Language**   Point out that the word *by* has many meanings. Explain that in the expression *came by, by* means "near" or "at." Share several examples of this usage, for example: *Yesterday, I stopped by the library to return a book.* Then call on volunteers to share their own example sentences, using *by* in this way.

Others liked lines and spots.
They made them thin and thick,
short and long, pink and black.

194

One painted simple flowers.

A little one just wanted to nibble
his brush.

195

# Monitor Comprehension

**PAGES 194–195**  Say: **These photographs show the elephants'
paintings. What do you see? Let's read to find out what the elephants paint.**

**1** **MAIN IDEA AND DETAILS**  **What are these two pages
mostly about?** (the different designs the elephants
paint) **What words does the author use to tell about the lines in
the elephants' paintings?** *(thin, thick, short, long, pink, black)*
**Which of these words name colors?** *(pink* and *black)* Review
color words with children by asking them to name other colors
they see in the paintings.

**2** **DRAW CONCLUSIONS**  **Why do you think the little elephant just
wanted to nibble his brush?** (Possible response: He was probably too young to understand how to use a brush.)

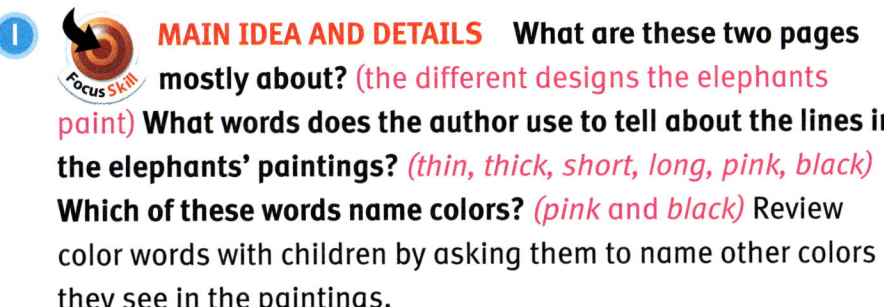

**BELOW-LEVEL**

**Pronoun Referents**  Discuss the
words *they, one,* and *his* on these
pages. Be sure children understand
that these words refer to one or more
than one elephant. Call on volunteers to read aloud each sentence
containing one of these words. Have
children replace the pronoun with a
naming word.

People saw this art and said,
"It's so nice!"
They wanted to **buy** the art.
They hung it in their homes.

"Thank you for helping us!"
Ning said to the artist.
Now they all had new jobs.

196

197

# Monitor Comprehension

**PAGES 196–197**   Say: **What do you think the elephants are doing here? Let's read to find out how the selection ends.**

**1 DRAW CONCLUSIONS**   **Do people like the elephants' art? How do you know?** (Yes, they say it is nice. They want to buy the art to hang in their homes, which shows that they like it.)

**2 EXPRESS PERSONAL OPINIONS**   **Do you think these paintings are amazing? Why or why not?** (Possible response: Yes, it is amazing that elephants can be taught to hold a brush and to paint.)

**3 AUTHOR'S PURPOSE**   **Why do you think the author wrote about the artist and the elephants?** (Possible responses: She wanted to show how a person's good idea can help to solve a problem. She wanted to show how special elephants are.)

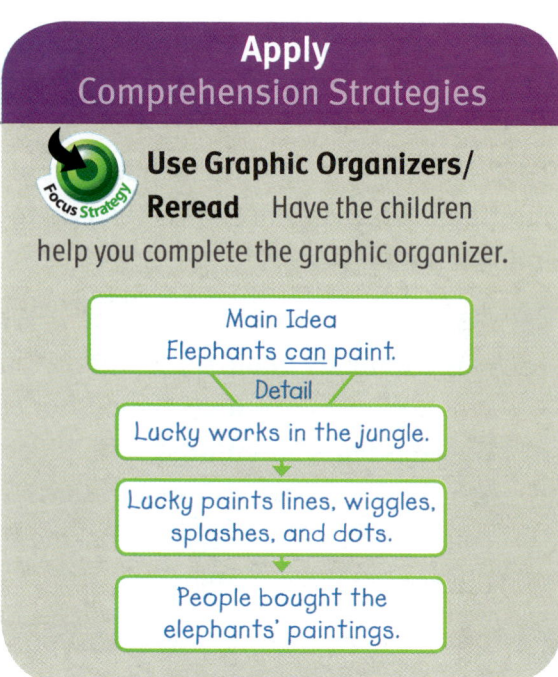

## Apply
### Comprehension Strategies

**Focus Strategy**   **Use Graphic Organizers/ Reread**   Have the children help you complete the graphic organizer.

Main Idea
Elephants _can_ paint.

Detail

Lucky works in the jungle.

Lucky paints lines, wiggles, splashes, and dots.

People bought the elephants' paintings.

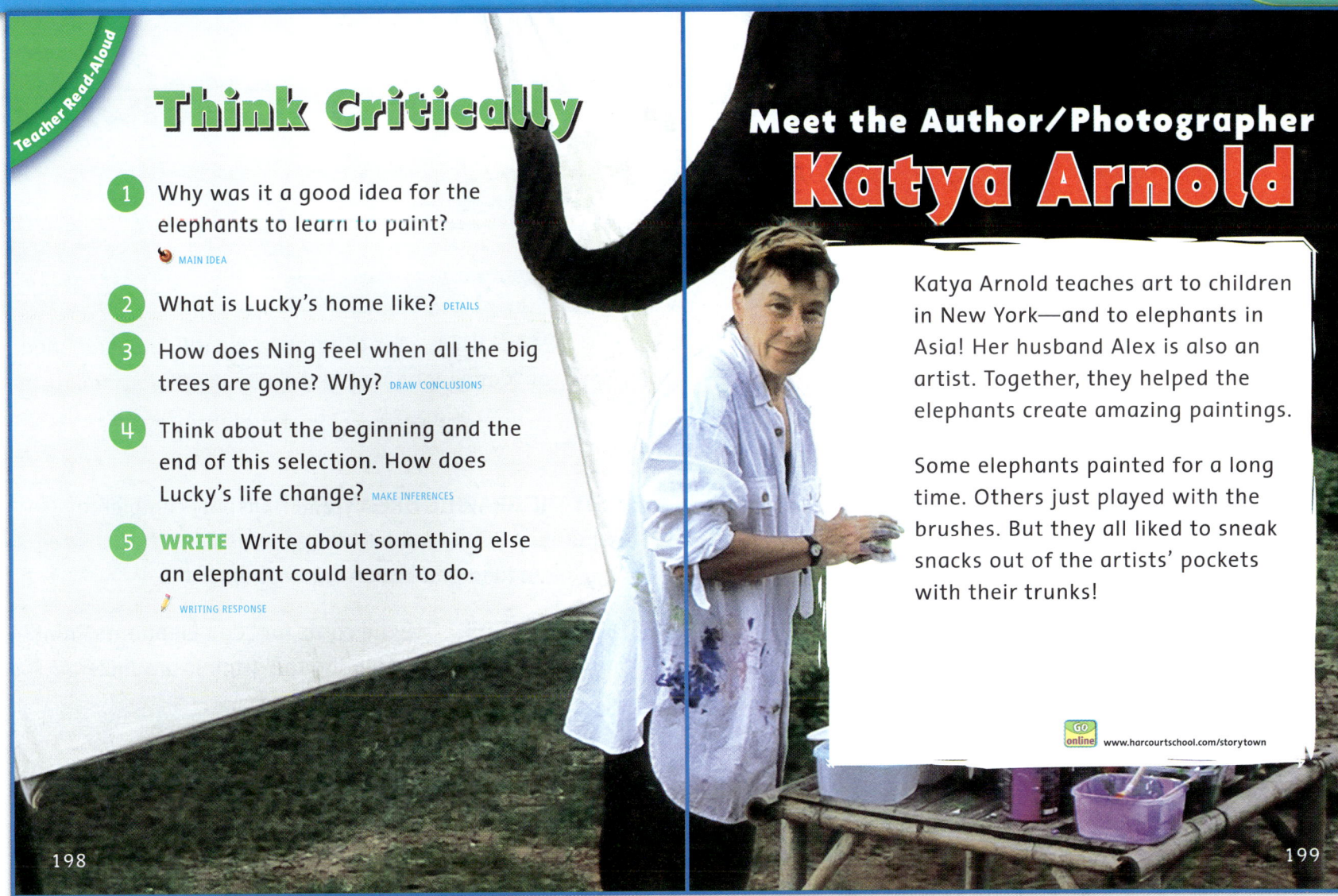

# Think Critically

1. Why was it a good idea for the elephants to learn to paint? **MAIN IDEA**

2. What is Lucky's home like? **DETAILS**

3. How does Ning feel when all the big trees are gone? Why? **DRAW CONCLUSIONS**

4. Think about the beginning and the end of this selection. How does Lucky's life change? **MAKE INFERENCES**

5. **WRITE** Write about something else an elephant could learn to do. **WRITING RESPONSE**

198

## Meet the Author/Photographer
# Katya Arnold

Katya Arnold teaches art to children in New York—and to elephants in Asia! Her husband Alex is also an artist. Together, they helped the elephants create amazing paintings.

Some elephants painted for a long time. Others just played with the brushes. But they all liked to sneak snacks out of the artists' pockets with their trunks!

**GO online** www.harcourtschool.com/storytown

199

# Think Critically

## Respond to the Selection

1. *FocusSkill* The elephants had no more work. They needed a way to help get money.
**MAIN IDEA**

2. Lucky's home is a farm in a jungle. **SETTING**

3. Ning feels worried when all the trees are gone because there is no more work and he needs to make money. **DRAW CONCLUSIONS**

4. Lucky's life gets easier because now she paints instead of carrying trees. **MAKE INFERENCES**

5. **WRITE** Responses will vary.
**WRITING RESPONSE**

# Meet the Author/ Photographer

**PAGE 199** Explain that this page tells about the person who wrote "Can Elephants Paint?" Identify Katya Arnold in the photograph on page 199. Remind children that an **author** does the writing and a **photographer** takes photographs to go with the writing. Explain that Katya Arnold wrote "Can Elephants Paint?" *and* took many of the photographs that accompany it. Read aloud page 199. Encourage children to follow along in their books as you read.

# Check Comprehension
## *Summarizing*

## Objectives
- *To practice summarizing a selection*
- *To read with proper intonation in a manner that sounds like natural speech*

### SUMMARIZING RUBRIC

| | |
|---|---|
| 4 | Uses details to clearly summarize the selection |
| 3 | Uses some details to summarize the selection |
| 2 | Summarizes the selection with some inaccuracies |
| 1 | Is unable to summarize the selection |

### Summarize

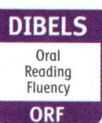  **MAIN IDEA** Ask children to identify the main idea of "Can Elephants Paint?" (Elephants learned to paint pictures that people bought. This gave the elephants and the villagers money that they needed.)

**REVISIT THE GRAPHIC ORGANIZER** Display completed **Transparency GO16.** Guide children to use the chart to identify the main idea and important details.

**STORY RETELLING CARDS** Use the cards for "Can Elephants Paint?" for a retelling or as an aid to completing the graphic organizer.

▲ Story Retelling Cards 1–6, "Can Elephants Paint?"

 Fluency

### Teach/Model

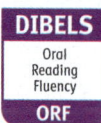 **REVIEW INTONATION** Remind children that good readers make their voices rise and fall so that their reading sounds like natural speech. They also let their voice get louder and softer, just like someone talking. Have children open to pages 184–185 and track the print as you read aloud with expressive intonation.

### Practice/Apply

**ECHO-READ** Read aloud the selection, one page at a time, modeling appropriate intonation, and have children echo-read.

### BELOW-LEVEL

**Fluency Practice** For fluency practice, have children read *Decodable Book 17,* the appropriate *Leveled Reader* (pp. T462–T465), or "Paint Your Dog!" in the *Book 1-3 Strategic Intervention Interactive Reader.*

# Build Robust Vocabulary

## Listening/Speaking: *Words from the Read-Aloud*

### Review Robust Vocabulary

**USE VOCABULARY IN DIFFERENT CONTEXTS** Remind children of the Student-Friendly Explanations of *agreement, unnoticed,* and *unthinkable.* Then discuss each word, using the following examples:

**agreement**

- How might you feel if one of your friends broke an agreement with you?

- If your friend wanted to go to the park and you wanted to watch a movie, would you be in agreement? Why or why not?

- Tell about an agreement you have with your parents.

**unnoticed**

- If you wore a colorful clown costume to school, would you go unnoticed? Why or why not?

- Which animal would go unnoticed at the beach, a polar bear or a seagull?

- If you spoke quietly in the library, would you go unnoticed? Would you go unnoticed if you sang loudly?

**unthinkable**

- Is it unthinkable that we will read a story in class today?

- Tell about an unthinkable event that would make you laugh.

- Is it unthinkable that rain made of chocolate milk will fall from the sky today? Why or why not?

## Objective

- *To review robust vocabulary through discussing ideas*

**REVIEW**

### Student-Friendly Explanations

**agreement** When you are in agreement with others, you all think the same thing.

**unnoticed** If you go unnoticed, no one sees you.

**unthinkable** An unthinkable event is something you never thought could or would happen.

### ON-LEVEL

**Discuss *un-*** Point out that the words *unnoticed* and *unthinkable* begin with the prefix *un-*. Explain that *un-* means "not." Guide children to understand that *unnoticed* means "not being noticed" and *unthinkable* means "something you cannot think of." Name other words that begin with *un-*, such as *unable, unopened,* and *unbelievable,* and help children define them.

# Grammar

## Possessives

**5-DAY GRAMMAR**

| | |
|---|---|
| **DAY 1** | Introduce Possessive Proper Nouns |
| **DAY 2** | Introduce Possessive Common Nouns |
| **DAY 3** | Introduce Possessive Pronouns *his, her, hers* |
| **DAY 4** | Introduce Pronouns *its, their, your, yours* |
| **DAY 5** | Review Possessives |

### Objective
• *To recognize possessive common nouns*

### Daily Proofreading

her name is jan.

(Her, Jan)

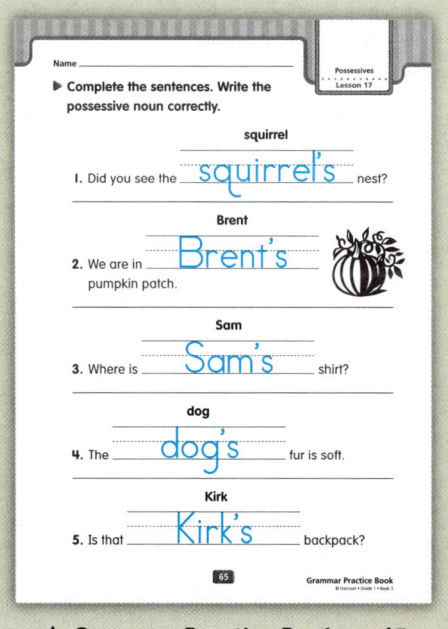

▲ **Grammar Practice Book, p. 65**

## Review

**USE A LITERATURE MODEL** Display "Elephant Song" from the *Big Book of Rhymes and Poems* page 33. Ask children to listen for an example of a possessive naming word. Track the print and read the poem, emphasizing the word *spider's* in the second line. Then reread the poem, encouraging children to join in.

**Elephant Song**

One elephant went out to play,
Out on a spider's web one day,
He had such enormous fun,
He called on another elephant
to come.

Ask a volunteer to point to the word that shows ownership. Write *spider's* on the board. Point to the apostrophe, and have children recall the name of this mark. Explain that *'s* can be added to many naming words, such as *spider,* to show ownership. Focus attention on the second line and ask a volunteer to tell what the spider owns.

## Practice/Apply

**GUIDED PRACTICE** Ask children where else an elephant could go to play, using the second line of "Elephant Song" as a model. Encourage them to use both proper and common nouns. Write children's contributions on the board and read them with children.

Out on Mary's bike one day,
Out on a big bird's nest one day,

**INDEPENDENT PRACTICE** Ask children to copy "Elephant Song" with one of the new second lines in place of the original. Have them read or sing the words and identify the possessive naming word. Have children respond in a way that reflects understanding and interpretation. Ask them to illustrate their poem.

# Shared Writing
*Friendly Letter*

**5-DAY** WRITING
| DAY 1 | Modeled Writing |
| DAY 2 | Shared Writing |
| DAY 3 | Shared Writing |
| DAY 4 | Independent Writing |
| DAY 5 | Independent Writing |

## Write Together

**REVIEW FRIENDLY LETTER** Remind children that a friendly letter has five parts: heading, greeting, body, closing, and signature.

**GENERATE IDEAS** Work with children to choose a person to write a class letter to. Have children brainstorm a list of school events to tell about, and choose a few to include.

**MODEL WRITING** Have volunteers dictate parts of a friendly letter as you record them on chart paper. Use the Step-by-Step Writing Instruction. Save the letter for Day 3.

### Step-by-Step Writing Instruction

**1** Say today's date for the heading. How does the name of a month begin?

> December 7, 20--

**2** Say *Dear* and the person's name for the greeting. How does a person's name begin? Then we add a comma.

> Dear Mike,

**3** What is the first sentence of our message? How do I write it?

> We just got two new fish for the class fish tank.

**WRITING TRAIT**

**4** What else do you think Mike would like to know?

> We named one Mike after you. We miss you!

**5** Write a closing to end the letter. Where do I write a capital letter? We add a comma at the end.

> Your friends,

**6** Our signatures belong under the closing. What kind of letter does a name begin with?

> Pia, Ann, Beth, Tran, Ricky, Phil

**7** Let's read our friendly letter together.

## Objectives

• *To review the parts of a friendly letter*

• *To contribute to the shared writing of a friendly letter*

 ### Writing Prompt

**Write About Feelings** Have children imagine that a good friend moves away and write about how they would feel.

▲ **Writer's Companion, Lesson 17**

### BELOW-LEVEL

**Review Friendly Letter** As you review the five parts of a friendly letter, display **Transparency LA34** from Day 1. Lead children to recall the purpose of each part of the letter and use the model to point out each part's characteristics. Keep the model on display so children can refer to it as they contribute to the Day 2 shared writing experience.

## Day at a Glance

### Day 3

**Phonemic Awareness**
- Phoneme Substitution

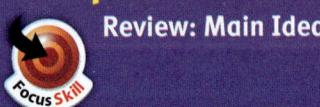 **and Spelling**
- Review: Syllable /əl/-*le*
- State the Generalization

**High-Frequency Words**
- Review: *buy*, *carry*, *money*, *other*, *paint*, *paper*, *would*

**Fluency**
- Intonation
- "Can Elephants Paint?" *Student Edition*, pp. 178–199

**Comprehension**
Review: Main Idea

**Reading**
- "An Elephant's Three T's," *Student Edition*, pp. 200–201

**Robust Vocabulary**
- Introduce: *rejoice, predicament, extraordinary*

**Grammar**
- Review: Possessives

**Shared Writing** ✏️
- Friendly Letter

# Warm-Up Routines

## Oral Language

**Objective** *To respond appropriately to oral communication*

> ### Question of the Day
> Where would you play with an elephant?
> What would you do?

Invite children to imagine that a friendly elephant wanted to play. Have them brainstorm where they would play. Then discuss what they would do. Have children help complete these sentence frames:

**I would take an elephant to ___. We would ___.**

## Read Aloud

**Objectives** *To understand concepts of print; to innovate on a rhyme*

**BIG BOOK OF RHYMES AND POEMS** Reread "Elephant Song," modeling reading left-to-right and top-to-bottom. Have children point to each capital letter and find the period. Explain that in many poems, the first word in each line begins with a capital letter even if it is not the beginning of a sentence. Have children check to see if this is true in "Elephant Song," and have them tell how they know. Invite children to elaborate on the poem by creating new verses.

▲ Big Book of Rhymes and Poems, p. 33

## Word Wall

**Objective** *To read high-frequency words*

**REVIEW HIGH-FREQUENCY WORDS** Review *buy, money, paint, would,* and other previously learned high-frequency words. Say each word, ask a volunteer to point to it, and have children read it aloud. Then point to words at random, and have children reread them. Repeat several times to reinforce instant recognition.

| buy | money | paint | would |

## Phonemic Awareness

**Objective** *To substitute medial phonemes to make new words*

**Routine Card 10** **PHONEME SUBSTITUTION: MEDIAL** Model by saying: **The word is** *pen.* **If I change /e/ to /i/, I make the new word** *pin.* Model another example and invite children to name the new word. Say: **The word is** *hat.* **Change /a/ to /o/. What is the new word?** (hot) Continue with these words:

must, /u/ to /a/ (mast)          sand, /a/ to /e/ (send)

tickle, /i/ to /a/ (tackle)      net, /e/ to /u/ (nut)

chap, /a/ to /i/ (chip)          flip, /i/ to /a/ (flap)

last /a/ to /i/ (list)           patch, /a/ to /i/ (pitch)

kettle, /e/ to /a/ (cattle)      lock, /o/ to /i/ (lick)

**net, /e/ to /u/ (nut)**

# Build Words

**phonics** *and Spelling*

| 5-DAY PHONICS | |
|---|---|
| DAY 1 | Introduce Syllable /əl/-*le* |
| DAY 2 | Word Building with Syllable /əl/-*le* |
| DAY 3 | Build Words |
| DAY 4 | Inflections -*ed*, -*ing* (double final consonant) |
| DAY 5 | Inflections -*ed*, -*ing* (double final consonant) |

## Objectives

- *To use /əl/-*le* and other known letter-sounds to decode words*
- *To add /əl/-*le* to one-syllable words or non-word syllables to read and write new words*
- *To recognize spelling patterns*

## Skill Trace

### Syllable /əl/-*le*

| | |
|---|---|
| Introduce | T392–T395 |
| Reteach | S42 |
| **Review** | **T408–T409, T432–T433, T445** |

---

**Syllable /əl/*le***

The class will have a talent night!
Seth plans to tell a riddle.
He says that it will make us giggle.
Ann plans to juggle purple balls.
She says that they will not fall.
Gilbert plans to play his fiddle.
We will sit still.
We will not wiggle!

Grade 1, Lesson 17    R33    Phonics: Syllable /əl/*le*

**Transparency R33**

---

## Word Building

**DIBELS** Nonsense Word Fluency **NWF**

**Routine Card 14**

**BUILD AND READ WORDS** Use a pocket chart and *Letter Cards*. Have children repeat each step with their *Word Builders* and *Word Builder Cards*.

Remind children that many two-syllable words end with the letters -*le* and the sounds /əl/. Build *riddle*. Run your hand under the letters as you slowly read the word. Pause briefly after *rid*, and then continue. Then read the word with children—*riddle*.

Lead children in building and reading other two-syllable words. Give the following directions and have children read the new words:

- **Change *r* to *m*.**
- **Change *mi* to *pu*.**
- **Change *dd* to *zz*.**
- **Change *pu* to *da*.**

Continue, having children substitute letters to build and read these words: *dabble, marble, gargle, giggle.*

## Read Words in Context

**READ SENTENCES** Display **Transparency R33** or write the sentences on the board or on chart paper. Have children choral-read each sentence as you track the print. Then ask volunteers to read each sentence aloud. Call on volunteers to underline or frame words that end with /əl/-*le*.

**5-DAY SPELLING**

| DAY 1 | Pretest |
| DAY 2 | Word Building |
| DAY 3 | **State the Generalization** |
| DAY 4 | Review |
| DAY 5 | Posttest |

### Review Spelling Words

**STATE THE GENERALIZATION**   List spelling words 1–6 on chart paper or on the board and have children read them. For words 1–2, ask: **What is the same about these words?** (*hand*) **What letters are added to the word *hand* to form *handle*?** (*le*) Repeat this procedure with spelling words 3–4. For words 5–6, elicit that each word has two-syllables and ends with the letters *-le* and the sounds /əl/.

**REVIEW WORDS**   List spelling words 7–8. Ask what is the same in both words. (Both words have /ûr/.) Ask what is different about the spelling of /ûr/ in the words. (*Turn* has *ur* and *girl* has *ir*.)

**HIGH-FREQUENCY WORDS**   List spelling words 9–10. Run your hand under *by* as you read it. Ask children to close their eyes, picture the word, and spell it with you. Repeat for the word *room*.

 **WRITE**   Have children write the spelling words in their note-books. Remind them to use their best handwriting.

## Handwriting

**LETTER SPACING**   Remind children to make sure their letters are not too close together or too far apart. In addition, emphasize the importance of having each letter sitting on the baseline.

---

### Spelling Words

| | | | |
|---|---|---|---|
| 1. | hand | 6. | little |
| 2. | handle | 7. | turn |
| 3. | wig | 8. | girl |
| 4. | wiggle | 9. | by |
| 5. | single | 10. | room |

### Decodable Book

- **Phonics**
  Syllable /əl/-*le*
- **Decodable Words**  See the list on page R11.

Decodable Book 17 ▲

Have children who need additional decoding practice read "Little Ann's Nap." See also *Decodable Books*, online (Take-Home Version).

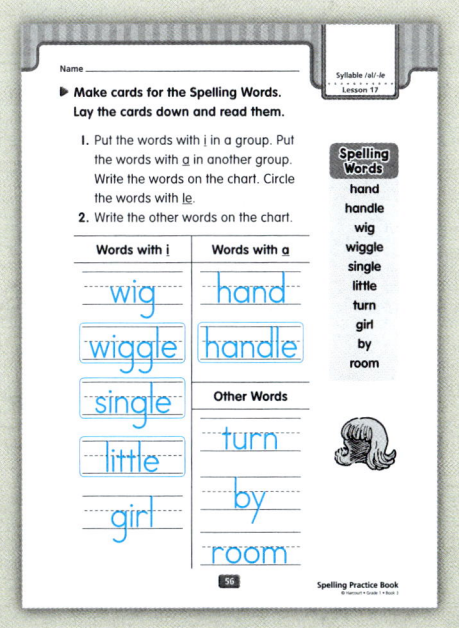

▲ Spelling Practice Book, p. 56

# High-Frequency Words

## Objective

- *To read high-frequency words*

### REVIEW  Tested

### High-Frequency Words

| | |
|---|---|
| buy | paint |
| carry | paper |
| money | would |
| other | |

**Usage**  Model the meaning of *would*. Say: **I would like to go to the movies tomorrow.** Have children use their own ideas to name a different place to go.

## Review

**DISPLAY THE WORDS**  Write the word *buy*. Have a volunteer read it. Erase the word, and ask children to spell it. Repeat this routine for *carry, money, other, paint, paper,* and *would*.

## Practice/Apply

**GUIDED PRACTICE**  Give each child a set of word cards (*Teacher Resource Book*, p. 141), and have children spread the cards out in front of them. Randomly call out one of the words, and have children hold up the matching card. Assess how well children are able to identify the words, and repeat until they can respond quickly and accurately.

**INDEPENDENT PRACTICE**  Have each child work with a partner. Have one partner turn a set of word cards face up and the other turn a set face down. Tell the child whose cards are face down to choose a card at random and read the word. The other partner should find the matching card. Then have children use the words in sentences and practice writing the words in their notebooks.

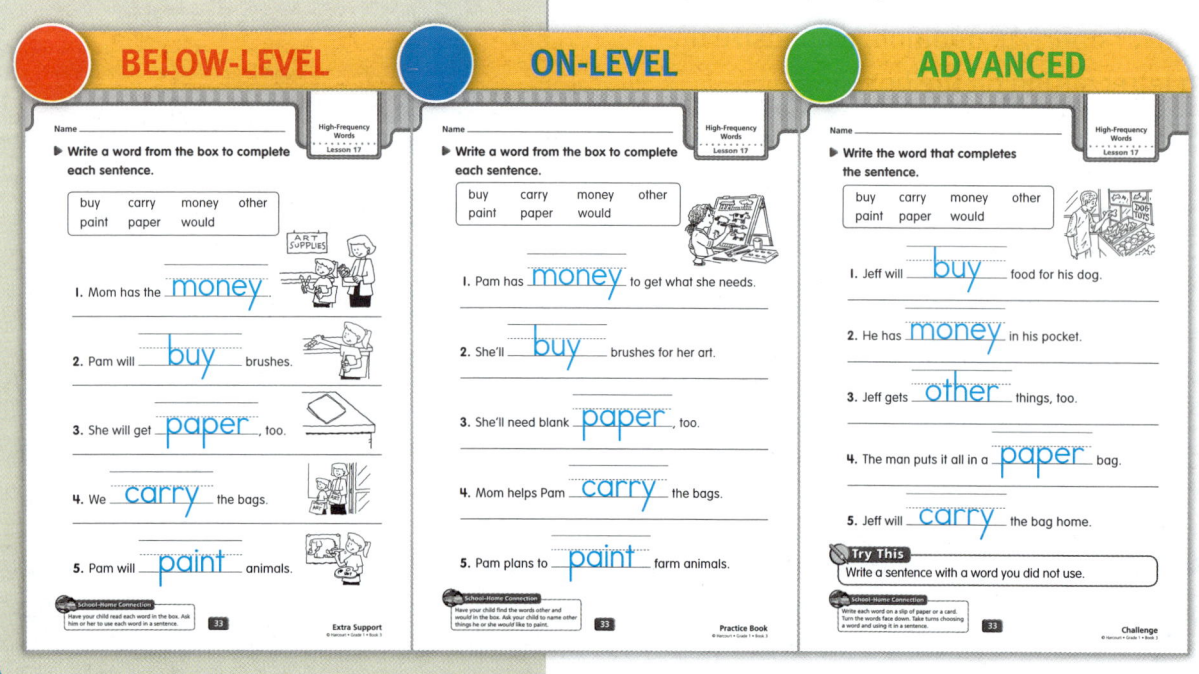

▲ Extra Support, p. 33    ▲ Practice Book, p. 33    ▲ Challenge, p. 33

- Group children according to academic levels, and assign one of the pages on the left.

- Clarify any unfamiliar concepts as necessary. See *ELL Teacher Guide*, Lesson 17, for support in scaffolding instruction.

# Fluency
*Intonation*

## Review

**DIBELS** Oral Reading Fluency **ORF**

**REVIEW PUNCTUATION** Have children open their *Student Edition* to page 187, and ask volunteers to name the end punctuation used for each sentence. Remind children that the exclamation point in the last sentence indicates that the sentence should be read with excitement. Model reading "Good! Let's paint, Lucky!" excitedly. Then remind children to pause briefly when they see a comma and to make a slightly longer pause when they see a period. Model reading the sentences on the page with proper intonation.

## Practice/Apply

**GUIDED PRACTICE** Call on volunteers to read aloud pages 187, 188, 189, or 190. Have children read aloud with fluency in a manner that sounds like natural speech. Remind them to use punctuation clues to help them determine how to read each sentence. After children read, ask them to tell how they knew how to say their lines. Provide feedback and encouragement.

**INDEPENDENT PRACTICE** Invite children to choose a page from the story and practice reading it. Then have children read orally from the familiar text with fluency, demonstrating good use of intonation as they read.

### Objective
• *To read with fluency and appropriate intonation*

### BELOW-LEVEL

**Discuss Dialogue** Remind children that quotation marks are used to show the exact words a character says. Point out the use of quotation marks in the story, and explain that children need to look at the end punctuation of the dialogue to help them determine how to read the text. For example, point out that the last sentence on page 187 includes two lines of dialogue that each end with an exclamation point.

### MONITOR PROGRESS

#### Fluency

| **IF** children have difficulty reading in a way that sounds like natural speech, | **THEN** model reading with proper intonation as you have children echo-read with you. |
|---|---|

**Small-Group Instruction, pp. S44–S45:**

● **BELOW-LEVEL:** Reteach
● **ON-LEVEL:** Reinforce
● **ADVANCED:** Extend

# Main Idea
*Comprehension*

## Objectives

- *To recognize the main idea and details in selections*
- *To listen to a selection read aloud for information*

## Skill Trace

 **Main Idea**

| | |
|---|---|
| Preview | T316 |
| Introduce | T324–T325 |
| Reteach | S36–S37, S46–S47 |
| **Review** | **T348, T360, T370, T402, T410–T411, T436, T448, T458** |
| Test | Bk 1-3 |
| Maintain | Monitor Comprehension, Bks 1-4, 1-5 |

## Review

 **REVIEW MAIN IDEA**   Remind children that the main idea of a selection is what the entire selection is about.

## Practice/Apply

**GUIDED PRACTICE**   Guide children to determine the main idea of stories and selections they have read this week and have them identify supporting details. Help children recall "Jungle Fun." Ask them to recall the main idea of the story, as well as some details. Then help children recall the main idea of "Can Elephants Paint?" plus some details from the selection.

**INDEPENDENT PRACTICE**   Have children apply their knowledge of main idea by completing *Practice Book* page 34.v

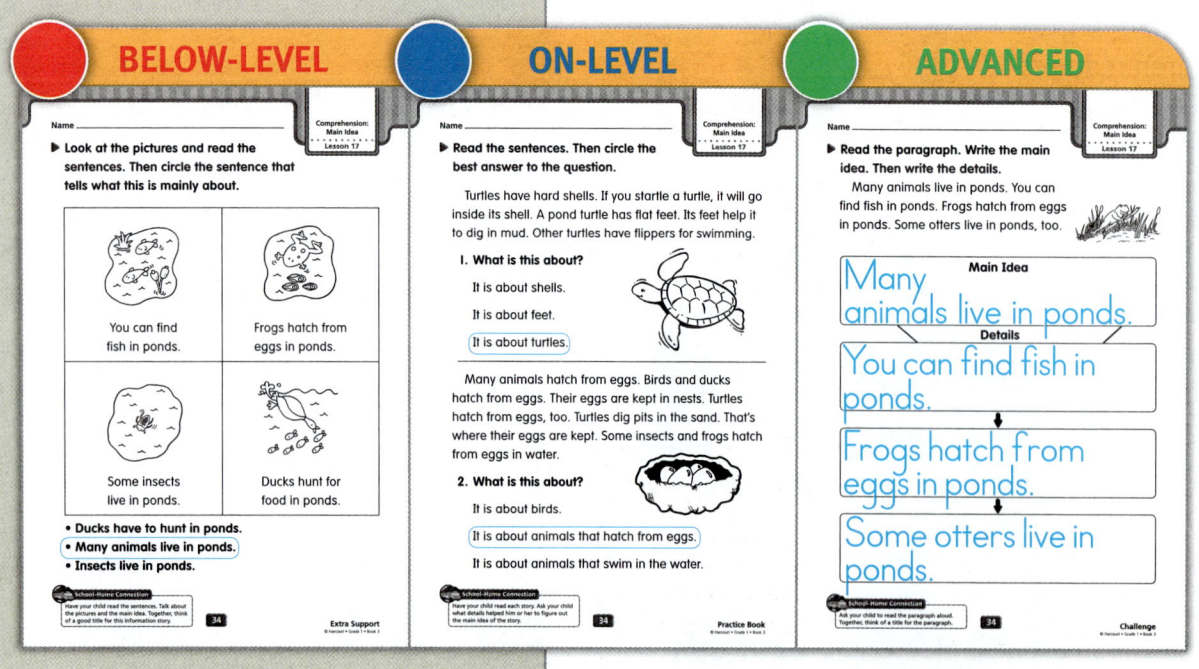

▲ Extra Support, p. 34      ▲ Practice Book, p. 34      ▲ Challenge, p. 34

### ELL

- Group children according to academic levels, and assign one of the pages on the left.
- Clarify any unfamiliar concepts as necessary. See *ELL Teacher Guide*, Lesson 17, for support in scaffolding instruction.

Science

An Elephant's Three T's

Nonfiction Article

Teacher Read-Aloud

## An Elephant's Three T's

200

### Teeth

Animals that eat plants have flat teeth. Elephants use their flat teeth to chew leaves, twigs, fruit, and bark.

### Tusks

Elephant tusks are long teeth. They are made of ivory. Elephants can use their tusks to help get food.

### Trunk

Elephants breathe through their trunks. They also use their trunks to put food and water in their mouths. They can even take a shower.

Best of all, elephants use their trunks to give each other a hug!

201

# Reading

## *Student Edition: Paired Selection*

### Read Aloud

**USE PRIOR KNOWLEDGE/SET A PURPOSE**  Guide children to use prior knowledge and set a purpose for listening.

**MONITOR LISTENING COMPREHENSION**  As you read, monitor listening comprehension by using the following questions:

- **SUMMARIZE**  What are an elephant's three T's? (teeth, tusks, trunk)

- **GENRE**  Is this selection fiction or nonfiction? (nonfiction) **How can you tell?** (It gives information.)

- **PERSONAL RESPONSE**  What would you do if you had a trunk like an elephant? (Responses will vary.)

## Connections

### Comparing Texts

**1** What is the most interesting thing you learned from the selection and the article?
*Possible response: Elephants can learn to paint with their trunks.*

**2** Tell about an elephant that you have seen. What did it do?
*Accept reasonable responses.*

**3** What is your favorite way to make pictures? Tell how you do it.
*Accept reasonable responses.*

### Writing

Write notes telling what you know about elephants. Then write sentences.

*Elephants can pick up things with their strong trunks.*

Main Idea
Things I know about elephants

Details

pick up things with their trunks

have teeth

some paint pictures

202

### Phonics

Make and read new words.

Start with **little**.

Change **l** to **w** and **t t** to **g g**.

Change **w** to **g**.

Change **gigg** to **cand**.

Change **c** to **h**.

### Fluency Practice

Read "Can Elephants Paint?" aloud to a partner. Pause when you see a comma or a period. Use your voice to show excitement when there is an exclamation point.

*Let's paint, Lucky!*

203

# Connections

## WRITING

 **Write Sentences** Guide children to recall the things they learned about elephants in "Can Elephants Paint?" and "An Elephant's Three T's." Record their responses on a graphic organizer. Invite children to write in their notebooks sentences about what they know about elephants.

*Elephants are strong. They can carry trees.*

## PHONICS

**Word Building** Distribute to children *Word Builder Cards a, c, d, e, g, g, g, h, i, l, n, l, t, t,* and *w.* Have children practice manipulating the cards to build and read *little, wiggle, giggle, candle,* and *handle.*

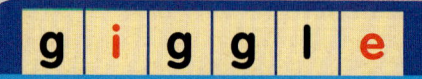

## FLUENCY

**Partner Reading** Have partners take turns reading aloud "Can Elephants Paint?" Remind children to look at the punctuation, including exclamation points, commas, and periods, to help them determine how to read each sentence.

*You can do it, Lucky!*

# Build Robust Vocabulary

## Listening/Speaking: *Words About the Selection*

### Teach/Model

**Routine Card 15**

**INTRODUCE ROBUST VOCABULARY**  Use *Routine Card 15* to introduce the words.

❶ Put the word in **selection context.**
❷ Provide for children the **Student-Friendly Explanation.**
❸ Have children **say the word** with you.
❹ Use the word in other contexts, and have children **interact with the word's meaning.**
❺ Say the Student-Friendly Explanation again, and ask children to **name the word** that goes with it.

❶ **Selection Context:** The artist began to **rejoice** when she saw that Lucky could paint.
❹ **Interact with Word Meaning:** What birthday present would make you rejoice?

❶ **Selection Context:** Ning and Lucky were in a **predicament** when all the trees were cut, and they had no way to make money.
❹ **Interact with Word Meaning:** Would you be in a predicament if you got to school on time or if you lost your homework?

❶ **Selection Context:** People thought that the elephants' art was **extraordinary**.
❹ **Interact with Word Meaning:** Would it be extraordinary to see a monkey play a musical instrument?

### Practice/Apply

**GUIDED PRACTICE**  Ask children to do the following:
- Imagine that you just received some good news. Show how you might rejoice.
- Describe a predicament that you have been in. Tell how you got out of it.
- Tell about an extraordinary talent you or someone you know has.

### Objective
- *To develop robust vocabulary through discussing a literature selection*

**Tested**

**INTRODUCE**

## Student-Friendly Explanations

**rejoice**  If you rejoice, you show that you are very happy.

**predicament**  If you have a predicament, you have a serious or difficult problem.

**extraordinary**  Something extraordinary is something that is very unusual or remarkable.

**E L L**

**Introduce Vocabulary**  Tell children that we often use the words *in* and *out* with *predicament*. Explain that when we have a predicament, or problem, we say we are "in a predicament." When we solve the predicament, we say we have gotten "out of a predicament." Have children use these phrases to first describe a predicament and then tell how they got out of it.

# Grammar
## Possessives

**5-DAY** GRAMMAR

| | |
|---|---|
| **DAY 1** | Introduce Possessive Proper Nouns |
| **DAY 2** | Introduce Possessive Common Nouns |
| **DAY 3** | Introduce Possessive Pronouns *his, her, hers* |
| **DAY 4** | Introduce Pronouns *its, their, your, yours* |
| **DAY 5** | Review Possessives |

## Objectives

- *To recognize possessive pronouns* his, her, hers
- *To use possessive common and proper nouns*

## Daily Proofreading

**this is Todds money.**

*(This; Todd's)*

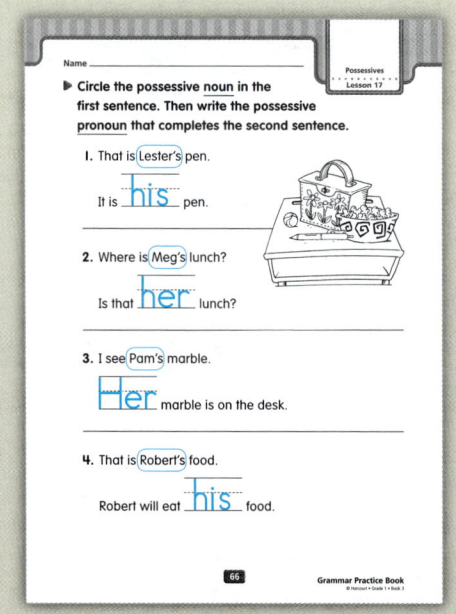

▲ Grammar Practice Book, p. 66

---

## Review

**DICTATE SENTENCES** Write the sentences below on the board, and have children read them. Review the *'s* possessive form.

> **That elephant's trunk can hold a brush.**
> **Lucky's painting is beautiful.**

Explain that some words, like *his, her,* and *hers,* can take the place of naming words and also show ownership. Write these sentences under the corresponding ones above. Underline *his, her,* and *hers.*

> **His trunk can hold a brush.**
> **Her painting is beautiful.**
> **The painting is hers.**

Track the print and have children read the sentences. Ask them to tell who *his, her,* and *hers* refers to.

## Practice/Apply

**GUIDED PRACTICE** Write the sentences below on the board. Track the print and have children read the first sentence. Ask a volunteer to tell how to write the first word correctly. *(Lucky's)* Ask what belongs to Lucky. *(trunk)* Follow a similar procedure to help children correct the remaining possessives, if needed.

> Luckys trunk picked up the brush.
> Her trunk is strong.
> The painting is her.
> The mans job was in the jungle.
> The elephants needed his help.

**INDEPENDENT PRACTICE** Have children write another sentence about an elephant that contains a possessive naming word or the word *his, her,* or *hers.*

# Shared Writing

*Friendly Letter*

**5-DAY** WRITING
**DAY 1** Modeled Writing
**DAY 2** Shared Writing
**DAY 3** Shared Writing
**DAY 4** Independent Writing
**DAY 5** Independent Writing

## Shared Writing

**REVIEW WITH A LITERATURE MODEL** Have children recall how people really liked the elephants' paintings. Tell children that people might have written to friends about the art. Read the following friendly letter as an example.

May 15, 20--

Dear Bill,

I went to an art show today. I saw amazing paintings made by elephants. Did you know that elephants can paint?

Your friend,
Sasha

Art Show

**PRACTICE WRITING** Reread with children the class letter from Day 2. Continue to help them add information to the body of the letter. Have children help spell words by supplying some or all of the letters.

**VOICE** Tell children to think about the person who will read the letter and to tell about things that would interest that person. Guide them to choose words that they would use when talking to a friend and classmate.

## Share

**DISCUSS THE FRIENDLY LETTER** Read the finished letter with children, tracking the print. Then ask children to

- identify each part of the letter and explain its purpose.
- check to make sure all names, dates, and places are capitalized.
- identify the main idea and details in the body of the letter.

Display the letter to use as a writing model for Days 4 and 5.

### Objectives

- *To contribute to the writing of a friendly letter*
- *To consider the audience and purpose of a friendly letter*

### Writing Prompt

**Write About Art** Have children draw and write about the kind of art that they like to look at or make.

### ADVANCED

**Audience** Remind children that a letter writer's voice is influenced by the letter's purpose and audience. Invite children to tell how the voice might change if Sasha were writing about the art show to the artist who taught the elephants.

# Warm-Up Routines

## Day at a Glance

### Day 4

**Phonemic Awareness**
• Phoneme Substitution

 **and Spelling**
• Review: Inflections *-ed, -ing*

**High-Frequency Words**
• Review: *buy, carry, money, other, paint, paper, would*

**Fluency**
• Intonation
• "Can Elephants Paint?" *Student Edition*, pp. 178–199

**Comprehension**
Review: Main Idea
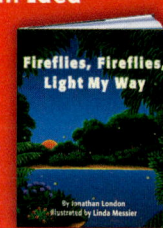
• Big Book: *Fireflies, Fireflies, Light My Way*

**Robust Vocabulary**
• Review: *rejoice, predicament, extraordinary*

**Grammar**
• Review: Possessives

**Independent Writing**
• Friendly Letter

## Oral Language

**Objective** *To respond appropriately to oral communication*

### Question of the Day

What does an elephant look like?
Describe it.

Encourage children to imagine that they are standing next to an elephant. Ask volunteers to describe what they would see, hear, feel, and so on. Then have children use these descriptions to complete the sentence frame:

**An elephant _____.**

## Read Aloud

**Objective** *To listen for a purpose*

**BIG BOOK OF RHYMES AND POEMS** Display the poem and read the title. Tell children to listen to find out how an elephant is described. After reading, ask children to recall two things named in the poem that let you know that you have seen an elephant. Then read aloud the poem several times, modeling appropriate intonation. Encourage children to join in. After children know the poem, recite it with them, using appropriate intonation.

▲ Big Book of Rhymes and Poems, p. 34

# Word Wall

**Objective** *To read high-frequency words*

**REVIEW HIGH-FREQUENCY WORDS** Review *carry, other, paper,* and other previously learned high-frequency words. Say each word, ask a volunteer to point to it, and have children read it aloud. Then point to words at random, and have children reread them. Repeat several times.

| carry | other | paper |
|---|---|---|

# Phonemic Awareness

**Objective** *To substitute medial phonemes to make new words*

**Routine Card 10**

**PHONEME SUBSTITUTION: MEDIAL** Tell children you will say a word and then make a new word by changing the middle sound. Say: **The word is *ship*. I change /i/ to /o/. The new word is *shop*.** Review the song with children, modeling the first example for them.

*(Sung to the tune of "A-Hunting We Will Go.")*

A-changing we will go; a-changing we will go.
Change /i/ to /a/ in *tingle,* my friend.
The new word now is *tangle!*

Have children make the following substitutions while singing the song:

**flush, /u/ to /a/** (flash)          **tackle, /a/ to /i/** (tickle)

**puddle, /u/ to /a/** (paddle)          **quick, /i/ to /a/** (quack)

**jangle, /a/ to /i/** (jingle)          **sung, /u/ to /i/** (sing)

**spell, /e/ to /i/** (spill)          **shatter, /a/ to /u/** (shutter)

**bubble, /u/ to /a/** (babble)          **rash, /a/ to /u/** (rush)

# Inflections -ed, -ing phonics

| 5-DAY PHONICS | |
|---|---|
| DAY 1 | Introduce Syllable /əl/-*le* |
| DAY 2 | Word Building with Syllable /əl/-*le* |
| DAY 3 | Word Building with Syllable /əl/-*le* |
| **DAY 4** | **Inflections -*ed*, -*ing* (double final consonant)** |
| DAY 5 | Inflections -*ed*, -*ing* (double final consonant) |

## Objectives

• *To recognize root words*

• *To read inflectional forms with* -ed *and* -ing *with a double final consonant.*

## Skill Trace

 **Inflections -*ed*, -*ing* (double final consonant)**

| | |
|---|---|
| Introduce | T270 |
| Review | T280, T444, T454 |
| Test | Bk 1-3 |
| Maintain | Bk 1-5, T98 |

 **Resources**

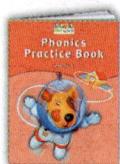 **Phonics Practice Book, pp. 95–96**

---

### Inflections -*ed*, -*ing* (double final consonant)

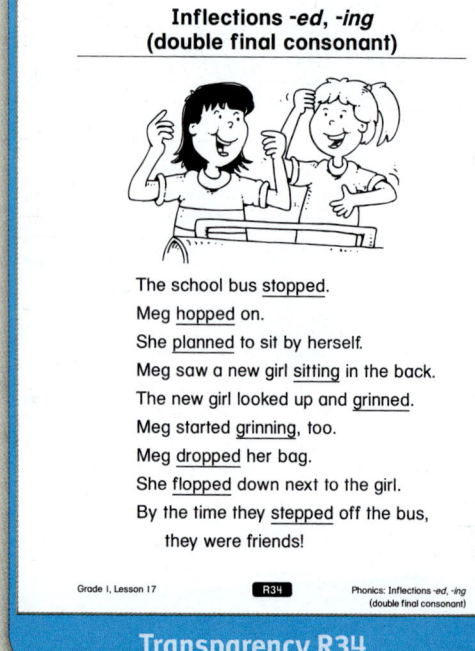

The school bus <u>stopped</u>.
Meg <u>hopped</u> on.
She <u>planned</u> to sit by herself.
Meg saw a new girl <u>sitting</u> in the back.
The new girl looked up and <u>grinned</u>.
Meg started <u>grinning</u>, too.
Meg <u>dropped</u> her bag.
She <u>flopped</u> down next to the girl.
By the time they <u>stepped</u> off the bus,
    they were friends!

Grade 1, Lesson 17    R34    Phonics: Inflections -*ed*, -*ing* (double final consonant)

**Transparency R34**

---

## Review

**REVIEW DOUBLING FINAL CONSONANT** Write these words on the board: *shop, shopped, shopping.* After you read the words, ask children to identify the root word and the endings added to it. Ask children how the root word changed when each ending was added. (The *p* was doubled.) Remind children that when the root word has a short vowel followed by one consonant, the final consonant is doubled before the ending is added. Frame the ending *ed* in *shopped* and have children identify the final sound in the word. Remind children that the ending *ed* can stand for the sound /t/ as in *shopped,* /d/ as in *fanned,* and /əd/ as in *nodded.*

## Working with Patterns

**READ WORDS WITH DOUBLED CONSONANTS** Make a chart as shown below. Track the print, and have children read the words. Ask them to identify the sound that the letters *ed* represent in the second column. Then point at random to the words and call on volunteers to read them aloud.

| Root Word | Double Consonant, Add ed | Double Consonant, Add ing |
|---|---|---|
| tap<br>grab<br>pet | tapped<br>grabbed<br>petted | tapping<br>grabbing<br>petting |

## Practice/Apply

**READ WORDS IN CONTEXT** Display **Transparency R34.** Have children read each sentence silently. Then ask a volunteer to read the sentence aloud. Point to the underlined word and have children identify how the root word changed when the ending was added. Then track the print as you lead children in choral-reading the sentences.

# Syllable /əl/-le

**phonics** *and Spelling*

| 5-DAY SPELLING | |
| --- | --- |
| DAY 1 | Pretest |
| DAY 2 | Word Building |
| DAY 3 | State the Generalization |
| DAY 4 | Review |
| DAY 5 | Posttest |

## Build Words

**MAP LETTERS TO SOUNDS** Use *Letter Cards* and a pocket chart to form words. Have children listen to your directions and change letters in each word to spell a spelling word. Then have a volunteer change the *Letter Cards* in the pocket chart.

- Form *wig* in the pocket chart and have children read it. Ask: **Which spelling word can you make by adding *gle*?** (wiggle)

- Leave *wiggle* in the pocket chart. Ask: **Which spelling word can you make by changing *w* and the first *g*?** (single)

| w | i | g | | |
| --- | --- | --- | --- | --- |
| w | i | g | g | l | e |
| s | i | n | g | l | e |
| l | i | t | t | l | e |

- Leave *single* in the pocket chart. Ask: **Which spelling word can you make by changing *s, n,* and *g*?** (little)

Follow a similar procedure with the following words: *hand* (handle), *burn* (turn), and *whirl* (girl).

**HIGH-FREQUENCY WORDS** Remind children that there are some other words they have to remember how to spell. Tell children that *by* is one such word. Tell children to picture the word and then write it. Continue with *room*.

### ADVANCED

**Create Word Clues** Read the following clues and have children use their *Word Builder Cards* to form the spelling word that answers each mystery-word riddle: **This mystery word is the opposite of *big*.** (little) **This mystery word names "only one."** (single) **This mystery word tells what a worm will do if you pick it up.** (wiggle) **This word names something you turn.** (handle)

## Objectives

- *To use /əl/-le and other known letter-sounds to spell and write words*

- *To spell and write known high-frequency words*

### Spelling Words

| | | | |
| --- | --- | --- | --- |
| 1. | hand | 6. | little |
| 2. | handle | 7. | turn |
| 3. | wig | 8. | girl |
| 4. | wiggle | 9. | by |
| 5. | single | 10. | room |

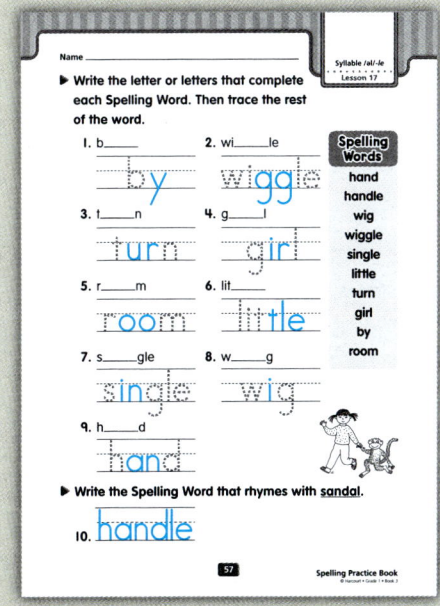

▲ Spelling Practice Book, p. 57

#  High-Frequency Words

## Objective
- *To read high-frequency words*

 REVIEW ✓ Tested

### High-Frequency Words

| | |
|---|---|
| buy | paint |
| carry | paper |
| money | would |
| other | |

---

### BELOW-LEVEL

**Review the Selection**  Give partners a set of high-frequency word cards. (*Teacher Resource Book,* p. 141). Have them track the text as you read aloud each page of "Can Elephants Paint?" Tell children to listen and look for high-frequency words as they follow along. When they locate one, have them hold up the word card to signal that they have found it. Continue in this manner until all the high-frequency word cards have been matched with words in the text.

---

## Review

**READ AND WRITE WORDS**  Duplicate and distribute an uncut story strip page for each child. (*Teacher Resource Book*, p. 227) Then do the following:

- Have children read the title in the first strip. Explain that the sentences tell about the selection, but some of them have missing words.

- Display *Word Cards* for the high-frequency words, or list the words on the board. Have children read each word.

## Practice/Apply

**GUIDED PRACTICE**  Direct children to read all the story strip sentences and to write the missing words in the blanks.

> When people saw the art, they wanted to _____ it.

**INDEPENDENT PRACTICE**  After children complete the story strip page, have them cut apart the strips. Have partners work together to read and match their story strips and then to arrange the events in the order in which they happen in the selection. Have children take the story strips home to share with family members.

◀ "A Pet for Me"
Practice Book, pp. 53–54

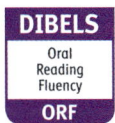 # Fluency
*Intonation*

## Review

DIBELS
Oral Reading Fluency
ORF

**MODEL READING WITH APPROPRIATE INTONATION** Remind children that when good readers read, they make sure that their voices rise and fall so their reading sounds like natural speech. Choose two or three selection pages to read aloud. Show children how to

▲ Student Edition, pp. 178–199

- make the voice fall at the end of a telling sentence or when a character is concerned or upset.

- make the voice rise at the end of a question or when a character is feeling happy or enthusiastic.

**Think Aloud** I'm going to read one page at a time. As I read, I'm going to pay attention to punctuation marks. I'm going to make my voice rise and fall so it sounds as if I am talking. Read each page after me, just the way I read it.

## Practice/Apply

**GUIDED PRACTICE** Have partners reread the selection aloud three or four times. Listen to partners read, giving feedback about intonation and providing guidance for improving fluency.

**INDEPENDENT PRACTICE** Organize children into small groups. Provide each group with the elephant character cutout (*Teacher Resource Book*, p. 196) or a stuffed elephant. As children pass the elephant around the group, have the "elephant keeper" read two pages of the story and ask several questions about what is happening on these pages. Have the rest of the group suggest answers. After the entire selection is read, invite each group member to identify his or her favorite part of the selection and tell why.

### Objectives
- *To build fluency through rereading a story*
- *To read in a manner that sounds like natural speech*

### Additional Related Reading
Guide children to self-select related books, such as these:
- *Splash!* by Flora McDonnell. Candlewick, 2003. **EASY**
- *Mouse Paint* by Ellen Stoll Walsh. Harcourt, 1995. **AVERAGE**
- *African Elephants* by Shannon Knudsen. Lerner, 2006. **CHALLENGE**

### BELOW-LEVEL
**Fluency Practice** Have children reread for fluency, using "Paint Your Dog!" in the *Book 1-3 Strategic Intervention Interactive Reader, Decodable Book 17,* or the appropriate *Leveled Readers.* (See pages T462–T465.) Guide them to select a small portion of a story and practice reading it several times.

# Main Idea
## Comprehension

### Objective

- *To recognize the main idea when listening to a story*

### Skill Trace

 **Tested** **Main Idea**

| | |
|---|---|
| Preview | T316 |
| Introduce | T324–T325 |
| Reteach | S36–S37, S46–S47 |
| Review | **T348, T360, T370, T402, T410–T411, T436, T448, T458** |
| Test | Bk 1-3 |
| Maintain | Monitor Comprehension, Bks 1-4, 1-5 |

### MONITOR PROGRESS

**Main Idea**

**IF** children have difficulty determining a story's main idea,

**THEN** have them suggest a favorite story and help them determine its main idea.

**Small-Group Instruction, pp. S46–S47:**

🔴 **BELOW-LEVEL:** Reteach

🔵 **ON-LEVEL:** Reinforce

🟢 **ADVANCED:** Extend

---

### Review

**TALK ABOUT MAIN IDEA** Review with children how to recognize a main idea. Ask them what a story's main idea is. (The story's main idea is what the story is mostly about.)

**USE PRIOR KNOWLEDGE/SET A PURPOSE** Display *Big Book Fireflies, Fireflies, Light My Way.* Guide children to use what they remember about the story to set a purpose for listening.

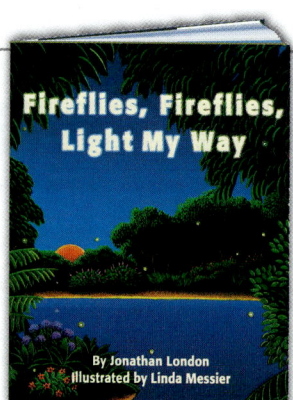

▲ **Big Book**

### Practice/Apply

**GUIDED PRACTICE** Monitor listening comprehension as you read, using the following questions:

- **Page 18:** **REREAD** If I wanted to find out more about muskrats, which page should I reread? What would I learn? (page 18; that they paddle far)

- **MAIN IDEA** What is the most important idea of this story? (Many animals lead the storyteller on a nighttime walk in the woods to a place where animals play.)

- **Page 27: DRAW CONCLUSIONS** When and how does the story pattern change? What makes you think this? (It changes when the storyteller meets the alligators. They don't lead the storyteller; instead, they chase and scare the storyteller.)

**INDEPENDENT PRACTICE** Remind children that story details can often help them to figure out the main idea. Have children recall the animals the storyteller meets. Then display the last illustrated spread, and have children identify where the animals are and what they are doing. Ask children how these details can help them figure out the story's main idea.

# Build Robust Vocabulary

## Listening/Speaking: *Words About the Selection*

### Review Robust Vocabulary

**USE VOCABULARY IN DIFFERENT CONTEXTS** Remind children of the Student-Friendly Explanations of *rejoice, predicament,* and *extraordinary.* Then discuss each word using the following examples:

**rejoice** Tell children that you will name some things. If they think the thing would make them rejoice, they should clap their hands and look happy. If not, they should do nothing.

| | |
|---|---|
| a trip to the beach | a rainy day |
| a broken toy | a new pet |
| a birthday gift | a new pencil |
| a big spider | a trip to the movies |

**predicament** Tell children that you will name some things. If they think the thing would put them in a predicament, they should say, "Oh no!" If not, they should say nothing.

| | |
|---|---|
| slipping on ice | reading a book |
| meeting a mean dog | losing a library book |
| ringing a doorbell | missing the school bus |
| breaking a friend's toy | shopping at the mall |

**extraordinary** Tell children that you will name some things. If they think the thing is extraordinary, they should say, "Wow!" If not, they should say nothing.

- a pet dinosaur
- a huge wave
- a pile of sand
- a double rainbow
- a singing cat
- a singing bird
- a shooting star
- a full moon

### Objective

- *To develop robust vocabulary to describe ideas*

**Tested**

**REVIEW**

### Student-Friendly Explanations

**rejoice** If you rejoice, you show that you are very happy.

**predicament** If you have a predicament, you have a serious or difficult problem.

**extraordinary** Something extraordinary is something that is very unusual or remarkable.

### ● ADVANCED

**Use Vocabulary in Different Contexts** Call on volunteers to describe an extraordinary predicament that they or someone they know might find themselves in. Then have them tell how and why they would rejoice if they managed to find a way out of this predicament.

# Grammar

*Possessives*

**5-DAY GRAMMAR**

| | |
|---|---|
| **DAY 1** | Introduce Possessive Proper Nouns |
| **DAY 2** | Introduce Possessive Common Nouns |
| **DAY 3** | Introduce Possessive Pronouns *his, her, hers* |
| **DAY 4** | **Introduce Pronouns *its, their, your, yours*** |
| **DAY 5** | Review Possessives |

## Objective

- *To recognize possessive nouns and possessive pronouns* its, their, your, yours

## Daily Proofreading

**is that book her**

(Is, hers?)

▲ **Grammar Practice Book, p. 67**

### Review

**IDENTIFY POSSESSIVES** Have children read the following sentences and review with them the possessive words. Ask children to explain who owns what in each sentence.

I see the <u>girl's</u> hat.   I see <u>her</u> hat.   The hat is <u>hers</u>.
That is <u>Jim's</u> cat.   That is <u>his</u> cat.

Then write these examples on the board to introduce the possessive pronouns *its, their, your,* and *yours*:

Mark has a dog.   <u>Its</u> fur is soft.
<u>Your</u> dog is big, Mark.   Is that small dog <u>yours</u>, too?
My friends like <u>their</u> pets.

Have children read each example. Ask them to identify the possessive words and tell who owns what. Mention that *your* and *yours* can refer to a boy or girl who owns something, while *its* refers to an animal or thing. *Their* can refer to people, animals, or things.

### Practice/Apply

**GUIDED PRACTICE** Write these sentence pairs on the board:

<u>The boy</u> has a cat.　　_____ cat is small.
<u>My friends</u> have a farm.　_____ farm is big.
<u>The cow</u> has big horns.　_____ horns are big!
<u>You</u> have a pig.　　　　_____ pig is pink.
Here is my <u>pet</u>.　　　　Where is ___?

Call on volunteers to read the sentences aloud. Then work with children to add *its, their, your,* and *yours* to complete the sentences.

**INDEPENDENT READING** Ask children to choose one sentence pair and to write both sentences correctly.

 # Independent Writing
*Friendly Letter*

| **5-DAY** WRITING | |
| --- | --- |
| DAY 1 | Modeled Writing |
| DAY 2 | Shared Writing |
| DAY 3 | Shared Writing |
| DAY 4 | Independent Writing |
| DAY 5 | Independent Writing |

## Write a Friendly Letter

**GENERATE IDEAS** Guide children to write for a familiar occasion, audience, or purpose. Tell them that they will write their own friendly letter to a relative or a friend about something interesting that has happened. Have them look again at the pictures they drew on Day 1 for ideas. Ask them to create a web with the topic, or main idea, in the center and important details around it.

tan fur · likes to be petted · **my new puppy** · Taffy · sleeps in my room

**WRITING TRAIT** **VOICE** Invite volunteers to dictate some of their sentences. Write them on the board and discuss whether or not they sound like something one would write to a friend or relative.

**WRITE** Ask children to draft their friendly letter, using their pictures and webs for ideas. Save the drafts to have children revise on Day 5.

January 22, 20--

Dear Grandpa,

We got a new puppy! Her fur is tan and soft. Her name is Taffy. Taffy likes to be petted. Her bed is in my room. When can you come see Taffy? You'll love her, just like we do!

Love,
Peter

Taffy

### Objectives

- *To identify the topic and voice of a friendly letter*
- *To draft a friendly letter*

### Writing Prompt

**Write About a Place** Have children write a brief message that could be on a postcard to a friend or relative about a favorite place.

 **BELOW-LEVEL**

**Write** Focus on having children draft the body of their message. Before they begin writing, check each child's web to make sure that the topic appears in the middle. Explain to children that the first sentence in their message should tell what the letter is about, and the next sentences should tell details that give more information.

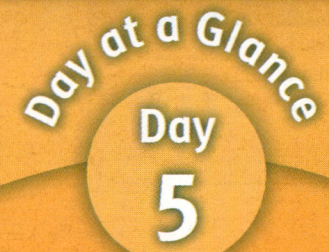

## Day at a Glance

### Day 5

**Phonemic Awareness**
- Phoneme Substitution

 **phonics and Spelling**
- Review: Inflections *-ed, -ing*
- Posttest: Syllable /əl/-*le*

**High-Frequency Words**
- Review

**Fluency**
- Intonation
  "Can Elephants Paint?"
  *Student Edition*, pp. 178–199

**Comprehension**
Focus Skill — Review: Main Idea

**Robust Vocabulary**
- Review

**Grammar**
- Review: Possessives

**Independent Writing**
- Friendly Letter

---

# Warm-Up Routines

## Oral Language

**Objective** *To respond appropriately to oral communication*

### Question of the Day

What can elephants do with their trunks?

Why is that amazing?

Write the following sentence frame and help children complete it.

**Elephants can use their trunks to _____.**

## Read Aloud

**Objectives** *To understand concepts of print; to read in a manner that sounds like natural speech*

**BIG BOOK OF RHYMES AND POEMS** Ask children what they remember about the poem. Then as you read, model left-to-right and top-to-bottom progression. Ask children to count the number of sentences in the poem and tell how they figured this out. Then have two groups choral-read the poem with you. One group should recite the first stanza and another group should recite the second stanza. Repeat, until children can recite the poem effortlessly.

▲ Big Book of Rhymes and Poems, p. 34

# Word Wall

**Objective** *To read high-frequency words*

**REVIEW HIGH-FREQUENCY WORDS** Review *carry, paint, way, would, your,* and other previously learned high-frequency words. Say each word, ask a volunteer to point to it, and have children read it aloud. Then point to words at random, and have children reread them. Repeat several times to reinforce instant recognition.

| carry | paint | way |
|-------|-------|-----|

# Phonemic Awareness

**Objective** *To substitute initial and medial phonemes to make words*

**Routine Card 10**

**PHONEME SUBSTITUTION: INITIAL AND MEDIAL** Tell children that they will sing a song and substitute the beginning or the middle sound they hear in a given word. Model the first example for them.

*(Sing to the tune of "A-Hunting We Will Go.")*

**A-changing we will go; a-changing we will go.
Change /h/ to /k/ in *handle*, my friend.
The new word now is *candle*!**

Have children make the following substitutions:

**nice, /n/ to /m/** (mice)  **soon, /s/ to /m/** (moon)

**jiggle, /j/ to /w/** (wiggle)  **tingle, /t/ to /s/** (single)

**crib, /i/ to /a/** (crab)  **cattle, /t/ to /m/** (camel)

**cuddle, /d/ to /p/** (couple)  **lock, /o/ to /i/** (lick)

# Inflections -ed, -ing phonics

**5-DAY SPELLING**

| | |
|---|---|
| DAY 1 | Introduce Syllable /əl/-le |
| DAY 2 | Word Building with Syllable /əl/-le |
| DAY 3 | Build Words |
| DAY 4 | inflections -ed, -ing (double final consonant) |
| DAY 5 | inflections -ed, -ing (double final consonant) |

## Objectives

• *To recognize root words*

• *To read inflectional forms with -ed and -ing with a double final consonant*

## Skill Trace

 **Tested** **Inflections -ed, -ing (double final consonants**

| | |
|---|---|
| Introduce | T270 |
| Review | T280, T444, T454 |
| Test | Bk 1-3 |
| Maintain | Bk 1-5, T98 |

## Review

**ROOT WORDS AND ENDINGS** Remind children that endings can be added to a root word to make new words.

• Write *pat* and read the word. Say: **The word *patted* is made by doubling the final consonant and adding *-ed* to the root word.** Write *patted* and read the word.

• Repeat this procedure to form *patting*.

## Work with Patterns

**ADDING ENDINGS** Display the chart from Day 4 (p. T444). Ask volunteers to underline root words and circle endings. Have children read the words.

| Root Word | Double Consonant, Add *-ed* | Double Consonant, Add *-ing* |
|---|---|---|
| tap<br>grab<br>pet | tapped<br>grabbed<br>petted | tapping<br>grabbing<br>petting |

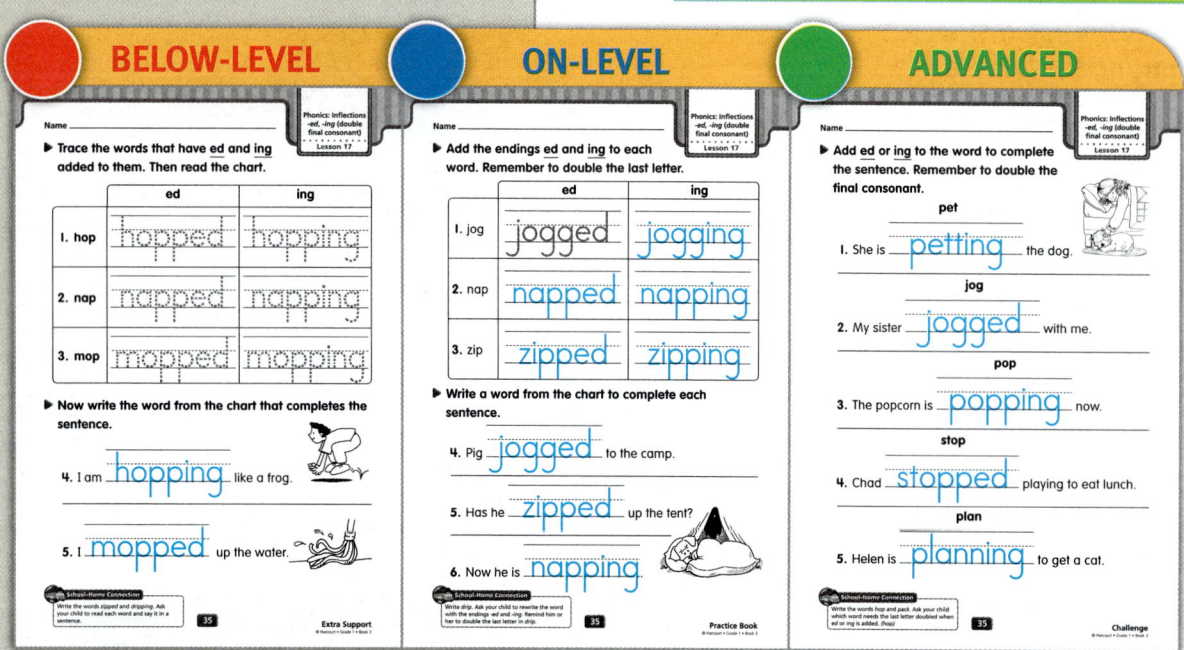

▲ Extra Support, p. 35    ▲ Practice Book, p. 35    ▲ Challenge, p. 35

 **E L L**

• Group children according to academic levels, and assign one of the pages on the left.

• Clarify any unfamiliar concepts as necessary. See *ELL Teacher Guide*, Lesson 17, for support in scaffolding instruction.

**5-DAY SPELLING**

DAY 1  Pretest
DAY 2  Word Building
DAY 3  State the Generalization
DAY 4  Review
DAY 5  Posttest

# Syllable /əl/-le

**phonics** *and Spelling*

## Assess

**POSTTEST** Assess children's progress. Use the dictation sentences from Day 1.

### Words with /əl/-le

1. hand     Raise your **hand** before you speak.
2. handle     Carry the basket by the **handle.**
3. wig     The clown wore a curly red **wig.**
4. wiggle     We watched the worm **wiggle.**
5. single     There isn't a **single** cracker left.
6. little     A new puppy is very **little.**

### Review

7. turn     Please **turn** off the television.
8. girl     Is that **girl** your sister?

### High-Frequency

9. by     Please sit **by** me.
10. room     Bob cleaned his messy **room.**

**WRITING APPLICATION** Have children complete and illustrate the following sentence frames:

**The little girl started to wiggle when \_\_\_\_\_.**
**I put my hand on the handle and \_\_\_\_\_.**

I put my hand on the handle and turned it.

The little girl started to wiggle when she laughed.

## Objectives

- *To use /əl/-le and other known letter-sounds to spell words*
- *To spell and write known high-frequency words*

### Spelling Words

| | | | |
|---|---|---|---|
| 1. | hand | 6. | little |
| 2. | handle | 7. | turn |
| 3 | wig | 8. | girl |
| 4. | wiggle | 9. | by |
| 5. | single | 10. | room |

**E L L**

**Writing Application** Remind children that one of the meanings of the word *single* is "one." Have children scan the list of spelling words, and guide them to identify the naming words in the list that name a single thing. (hand, handle, wig, girl, room) Have each child choose one of these words and write a sentence using this word. As an example, share this sentence: *A girl sat down.* Invite volunteers to read their sentence aloud.

# High-Frequency Words

## Objectives

- *To read high-frequency words*
- *To explore word relationships*

**REVIEW** Tested

### High-Frequency Words

| | |
|---|---|
| buy | other |
| carry | night |
| does | paint |
| how | paper |
| line | water |
| money | would |

### Review

**REINFORCE WORD RECOGNITION** Display *Word Cards* for all the words in a pocket chart. Point to words at random and ask volunteers to read them.

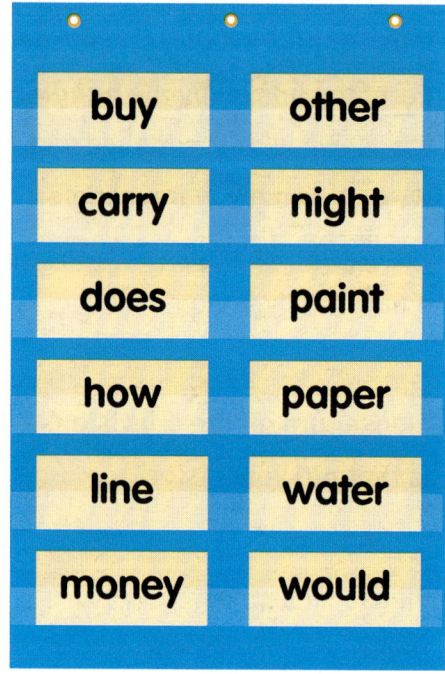

**SORT WORDS** Guide children in sorting the words into columns according to the number of letters. Then have them read aloud the words in each column.

- Have children look at the five-letter words—*carry, money, other, night, paint, paper, water, would.* Have them identify and segment these words by clapping out the syllables. Then ask: **Which words have one syllable?** (night, paint, would) **Which words have two syllables?** (carry, money, other, paper, water)

- Have children look at the three-letter and four-letter words—*buy, how; does, line.* Ask: **Which words have the sound /ī/?** (buy, line) **Which words have the letter *o*?** (how, does)

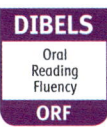

# Fluency

*Intonation*

## Readers' Theater

**DIBELS**
Oral Reading Fluency
**ORF**

**PERFORM "CAN ELEPHANTS PAINT?"** To help children improve their fluency, have them perform "Can Elephants Paint?" as Readers' Theater. Use the following procedures:

- Read aloud several pages of "Can Elephants Paint?" Model fluent reading with appropriate intonation as children follow along.

- Assign children to groups of four and have them read the selection together. Then have two children take turns as the narrator while the others choose the part of Ning or the artist. Have them practice reading the selection aloud with appropriate intonation in a manner that sounds like natural speech.

- Listen to each group read. Provide feedback and support.

- Invite each group to read the selection to another group. Remind them to focus on reading with appropriate intonation.

### ADVANCED

**Television News** Discuss why "Can Elephants Paint?" would make a good feature story on the news. Have small groups read the selection as if they were news reporters. Provide toy elephants, paper, paint, and brushes for children to use as props for the newscast.

## Objective

- *To read fluently with appropriate intonation*

### ASSESSMENT

**Monitoring Progress** Periodically, take a timed sample of children's oral reading and measure the number of words read correctly per minute. Children should be accurately reading approximately 60 words per minute by the end of Grade 1.

## Fluency Support Materials

**Fluency Builders, Grade 1,** Lesson 17

**Audiotext** *Student Edition* selections are available on *Audiotext Grade 1,* CD 3.

**Strategic Intervention Teacher Guide,** Lesson 17

# Main Idea
## Comprehension

**Objective**
- *To identify the main idea of a story*

**Skill Trace**

 **Main Idea**

| | |
|---|---|
| Preview | T316 |
| Introduce | T324–T325 |
| Reteach | S36–S37, S46–S47 |
| Review | T348, T360, T370, T402, T410–T411, T436, T448, T458 |
| Test | Bk 1-3 |
| Maintain | Monitor Comprehension, Bks 1-4, 1-5 |

**BELOW-LEVEL**

**Guided Practice** Review the reading selections with children before meeting with the whole group. Page through the *Big Book* and the *Student Edition* selections. Help children recall important details by prompting them with questions such as these: **What did Lucky learn to do? Where did the storyteller go on the walk? What helped the storyteller see in the dark?**

## Review

**REVIEW THE SKILL** Review main idea with children. Guide them to determine the main idea of the stories and selections they read this week and identify the supporting details. Draw a four-column chart on the board. Enter the selection titles in the first row as shown. Enter the headings in the first column as shown. Read aloud the titles. Remind children that these are selections they heard or read this week. Read aloud the headings in the first column. Write the main idea of and one detail from the read-aloud in the second column.

## Practice/Apply

**GUIDED PRACTICE** Ask volunteers to name the main idea and identify a supporting detail for "Can Elephants Paint?" Write their responses in the third column of the chart. Then help them do the same for *Fireflies, Fireflies, Light My Way,* and record responses in the last column.

| | "How the Rainbow Came to Be" | "Can Elephants Paint?" | Fireflies Fireflies, Light My Way |
|---|---|---|---|
| **Main Idea** | Earth is made of many colors. | Elephants can make amazing art. | The narrator meets many animals during a walk. |
| **Detail** | Blue painted the oceans, rivers, and sky. | Lucky learned to paint with a brush. | Fireflies light the way. |

**INDEPENDENT PRACTICE** Have children page through their *Student Edition* to help them recall selections they have read. Ask each child to name one of the selections and identify the main idea and one supporting detail.

# Build Robust Vocabulary

## Listening/Speaking

### Review

**REINFORCE MEANINGS** Ask children the following questions:

- If you were in a *predicament,* how might you feel? Why?

- If you saw something *extraordinary,* would you keep it a secret or tell your friend about it? Why?

- Name something that would make you *rejoice.*

**CLOZE SENTENCES** Guide children to develop their vocabulary by discussing the meanings of *agreement, unnoticed, unthinkable, extraordianary,* and *predicament.* Read the following sentences aloud. Pause and invite volunteers to finish the sentences with the appropriate Vocabulary Words.

Kim and Alysha are spending the day together. Kim wants to go to the park. Alysha also wants to go to the park. The two friends want to go to the park. They are in _____. (agreement)

It is late at night. A black cat walks silently across the lawn. The mice in the bushes don't even know the cat is there. The cat passes by _____. (unnoticed)

Pablo imagined a place where it snowed every day of the year. People used sleds and skis to get around, even in summer. A place like this is _____. (unthinkable, extraordinary)

Trent was late for school. He grabbed his backback and rushed out the door. When he got to school, Trent realized he was still wearing his pajamas. He was in quite a _____! (predicament)

### Objective

- *To review robust vocabulary*

**REVIEW**   Tested

**Build Robust Vocabulary**

| | |
|---|---|
| agreement | rejoice |
| extraordinary | unnoticed |
| predicament | unthinkable |

 **MONITOR PROGRESS**

**Build Robust Vocabulary**

| **IF** children do not demonstrate understanding of the words and have difficulty using them, | **THEN** model using each word in several sentences and have children repeat each sentence. |
|---|---|

**Small-Group Instruction, pp. S48–S49:**

- 🔴 **BELOW-LEVEL:** Reteach
- 🔵 **ON-LEVEL:** Reinforce
- 🟢 **ADVANCED:** Extend

# Grammar
## Possessives

**5-DAY GRAMMAR**

| DAY 1 | Introduce Possessive Proper Nouns |
| DAY 2 | Introduce Possessive Common Nouns |
| DAY 3 | Introduce Possessive Pronouns *his, her, hers* |
| DAY 4 | Introduce Pronouns *its, their, your, yours* |
| DAY 5 | Review Possessives |

## Objective
- *To write and speak using possessive nouns and pronouns*

## Daily Proofreading

**is their plant as big as your**
(Is, yours?)

## Language Arts Checkpoint

If children have difficulty with the concepts, see pages S50–S51 to reteach.

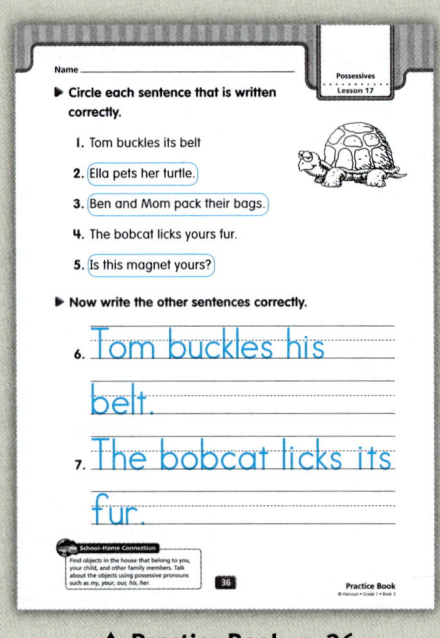

▲ Practice Book, p. 36

---

### Review

**COMPOSE A LOST-AND-FOUND NOTICE**  Tell children that possessives are often used in lost-and-found notices. Model for children several sentences for a notice that the artist might have written if Lucky had wandered away from the farm. Read the notice with children, and have them point out the possessives. Discuss who owns what.

> **Lost: Ning's Elephant!**
>
> The elephant's name is Lucky.
>
> She can pick up logs with her trunk.
>
> His elephant can also paint with her trunk.

### Practice/Apply

**GUIDED PRACTICE**  Have volunteers dictate sentences for a lost-and-found notice describing a belonging they have lost. Write these sentences on the board with errors in the possessives. Work with children to correct the errors.

**INDEPENDENT PRACTICE**  Have children work independently to write a short lost-and-found notice about something belonging to a friend or family member. Encourage them to correctly use possessive nouns and possessive pronouns such as *his, her, hers, its, their, your,* and *yours*.

Have children illustrate their writing with a picture of the lost item. Invite children to share their work with the group. Have the group identify the possessives.

> **Lost: Ann's Lunchbox!**
>
> Ann's lunchbox is missing.
>
> It has pink ducks painted on its lid.

# Independent Writing

*Friendly Letter*

| **5-DAY** WRITING | |
|---|---|
| **DAY 1** | Modeled Writing |
| **DAY 2** | Shared Writing |
| **DAY 3** | Shared Writing |
| **DAY 4** | Independent Writing |
| **DAY 5** | Independent Writing |

## Write a Friendly Letter

**WRITE** Have children continue writing their friendly letters from Day 4. Remind them that the body of their letters should share something interesting that has happened.

 **VOICE** Remind children to use friendly words since they are writing to a friend or relative, and to tell about things that will interest that person.

### Friendly Letter

- The <u>heading</u> gives the date.
- The <u>greeting</u> tells who gets the letter.
- The <u>body</u> is the message.
- The <u>closing</u> says good-bye.
- The <u>signature</u> is the writer's name.

**REVISE** Have children read their friendly letters to a partner to see that the body of the letter is about something interesting that has happened. Read the list of critiera for a friendly letter to children, and have them use the list to make sure they have included all five parts in their letter. Guide children to map sounds as they write. For instance, say the word *hamster.* Ask children how many sounds they hear. Have children name the letter that stands for each sound as they write the word. Have children do a final read of their friendly letter to check that they have correctly used basic capitalization and punctuation. Then have them make a clean copy of their letter.

## Share

**BULLETIN BOARD DISPLAY** Have children read their letters aloud to the group. Guide them to choose and adapt their spoken language so that it will be appropriate for their audience. Help them to speak clearly and at an appropriate rate and volume. Then have children help you create a mailbox bulletin board display that features the letters they wrote.

## Objectives

- *To draft and revise a friendly letter*
- *To publish a friendly letter*

## Writing Prompt

**Self-Selected Writing** Have children draw a picture to generate ideas about a topic of their choice and then write about it.

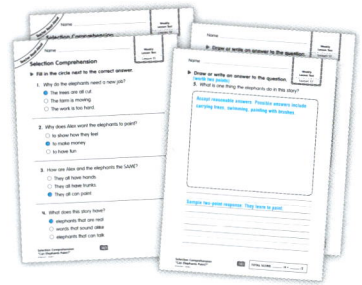

**WEEKLY LESSON TEST**

▲ Weekly Lesson Tests pp. 171–180

- Selection Comprehension with Short Response
- Phonics and Spelling
- High-Frequency Words
- Focus Skill
- Robust Vocabulary
- Grammar Skill
- Fluency

**GO online** For prescriptions, see p. A6. Also available electronically on *StoryTown* Online Assessment and ExamView.®

 **Podcasting:** Assessing Fluency

# Leveled Readers
*Reinforcing Skills and Strategies*

**Genre: Nonfiction**

### BELOW-LEVEL

## The Animal Painter

**SUMMARY** Sandra is an artist who likes to paint animals. She is happy when people want to buy her paintings.

- **phonics** Syllable /əl/-*le*
- **High-Frequency Words:** *buy, carry, money, other, paint, paper, would*
- **Main Idea**

### Before Reading

**BUILD BACKGROUND/SET A PURPOSE** Encourage children to tell about their artistic endeavors. Ask: **Do you like to draw, paint, or make sculptures? What materials do you like to work with? How do you decide what to draw, paint, or make? Do you have a favorite artwork? Would you sell it if someone wanted to buy it?** Then guide children to preview the book and set a purpose for reading it.

### Reading the Book

**PAGES 2–8  MAIN IDEA  What does this book tell you about Sandra?** (Possible response: She likes to paint birds. She sells her paintings.)

**PAGES 2–8  DETAILS, PERSONAL RESPONSE  What do you know about Sandra?** (Possible responses: She likes to paint birds. She sells her paintings.) **What else would you like to know about her?** (Responses will vary.)

**REREAD FOR FLUENCY** Have partners read alternate pages of the selection several times so that it sounds like natural speech.

### Think Critically  *(See inside back cover for questions.)*

1. **NOTE DETAILS** Sandra has a bag to carry her paint and paper.

2. **MAIN IDEA** Sandra paints and sells her work.

3. **NOTE DETAILS** People buy Sandra's paintings.

4. **SPECULATE** Possible responses: People buy them because they like them and because they like birds.

5. **PERSONAL RESPONSE** Responses will vary.

**LEVELED READER TEACHER GUIDE**

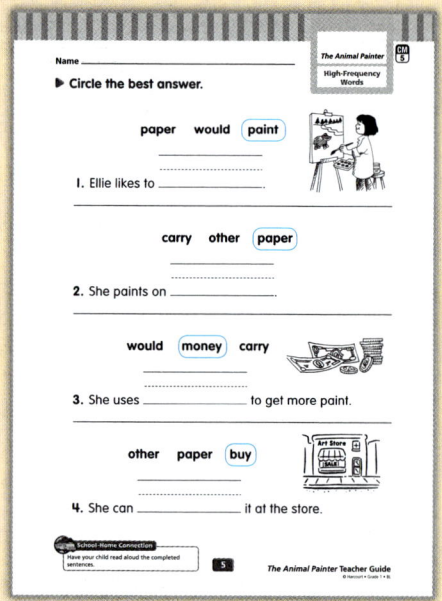

▲ High-Frequency Words, p. 5

▲ Comprehension, p. 6

**www.harcourtschool.com/storytown**

⭐ **Leveled Readers, online**
*Searchable by genre, skill, vocabulary, level, or title*
⭐ **Student Activities and Teacher Resources, online**

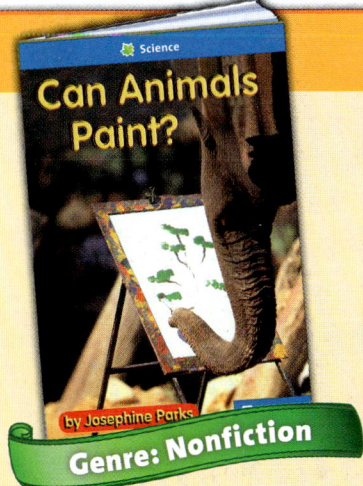
by Josephine Parks
**Genre: Nonfiction**

## ON-LEVEL

# Can Animals Paint?

**SUMMARY** Readers learn that elephants can actually learn to paint and that people buy their paintings.

 **phonics** Syllable /əl/-*le*
• **High-Frequency Words:**
*buy, carry, money, other, paint, paper, would*
 **Main Idea**

### Before Reading

**BUILD BACKGROUND/SET A PURPOSE** Have children share their artistic experiences with painting, telling what materials they use and how they use them. Ask if they know of any animals that can paint. Then guide children to preview the book and set a purpose for reading it.

### Reading the Book

**PAGES 2–8** ⬤ **MAIN IDEA** What kinds of animals can paint? (elephants) **What did you mostly learn from this book?** (Possible response: that these elephants can paint and people buy their paintings)

**PAGES 2–8 COMPARE AND CONTRAST** Why do you think dogs and birds can't paint, but elephants can? (Possible response: It would be hard for dogs and birds to hold a brush. Elephants can easily hold a brush with their trunk.)

**REREAD FOR FLUENCY** Have partners choose the pages they think are interesting and read them several times with appropriate intonation.

### Think Critically

① **NOTE DETAILS** A dog can carry a ball to the park.

② ⬤ **MAIN IDEA** Possible response: It is about elephants who paint.

③ **NOTE DETAILS** People sell them to get money for paint and other things.

④ **NOTE DETAILS** It paints with a brush and its trunk.

⑤ **PERSONAL RESPONSE** Responses will vary.

**LEVELED READER TEACHER GUIDE**

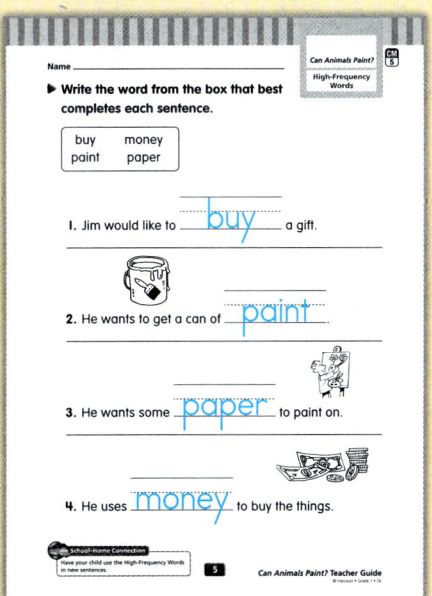

▲ High-Frequency Words, p. 5

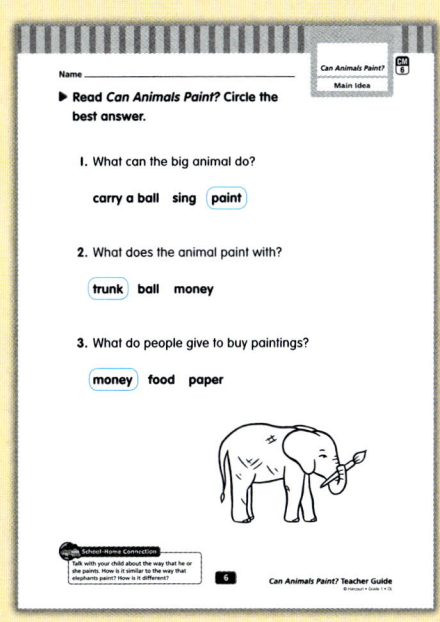

▲ Comprehension, p. 6

# Leveled Readers
## Reinforcing Skills and Strategies

 **ADVANCED**

## Congo the Painter

**SUMMARY** Although most animals can't paint, readers learn that Congo, a chimpanzee, is one who can.

-  **phonics** Syllable /əl/-*le*
- **High-Frequency Words:** *buy, carry, money, other, paint, paper, would*
- **Main Idea**

### Before Reading

**BUILD BACKGROUND/SET A PURPOSE** Have children name some wild animals. List them on the board. Ask: **Do you think any of the animals on the list can paint a picture? Why or why not?** Then have children preview and set a purpose for reading the book.

### Reading the Book

**PAGES 2–8** **MAIN IDEA** **What is the most important thing you learn about Congo?** (Possible response: that he is a chimpanzee that can paint)

**PAGES 7–8** **DRAW CONCLUSIONS** **Why do you think people like to buy Congo's paintings?** (Possible responses: because they like the way they look; because they are amazed that an animal can paint.)

**REREAD FOR FLUENCY** Have partners alternate reading pages aloud several times with appropriate intonation and at a speech-like pace.

### Think Critically *(See inside back cover for questions.)*

1. **GENRE** Possible response: It gives true information and has photographs.

2. **MAIN IDEA** Possible response: Most animals can't paint, but Congo is a good painter.

3. **NOTE DETAILS** Congo painted with lots of paint and a brush.

4. **AUTHOR'S PURPOSE** Possible response: She wanted to show how special Congo was, since he was an animal who could paint.

5. **PERSONAL RESPONSE** Responses will vary.

**LEVELED READER TEACHER GUIDE**

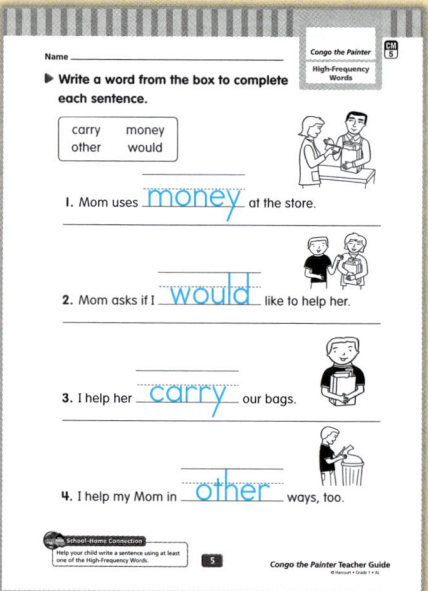

▲ High-Frequency Words, p. 5

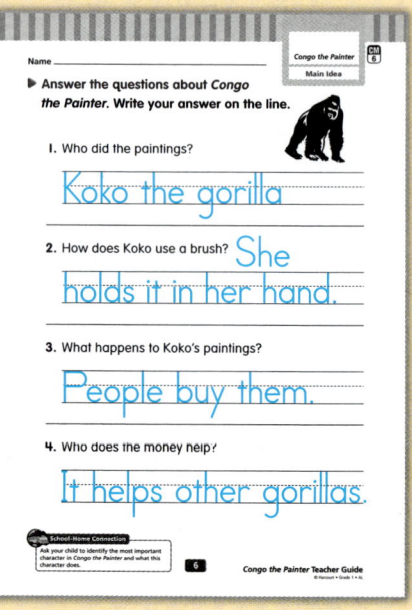

▲ Comprehension, p. 6

**Genre: Nonfiction**

# What Is This Animal?

**SUMMARY** Readers put together word and picture clues—feet, legs, ears, back, trunk, and tusks—to answer the question "What is this animal?" It is an elephant!

- **Strong Picture Support**
- **Concept Vocabulary**
- **Scaffolded Language Development**

## Before Reading

**BUILD BACKGROUND/SET A PURPOSE** Display a picture of an animal so that only one part is visible, such as the tail of a cat. Have children name the part they see. Ask: **Do you know what the animal is?** Have them tell the other parts they would need to see in order to identify the animal. Then guide children to preview the book and set a purpose for reading it.

## Reading the Book

**PAGES 2–7 MAIN IDEA What is this animal?** (elephant)

**PAGES 2–8 DETAILS, GRAPHIC AIDS Name and tell about the different parts of the elephant.** (Its feet are big and thick, with toes. Its legs are thick and long. Its ears are large and fan-like. Its trunk is long. Its tusks curve and come to a point.)

**REREAD FOR FLUENCY** Have children choral-read with you, using the same intonation.

## Scaffolded Language Development    *(See inside back cover for teacher-led activity.)*

Provide additional examples and explanation as needed.

**LEVELED READER TEACHER GUIDE**

▲ Build Background, p. 5

▲ Scaffolded Language Development, p. 6

# Lesson 18

## WEEK AT A GLANCE

### Phonemic Awareness
Phoneme Blending and Substitution

### ✓ Phonics
Long Vowel /ō/ow, oa
Phonograms -ow, -oat, -own, -oast

### ✓ Spelling
*low, slow, grow, road, soap, boat, little, handle, carry, would*

### ✓ High-Frequency Words
*mouse, our, over, pretty, surprise, three*

### Reading
**"Snow Surprise"** by Lisa Campbell Ernst
REALISTIC FICTION

**"The Snowflake Man"** NONFICTION

### ✓ Fluency
Reading Rate

### ✓ Comprehension
 Author's Purpose/Point of View
 Monitor Comprehension: Make Inferences

### ✓ Robust Vocabulary
*bulged, jostled, argue, command, labored, wary*

### ✓ Grammar
Homophones

### Writing
Form: Thank-You Letter
Trait: Word Choice

### Weekly Lesson Test

 = Focus Skill     = Focus Strategy    ✓ = Tested Skill

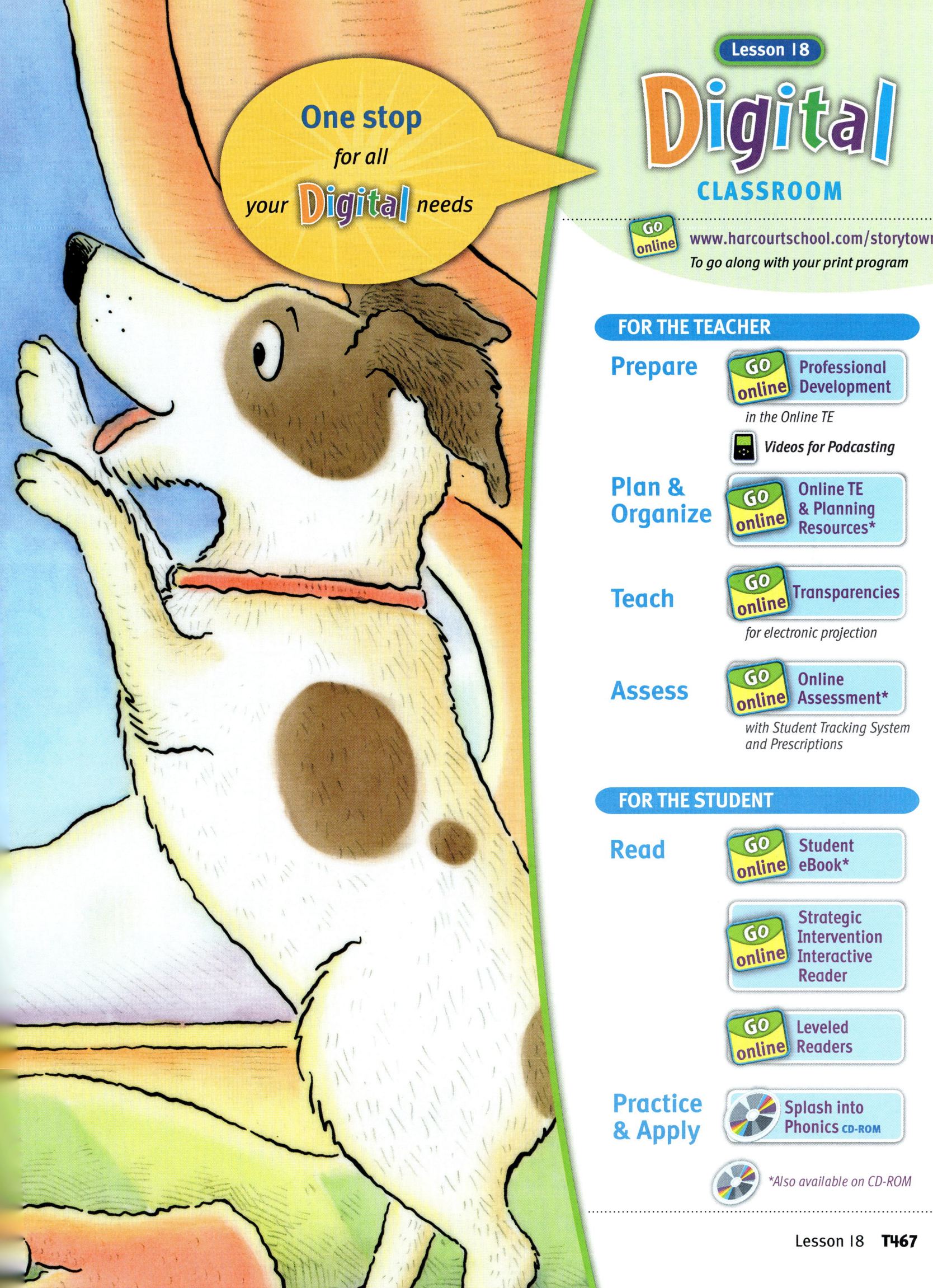

**One stop** *for all* *your* **Digital** *needs*

# Digital
## CLASSROOM

**Go online** www.harcourtschool.com/storytown
*To go along with your print program*

### FOR THE TEACHER

**Prepare**

**Go online** Professional Development
*in the Online TE*

**Videos for Podcasting**

**Plan & Organize**

**Go online** Online TE & Planning Resources*

**Teach**

**Go online** Transparencies
*for electronic projection*

**Assess**

**Go online** Online Assessment*
*with Student Tracking System and Prescriptions*

### FOR THE STUDENT

**Read**

**Go online** Student eBook*

**Go online** Strategic Intervention Interactive Reader

**Go online** Leveled Readers

**Practice & Apply**

Splash into Phonics CD-ROM

*Also available on CD-ROM

# Literature Resources

## STUDENT EDITION

Go online eBook STUDENT EDITION

**Get Started Story**

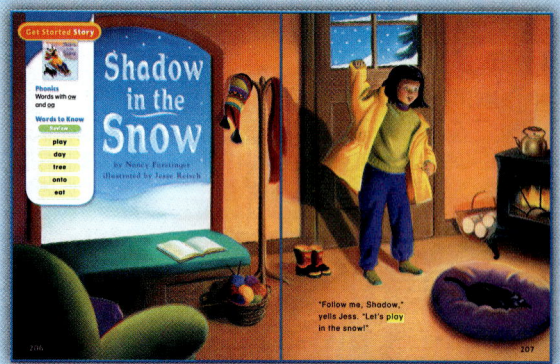

**Shadow in the Snow, pp. 206–213**

**Genre: Realistic Fiction**

**SOCIAL STUDIES** **Snow Surprise, pp. 218–239**

*by Lisa Campbell Ernst*  Joan's dog accidentally knocks over the snowman she has built, turning it into a snow surprise.

**Accelerated Reader**

*Practice Quizzes for the Selection*

**Audiotext**  *Student Edition selections are available on Audiotext Grade 1, CD 3 and 6.*

**Paired Selections**

◀ **Reading Across Texts**
**Comparing Realistic Fiction and Nonfiction**

**Genre: Nonfiction**

## ADDITIONAL READING

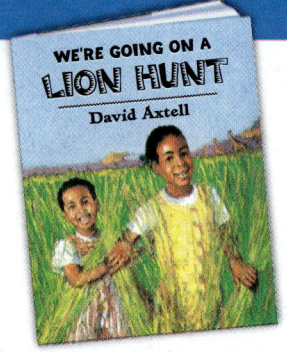

**Big Book**
*We're Going on a Lion Hunt*

**Decodable Book**
**"The Little Yellow Tugboat"**
★ Applies Long Vowel /ō/*ow, oa*

# Support for Differentiated Instruction

 LEVELED READERS

**Muffin Surprise**
by Jack Lewis
illustrated by Anna Walker

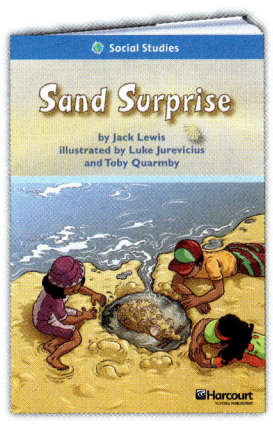

**Sand Surprise**
by Jack Lewis
illustrated by Luke Jurevicius and Toby Quarmby

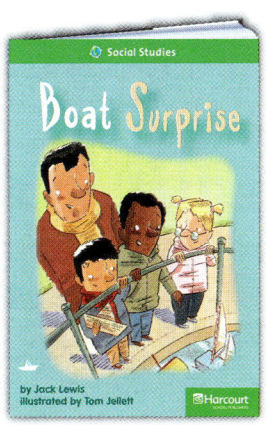

**Boat Surprise**
by Jack Lewis
illustrated by Tom Jellett

**Snow Play**
by Jack Lewis

● **BELOW-LEVEL**　　● **ON-LEVEL**　　● **ADVANCED**　　E L L

## LEVELED PRACTICE

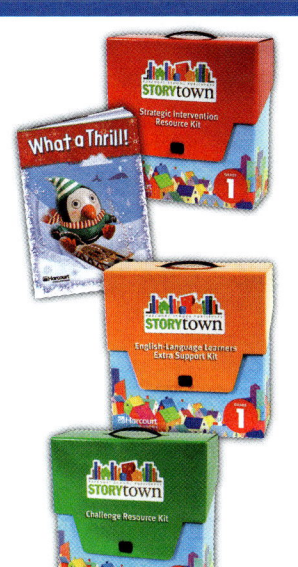

◄ **Strategic Intervention Resource Kit, Lesson 18**

◄ **Strategic Intervention Interactive Reader, Lesson 18**
Strategic Intervention Interactive Reader Online

◄ **ELL Extra Support Kit, Lesson 18**

◄ **Challenge Resource Kit, Lesson 18**

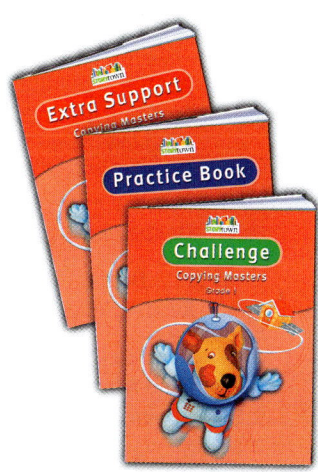

● **BELOW-LEVEL**
Extra Support Copying Masters, pp. 37–42

● **ON-LEVEL**
Practice Book, pp. 37–43

● **ADVANCED**
Challenge Copying Masters, pp. 37–41

## ADDITIONAL RESOURCES

boat

- Spelling Practice Book, pp. 58–62
- Grammar Practice Book, pp. 69–72
- Reading Transparencies R35–R36
- Language Arts Transparencies LA35–LA36
- Test Prep System
◄ **Literacy Center Kit, Cards 86–90**
◄ **Sound/Spelling Card**
- Fluency Builders
◄ **Photo Cards**
- Read-Aloud Anthology, p. 68

## ✅ ASSESSMENT

✔ **Weekly Lesson Tests**
- Comprehension
- Phonics and Spelling
- Focus Skill
- Robust Vocabulary
- High-Frequency Words
- Grammar
- Fluency

 **www.harcourtschool.com/storytown**
- Online Assessment
*Also available on CD-ROM—ExamView®*

# Suggested Lesson Planner

## Step 1 | Whole Group

### Daily Language
- Oral Language
- High-Frequency Words
- Shared Reading
- Phonemic Awareness

### Word Work
-  phonics
- Spelling
- High-Frequency Words

### Skills and Strategies
- Reading
- Fluency
- Comprehension
- Build Robust Vocabulary

## Step 2 | Small Groups

## Step 3 | Whole Group

### Language Arts
- Grammar
- Writing

## Day 1

**QUESTION OF THE DAY,** p. T478
*What are some places you might go hiking?*

**READ ALOUD,** p. T478
*Big Book: We're Going on a Lion Hunt*

**WORD WALL,** p. T479

**PHONEMIC AWARENESS,** p. T479
Phoneme Blending

▲ Big Book

**phonics,** p. T480
Introduce: Long Vowel /ō/ow, oa

**SPELLING,** p. T483
Pretest: *low, slow, grow, road, soap, boat, little, handle, carry, would*

**HIGH-FREQUENCY WORDS,** p. T485
Review: *play, day, tree, onto, eat*

**READING,** p. T484
Get Started Story, "Shadow in the Snow"
Decodable Text
*Options for Reading*

▲ Student Edition

**FLUENCY,** p. T489
Reading Rate

**COMPREHENSION,** p. T490
Read-Aloud: "The Mitten"
Review: Author's Purpose/Point of View

**BUILD ROBUST VOCABULARY,** p. T491
Introduce: *bulged, jostled, argue*

**GRAMMAR,** p. T492
Introduce: Troublesome Words: Homophones

***Daily Proofreading***
Jess tossed a snowball at shadow (Jess, Shadow.)

 **MODELED WRITING,** p. T493
Introduce: Thank-You Letter
Writing Trait: Word Choice

**Writing Prompt** *Make a list of helpful things people have done for you.*

## Day 2

**QUESTION OF THE DAY,** p. T494
*What are some ways to play in snow?*

**SHARED READING,** p. T494
*Big Book of Rhymes and Poems,* "A Sound Riddle"

**WORD WALL,** p. T495

**PHONEMIC AWARENESS,** p. T495
Phoneme Substitution

**phonics,** p. T496
Review: Long Vowel /ō/ow, oa

**SPELLING,** p. T496
Word Building

**HIGH-FREQUENCY WORDS**
Words to Know, p. T500
Introduce: *mouse, our, over, pretty, surprise, three*

**READING,** p. T502
"Snow Surprise"
*Options for Reading*

**COMPREHENSION,** pp. T499, T502
Review: Author's Purpose/Point of View
Introduce: Make Inferences

▲ Student Edition

**RETELLING/FLUENCY,** p. T514
Reading Rate

**BUILD ROBUST VOCABULARY,** p. T515
Review: *bulged, jostled, argue*

### Suggestions for Differentiated Instruction *(See pp. T472–T473.)*

**GRAMMAR,** p. T516
Review: Troublesome Words: Homophones

***Daily Proofreading***
Would you like two eat now (to, now?)

 **SHARED WRITING,** p. T517
Review: Thank-You Letter
Writing Trait: Word Choice

**Writing Prompt** *Make a list of closings you can use to end your thank-you letter.*

 = **Focus Skill**      = **Focus Strategy**      = **Tested Skill**

**Skills at a Glance**

 **phonics**
Long Vowel /ō/ *ow*, *oa*
• Phonograms –*ow*, –*oat*, –*own*, –*oast*

**Comprehension**
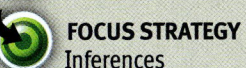 **FOCUS SKILL** Author's Purpose/Point of View
**FOCUS STRATEGY** Make Inferences

**Phonemic Awareness**
Phoneme Blending and Substitution
**Fluency**
Reading Rate

**Vocabulary**
**HIGH-FREQUENCY:** *mouse, our, over, pretty, surprise, three*
**ROBUST:** *bulged, jostled, argue, command, labored, wary*

## Day 3

**QUESTION OF THE DAY,** p. T518
*What does a snowball look like? What can you do with one?*

**SHARED READING,** p. T518
*Big Book of Rhymes and Poems,* "A Sound Riddle"

**WORD WALL,** p. T519

✓ **PHONEMIC AWARENESS,** p. T519
Phoneme Blending

✓  **phonics**, p. T520
Review: Long Vowel /ō/ *ow, oa*
Short Vowel /o/ *o*

✓ **SPELLING,** p. T521
State the Generalization

✓ **HIGH-FREQUENCY WORDS,** p. T522
Review: *mouse, our, over, pretty, surprise, three*

✓ **FLUENCY,** p. T523
Reading Rate: "Snow Surprise"

✓ **COMPREHENSION,** p. T524
Review: Author's Purpose/Point of View
Paired Selection: "The Snowflake Man"

**CONNECTIONS,** p. T528

✓ **BUILD ROBUST VOCABULARY,** p. T529
Introduce: *command, labored, wary*

## Day 4

**QUESTION OF THE DAY,** p. T532
*Have you heard a dog bark? What do you think a dog barks at?*

**SHARED READING,** p. T532
*Big Book of Rhymes and Poems,* "My Dog"

**WORD WALL,** p. T533

✓ **PHONEMIC AWARENESS,** p. T533
Phoneme Substitution

✓  **phonics**, p. T534
Introduce: Phonograms –*ow*, –*oat*
Review: Initial Blends with *l, s, r*

✓ **SPELLING,** p. T535
Review Spelling Words

✓ **HIGH-FREQUENCY WORDS,** p. T536
Review: *mouse, our, over, pretty, surprise, three*

✓ **FLUENCY,** p. T537
Reading Rate: "Snow Surprise"

✓ **COMPREHENSION,** p. T538
Review: Author's Purpose/Point of View
*Big Book: We're Going on a Lion Hunt*

✓ **BUILD ROBUST VOCABULARY,** p. T539
Review: *command, labored, wary*

▲ Student Edition

## Day 5

**QUESTION OF THE DAY,** p. T542
*What things have you done just because you like to do them?*

**SHARED READING,** p. T542
*Big Book of Rhymes and Poems,* "My Dog"

**WORD WALL,** p. T543

✓ **PHONEMIC AWARENESS,** p. T543
Phoneme Blending

✓  **phonics**, p. T544
Review: Phonograms –*own*, –*oast*

✓ **SPELLING,** p. T545
Posttest

✓ **HIGH-FREQUENCY WORDS,** p. T546
Review: *mouse, our, over, pretty, surprise, three*

✓ **FLUENCY,** p. T547
Reading Rate: "Snow Surprise"

✓ **COMPREHENSION,** p. T548
Review: Author's Purpose/Point of View

✓ **BUILD ROBUST VOCABULARY,** p. T549
Review

▲ Student Edition

---

 **BELOW-LEVEL**  **ON-LEVEL**  **ADVANCED**

---

✓ **GRAMMAR,** p. T530
Review: Troublesome Words: Homophones

*Daily Proofreading*
i one the contest! (I, won)

 **SHARED WRITING,** p. T531
Review: Thank-You Letter
Writing Trait: Word Choice

**Writing Prompt** *Write a list of things for which you would like to thank your parents.*

✓ **GRAMMAR,** p. T540
Review: Troublesome Words: Homophones

*Daily Proofreading*
We have to pup (two, pups.)

**INDEPENDENT WRITING,** p. T541
Review: Thank-You Letter
Writing Trait: Word Choice

**Writing Prompt** *Write about a gift you gave to someone.*

✓ **GRAMMAR,** p. T550
Review: Troublesome Words: Homophones

*Daily Proofreading*
Do you sea my backpack. (see, backpack?)

**INDEPENDENT WRITING,** p. T551
Review: Thank-You Letter
Writing Trait: Word Choice

**Writing Prompt** *Write a thank-you letter to a friend for being such a good friend.*

# Suggested Small Group Planner

45-60+ Minutes

## Day 1 | Day 2

### ● BELOW-LEVEL
15+ Min. each

**Day 1**

**Teacher-Directed**
*Student Edition:*
Get Started Story,
"Shadow in the Snow,"
p. T484

**Independent**
 Listening/Speaking Center, p. T476
Extra Support Copying Masters, p. 37

▲ Student Edition

**Day 2**

**Teacher-Directed**
*Student Edition:*
"Snow Surprise,"
p. T502

**Independent**
 Reading Center, p. T476
Extra Support Copying Masters, p. 39

▲ Student Edition

### ● ON-LEVEL
15+ Min. each

**Day 1**

**Teacher-Directed**
*Student Edition:*
Get Started Story,
"Shadow in the Snow,"
p. T484

**Independent**
 Reading Center, p. T476
Practice Book, p. 37

▲ Student Edition

**Day 2**

**Teacher-Directed**
*Student Edition:*
"Snow Surprise," p. T502

**Independent**
 Letters and Sounds
Center, p. T477
Practice Book, p. 39

▲ Student Edition

### ● ADVANCED
15+ Min. each

**Day 1**

**Teacher-Directed**
Leveled Reader:
"Boat Surprise," p. T554
Before Reading

**Independent**
 Letters and Sounds
Center, p. T477
Challenge Copying Masters, p. 37

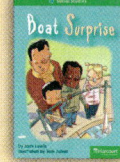 ▲ Leveled Reader

**Day 2**

**Teacher-Directed**
Leveled Reader:
"Boat Surprise," p. T554
Read the Book

**Independent**
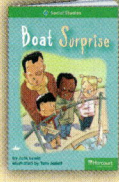 Word Work Center,
p. T477
Challenge Copying Masters, p. 39

▲ Leveled Reader

### ELL

**English-Language Learners**

*In addition to the small-group suggestions above, use the ELL Extra Support Kit to promote language development.*

**Day 1**

**LANGUAGE DEVELOPMENT SUPPORT**
**Teacher-Directed**
ELL TG, Day 1

**Independent**
ELL Copying Masters, Lesson 18

**Day 2**

**LANGUAGE DEVELOPMENT SUPPORT**
**Teacher-Directed**
ELL TG, Day 2

**Independent**
ELL Copying Masters, Lesson 18

### Intervention

 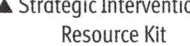 

▲ Strategic Intervention
Resource Kit

▲ Strategic Intervention
Interactive Reader

**Day 1**

Strategic Intervention TG, Day 1
Strategic Intervention Practice Book, Lesson 18

**Day 2**

Strategic Intervention TG, Day 2
Strategic Intervention
Interactive Reader, Lesson 18

▲ Strategic Intervention
Interactive Reader

 = Literacy Center Cards

| MONITOR PROGRESS Small-Group Instruction | Phonemic Awareness/ Phonics | High-Frequency Words | Fluency | Comprehension | Robust Vocabulary | Language Arts Checkpoint |
|---|---|---|---|---|---|---|
| | Long Vowel /ō/ow, oa p. S52 | *mouse*, *our*, *over*, *pretty*, *surprise*, *three* p. S53 | Reading Rate pp. S54–S55 | Focus Skill Author's Purpose/Point of View pp. S56–S57 | *pleased*, *joy*, *stammered*, *puzzling*, *probing*, *unrelenting* pp. S58–S59 | **Grammar:** Troublesome Words: Homophones **Writing:** Thank-You Letter pp. S60–S61 |

# Day 3

**Teacher-Directed**
Leveled Reader:
"Muffin Surprise," p. T552
Before Reading; Read the Book

**Independent**
⭐ Word Work Center, p. T477
Extra Support Copying Masters, p. 40

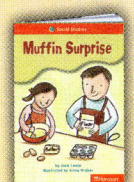
▲ Leveled Reader

**Teacher-Directed**
Leveled Reader:
"Sand Surprise," p. T553
Before Reading; Read the Book

**Independent**
⭐ Writing Center, p. T477
Practice Book, p. 40

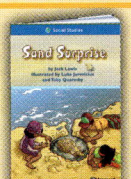
▲ Leveled Reader

**Teacher-Directed**
Leveled Reader:
"Boat Surprise," p. T554
Think Critically

**Independent**
⭐ Listening/Speaking Center, p. T476
Challenge Copying Masters, p. 40

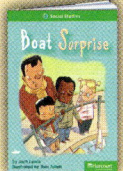
▲ Leveled Reader

**LANGUAGE DEVELOPMENT SUPPORT**
**Teacher-Directed**
Leveled Reader:
"Snow Play," T555
Before Reading; Read the Book
ELL TG, Day 3

**Independent**
ELL Copying Masters, Lesson 18

▲ Leveled Reader

Strategic Intervention TG, Day 3
Strategic Intervention Interactive Reader, Lesson 18
Strategic Intervention Practice Book, Lesson 18

▲ Strategic Intervention Interactive Reader

# Day 4

**Teacher-Directed**
Leveled Reader:
"Muffin Surprise," p. T552
Reread for Fluency

**Independent**
⭐ Letters and Sounds Center, p. T477
Cut-Out/Fold-Up Book, Practice Book, pp. 55–56

▲ Leveled Reader

**Teacher-Directed**
Leveled Reader:
"Sand Surprise," p. T553
Reread for Fluency

**Independent**
⭐ Word Work Center, p. T477
Cut-Out/Fold-Up Book: Practice Book, pp. 55–56

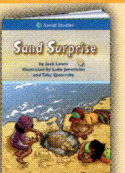
▲ Leveled Reader

**Teacher-Directed**
Leveled Reader:
"Boat Surprise," p. T554
Reread for Fluency
Self-Selected Reading: Classroom Library Collection

**Independent**
⭐ Writing Center, p. T477
Cut-Out/Fold-Up Book: Practice Book, pp. 55–56

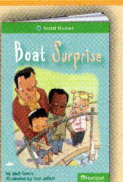

▲ Leveled Reader

**LANGUAGE DEVELOPMENT SUPPORT**
**Teacher-Directed**
Leveled Reader:
"Snow Play," T555
Reread for Fluency
ELL TG, Day 4

**Independent**
ELL Copying Masters, Lesson 18

▲ Leveled Reader

Strategic Intervention TG, Day 4
Strategic Intervention Interactive Reader, Lesson 18

▲ Strategic Intervention Interactive Reader

# Day 5

**Teacher-Directed**
Leveled Reader:
"Muffin Surprise," p. T552
Think Critically

**Independent**
⭐ Writing Center, p. T477
Leveled Reader: Reread for Fluency
Extra Support Copying Masters, p. 42

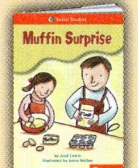
▲ Leveled Reader

**Teacher-Directed**
Leveled Reader:
"Sand Surprise," p. T553
Think Critically

**Independent**
⭐ Listening/Speaking Center, p. T476
Leveled Reader: Reread for Fluency
Practice Book, p. 42

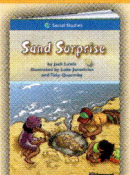
▲ Leveled Reader

**Teacher-Directed**
Leveled Reader:
"Boat Surprise," p. T554
Reread for Fluency
Self-Selected Reading: Classroom Library Collection

**Independent**
⭐ Reading Center, p. T476
Leveled Reader: Reread for Fluency
Challenge Copying Masters, p. 42

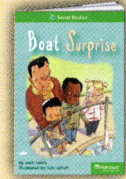
▲ Leveled Reader

**LANGUAGE DEVELOPMENT SUPPORT**
**Teacher-Directed**
Leveled Reader:
"Snow Play" p. T555
Think Critically
ELL TG, Day 5

**Independent**
Leveled Reader:
Reread for Fluency
ELL Copying Masters, Lesson 18

▲ Leveled Reader

Strategic Intervention TG, Day 5
Strategic Intervention Interactive Reader, Lesson 18

▲ Strategic Intervention Interactive Reader

# Leveled Readers & Leveled Practice
## *Reinforcing Skills and Strategies*

## LEVELED READERS SYSTEM

- **Leveled Readers**
- **Leveled Readers CD**
- **Leveled Reader Teacher Guides**
  - *Comprehension*
  - *High-Frequency Words*
  - *Oral Reading Fluency Assessment*
- **Response Activities**
- **Leveled Readers Assessment**

See pages T552–T555 for lesson plans.

### BELOW-LEVEL

- **phonics** Long Vowel /ō/*ow, oa*
- High-Frequency Words: *mouse, our, over, pretty, surprise, three*
- Author's Purpose/Point of View

**LEVELED READER TEACHER GUIDE**

▲ High-Frequency Words, p. 5

▲ Comprehension, p. 6

### ON-LEVEL

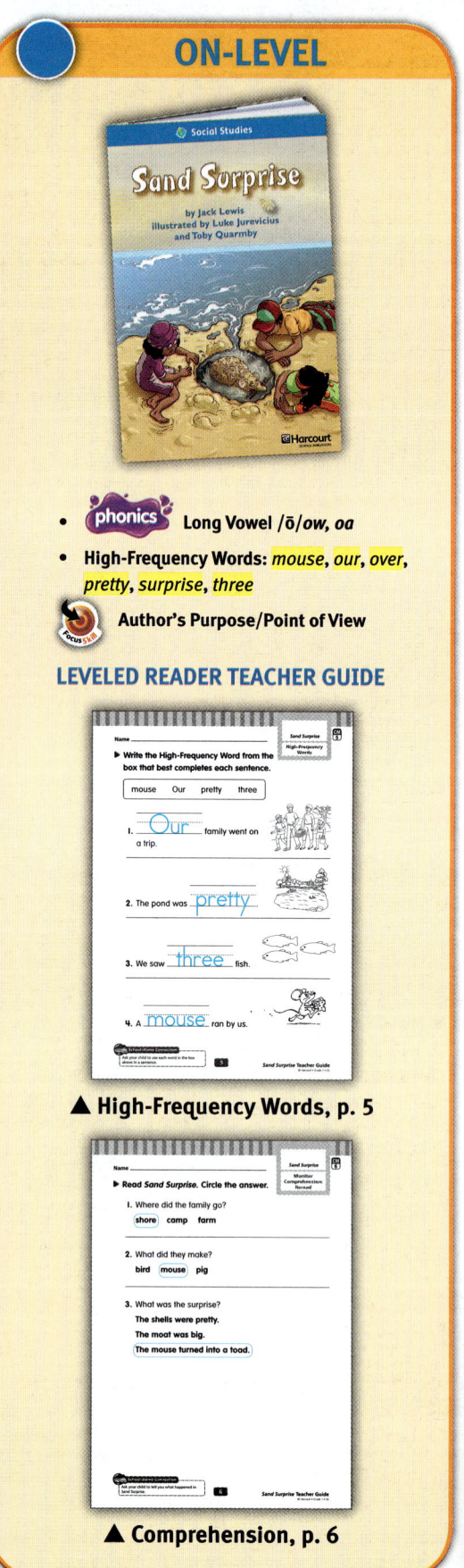

- **phonics** Long Vowel /ō/*ow, oa*
- High-Frequency Words: *mouse, our, over, pretty, surprise, three*
- Author's Purpose/Point of View

**LEVELED READER TEACHER GUIDE**

▲ High-Frequency Words, p. 5

▲ Comprehension, p. 6

## ADVANCED

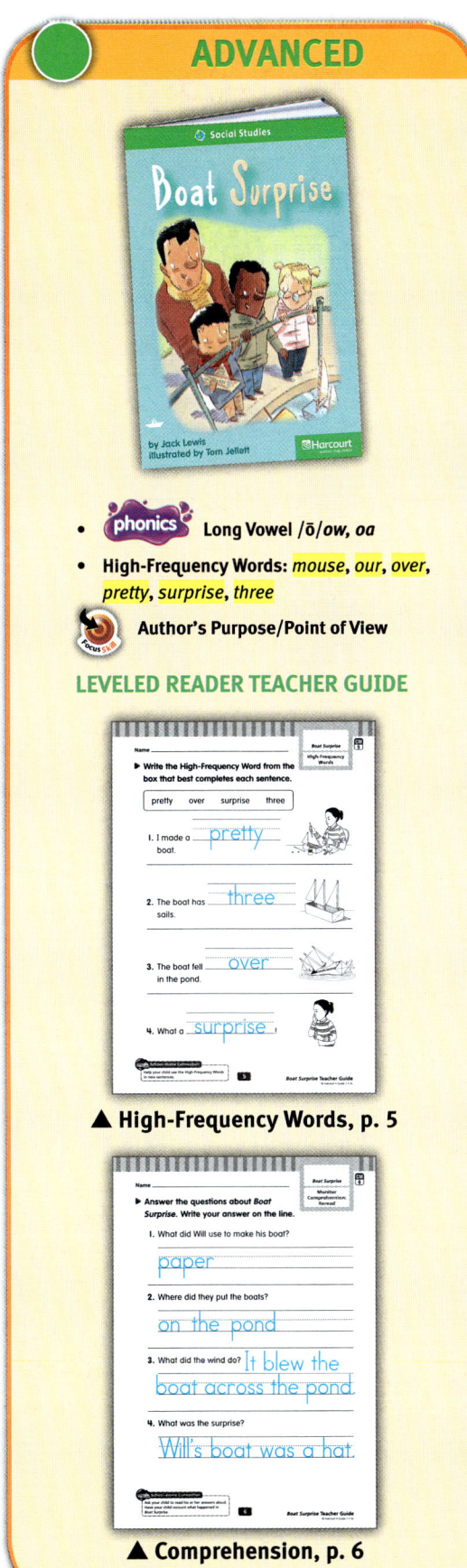

- **phonics** Long Vowel /ō/*ow*, *oa*
- **High-Frequency Words:** *mouse*, *our*, *over*, *pretty*, *surprise*, *three*
- Author's Purpose/Point of View

### LEVELED READER TEACHER GUIDE

▲ High-Frequency Words, p. 5

▲ Comprehension, p. 6

## E L L

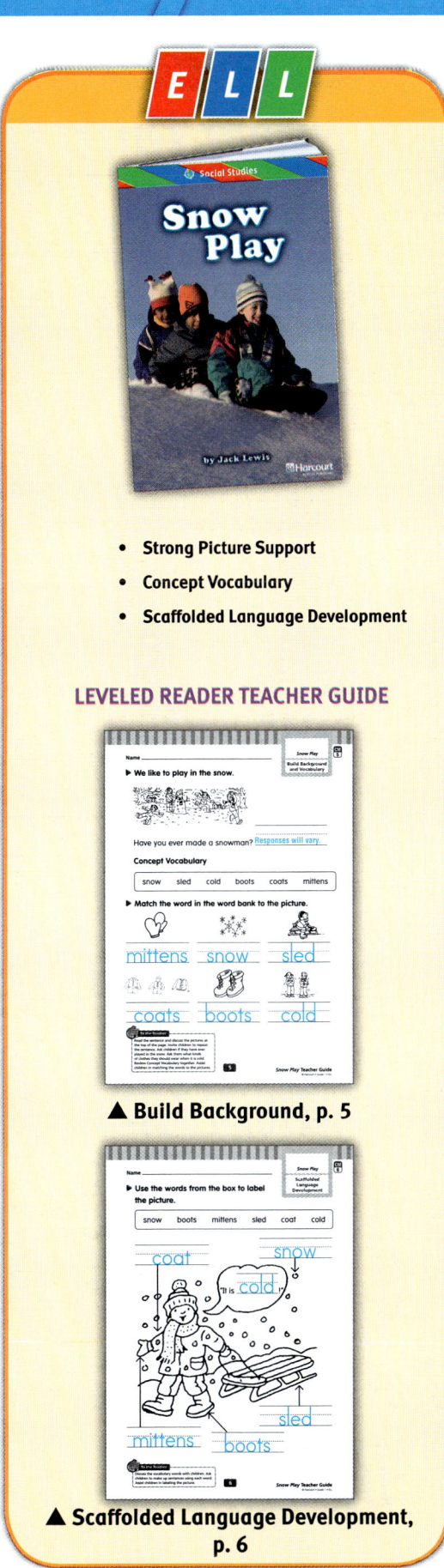

- **Strong Picture Support**
- **Concept Vocabulary**
- **Scaffolded Language Development**

### LEVELED READER TEACHER GUIDE

▲ Build Background, p. 5

▲ Scaffolded Language Development, p. 6

## CLASSROOM LIBRARY

### for Self-Selected Reading

**EASY**

▲ *Maxwell Mouse* by Sharon Gordon. **FANTASY**

**AVERAGE**

▲ *Hello, House!* by Linda Hayward. **FOLKTALE**

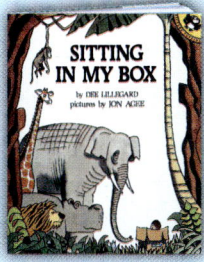

**AVERAGE**

▲ *Sitting in My Box* by Dee Lillegard. **FANTASY**

▲ Classroom Library Books Teacher Guide, pp. 16–19, 40–47

# Literacy Centers

*15 Min. each*

## Management Support

While you provide direct instruction to individuals or small groups, other children can work on literacy center activities.

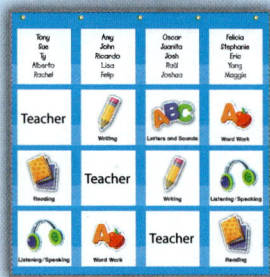

▲ **Literacy Centers Pocket Chart**

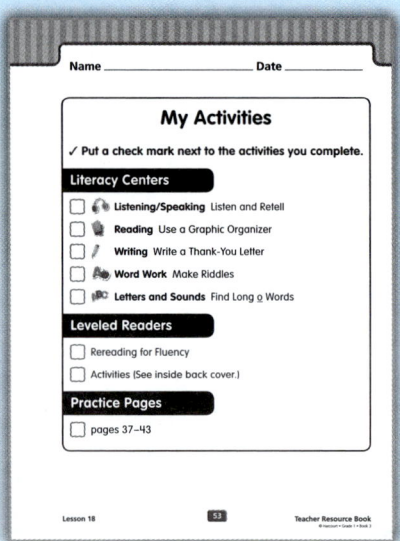

▲ **Teacher Resource Book, p. 53**

## Homework for the Week

**TEACHER RESOURCE BOOK, PAGE 22**

The *Homework Copying Master* provides activities to complete for each day of the week.

**www.harcourtschool.com/storytown**

---

### LISTENING/SPEAKING

## Listen and Retell

*Objectives* To listen to a story; to record details and retell a story

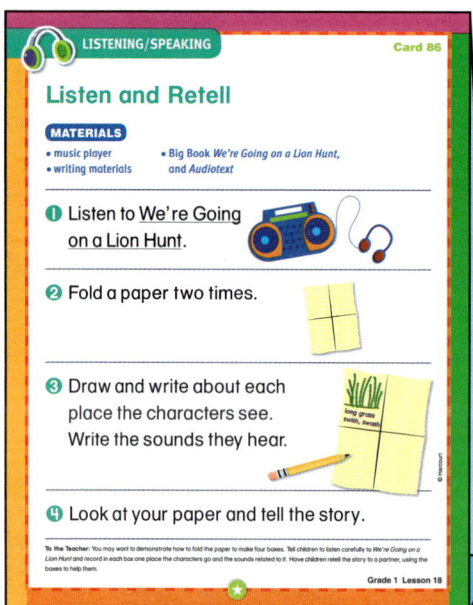

**LISTENING/SPEAKING** — Card 86

### Listen and Retell

**MATERIALS**
- music player
- writing materials
- Big Book *We're Going on a Lion Hunt*, and Audiotext

❶ Listen to We're Going on a Lion Hunt.

❷ Fold a paper two times.

❸ Draw and write about each place the characters see. Write the sounds they hear.

❹ Look at your paper and tell the story.

⭐ **Literacy Center Kit • Card 86**

---

### READING

## Use a Graphic Organizer

*Objective* To improve comprehension by reading a story and using a story map

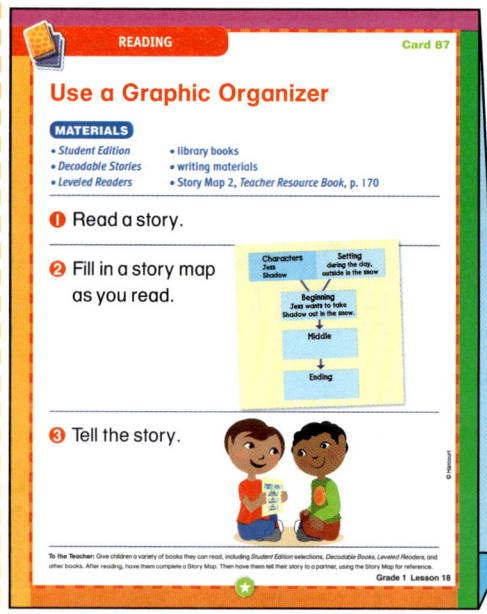

**READING** — Card 87

### Use a Graphic Organizer

**MATERIALS**
- Student Edition
- Decodable Stories
- Leveled Readers
- library books
- writing materials
- Story Map 2, Teacher Resource Book, p. 170

❶ Read a story.

❷ Fill in a story map as you read.

❸ Tell the story.

⭐ **Literacy Center Kit • Card 87**

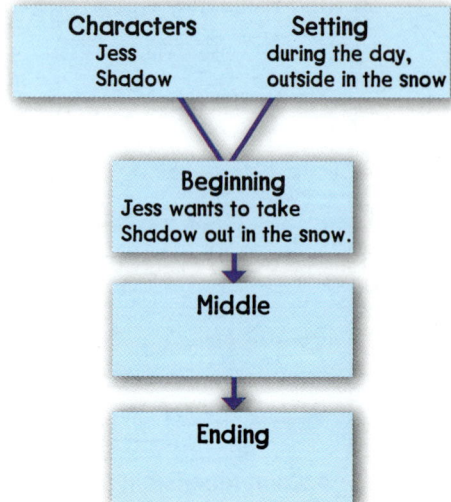

| Characters | Setting |
|---|---|
| Jess Shadow | during the day, outside in the snow |

**Beginning**
Jess wants to take Shadow out in the snow.

**Middle**

**Ending**

## WRITING

# Write a Thank-You Letter

**Objective** To write a thank-you letter to a person who was helpful

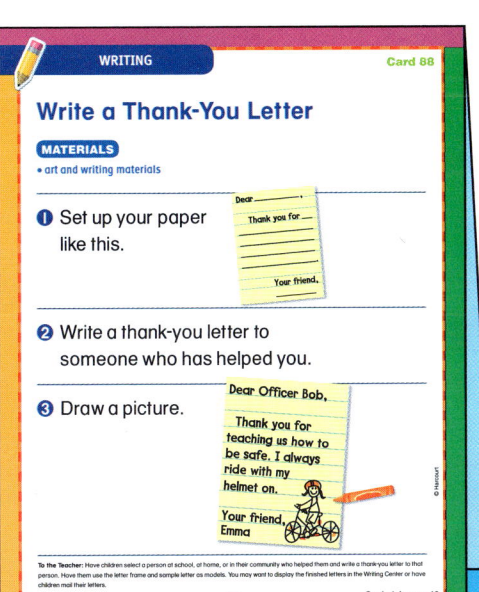

⭐ **Literacy Center Kit • Card 88**

## WORD WORK

# Make Riddles

**Objective** To create riddles for high-frequency words

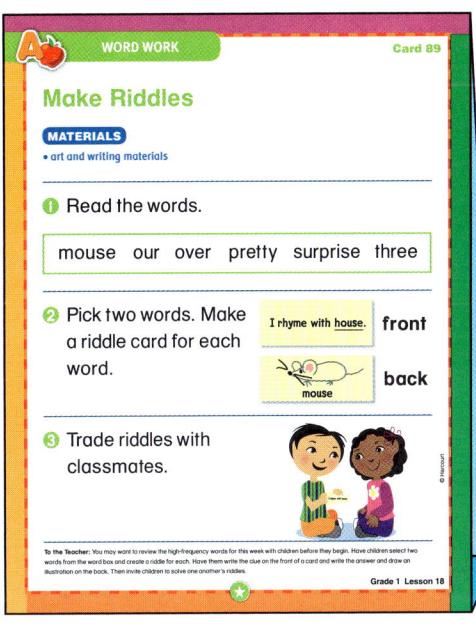

⭐ **Literacy Center Kit • Card 89**

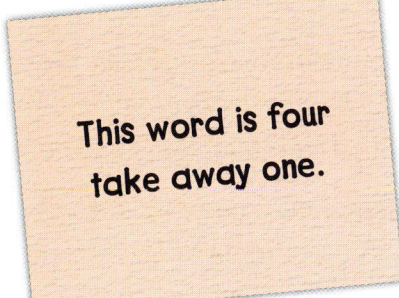

## LETTERS AND SOUNDS

# Find Long o Words

**Objective** To identify and sort long o words spelled with oa, ow

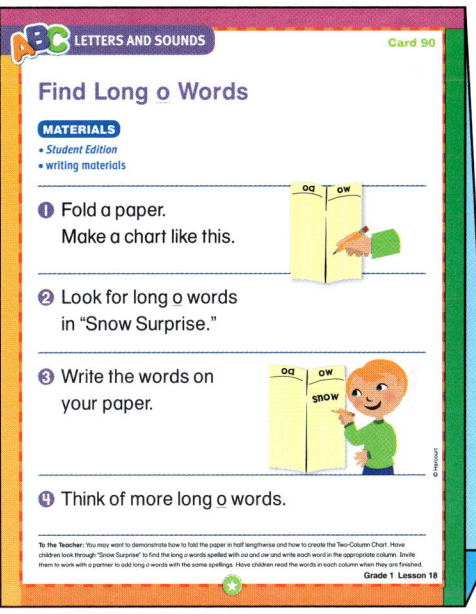

⭐ **Literacy Center Kit • Card 90**

# Warm-Up Routines

## Day at a Glance

### Day 1

**Phonemic Awareness**
- Phoneme Blending

 **phonics and Spelling**
- Introduce: Long Vowel /ō/ *ow*, *oa*
- Pretest

**Reading**

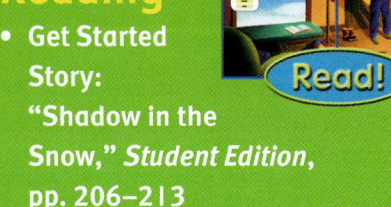

- Get Started Story: "Shadow in the Snow," *Student Edition*, pp. 206–213

**Comprehension**
- *Read-Aloud Anthology:* "The Mitten"

 Review: Author's Purpose/ Point of View

**Fluency**
- Reading Rate

**Robust Vocabulary**
- Introduce: *argue, bulged, jostled*

**Grammar**
- Introduce: Troublesome Words: Homophones

**Modeled Writing**
- Thank-You Letter

---

## Oral Language

**Objective** *To listen attentively and respond appropriately to oral communication*

### Question of the Day

**Where are some places you might go hiking?**

Write the following sentence frame and help children complete it. Then have children practice choral-reading the responses fluently with you.

**I went _____ on my hike.**

## Read Aloud

**Objectives** *To listen for a purpose; to respond to literature through drama*

 **Routine Card 17**

**BIG BOOK** Help children identify the story title, and the name of the author and illustrator. Ask children to explain their roles.

- **Set a purpose and read.** Teach children direction words such as *over*, *under*, *around*, and *through*. Ask children to listen for these words as you read.

- **Respond.** After you read, lead children to respond through drama in a way that reflects understanding and interpretation. Have them show how they would move through each place.

▲ Big Book *We're Going on a Lion Hunt*

# Word Wall

**Objective** *To read high-frequency words*

**REVIEW HIGH-FREQUENCY WORDS** Review *carry, would, play, day, tree, onto, eat,* and other previously learned high-frequency words. Say each word, ask a volunteer to point to it, and have children read it aloud. Then point to words at random, and have children reread them. Repeat several times.

| carry | would | play | day |
|-------|-------|------|-----|

| tree | onto | eat |
|------|------|-----|

# Phonemic Awareness

**Objective** *To blend phonemes to say words*

**Routine Card 1**

**PHONEME BLENDING** Tell children that you are going to say a word very slowly. Challenge them to guess the word and say it naturally. Model by slowly saying: /k/ /ō/ /t/, **coat.** Slowly say the following phonemes and have children blend the sounds to say the word.

/s/ /ō/ /k/ (soak)   /l/ /ō/ (low)   /k/ /u/ /t/ (cut)

/k/ /a/ /p/ (cap)   /s/ /ā/ /l/ (sail)   /s/ /l/ /e/ /d/ (sled)

/s/ /n/ /ō/ (snow)   /f/ /l/ /ō/ /t/ (float)

/h/ /i/ /l/ (hill)   /h/ /o/ /t/ (hot)

/d/ /ē/ /p/ (deep)   /ī/ /s/ (ice)

 **Podcasting: Phoneme Blending**

# Long Vowel /ō/ *ow, oa*

 **phonics** *and Spelling*

## Objectives

- *To recognize and generate the sound of /ō/*
- *To build and blend words with /ō/ow, oa and other known letter-sounds*
- *To use /ō/ow, oa and other known letter-sounds to spell words*

## Skill Trace

**Tested** ✓ **Long Vowel /ō/ *ow, oa***

| | |
|---|---|
| **Introduce** | **T480–T483** |
| Reteach | S52 |
| Review | T496–T498, T520–T521, T535 |
| Test | Bk 1-3 |
| Maintain | Bk 1-4, T76–T77; Bk 1-5, T436–T437 |

Refer to *Sounds of Letters CD* Track 17 for pronunciation of /ō/.

float

## Connecting Letter to Sound

**Routine Card 12** **DEVELOP PHONEMIC AWARENESS OF /ō/** Say the word *oats*. Have children say the word. Repeat with *bowl* and *snow*. Say: **The words *oats*, *bowl*, and *snow* all have /ō/, the long o sound.** Have children say /ō/.

**CONNECT LETTER AND SOUND** Display *Sound/ Spelling Card Oo*. Say the letter name. Explain that two letters can work together to stand for one sound. In the word *oats*, the letters o and *a* stand for /ō/. In *snow*, the letters o and *w* stand for the long o sound.

**DISCRIMINATE /ō/** Say: **When I say a word that begins with /ō/, form an *o* with your thumb and index finger. When I say a word that does not begin with /ō/, keep your hand on your desk.** Say these words:

oak    oat    rod    cot    own    fall    coat

Tell children that some words have the sound /ō/ in the middle. Say *boat*, elongating the /ō/ sound. Tell children that *boat* has /ō/ in the middle. Then say the following words, elongating the medial sound and having children name that sound.

toad    lot    float    hall    load    coach

▲ Sound/Spelling Card 39

oa__
__ow
o__e
o

## Word Blending

**DIBELS** Nonsense Word Fluency **NWF**

**WORDS WITH /ō/ow, oa** Demonstrate each step with *Letter Cards* and a pocket chart. Have children repeat each step after you, using their *Word Builder Cards* and *Word Builders*.

**Routine Card 13** **BLEND AND READ** *goat* Hold up *c* and say /k/. Hold up *o* and say /o/. Hold up *t* and say /t/. Read the word *cot*. Now add an *a* after the *o*. Blend and read the word /kōt/—*coat*. Remind children that the letters *o* and *a* work together to spell one sound—/ō/.

- Then place the letters *g, o, a, t* in the pocket chart. Have children do the same with their letters and *Word Builders*.

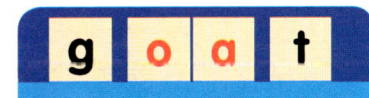

- Point to *g* and say /g/. Point to *oa* and say /ō/. Point to *t* and say /t/. Prompt children to repeat after you.

- Slide *g* and *oa* together. Run your hand under the letters as you blend the sounds, elongating the long o sound—/gō/. Have children repeat.

- Slide *t* next to *goa*. Run your hand under *goat* as you blend the sounds. Emphasize the long vowel sound: /gōt/. Have children repeat.

- Read *goat* naturally. Repeat, having children read the word with you.

Follow the same procedures for *roam, coal, row,* and *crow.*

### Professional Development

 **Podcasting:** Word Building, Gr. 1

**E L L**

**Support Word Meaning** Use *Photo Cards* to support word meaning. For example, as children blend *coat*, display the *Photo Card* for *coat*.

coat

▲ Photo Card 38

### ● BELOW-LEVEL

**Sort Words with /ō/ and /o/** Write the following words on cards and have children sort them by vowel sound: *flow, soak, flop, coach, show, float, not, glow, pop.* Have children name the letters that spell /ō/ in the long o words.

| flow | soak | coach |
|---|---|---|
| show | float | glow |

# Long Vowel /ō/ ow, oa

 **phonics** *and Spelling*

## Word Building

**Routine Card 14** **BUILD SPELLING WORDS** Use *Letter Cards* and a pocket chart. Have children use their *Word Builder Cards* and *Word Builders*.

Place the *Letter Cards l, o,* and *w* in the pocket chart. Then read the word naturally—*low*.

Have children build and read new words. As they build each word, write it on the board. Say:

- **Add *s* before *l*. What word is it?**
- **Change *sl* to *gr*. What word is it?**
- **Take away *g*. Change *ow* to *oa*. Add *d* on the end. What word is it?**

Continue in a similar manner to build and read *soap* and *boat*. Then have children read the words on the board.

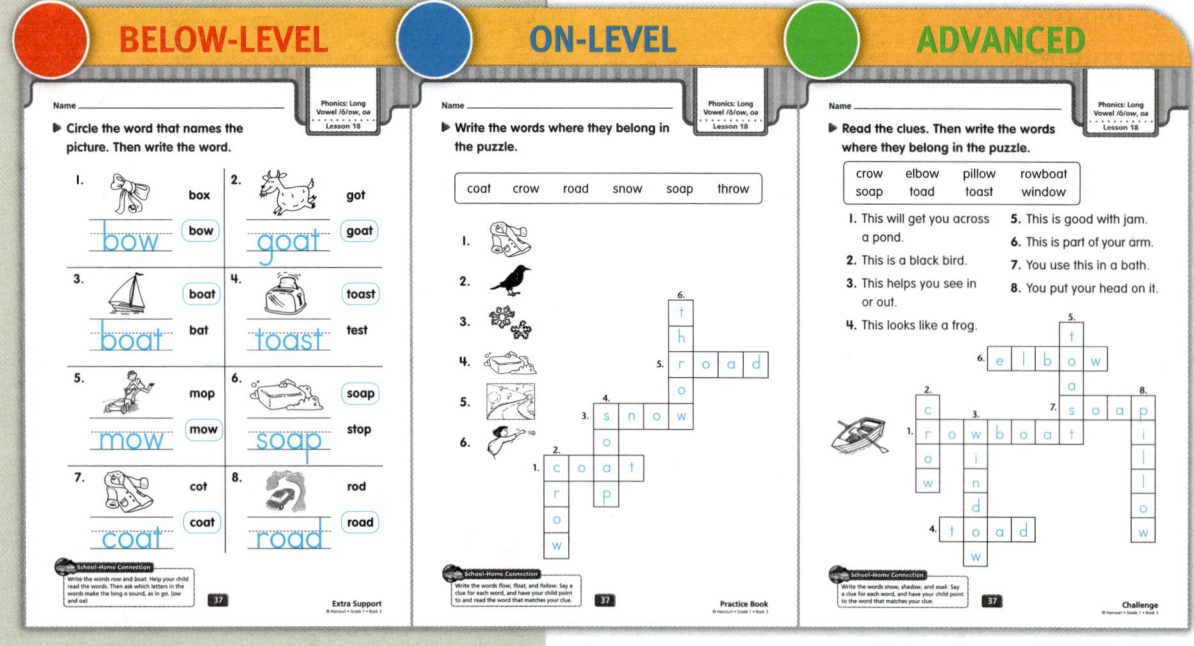

▲ Extra Support, p. 37    ▲ Practice Book, p. 37    ▲ Challenge, p. 37

**ELL**

- Group children according to academic levels, and assign one of the pages on the left.

- Clarify any unfamiliar concepts as necessary. See *ELL Teacher Guide,* Lesson 18, for support in scaffolding instruction.

**5-DAY SPELLING**

| DAY 1 | Pretest |
|---|---|
| DAY 2 | Word Building |
| DAY 3 | State the Generalization |
| DAY 4 | Review |
| DAY 5 | Posttest |

## Introduce Spelling Words

**PRETEST** Say the first word and read the dictation sentence. Repeat the word as children write it. Write the word on the board and have children check their spelling. Tell them to circle the word if they spelled it correctly or write it correctly if they did not. Repeat for words 2–10.

### Words with /ō/*ow, oa*

1. low    The pup easily hopped over the **low** fence.

2. slow    I was too **slow** to win the race.

3. grow    We **grow** flowers in our garden.

4. road    The big trucks roared down the busy **road.**

5. soap    Use lots of **soap** when you wash your hands.

6. boat    We sailed around the lake in our **boat.**

### Review

7. little    A newborn kitten is very **little.**

8. handle    Always hold the pitcher by its **handle.**

### High-Frequency

9. carry    Jack will **carry** his lunch in his backpack.

10. would    What **would** you like to do today?

### Spelling Words

| | |
|---|---|
| 1. **low** | 6. **boat** |
| 2. **slow** | 7. **little** |
| 3. **grow** | 8. **handle** |
| 4. **road** | 9. **carry** |
| 5. **soap** | 10. **would** |

---

## ✓ MONITOR PROGRESS

### Phonics: Long Vowel /ō/*ow, oa*

**IF** children have difficulty building and reading words with /ō/*ow, oa,*

**THEN** help them blend and read the words *blow, own, toad,* and *float* individually.

### Small-Group Instruction, p. S52:

● **BELOW-LEVEL:** Reteach    ● **ON-LEVEL:** Reinforce    ● **ADVANCED:** Extend

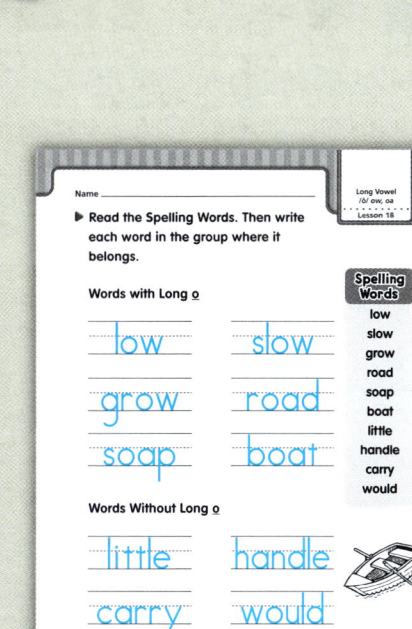

▲ Practice Book, p. 38

# Reading

*Get Started Story:* **Shadow in the Snow**

## Objectives

- *To use letter-sound knowledge to read decodable text*
- *To develop fluency*
- *To review high-frequency words*

 **Podcasting:** Reading Decodable Text, Gr. I

## Options for Reading

 **BELOW-LEVEL**

**Echo-Reading** Have children echo-read each sentence. Pause to discuss it using the Monitor Comprehension questions. Have children frame and read long /ō/*ow, oa* words.

 **ON-LEVEL**

**Monitor Comprehension** Have children read the story aloud, page by page. Ask the Monitor Comprehension questions as you go. Then lead children in retelling the story and describing their favorite parts.

 **ADVANCED**

**Independent Reading** Have children read each page silently, looking up each time they finish a page. Ask the Monitor Comprehension questions as you go; then lead them in a discussion about what things they think are funny in the story.

### Apply Long Vowel /ō/*ow, oa*

**READ DECODABLE TEXT** Write the following sentences on the board. Tell children they will read a story about a girl and her dog Shadow.

**Shadow follows Jess.**

**Shadow spots a black crow.**

- Have children read the first sentence as you track the print.
- Have children frame and read the long *o* words.
- Tell children that many words in the story have the long *o* sound.

**Routine Card 17** **INTRODUCE THE STORY** Have children look at the first page and read aloud the title. Ask children to point to the names of the author and illustrator as you read them aloud. Review that the author writes the story and the illustrator draws the pictures. Tell children they will read to find out what a girl and her dog do.

**Preview** Preview the story with a picture walk. Use the illustrations to develop meaning for the text. Then guide children through the story, using the Monitor Comprehension questions.

**Get Started Story**

**Phonics**
Words with <u>ow</u> and <u>oa</u>

**Words to Know**

**Review**

play

day

tree

onto

eat

## Shadow in the Snow

by Nancy Furstinger
illustrated by Jesse Reisch

206

207

"Follow me, Shadow,"
yells Jess. "Let's play
in the snow!"

# Monitor Comprehension

**PAGES 206–207** Have children look at the title page and the first page of the story. Say: **It looks cold outside. What do you think the girl is doing? Let's read to find out.**

**1** **NOTE DETAILS** What does Jess want to do? (go outside and play in the snow)

**2** **APPLY PHONICS** What is the dog's name? (Shadow) **Read the sentence that tells.**

**E L L**

**Context Clues** Model how to use the illustrations to find meanings of unfamiliar nouns, such as *crow, squirrels, rowboat,* and *sled.*

**TECHNOLOGY**

 **eBook** "Shadow in the Snow" is available in an eBook.

 **Audiotext** "Shadow in the Snow" is available on *Audiotext Grade 1,* CD 6 for subsequent readings.

"Look at that black crow," Jess grins. "He soaks up sun and sings all **day**."

A rabbit rests by an oak **tree**. Shadow sniffs the snow. He thinks he is on a hunt.

208

209

# Monitor Comprehension

**PAGES 208–209** Say: **I see Jess and Shadow outside in the snow. Let's read to find out what they will do.**

1 **MAKE INFERENCES** **How do you think it feels outside in the snow?** (It is cold.) **How do you know?** (Jess is wearing warm clothes. Snow only falls when the weather is cold.)

2 **RELATE PICTURES TO TEXT** **Whose tracks is Shadow sniffing?** (the rabbit's tracks)

A rowboat sits on a pond. "In spring, we'll row that boat on the water," Jess tells Shadow.

Jess tucks her chin under her yellow coat. Snow blows off a branch and <mark>onto</mark> her hat. "Shadow!" she calls.

210

211

# Monitor Comprehension

**PAGES 210–211 Say: It looks like Jess and Shadow are having fun. Let's read to find out what they are doing.**

**1** **MAKE INFERENCES** **Why does Jess tuck her chin under her coat?** (to keep warm)

**2** **DRAW CONCLUSIONS** **Why can't Jess and Shadow row the rowboat?** (The pond is frozen.)

**3** **MAKE PREDICTIONS** **What do you think Jess and Shadow will do next?** (Responses will vary.)

## STRATEGIC READING

**Words with /ō/ow, oa** Remind children that the letter pairs *ow* and *oa* both stand for the same sound, /ō/, the long *o* sound. Have children locate and read long *o* words with each spelling on the pages.

Jess zips along a hilltop on her sled.
Shadow runs with Jess.

212

"Let's have a snack, Shadow. I will eat an apple muffin, and you can drink a bowl of milk. Then let's go back and play in the snow!"

213

# Monitor Comprehension

**PAGES 212–213** Have children look at the illustrations. Ask: **Do you think Jess and Shadow are still having fun in the snow? Let's read to find out.**

**1** **DRAW CONCLUSIONS** **Do Jess and Shadow like playing in the snow? How do you know?** (Yes; they both look happy; they will go back outside after their snack.)

**2** **PERSONAL RESPONSE** **Would you enjoy spending time in the snow with Jess and Shadow? Why or why not?** (Responses will vary.)

## HIGH-FREQUENCY WORDS

**Review** Remind children that there are some words they have to remember because they have not learned all of the letter-sounds yet. Have children find, frame, and read the words *go, have,* and *of* on page 213.

# Check Comprehension

*Retelling*

## Retell

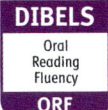
**DIBELS** Oral Reading Fluency **ORF**

**RETELL "SHADOW IN THE SNOW"** Ask children to name the characters in "Shadow in the Snow." Then have volunteers tell what happens in the beginning, middle, and end of the story. Write their responses in a chart such as the one below.

| Beginning | Middle | Ending |
|---|---|---|
| Jess sees snow and wakes Shadow. | Jess and Shadow see a crow, a rabbit, and a rowboat. Jess has fun riding on a sled while Shadow follows. | Jess and Shadow go inside for a snack. |

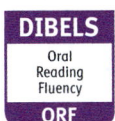

# Fluency

*Reading Rate*

## Repeated Reading

**DIBELS** Oral Reading Fluency **ORF**

**READ WITH A PARTNER** Have partners reread "Shadow in the Snow" three or four times. Suggest that they read one page at a time and try to increase their reading rate each time. Readers should pay attention to the words and try to read each one correctly without pausing to sound them out. Listeners should follow along and make sure the reader does not skip, add, or misread words. Visit partners and listen to them read. Give children feedback about reading at an appropriate rate with accuracy. Guide them to improve their fluency.

## Objectives
- *To practice retelling a story*
- *To read fluently in a manner that sounds like natural speech*

### RETELLING RUBRIC

| | |
|---|---|
| 4 | Uses details to clearly retell the story |
| 3 | Uses some details to retell the story |
| 2 | Retells the story with some inaccuracies |
| 1 | Is unable to retell the story |

## Professional Development

**Podcasting:** Auditory Modeling

# Comprehension
## *Read Aloud*

### Objective
- *To understand characteristics of a folktale*

### Daily Comprehension
 **Author's Purpose/ Point of View**

| | |
|---|---|
| **DAY 1:** | Review Author's Purpose/ Point of View *Read-Aloud Anthology* |
| **DAY 2:** | Review Author's Purpose/Point of View *Student Edition* |
| **DAY 3:** | Review Author's Purpose/ Point of View *Paired Selection Student Edition* |
| **DAY 4:** | Review Author's Purpose/ Point of View *Big Book* |
| **DAY 5:** | Review Author's Purpose/ Point of View *Comparing Texts* |

**E L L**

**Vocabulary** To make sure children understand the humor, before reading, show pictures of the animals that appear in the story. If any of the animals are unfamiliar to the children, explain and then talk about the size of each animal.

---

### Before Reading

**CONNECT TO PRIOR KNOWLEDGE** Tell children they will be listening to an old story called a **folktale**. This folktale starts out like a true story but then gets sillier and sillier. The story is about animals who curl up in a mitten to keep warm. Ask children to name animals that could fit in a mitten and animals that could not.

▲ Read-Aloud Anthology, "The Mitten," p. 68

**GENRE STUDY: FOLKTALE** Explain that "The Mitten" is a kind of story called a folktale. Say:

> **Think Aloud** **A folktale is an old story that people have told each other over and over again. The author liked the story, so she made it into a book. As in many folktales, the animals in this story can talk.**

 **REVIEW THE SKILL: AUTHOR'S PURPOSE/POINT OF VIEW** Remind children that authors write because they have ideas to share. Say: **Sometimes authors write to entertain the reader, and sometimes they write to inform, or help readers learn. The reason for writing is called the author's purpose. Authors also have a point of view, or how they feel about an idea.** Tell children that they will be discussing the author's purpose and point of view for "The Mitten" later in the week. Then read the story to them.

### After Reading

**RESPOND** Have children tell which parts of the story could really happen and which parts could not.

 # Build Robust Vocabulary

## Listening/Speaking: *Words from the Read-Aloud*

### Teach/Model

**Routine Card 15** **INTRODUCE ROBUST VOCABULARY** Use *Routine Card 15* to introduce the words.

❶ Put the word in **selection context**.
❷ Provide the **Student-Friendly Explanation** for children.
❸ Have children **say the word** with you.
❹ Use the word in other contexts, and have children **interact with the word's meaning**.
❺ Say the Student-Friendly Explanation again, and ask children to **name the word** that goes with it.

❶ **Selection Context:** When the mitten was empty, it was flat, but when the animals crawled inside, it **bulged**.
❹ **Interact with Word Meaning:** My suitcase bulged when I put too much in it. When your backpack bulged, what was inside?

❶ **Selection Context:** The hedgehog **jostled** the mole and rabbit to make room for itself in the mitten.
❹ **Interact with Word Meaning:** When might you need to jostle someone to make them move over and give you some space?

❶ **Selection Context:** The animals did not **argue** when the bear came in because they did not want to make him mad.
❹ **Interact with Word Meaning:** If you said it was snowing when it was really warm and sunny, your classmates might argue with you. What else do people argue about?

### Practice/Apply

**GUIDED PRACTICE** Ask children to do the following:
• Close your mouth and make your cheeks bulge.
• Show how you might gently jostle people on a crowded bus as you walk up the aisle.
• Show a partner how you look when you argue.

### Objective
• *To develop robust vocabulary through discussing a literature selection*

 **Tested**

### Student-Friendly Explanations

**bulged** If a container bulged, its sides stuck out as if it were going to burst.

**jostled** When you have jostled people, you have bumped them or poked them to make them move.

**argue** When you argue with someone, you disagree loudly.

 **E L L**

**Introduce Vocabulary** Help children understand the meaning of *bulged* by stuffing a toy into a mitten and having children guess what is inside. Guide children to understand that the mitten only bulged after the large object was placed inside.

# Grammar

## Troublesome Words: Homophones

**5-DAY GRAMMAR**

**DAY 1** Introduce Homophones
**DAY 2** Use a Literature Model
**DAY 3** Recognize Incorrect Homophones
**DAY 4** Identify Homophones
**DAY 5** Write Sentences with Homophones

### Objective
- *To identify homophones and use them correctly*

### Daily Proofreading

**jess tossed a snowball at shadow**

(Jess, Shadow.)

---

**Troublesome Words: Homophones**

Jack will _____ the tickets.
    by    buy

My dog ran _____ with a stick.
    by    buy

I _____ my friend Pam well.
no    know

We went _____ the park.
    to    too

Ming wants a sticker, _____.
        to    too

I use _____ hands to catch the ball.
   to  two  too

Grade 1, Lesson 18    **LA35**    Grammar: Troublesome Words: Homophones

**Transparency LA35**

---

### Teach/Model

**INTRODUCE THE CONCEPT** Write the following sentences on the board. Read them aloud and then with children.

**I knew I would lose my new mitten.**
**When you write a letter, spell the words right.**

Ask which words sound alike in the first sentence. Underline *knew* and *new,* and explain that these words are called **homophones** because they sound alike but have different spellings and meanings. Follow the same procedure with *write* and *right.*

### Guided Practice

**IDENTIFY HOMOPHONES** Display **Transparency LA35.** Read aloud the sentences with children, tracking the print. Have volunteers circle the correct homophone to use in each sentence. Read each sentence as a group, and then have children spell the correct homophone.

### Practice/Apply

**WRITE SENTENCES WITH HOMOPHONES** Write on the board a pair of homophones, and have children dictate a sentence for each word. Track the print as you read the sentences aloud. Have children identify the homophones and tell what they mean. Underline the words and talk about the different spellings.

# Modeled Writing

*Thank-You Letter*

**5-DAY WRITING**

| DAY 1 | Modeled Writing |
|-------|-----------------|
| DAY 2 | Shared Writing |
| DAY 3 | Shared Writing |
| DAY 4 | Independent Writing |
| DAY 5 | Independent Writing |

## Teach/Model

**INTRODUCE THANK-YOU LETTERS** Remind children that they have learned how to write a friendly letter. Tell them that a thank-you letter is a special kind of friendly letter and has the same parts. Display **Transparency LA36,** read the letter to children, and talk about the parts. Together, develop a list of characteristics of a well-written thank-you letter.

### Thank-You Letter

- It is written to thank someone.
- The <u>heading</u> is the date.
- The <u>greeting</u> tells who gets the letter.
- The <u>body</u> is the message. It tells why you are thankful.
- The <u>closing</u> says good-bye.
- The <u>signature</u> is your name.

**WRITING TRAIT** **WORD CHOICE** Have children identify specific words that tell why the writer of the student model is thankful. Talk about other words children could use in thank-you letters.

## Guided Practice

**DRAFT A THANK-YOU LETTER** Model saying sentences about something you are thankful for, such as *Thank you for the pretty flowers. I feel happy every time I look at them!* Have children add sentences about being thankful.

## Practice/Apply

**PRACTICE SAYING THANK YOU** Have children draw a picture of a person giving them a gift or helping them. Ask partners to share their pictures and tell what they would say to thank the person. Save the pictures for Days 4–5.

### Objectives

- *To develop a list of criteria for writing a thank-you letter*
- *To generate ideas for writing*

### Writing Prompt

**Write a List** Have children begin a list of helpful things people have done for them that they could write a thank-you letter for.

**Student Model: Thank-You Letter**

November 15, 20—

Dear Pam,

Thank you for the yellow backpack you gave me for my birthday. It is the perfect gift. I will use it at school. I can fit my lunch and lots of books in it. It was nice of you to give it to me.

Your friend,
Tom

Grade 1, Lesson 18    LA36    Writing: Thank-You Letter

**Transparency LA36**

# Warm-Up Routines

## Day at a Glance

### Day 2

**Phonemic Awareness**
- Phoneme Substitution

 **phonics and Spelling**
- Review: Long Vowel /ō/ *ow, oa*
- Build Words

**Comprehension**
Review: Author's Purpose/Point of View

**High-Frequency Words**
- Introduce: mouse, our, over, pretty, surprise, three

**Reading**
- "Snow Surprise," *Student Edition,* pp. 218–239

**Fluency**
- Reading Rate

**Robust Vocabulary**
- Review: *argue, bulged, jostled*

**Grammar**
- Review: Troublesome Words: Homophones

**Shared Writing**
- Thank-You Letter

---

## Oral Language

**Objective** *To listen attentively and respond appropriately to oral communication*

### Question of the Day

**What are some ways to play in snow?**

Talk about snow and the effects of a big snowfall. Then help children brainstorm ways to enjoy snow. Have children complete the following sentence frame.

**I like to _____ in the snow.**

## Read Aloud

**Objective** *To listen for a purpose*

**BIG BOOK OF RHYMES AND POEMS** Display the poem and read the title and the poet's name. Explain that the poem is also a riddle. Ask children to listen attentively for clues that will help them answer the riddle. Then read the poem aloud, stopping just before the last line to allow volunteers to guess the answer. Then reread the poem for children to enjoy. Ask them what sound words they hear.

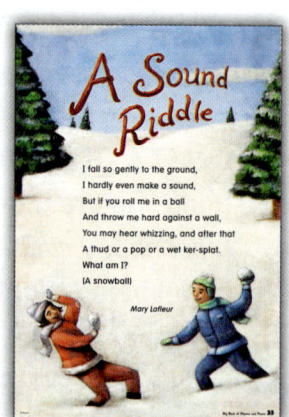

▲ **Big Book of Rhymes and Poems, p. 35**

## Word Wall

**Objective** *To read high-frequency words*

**REVIEW HIGH-FREQUENCY WORDS** Review *buy, carry, money, other, paint, paper, would,* and other previously learned high-frequency words. Say each word, ask a volunteer to point to it, and have children read it aloud. Then point to words at random, and have children reread them. Repeat several times to reinforce instant recognition.

| buy | carry | money | other |
|-----|-------|-------|-------|

| paint | paper | would |
|-------|-------|-------|

## Phonemic Awareness

**Objective** *To substitute phonemes to make new words*

**Routine Card 10** **PHONEME SUBSTITUTION** Tell children they are going to sing a song and substitute one sound for another to make a new word. Model the first one for them.

*(Sung to the tune of "Row, Row, Row Your Boat")*

***Mouse, mouse, mouse* is the word. Change /m/ to /h/. Now I have a new word, tell me what it is.** (house)

**snow, /n / to /l/** (slow)          **ran, /n/ to /t/** (rat)

**munch, /m/ to /l/** (lunch)          **road, /ō/ to /ī/** (ride)

**tap, /t/ to /k/** (cap)          **crow, /ō/ to /ī/** (cry)

**fell, /f/ to /y/** (yell)          **coat, /ō/ to /a/** (cat)

# Long Vowel /ō/ow, oa

 **phonics** *and Spelling*

## Objectives

- *To blend sounds into words*
- *To spell three- and four-letter long vowel words with /ō/ow, oa, and high-frequency words*

## Skill Trace

 **Tested** **Long Vowel /ō/ow, oa**

| | |
|---|---|
| Introduce | T480–T483 |
| Reteach | S52 |
| **Review** | **T496–T497, T520–T521** |
| Test | Bk 1-3 |
| Maintain | Bk 1-4, T76–T77 |
| | Bk 1-5, T436–T437 |

## Spelling Words

| | |
|---|---|
| 1. low | 6. boat |
| 2. slow | 7. little |
| 3. grow | 8. handle |
| 4. road | 9. carry |
| 5. soap | 10. would |

---

### Word Building

**DIBELS** Nonsense Word Fluency **NWF** | **Routine Card 14** | **BUILD AND READ A SPELLING WORD** Place the *Letter Cards l, o, w* in the pocket chart. Ask children to say the name of each letter and the sounds *l* and *ow* stand for. Then read the word naturally—*low*. Have children do the same.

**BUILD SPELLING WORDS** Ask children what letter you should add to turn *low* into *slow*. (Add *s* to the beginning.) Ask them which letters you should change to make *slow* become *grow*. (Change *sl* to *gr*.) Continue building spelling words 4–6 in this manner. Have children repeat each step after you and then read the words.

---

 **E L L**

**Build Spelling Words** Have children make up an action to show the meaning of each word. Children can place their hand near the ground for *low*, move in slow motion for *slow*, crouch down and then stand up for *grow*, pantomime driving for *road*, pantomime hand washing for *soap*, and move their hand up and down like a boat on waves for *boat*.

 **ADVANCED**

**Spelling Pattern** Point out that the *ow* spelling appears most often at the end of a word, while the *oa* spelling usually occurs in the middle. (Exceptions include *bowl* and *whoa*.) Have children work together to sort the spelling words according to their long *o* spelling and then list other words that follow the same pattern.

| 5-DAY PHONICS/SPELLING | |
|---|---|
| DAY 1 | Pretest |
| DAY 2 | Word Building |
| DAY 3 | State the Generalization |
| DAY 4 | Review |
| DAY 5 | Posttest |

## Read Words in Context

**APPLY PHONICS** Write the following sentences on the board or on chart paper. Have children read each sentence silently. Then track the print as children read the sentences aloud.

> **Low** plants **grow** next to the **road**.
>
> You must hold the **little** bag by its **handle**.
>
> Did you buy me a bar of **soap**?
>
> The big **boat** is **slow**.

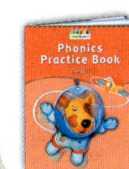

 **Resources**

**Phonics Practice Book, pp. 97–100**

**WRITE** Dictate several words from the pocket chart. Have children write the words on a dry-erase board or in their notebook.

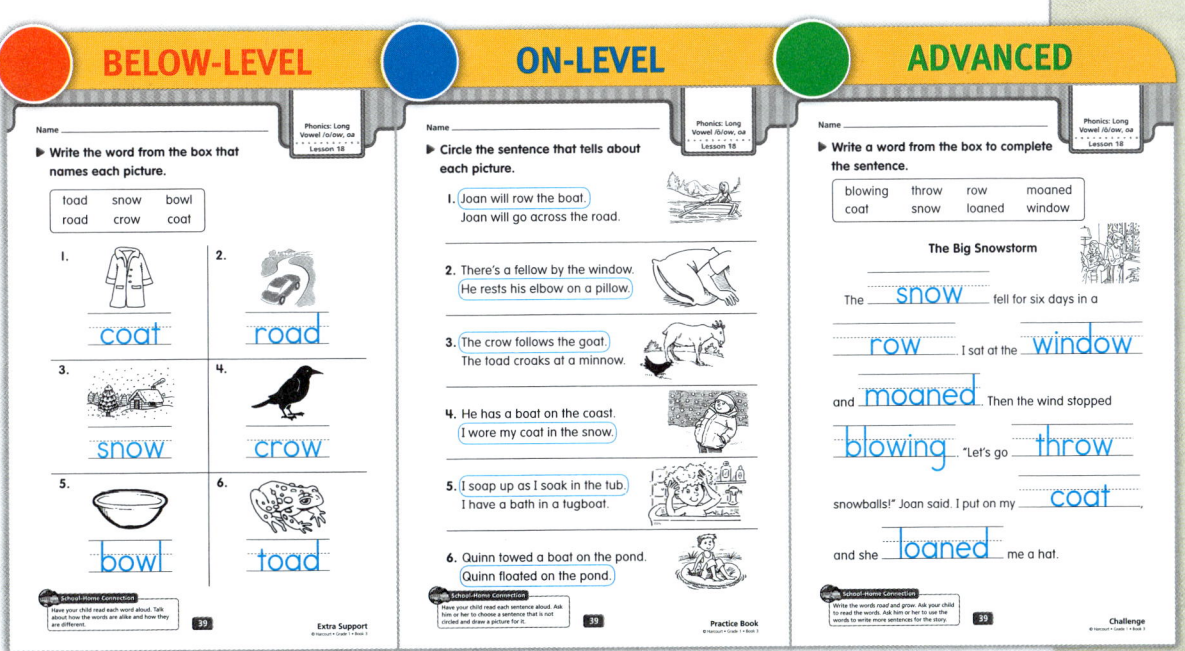

▲ Extra Support, p. 39    ▲ Practice Book, p. 39    ▲ Challenge, p. 39

**E L L**

- Group children according to academic levels, and assign one of the pages on the left.

- Clarify any unfamiliar concepts as necessary. See *ELL Teacher Guide*, Lesson 18, for support in scaffolding instruction.

Teacher Read-Aloud

## Phonics Skill

### Words with ow and oa

The letters **ow** can stand for the long **o** sound, as in the words **bowl** and **snow**.

**bowl**

**snow**

The letters **oa** can also stand for the long **o** sound, as in the words **goat** and **road**.

**goat**

**road**

214

Look at each picture. Read the words. Tell which word names the picture.

toad
boat
coat

bowl
blow
bow

**GO online** www.harcourtschool.com/storytown

**Try This!**

**Read the sentences.**

I put on my coat to go out. I could see the wind blow the trees. I could see snow on the road. I was glad I had my coat.

215

### Practice/Apply

**GUIDED PRACTICE** Have children turn to page 214 in their *Student Edition*. Read the information about the long *o* sound. Then lead them through the activity at the top of page 215.

**Try This!** **INDEPENDENT PRACTICE** Tell children that they will read some sentences, and that they should use what they know about the long *o* sound to help them figure out words. Have them read silently and then aloud. Talk about what the sentences are about, and ask volunteers to identify long *o* words.

**E L L**

**Try This!** Help children with the Try This! activity by sharing photographs of a coat, a tree, snow, and a road.

▲ Photo Card 119

# Author's Purpose/
# Point of View *Comprehension*

## Teach/Model

**REVIEW THE SKILL** Remind children that authors write for a reason, or purpose. They may want to entertain or to teach. Read aloud the following excerpt from "The Mitten" (*Read-Aloud Anthology*, p. 68).

> **A great bear lumbered by. He spied the mitten all plumped up. Not being one to be left out in the cold, he began to nose his way in. The animals were packed in as tightly as could be. But what animal would argue with a bear?**

Then model for children how to recognize the author's purpose.

( **Think Aloud** ) **In this passage, the author tells about a very silly situation. Can you picture all those animals in one little mitten? It makes me laugh. The author's purpose here is to entertain.**

## Practice/Apply

**GUIDED PRACTICE** Read *Student Edition* page 210 as children follow along. Guide children to use the illustration and the text to determine that the author's purpose was to entertain. Then ask how children think the author feels about snow. Have children locate sentences that show the author's point of view.

### Objective
- *To identify author's purpose and point of view*

### Skill Trace
 **Tested** **Author's Purpose/ Point of View**

| Preview | T142 |
|---|---|
| Introduce | T151 |
| Reteach | S16-S17, S56-S57 |
| Review | T176, T188, T198, T490, T499, T524, T538, T548 |
| Test | Bk 1-3 |
| Maintain | Monitor Comprehension, Bk 1-4, 1-5 |

# High-Frequency Words
**Words to Know**

## Objective
• *To read high-frequency words*

**INTRODUCE** *Tested* ✓

### High-Frequency Words

| | |
|---|---|
| mouse | pretty |
| our | surprise |
| over | three |

---

### ✓ MONITOR PROGRESS

**High-Frequency Words**

| **IF** children have difficulty reading and spelling the words, | **THEN** display two sets of word cards, and have them read and match the words. |
|---|---|

**Small-Group Instruction, p. S53:**

● **BELOW-LEVEL:** Reteach
● **ON-LEVEL:** Reinforce
● **ADVANCED:** Extend

---

### Teach/Model

**Routine Card 16** **INTRODUCE WORDS** Write the words *mouse, our, over, pretty, surprise,* and *three* on the board.

• Point to and read *mouse.* Repeat it, having children say it with you.

• Say: **A *mouse* is a little animal with a long tail.**

• Point to each letter as you spell the word. Have children spell the word with you.

• Have children reread the word.

Repeat for the remaining words. Use the following sentences:

• **We are all proud of *our* school.**

• **The glass fell *over* when Ted bumped the table.**

• **I love your shirt because it is such a *pretty* color.**

• **The party was a big *surprise.***

• **Two plus one equals *three.***

### Guided Practice

**STUDENT EDITION PAGES 216–217** Have children point to and read aloud each of the highlighted words. Talk about the artwork. Then ask volunteers to read aloud the sentences.

**STORY WORDS** List *brother, rolling,* and *trouble* on the board. Read the words aloud. Repeat, having children read the words with you. Explain that a *brother* is a boy in your family. In "Snow Surprise," Ben is Joan's little brother. Explain that Joan is *rolling* something into a ball. Then tell children that *trouble* is something bad that happens. In the story, the wild animals cause trouble. Point to the words again, and have children read them aloud.

## Words to Know

**High-Frequency Words**

our

pretty

surprise

over

three

mouse

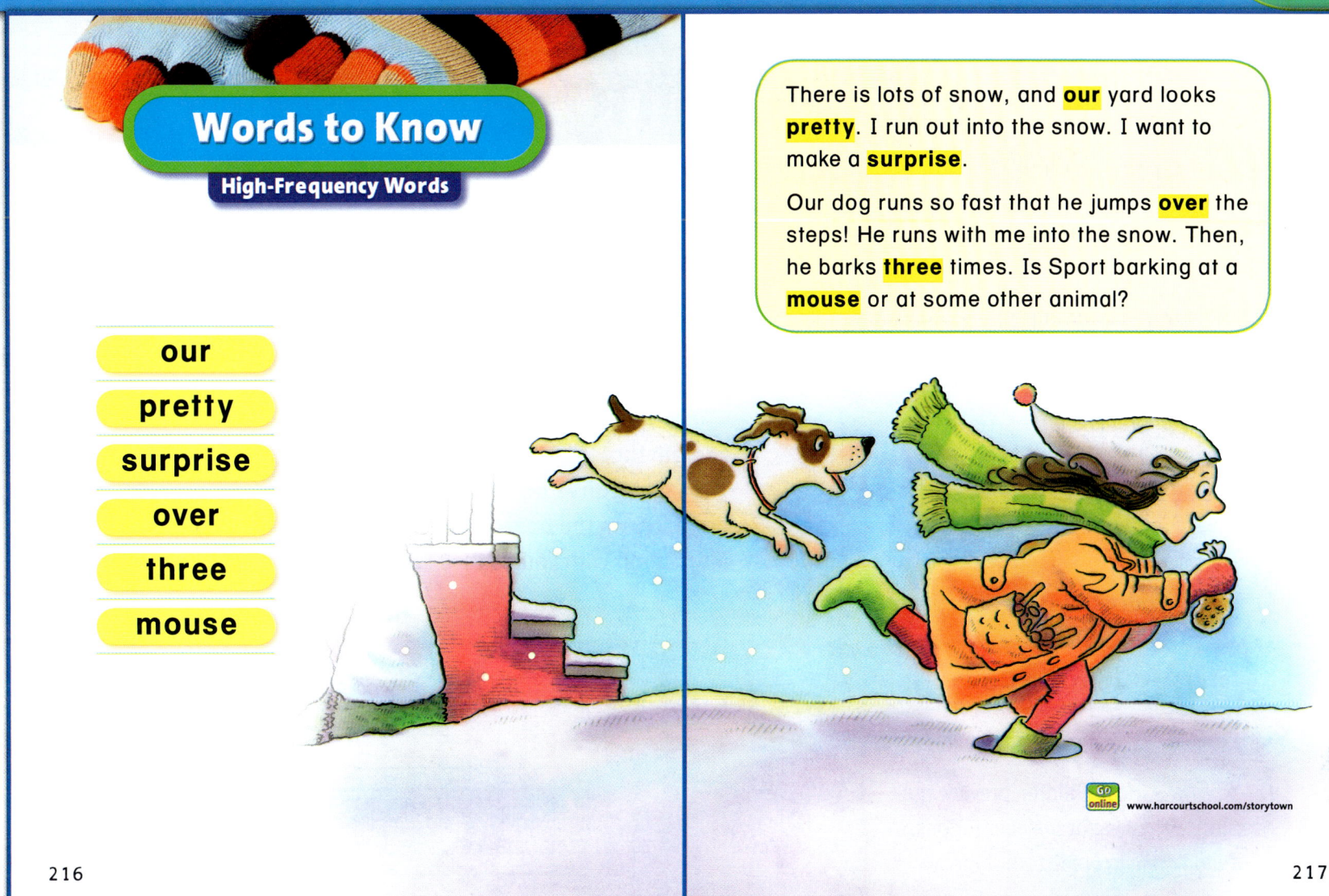

There is lots of snow, and **our** yard looks **pretty**. I run out into the snow. I want to make a **surprise**.

Our dog runs so fast that he jumps **over** the steps! He runs with me into the snow. Then, he barks **three** times. Is Sport barking at a **mouse** or at some other animal?

www.harcourtschool.com/storytown

216

217

**Reinforce Words** Collect small classroom objects in sets of three. Then use this pattern to help children practice the word *three*. Give a child three pencils and ask: **Do you have three pencils?** Have the child respond by counting the objects and saying: **Yes, I have three pencils.** Repeat the activity, varying the objects and the number of objects so children will sometimes respond negatively: **No, I don't have three books.**

See *ELL Teacher Guide,* Lesson 18, for support in scaffolding instruction.

#  Reading

*Student Edition:* Snow Surprise

## Objectives

- *To recognize the characteristics of realistic fiction*
- *To make inferences as a strategy for comprehension*
- *To apply word knowledge to the reading of a text*

 **Podcasting:** Use Story Structures, Gr. I

## Options for Reading

 **BELOW-LEVEL**

**Preview** Have children preview the story by looking at the illustrations. Guide them to predict what the author's purpose or point of view is. Read each page of the story to children, and have them echo-read.

 **ON-LEVEL**

**Monitor Comprehension** Have children read the story aloud, page by page. Ask the Monitor Comprehension questions as you go. Then lead them in retelling the story and describing their favorite part.

 **ADVANCED**

**Independent Reading** Have children read each page silently, looking up each time they finish a page. Ask the Monitor Comprehension questions as you go. Discuss how the snow surprise was created.

## Genre Study

**DISCUSS REALISTIC FICTION: PAGE 218** Point to the genre label on *Student Edition* page 218 and tell children that this is *realistic fiction*. Read the explanation below the genre label. Explain that this story is about something that could really happen. Then use **Transparency GO13** or copy the graphic organizer from page 218 on the board. Tell children that they will complete this story map along with you as they read "Snow Surprise."

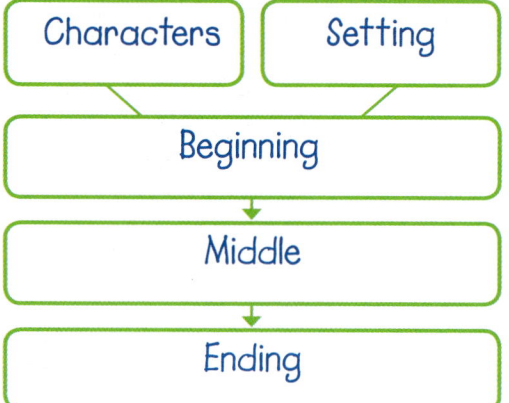

## Comprehension Strategies

**MAKE INFERENCES: PAGE 218** Tell children that good readers use what they already know to make inferences about things the author doesn't say. To make inferences, think about what the author says. Then think about what you know from your own experience. Provide this example:

**Think Aloud** In "The Mitten," the author writes that the hedgehog spent the day looking under wet leaves for things to eat, and got into the mitten to warm himself. I think the hedgehog was wet, cold, and hungry because the story said that it had been looking for food under wet leaves.

Then read aloud the text under Comprehension Strategy on page 218. Point out to children that thinking about these ideas can help them understand the story better.

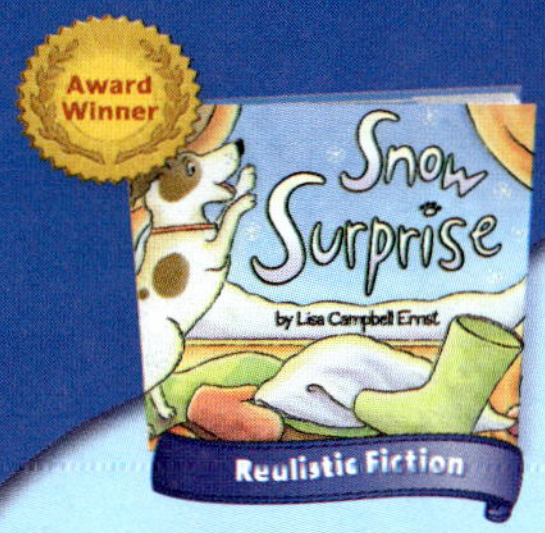

## Genre Study
**Realistic fiction** stories are made-up, but the events could happen in real life.

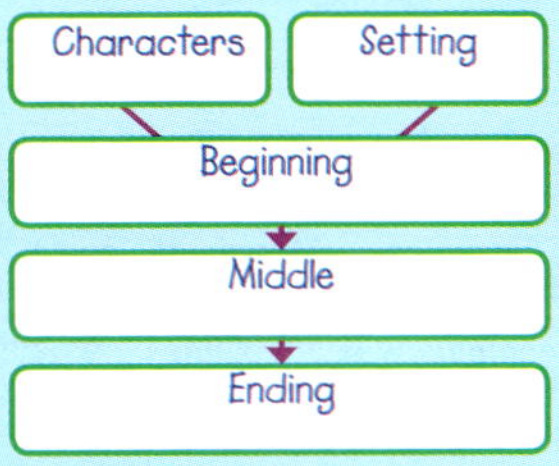

Characters → Setting

Beginning

Middle

Ending

## Comprehension Strategy
**Monitor Comprehension: Make Inferences** Use clues from what you are reading and what you already know to help you understand the story.

218

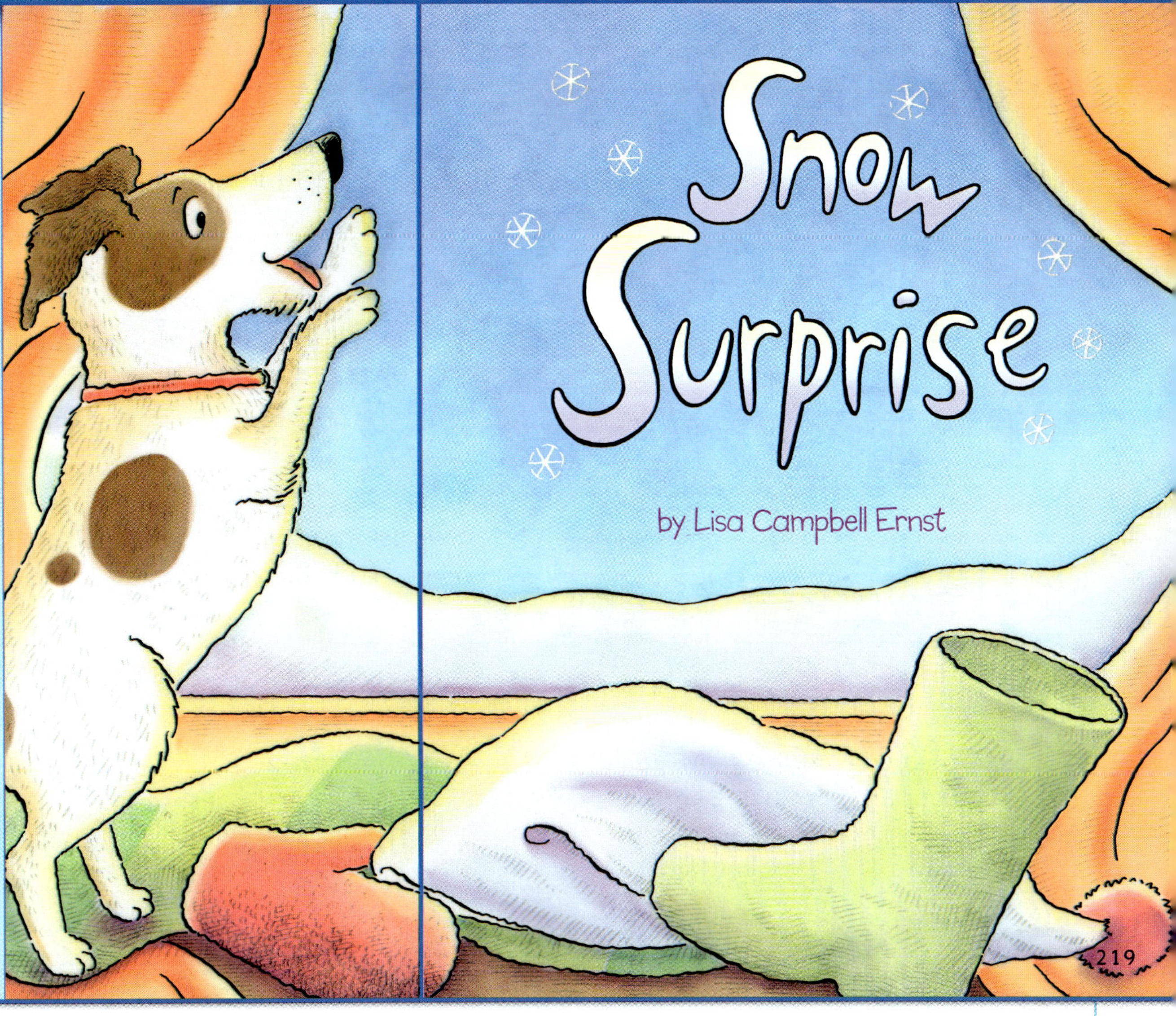

Snow Surprise

by Lisa Campbell Ernst

219

---

### Build Background

**DISCUSS SNOW** Tell children they are going to read a story about a girl who makes something with snow. Ask them to tell about their own experiences with snow or things they have read about snow.

 **SET A PURPOSE AND PREDICT** Tell children that this is a story they will read to be entertained.

Routine Card **17**

- Point to the high-frequency word *Surprise* in the title and have a volunteer read it. Then read the title to children.

- Ask children to predict what the surprise will be.

- List the predictions on the board.

- Invite children to read to find out what the surprise is.

### TECHNOLOGY

 **eBook** "Snow Surprise" is available in an eBook.

 **Audiotext** "Snow Surprise" is available on *Audiotext Grade 1*, CD 3 for subsequent readings.

"Surprise! Look at the snow, Joan!" yelled her little brother, Ben.

220

Joan looked out. The snow was so pretty! Sport barked.

"I saw the snow first! I saw the snow first!" Ben sang.

221

# Monitor Comprehension

**PAGES 220–221** Say: **The boy looks excited. Let's read to find out why.**

1. **NOTE DETAILS** Why is Ben excited? (It snowed.)

2. **DRAW CONCLUSIONS** Do you think Ben likes snow? Why do you think so? (Yes; he looks happy and is yelling and singing about it.)

3. **AUTHOR'S PURPOSE/POINT OF VIEW** How do you think the author feels about snow? Why do you think so? (The author probably likes snow because the characters she wrote about like it.)

*Focus Skill*

## Apply
### Comprehension Strategies

**Recognize Story Structure** Demonstrate how to use the graphic organizer to comprehend the story.

**Think Aloud** After looking at the pictures and reading, I know that the characters are Joan, Ben, and Sport. They are excited about the snow outside. Let's add this information to the story map.

**Characters:** Joan, Ben, and Sport

Joan ran for her coat. "I'll show you a snow surprise," she called to Ben. Joan loaded her pockets with all sorts of things.

"Don't look!" she said. Then she ran out with Sport.

222

223

# Monitor Comprehension

**PAGES 222–223** Say: **It looks like Joan is gathering things from the kitchen. Let's read to find out what is happening.**

**1** **NOTE DETAILS/APPLY PHONICS** **What article of clothing does Joan run for?** (her coat) **Find and read the sentence that tells.**

**2** **DRAW CONCLUSIONS** **Why is Joan gathering things?** (She is going to use them to make a snow surprise.)

**3** **MAKE INFERENCES** **Why do you think Joan says, "Don't look"?** (She doesn't want Ben to see the surprise until it's finished.)

## Use Multiple Strategies

**Ask Questions** Say: Asking questions about a story helps me think about what I read. I can ask myself, "What will Joan make with the things she gathers from the kitchen?" I will read more to find out.

Student Edition, pp. 224–225

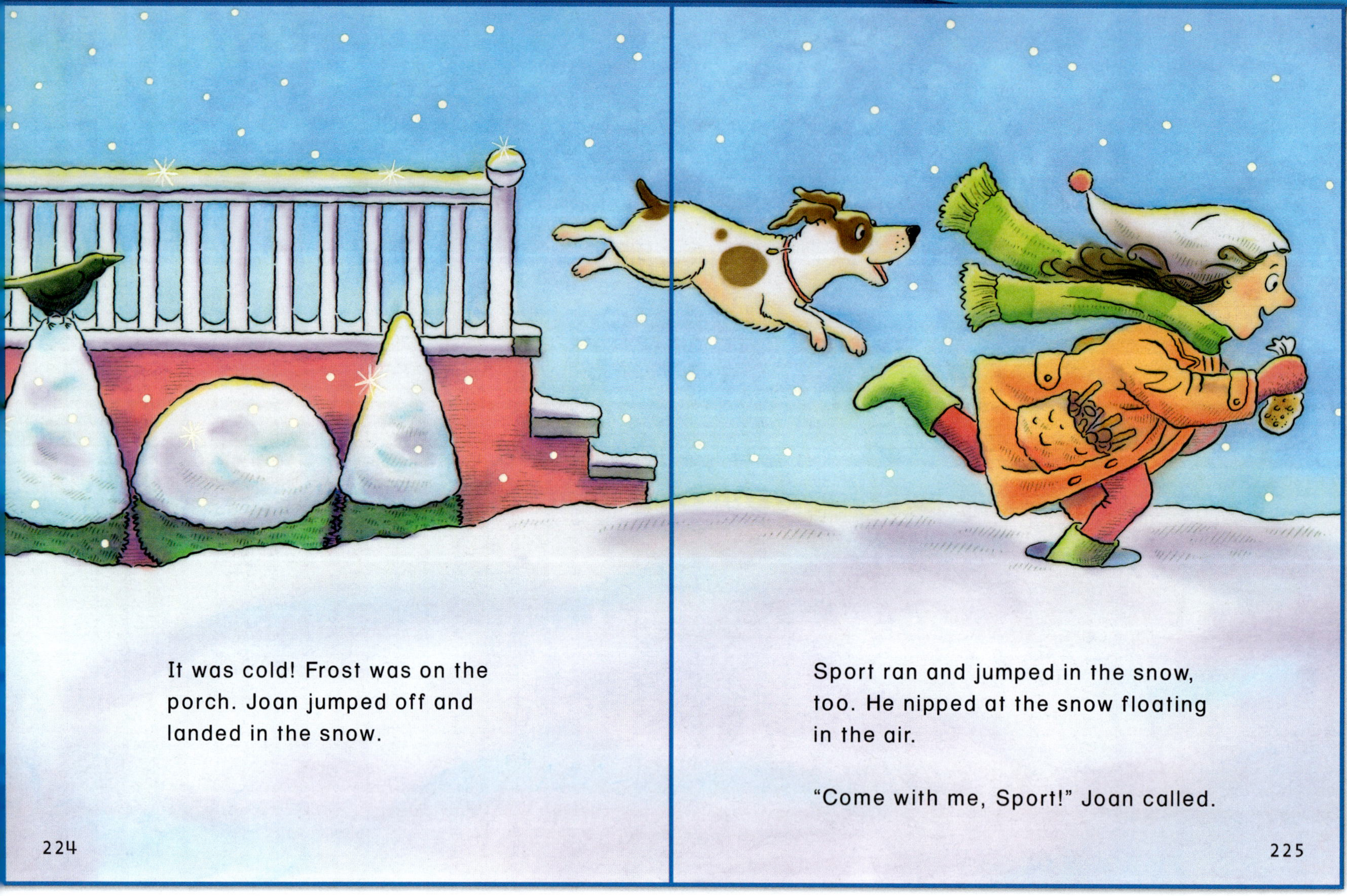
It was cold! Frost was on the porch. Joan jumped off and landed in the snow.
224
Sport ran and jumped in the snow, too. He nipped at the snow floating in the air.
"Come with me, Sport!" Joan called.
225

# Monitor Comprehension

**PAGES 224–225** Say: **Joan and Sport are outside. Let's read to find out what they are doing.**

1. **NOTE DETAILS** **What are Joan and Sport doing?** (They are jumping and running in the snow.)
2. **MAKE PREDICTIONS** **What do you think Joan and Sport will do next?** (Responses will vary.)

**ELL**

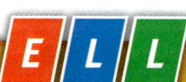

**Develop Vocabulary** Point to and name the articles of clothing that Joan is wearing. Have children repeat the names after you. Then point to each article of clothing again and have children say its name.

Joan packed snow into a small ball. Then she started rolling the ball.

"It's growing!" Joan yelled.

226

Joan made three snowballs. They were all in a row—big, bigger, and biggest.

227

# Monitor Comprehension

**PAGES 226–227** Say: It looks like Joan is making snowballs. I wonder what she will do with them. Let's read to find out.

1. **NOTE DETAILS** How many snowballs does Joan make? (three) Point to the word that tells the answer.

2. **NOTE DETAILS** What does Joan do with the snowballs? (She lines them up from smallest to biggest.)

3. **PERSONAL RESPONSE** Have you ever made snowballs? What did you do with them? (Responses will vary.)

**SCIENCE**

## SUPPORTING STANDARDS

**The Equator** Show a globe and explain that a globe is a model of Earth. Point out the equator and the North and South Poles. Explain that, in general, places near the equator are hot and do not get snow, while places near the poles are cold and are often covered with snow. The farther a place is from the equator, the more snow it is likely to get. Have children find the equator on a globe.

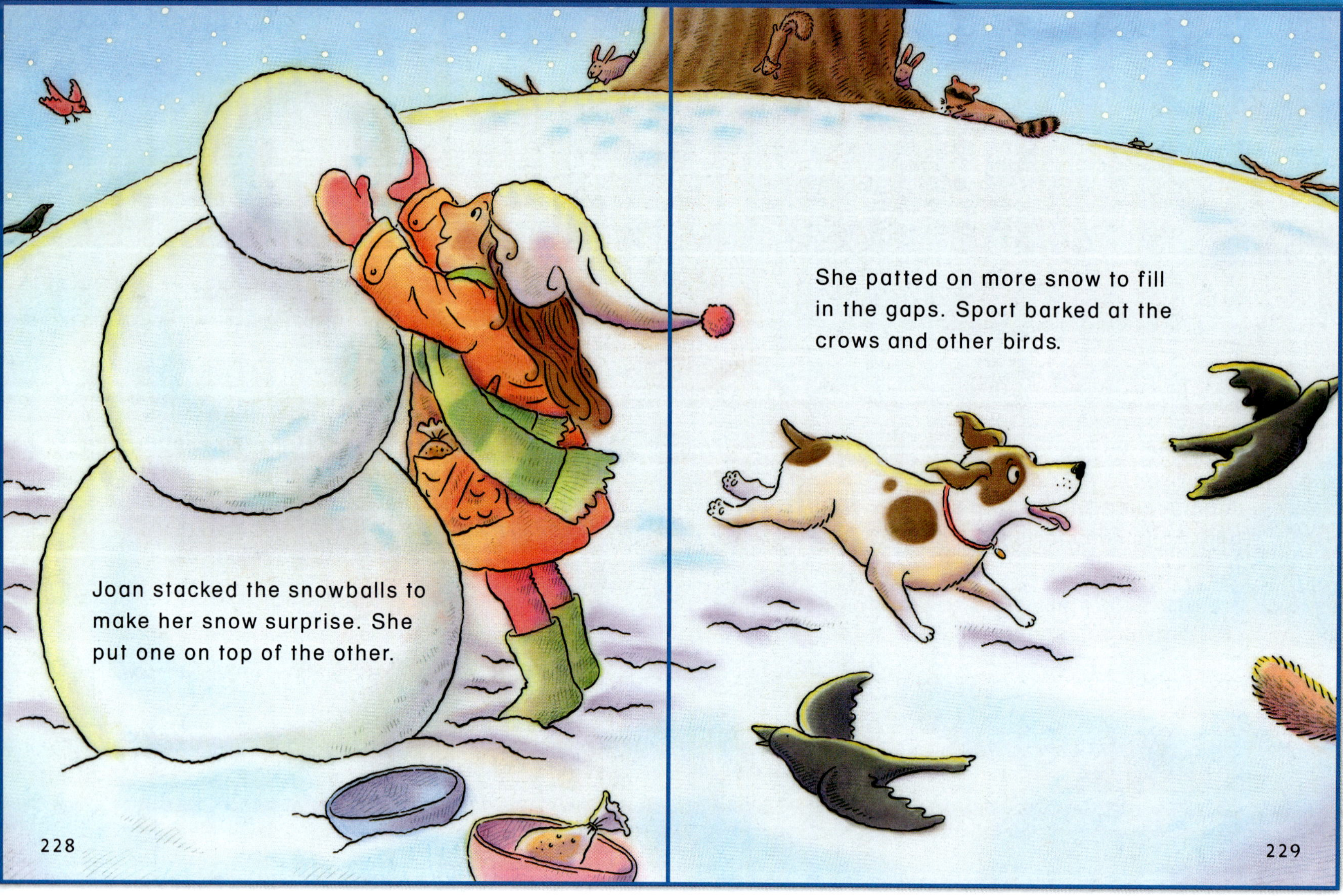

Joan stacked the snowballs to make her snow surprise. She put one on top of the other.

228

She patted on more snow to fill in the gaps. Sport barked at the crows and other birds.

229

# Monitor Comprehension

**PAGES 228–229** Say: **Now Joan is stacking the snowballs. Let's read to find out what she is making.**

 **1** **MAKE INFERENCES** **What is Joan making?** (a snowman)

**2** **NOTE DETAILS** **What does Sport do?** (Sport chases the birds.)

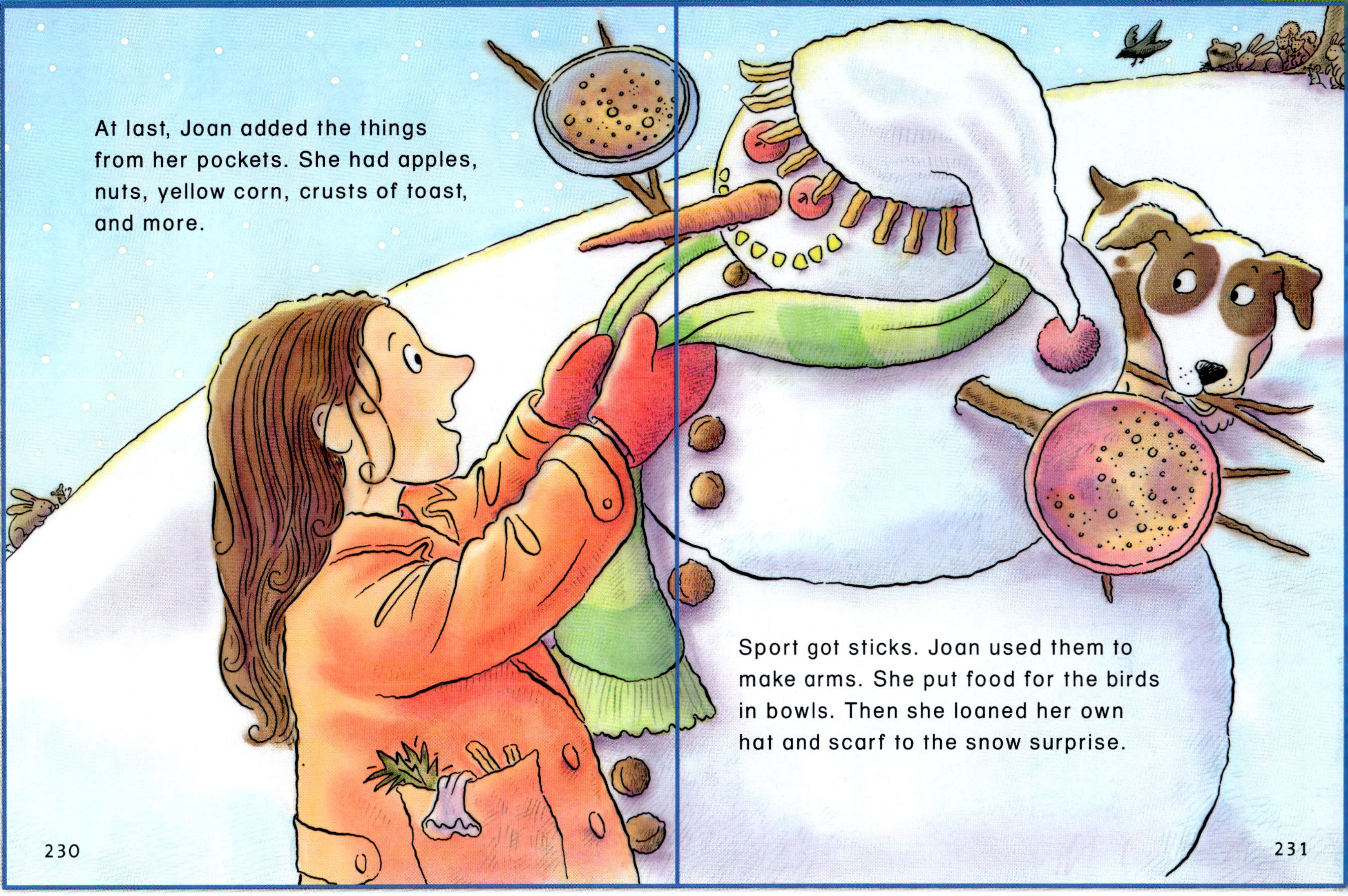

At last, Joan added the things from her pockets. She had apples, nuts, yellow corn, crusts of toast, and more.

230

Sport got sticks. Joan used them to make arms. She put food for the birds in bowls. Then she loaned her own hat and scarf to the snow surprise.

231

# Monitor Comprehension

**PAGES 230–231** Say: **I can see that Joan is adding things to the snowman. Let's read to find out what is happening.**

**1** **NOTE DETAILS** **What does Joan use to decorate the snowman?** (the food from her pockets, sticks, and her scarf and hat)

**2** 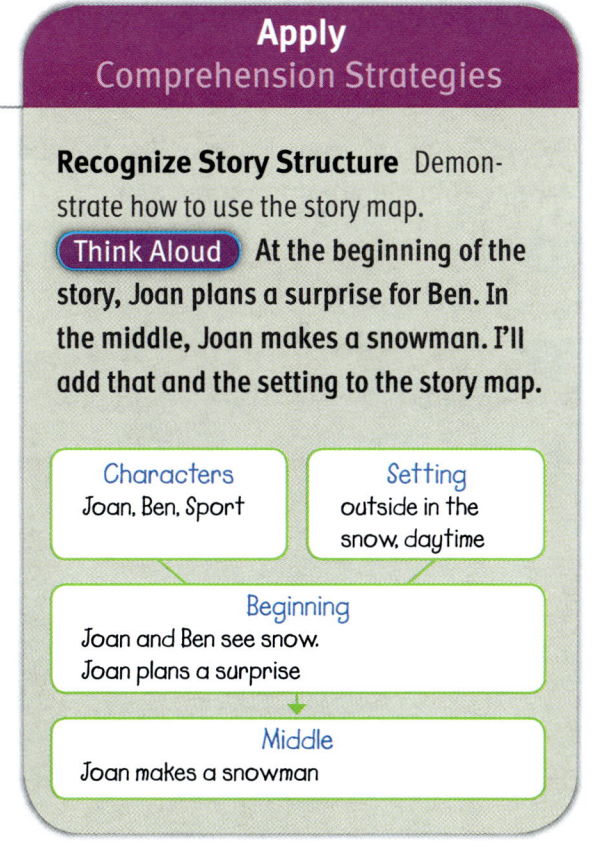 **MAKE INFERENCES** **Why does Joan put food for the birds in a bowl?** (Possible response: She wants to feed them. It is harder for the birds to find food in the snow.)

**3** **PERSONAL RESPONSE** **Have you ever made a snowman? What did you use to decorate it?** (Responses will vary.)

## Apply
### Comprehension Strategies

**Recognize Story Structure** Demonstrate how to use the story map.

**Think Aloud** At the beginning of the story, Joan plans a surprise for Ben. In the middle, Joan makes a snowman. I'll add that and the setting to the story map.

| Characters | Setting |
|---|---|
| Joan, Ben, Sport | outside in the snow, daytime |

**Beginning**
Joan and Ben see snow. Joan plans a surprise

**Middle**
Joan makes a snowman

Lesson 18 (*Student Edition*, pp. 230–231) **T509**

Student Edition, pp. 232–233

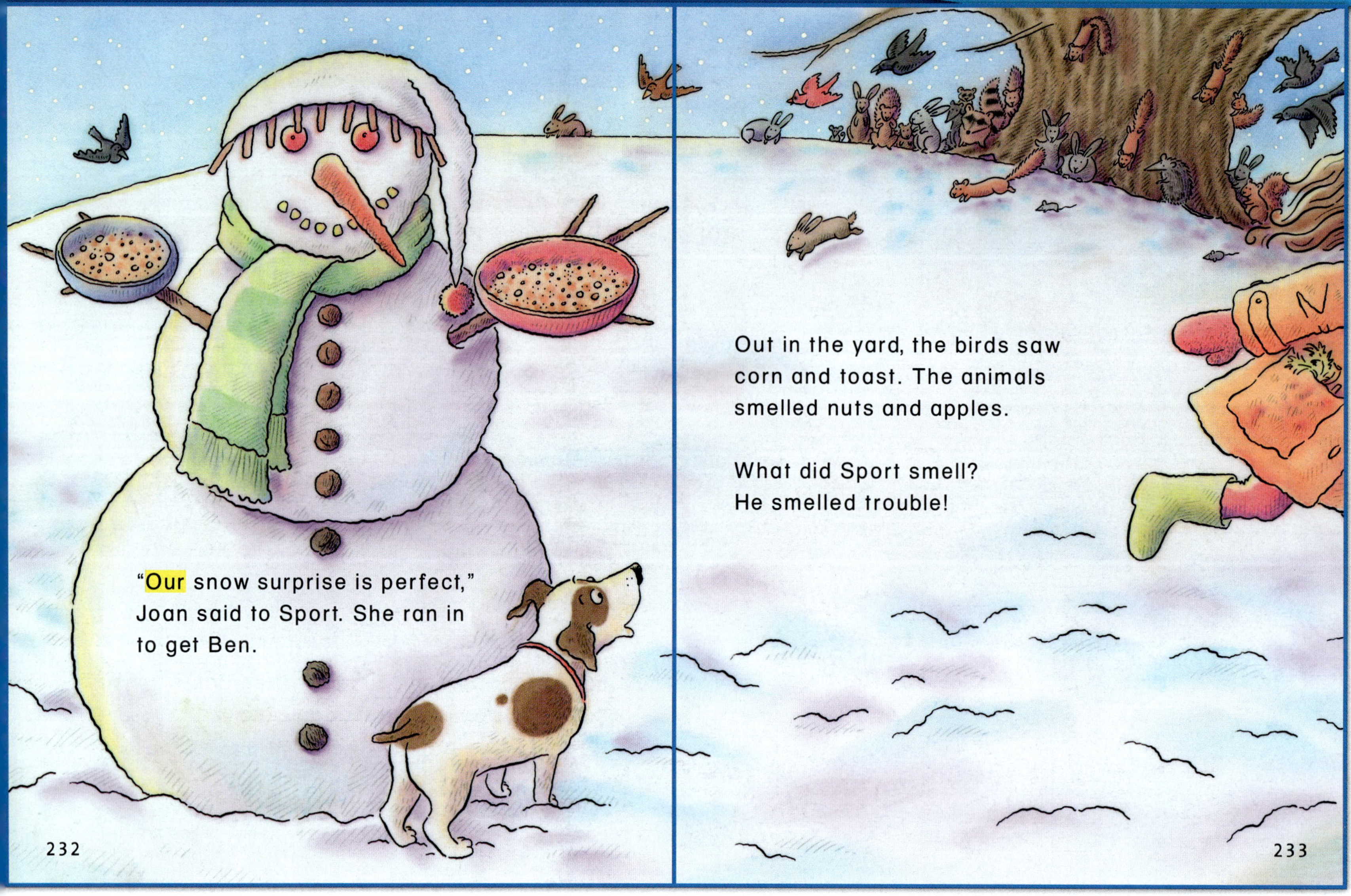
"Our snow surprise is perfect," Joan said to Sport. She ran in to get Ben.
232
Out in the yard, the birds saw corn and toast. The animals smelled nuts and apples.
What did Sport smell? He smelled trouble!
233

# Monitor Comprehension

**PAGES 232–233** Say: **It looks like the snow surprise is ready. Let's read to find out what happens next.**

1. **DRAW CONCLUSIONS** **Does Joan like the snowman? How do you know?** (Yes; she says it is perfect.)
2. **RELATE PICTURES TO TEXT** **Why do you think Sport smells trouble?** (He sees the animals running towards the food.)
3. **MAKE PREDICTIONS** **What do you think will happen next?** (Responses will vary.)

**ELL**

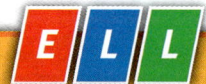

**Explain Idiomatic Expressions**
Explain that when the author says that Sport smelled trouble, she does not mean that Sport actually used his nose to smell something. She is using an expression that means that Sport has a feeling that something bad is about to happen.

In a flash, there <u>was</u> trouble. The birds snatched the food. The animals munched. It was a mad dash for the snacks!

234

Sport jumped at them all. The snow surprise tipped. Then it fell <mark>over</mark> with a THUD!

235

# Monitor Comprehension

**PAGES 234–235** Say: **What a mess! Let's read to find out what is happening.**

**1** **NOTE DETAILS** **What are the animals trying to do?** (They are trying to get the food to eat it.)

**2** **NOTE DETAILS** **What happens to the snowman?** (It falls over when Sport jumps at the animals.)

**3** **MAKE PREDICTIONS** **How do you think Joan will feel when she sees the snowman? Why?** (Possible responses: sad, upset; because she worked hard to build it and was excited to surprise Ben.)

**ADVANCED**

**Speculate** Have children think about how they might have avoided the problem. For example, ask what other things Joan might have used to build the snowman.

## Student Edition, pp. 236–237

Joan led Ben out to show him the surprise. She gasped. It was not there!
"Oh, no," Joan groaned.
236
Ben clapped his hands. "A mouse!" he sang. "It's a snow mouse!"
Joan looked again. It was a mouse.
"Surprise!" she said.
237

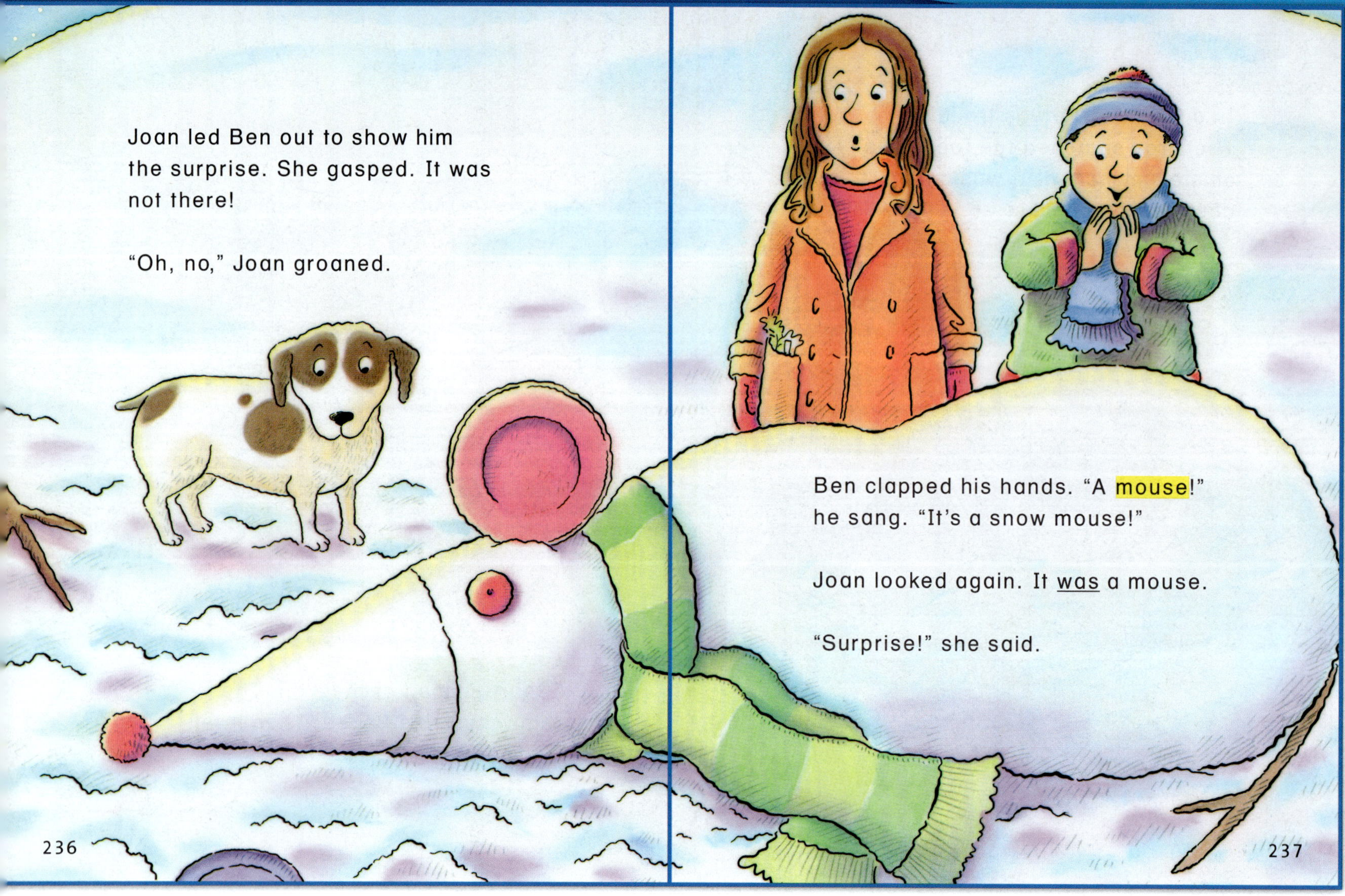

# Monitor Comprehension

**PAGES 236–237** Say: **The snowman is lying on the ground. I see that Joan looks surprised and Ben looks happy. Let's read to find out what is happening.**

1. **DETERMINE CHARACTERS' EMOTIONS** **Does Ben like the surprise? How do you know?** (Yes; he claps and sings.)

2. **NOTE DETAILS** **Who else is surprised? Why?** (Joan, because she thought the snowman was ruined, but she realizes it is still a snow surprise)

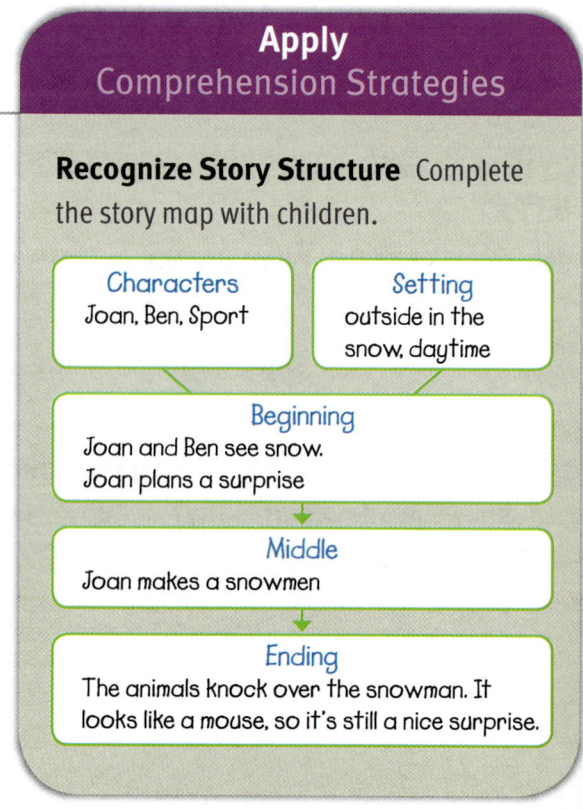

### Apply
### Comprehension Strategies

**Recognize Story Structure** Complete the story map with children.

| Characters | Setting |
|---|---|
| Joan, Ben, Sport | outside in the snow, daytime |

**Beginning**
Joan and Ben see snow.
Joan plans a surprise

**Middle**
Joan makes a snowmen

**Ending**
The animals knock over the snowman. It looks like a mouse, so it's still a nice surprise.

## Think Critically

1. Why do you think the author wrote this story? 🐾 AUTHOR'S PURPOSE/POINT OF VIEW

2. What are the steps for making Joan's snow surprise? DETAILS

3. Do you think the animals are happy that Joan is making a snow surprise? Why or why not? DRAW CONCLUSIONS

4. Think about the ending. What do you think Joan and Ben will do next? MAKE INFERENCES

5. **WRITE** Write about something you made to surprise someone, or about a time someone surprised you. ✏ WRITING RESPONSE

### Meet the Author/Illustrator
# Lisa Campbell Ernst

Lisa Campbell Ernst grew up in a family that loved books and sharing stories. So, she would draw pictures and make up stories about the animals in her neighborhood.

"I still love drawing animals! To know how to draw Sport, I watched my pets Fred and Elmo playing outside. I watched the wildlife in my backyard for the other animals, and my daughter Allison to draw Joan."

www.harcourtschool.com/storytown

238

239

# Think Critically

## Respond to the Literature

1.  to entertain   **AUTHOR'S PURPOSE/ POINT OF VIEW**

2. First, make three snowballs. Then, stack the snowballs one on top of the other. Fill in the gaps with snow. Last, decorate it with sticks, food, and a hat and scarf.   **DETAILS**

3. Possible response: Yes; the surprise includes food.   **DRAW CONCLUSIONS**

4. Possible response: They will make more snow mice.   **MAKE INFERENCES**

5. **WRITE**  Responses will vary   **WRITING RESPONSE**

# Meet the Author/Illustrator

**PAGE 239** Explain that this page tells about the person who wrote and illustrated the story "Snow Surprise." Identify Lisa Campbell Ernst in the photograph on page 239. Encourage children to point to the author's name as you read it aloud. Remind children that an author writes a story, and an illustrator creates pictures to go with the writing. Explain that Lisa Campbell Ernst is both the author and the illustrator. Read aloud page 239. Encourage children to track the print as you read.

Lesson 18 (*Student Edition*, pp. 238–239)   **T513**

# Check Comprehension

## *Retelling*

## Objectives

- *To practice retelling a story*
- *To read at an appropriate rate in a manner that sounds like natural speech*

### RETELLING RUBRIC

| 4 | Uses details to clearly retell the story |
|---|---|
| 3 | Uses some details to retell the story |
| 2 | Retells the story with some inaccuracies |
| 1 | Is unable to retell the story |

### Retell

**DIBELS** Oral Reading Fluency **ORF**

 **AUTHOR'S PURPOSE/POINT OF VIEW** Ask children to tell why the author wrote the story. (to entertain) Have them describe the author's feelings about snow. (She probably thinks snow is fun.)

 **REVISIT THE GRAPHIC ORGANIZER** Display completed **Transparency GO13.** Have children work in small groups to retell the story.

**STORY RETELLING CARDS** The cards for "Snow Surprise" can be used for a retelling or as an aid to completing the story map.

▲ Story Retelling Cards 1–6, "Snow Surprise"

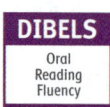 # Fluency

### Teach/Model

**DIBELS** Oral Reading Fluency **ORF**

**READING RATE** Have children turn to pages 220–221 of "Snow Surprise" and track the print as you read aloud at a consistent rate. Remind children that their goal is to read as naturally as they talk without stopping to correct mistakes or to sound out words.

### Practice/Apply

**ECHO-READ** Read aloud the rest of the story, one page at a time. Model reading at an appropriate reading rate and have children echo-read.

### BELOW-LEVEL

**Fluency Practice** For fluency practice, have children read *Decodable Book 18,* the appropriate *Leveled Reader* (pp. T552–T555), or "First Snow" in the *Book 1-3 Strategic Intervention Interactive Reader.*

# Build Robust Vocabulary

**Listening/Speaking:** *Words from the Read-Aloud*

## Review Robust Vocabulary

**USE VOCABULARY IN DIFFERENT CONTEXTS** Remind children of the Student-Friendly Explanations of *bulged, jostled,* and *argue.* Then discuss each word using the following examples:

### bulged
- If your friend's lunch bag bulged, would the bag be full or empty? Tell why.
- What might you put in your pocket to make it bulge?

### jostled
- Are you more likely to jostle someone when you are in the middle of a crowd or when you are standing in an empty hallway? Tell why.
- Would you get mad if someone jostled you? Why or why not?
- Tell about a time when you jostled someone.

### argue
- If your friend told you to get out of the way because a car was coming, would you argue? Why or why not?
- What kinds of things do children argue about?
- How can friends make up after they argue?

## Objective
- *To review robust vocabulary to describe ideas*

### REVIEW
### Student-Friendly Explanations

**bulged** If a container bulged, its sides stuck out as if it were going to burst.

**jostled** When you have jostled people, you have bumped them or poked them to make them move.

**argue** When you argue with someone, you disagree loudly.

# Grammar

## Troublesome Words: Homophones

**5-DAY GRAMMAR**

| | |
|---|---|
| **DAY 1** | Introduce Homophones |
| **DAY 2** | Use a Literature Model |
| **DAY 3** | Recognize Incorrect Homophones |
| **DAY 4** | Identify Homophones |
| **DAY 5** | Write Sentences with Homophones |

### Objectives

- To understand the concept of homophones
- To identify homophones

### Daily Proofreading

**Would you like two eat now**

(to, now?)

▲ Grammar Practice Book, p. 69

---

## Review

**USE A LITERATURE MODEL** Challenge children to learn a tongue twister. Slowly read aloud the tongue twister below. Reread it a few times and encourage children to join in when they can.

**Tongue Twister**

How much wood
would a woodchuck chuck
if a woodchuck
could chuck wood?

Write the tongue twister on the board. Track the print as you read it with children. Ask volunteers to underline the two words that sound the same but are spelled differently and have different meanings. *(wood, would)* Remind children that these words are called homophones.

## Practice/Apply

**GUIDED PRACTICE** Write the following sentences on the board. Read them with children, and have volunteers underline the homophones. Reread the words with children, and discuss the meaning of each one.

> The <u>tale</u> is about a cat with a long <u>tail</u>.
> Rick <u>sent</u> one <u>cent</u> to his sister.
> Jan <u>read</u> the book with the <u>red</u> cover.
> Abby <u>won</u> <u>one</u> race.

**INDEPENDENT PRACTICE** Have children write a homophone pair at the bottom of a sheet of paper and draw a picture to illustrate one of the words. Children can challenge a partner to look at the picture and point to the correct homophone.

**5-DAY WRITING**

| | |
|---|---|
| DAY 1 | Modeled Writing |
| DAY 2 | Shared Writing |
| DAY 3 | Shared Writing |
| DAY 4 | Independent Writing |
| DAY 5 | Independent Writing |

# Shared Writing

*Thank-You Letter*

## Write Together

**REVIEW THANK-YOU LETTERS** Remind children that a thank-you note is a special kind of friendly letter. Review reasons for writing a thank-you letter and the parts of a letter.

**GENERATE IDEAS** Brainstorm with children about people in the school who deserve thanks. List each person's name and a note or picture about their deed. Have children vote for a recipient for the letter.

**MODEL WRITING** Have volunteers dictate their sentences as you write them on chart paper, using the Step-by-Step Writing Instruction as a guide. Then track the print and read the sentences with children. Save the sentences for Day 3.

### Step-by-Step Writing Instruction

| | | |
|---|---|---|
| **1** | How does a letter begin? How do I write the first letter in the name of the month? | October 12, 20-- |
| **2** | What should the greeting say? Where do I need capital letters? Where does the comma go? | Dear Mr. Chapman, |
| **3** *WRITING TRAIT* | Mr. Chapman was very nice to us. What should we say to him? | Thank you for getting our ball off the roof. |
| **4** | What should we write for our closing? Which letter is a capital? What mark comes at the end? | Your friends, |
| **5** | How do we write the name of our class? What mark do we use to show the class belongs to the teacher? | Mrs. Hill's Class |
| **6** | Let's read our letter together. | |

## Objectives

- *To generate ideas for writing*
- *To draft a thank-you letter*

## Writing Prompt

**Closings** Help children begin a list of closings they can use when they write thank-you letters, such as *Your friend, Your son, Love, Yours truly,* and *Sincerely.*

▲ **Writer's Companion, Lesson 18**

### BELOW-LEVEL

**Use a Letter Form** If children have difficulty remembering letter format, duplicate forms that have lines for the heading, greeting, body, closing, and signature. Have children write letters on this special paper until they master letter format.

# Warm-Up Routines

## Day at a Glance

### Day 3

### Phonemic Awareness
- Phoneme Blending

###  phonics and Spelling
- Long Vowel /ō/ *ow, oa*; /o/ *o*
- State the Generalization

### High-Frequency Words
- Review: *mouse, our, over, pretty, surprise, three*

### Fluency
- Reading Rate
- "Snow Surprise," *Student Edition*, pp. 218–239

### Comprehension

Review: Author's Purpose/Point of View

### Reading
- "The Snowflake Man," *Student Edition*, pp. 240–245

### Robust Vocabulary
- *command, labored, wary*

### Grammar
- Troublesome Words: Homophones

### Shared Writing ✏️
- Thank-You Letter

---

## Oral Language

**Objective** To listen attentively and respond appropriately to oral communication

### Question of the Day

**What does a snowball look like?**

**What can you do with one?**

Help children brainstorm what a snowball looks like and things they would do with one. Have children help you complete the following sentence frame.

**A snowball _____.**

## Read Aloud

**Objectives** *To understand concepts of print; to innovate on a poem*

**BIG BOOK OF RHYMES AND POEMS** Ask children to tell what they remember about the poem. Then read it, demonstrating how to read from left to right and from top to bottom. Ask children to identify individual words, spaces between letters and words, and punctuation. After you read, encourage children to think of other sounds the snowball could make. Work together to create new lines beginning with *You may hear. . . .* Then recite the new verse together.

▲ Big Book of Rhymes and Poems, p. 35

# Word Wall

**Objective** *To read high-frequency words*

**REVIEW HIGH-FREQUENCY WORDS** Review *mouse, our, over, pretty, surprise, three,* and other previously learned high-frequency words. Say each word, ask a volunteer to point to it, and have children read it aloud. Then point to words at random, and have children reread them. Repeat several times.

| mouse | our | over |
|-------|-----|------|
| pretty | surprise | three |

# Phonemic Awareness

**Objective** *To blend phonemes into recognizable words*

**Routine Card 1** **PHONEME BLENDING** Tell children that you are going to say some words very slowly. Model by saying /b/ /ō/ /t/, then say the word naturally—*boat.* Say the following phonemes, having children blend the sounds to say the words:

| | | |
|---|---|---|
| /k/ /ō/ /t/ (coat) | /f/ /o/ /g/ (fog) | /g/ /r/ /ō/ /n/ (groan) |
| /d/ /i/ /m/ (dim) | /s/ /u/ /n/ (sun) | /v/ /a/ /n/ (van) |
| /f/ /ō/ /m/ (foam) | /w/ /a/ /l/ (wall) | /c/ /r/ /ō/ /k/ (croak) |
| /l/ /ō/ (low) | /f/ /i/ /g/ (fig) | /g/ /l/ /ō/ (glow) |

## /b/ /ō/ /t/ boat

 Podcasting: Phoneme Blending

# Build Words

**phonics** *and Spelling*

| 5-DAY PHONICS | |
|---|---|
| **DAY 1** | Introduce /ō/ow, oa |
| **DAY 2** | Review /ō/ow, oa |
| **DAY 3** | Word Building with /ō/ow, oa and /o/o |
| **DAY 4** | Phonograms -ow, -oat |
| **DAY 5** | Phonograms -own, -oast |

## Objectives

- *To discriminate between the letter-sound associations /ō/ow, oa and /o/o*
- *To use /ō/ow, oa and other known letter-sounds to decode words*
- *To recognize spelling patterns*

## Skill Trace

| **Tested** ✓ | Long /ō/*ow, oa* | Short /o/*o* |
|---|---|---|
| Introduce | T480–T483 | Bk 1-1, T408–T411 |
| Reteach | S52 | Bk 1-1, S42 |
| **Review** | **T496–T498, T520–T521** | Bk 1-1; T424–T425 T446–T447 T532–T533 |
| Test | Bk 1-3 | Bk 1-1 |
| Maintain | Bk 1-4, T76; Bk 1-5, T436 | Bk 1-2, T74, T434; Bk 1-3, T520; Bk 1-4, T438 |

### Long Vowel /ō/*ow, oa*

Jon has a goat.
Her name is Joan.
Joan has spots on her fur.
Joan likes to run on the road.
She has on a bow for the show.
Oh, no, Joan! Do not eat the box!

Grade 1, Lesson 18 · **R35** · Phonics: Long Vowel /ō/ow, oa; Short Vowel /o/o

**Transparency R35**

## Word Building

**Routine Card 14**

**BUILD AND READ WORDS** Use a pocket chart and *Letter Cards.* Have children repeat each step with their *Word Builders* and *Word Builder Cards.*

Build the word *lot.* Then have children read the word naturally—*lot.*

Lead children in building and reading new words by saying:

- **Change *t* to *w*. Read the word.**
- **Add *s* before *l*. Read the word.**
- **Change *w* to *t*. Read the word.**

Continue in a similar manner to have children build and read these words: *got, grow, rod, road.*

## Read Words in Context

**READ SENTENCES** Display **Transparency R35** or write the sentences on the board or on chart paper. Have children choral-read the story as you track the print. Review with children how to distinguish long- and short-vowel sounds in single-syllable words. Say these words: *cost/coast, shop/show, box/bow.*

Then ask volunteers to read each sentence aloud. Call on other volunteers to underline words that have the long *o* sound and circle words with the short *o* sound.

**5-DAY** SPELLING
| | |
|---|---|
| **DAY 1** | Pretest |
| **DAY 2** | Word Building |
| **DAY 3** | State the Generalization |
| **DAY 4** | Review |
| **DAY 5** | Posttest |

## Review Spelling Words

**STATE THE GENERALIZATION** List spelling words 1–6 on chart paper or the board and have children read them. Ask: **What is the same in each word?** (Each word has the /ō/ sound.) Have volunteers read each word and underline the letters that stand for the /ō/ sound. Tell children that *ow* and *oa* can stand for the /ō/ sound.

**REVIEW WORDS** List spelling words 7–8. Talk about what is the same in both words. (Both words end with the /əl/ sound and the letters *le.*) Have children read and spell the words.

**HIGH-FREQUENCY WORDS** List spelling words 9–10. Remind children that they have seen and read these words many times. Run your hand under *carry* as you read it and ask children to look carefully at the letters. Ask them to close their eyes, picture the word, and spell it with you. Repeat for *would.*

**WRITE** Have children write the spelling words in their notebooks. Remind them to use their best handwriting and to use the list to check spelling.

# Handwriting

**LETTER SPACING** Remind children to make sure their letters are not too close together or too far apart.

---

### Spelling Words

| | |
|---|---|
| 1. low | 6. boat |
| 2. slow | 7. little |
| 3. grow | 8. handle |
| 4. road | 9. carry |
| 5. soap | 10. would |

---

### Decodable Book

- **Phonics**
  Long Vowel /ō/
  *ow, oa*
- **Decodable Words** Decodable Book 18 ▲
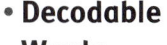

See the list on page R11.

Have children who need additional decoding practice read "The Little Yellow Tugboat" from *Decodable Book 18.* See also *Decodable Books* online (Take-Home Version).

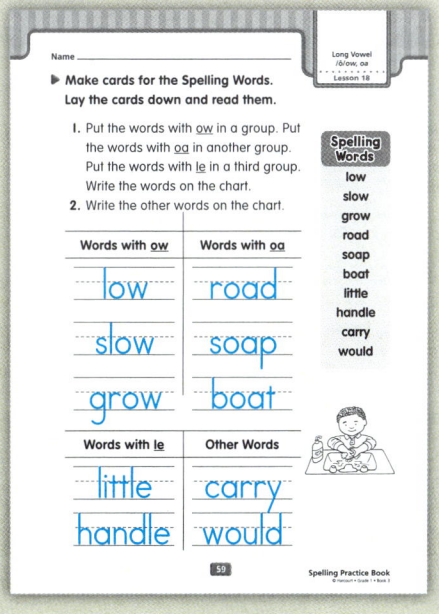

▲ **Spelling Practice Book, p. 59**

# High-Frequency Words

## Objective
• *To read high-frequency words*

**REVIEW** Tested ✓

### High-Frequency Words

| | |
|---|---|
| mouse | pretty |
| our | surprise |
| over | three |

**Model Usage** Tell children that the word *over* can mean "above." Hold a book over your head and say: **The book is *over* my head.** Explain that *over* can also mean "finished or done." Say: **Our day at school is *over* at two o'clock.**

## Review

**DISPLAY THE WORDS** Write the word *mouse*. Have a volunteer read it. Erase the word, and ask children to spell it. Repeat this routine for *our, over, pretty, surprise,* and *three*.

## Practice/Apply

**GUIDED PRACTICE** Give each child a set of word cards (*Teacher Resource Book*, p. 142), and have children spread the cards out in front of them. Randomly call out one of the words, and have children hold up the matching card. Assess how well children are able to identify the words, and repeat until they can respond quickly and accurately.

**INDEPENDENT PRACTICE** Have children work with partners. Have one partner set aside his or her word cards, leaving one set for the pair. Tell them they will take turns giving clues about a word for their partner to identify. Model several examples, such as: **This word has five letters. It rhymes with *me*. What is the word?** *(three)* Finally, have children practice writing the words in their notebooks.

mouse

surprise

over

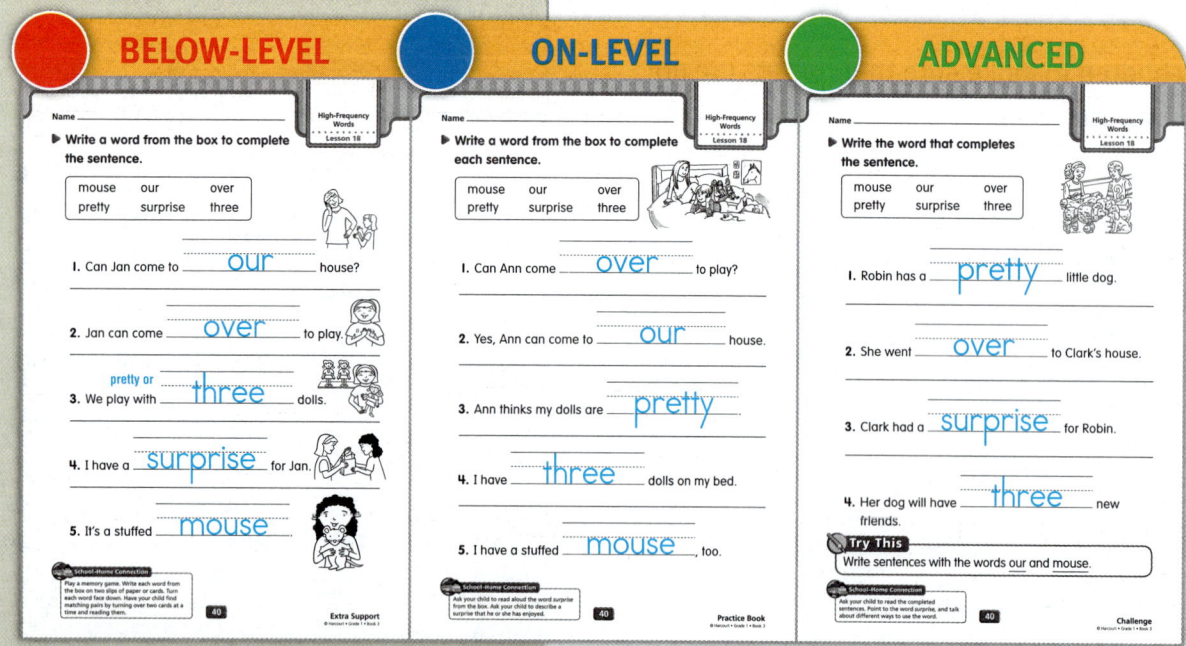

▲ Extra Support, p. 40      ▲ Practice Book, p. 40      ▲ Challenge, p. 40

**ELL**

• Group children according to academic levels, and assign one of the pages on the left.

• Clarify any unfamiliar concepts as necessary. See *ELL Teacher Guide,* Lesson 18, for support in scaffolding instruction.

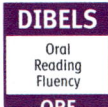 # Fluency
## *Reading Rate*

## Review

**DIBELS** Oral Reading Fluency **ORF**

**REVIEW PUNCTUATION** Have children open their *Student Edition* to page 225, and invite a volunteer to name the punctuation marks they see on that page. Remind children that they should pause briefly at commas and a slight bit longer when there is end punctuation such as a period or an exclamation point. Remind children that when they read, they should not read too fast or too slowly.

## Practice/Apply

**GUIDED PRACTICE** Invite volunteers to read aloud pages 226, 227, 228, or 229. After they read, provide feedback and encouragement. Ask them how they decided how fast to read and when to pause.

**INDEPENDENT PRACTICE** Have each child select a page from the story and practice reading it aloud. Then invite children to reread the same page to practice reading at an appropriate rate. If children are reading too slowly, have them reread to increase their rate. If they are reading too quickly, ask them to slow down and pause at the punctuation marks. Remind them that they should read at the same rate they talk. Have them continue practicing reading aloud until they are reading at an appropriate rate.

### Objective
• *To read with fluency at an appropriate rate*

 **ON-LEVEL**

**Partner Reading** Have children practice reading aloud with a partner. Ask partners to take turns reading a page from a story. Have children give each other feedback on their reading rate.

 **MONITOR PROGRESS**

**Fluency**

| | |
|---|---|
| **IF** children have difficulty reading at an appropriate rate, | **THEN** model reading as you have children echo-read the story with you. |

**Small-Group Instruction, pp. S54–S55:**

🔴 **BELOW-LEVEL:** Reteach
🔵 **ON-LEVEL:** Reinforce
🟢 **ADVANCED:** Extend

# Author's Purpose/Point of View *Comprehension*

## Objectives

- *To identify the author's purpose/point of view*
- *To listen to an article read aloud for information*

## Skill Trace

 **Tested** Author's Purpose/Point of View

| | |
|---|---|
| Preview | T142 |
| Introduce | T151 |
| Reteach | S16–S17, S56–S57 |
| Review | T176, T188, T198, T490, T499, T524, T538, T548 |
| Test | Bk 1-3 |
| Maintain | Monitor Comprehension, Bks 1-4, 1-5 |

## Review

**REVIEW AUTHOR'S PURPOSE/POINT OF VIEW** Remind children that authors write for a reason or a purpose. Help them recall the story "The Mitten" from the *Read-Aloud Anthology*. Ask the children to tell the author's purpose/point of view for writing the story.

## Practice/Apply

**GUIDED PRACTICE** Ask children to recall the author's purpose/point of view for writing "The Snow Surprise." Guide them to determine author's purpose and point of view when they read the article "The Snowflake Man."

**INDEPENDENT PRACTICE** Have children apply their knowledge of author's purpose/point of view by completing *Practice Book* page 41.

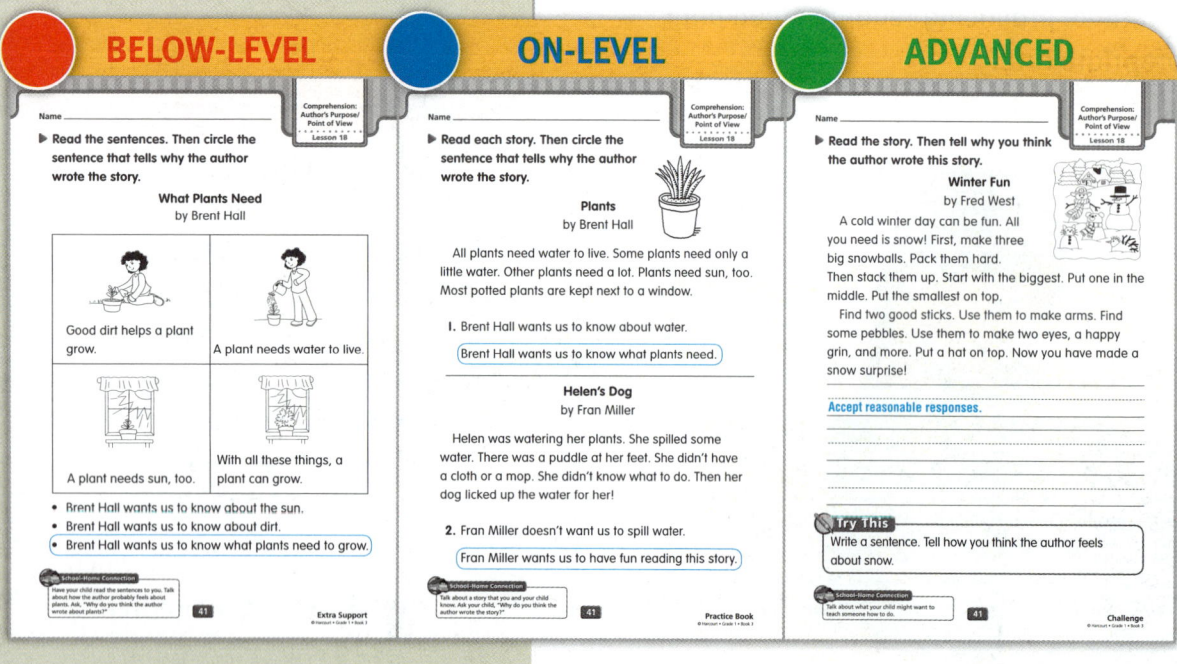

▲ Extra Support, p. 41    ▲ Practice Book, p. 41    ▲ Challenge, p. 41

- Group children according to academic levels, and assign one of the pages on the left.

- Clarify any unfamiliar concepts as necessary. See *ELL Teacher Guide*, Lesson 18, for support in scaffolding instruction.

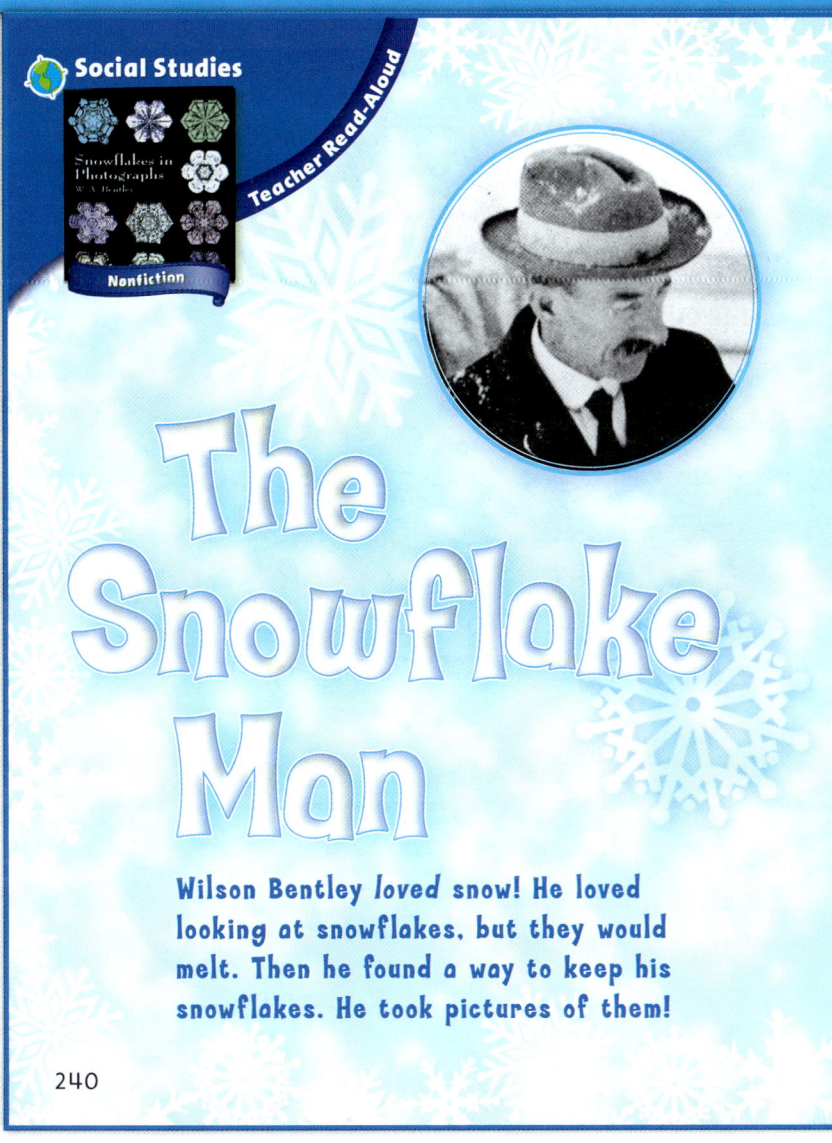

**Social Studies**

Teacher Read-Aloud

Snowflakes in Photographs

**Nonfiction**

# The Snowflake Man

Wilson Bentley *loved* snow! He loved looking at snowflakes, but they would melt. Then he found a way to keep his snowflakes. He took pictures of them!

240

**Read what Wilson Bentley said about snow.**

"I was born in 1865, and I can't remember a time I didn't love the snow."

▼ Wilson Bentley is using an old camera to take his famous pictures. He is known as "Snowflake Bentley."

241

# Reading

*Student Edition: Paired Selection*

## Read Aloud

**Routine Card 17**

**USE PRIOR KNOWLEDGE/SET A PURPOSE** Guide children to use prior knowledge and set a purpose for reading. As you read, monitor listening comprehension by using the following questions:

- **PROBLEM/SOLUTION** **What was Wilson Bentley's problem?** (He loved looking at snowflakes, but they would melt.) **How did he solve his problem?** (He took pictures of the snowflakes.)

- **PERSONAL RESPONSE** **What would you like to take pictures of? Why?** (Responses will vary.)

**E L L**

**Build Background** Have children make a paper snowflake. Show them how to fold the paper and then cut out the design. Display the snowflakes and point out how each one is different.

"A snowstorm is always so exciting to me. I never know when I am going to find some wonderful prize."

"You asked how I catch my crystals. I do it with this little wooden tray. It is painted black so that the flakes will show against it."

242

243

# Monitor Comprehension

1. **DRAW CONCLUSIONS** **What prize does Wilson Bentley hope to find during a snowstorm?** (a beautiful snowflake)

2. **NOTE DETAILS** **Why did Wilson Bentley catch snowflakes in a black tray?** (It was easier to see the white snowflakes.)

## STRATEGIC READING

Write *snowflake, 1865, prize, crystals,* and *exciting* on the board. Tell children that these are in the selection. Read aloud each one, and have children repeat after you. Talk briefly about the meaning of each. For example, explain that 1865 names the year Wilson Bentley was born. This means that he was born over 100 years ago. Explain that *crystals* is what Bentley calls snowflakes. He may have used this word because each snowflake is made up of very small pieces of snow that shine and look like tiny pieces of glass.

"Usually they have six sides or six branches. And the six sides will be exactly the same."

"Each snowflake is as different from its fellows as we are from each other."

244

245

# Monitor Comprehension

① **COMPARE AND CONTRAST  How are all snowflakes the same?** (They usually have six sides or branches. All six sides look the same.) **How are they different?** (Each one has a different design.)

② **AUTHOR'S PURPOSE/POINT OF VIEW  Why do you think the author chose to write this selection about Wilson Bentley?** (Possible responses: he is interesting; to give information about snowflakes)

**SOCIAL STUDIES**

**Snowflake Bentley**  Wilson A. Bentley was born in a small town in Vermont. He was amazed at the beauty of snowflakes. He wanted others to see and appreciate these tiny works of art. Bentley discovered that he could attach a microscope to a camera. After many years, he learned how to take pictures of snowflakes. Tell children that the photographs in this selection are copies of ones actually taken by Mr. Bentley.

## Connections

### Comparing Texts

**1** What was the most interesting thing you learned about snow from "Snow Surprise" or "The Snowflake Man"? (Possible response: You can make fun things with snow.)

**2** What other things do people do in the snow for fun? (Possible responses: make a snow fort, sledding, skiing)

**3** Tell about something you made that did not turn out the way you expected. Responses will vary.

#### ✏ Writing

Pretend that Joan made the snow surprise for you. Write a note to thank her for it.

> January 17, 20--
> Dear Joan,
> Thank you for making the snow surprise for me. It looks like a giant mouse! How did you make it?
> Your Pal,
> Emma

246

### Phonics

Make and read new words.

Start with **slow**.

Change `s` `l` to `r`.

Change `w` to `a` `d`.

Change `r` to `t`.

Change `d` to `s` `t`.

### Fluency Practice

Take turns reading pages of "Snow Surprise." Make the characters sound as if they are really talking to you.

"Come with me, Sport!"

247

---

# Connections

## ⏱ WRITING

**Write a Note** Remind children of the features of a thank-you note, including the greeting and closing. Have them write a thank-you note to Joan from "Snow Surprise."

> Thank you for the snow surprise. I really like it!

## ⏱ PHONICS

**Word Building** Distribute to children *Word Builder Cards a, d, l, o, r, s, t, t,* and *w*. Have children practice manipulating the cards to build and read *slow, row, road, toad,* and *toast*.

`r` `o` `a` `d`

## ⏱ FLUENCY

**Small-Group Reading** Organize children into small groups. Ask children to take turns reading one page of "Snow Surprise." Remind them to think about how quickly or slowly they should read each character's words. Tell them to make it sound as if the characters are really talking.

"I saw the snow first!"

# Build Robust Vocabulary

## Listening/Speaking: *Words About the Selection*

### Teach/Model

 **Routine Card 15**

**INTRODUCE ROBUST VOCABULARY** Use *Routine Card 15* to introduce the words.

---

❶ Put the word in **selection context.**
❷ Provide the **Student-Friendly Explanation** for children.
❸ Have children **say the word** with you.
❹ Use the word in other contexts, and have children **interact with the word's meaning.**
❺ Say the Student-Friendly Explanation again, and ask children to **name the word** that goes with it.

---

❶ **Selection Context:** Joan <mark>commands</mark> her dog Sport to come along when she says, "Come with me."
❹ **Interact with Word Meaning:** I can command my dog to sit. Would you command a dog or a goldfish to roll over? Why?

❶ **Selection Context:** Joan <mark>labored</mark> to make the snowman, using snow, sticks, and food.
❹ **Interact with Word Meaning:** On Saturday, I labored all day to clean my home. Would you have labored if you built a sand castle or if you took a nap? Why?

❶ **Selection Context:** The animals are <mark>wary</mark> of Joan and do not go near the snowman until she goes inside the house.
❹ **Interact with Word Meaning:** I would be wary if I heard a strange noise outside my door. Would you be more wary about going into a dark cave or a bright room? Why?

### Practice/Apply

**GUIDED PRACTICE** Ask children to do the following:
- Name something your parents might command you to do.
- Tell how you would feel if you labored all day cleaning.
- Name an animal you would be wary of.

### Objective

- *To develop robust vocabulary through discussing a literature selection*

**INTRODUCE** **Tested** ✓

### Student-Friendly Explanations

<mark>command</mark> When you command someone, you tell him or her what to do.

<mark>labored</mark> If you labored, you worked very hard.

<mark>wary</mark> When you are cautious and unsure about something that might be dangerous, you are wary.

**Introduce Vocabulary** Use body language, facial expressions, and tone of voice to help demonstrate the meaning of each word. For example, slouch and say in a tired voice: **I am so tired. I labored all day to clean up my yard.** Shake and say in a scared voice: **W-what is that noise? I am wary of going into this dark room.**

# Grammar

## Troublesome Words: Homophones

### Objective

- To identify homophones and use them correctly

### Daily Proofreading

**i one the contest!**

(I, won)

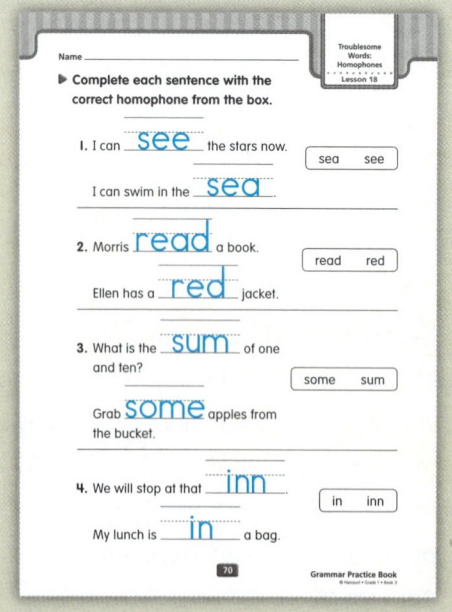

▲ Grammar Practice Book, p. 70

### Review

**DICTATE SENTENCES** Remind children that they have learned about homophones, words that sound alike but have different spellings and meanings. Write on the board some of the homophone pairs that children have worked with this week, including *by/buy, to/two, tale/tail, red/read, new/knew, right/write,* and *one/won.* Review the meaning of each word with children, and then invite volunteers to dictate sentences that include these words. Record their sentences using the incorrect homophone.

My hat is read.

We one the game.

Max has a knew bike.

I can right my name.

### Practice/Apply

**GUIDED PRACTICE** Reread the first sentence to children, tracking the print. Model how to use context clues to identify the incorrect homophone and replace it with the correct one. Say: **The word *read*, *r-e-a-d*, means "to have learned from something in print." This does not make sense in this sentence. The word should be *red*, *r-e-d*, which is the name of a color.**

Follow a similar procedure to help children identify and correct the homophones in the remaining sentences. Guide them to use context clues to determine the correct word to use. Then track the print and read aloud the finished text with children.

**INDEPENDENT PRACTICE** Have children write their own sentence, using one of the homophones on the board. Have partners trade papers. Ask children to underline the homophone in their partner's sentence and talk about whether it is the correct word.

# Shared Writing

*Thank-You Letter*

| 5-DAY WRITING | |
|---|---|
| DAY 1 | Modeled Writing |
| DAY 2 | Shared Writing |
| DAY 3 | Shared Writing |
| DAY 4 | Independent Writing |
| DAY 5 | Independent Writing |

## Write Together

**REVIEW WITH A LITERATURE MODEL** Have children open their *Student Edition* to "Snow Surprise" and read aloud these sentences:

p. 222: **Joan ran for her coat. "I'll show you a snow surprise," she called to Ben.**

p. 237: **Ben clapped his hands, "A mouse!" he sang. "It's a snow mouse!"**

After reading, guide children to talk about what Ben would thank Joan for if he were to write her a thank-you letter.

**PRACTICE WRITING** Reread the group thank-you letter from Day 2. Guide children to consider the needs of their audience as they write. Since they are writing to an adult, tell them to make sure the letter is a little more formal. Explain that they should write about things they would say politely to Mr. Chapman. Work with children to add to the body of the letter and to make revisions as needed to improve it.

**WORD CHOICE** Read the letter with children, tracking the print. Point out words and sentences that will help the reader know how thankful they are. Encourage children to add words to make their message clearer.

WRITING TRAIT

## Share

**DISCUSS THE THANK-YOU LETTER** Read the finished letter with children, tracking the print. Then ask them to

- identify words and sentences about thanking the person.

- identify the parts of a thank-you letter.

- identify capital letters and punctuation marks and tell why they are used.

Display the thank-you letter. Children can use it as a writing model for Days 4 and 5.

## Objectives

- *To write a thank-you letter*
- *To identify the distinguishing features of a thank-you letter*

## Writing Prompt

**Write a List** Have children create a list of things they would like to thank their parents for.

> Oct 12, 20--
>
> Dear Mr. Chapman,
>
> Thank you for getting our ball off the roof.
>
> Your friends,
> Mrs. Hill's Class

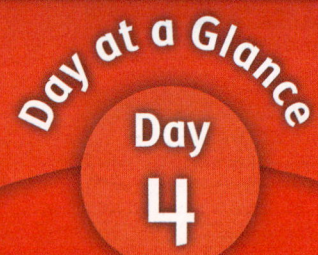

## Day at a Glance
### Day 4

**Phonemic Awareness**
- Phoneme Substitution

 **and Spelling**
- Introduce: Phonograms *-ow, -oat*
- Maintain: Initial Blends with *l, s, r*
- Review: Long Vowel /ō/*ow, oa*

**High-Frequency Words**
- Review: *mouse, our, over, pretty, surprise, three*

**Fluency**
- Reading Rate
- "Snow Surprise," *Student Edition,* pp. 218–239

**Comprehension**
 Review: Author's Purpose/ Point of View

- Big Book: *We're Going on a Lion Hunt*

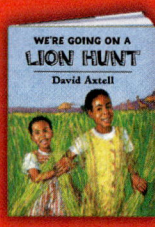

**Robust Vocabulary**
- Review: *command, labored, wary*

**Grammar**
- Review: Troublesome Words: Homophones

**Independent Writing**
- Thank-You Letter

# Warm-Up Routines

## Oral Language

**Objective** *To listen attentively and respond appropriately to oral communication*

### Question of the Day

Have you heard a dog bark? What do you think a dog barks at?

Help children brainstorm things that might make a dog bark. Write the following sentence frame and have children complete it.

**A dog barks at _____.**

## Read Aloud

**Objective** *To appreciate the rhythm and rhyme of a poem*

**BIG BOOK OF RHYMES AND POEMS** Display the poem and read the title and the poet's name. Ask children to describe the poet's role. Then read the poem aloud, and have them listen for words that rhyme. After you read, ask children to name rhyming words. Reread the poem, and have children clap the rhythm with you and join in on the parts they know.

▲ Big Book of Rhymes and Poems, p. 11

## Word Wall

**Objective** *To read high-frequency words*

**REVIEW HIGH-FREQUENCY WORDS** Review *over, tree, mouse, our, play, day, onto, eat,* and other previously learned high-frequency words. Say each word, ask a volunteer to point to it, and have children read it aloud. Then point to words at random, and have children reread them. Repeat several times to reinforce instant recognition.

| | | | |
|---|---|---|---|
| mouse | our | over | play |
| day | tree | onto | eat |

## Phonemic Awareness

**Objective** *To substitute phonemes to make new words*

**Routine Card 10**

**PHONEME SUBSTITUTION** Tell children that you will say a word and they will change the middle sound to make a new word. Model by saying: *coat.* /k/ /ō/ /t/. **If I change /ō/ to /u/, I get** *cut.* Continue with the following words:

**man,** /a/ to /ō/ (moan)    **hit,** /i/ to /a/ (hat)

**load,** /ō/ to /i/ (lid)    **crush,** /u/ to /a/ (crash)

Tell children that you will say a word and they will change the ending sound to make a new word. Model by saying: *cap.* /k/ /a/ /p/. **If I change /p/ to /t/, I get** *cat.* Continue with the following words:

**pork,** /k/ to /t/ (port)    **roam,** /m/ to /st/ (roast)

**coach,** /ch/ to /t/ (coat)    **chug,** /g/ to /m/ (chum)

# Phonograms -ow, -oat

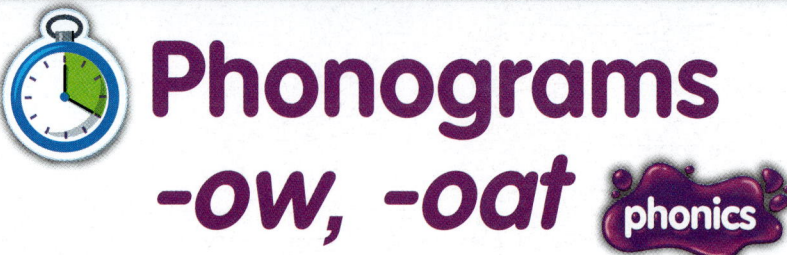

| 5-DAY PHONICS | |
|---|---|
| **DAY 1** | Introduce /ō/ow, oa |
| **DAY 2** | Review /ō/ow, oa |
| **DAY 3** | Word Building with /ō/ow, oa and /o/o |
| **DAY 4** | Phonograms -ow, -oat |
| **DAY 5** | Phonograms -own, -oast |

## Objectives

- *To recognize root words*
- *To read and use phonograms -ow, -oat*

## Skill Trace

**Phonograms -ow, -oat**

Introduce   T534–T535

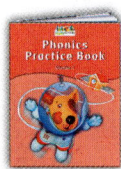 **Resources**

**Phonics Practice Book, pp. 101–102**

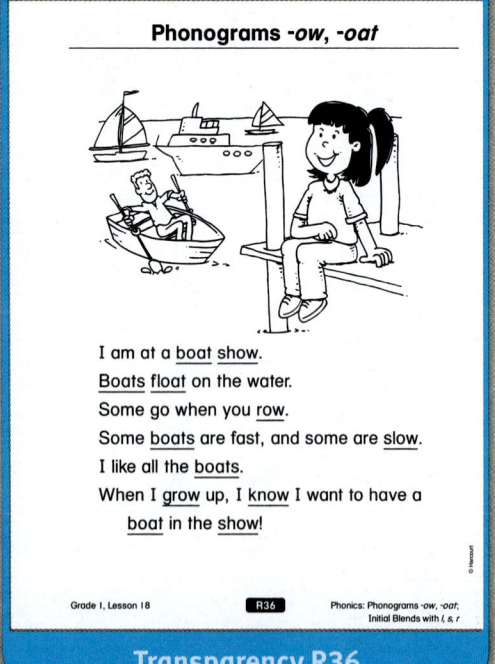

**Phonograms -ow, -oat**

I am at a <u>boat</u> show.
<u>Boats</u> <u>float</u> on the water.
Some go when you <u>row</u>.
Some <u>boats</u> are fast, and some are <u>slow</u>.
I like all the <u>boats</u>.
When I <u>grow</u> up, I <u>know</u> I want to have a <u>boat</u> in the show!

Grade 1, Lesson 18      R36      Phonics: Phonograms -ow, -oat;
Initial Blends with l, s, r

**Transparency R36**

## Teach/Model

**LISTEN FOR RHYMING WORDS**  Say the words *slow, snow,* and *row.* Ask children how the words are the same. (They both end with /ō/. They rhyme.) Write *slow, snow,* and *row* on the board and have children read them aloud. Underline *-ow* in each word, and remind children that these letters can stand for the long *o* sound.

Say the words *coat, goat,* and *boat.* Ask how these words are the same. (They both end with /ōt/. They rhyme.) Write *coat, goat,* and *boat* on the board and have children read them aloud. Underline *-oat* in each word. Remind children that the letters *-oa* can also spell long *o*.

## Guided Practice

**FORM WORDS**  Write *-ow* and *-oat* at the head of two columns on chart paper. Have children suggest words that end with either *-ow* or *-oat* and name the beginning letter or letters. Have children read each word as it is added to the chart. Then have children read both sets of words in the final list. Randomly point to words and have children read the word that you point to.

| -ow | -oat |
|---|---|
| flow | float |
| slow | goat |
| know | boat |

## Practice/Apply

**READ WORDS IN CONTEXT**  Display **Transparency R36.** Have children read each sentence silently. Then ask a volunteer to read the first sentence aloud. Point out the underlined words with phonograms *-ow* or *-oat.* If the words are not on the chart, add them to the list. Then track the print as you lead children in choral-reading the sentences.

# Long Vowel /ō/ ow, oa  and Spelling

## Build Words

**MAP LETTERS TO SOUNDS** Use *Letter Cards* and a pocket chart to form words. Have children listen to your directions and change one letter in each word to spell a spelling word. Have them write the word on a sheet of paper or in their notebook. Then have a volunteer change the *Letter Card* in the pocket chart so that children can self-check their spelling.

- Form *lot* in the pocket chart and have children read it. Ask: **Which spelling word can you make by changing the last letter?** (low)

- Form *grew* in the pocket chart and have children read it. Ask: **Which spelling word can you make by changing the *e*?** (grow)

- Form *load* in the pocket chart and have children read it. Ask: **Which spelling word can you make by changing the first letter?** (road)

Follow a similar procedure with the following words: *slot* (slow), *sap* (soap), *bat* (boat), *lit* (little), *candle* (handle).

**HIGH-FREQUENCY WORDS** Remind children that there are some other words they have to remember how to spell. Tell them that *carry* is one such word. Tell children to picture the word and then write it. Continue with *would*.

> ### BELOW-LEVEL
>
> **Map Letters to Sounds** Display *Letter Cards* for each word in random order. For each word, help children connect each sound to its letter or letters by having them arrange the letters to spell the word. Then have them write the word.

### Objectives

- *To use /ō/ow, oa and other known letter-sounds to spell and write words*

- *To spell and write known high-frequency words*

### Spelling Words

| | | | |
|---|---|---|---|
| 1. | low | 6. | boat |
| 2. | slow | 7. | little |
| 3. | grow | 8. | handle |
| 4. | road | 9. | carry |
| 5. | soap | 10. | would |

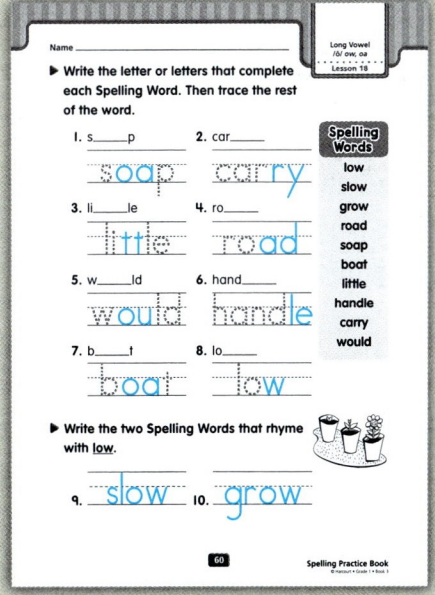

▲ Spelling Practice Book, p. 60

# High-Frequency Words

## Objective

- *To read high-frequency words*

### REVIEW | Tested

### High-Frequency Words

| | |
|---|---|
| mouse | pretty |
| our | surprise |
| over | three |

### Review Story Events
Read aloud the sentences. Have children act out sentences to demonstrate understanding of the high-frequency words.

 **BELOW-LEVEL**

**Read and Write Words** Read aloud the story strips as children track the print. When you come to a blank, say: **blank.** Reread, but this time when you come to a blank, pause for children to say the word that makes sense. Point to the displayed word and have children write it. Have children echo-read the sentences to check their work.

## Review

**READ AND WRITE WORDS** Duplicate and distribute an uncut story strip page (*Teacher Resource Book*, p. 228) to each child. Then:

- Have children read the story title in the first strip. Explain that the sentences tell the story, but some have missing words.

- Display *Word Cards* for the high-frequency words, or list the words on the board. Have children read each word.

## Practice/Apply

**GUIDED PRACTICE** Direct children to read all the story strip sentences and to write the missing words in the blanks.

> Joan looked out and saw the _____ snow.

**INDEPENDENT PRACTICE** After children complete the story strip page, have them cut apart the strips. Have partners work together to read and match their story strips and then to arrange the events in the order in which they happen in the story. Have children take the story strips home to share with family members.

Children read the words in context in the Cut-Out/Fold-Up Book.

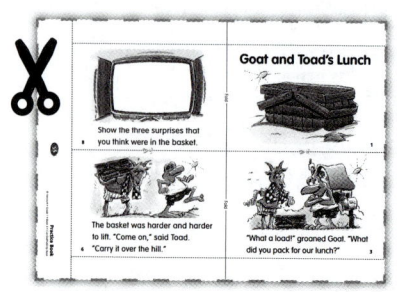

◄ **"Goat and Toad's Lunch" Practice Book, pp. 55–56**

# Fluency
## *Reading Rate*

### Review

**DIBELS** Oral Reading Fluency **ORF** **MODEL READING AT AN APPROPRIATE RATE** Remind children that when good readers read, it sounds like talking. They do not speak too fast or too slowly. They speak at a rate that can be understood by the listener.

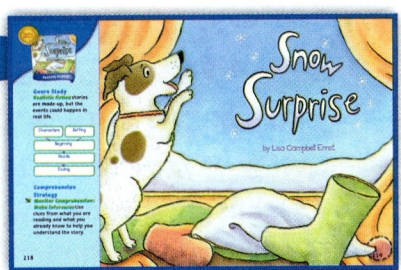

▲ Student Edition, pp. 218–239

**Think Aloud** **I am going to read "Snow Surprise" one page at a time. I am going to notice the commas and end marks so I know when to pause as I read. Read each page after me, just the way I read it.**

### Practice/Apply

**GUIDED PRACTICE** Have partners reread "Snow Surprise" aloud three or four times. Remind them to use the punctuation to signal them when to pause. Tell them that their reading rate should increase with each reading because they will be more familiar with the words they are reading. Listen to partners read, giving them feedback about their reading rate and guidance for improving fluency.

**INDEPENDENT PRACTICE** Have partners take the parts of Joan and Ben and practice reading "Snow Surprise" fluently at an appropriate rate. Then have partners make stick puppets with the character cutouts (*Teacher Resource Book*, p. 197) and use them to act out the story as they read it aloud to the group. Remind the audience to listen carefully and quietly and to clap for the performers when they have finished.

### Objectives
- *To build fluency through rereading a story*
- *To read in a manner that sounds like natural speech*

### Additional Related Reading

Guide children to self-select related books, such as:

- *Tiny the Snow Dog* by Cari Meister. Viking, 2001. **EASY**

- *A Little Bit of Winter* by Paul Stewart. HarperCollins, 2000. **AVERAGE**

- *The Mitten* adapted and illustrated by Jan Brett. Penguin, 1996. **CHALLENGE**

### BELOW-LEVEL

**Fluency Practice** Have children reread for fluency, using "First Snow" in the *Book 1-3 Strategic Intervention Interactive Reader, Decodable Book 18,* or the appropriate *Leveled Reader* (see pages T552–T555). Guide them to select a small portion of a story and practice reading it several times.

# Author's Purpose/Point of View *Comprehension*

## Objective

- *To determine the author's purpose and point of view while listening to a story*

## Skill Trace

 **Tested** **Author's Purpose/ Point of View**

| | |
|---|---|
| Preview | T142 |
| Introduce | T151 |
| Reteach | S16–S17, S56–S57 |
| **Review** | **T176, T188, T198, T490, T499, T524, T538, T548** |
| Test | Bk 1-3 |
| Maintain | Monitor Comprehension, Bks 1-4, 1-5 |

---

 **MONITOR PROGRESS**

### Author's Purpose/Point of View

| **IF** children have difficulty determining the author's purpose, | **THEN** have them suggest a favorite story and help them identify the author's purpose. |
|---|---|

**Small-Group Instruction, pp. S56–S57:**

🔴 **BELOW-LEVEL:** Reteach
🔵 **ON-LEVEL:** Reinforce
🟢 **ADVANCED:** Extend

---

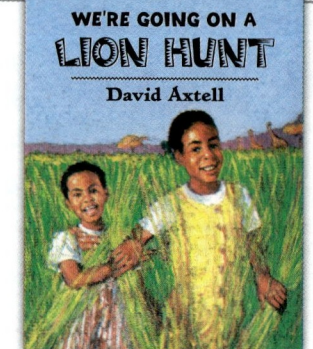

▲ **Big Book**

### Review

**TALK ABOUT AUTHOR'S PURPOSE/POINT OF VIEW** Invite children to identify the purposes that authors have when writing a story. (to inform, to entertain, to teach a lesson)

**USE PRIOR KNOWLEDGE/SET A PURPOSE** Display *Big Book We're Going on a Lion Hunt*. Guide children to use prior knowledge and set a purpose for listening. Have children chime in on the repeated text.

**DISCUSS HOMOPHONES** As you read aloud, point out homophones. Point out the word *one* on page 5. Say: **The word *one*, o-n-e, is a number word, as in "I have *one* nose." A homophone for *one* is *won*, w-o-n, as in "I *won* the race."** Call attention to other homophones throughout the story, such as *through, not, to, nose, mane, four.*

### Practice/Apply

**GUIDED PRACTICE** Monitor listening comprehension as you read, using the following questions:

- **PAGE 14: MAKE INFERENCES** Why do you think the girls tiptoe through the cave? (They tiptoe so the lion won't hear them.)

- 🌀 **AUTHOR'S PURPOSE/POINT OF VIEW** What is the author's purpose? (to entertain) How do you think the author feels about lions? (He thinks they are big and scary.)

- **CHARACTERS' EMOTIONS** How do you think the girls feel when they get back home? Why do you think this? (Possible responses: relieved; they got home safely.)

**INDEPENDENT PRACTICE** Remind children that authors have different purposes for writing a story. Lead children in a discussion of how the story might be different if the author's purpose were to give information about lions.

# Build Robust Vocabulary

## Listening/Speaking: *Words About the Selection*

### Review Robust Vocabulary

**USE VOCABULARY IN DIFFERENT CONTEXTS** Remind children of the Student-Friendly Explanations of *command, labored,* and *wary.* Then discuss each word using the following examples:

**command** Tell children that you will say some sentences. When you command them to do something, they should perform the action. Otherwise, they should do nothing.

| | |
|---|---|
| **Touch your toes.** | **Who is wearing a red shirt?** |
| **Today is Tuesday.** | **Say your name.** |

**labored** Tell children you will name some activities. If the activity is something a person would labor to do, children should sit down. If it is not, they should remain standing.

| | |
|---|---|
| **Take a nap.** | **Color in a coloring book.** |
| **Build a house.** | **Climb a mountain.** |

**wary** Tell children you will name some things. If children would be wary of those things, they should cover their eyes. If not, they should put their hands at their sides.

| | |
|---|---|
| snake | friend |
| rock | campfire |
| sand | ladybug |
| flower | bumblebee |
| lion | hat |

### Objective
- *To review robust vocabulary*

**REVIEW** — Tested

#### Student-Friendly Explanations

**command** When you command someone, you tell him or her what to do.

**labored** If you labored, you worked very hard.

**wary** When you are cautious and unsure about something that might be dangerous, you are wary.

#### ON-LEVEL

**Extend the Activity** Invite volunteers to give the class commands or to name things and ask children which ones they would be wary of.

#  Grammar

## Troublesome Words: Homophones

**5-DAY GRAMMAR**

| | |
|---|---|
| DAY 1 | Introduce Homophones |
| DAY 2 | Use a Literature Model |
| DAY 3 | Recognize Incorrect Homophones |
| DAY 4 | **Identify Homophones** |
| DAY 5 | Write Sentences with Homophones |

### Objective
• To identify and use homophones correctly

### Daily Proofreading

**We have to pup**
(two, pups.)

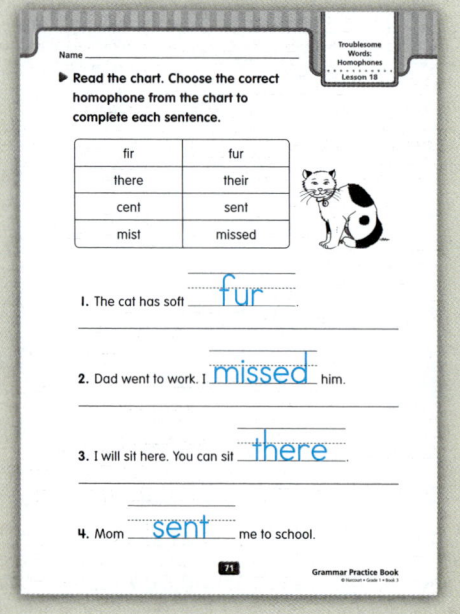

▲ Grammar Practice Book, p. 71

### Review

**IDENTIFY HOMOPHONES** Review the definition of homophones with children. Write on the board some of the homophones they have learned this week as well as some words that are not homophones. Work with children to identify the homophones. Leave the list of homophones on the board.

### Practice/Apply

**GUIDED PRACTICE** Write the following sentences on the board.

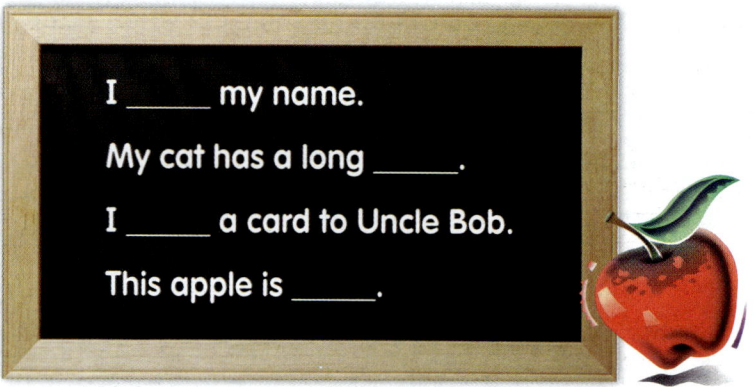

I _____ my name.

My cat has a long _____.

I _____ a card to Uncle Bob.

This apple is _____.

Call on volunteers to read the sentences aloud. Have children use context clues and their knowledge of word meanings to identify the homophone that correctly completes each sentence. Ask children to spell the word for you as you write it in the blank. Have them refer to the word list on the board as needed. *(read or write, tail, write, red)*

**INDEPENDENT PRACTICE** Ask children to choose one sentence to write. Have them underline the homophone and then illustrate their sentence.

# Independent Writing

*Thank-You Letter*

**5-DAY WRITING**
| | |
|---|---|
| **DAY 1** | Modeled Writing |
| **DAY 2** | Shared Writing |
| **DAY 3** | Shared Writing |
| **DAY 4** | Independent Writing |
| **DAY 5** | Independent Writing |

## Write a Thank-You Letter

**GENERATE IDEAS** Tell children they will write their own thank-you letters. Ask them to look again at the pictures they drew on Day 1. Ask them to write a list of words that they could use when they thank the person who gave them the gift or helped them.

happy
lucky
new
helpful
thank
gift

**REVIEW CHARACTERISTICS** Display the list of characteristics of a well-written thank-you letter from Day 1, and read it with children.

 **WORD CHOICE** Write on the board *It is nice.* Ask children to suggest more specific words they could use to replace *nice.* Remind them to use clear words in their writing to tell how things look, sound, smell, feel, or taste.

### Thank-You Letter

- It is written to thank someone.
- The <u>heading</u> is the date.
- The <u>greeting</u> tells who gets the letter.
- The <u>body</u> is the message. It tells why you are thankful.
- The <u>closing</u> says good-bye.
- The <u>signature</u> is your name.

 **WRITE** Review with children how to use margins to make their writing readable. Before they begin writing, have them place two fingers down on the left side of the page and make a light pencil mark down the page. Tell them that this is the area in which there should be no writing. Have them do the same on the right side. Then ask children to write a draft of their thank-you letter. Have them use their prewriting pictures and word lists for ideas.

### Objectives

- *To select a focus when writing*
- *To write a thank-you letter*
- *To use sensory details in writing*

### Writing Prompt

**Write About a Gift** Have children write about a gift they gave to someone. Have them tell what the gift was and why they gave it to that person.

### ADVANCED

**Elaborate** Encourage children to elaborate on their thank-you letters, describing in detail why they are thankful. Have them add descriptive words to make their writing clear. They can also add sentences to give additional reasons why they like the gift or are thankful for the help.

## Phonemic Awareness
- Phoneme Blending

 **and Spelling**
- Introduce: Phonograms -*own*, -*oast*
- Posttest: Long Vowel /ō/*ow*, *oa*

## High-Frequency Words
- Review

## Fluency
- Reading Rate
- "Snow Surprise," *Student Edition*, pp. 218–239

## Comprehension
 Review: Author's Purpose/ Point of View

## Robust Vocabulary
- Review

## Grammar
- Review: Troublesome Words: Homophones

## Independent Writing
- Thank-You Letter

# Warm-Up Routines

## Oral Language

**Objectives**  *To express feelings; to listen attentively*

### Question of the Day

**What things have you done, just because you like to do them?**

Talk with children about enjoyable things they have done. Help children complete this sentence frame.

**One time I _____ just because I liked to.**

## Read Aloud

**Objectives**  *To understand concepts of print; to listen for enjoyment to a contemporary poem*

**BIG BOOK OF RHYMES AND POEMS**  Ask children to tell what they remember about the poem. Then read it, modeling reading from left to right and from top to bottom. Ask children to identify individual words, spaces between letters and words, capital letters, and periods. Reread the poem several times, encouraging children to join in.

▲ **Big Book of Rhymes and Poems, p. 11**

## Word Wall

**Objective** *To read high-frequency words*

**REVIEW HIGH-FREQUENCY WORDS** Review *pretty, surprise, three, carry, would,* and other previously learned high-frequency words. Say each word, ask a volunteer to point to it, and have children read it aloud. Then point to words at random, and have children reread them. Repeat several times. Then read all the words displayed, one word at a time.

**pretty**   **surprise**   **three**   **carry**   **would**

## Phonemic Awareness

**Objective** *To blend phonemes into recognizable words*

**Routine Card 1** **PHONEME BLENDING** Tell children that you will say each sound in a word slowly and they will blend the sounds to say the word. Segment the word *low* into phonemes—/l/ /ō/. Then say it naturally—*low*. Continue with the following words:

/s/ /l/ /ō/ (slow)   /s/ /n/ /ō/ (snow)   /g/ /ō/ /t/ (goat)

/g/ /r/ /ō/ (grow)   /r/ /ō/ /m/ (roam)   /f/ /l/ /ō/ /t/ (float)

/k/ /r/ /ō/ (crow)   /t/ /ō/ (tow)   /t/ /ō/ /s/ /t/ (toast)

**Ask children how all the words are alike.** (They all have /ō/.)

### /g/ /ō/ /t/ (goat)

 Podcasting: Phoneme Blending

# Phonograms -own, -oast

**phonics**

| DAY 1 | Introduce /ō/ow, oa |
|---|---|
| DAY 2 | Review /ō/ow, oa |
| DAY 3 | Word Building with /ō/ow, oa and /o/o |
| DAY 4 | Phonograms -ow, -oat |
| DAY 5 | Phonograms -own, -oast |

## Objectives

- *To discriminate between words with different patterns*
- *To use common vowel spelling patterns to read words.*

## Skill Trace
**Phonograms -own, -oast**

Introduce   T544

## Review

**RHYMING WORDS** Tell children that words that rhyme often have the same ending letters.

- Write *shown*. Say: **A word that rhymes with *shown* and ends with the same letters is *grown*.** Write *grown*.

- Write *toast*. Say: **A word that rhymes with *toast* and ends with the same letters is *coast*.** Write *coast*.

## Work with Patterns

**BUILD WORDS** Draw a two-column chart with the heads -*own*  and -*oast*. Have children suggest words that end with either -*own* or -*oast* and say what letter or letters are needed to begin the words. Have children read each word as it is added to the chart.

| -own | -oast |
|---|---|
| grown | toast |
| shown | coast |
| flown | roast |

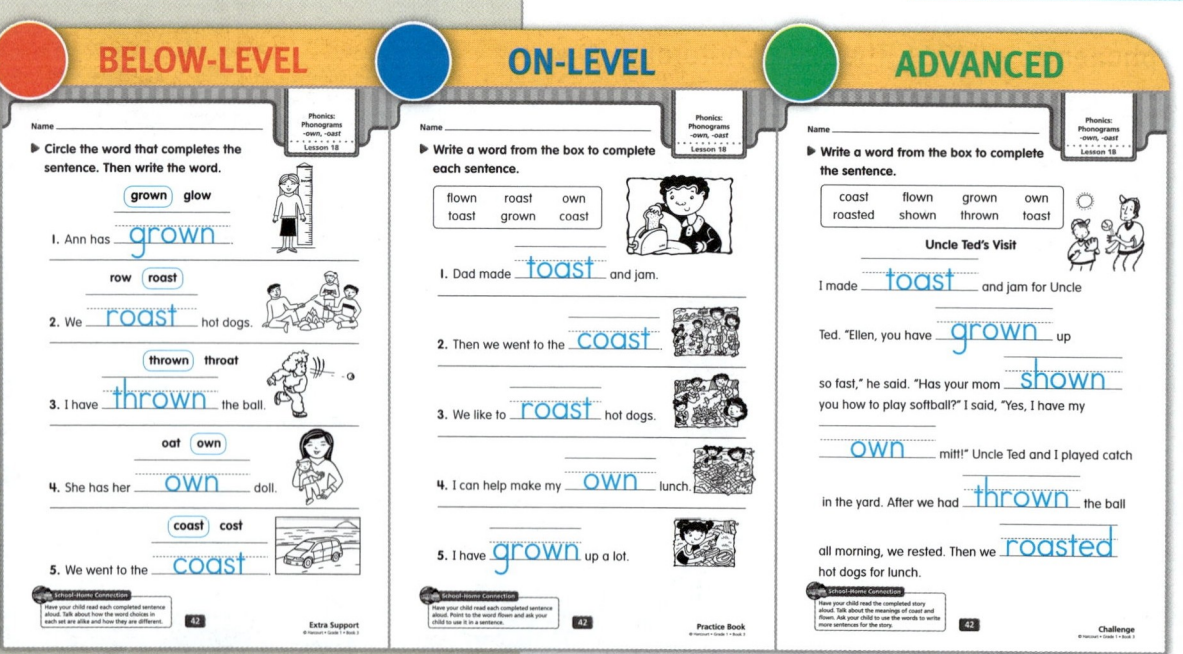

**BELOW-LEVEL**  ▲ Extra Support, p. 42

**ON-LEVEL**  ▲ Practice Book, p. 42

**ADVANCED**  ▲ Challenge, p. 42

**E L L**

- Group children according to academic levels, and assign one of the pages on the left.

- Clarify any unfamiliar concepts as necessary. See *ELL Teacher Guide*, Lesson 18, for support in scaffolding instruction.

# Long Vowel /ō/ ow, oa  and Spelling

**5-DAY SPELLING**
| | |
|---|---|
| **DAY 1** | Pretest |
| **DAY 2** | Word Building |
| **DAY 3** | State the Generalization |
| **DAY 4** | Review |
| **DAY 5** | Posttest |

## Objectives

- *To use /ō/ow, oa and other known letter-sounds to spell and write words*
- *To spell and write known high-frequency words*

### Spelling Words

| | |
|---|---|
| 1. **low** | 6. **boat** |
| 2. **slow** | 7. **little** |
| 3. **grow** | 8. **handle** |
| 4. **road** | 9. **carry** |
| 5. **soap** | 10. **would** |

## Assess

**POSTTEST** Assess children's progress. Use the dictation sentences from Day 1.

### Words with /ō/ ow, oa

1. low     The pup easily hopped over the **low** fence.
2. slow    I was too **slow** to win the race.
3. grow    We **grow** flowers in our garden.
4. road    The big trucks roared down the busy **road.**
5. soap    Use lots of **soap** when you wash your hands.
6. boat    We sailed around the lake in our **boat.**

### Review

7. little   A newborn kitten is very **little.**
8. handle   Always hold the pitcher by its **handle.**

### High-Frequency

9. carry    Jack will **carry** his lunch in his backpack.
10. would   What **would** you like to do today?

**WRITING APPLICATION** Have children complete and illustrate the following sentence frames.

I would sail a boat on a \_\_\_\_\_.
I carry the \_\_\_\_\_ by the handle.

I would sail a boat on a lake.

I carry the basket by the handle.

# High-Frequency Words

## Objectives

- *To read high-frequency words*
- *To explore word relationships*

**REVIEW** **Tested** ✓

### High-Frequency Words

| | | |
|---|---|---|
| buy | mouse | pretty |
| feel | our | surprise |
| loud | over | their |
| money | paint | three |

---

### BELOW-LEVEL

**Reinforce Word Recognition** If children are having difficulty with a high-frequency word, have them spell it aloud as they write it on paper.

---

## Review

**REINFORCE WORD RECOGNITION** Display *Word Cards* for all of the words in a pocket chart. Point to words at random and ask volunteers to read them.

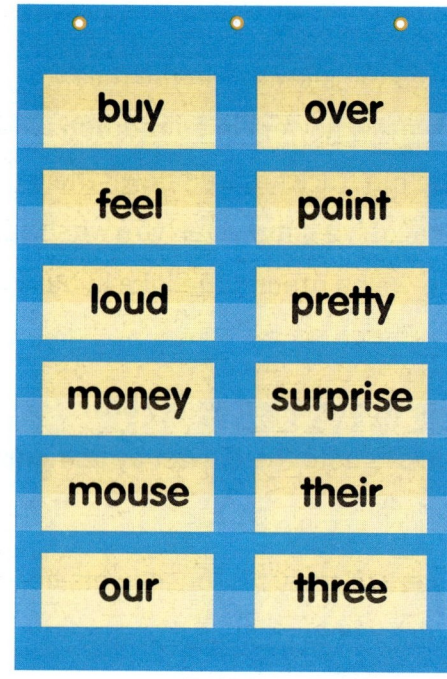

**SORT WORDS** Guide children in sorting the words into columns according to the number of letters. Then have them read the words in each column aloud.

- Have children look at the four-letter words: *feel, loud,* and *over.* Ask: **Which of these words is a direction word?** (over)

- Have children find and read the word *buy.* Ask: **Which word names what you need in order to buy something?** (money)

- Ask: **Which word rhymes with *house?*** (mouse) **Which word tells how many?** (three)

# 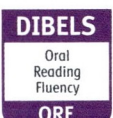 Fluency
## *Reading Rate*

### Readers' Theater

**▲ Student Edition, pp. 218–239**

**DIBELS**
Oral Reading Fluency
**ORF**

**PERFORM "SNOW SURPRISE"** To help children improve their fluency, have them perform "Snow Surprise" as Readers' Theater. Use the following procedures:

- Read "Snow Surprise" aloud. Model reading fluently and at an appropriate rate.

- Discuss the importance of reading at an appropriate rate so that the audience will be able to understand what is being read.

- Have partners read the story together. Then have them choose the part of Joan or Ben and practice rereading the story at an appropriate rate.

- Listen to sets of partners read. Provide feedback and support.

- Invite partners to read the story to classmates. Remind them to focus on reading at an appropriate rate.

**BELOW-LEVEL**

**Echo-Read** Read a page from the story at an appropriate rate, and have children read exactly as you did. Continue to have children echo-read each page.

## Objective
- *To read fluently at an appropriate rate*

 **ASSESSMENT**

**Monitoring Progress** Periodically, take a timed sample of children's oral reading and measure the number of words read correctly per minute. Children should be accurately reading approximately 60 words per minute by the end of Grade 1.

### Fluency Support Materials

 **Fluency Builders, Grade 1,** Lesson 18
● ● ●

 **Audiotext** *Student Edition* selections are available on *Audiotext Grade 1,* CD 3.

 **Strategic Intervention Teacher Guide,** Lesson 18

# Author's Purpose/Point of View *Comprehension*

## Objective
- *To identify and describe the author's purpose/point of view*

## Skill Trace

**Tested**  **Author's Purpose/ Point of View**

| | |
|---|---|
| Preview | T142 |
| Introduce | T151 |
| Reteach | S16–S17, S56–S57 |
| **Review** | **T176, T188, T198, T490, T499, T524, T538, T548** |
| Test | Bk 1-3 |
| Maintain | Monitor Comprehension Bk 1-4, 1-5 |

## ADVANCED

**Identify Author's Purpose/Point of View** Invite children to choose a favorite story. Have them share the story with the group and tell why they think the author wrote it and what the author's point of view is.

### Review

**REVIEW THE SKILL** Ask children to explain different reasons that authors write stories and articles. (to entertain, to inform, to teach a lesson) Draw a three-column chart on the board with the titles "The Mitten," "Snow Surprise," and *We're Going on a Lion Hunt* each at the top of one column. Remind children that these are the read-aloud, the *Student Edition* selection, and the *Big Book* that they read this week. Write the author's purpose for writing "The Mitten" in the first column.

**GUIDED PRACTICE** Ask volunteers to tell why the author wrote "Snow Surprise." Write their responses in the second column of the chart. Then have them repeat the process for *We're Going on a Lion Hunt*.

| | "The Mitten" | "Snow Surprise" | We're Going on a Lion Hunt |
|---|---|---|---|
| **Author's Purpose** | To entertain | To entertain | To entertain |

**INDEPENDENT PRACTICE** Have children page through their *Student Edition* to help them recall selections they have already read. Ask each one to name one of the selections and tell why they think the author wrote it.

# Build Robust Vocabulary

## Listening/Speaking

### Review

**REINFORCE MEANINGS** Ask children the following questions:

- Would you be *wary* of a teacher who gave you a *command?* Why or why not? Would you be *wary* of a growling bear? Tell why or why not.

- If you stuff three pairs of socks in your pocket, would your pocket *bulge?* Would it *bulge* if you put three pennies in it? Tell why or why not.

- Would you be tired if you had *labored* all day doing yard work? Why or why not?

- Would you *argue* with someone who *jostled* you while you were waiting in line? Why or why not?

**ACT OUT WORDS** Prompt children to work in pairs to act out scenes that illustrate their understanding of the words. Use the following prompts as models.

- Your partner is your pet dog. Command him or her to do a trick.

- You and your partner are at the doorway of a dark room. Show how you would look if you were wary of going inside.

- Pretend to argue with your partner about who should get to play with a favorite toy.

- Pretend that you and your partner are in a tight space, such as an elevator, with several other people. Show how you might get jostled.

**REVIEW** Tested ✓

### Build Robust Vocabulary

| | |
|---|---|
| argue | jostled |
| bulged | labored |
| command | wary |

**MONITOR PROGRESS**

### Build Robust Vocabulary

| **IF** children do not demonstrate understanding of the words and have difficulty using them, | **THEN** model using each word in several sentences. Have children repeat each sentence. |
|---|---|

**Small-Group Instruction, pp. S58–S59:**

🔴 **BELOW-LEVEL:** Reteach
🔵 **ON-LEVEL:** Reinforce
🟢 **ADVANCED:** Extend

# Grammar

## *Troublesome Words: Homophones*

### Objective
- *To identify and use homophones correctly*

### Daily Proofreading

**Do you sea my backpack.**
(see, backpack?)

### ✓ Language Arts Checkpoint

If children have difficulty with the concepts, see pages S60–S61 to reteach.

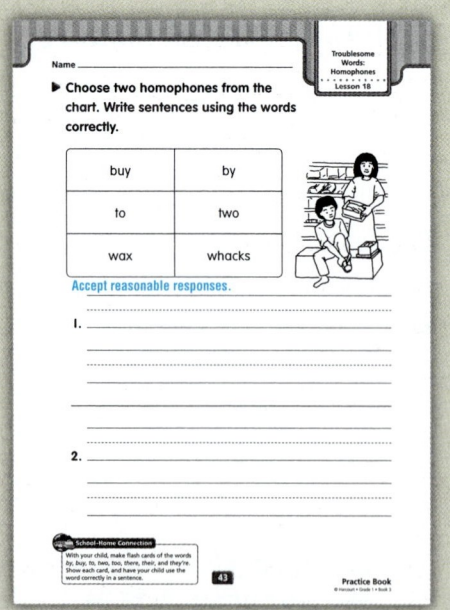

▲ Practice Book, p. 43

---

### Review

**IDENTIFY HOMOPHONES** Remind children that homophones are words that sound alike but have different spellings and meanings. Write the following sentences on the board with the homophones underlined. Read them with children, and ask them to tell which sentence has the correct word.

| | |
|---|---|
| I <u>see</u> a clock. | I <u>write</u> a letter. |
| I <u>sea</u> a clock. | I <u>right</u> a letter. |

Then have children help you brainstorm a list of other homophone pairs. Write the words on the board.

### Practice/Apply

**GUIDED PRACTICE** Have volunteers say new sentences using the homophones on the board. Write each sentence and guide children to spell the homophone correctly.

The fish is in the sea.

I water the red flower.

**INDEPENDENT PRACTICE** Organize children into pairs. Have children choose a pair of homophones and write a sentence for each word on a sheet of paper. Have them illustrate their work. Then have partners check one another's work. Encourage them to refer to the words on the board if they need help with spelling.

Invite partners to share their sentences and drawings with the group. Ask volunteers to identify the homophone in each sentence. You may want to collect children's papers, and bind them into a class book.

# Independent Writing
*Thank-You Letter*

| 5-DAY WRITING | |
|---|---|
| DAY 1 | Modeled Writing |
| DAY 2 | Shared Writing |
| DAY 3 | Shared Writing |
| DAY 4 | Independent Writing |
| DAY 5 | Independent Writing |

## Write a Thank-You Letter

**WRITE** Have children continue writing their thank-you letters from Day 4. Remind them that the purpose of the letter is to thank someone.

**WRITING TRAIT** **WORD CHOICE** Remind children to write about things their reader would like to know. Have children check that they have used words that tell how they feel, such as *happy* or *surprised*.

**REVISE** Have children read their thank-you letter to a partner. Read the list of criteria for a thank-you letter to children, and have them use it to improve their writing. Guide them to add details to explain why they are thankful. Also, work with children to check their spelling. Help them write with more proficient spelling of regularly spelled patterns, such as long *o* spelled *-ow* or *-oa*.

### Thank-You Letter

- It is written to thank someone.
- The <u>heading</u> is the date.
- The <u>greeting</u> tells who gets the letter.
- The <u>body</u> is the message. It tells why you are thankful.
- The <u>closing</u> says good-bye.
- The <u>signature</u> is your name.

## Share

**AUTHOR'S CHAIR** Have children write a clean copy of their letters or type them, using a computer, to share with classmates. Before they begin, have children determine their purpose for listening, such as to find out whom their classmate is thanking and why. After children have shared, help children determine how their writing achieves its purposes. Ask: **Did you explain why you are thankful? Did you tell why you liked the gift or why you appreciate what that person has done?**

Author's Chair

## Objectives
- *To write a thank-you letter*
- *To evaluate and revise a thank-you letter*

### Writing Prompt

**Thank a Friend** Have children write a thank-you letter to a friend to thank them for being a good friend.

### WEEKLY LESSON TEST

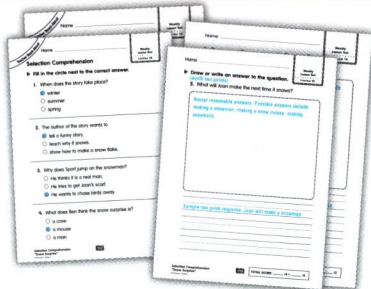

▲ Weekly Lesson Tests, pp. 181–191

- Selection Comprehension with Short Response
- Phonics and Spelling
- High-Frequency Words
- Focus Skill
- Robust Vocabulary
- Grammar
- Fluency

**GO online** For prescriptions, see p. A7. Also available electronically on *StoryTown* Online Assessment and ExamView®.

 **Podcasting:** Assessing Fluency

# Leveled Readers

*Reinforcing Skills and Strategies*

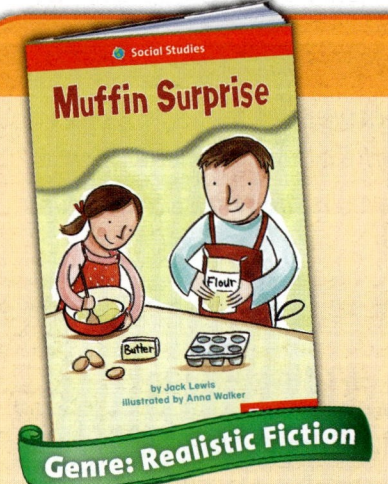

Genre: Realistic Fiction

## BELOW-LEVEL

### Muffin Surprise

**SUMMARY** When muffins do not turn out as expected, a child and her father transform them into works of art to surprise her mom.

 **phonics** Long /ō/*ow, oa*

- **High-Frequency Words:** *mouse, our, over, pretty, surprise, three*

- **Author's Purpose/Point of View**

### Before Reading

**BUILD BACKGROUND/SET A PURPOSE** Have children tell about a time when they made something that didn't turn out as they expected. Ask: **What did you try to make? What went wrong? What did you do?** Then guide children to preview the story and set a purpose for reading it.

### Reading the Book

**PAGE 2 MAKE PREDICTIONS What do you think that Dad and Joan will make for Mom?** (Possible response: Muffins, because that's the name of the book and muffins are a good breakfast food.)

**PAGES 4–8 AUTHOR'S PURPOSE/POINT OF VIEW Why do you think the author has Joan suggest another way to use the muffins instead of throwing them out?** (Possible response: To show that she can take the flat muffins and use them to make something special.)

**REREAD FOR FLUENCY** Have partners read alternate pages of the story aloud several times with expression at a speech-like pace.

### Think Critically    *(See inside back cover for questions.)*

**1 NOTE DETAILS** Mom was in bed.

**2 PROBLEM/SOLUTION** Joan turned them into mouse muffins.

**3 CHARACTERS' EMOTIONS** Possible responses: happy, surprised

**4 AUTHOR'S PURPOSE/POINT OF VIEW** Joan is not telling the story because the author uses the words "said Joan," not "I said."

**5 PERSONAL RESPONSE** Responses will vary.

**LEVELED READER TEACHER GUIDE**

▲ High-Frequency Words, p. 5

▲ Comprehension, p. 6

www.harcourtschool.com/storytown

★ **Leveled Readers, online**
*Searchable by genre, skill, vocabulary, level, or title*
★ **Student Activities and Teacher Resources, online**

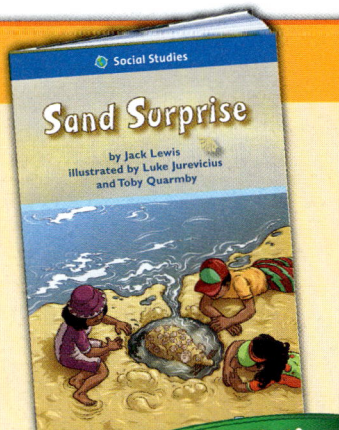

**Genre: Realistic Fiction**

## ON-LEVEL

# Sand Surprise

**SUMMARY** Three children are surprised when a mouse sculpture they make in the sand is transformed into a toad as the tide comes in.

-  **phonics** Long /ō/ *ow, oa*
- **High-Frequency Words:** *mouse, our, over, pretty, surprise, three*
- **Author's Purpose/Point of View**

### Before Reading

**BUILD BACKGROUND/SET A PURPOSE** Have children share experiences they may have had at the shore, digging and building in the sand. Ask: **What did you make? How? Did you use shells and sticks? What happened at the end of the day?** Then guide children to preview the story and set a purpose for reading it.

### Reading the Book

**PAGES 2–8 AUTHOR'S PURPOSE/POINT OF VIEW Why do you think the author chooses to turn the sand mouse into a toad?** (Possible response: to show that a spoiled idea can turn out to be a nice surprise)

**PAGES 4–5 BEGINNING, MIDDLE, ENDING What happens in the middle of the story?** (The family decorates the mouse with shells and adds a moat around the mouse.)

**REREAD FOR FLUENCY** Have partners read alternate pages of the story aloud several times with expression at a speech-like pace.

### Think Critically
*(See inside back cover for questions.)*

1. **NOTE DETAILS** The children made a sand mouse.

2. **CAUSE/EFFECT** The mouse changed into a toad.

3. **CHARACTERS' EMOTIONS** Possible responses: surprised, upset

4. **AUTHOR'S PURPOSE/POINT OF VIEW** One of the sisters is telling the story. The author uses words like "I said" and "we made."

5. **PERSONAL RESPONSE** Responses will vary.

**LEVELED READER TEACHER GUIDE**

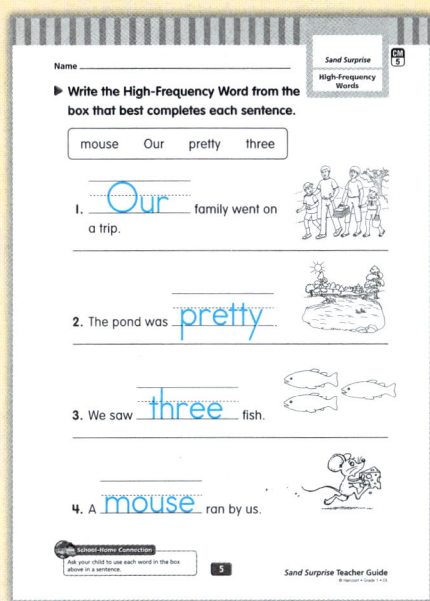

▲ High-Frequency Words, p. 5

▲ Comprehension, p. 6

# Leveled Readers

## *Reinforcing Skills and Strategies*

## ADVANCED

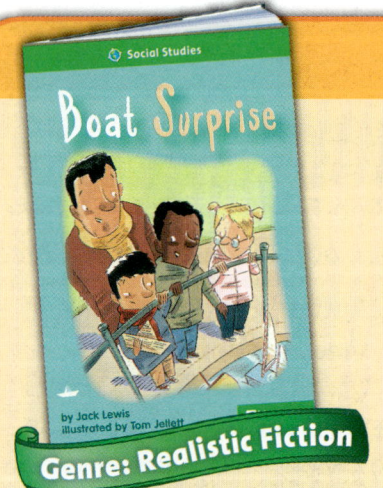
**Genre: Realistic Fiction**

### Boat Surprise

**SUMMARY** Children make boats and test them out on a pond, but one boy decides to wear his boat as a hat because he doesn't want it to soak up water and tip over.

- **phonics** Long /ō/ *ow, oa*
- **High-Frequency Words:** *mouse, our, over, pretty, surprise, three*
- **Author's Purpose/Point of View**

### Before Reading

**BUILD BACKGROUND/SET A PURPOSE** Ask children if they have ever made a model boat. Ask: **What did you use to make it? Did you test it out? What happened? Did it float? Sink? Soak up water? Tip over?** Then have children set a purpose for reading the story.

### Reading the Book

**PAGES 2–8 AUTHOR'S PURPOSE/POINT OF VIEW** **What does the author want the reader to learn from the story?** (Possible response: Good ideas can come from things that don't work out as planned.)

**PAGE 5 NOTE DETAILS** **What kind of boat does Mitch make?** (a house boat) **What does he call it?** (*Mouse Boat*)

**REREAD FOR FLUENCY** Have children reread the story aloud several times with expression at a speech-like pace.

### Think Critically
*(See inside back cover for questions.)*

1. **NOTE DETAILS** Will used paper to make his boat.

2. **BEGINNING, MIDDLE, ENDING** He picked it up and put it on his head.

3. **MAKE PREDICTIONS** Possible responses: Yes, because it was light, and the wind could blow it along; No, because it was made of paper, and the water would soak into the paper.

4. **AUTHOR'S PURPOSE/POINT OF VIEW** One of the students in the class told the story. The student used the word "we."

5. **PERSONAL RESPONSE** Responses will vary.

**LEVELED READER TEACHER GUIDE**

▲ High-Frequency Words, p. 5

▲ Comprehension, p. 6

**www.harcourtschool.com/storytown**

**Go online**

★ **Leveled Readers, online**
*Searchable by genre, skill, vocabulary, level, or title*
★ **Student Activities and Teacher Resources, online**

# Snow Play

**SUMMARY** Three children put on their boots, coats, and mittens and go out to play in the snow.

*by Jack Lewis*

**Genre: Nonfiction**

- **Strong Picture Support**
- **Concept Vocabulary**
- **Scaffolded Language Development**

## Before Reading

**BUILD BACKGROUND/SET A PURPOSE** Have children tell what they would wear to go outside on a cold, snowy, winter day, and what fun things they would do in the snow. Guide children to preview the story and set a purpose for reading it.

## Reading the Book

**PAGES 4–6 NOTE DETAILS** What do the children put on before they go outside to play? Why do you think so? (They put on boots, coats, and mittens to stay warm and keep their feet dry.)

**PAGES 2–8 AUTHOR'S PURPOSE/POINT OF VIEW** What do you think the author wants readers to know about snow? (Possible response: Sledding is one way to have fun on a cold and snowy day.)

**REREAD FOR FLUENCY** Model reading each page at an appropriate speed. Have children repeat the reading three or four times until they are reading at a speech-like pace.

## Scaffolded Language Development    *(See inside back cover for teacher-led activity.)*

Provide additional examples and explanation as needed.

**LEVELED READER TEACHER GUIDE**

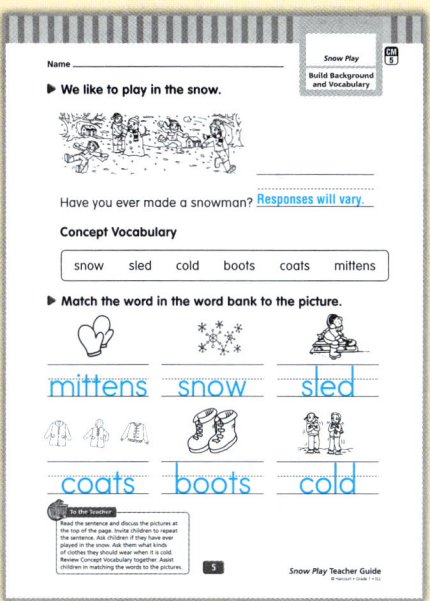

▲ Build Background, p. 5

▲ Scaffolded Language Development, p. 6

# READERS' THEATER

## Help Yourself

### Objectives
- *To read in a manner that sounds like natural speech*
- *To adjust rate and volume of spoken language appropriate to the audience and purpose*

### READERS' THEATER

 *Phonics Review*
- Digraphs /ch/ *ch, tch*
- *r*-Controlled Vowel /är/ *ar*
- Digraphs /kw/ *qu*, /hw/ *wh*
- *r*-Controlled Vowels /ûr/ *er, ir, ur*
- Syllable /əl/ *-le*
- Long Vowel /ō/ *ow, oa*

High-Frequency Words Review
*rain, need, watch, again, know, feel, family, people, always, nice, please, would, other, lucky, three, our, over*

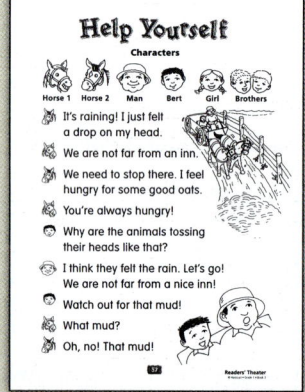

▲ Practice Book, pages 57–60

---

## DAY 1

### ■ Build Background
Tell children that this play is about a man who asks others for help with a problem and then realizes he could help too. Ask: *What are some ways a person could help solve their own problem while asking others for help too?*

### ■ Preview/Model
Give each child a copy of "Help Yourself." Guide them to preview the illustrations and predict what the play will be about. Then read aloud to them with appropriate expression.

### ■ Read Together
Read through the play with children, inviting a different volunteer to read each line. Tell children that they will be practicing and performing the play over the next few days.

---

## DAY 2

### ■ Assign Roles
Organize children into groups for performing the play. Assign roles to children within each group, and have each child highlight his or her lines. Ask groups to read through the play together. Monitor their progress and offer feedback as they do.

### E L L

**Sentence Structures** Assign the more repetitive roles to children with lower English proficiency so they can practice oral sentence structure.

---

### Focus on

## Fluency

*Use the Readers' Theater to reinforce fluency concepts taught within the theme.*

**Intonation** *Remind children that they may need to change their tone when they see the end marks of a sentence.*

**Reading Rate** *Remind children that when they read, it should sound like someone speaking.*

## DAY 3

### ■ Rehearse

Have children practice reading their assigned parts from highlighted scripts. Circulate among the groups, providing feedback as necessary.

### ■ Build Fluency

Ask children to concentrate on reading the text with appropriate pacing, expression, and intonation. Have them think about how the characters would actually sound and then try to project that as they practice.

## DAY 4

### ■ Rehearse

Have children continue practicing the play. Remind them to focus on reading their parts with appropriate pacing, expression, and intonation.

### ■ Prepare to Perform

Give each group copies of pages 57–60, and invite them to make nametags to wear during their performance. Punch holes in the upper corner of each child's nametag, and tie yarn through the holes so children can wear the nametags as necklaces.

## DAY 5

### ■ Perform

Have children perform the play for classmates, children at the same grade level, or younger children. Help children introduce the play to the audience and tell the audience what to listen for.

### ■ Evaluate

Afterward, ask children the following questions to help them evaluate their performance:

- Did you read too fast, too slowly, or just right?
- Did you read fluently, as if you were really the character?
- Do you think the audience enjoyed your performance?
- How could you improve your performance for next time?

# Theme Wrap-Up & Review

## Making Connections

**STUDENT EDITION** Page through the stories with children. Invite volunteers to identify characters and story events. Discuss: *If you could meet one of the characters in the story, which one would you choose? Why?* Suggest that children draw and write about their choices. Small groups can share and compare their ideas.

**BIG BOOKS** Ask children to tell what they remember about each story. Page through the books to confirm recollections. Discuss: *What is your favorite part of each book? Why?* Encourage volunteers to turn to specific pages and explain the reasons for their choices. Ask other children to share their choices and tell why.

*Visit the various centers and review activities in which children participated during this theme.*

## Theme Project

**CONSTRUCTION WITH FOUND OBJECTS** Review the constructions children made and their storyboards with the class. Divide the class into groups and have each group choose a construction that seems especially creative to them. Encourage the group to discuss what makes the construction creative. Then have them write about a sentence. You may provide the story starter: This construction is creative because_____. You also may invite children to dictate their thoughts. Invite the group to share the construction they chose with the class and read aloud the sentences they wrote. Place the sentences behind the storyboard for the construction.

▲ Fireflies, Fireflies,
Light My Way

▲ We're Going on
a Lion Hunt

# Phonics

**WRITE A CAPTION**   Write on index cards words that have the phonics elements taught in this theme. Have children draw a picture illustrating two or more words. For example, a child might use the words *fort*, *swing*, and *deck* to draw a play fort with a swing and a deck.

# Comprehension

**MAIN IDEA**   Review the concept of main idea—what a story is mostly about. Have partners choose a favorite book from the classroom library and read it aloud together. Provide each pair with an index card and have them write a sentence on it that tells the main idea of the story.

# Grammar

**NAMES OF HOLIDAYS**   Write several names of holidays on pieces of paper and place them in a box. Have partners draw one of the pieces of paper from the box. Then have them write a riddle about the holiday they drew. Have the rest of the class guess the holiday. The person who guesses the answer to the riddle writes the name of the holiday on the chalkboard. Continue guessing until all of the riddles have been solved.

# High-Frequency Words

**CHAIN OF WORDS STORY**   Duplicate the cards for the high-frequency words from pages 137–142 and place them face down. Have each child select one card. Then tell children they will use their words in a story. Have a volunteer start the story by using his or her word in a sentence. Have the next volunteer continue the story by using his or her word in a sentence. Continue until all selected words have been used.

# Spelling

**WORD BUILDING**   Have children use their Word Builders and Word Builder Cards to review spelling words. Start with the sequence *chip, inch, farm, part, quiz, turn,* and *put.* Then have children build *hand, room, wiggle, single, grow, soap,* and *carry.*

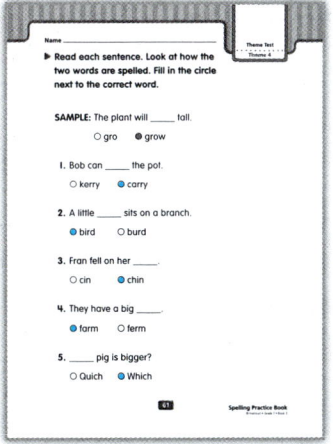

**Spelling Practice Book, pp. 61–62**

# Monitor Progress
## at the End of Theme 4

**THEME 4 TEST**    After instruction for Theme 4, assess student progress in the following areas:

- Phonics /Spelling
- Comprehension of grade-level text
- Vocabulary
- High-Frequency Words
- Grammar
- Fluency*

*(*Note on Fluency: Assessment can be staggered to make sure all students can be individually assessed.)*

## GO online  ASSESSMENT

✔ Weekly Lesson Tests
✔ Theme 4 Test
✔ Mid-Year Benchmark Assessment
✔ Student Profile System to track student growth
✔ Prescriptions for Reteaching

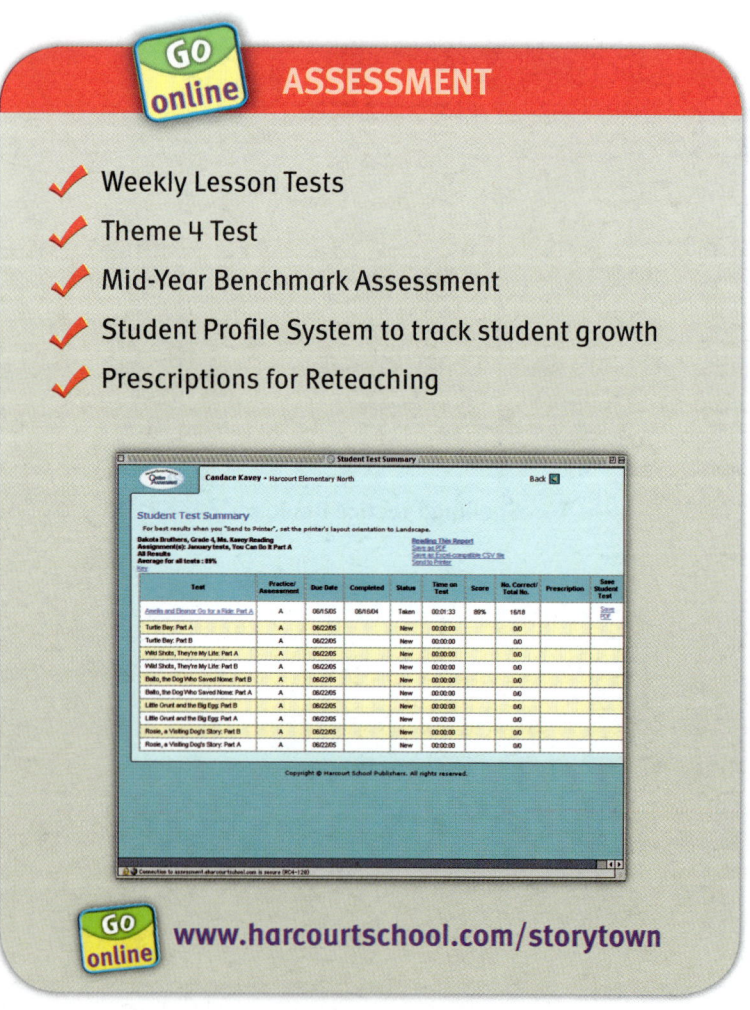

**GO online**   **www.harcourtschool.com/storytown**

## ✔ MONITOR PROGRESS

### Use Data to Inform Instruction for Theme 5

| IF performance is | THEN, in addition to core instruction, use these resources: |
|---|---|
| 🔴 **BELOW-LEVEL: Reteach** | • Below-Level Leveled Readers<br>• Leveled Readers System<br>• Extra Support Copying Masters<br>• Strategic Intervention Resource Kit<br>• Intensive Intervention Program |
| 🔵 **ON-LEVEL: Reinforce** | • On-Level Leveled Readers<br>• Leveled Readers System<br>• Practice Book |
| 🟢 **ADVANCED: Extend** | • Advanced Leveled Readers<br>• Leveled Readers System<br>• Challenge Copying Masters<br>• Challenge Kit |

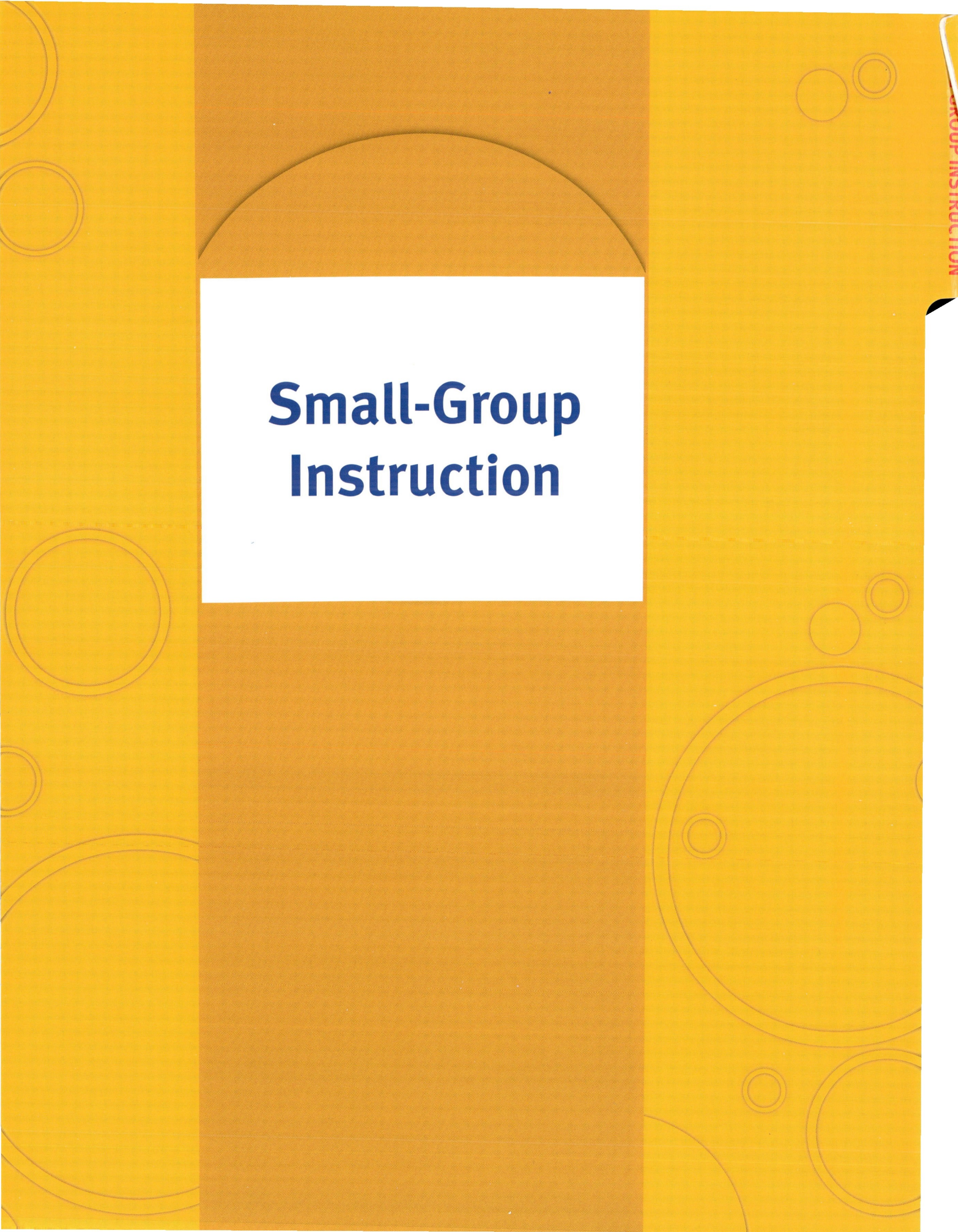

# Small-Group Instruction

# SMALL-GROUP INSTRUCTION

# Phonemic Awareness/Phonics

## Objective

*To practice and apply knowledge of digraph /ch/ch, tch*

### Decodable Book 13

"Ranch Pals" ▲

## MONITOR PROGRESS

**Phonemic Awareness/Phonics**

After small-group instruction, are children able to blend and read words with the digraph?

If not, provide additional small-group practice with the sound. See the *Strategic Intervention Resource Kit* for additional support.

**Strategic ▶ Intervention Resource Kit**

---

BELOW-LEVEL · RETEACH

### Word Blending

**Routine Card 12** Reintroduce /ch/ch, tch using *Routine Card 12*. Make sure children recognize *ch* and *tch* as a unit. Then hold up a variety of *Letter Cards*, including the *ch* and *tch* cards, at random, and have children name the sound. Once children can easily recognize the digraph, use *Routine Card 1* to practice word blending. Begin with the four-letter words *chin* and *chip,* and then blend *inch, watch,* and *catch.* End by guiding children through *Decodable Book 13,* "Ranch Pals."

ON-LEVEL · REINFORCE

### Read Words with *ch* and *tch*

Build *inch, such,* and *catch* in the pocket chart and have children read each one. Then write sentences for children to read:

**That fish is an inch longer.**

**That fish is such a catch!**

Then have children read *Decodable Book 13,* "Ranch Pals," aloud. Ask questions to make sure children understand what they have read.

ADVANCED · EXTEND

### Telling Stories

Give pairs of children several *Word Cards* with the digraph /ch/ch, tch. Have the group use all the words in a story they compose. Ask the children to tell their stories to the group, displaying each *Word Card* as they say it in the story.

# High-Frequency Words

## BELOW-LEVEL RETEACH

### Match Words

Reintroduce the words using *Routine Card 16*. Display two sets of *Word Cards* and ask children to match the words from the two sets. Have children say the word when they match the cards. Randomly display all the cards and ask children to call out each word. Continue until children are able to recognize each word quickly.

air

fly

friends

grew

need

play

rain

watch

## ON-LEVEL REINFORCE

### Reinforce Instant Recognition

Hold up the *Word Cards* for each of the lesson's high-frequency words, one at a time, and have children read each word. Then display the cards in a pocket chart. Point to words at random and have children read them. Repeat several times. Finally, ask children to write each word on the board, on chart paper, or in their notebooks.

## ADVANCED EXTEND

### Concentration

Display the eight *Word Cards* from this lesson along with several words from previous lessons. Then play Concentration. Have children take turns reciting the line shown below in rhythm with a lap-hands-lap-hands clapping rhythm. At the end of the sentence, each child should say the word on the *Word Card* you are holding up.

**Here's a word that I can read: [fly].**

E L L

Write these sentences on the board and then read them to children:

*Look up in the **air**.*

*A hen cannot **fly**.*

*I like my **friends**.*

*The plant **grew** tall.*

*I **need** to find my dog.*

*Will you **play** with me?*

*Do you see the **rain** fall?*

***Watch** me run.*

Have children repeat each sentence.

## MONITOR PROGRESS

**High-Frequency Words** After small-group instruction, are children able to recognize and read the words *air, fly, friends, grew, need, play, rain,* and *watch*?

If not, provide additional small-group practice with the words. See the *Strategic Intervention Resource Kit* for additional support.

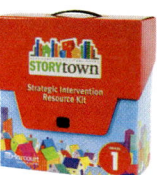

Strategic ▶
Intervention
Resource Kit

# Fluency

## Objective
*To read with appropriate intonation*

**Intonation**   Point out that when we speak, we use intonation. Ask a question and note how your voice rose at the end. Have children repeat the question. Make a statement. Note how your voice stayed the same. Then say several sentences, both statements and questions, and have children repeat them. Then indicate whether their voices rose at the end or stayed the same.

## MONITOR PROGRESS

After small-group instruction, are children able to read their *Leveled Reader* with appropriate intonation?

If not, provide additional small-group practice with the *Leveled Reader*. See the *Strategic Intervention Resource Kit* for additional support.

**Strategic ▶
Intervention
Resource Kit**

BELOW-LEVEL   RETEACH

## Model Fluent Reading

Demonstrate to children good intonation by reading the following sentence once in a monotone and then with intonation that shows understanding of how a good reader's voice rises and falls in response to punctuation and word emphasis: "Hey! Where are you going?"

Distribute copies of *From Chick to Hen* to children. Read the book aloud to them using appropriate intonation. Ask children to repeat some sentences after you, copying your intonation. Then have children read the story with a partner, practicing reading with intonation.

## Echo-Reading

Distribute *A Kitten Grows* to children. Explain that they will be practicing reading fluently. Read each page aloud to children, modeling appropriate intonation, and have them read it aloud after you, imitating your intonation. After reading the story through in this way, have children practice reading the story with partners. Listen to them read, offering comments to help them read more fluently.

## Independent Reading

Remind children that a good reader makes reading aloud sound like talking. Distribute *A Frog's Life* to children, and tell them that they will be reading the book, practicing reading in a way that sounds like normal speech. Have children pair off and have one child read the story aloud while the other listens. Then have the listener offer constructive comments about the reader's fluency and intonation. Finally, have partners switch roles.

**LEVELED READERS**

● **BELOW-LEVEL**

▲ From Chick to Hen

● **ON-LEVEL**

▲ A Kitten Grows

● **ADVANCED**

▲ A Frog's Life

# Comprehension
## *Sequence*

### Objective
*To identify sequence of events in a story*

**Demonstrate Sequence** Put on a jacket using a step-by-step approach. Say "first" and put your arm in one sleeve, "next" while you put your arm in the other sleeve, and "last" as you straighten the jacket. Have children do other actions in sequence as they say those words.

After small-group instruction, are children able to identify and describe the sequence of events in a story?

If not, provide additional small-group practice with the skill. See the *Strategic Intervention Resource Kit* for additional support.

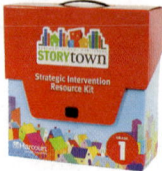

**Strategic ▶ Intervention Resource Kit**

## Identify Sequence

Ask children to open the *Student Edition* to pages 24–25 and review sequence of events. Then ask children to turn to the story "A Butterfly Grows," on page 28. Go through the illustrations with children, using words such as *first* and *next* to tell the sequence of events as you point to the pictures. Then ask children to tell the sequence of events in the following activities, using words such as *first* and *last*:

- brushing teeth
- dressing to go outside
- pouring a glass of water
- getting ready for school
- drawing a picture

## ON-LEVEL REINFORCE

### Identify Sequence of Events

Remind children that a sequence of events is the order in which things happen. Talk through the sequence of events in "A Butterfly Grows." Then ask children to tell the sequence of events in one of these stories: "Dot and Bob," "Little Red Hen Gets Help," "Beth's Job," "Soccer Song," or "King Midas and His Gold." Remind children to use words that help make the sequence of events clear, such as *first, second, next,* and *last.*

## ADVANCED EXTEND

### Explain a Sequence

Ask children to think of something they do every day that takes several steps. Ask them to think about the sequence of events involved in this task. Then have children explain to classmates the steps they use to complete the task, using signal words such as *first, then, next,* and *last.*

# Robust Vocabulary

## Objective
*To review robust vocabulary*

**REVIEW** | Tested ✓

### Build Robust Vocabulary

| | |
|---|---|
| astonishing | doubt |
| continue | examine |
| devour | transform |

## MONITOR PROGRESS

After small-group instruction, are children able to use and understand robust vocabulary words?

If not, provide additional small-group practice with the words. See the *Strategic Intervention Resource Kit* for additional support.

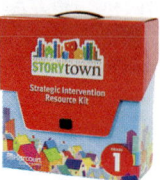
**Strategic** ▶
**Intervention**
**Resource Kit**

---

BELOW-LEVEL   RETEACH

## Reintroduce the Words

**Routine Card 15** Use *Routine Card 15* to reintroduce all six words to children. Review the Student-Friendly Explanations until they are familiar with the words. Then ask *yes* or *no* questions, such as the following, to check for understanding. Ask children to explain their answers.

**astonishing** — If you saw a cat talk, would you think that was astonishing?

**continue** — If you were in the middle of lunch and you were still hungry, would you continue to eat?

**devour** — If you were hungry and someone gave you a delicious meal, would you devour it?

**doubt** — If a friend told you he was king of America, would you doubt him?

**examine** — If your dog had a hurt paw and you wanted to help it, would you examine the paw?

**transform** — Can a caterpillar transform into a truck?

## Guess the Word

Review for children the Student-Friendly Explanation for each word and use each in a sentence. Then ask each child to choose a word and give clues about it to the other children. Children can describe the word or act it out until the others in the group guess the word. For example, for *astonishing,* a child might offer the word "surprising" or say "What!" and show an expression of astonishment on his or her face.

**Comprehension**   Create less-complicated sentences to gauge comprehension, such as "If you eat something quickly, do you *devour* it?" and "Does *transform* mean to change?" Children can respond by putting a thumb up for *yes* and a thumb down for *no*.

## Apply Word Knowledge

Write each word on the board or on chart paper and say it for children. Then challenge children to make up sentences using the words. Each child should say his or her sentence, leaving a blank where the robust vocabulary word fits. Have a volunteer repeat the sentence, filling in the correct word.

# Grammar and Writing
## Language Arts Checkpoint

## Objectives

- *To recognize names of days and months*
- *To compose a sequence story*

---

**Student Model: Sequence Story**

It was raining on Saturday. I had to stay inside. Mom said, "Let's make sock puppets!" First, we found old socks and added bits of cloth and string to make the puppets. Next, we drew faces on the socks. Last, we made up a puppet show. We added some songs and put on the show for Dad. Sock puppets are fun!

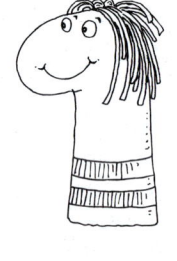

Grade 1, Lesson 13          LA26          Writing: Sequence Story

**Transparency LA26**

---

### Review Days and Months

Display the classroom calendar. Go through the days and months, saying the name of each and having children repeat it. Then display a yearly calendar that has days and months spelled out.

- Reinforce the sequential nature of the days of the week and months of the year by having children say the names in sequence.

- With the calendar in view, ask children questions that reinforce the order of days and months. For example, "What is the day after Tuesday?" and "What month is before September?"

- Have children take turns coming to the calendar and pointing to days of the week and months of the year and having the group repeat them.

**REVIEW A SEQUENCE STORY**   Remind children that a sequence is the order in which something happens. On **Transparency LA26**, underline *first, next,* and *last* as you read the story to children. Explain that the underlined words tell the sequence—the order in which things happen. Emphasize the sequence by creating a numbered list and recording each event in the story. Next to the appropriate events, write the sequence words *first, next,* and *last*. Read the story aloud again. Have children raise their hand when they hear the words *first, next,* and *last*.

## ON-LEVEL REINFORCE

## Days and Months

Have children use cards with the months and days written on them. Shuffle the cards and place them face down. Ask children to take a card in turns and give clues that identify the day or month, such as "This day comes after Monday," and "This is the first month of the year."

**SEQUENTIAL STORY**   Ask a volunteer to read the sequential story he or she wrote. Relate the sequence of events in the story for children, using words such as *first* and *next.* Then have group members take turns reading their stories while other members of the group describe the sequence of events they hear in each story.

## ADVANCED EXTEND

## Calendar Story

Ask children to use the days of the week and months of the year to tell a sequential story that also uses words that tell sequence.

- Offer an example, telling a story in which a child and her family go on a driving trip to visit Grandma, first leaving on Monday, traveling the next 200 miles on Tuesday, and arriving at Grandma's at last on Wednesday.

- As children tell the story, have a calendar with months and days visible for reference and a list of sequential words such as *first, then, next,* and *last.*

- Use this starter sentence, if children need one: "On Monday, Matt woke up and the first thing he did was put on his school clothes."

**E L L**

**Calendar Work**   Reinforce with children that the same concepts of days of the week and months of the year exist in their home language. As in English, the days and months occur in the same sequence: Monday is always the next day after Sunday, for example.

# Phonemic Awareness/Phonics

## Objective

*To practice and apply knowledge of r-controlled vowel /är/ar*

### Decodable Book 14

"Charming Carmel" ▲

**MONITOR PROGRESS**

**Phonemic Awareness/ Phonics**   After small-group instruction, are children able to blend and read words with the *r*-controlled vowel /är/*ar*?

If not, provide additional small-group practice. See the *Strategic Intervention Resource Kit* for additional support.

**Strategic ▶ Intervention Resource Kit**

---

**BELOW-LEVEL   RETEACH**

## Word Blending

**Routine Card 12**   Reintroduce /är/*ar* using *Routine Card 12.* Then hold up a variety of *Sound/Spelling Cards,* including *ar,* at random, and have children name the sounds. Once children can easily recognize the letters and sounds, use *Routine Card 1* to help them practice word blending with /är/*ar.* Begin with the three-letter words *far* and *car,* and then blend *cart, part,* and *park.* End by guiding children through *Decodable Book 14,* "Charming Carmel."

---

**ON-LEVEL   REINFORCE**

## Word Building

**Routine Card 14**   Build *arm, farm, part,* and *far* in the pocket chart and have children read each one. Then write sentences for children to read:

**The farm is far.**

**That part of my arm is wet.**

Then have children read *Decodable Book 14,* "Charming Carmel," aloud. Ask questions to make sure children understand what they have read.

---

**ADVANCED   EXTEND**

## Making Words

Give children *Sound/Spelling Cards,* including the *ar* card for the sound /är/. Challenge children to make as many words using the /är/ sound as they can. Ask children to write each word they make and then read it to you.

# High-Frequency Words

● BELOW-LEVEL RETEACH

## Match Words

 Reintroduce the lesson's high-frequency words using *Routine Card 16*. Display two sets of *Word Cards* and ask children to match the words from the two sets. Have children say the word when they match its two cards. Then randomly display all the cards and ask children to call out each word. Run through the cards until children are able to recognize each word quickly.

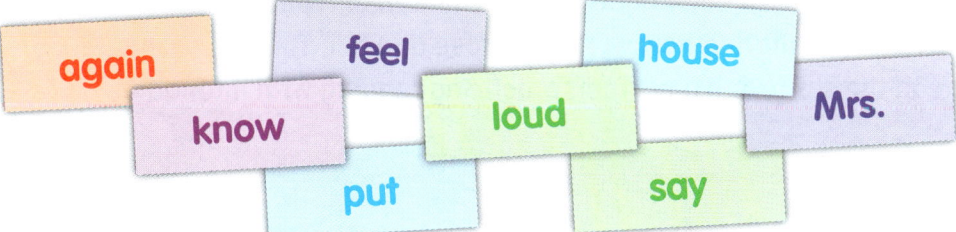

● ON-LEVEL REINFORCE

## Reinforce Instant Recognition

Hold up *Word Cards* for each of the lesson's high-frequency words, one at a time. Have children read each word. Then display the cards in a pocket chart. Point to words at random and have children read them. Repeat several times. Finally, ask children to write each word on the board, on chart paper, or in their notebooks.

● ADVANCED EXTEND ✏

## Missing Word

Shuffle *Word Cards* from this lesson and several words from previous lessons and place them face down. Have children in the group take a *Word Card* at random and then write a sentence using the word but leaving a blank for the word. Collect the *Word Cards* and spread them face up. Have children take turns showing and reading their sentences while other members of the group decide which word correctly fits in the blank.

## Objective
*To read high-frequency words*

Write sentences such as these on the board and then read them to children:

Sing that ***again!***

I ***feel*** cold.

Her ***house*** is next to mine.

Do I ***know*** you?

That band is ***loud!***

***Mrs.*** Lee is here.

***Put*** that down, please.

Did you ***say*** something?

Ask children to repeat each sentence as you trace under it.

### ✓ MONITOR PROGRESS

**High-Frequency Words** After small-group instruction, are children able to recognize and read the words *again, feel, house, know, loud, Mrs., put,* and *say*?

If not, provide additional small-group practice with the words. See the *Strategic Intervention Resource Kit* for support.

**Strategic ▶ Intervention Resource Kit**

# Fluency

## Objective
*To read with appropriate intonation in a manner that sounds like natural speech*

**End Marks**   Write these sentences on the board: *Stop! Is someone there? Here it is.* Read each sentence, demonstrating how end marks affect the sound of your voice. Find other sentences with different end marks and have children read them to show they understand.

**Intonation**   After small-group instruction, are children able to read their *Leveled Reader* with appropriate intonation and in a manner that sounds like natural speech?

If not, provide additional small-group practice with the *Leveled Reader*. See the *Strategic Intervention Resource Kit* for additional support.

**Strategic ▶
Intervention
Resource Kit**

## Model Fluent Reading

Explain that good readers read aloud so their reading sounds like natural speech. Demonstrate by reading several pages of *Mark's Big Day* and asking children to notice how your reading sounds like normal conversation.

Then distribute copies of *Carl Can Run* to children. Read the book aloud to them using good intonation. Ask children to repeat some sentences after you, imitating how your voice rose and fell. Then have children read the story with a partner, practicing reading with intonation.

## ON-LEVEL REINFORCE

### Echo-Reading

Distribute *A Card for Mark* to children. Explain that they will be practicing reading aloud so their reading sounds like natural speech. Read each page aloud to children, modeling appropriate intonation, and have them read it aloud after you, imitating how you speak. After reading the story through in this way, have children practice reading the story with partners. Listen to them read, offering comments to help them read more fluently.

## ADVANCED EXTEND

### Independent Reading

Remind children that a good reader makes reading aloud sound just like people talk every day. Distribute *Scarlet's Muffins* to children. Tell them that they will be reading the book aloud and practicing reading in a way that sounds like a conversation they might have with a friend. Have them pair off and have one child read the story aloud while the other listens. Have the listener offer constructive comments about the way his or her partner read aloud. Then ask partners to reverse roles. When children finish, discuss how reading fluently so their reading sounds like natural speech helps children understand and appreciate the story.

**LEVELED READERS**

● **BELOW-LEVEL**

▲ Carl Can Run

● **ON-LEVEL**

▲ A Card for Mark

● **ADVANCED**

▲ Scarlet's Muffins

Lesson 14   S15

# Comprehension
## Author's Purpose/Point of View

### Objective
*To identify author's purpose and point of view*

**Explain Point of View**  Help children understand that all stories are "told" by someone. Note that this is different from who *writes* the story. Review "Mark's Big Day." Tell children that in this story, the author is acting as the storyteller. We know this because he uses the characters' names when he tells what they do and say.

**Author's Purpose/Point of View**  After small-group instruction, are children able to identify and describe author's purpose and point of view?

If not, provide additional small-group practice with the skill. See the *Strategic Intervention Resource Kit* for additional support.

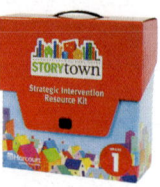

**Strategic ▶ Intervention Resource Kit**

## Identify Author's Purpose and Point of View

Remind children that whenever an author writes, he or she has a purpose—a reason for writing. For stories, the purpose is to entertain. Hold up "Mark's Big Day" as an example. Then say that some authors write to give information, or inform. "A Butterfly Grows" was written to inform. Page through familiar selections in the *Student Edition* and help children determine whether each was written to entertain or to inform.

Review point of view with children. Explain that point of view is who tells the story. Say this story sentence: **I felt sad because I couldn't go to school.** Help children understand that the person telling the story is a character. Then say this story sentence: **In the woods, Tad walked slowly.** Guide children to understand that the author is acting as the storyteller.

## Identify Author's Purpose and Point of View

Ask children to explain two reasons an author might write a book. (to entertain, to give information) Read a few lines from "Ann's Trip to the Stars" (*Student Edition*, pages 54–61) and "A Butterfly Grows" (*Student Edition*, pages 28–45) and discuss the author's purpose for each. Then refer to "Ann's Trip to the Stars" again and ask children who is telling the story. (a character in the story) Compare the story with "Mark's Big Day" and help children notice what is different when the author serves as storyteller.

## Using Author's Purpose and Point of View

Briefly review author's purpose and point of view. Then have children go through their *Student Edition* and review stories and selections they have already read. Ask them to list selections written to entertain and selections written to give information. Also have them list selections written from the point of view of a character and those written from the point of view of the author as storyteller. After children have made their lists, have them share them and explain why they placed selections where they did.

# Robust Vocabulary

## Objective
*To review robust vocabulary*

**REVIEW** | Tested ✓

### Build Robust Vocabulary

| | |
|---|---|
| approached | excel |
| blunder | pace |
| energetic | reassure |

**MONITOR PROGRESS**

**Vocabulary**  After small-group instruction, are children able to use and understand the robust vocabulary words?

If not, provide additional small-group practice with the words. See the *Strategic Intervention Resource Kit* for additional support.

**Strategic ▶ Intervention Resource Kit**

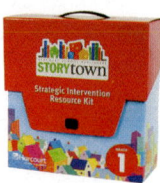

**BELOW-LEVEL   RETEACH**

## Reintroduce the Words

**Routine Card 15**  Use *Routine Card 15* to reintroduce all six words to children. Review the Student-Friendly Explanations until they are familiar with the words. Then ask questions such as these to check for understanding. Be sure children explain their answer each time.

**approached**  If you approached a friend, did you go up to the friend or back away from the friend?

**blunder**  Would it be a blunder to call a friend by the wrong name or to give the friend a snack?

**energetic**  Which is energetic, a dog racing around a yard or a dog sleeping in the sun?

**excel**  If you excel at something, are you good at it or bad at it? At what do you excel?

**pace**  If you wanted to hurry, would you go at a slow pace or at a fast pace?

**reassure**  If you wanted to reassure a friend, would you pat his or her shoulder or walk away?

## ON-LEVEL REINFORCE

## Apply Word Knowledge

Review for children the Student-Friendly Explanation for each word and give an example of the usage of each. Then randomly call out words and ask children to give more examples. Write the examples on the board randomly and when children have finished, have them match those examples with the words.

**Alternate Questions** Create yes-or-no questions from the Reteach questions. For example, ask, "If you *excel* at something, are you good at it?" Children can nod or shake their heads to indicate a response.

## ADVANCED EXTEND

## Tell a Story

Review for children the Student-Friendly Explanation for each word and give an example of each. Write the words on the board, making sure children can identify them by sight. Then ask children to make up a story using all the words. You may want to give them some ideas for stories:

- a bike race

- a lost puppy

- going on a picnic

- having a dream

When children have finished their story, have them tell it to the class.

# Grammar and Writing
## Language Arts Checkpoint

### Objectives
- *To recognize names of holidays*
- *To compose an e-mail*

**Names of Holidays**

Valentine's Day    Fourth of July

Presidents' Day    Thanksgiving Day

Grade 1, Lesson 14    LA27    Grammar: Names of Holidays

**Transparency LA27**

**BELOW-LEVEL RETEACH**

### Review Holidays

Display Grammar **Transparency LA27.** Ask children to identify each holiday as you say its name.

- Trace under the capital letter that begins the name of each holiday as you say its name. Explain that names of holidays begin with a capital letter.

- Ask how each picture relates to that holiday.

- Ask children to name other holidays.

- Ask children for scenes that go along with those holidays, just as the pictures on the transparency go along with the names of the holidays. Encourage children to think of ways they celebrate holidays.

**REVIEW WRITING AN E-MAIL** Write a sample e-mail about a holiday on the board or on chart paper. Read the message to children and identify parts of the e-mail such as the address, the subject line, and the body of the message. Help children understand the difference between an e-mail address and a conventional letter address. Review with children that e-mail messages are usually shorter than letters that are sent through the mail.

## Connect Grammar and Writing

Review the important parts of an e-mail and the use of each. Tell children to imagine they have just been invited to a Fourth-of-July picnic. Create an e-mail form on the board or on chart paper. Have children compose a message in response to the invitation. Provide a made-up e-mail address for the "To" line. Remind children that names of holidays are capitalized. Guide them to enter a subject line that accurately reflects the message they compose.

### Understanding Holidays

Many of the holidays we celebrate are particular to the United States. Go through major holidays with children, offering simple explanations for any with which children are not familiar.

## Holiday Clues

Ask children to think of all the holidays they can and list them on the board. Point out to children that all the holidays begin with capital letters.

- Have children take turns telling something associated with a holiday on the list.

- Other children can guess which holiday is being described.

- When everyone has had a turn, have children compose an e-mail message to a friend about an imaginary holiday celebration they attended. Suggest that children use one of the descriptions they heard from classmates.

# Phonemic Awareness/Phonics

## Objective

*To practice and apply knowledge of digraphs /kw/qu, /hw/wh*

### Decodable Book 15

"Quint and the Squids";▲
"What Is It?";
"Wham!"

MONITOR PROGRESS

**Phonemic Awareness/ Phonics** After small-group instruction, are children able to blend and read words with digraphs /kw/*qu* and /hw/*wh*?

If not, provide additional small-group practice with the sounds. See the *Strategic Intervention Resource Kit* for additional support.

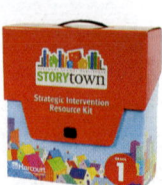

**Strategic ▶ Intervention Resource Kit**

---

● **BELOW-LEVEL** **RETEACH**

## Word Blending

  Reintroduce /kw/*qu*, /hw/*wh* using *Routine Card 12*. Then hold up pairs of *Letter Cards qu* and *wh*. Have children name the letters and the sounds the letter combinations stand for. Then use *Routine Card 13* to help them practice word blending with /kw/*qu* and /hw/*wh*. Begin with the words *quilt* and *when*. Then blend *quiz, whim,* and *what*. End by guiding children through the stories in *Decodable Book 15*.

**w h e n**

---

● **ON-LEVEL** **REINFORCE**

## Word Building

Build *quick, which,* and *when* in the pocket chart and have children read each one. Then write sentences for children to read:

**When will Dean be quiet?**

**When Meg was little, she was very quick.**

Then have children read the stories in *Decodable Book 15* aloud. Ask questions to make sure children understand what they have read.

---

● **ADVANCED** **EXTEND** 🖉

## Write with Digraphs /kw/*qu*, /hw/*wh*

Create word webs for the digraphs /kw/*qu* and /hw/*wh* on the board. Have volunteers help complete each web with words that contain one of the digraphs. Then invite children to think of sentences that use two or more of the words. Challenge them to create sentences with as many /kw/*qu* and /hw/*wh* digraphs as possible.

# High-Frequency Words

 **BELOW-LEVEL** **RETEACH**

## Match Words

Routine Card 16

Reintroduce the lesson's high-frequency words by using *Routine Card 16*. Display two sets of *Word Cards* and ask children to match the words from the two sets. Have them say the word when they form a match. Then randomly display all the cards and ask children to say each word. Continue displaying the cards until children are able to recognize each word quickly.

about   books   family   name   read   work   writing   people

---

 **ON-LEVEL** **REINFORCE**

## Rapid Word Naming

Hold up the *Word Cards* for the lesson's high-frequency words, one at a time, and guide children to read each word. Then randomly display the cards, having children name each word. Finally, ask children to write each word on the board, on chart paper, or in their notebook.

---

 **ADVANCED** **EXTEND**

## Find Similarities

Select the *Word Cards* from Lesson 15 along with several cards from previous lessons. Randomly hold up the cards and have children name each word. Then have a volunteer think of some kind of similarity or matching element in two or more of the cards. Invite the other children to figure out how the words match or are similar.

**I can match *say* and *name*.** (both words have the long *a* sound)

**I can match *books* and *people*.** (both words name more than one)

---

## Objective
*To read high-frequency words*

**E L L**

Model usage of each word with sentences such as the following:

*The book was **about** dogs.*

*All **books** have pages.*

*My **family** went to Chicago.*

*Everyone has a **name**.*

*I like to **read** scary stories.*

*It is important to **work** hard.*

*Jan was **writing** a letter.*

*Most **people** are friendly.*

Scary Stories

Have children repeat each sentence.

---

 **MONITOR PROGRESS**

**High-Frequency Words** After small-group instruction, are children able to recognize and read the words *about, books, family, name, read, work, writing,* and *people*?

If not, provide additional small-group practice with the words. See the *Strategic Intervention Resource Kit* for additional support.

**Strategic ▶ Intervention Resource Kit**

# Fluency

## Objective
*To read at a rate appropriate for the text*

**Expression** Remind children that in addition to choosing a pace, it is important to read with expression. Model the following sentences using expression:

Watch out!

Do you want to play, too?

Mary ran as fast as she could!

After small-group instruction, are children able to read their *Leveled Reader* accurately and with an appropriate reading rate?

If not, provide additional small-group practice with the *Leveled Reader*. See the *Strategic Intervention Resource Kit* for additional support.

**Strategic ▶ Intervention Resource Kit**

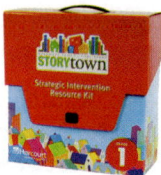

**BELOW-LEVEL   RETEACH**

## Model Fluent Reading

Remind children that it is important to adjust reading rate according to the text. Distribute copies of *Susan L. Roth* to children. Read the book aloud to them, modeling a reading rate that is appropriate to the text. After reading, review several sentences, explaining why it was appropriate to speed up or slow down. Have children repeat these sentences, imitating a similar rate. Then have them read the story with a partner, practicing an appropriate reading rate.

## Echo-Reading

Distribute *Amy Hest* to children. Explain to them that they will practice reading the story fluently, at a reading rate that is appropriate to the text. Read each page aloud to children, modeling the appropriate rate. Then have children read aloud after you, imitating your rate. After reading the story in this manner, have children reread the story with a partner. Listen to them read and provide feedback about how they adjusted their reading rate according to the text.

## Independent Reading

Ask a volunteer to explain what it means to adjust reading rate according to the text. Distribute *Joseph Bruchac* to children and have them read the book, using a reading rate that is appropriate to the text. Have children choose partners, and ask one child to read the story aloud while the other listens. Then have the listener offer constructive feedback about the reader's fluency and rate. Finally, reverse the partners' roles.

### LEVELED READERS

**BELOW-LEVEL**

▲ Susan L. Roth

**ON-LEVEL**

▲ Amy Hest

**ADVANCED LEVEL**

▲ Joseph Bruchac

# Comprehension
## *Sequence*

### Objective
*To determine the sequence of events in a selection*

**Clarify Meaning** The word *sequence* may be unfamiliar to children. Provide examples of familiar events that take place in order, such as morning routines or school dismissal. Then ask the children to repeat the sequence of events in each example.

**Comprehension** After small-group instruction, are children able to identify and describe a story's sequence?

If not, provide additional small-group practice with the skill. See the *Strategic Intervention Resource Kit* for additional support.

**Strategic ▶**
**Intervention**
**Resource Kit**

### Review Sequence

Have children open their *Student Edition* to pages 102–103, and review with them the concept of sequence. Write the words *first, next,* and *last* on the board and talk about the things that happen first, next, and last in the pictures, pointing to each word in turn. Hold up a familiar story or book and tell what happens first, next, and last. Then have children follow your model and tell about another familiar story of their own choosing.

## Identify Sequence

Remind children of the definition of *sequence* and ask a volunteer to name and describe the sequence of events in "The Best Apple Crisp in the World" from the *Read-Aloud Anthology*, page 58. Then present three other familiar stories to the children, asking them to describe the sequence of events in each story. Finally, discuss the importance of sequence and how it pertains to the understanding of a story.

## Explore the Importance of Sequence

Ask children to tell what sequence is. Ask why it is important to tell about events in the order in which they happened. Then tell children to think about the sequence of events in the familiar story "Goldilocks and the Three Bears." If events were told in a different sequence, would the story make sense? Talk about possible changes in sequence and how they would affect this story.

# Robust Vocabulary

## Objective
*To review robust vocabulary*

**REVIEW**

## Build Robust Vocabulary

| | |
|---|---|
| accomplishment | cozily |
| admire | interrupted |
| ambition | triumphantly |

**MONITOR PROGRESS**

**Robust Vocabulary** After small-group instruction, are children able to use and understand the robust vocabulary words?

If not, provide additional small-group practice with the words. See the *Strategic Intervention Resource Kit* for additional support.

**Strategic ▶ Intervention Resource Kit**

---

**BELOW-LEVEL   RETEACH**

## Reintroduce the Words

**Routine Card 15** Use *Routine Card 15* to reintroduce all six words to children. Review the Student-Friendly Explanations until children are familiar with the words. Then ask questions, such as the following, to check for understanding. Be sure children explain their answers.

**accomplishment**  What is one recent accomplishment that you made at school?

**admire**  Would you be more likely to admire a helpful class-mate or a bully?

**ambition**  What ambitions do you have about your future?

**cozily**  Would you lie cozily in bed if you were warm and comfortable, or if you were hot and annoyed?

**interrupted**  Would you be pleased or upset if someone interrupted you while playing your favorite game?

**triumphantly**  Would you shout triumphantly after you found out some sad news or after you won a baseball game?

## ON-LEVEL REINFORCE

### Apply Word Knowledge

Review for children the Student-Friendly Explanation for each word. Play a word game, using clues about each word. For example, say: **I'm thinking of a word that I would use to tell how I feel about my favorite football player.** (admire) Continue until children display an understanding of each Student-Friendly Explanation.

## ADVANCED EXTEND

### Skits

Write the six words on the board or on chart paper and read each one to children. Have them repeat the words, making sure they can identify them by sight. Then review the Student-Friendly Explanations. Allow groups of two or three children to perform a brief skit about one of the words and invite other children to guess which word is being dramatized. After each performance, have children discuss other situations in which they might use the word.

### ELL

**Consonant Sounds** The /sh/ sound can be troublesome for some children because it does not occur in their home language. Help children practice saying *accomplish*. Then add the *-ment* ending. Point out the *-tion* ending of *ambition*, which also has the /sh/ sound. Have children practice saying *shun* before they pronounce the whole word: *ambition*.

# Grammar and Writing
## Language Arts Checkpoint

## Objectives

- *To understand that the words* I *and* me *take the place of some naming words*

- *To understand that a personal narrative tells about someone's experiences*

**Using *I* and *Me***

1. I lost my ball in the park.
2. Mom helped me look for it.
3. I tossed the ball to Mom.
4. Mom tossed the ball to me.

Grade 1, Lesson 15 · LA29 · Grammar: Using *I* and *Me*

**Transparency LA29**

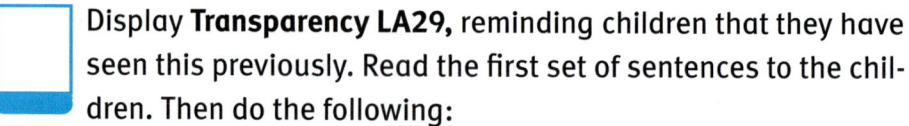

BELOW-LEVEL RETEACH

## Review Using *I* and *Me*

Display **Transparency LA29,** reminding children that they have seen this previously. Read the first set of sentences to the children. Then do the following:

- Explain that *I* is used in the naming part of the sentence, and *me* is used in the telling or action part of the sentence.

- Point out that *I* and *me* take the place of naming words and are used when talking about oneself.

- Point out that *I* is always written with a capital letter.

Guide children in repeating these steps for the remaining sentences.

**REVIEW PERSONAL NARRATIVE**     Remind children that a personal narrative is about something that has actually happened to the writer. Tell children you are going to write a personal narrative. Ask which of these sentences you might use as the first sentence:

**I'll never forget my trip to Mars.**

**I have fond memories of those years when I used to teach first grade.**

**I'll always remember my first day of teaching.**

Point out that the words *I, me,* and *my* help readers know that they are reading a personal narrative. Have students think of a beginning sentence for their own personal narrative. Suggest one of these sentence frames:

**I have fond memories of _____.**

**I'll always remember _____.**

## Connect Grammar and Writing

Ask a volunteer to dictate a sentence that includes *I* or *me*. Write the sentence on the board. Remind children that the word *I* is used in the naming part of a sentence and *me* is used in the telling part. Ask a volunteer to identify those elements of the sentence. Continue by asking children if we use *I* and *me* when writing personal narratives. Display the characteristics of a well-written personal narrative (from Day 1 writing) and review the criteria for this type of writing. Ask children to review the personal narratives they wrote and discuss how they incorporated the chart's criteria.

**Capitalization**   Remind students that no matter where the word *I* is placed in a sentence, it is always capitalized. Model and discuss the following examples on the board:

**I like to eat carrots.**

**Jay and I walk fast.**

## Apply the Skills

Display a volunteer's personal narrative on the overhead projector or rewrite it on the board. Read the narrative aloud to the children. Have volunteers identify the following in the narrative:

- the personal experience or event that has happened in this person's life

- the beginning, middle, and ending of the narrative

- the usage and location of *I* and *me* (naming or telling part of the sentence)

Repeat with other children's narratives.

*In the beginning I was born.*

# Phonemic Awareness/Phonics

## Objective

*To practice and apply knowledge of r-controlled vowels /ûr/er, ir, ur*

### Decodable Book 16

"Helping Bird";
"King Arthur Hurt His Leg";
"Curt's Bag" ▲

### MONITOR PROGRESS

**Phonemic Awareness/ Phonics**   After small-group instruction, are children able to blend and read words with *r*-controlled vowels /ûr/er, ir, ur?

If not, provide additional small-group practice with the sound. See the *Strategic Intervention Resource Kit* for additional support.

**Strategic ▶ Intervention Resource Kit**

---

## Word Blending

  Reintroduce /ûr/er, ir, ur using *Routine Card 12*. Then randomly hold up the letter combinations *er, ir,* and *ur,* and have children name the sound and the letter combinations each time. Then use *Routine Card 13* to help them practice word blending with /ûr/er, ir, ur. Begin with the words *fern* and *sir*. Then blend *stir, hurt,* and *shirt*. End by guiding children through the stories in *Decodable Book 16*.

---

 ON-LEVEL   REINFORCE

## Word Building

Build *burn, third, surf,* and *thirst* in the pocket chart and have children read each one. Then write sentences for children to read:

**This is the third time I have burned the toast.**

**Her skirt has ferns on it.**

Have children read aloud the stories in *Decodable Book 16*. Ask questions about the stories to make sure children understand.

---

## Use *r*-Controlled Vowels /ûr/er, ir, ur

Brainstorm a list of /ûr/er, ir, ur words with children and write them on the board. Ask a volunteer to say a sentence that includes the first two words on the list. The next child should say a sentence that includes the second and third words, the next uses the third and fourth words, and so on. Then challenge children to expand the sentences to three words from the list.

# High-Frequency Words

## BELOW-LEVEL RETEACH

### Match Words

Routine Card 16

Reintroduce the lesson's high-frequency words by using *Routine Card 16*. Display two sets of *Word Cards* and ask children to match the words from the two sets. Have them say a word when they match its two cards. Then randomly display all the cards and ask children to say each word. Continue displaying the cards until children are able to recognize each word quickly.

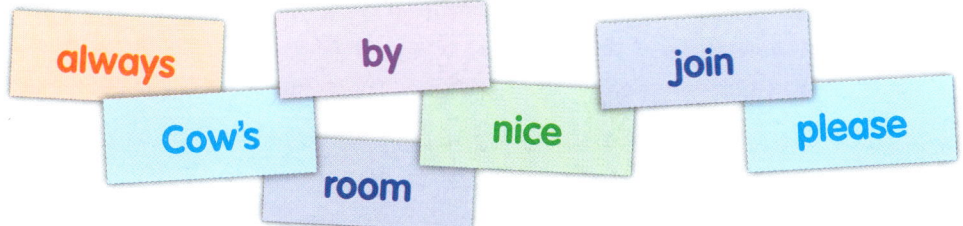

always

by

join

Cow's

nice

please

room

## ON-LEVEL REINFORCE

### Rapid Word Naming

Hold up the *Word Cards* for the lesson's high-frequency words, one at a time, and guide children to read the words. Then randomly display the cards, having children name the word each time. Finally, ask children to write each word on the board, on chart paper, or in their notebook.

## ADVANCED EXTEND

### Sentence Challenge

Select *Word Cards* for Lesson 16's high-frequency words along with several cards with words from previous lessons. Randomly hold up the cards and have children name each word. Then hold up two cards at a time and tell children to say a sentence that includes both words. When everyone has had a turn, hold up three cards at a time and have children say sentences that contain all three words.

### E L L

Model usage of each word with sentences, such as the following:

I **always** drink milk.

I will sit **by** Kim.

I hear **Cow's** bell.

Theresa will **join** the game.

You look **nice** today.

**Please** raise your hand.

The **room** is big.

Have children repeat each sentence.

### MONITOR PROGRESS

**High-Frequency Words** After small-group instruction, are children able to recognize and read the words *always, by, Cow's, join, nice, please,* and *room*?

If not, provide additional small-group practice with the words. See the *Strategic Intervention Resource Kit* for additional support.

**Strategic ▶
Intervention
Resource Kit**

# Fluency

## Objective
*To read fluently and at a rate appropriate for the text*

**Use Punctuation** Remind children that punctuation can help them know when to pause during reading. Point out that punctuation marks often remind us to take a breath and then continue reading.

### MONITOR PROGRESS

After small-group instruction, are children able to read their *Leveled Reader* fluently and at an appropriate rate?

If not, provide additional small-group practice with the *Leveled Reader*. See the *Strategic Intervention Resource Kit* for additional support.

**Strategic ▶ Intervention Resource Kit**

BELOW-LEVEL RETEACH

## Model Fluent Reading

Remind children that it is important to adjust reading rate according to the text. Distribute copies of *Room for a Friend* to children. Read the book aloud to them, modeling an appropriate reading rate based on the text. After reading, review a few sentences, reading them aloud at an appropriate rate. Have children repeat these sentences, imitating your rate. Then have children read the story with a partner, practicing reading aloud at an appropriate rate.

## ON-LEVEL REINFORCE

## Echo-Reading

Distribute *Always Room for More* to children. Explain to them that they will practice reading the story fluently and at the appropriate reading rate for the text. Read one page aloud to children, modeling the appropriate rate. Then have children read aloud after you, imitating your reading rate and expression. After reading the entire story in this manner, have children reread the story with a partner. Listen to them read and provide feedback about fluency and reading rate.

## ADVANCED EXTEND

## Independent Reading

Ask a volunteer to explain the meaning of adjusting reading rate according to the text. Distribute *A New Friend* to children and have them read the book, adjusting reading rate to fit the text. Have children choose a partner, and have one child read the story aloud while the other listens. Then have the listener offer constructive feedback about the reader's fluency and rate. Finally, reverse the partners' roles.

**LEVELED READERS**

● **BELOW-LEVEL**

▲ Room for a Friend

● **ON-LEVEL**

▲ Always Room for More

● **ADVANCED**

▲ A New Friend

# Comprehension
## *Main Idea*

### Objective
*To understand main idea*

**Reinforce the Concept** Use pictures from magazines or illustrations from unfamiliar story books to reinforce the concept of main idea. Display the pictures and ask: **What's happening?** Guide children to state a main idea. If necessary, point out the details children name and guide them to the main idea.

After small-group instruction, are children able to identify and describe a main idea?

If not, provide additional small-group practice with the skill. See the *Strategic Intervention Resource Kit* for additional support.

**Strategic ▶ Intervention Resource Kit**

### Review Main Idea

Have children open their *Student Edition* to pages 138–139 and review with them the concept of main idea. Then discuss the pictures and questions on the pages. Point out that we can find the main idea in a picture or in something that we read. Emphasize that the main idea in something that we read is the most important idea in the story or selection. Hold up a picture from the newspaper and state the main idea. Model your thought process to help children understand how you used the details of the picture to arrive at the main idea. Display other newspaper or magazine pictures and help children go through the same process and state the main ideas.

## Identify Main Idea

Review the definition of main idea. Ask a volunteer to name and describe the main idea in "The Lion and the Mouse" from the *Read-Aloud Anthology*, page 62. Then display a simple children's picture book. Ask children what they think the main idea is, based on the cover illustration. Write their ideas on the board. Then read the story aloud and have children revisit their ideas. What details in the story might make them revise their main idea statements?

## Explore the Importance of Main Idea

Ask a volunteer to identify the main idea of a recently read class selection. Discuss the difference between the main idea of a story versus the details of a story. Then allow volunteers to give a brief "book review" of books they have recently read. Children should share the titles, the main ideas, and their opinions of the books.

# Robust Vocabulary

## Objective
*To review robust vocabulary*

### REVIEW
### Build Robust Vocabulary

| | |
|---|---|
| **amiable** | **mercy** |
| **captured** | **relax** |
| **compatible** | **struggling** |

**MONITOR PROGRESS**

After small-group instruction, are children able to use and understand the robust vocabulary words?

If not, provide additional small-group practice with the words. See the *Strategic Intervention Resource Kit* for additional support.

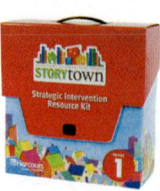

**Strategic ▶**
**Intervention**
**Resource Kit**

---

**BELOW-LEVEL  RETEACH**

## Reintroduce the Words

**Routine Card 15** Use *Routine Card 15* to reintroduce all six words to children. Review the Student-Friendly Explanations until children are familiar with the words. Then ask questions such as the following to check for understanding. Be sure children explain their answers.

**amiable**     Would friends describe you as amiable?

**captured**     Would you be more likely to capture a frog or a shark?

**compatible**     If you are compatible with a classmate, do you work well together or work poorly together?

**mercy**     If you show mercy to someone who has hurt your feelings, would others consider you a kind person or a mean person?

**relax**     Would you be able to relax in a sunny meadow? In a swamp filled with alligators?

**struggling**     If you are struggling on a test, are you finding it easy or hard to complete the test?

## ON-LEVEL REINFORCE

### Apply Word Knowledge

Review for children the Student-Friendly Explanation for each word and model sample sentences incorporating each one. Then encourage students to think of their own sentences using the words. Allow volunteers to come to the front of the class and share their sentence. Discuss how each of these words can be used in a variety of ways.

## ADVANCED EXTEND

### Everyday Use

Write the six words on the board or on chart paper and read each one to children. Have them repeat the words, making sure that they can identify them by sight. Then review the Student-Friendly Explanations. Next, allow children an opportunity to incorporate the words into their everyday vocabulary. Ask them to role-play a conversation with a friend on the playground. Have volunteers pretend to talk to a friend, correctly using as many robust vocabulary words as possible as they speak.

### E L L

**Clarify Pronunciation**    Point out that the letter *c* can make the sound /k/ or the sound /s/. It makes the /k/ sound in *captured* and *compatible*. It makes the /s/ sound in *mercy*. Write these words on the board and say them for children. Note that when *c* is the first letter of a word, it usually makes the /k/ sound, but not always.

# Grammar and Writing
## Language Arts Checkpoint

### Objectives
- *To use* he, she, it, *and* they *correctly*
- *To understand the parts of an invitation and to write an invitation*

**Using *He*, *She*, *It*, and *They***

Grade 1, Lesson 16    **LA31**    Grammar: Using *He, She, It, and They*

**Transparency LA31**

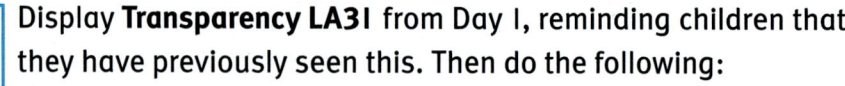

### Review *he*, *she*, *it* and *they*

Display **Transparency LA31** from Day I, reminding children that they have previously seen this. Then do the following:

- Remind children that *he, she, it,* and *they* can take the place of names of people, animals, places, and things.

- Share a sentence about a person, place, or thing in the school. Then ask volunteers to repeat your sentence, substituting *he, she, it,* or *they.*

- Allow students an opportunity to develop their own sentences, always demonstrating how to substitute the appropriate pronouns.

**REVIEW PARTS OF AN INVITATION**    Remind children about the importance of a well-written invitation. Invite volunteers to recall the characteristics of a well-written invitation. Then create a simple invitation on the board, having children help you place pertinent pieces of information in the correct places.

## ON-LEVEL REINFORCE

### Recall Grammar

Ask a volunteer to recall when we use *he, she, it,* and *they.* Place a variety of sentences on the board, using the wrong pronoun in each sentence. Allow volunteers to correct your sentences, substituting the appropriate pronoun.

**RECALL WRITING** Distribute the children's completed Day 5 invitations. Ask children to recall the characteristics of a well-written invitation. Then have volunteers display their invitations, explaining how their invitations display those characteristics.

### Word Substitution

**Word Substitution** Display sentences such as the ones below on the board or chart paper. Ask students to substitute *he, she, it,* and *they* as needed.

- Mary is very nice.
- Alan, Don, and Mae will go to the park.
- The shark was large.

## ADVANCED EXTEND

### Apply the Skills

Invite volunteers to read their completed invitations from Day 5. Have volunteers identify the elements of their well-written invitations. Then ask them to share a few details about their events. When they share, encourage them to use the pronouns *he, she, it,* and *they* as appropriate. Have listeners participate by showing a "thumbs up" each time they hear a classmate say one of these pronouns.

# Phonemic Awareness/Phonics

## Objective

*To practice and apply knowledge of the syllable /əl/-le*

### Decodable Book 17

"Little Ann's Nap" ▲

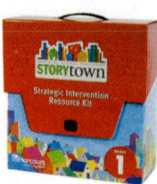

### BELOW-LEVEL  RETEACH

## Listen for Syllable -*le*

List these words on the board: *little, jungle, wiggle.* Have children say each word after you and listen for /əl/ at the end. Reread the words with children and have volunteers underline the letters that stand for the /əl/ sound. Emphasize that /əl/ adds another word part, or syllable, to the word. Read the words again with children, clapping the word parts. Then have children turn to "Little Ann's Nap" in *Decodable Book 17.* Have them echo-read each sentence. Help them frame and read words that end in /əl/-*le.*

### ON-LEVEL  REINFORCE

## Word Building

Build *juggle, fiddle,* and *riddle* in the pocket chart and have children read each word. Then write sentences for children to read:

**Angie can juggle and play the fiddle.**

**Angie can solve a riddle.**

Have children read aloud *Decodable Book 17,* "Little Ann's Nap." Ask questions to make sure children understand what they have read.

### ADVANCED  EXTEND ✏️

## Write with the Syllable /əl/-*le*

Brainstorm a list of /əl/-*le* words with the children and write them on the board. Have partners create sentences using words from the list. Challenge partners to see who can develop a sentence with the most /əl/-*le* words.

# High-Frequency Words

**Objective**
*To read high-frequency words*

---

 **BELOW-LEVEL · RETEACH**

## Match Words

**Routine Card 16** Reintroduce the lesson's high-frequency words by using *Routine Card 16*. Display two sets of *Word Cards* and ask children to match the words from the two sets. Have them say a word when they form a match. Then randomly display all the cards and ask children to say each word again. Continue displaying the cards until children are able to recognize each word quickly.

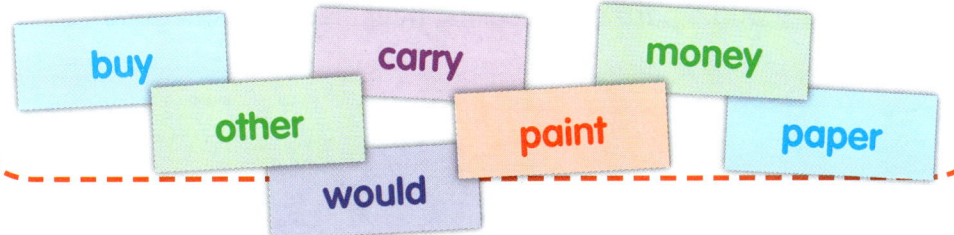

---

 **ON-LEVEL · REINFORCE**

## Rapid Word Naming

Hold up the *Word Cards* for the lesson's high-frequency words, one at a time, and guide children to read the words. Then randomly display the cards, having children name each word. Finally, ask children to write each word on the board, on chart paper, or in their notebook.

---

 **ADVANCED · EXTEND**

## Play "Speed"

Select the seven *Word Cards* from Lesson 17 along with several cards from previous lessons. Randomly hold up the cards and have children name each word. Encourage children to recognize these words quickly. Try to quicken the pace with which you display each card. Then have children work with partners, holding up word cards for each other, continually trying to increase their speed. Suggest that children clock their partners' overall time.

---

 **E L L**

Model usage of each word with sentences, such as the following:

> Tom will **buy** the flowers.
>
> I can **carry** the bag.
>
> Billy kept the **money** in his pocket.
>
> The **other** pocket has a hole in it.
>
> I like to **paint** pictures.
>
> The teacher has a stack of **paper**.
>
> I **would** like to play the game.

Have children repeat each sentence.

---

✓ **MONITOR PROGRESS**

**High-Frequency Words**  After small-group instruction, are children able to recognize and read the words *buy, carry, money, other, paint, paper,* and *would*?

If not, provide additional small-group practice with the words. See the *Strategic Intervention Resource Kit* for additional support.

**Strategic ▶
Intervention
Resource Kit**

# Fluency

## Objective

*To read fluently using intonation in a manner that sounds like natural speech*

**Use Punctuation** Remind children that noticing punctuation can help them with intonation. Call attention to how your voice rises and falls as you speak. Then say these sentences and have children repeat:

**Where would you like to go?**

**I smell fire!**

**My dog is brown.**

**MONITOR PROGRESS**

After small-group instruction, are children able to read their *Leveled Reader* fluently and with good intonation?

If not, provide additional small-group practice with the *Leveled Reader*. See the *Strategic Intervention Resource Kit* for additional support.

**Strategic ▶ Intervention Resource Kit**

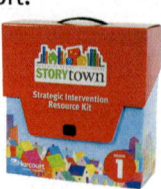

BELOW-LEVEL RETEACH

## Model Fluent Reading

Remind children that good readers make their voices rise and fall as they read so their reading sounds like natural speech. Distribute copies of *The Animal Painter* to children. Read the book aloud to them, modeling proper intonation. After reading, review several sentences, explaining the reasoning for the rise and fall in your voice. Have children repeat these sentences, imitating your intonation. Then have children read the story with a partner, practicing fluent reading with good intonation.

**ON-LEVEL REINFORCE**

## Echo-Reading

Distribute *Can Animals Paint?* to children. Explain to them that they will practice reading the story fluently and using appropriate intonation. Read one page aloud to children, modeling a rise and fall in your voice as you read. Then have children read aloud after you, imitating the same intonation. After reading the entire story in this manner, have children reread the story with a partner. Listen to them read and give them feedback about how they adjusted the rise and fall of their voice, according to the text.

 **ADVANCED EXTEND**

## Independent Reading

Ask a volunteer to explain the meaning of intonation. Distribute *Congo the Painter* to children and tell them they will read the book to practice fluency and proper intonation. Have them choose a partner and have one child read while the other follows along and listens. Then have the listener offer constructive feedback about the reader's fluency and intonation. Finally, reverse the partners' roles.

**LEVELED READERS**

● **BELOW-LEVEL**

▲ The Animal Painter

● **ON-LEVEL**

▲ Can Animals Paint?

● **ADVANCED LEVEL**

▲ Congo the Painter

# Comprehension
*Main Idea*

## Objective
*To understand the main idea of a story*

**Check Understanding** Display the cover of a picture book. Ask: *What's happening?* After children answer, tell them that they have just stated the main idea of the picture. Repeat with several other picture books. Point out that answering *What's happening?* will also lead them to the main idea of a story.

**Comprehension** After small-group instruction, are children able to identify the main idea of a picture or story?

If not, provide additional small-group practice with the skill. See the *Strategic Intervention Resource Kit* for additional support.

**Strategic ▶ Intervention Resource Kit**

## Review Main Idea

Have children open their *Student Edition* to pages 174–175, and review with them the concept of main idea. Review the three pictures on the pages and have children state the main idea of each. Point out that a story has a main idea just as a picture or illustration does. Have children practice finding the main idea with several more pictures from magazines or illustrations in picture books. Then ask children to recall a simple, familiar story, such as "The Three Little Pigs." Guide them to state the main idea of the story. You may need to help children sort through details that are not needed in the main idea statement.

## Identify Main Idea

Review the definition of main idea. Ask a volunteer to identify the main idea of "Can Elephants Paint?" Then ask children to recall "One More Friend" (*Student Edition*, pages 142–159). Help children to determine the main idea of that story. Finally, allow children to page through the *Student Edition* and look at stories they have already read. Have each child choose one story and state its main idea.

## Explore the Importance of Main Idea

Ask children what a main idea is. Then have a volunteer identify the main idea of a recently read class selection. Discuss the difference between the main idea of a story and the many details in the story. Then allow volunteers to state the main idea of other stories they have read recently. Continue until each child has had a turn.

# Robust Vocabulary

## Objective

*To review robust vocabulary*

**Tested**

**REVIEW** ✓

### Build Robust Vocabulary

| | |
|---|---|
| **agreement** | **rejoice** |
| **extraordinary** | **unnoticed** |
| **predicament** | **unthinkable** |

**MONITOR PROGRESS**

**Robust Vocabulary** After small-group instruction, are children able to use and understand the robust vocabulary words?

If not, provide additional small-group practice with the words. See the *Strategic Intervention Resource Kit* for additional support.

**Strategic ▶ Intervention Resource Kit**

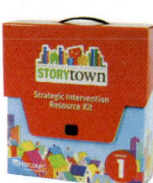

---

## Reintroduce the Words

**Routine Card 15** Use *Routine Card 15* to reintroduce all six words to children. Review the Student-Friendly Explanations until children are familiar with the words. Then ask questions such as the following to check for understanding. Be sure children explain their answers.

**agreement** — If a group is in agreement, do they all want to do the same thing or different things?

**extraordinary** — Would it be more extraordinary to see a barking dog or a shooting star?

**predicament** — If you were in a predicament, might you need help or would you not need help?

**rejoice** — If you rejoice, are you most likely happy or sad?

**unnoticed** — Would you be more likely to go unnoticed at a friend's party or at an amusement park?

**unthinkable** — If something is unthinkable, would you be more likely to describe it as normal or as unusual?

## Apply Word Knowledge

Review with children the Student-Friendly Explanation for each word. Model the usage of each word. Then encourage students to think of their own sentences using the words. Allow volunteers to stand and share their sentences in front of the group. Encourage them to role-play or dramatize the sentences when possible.

## Complete the Sentence

Write the six words on the board or on chart paper and read each one to children. Have them repeat the words, making sure that they can identify them by sight. Then review the Student-Friendly Explanations. Next, create a sentence frame, such as the following: **I was in _____ with my friends about what game to play at recess.** (agreement) After giving the example, have children take turns selecting a word and composing a sentence. Have others guess which word belongs in the blank.

**Clarify Prefixes**   Point out that *unnoticed* and *unthinkable* both begin with *un-*. Tell children that in these two words, the *un-* beginning means "not." So, they can think of the words as "not noticed" and "not thinkable."

# Grammar and Writing
## Language Arts Checkpoint

### Objectives
- *To recognize and use possessive nouns and pronouns*
- *To understand the purpose of each part of a friendly letter*

**Student Model: Friendly Letter**

April 10, 20—

Dear Russ,

I miss you! How do you like your new house? How is your new school? I have a new dog. His name is Gus. He likes to run and play all the time. Please send me a card or call me.

Your friend,
Todd

Grade 1, Lesson 17    LA34    Writing: Friendly Letter

**Transparency LA34**

**BELOW-LEVEL  RETEACH**

### Review Possessive Nouns

Remind children that a noun names a person, place, or thing. A possessive noun shows who has or owns something. For most words, the addition of *'s* shows possession. Write these examples on the board:

- **Martin's desk**
- **the chair's leg**

Have volunteers identify the noun that shows possession and circle the *'s* ending. Then remind children that a pronoun is a word that stands for a noun. A pronoun can also tell who has or owns something. Write these possessive pronouns on the board: *his, her, hers, its, their, your, yours.* Point out that possessive pronouns do not have apostrophes, and some of them do not end with *s.* Say several sentences using these pronouns. Write the possessive parts on the board, such as *his jacket* or *their books.* Talk about who has or owns each object.

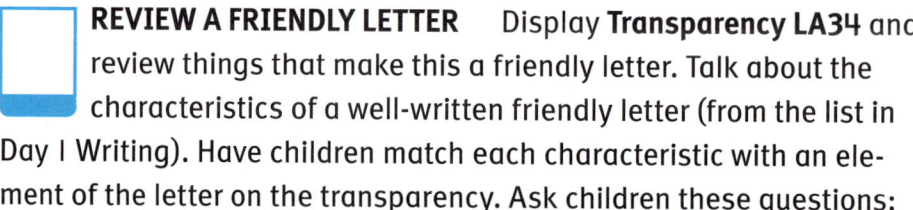

**REVIEW A FRIENDLY LETTER**    Display **Transparency LA34** and review things that make this a friendly letter. Talk about the characteristics of a well-written friendly letter (from the list in Day 1 Writing). Have children match each characteristic with an element of the letter on the transparency. Ask children these questions:

- **Where is the date? What is the date?**
- **What part tells who will receive the letter?**
- **What happens in the body of the letter?**
- **Where is the closing? What punctuation mark goes after the closing?**
- **Where is the signature?**

## ON-LEVEL REINFORCE

### Recall Possessive Nouns and Pronouns

Ask a volunteer to define what a possessive noun is. Then ask volunteers to share sentences that include at least one possessive noun. Record their sentences on the board. Have volunteers help you explain the possessive forms. Repeat a similar exercise with the possessive pronouns *his, her, hers, its, their, your, yours.*

**RECALL FRIENDLY LETTER FORMAT**    Distribute children's completed friendly letters from Day 5. Ask children to recall the characteristics of a well-written friendly letter. For each element of a friendly letter, have volunteers point out the corresponding part of their own friendly letter and say what it is. Guide children to give feedback or to correct other children's mistakes in a constructive manner.

### Identify Possessive Pronouns

Review with children what a pronoun is. Tell children that possessive pronouns have different forms and that they will need to remember them. They might want to keep a list in their notebook.

## ADVANCED EXTEND

### Apply the Skills

Invite volunteers to show and/or read their completed friendly letters from Day 5. Have group members evaluate the elements of the letters using these questions:

- **Where is the date?**
- **Where is the greeting? Does a comma follow the greeting?**
- **Does the body contain complete sentences?**
- **Where is the closing? Does a comma follow the closing?**
- **Where is the signature? Has the writer signed his or her name?**
- **Does the letter contain any possessive nouns or pronouns? Are they formed and used correctly?**

# Phonemic Awareness/Phonics

## Objective
*To practice and apply knowledge of long vowel /ō/ow, oa*

### Decodable Book 18

**"The Little Yellow Tugboat"** ▲

**MONITOR PROGRESS**

**Phonemic Awareness/Phonics** After small-group instruction, are children able to blend and read words with long vowel /ō/*ow, oa*?

If not, provide additional small-group practice. See the *Strategic Intervention Resource Kit* for additional support.

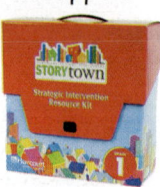

**Strategic ▶ Intervention Resource Kit**

**BELOW-LEVEL   RETEACH**

## Word Blending

**Routine Card 12** List these words on the board: *coat, boat, toad*. Have children say each word after you and listen for the /ō/ sound in the middle. Reread the words with children and have volunteers underline the letters that stand for the /ō/ sound. Repeat for /ō/ at the end of these words: *row, snow, grow*. Emphasize that /ō/ is called the long *o* sound. Then have children turn to "The Little Yellow Tugboat" in *Decodable Book 18*. Have them echo-read each sentence. Help them frame and read long *o* words.

**ON-LEVEL   REINFORCE**

## Read Long *o* Words

Build *bow, goat, slow,* and *road* in the pocket chart and have children read each word. Then write sentences for children to read:

**I tied a row of bows in my hair.**

**Mary walked slowly down the road with a goat.**

Have children read *Decodable Book 18,* "The Little Yellow Tugboat," aloud. Ask questions to make sure children understand what they have read.

**ADVANCED   EXTEND** ✏

## Write with Long Vowel /ō/*ow, oa*

Brainstorm a list of long vowel /ō/*ow, oa* words with the children and write them on the board. Challenge children to think of two-syllable words, such as *oatmeal* and *follow*. Ask children to create sentences using a variety of these words and record them in their notebooks.

# High-Frequency Words

## BELOW-LEVEL RETEACH

### Match Words

 Reintroduce the lesson's high-frequency words by using *Routine Card 16*. Display two sets of *Word Cards* and ask children to match the words from the two sets. Have them say a word when they match its two cards. Then randomly display all the cards and ask children to say each word again. Continue displaying the cards until children are able to recognize each word quickly.

mouse   our   three   over   pretty   surprise

## ON-LEVEL REINFORCE

### Reinforce Instant Recognition

Hold up the *Word Cards* for the lesson's high-frequency words, one at a time, and have children read the words. Then display the *Word Cards* in a pocket chart. Point to words at random and have children read them. Repeat several times. Finally, ask children to write each word on the board, on chart paper, or in their notebooks.

## ADVANCED EXTEND

### Form Sentences

Gather the six *Word Cards* from Lesson 18 along with several words from previous lessons. Randomly hold up the cards and have children name each word. Then continue displaying the cards, asking children to name each word and to use the word in a sentence.

 **E L L**

Model usage of each word with sentences, such as the following:

The **mouse** ran across the room.

**Our** house is red.

Rudy ran **over** the hill.

I wore a **pretty** dress.

This party was such a **surprise**!

There were **three** other girls in line.

Have children repeat each sentence.

**High-Frequency Words**   After small-group instruction, are children able to recognize and read the words *mouse, our, over, pretty, surprise,* and *three*?

If not, provide additional small-group practice with the words. See the *Strategic Intervention Resource Kit* for support.

**Strategic ▶ Intervention Resource Kit**

# Fluency

## Objective

*To read fluently and at an appropriate rate*

### BELOW-LEVEL

**Emphasize Steadiness** Tell children that a good reading rate is not too slow and not too fast. Note that the best reading rate is a steady rate that is good for both the reader and for listeners. It may be confusing for listeners if a reader slows down and speeds up too much. Model a steady reading rate and have children echo-read. Remember to be expressive.

### MONITOR PROGRESS

**Fluency** After small-group instruction, are children able to read their *Leveled Reader* fluently and at an appropriate rate?

If not, provide additional small-group practice with the *Leveled Reader*. See the *Strategic Intervention Resource Kit* for additional support.

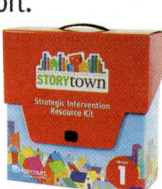

**Strategic ▶ Intervention Resource Kit**

BELOW-LEVEL   RETEACH

## Model Fluent Reading

Remind children that it is important to read at a steady rate that is neither too slow nor too fast. Distribute copies of *Muffin Surprise* to children. Read the book aloud to them, modeling an appropriate reading rate. After reading, review several sentences, explaining the reasoning for speeding up or slowing down. Have children repeat these sentences, imitating your reading rate and expression. Then have children read the story with a partner, practicing an appropriate reading rate. Provide feedback to help children find a reading rate that is comfortable.

## Echo-Reading

Distribute *Sand Surprise* to children. Explain to them that they will practice reading the story fluently and at an appropriate reading rate. Read one page aloud to children, modeling an appropriate rate. Then have children read aloud after you, imitating your rate and expression. After reading the entire story in this manner, have children reread the story with a partner. Listen to the children read and provide feedback about their fluency and reading rate.

## Independent Reading

Ask children why it is important to read at a steady and appropriate rate for the text. Distribute *Boat Surprise* to children and tell them that they will use it to practice reading fluently and at an appropriate rate. Have children choose a partner, and ask one child to read the story aloud while the other listens. Then have the listener offer constructive feedback about the reader's rate. Finally, switch the partners' roles. Remind children that reading too fast may cause the reader to skip or mispronounce words. Also, fast reading makes it hard for listeners to understand well.

**LEVELED READERS**

🔴 **BELOW-LEVEL**

▲ Muffin Surprise

🔵 **ON-LEVEL**

▲ Sand Surprise

🟢 **ADVANCED**

▲ Boat Surprise

# Comprehension
## *Author's Purpose/Point of View*

### Objective
*To understand author's purpose and point of view*

**Clarify Meaning** The phrase "point of view" may be confusing. Tell children that "point of view" means "who is telling the story." If a character is telling the story, readers will see words such as *I, me,* and *my.* If the author is telling the story, the characters will be called by name. It will seem as if someone who is watching all the action is telling the story.

**Author's Purpose/Point of View** After small-group instruction, are children able to identify author's purpose and point of view?

If not, provide additional small-group practice with the skill. See the *Strategic Intervention Resource Kit* for additional support.

**Strategic ▶ Intervention Resource Kit**

## Review Author's Purpose/Point of View

Help children remember the purposes authors have for writing—to entertain, to inform, to teach a lesson. Remind children that they just read "Snow Surprise" and "The Snowflake Man." Talk about how the two readings were similar. Then help children conclude that "Snow Surprise" is a made-up story and was written to entertain. "The Snowflake Man" is about a real person and was written to inform readers about that person. Note that when writers write to inform, readers may also be entertained.

Remind children that in "Snow Surprise," the characters are Joan and Ben. We know that because the author is telling the story and uses each of their names. Refer children to the *Big Book, We're Going on a Lion Hunt,* and guide them to determine the point of view. (The characters tell the story.)

## Identify Author's Purpose/Point of View

Review the definitions of author's purpose and point of view. Ask a volunteer to describe the author's purpose and point of view in "Shadow in the Snow," *Student Edition* pages 206–213. Then have children page through the *Student Edition* and look at selections they have already read. Have each child choose a story and identify the author's purpose and the point of view. If children need help with point of view, pose this question: **Is a character telling the story or is the author telling the story?**

## Explore the Importance of Author's Purpose/Point of View

Have a volunteer identify the author's purpose and point of view in a recently read class selection. Then challenge children to brainstorm ideas about possible stories they would like to write. Discuss what the stories' purposes and points of view would be. Then allow children an opportunity to record one idea in their notebooks. Ask them to create a picture or write a few sentences about the idea.

# Robust Vocabulary

## Objective

*To review robust vocabulary*

### REVIEW

**Build Robust Vocabulary**

| | |
|---|---|
| argue | jostled |
| bulged | labored |
| command | wary |

### MONITOR PROGRESS

**Vocabulary** After small-group instruction, are children able to use and understand the robust vocabulary words?

If not, provide additional small-group practice with the words. See the *Strategic Intervention Resource Kit* for additional support.

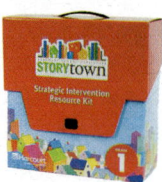

**Strategic ▶**
**Intervention**
**Resource Kit**

---

**BELOW-LEVEL   RETEACH**

## Reintroduce the Words

**Routine Card 15** Use *Routine Card 15* to reintroduce all six words to children. Review the Student-Friendly Explanations until children are familiar with the words. Then ask questions such as the following to check for understanding. Be sure children explain their answers.

**argue** — If you argue with a friend, are you agreeing or disagreeing with your friend?

**bulged** — If your backpack bulged, would you be more likely to carry your sweatshirt in your hand or place it in your backpack?

**command** — If you command your dog, do you tell the dog what to do or do you let the dog do whatever it wants?

**jostled** — If you were being jostled in a crowd, would you be comfortable or uncomfortable?

**labored** — If you labored on a test, did you put forth a lot of effort or a little effort?

**wary** — If you were wary about entering a building, would you run inside immediately or go in carefully?

## Apply Word Knowledge

Review with children the Student-Friendly Explanation for each word. Model sample sentences using each of the words. Then encourage students to think of their own sentences using the words. Allow volunteers to come to the front of the group and share their sentences. Encourage them to role-play or dramatize the sentences when possible.

## Word Descriptions

Write the six words on the board or on chart paper and read each one to children. Have them repeat the words, making sure that they can identify them by sight. Then review the Student-Friendly Explanations. Next, describe one of the words to children, without saying the word. You might say: **If I were watching you disagree with a friend about what game to play, I would be watching you _____?** (argue) Ask children to guess the word. Continue with all the robust vocabulary words.

### Understand Word Endings

Note that *bulged, jostled,* and *labored* all have an *–ed* ending. Remind children that verbs with this ending tell about things that happened in the past. Model both the present and past tenses of these three words.

**I labor today.**

**I labored yesterday.**

# Grammar and Writing

## Language Arts Checkpoint

### Objectives

- To identify homophones and use them correctly
- To understand how to write a thank-you letter

**Reinforce Homophones**   For those homophones that arise regularly in everyday school work, establish a list on the board or on chart paper. For each homophone pair, show the words in simple sentences that exemplify the words' meanings.

**Come here.     I hear the bell.**

**Troublesome Words: Homophones**

Jack will _____ the tickets.
　　　　by    buy
My dog ran _____ with a stick.
　　　　　by    buy
I _____ my friend Pam well.
　no    know
We went _____ the park.
　　　　to    too
Ming wants a sticker, _____.
　　　　　　to    too
I _____ use hands to catch the ball.
　to   two   too

Grade 1, Lesson 18       LA35       Grammar: Troublesome Words: Homophones

**Transparency LA35**

**BELOW-LEVEL    RETEACH**

## Review Troublesome Words: Homophones

Display **Transparency LA35,** reminding children that they have seen it before. Remind children that homophones are words that sound the same but have different spellings and different meanings. For example, *hi/high, be/bee,* and *deer/dear* are homophones.

Write the following sentences on the board. Have children choose the correct homophone to complete the sentence.

- Did you hear/here that dog bark?
- Dad burned wood/would in the campfire.

Extend the activity by having children make up sentences that contain the unused homophones from the sentences above. Write children's sentences so children can see which word is being used.

**REVIEW THANK-YOU LETTERS**   Remind children that a thank-you letter is a special kind of friendly letter. Invite volunteers to recall the criteria used to write a thank-you letter (see Day 1 Writing). Then model by writing a brief thank-you letter on the board. As you write, allow volunteers to guide you, offering suggestions that help you meet the criteria needed for a thank-you letter.

## Recall Grammar

Ask a volunteer to tell what a homophone is. Place a variety of sentences on the board, using homophones correctly and incorrectly. Use the words *be/bee, see/sea, meet/meat,* and *son/sun.* Allow volunteers to underline correctly used homophones and to correct incorrect homophones.

**RECALL WRITING**    Distribute the children's completed thank-you letters from Day 5. Ask children to recall the characteristics of a well-written thank-you letter (see Day 1 Writing). Then have volunteers identify elements that display those characteristics in their letters. Encourage group discussion of the various elements and guide children to revise their letters as necessary.

## Apply the Skills

Invite volunteers to read their completed thank-you letters from Day 5. Allow listeners to look at each volunteer's letter so that they can comment on format as well as content. Have children identify elements that display the characteristics of a well-written thank-you letter. Then ask children to read their own letters and identify any homophones that they find. Allow volunteers to share sentences that contain homophones. Discuss whether each homophone was used correctly in the sentence.

# Teacher's Notes

# Assessment

# Assessment

## Good assessment tells you what your students need to learn to meet grade-level standards.

It's not just about scoring the students—or the teacher, for that matter. It's about helping teachers **know what to teach and how much.**

Reading education is a **growing science.** We know more about how children learn to read than we did in the past. This **knowledge gives us the power** to use assessment to inform instruction. Assessment exposes the missing skills so that teachers can fill in the gaps.

## Good assessment is part of instruction.

Think about it: if you are testing what you are teaching, then the test is another **practice and application** opportunity for children. In addition, when tests focus on the skills that are essential to better reading, testing informs teachers about which students need more instruction in those essential skills.

## What is the best kind of assessment to use?

Using more than one kind of assessment will give you the clearest picture of your students' progress. **Multiple measures** are the key to a well-rounded view.

First, consider the assessments that are already **mandated** for you: your school, your district, and your state will, of course, tell you which tests you must use, and when. In addition to these, you should use **curriculum-based assessments** to monitor your students' progress in *StoryTown.*

The following curriculum-based assessments are built into *StoryTown.*

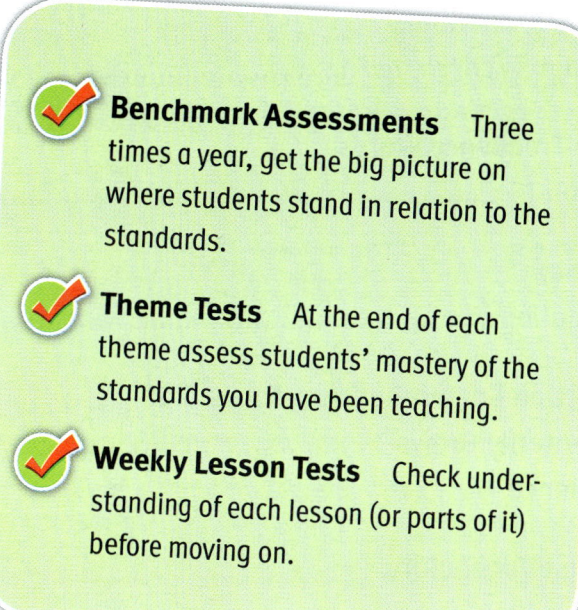

**Benchmark Assessments**   Three times a year, get the big picture on where students stand in relation to the standards.

**Theme Tests**   At the end of each theme assess students' mastery of the standards you have been teaching.

**Weekly Lesson Tests**   Check understanding of each lesson (or parts of it) before moving on.

On a daily basis, point-of-use **Monitor Progress** notes help you check understanding and reteach or extend instruction. Additional checklists and rubrics are provided to help you monitor students' comprehension, writing, listening, and speaking.

The *Benchmark Assessments,* the *Theme Tests,* and the *Weekly Lesson Tests* are all available online. Students can take the tests on the computer, or you can use pencil and paper and enter the scores into the database later. Either way, *StoryTown Online Assessment* will help you track students' progress and share their growth with administrators and families.

 *StoryTown Online Assessment*

## Lesson 13  Weekly Test

### ☑ Tested Skills

**Prescriptions**

**Phonics/Spelling**
Digraphs /ch/*ch, tch* ....................................................... Reteach, p. S2

**High-Frequency Words**
Lesson 13................................................................. Reteach, p. S3

**Fluency**
Intonation................................................................. Reteach, pp. S4–S5

**Selection Comprehension/Focus Skill**
"A Butterfly Grows" ....................................................... Reteach, pp. S6–S7
Sequence

**Robust Vocabulary**
Lesson 13................................................................. Reteach, pp. S8–S9

**Grammar**
Names of Days and Months ........................................... Reteach, pp. S10–S11

# Weekly Test

## ✔ Tested Skills

## Prescriptions

**Phonics/Spelling**

*r*-Controlled Vowel /är/*ar* ............................................... Reteach, p. S12

**High-Frequency Words**

Lesson 14................................................................ Reteach, p. S13

**Fluency**

Intonation................................................................ Reteach, pp. S14–S15

**Selection Comprehension/Focus Skill**

"Mark's Big Day" ........................................................ Reteach, pp. S16–S17

Author's Purpose/Point of View

**Robust Vocabulary**

Lesson 14................................................................ Reteach, pp. S18–S19

**Grammar**

Names of Holidays ...................................................... Reteach, pp. S20–S21

## Lesson 15 — Weekly Test

### ☑ Tested Skills            Prescriptions

**Phonics/Spelling**
Digraphs /kw/*qu*; /hw/*wh*................................................ Reteach, p. S22

**High-Frequency Words**
Lesson 15 ................................................................. Reteach, p. S23

**Fluency**
Reading Rate ............................................................. Reteach, pp. S24–S25

**Selection Comprehension/Focus Skill**
"Tomás Rivera" ......................................................... Reteach, pp. S26–S27
Sequence

**Robust Vocabulary**
Lesson 15.................................................................. Reteach, pp. S28–S29

**Grammar**
Using *I* and *Me*........................................................ Reteach, pp. S30–S31

# Weekly Test

## ✔ Tested Skills    Prescriptions

**Phonics/Spelling**

*r*-Controlled Vowels /ûr/*er, ir, ur* ..................................... Reteach, p. S32

**High-Frequency Words**

Lesson 16.................................................................. Reteach, p. S33

**Fluency**

Reading Rate ............................................................. Reteach, pp. S34–S35

**Selection Comprehension/Focus Skill**

"One More Friend" ...................................................... Reteach, pp. S36–S37

Main Idea

**Robust Vocabulary**

Lesson 16.................................................................. Reteach, pp. S38–S39

**Grammar**

Using *He, She, It,* and *They* ........................................... Reteach, pp. S40–S41

## Lesson 17 — Weekly Test

### ✔ Tested Skills       Prescriptions

**Phonics/Spelling**

Syllable /əl/-*le*................................................. Reteach, p. S42

**High-Frequency Words**

Lesson 17............................................................ Reteach, p. S43

**Fluency**

Intonation........................................................... Reteach, pp. S44–S45

**Selection Comprehension/Focus Skill**

"Can Elephants Paint?" .................................... Reteach, pp. S46–S47
Main Idea

**Robust Vocabulary**

Lesson 17............................................................ Reteach, pp. S48–S49

**Grammar**

Possessives ....................................................... Reteach, pp. S50–S51

## Lesson 18 Weekly Test

☑ **Tested Skills**                                    **Prescriptions**

**Phonics/Spelling**
Long Vowel /ō/ *ow, oa*.................................................... Reteach, p. S52

**High-Frequency Words**
Lesson 18................................................................ Reteach, p. S53

**Fluency**
Reading Rate ............................................................ Reteach, pp. S54–S55

**Selection Comprehension/Focus Skill**
"Snow Surprise" .......................................................... Reteach, pp. S56–S57
Author's Purpose/Point of View

**Robust Vocabulary**
Lesson 18................................................................ Reteach, pp. S58–S59

**Grammar**
Troublesome Words: Homophones................................ Reteach, pp. S60–S61

# Theme 4 Test

| ✔️ **Tested Skills** | **Prescriptions** |
| --- | --- |
| Phonics/Spelling ........................................... | Small-Group Instruction, pp. S2, S12, S22, S32, S42, S52 |
| High-Frequency Words ..................................... | Small-Group Instruction, pp. S3, S13, S23, S33, S43, S53 |
| Reading Comprehension ................................... | Small-Group Instruction, pp. S6–S7, S16–S17, S26–S27, S36–S37, S46–S47, S56–S57 |
| Robust Vocabulary ......................................... | Small-Group Instruction, pp. S8–S9, S18–S19, S28–S29, S38–S39, S48–S49, S58–S59 |
| Grammar .................................................... | Small-Group Instruction, pp. S10–S11, S20–S21, S30–S31, S40–S41, S50–S51, S60–S61 |
| Fluency ..................................................... | Small-Group Instruction, pp. S4–S5, S14–S15, S24–S25, S34–S35, S44–S45, S54–S55 |

**BELOW-LEVEL  RETEACH**

- Below-Level Leveled Readers
- Leveled Reader System
- Extra Support Copying Masters
- Strategic Intervention Kit
- Intensive Intervention Program

**ON-LEVEL  REINFORCE**

- On-Level Leveled Readers
- Leveled Reader System
- Practice Book

**ADVANCED  EXTEND**

- Advanced Leveled Readers
- Leveled Reader System
- Challenge Copying Masters
- Challenge Resource Kit

To determine whether children need even more support, use your district-approved diagnostic and screening assessments.

# Resources

RESOURCES

# ADDITIONAL RESOURCES

# Handwriting

Individual children come to first grade with various levels of handwriting skills, but they all have the desire to communicate effectively. To learn correct letter formation, they must be familiar with concepts of

- position (top, middle, bottom; on, above, below).
- size (tall, short).
- direction (left, right; up, down; over, around, across).
- order (first, next, then, last).
- open and closed.
- spacing.

The lessons in *StoryTown* build on these concepts in both formal and informal handwriting lessons so that children develop the skills they need to become independent writers. To assess children's handwriting skills, have them write each capital and lowercase letter of the alphabet. Note whether children use correct formation, appropriate size and spacing.

## Stroke and Letter Formation

The shape and formation of letters taught in *StoryTown* are based on the way experienced writers write their letters. Most are formed with a continuous stroke, so children do not often pick up their pencils when writing a single letter. Letter formation is simplified through the use of "letter talk"—an oral description of how the letter is formed. Models for manuscript and D'Nealian Handwriting are used in this program to support different writing systems.

## Learning Modes

A visual, kinesthetic, tactile, and auditory approach to handwriting is used throughout *StoryTown*. To help children internalize letter forms, each letter is taught in the context of how it looks, the sound it stands for, and how it is formed.

## Position for Writing

Establishing the correct posture, pencil grip, and paper position for writing will help prevent handwriting problems later on.

**Posture** Children should sit with both feet on the floor and with hips to the back of the chair. They can lean forward slightly but should not slouch. The writing surface should be smooth and flat and at a height that allows the upper arms to be perpendicular to the surface and the elbows to be under the shoulders.

**Writing Instrument** An adult-sized number-two lead pencil is a satisfactory writing tool for most children. However, use your judgment in determining what type of instrument is most suitable for a child, given his or her level of development.

**Hand Dominance** To determine each child's hand dominance, observe him or her at play and note which hand is the preferred hand. Watching the child turn a doorknob, roll a ball, build a block tower, or turn the pages in a book will help you note hand dominance.

**Paper Position and Pencil Grip**  The paper is slanted along the line of the child's writing arm, and the child uses his or her nonwriting hand to hold the paper in place. The child holds the pencil slightly above the paint line—about 1 inch from the lead tip.

## Reaching All Learners

The best instruction builds on what children already know and can do. Given the tremendous range in children's experience with writing materials prior to first grade, a variety of approaches will be needed. Throughout *StoryTown*, viable alternatives are suggested for reaching all learners.

**Extra Support**  For children with limited print concepts, one of the first and most important understandings is that print carries meaning and that writing has real purpose. Provide many opportunities for writing in natural settings. For example, children can

- **make a class directory listing names and phone numbers of their classmates.**
- **record observations in science.**
- **write and illustrate labels for art materials.**
- **draw and label maps, pictures, graphs, and picture dictionaries.**

**ELL**  English-Language Learners can also participate in meaningful print experiences. They can

- **write signs, name tags, and messages.**
- **label pictures.**
- **join in shared writing experiences.**

**Challenge**  To ensure the continued rapid advancement of children who come to first grade already writing, provide

- **exposure to a wide range of reading materials.**
- **opportunities for independent writing on self-selected and assigned topics.**
- **explicit instruction in print conventions (punctuation, use of capital letters).**
- **introduce simple editing marks and encourage children to proofread and edit their own work.**

The handwriting strand in *StoryTown* teaches correct letter formation and spacing and provides a variety of opportunities to help children become fluent, confident writers. Materials and activities include

- **handwriting activities in the Teacher Edition.**
- **reproducible models for manuscript and D'Nealian Handwriting.**

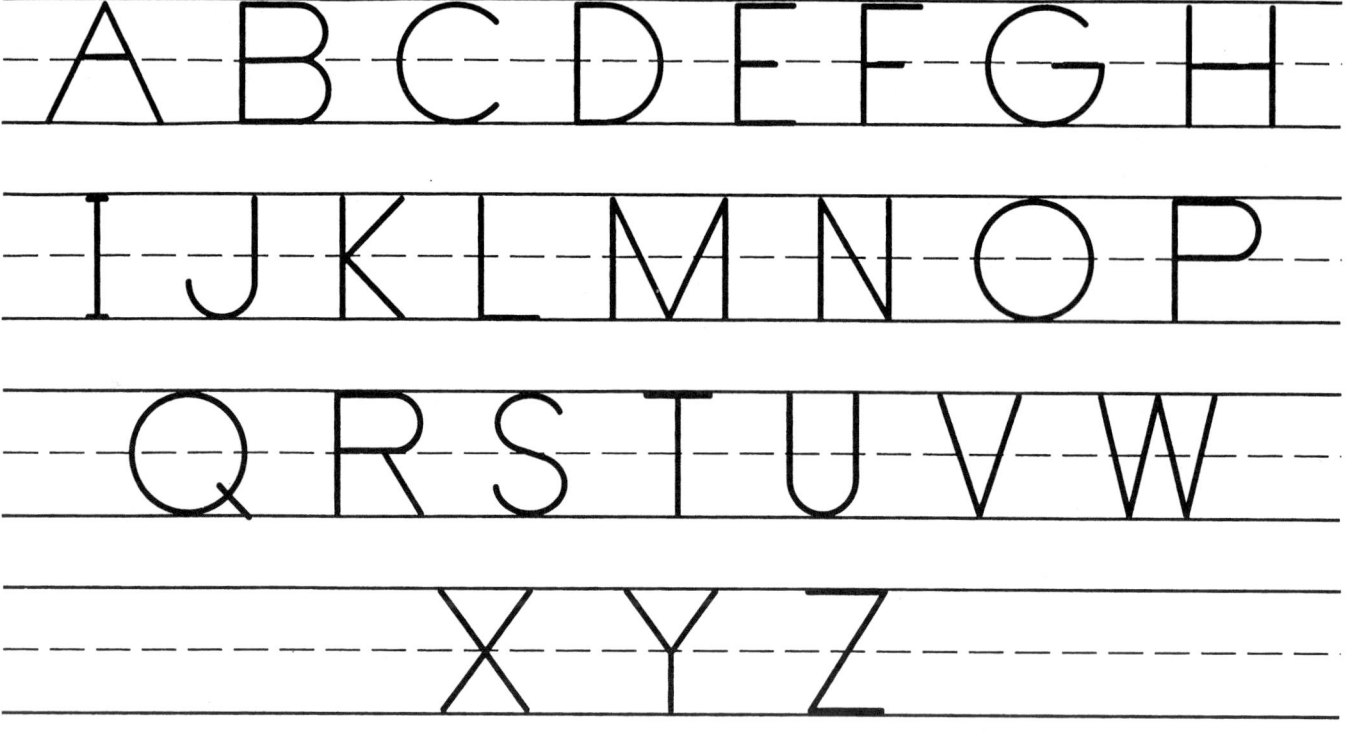

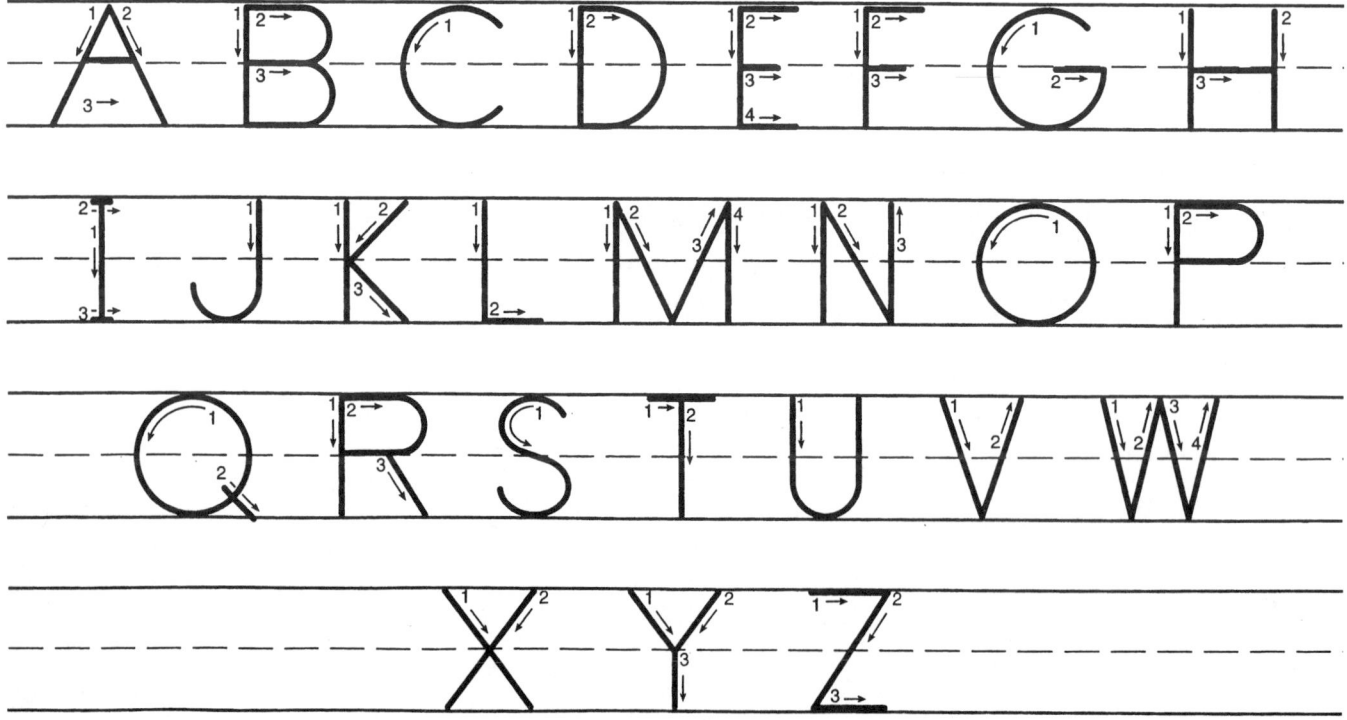

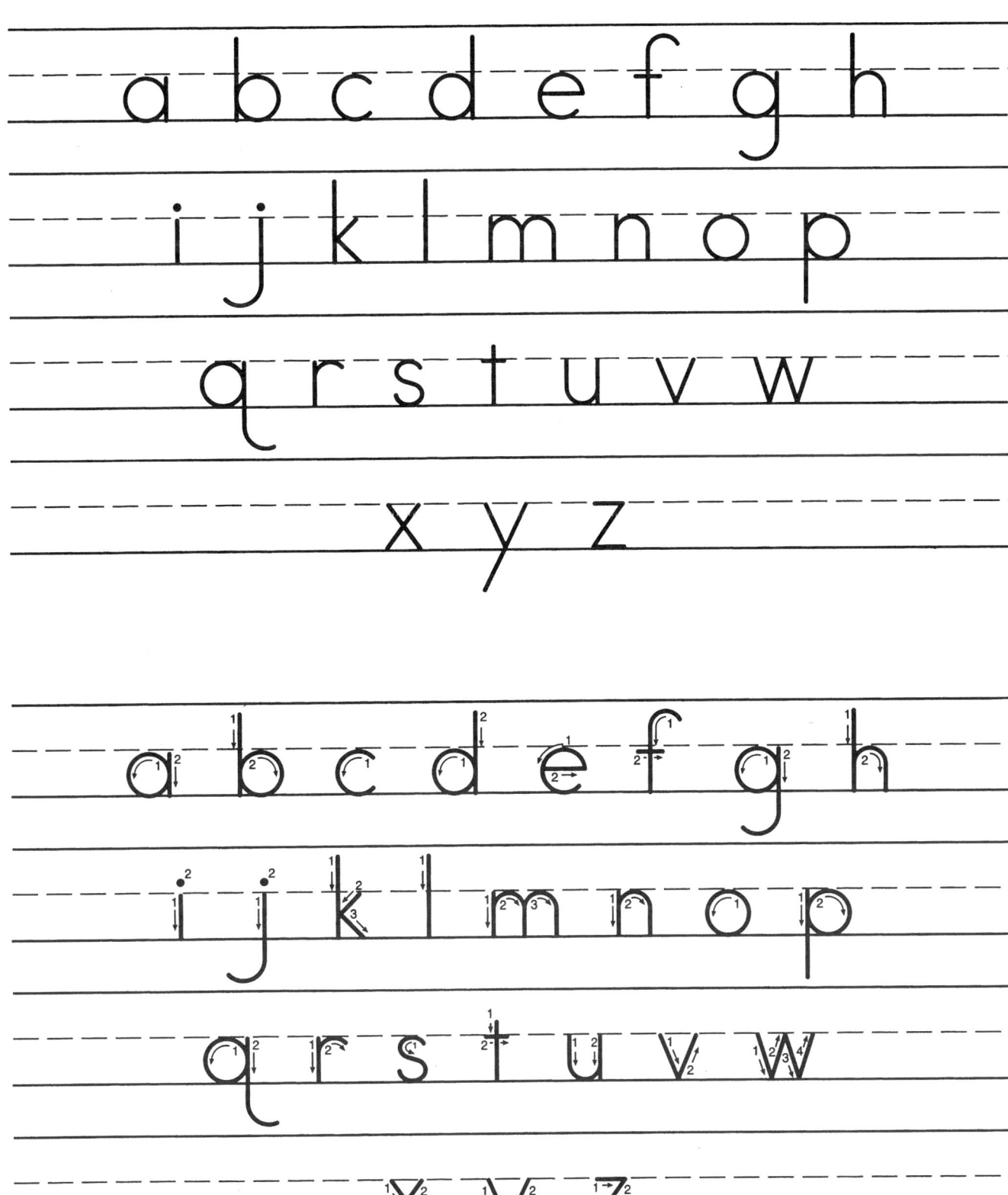

A B C D E F G H

I J K L M N O P

Q R S T U V W

X Y Z

a b c d e f g h

i j k l m n o p

q r s t u v w

x y z

# Additional Reading

**WILD AND WONDERFUL** This list is a compilation of the additional theme- and topic- related books cited in the lesson plans. You may wish to use this list to provide children with opportunities **to read at least twenty minutes a day** outside of class

**Theme 4**    WILD AND WONDERFUL

**Allen, Pamela.**
*Who Sank the Boat?* Putnam, 1996. The reader is invited to guess who causes the boat to sink when five animals of varying sizes decide to go for a row. *Children's Choice.* **AVERAGE**

**Brett, Jan.**
*The Mitten.* Penguin, 1996. Several animals sleep snugly in Nicki's lost mitten until the bear sneezes. *Award-Winning Author.* **CHALLENGE**

**Ehlert, Lois.**
*In My World.* Harcourt, 2006. This book describes some of the many things in the natural world—such as worms, seashells, flowers, and stars—that a child can appreciate. *Award-Winning Author/ Illustrator.* **EASY**

**Ehlert, Lois.**
*Waiting for Wings.* Harcourt, 2001. This dynamic, larger-than-life book tells about the growth of a beautiful butterfly. *ALA Notable Book; Notable Children's Book in the Language Arts.* **CHALLENGE**

**Fowler, Allan.**
*It's a Good Thing There Are Insects.* Children's Press, 1991. This book identifies the characteristics of insects and describes some of their useful activities and products. **AVERAGE**

**Keo, Ena.**
*I Can Be Anything.* Steck-Vaughn, 1997. Two children imagine various professions that they can have when they grow up— because they can do anything! **AVERAGE**

**Knudsen, Shannon.**
*African Elephants.* Lerner, 2006. What do African elephants do all day? Readers find out in this exciting book about Earth's largest land animals. **CHALLENGE**

**Larrañaga, Ana.**
*Beautiful Bugs.* Polka Dot, 2000. Meet a variety of vibrant bugs in this colorfully illustrated introduction to the insect world. **EASY**

**McDonnell, Flora.**
*Splash!* Candlewick, 2003. When the jungle animals are hot, a baby elephant has a good solution involving the squirting and splashing of water at the watering hole. **EASY**

**Meister, Cari.**
*Tiny the Snow Dog.* Viking, 2001. Tiny and his owner play in the snow, and Tiny becomes a snow dog. **EASY**

**Parr, Todd.**
*Reading Makes You Feel Good.* Little, Brown, 2005. This book describes the characteristics and various advantages of reading. **EASY**

**Parr, Todd.**
*The Feelings Book.* Megan Tingley, 2005. Children express different moods, including "I feel very mad," "I feel like reading books all day," and "I feel like trying something new." **EASY**

**Schlepp, Tammy J.**
*Going to School (My World).* Copper Beech, 2001. Thinking about his first day at school gives Alex butterflies, but his parents, teacher, and friends make it easier. **AVERAGE**

**Shepard, Daniel.**
*All Kinds of Farms.* Capstone, 2004. Simple text and photographs introduce crops that grow in a variety of locations and climates. **CHALLENGE**

**Stewart, Paul.**
*A Little Bit of Winter.* HarperCollins, 2000. Before hibernating, Hedgehog asks Rabbit to save him "a little bit of winter." How will Rabbit manage to save some of the season for his friend? **AVERAGE**

**Walsh, Ellen Stoll.**
*Mouse Paint.* Harcourt, 1995. Three white mice discover jars of red, blue, and yellow paint and explore the world of color. *Children's Choice.* **AVERAGE**

**Wells, Rosemary.**
*The School Play.* Hyperion, 2001. When Yoko's class puts on a play about taking care of teeth, not everyone is happy with his or her part. *Award-Winning Author/ Illustrator.* **CHALLENGE**

**Wood, Audrey.**
*The Napping House.* Harcourt, 2004. In this cumulative tale, a wakeful flea atop a number of sleeping creatures causes a commotion, with just one bite. *ALA Notable Book; Children's Choice; New York Times Best Illustrated Book.* **CHALLENGE**

# Student Edition Word Lists

The following words appear in the *Student Edition* stories in Book 1–3.

## A Butterfly Grows

a
air*
all
am
an
and
at
beautiful
big
branch
*butterfly*
can
*caterpillar*
chomp
*chrysalis*
come
crunch
days
don't
drink
drops
eat
egg
falls
fills
find
fly*
food
for
friends*
go
grew*
grow
hang
hatched
have
help
I
I'm
in
inch
insect
is
it
last
legs
like
little
long
look
lunch
me
munch
my
need*
now
on
onto
out
plant
plants
play*
plips
plops
rain*
rest
see
shed
sip
six
skin
small
snug
so
soon
spot
ten
the
then
this
to
us
watch*
water
will
wind
wings
with
you

## Mark's Big Day

a
act
again*
and
are
asked
at
bad
barked
big
bing
*blow*
but
called
can
champ
children
clock
day
did
do
dog
don't
dressed
feel*
felt
for
from
get
good
got
grin
had
hard
hat
he
him
his
house*
huff
hug
I
I'll
in
is
it
it's
jacket
just
know*
like
looked
loud*
luck
made
Mark
Mark's
me
*mistake*
mom
Mrs.*
not
of
oh
on
out
parks
part
parts
play
puff
put*
said
say*
scarf
school
*shy*
snarl
soft
soon
started
thanks
the
their
thinking
this
time
to
too
up
want
was
wasn't
went
wish
with
*wolf*
yes
you
your

## Tomás Rivera

a
about*
all
and
as
asked
at
best
big
books*
born
bugs
called
can
cars
children
clapped
come
crops
day
did
family*
farm
for
from
fun
gasped
get
go
good
got
Grandpa
grew
had
hands
hard
he
help
helped
his
hop
I
in
is
it
it's
job
just
kept
let's
*library*
look
lots
many
name*
night
now
of
on
people*
pick
picking
quick
read*
Rivera
Rivera's
said
stars
started
still
*stories*
*teacher*
tell
telling
*Texas*
the
them
then
they
think
thinking
this
time
to
*Tomás Rivera*
too
up
visit
want
was
we
went
when
will
wink
with
work*
writing*
you

## One More Friend

a
all
always*
an
and
ant
are
baa
backyard
bark
be
Bird
but
by*
calls
can't
cat
chick
chirp
cluck
come
Cow's*
curl
Dog
don't
Duck
*elephant*
first
flaps
for
friend
Frog
good
*hammock*
happy
hen
his
hops
in
is
it's
join*
jump
jumps

**Key:**
\* High-Frequency Word in Book 1–3
*italics* Story Word in Book 1–3
red Word appears for the first time in Book 1–3.
**normal type** Decodable Word or Known Word*
*Known words were taught in the Kindergarten Program, in the Inventory Unit, in Book 1–1, or in Book 1–2.*

*kindness*
*Lamb*
little
more
my
nice*
no
now
oh
one
out
play
please*
purr
quack
rest
ribbit
room*
run
say
*shade*
she
sir
skips
slinks
steps
the
then
there
there's
third
this
to
turn
up
us
way
what
when
who
will
wings
you
your

**Can Elephants Paint?**

a
all
an

and
art
artist
asked
back
big
black
blinked
brush
brushed
buy*
by
came
can
carry*
cut
darling
day
days
dipped
do
dot
dots
dragged
elephant
elephants
farm
flowers
for
get
giggle
good
grabbed
had
handed
handle
hands
hard
head
held
help
helped
helping
her
his
homes
how
hung
I
*idea*
in

it
it's
jobs
jungle
just
let's
liked
lines
little
lived
long
lots
*Lucky*
Lucky's
made
marks
me
middle
money*
more
my
new
nibble
Ning
no
not
now
of
off
on
one
other*
others
paint*
painted
paper*
people
pink
purple
said
saw
she
short
simple
splashes
spot
spots
started
strong
swim
thank

that
the
their
them
then
there
they
thick
thin
think
this
thinking
to
trees
trunk
trunks
us
use
wanted
was
watch
we
went
were
what
when
will
with
worked
would*
you
you're
your

**Snow Surprise**

a
added
again
air
all
and
animals
apples
arms
at
ball
barked
Ben
big
bigger

biggest
birds
bowl
*brother*
called
clapped
coat
cold
come
corn
crows
crusts
dash
did
don't
fell
fill
first
flash
floating
food
for
from
frost
gaps
gasped
get
got
groaned
growing
had
hands
hat
he
her
him
his
I
I'll
in
into
is
it
it's
Joan
jumped
landed
last
led
little
loaded

loaned
look
looked
mad
made
make
me
more
mouse*
munched
nipped
no
not
nuts
of
off
oh
on
one
other
our*
out
over*
own
packed
patted
perfect
pockets
porch
pretty*
put
ran
rolling
row
said
sang
saw
scarf
she
show
small
smell
smelled
snacks
snatched
snow
snowballs
so
sorts
sport
stacked

started
sticks
surprise*
the
them
then
there
they
things
three*
thud
tipped
to
toast
too
top
*trouble*
used
was
were
what
with
yard
yelled
yellow
you

# Get Started Story and Decodable Book Word Lists

The following words appear in the *Get Started Stories* and *Decodable Books* in Book 1–3.

**Get Started Story 13: Rich Gets Big**

a
an
be*
big
branch
brings
calls
cannot
cat
check
chest
for
get
gets
grow*
has
he*
his
I*
inch
it
just
long
mitt
Mom
more
not
of*
on
porch
Rich
says
shelf
sits
small
snapshot
stands
tells
that
the*
thinks
to*
too*
top
wants*

was*
will
wish
with
yes
you*

**Decodable Book 13: Ranch Pals**

a
and
are*
at
big
Blanch
Blanch's
branch
bunch
catch
chat
checks
chick
chickens
children
chill
chops
chore
chores
comes*
Dad
do*
eggs
fetch
for
fun
get
hatching
in
is
latch
lifts
likes*
live*
logs
lunch
Mitch
Mitch's
Mom
much
munch

nest
on
ox
pals
pen
piglets
pigs
ranch
so*
stack
the*
there*
they*
think
to*
will

**Get Started Story 14: Ann's Trip to the Stars**

a
along
am
and
Ann
Ann's
asks
back
bark
barks
Ben
big
blast
block
can
Carl
claps
cold
crash
Dad
dark
end
far
fix
flash
get
go*
grin

grins
hall
hangs
has
help
her
hot
I*
in
is
it
kit
long
Mars
Mom
my*
not
off
path
play
red
rocks
says
scarf
sharp
ship
stands
stars
start
starts
sun
thanks
the*
to*
trip
will
with
yes
you*

**Decodable Book 14: Charming Carmel**

a
all
along
art
artists
at

bark
bring
can
Carmel
charming
cling
contest
dark
day*
dogs
dot
fish
grand
has
have*
here*
I
in
is
it
jacket
just
like*
look*
lot
lots
map
much
not
of
off
on
out*
postcard
rocks
run
sand
scarf
see*
sharp
shore
small
spend
starfish
started
the*
then
there*
they*
this
time*

to*
visit
warm
water
will
you*

**Get Started Story 15: A Quiz for Brent**

a
backyard
bed
big
Brent
bucket
check
cloth
Dad
desk
find*
finishes
for
gets
glad
got
granddad
he*
him
hint
is
it's
Mom
not
on
quick
quilt
quit
quiz
red
small
soft
tan
tells
that
the*
think
to*

too*
what*
will

**Decodable Book 15: Quint and the Squids**

all
and
are*
arms
asked
at
be*
big
can
cannot
dad
dark
do*
fish
from*
gasped
getting*
grab
has
his
I
ink
is
it
liquid
long
look*
looked*
lunch
must
not
now*
one*
quick
Quint
Quint's

**Key:**

\* High-Frequency Word in Book 1–3

**normal type** Decodable Word

red
said*
see*
six
small
squid
squid's
squids
swim
ten
that
the*
them
we*
with
yes

**Decodable Book 15: Which Animal Is It?**

a
and
animal*
big
can
do*
dog
farm
fast
flash
frog
grunt
happy*
hints
hop
hot
in
is
it
jumps
licks
lives*
mud
on
past
pen
pig
pond

runs
sits
small
swim
the*
think
this
use*
water*
when
where*
which
whippet
whiz
you*

**Decodable Book 15: Whack! Wham!**

a
and
are*
asked
at
back
ball
basket
basketball
big
can
do*
forth
fun
got
hard
hit
I
in
is
it
kept
kick
kicked
kicking
landed
let's
net
now*
on

Pam
past
porch
said*
sat
soccer
stop
thanks
that
the*
this
we*
whack
wham
what*
when
whiz
will
yelled
yes
you*
zipped

**Get Started Story 16: A Perfect Lunch**

a
all
and
ask
Ben
Bert
best
bird
bumps
can
come*
comes*
corn
dirt
dishes
do*
drink
drops
fills
first
for
friends*

glass
have*
he*
her
his
in
is
It's
Jen
Kit
Let's
Liz
lunch
Meg
muffin
muffins
my*
next
no*
now*
oh*
out*
perfect
perhaps
picks
picnic
says*
serving
sets
she*
sips
sit
sits
skirt
squirts
tap
the*
they*
third
this
trick
up
where*
will
with

**Decodable Book 16: Helping a Bird**

a
all
and
animal*
asked
at
Bert
better
bird
can
can't
car
chirp
crossed
dirt
fell
Fern
first
fly*
for
get
gets
go*
got
held
help
helping
her
his
hurt
I'll
in
is
it
it's
its
leg
let
let's
look*
Mom
on
onto*
out*
perch
perfect
perhaps
plant
river
said*
shelter

shirt
sister
sit
skirt
slid
spot
that
the*
they*
this
to*
tuck
under
up
when
whispered
will
yes

**Decodable Book 16: King Curtis and Shirl**

a
and
as
asked
bed
better
big
but
can
curls
Curtis
dad
dad's
day*
fell
felt
get
gets
had
has
hat
have*
he*
help
her
his
hurt

I
in
is
job
king
land
leg
must
not
now*
of*
one*
or
rest
sad
said*
Shirl
still
the*
then
to*
too*
tripped
turned
up
will
with
yard
you*
your*

**Decodable Book 16: Burt's Bag**

a
all
am
and
animals*
bag
ball
better
big
burst
Burt
can
cars
did
first
for

fun
fur
get
go*
going*
Gramps
grin
had
hat
have*
he*
his
hurt
I
if
in
is
it
let's
lift
Mom
my*
not
now*
one*
pack
packed
pants
pick
said*
shirts
soccer
started
stuff
stuffed
then
thing
this
to*
trucks
turn
visiting
was*
went
what*
will
with
yelled
you*

**Get Started Story 17: Jungle Fun**

a
an
and
animals*
balls
bells
best
big
birds
bubbles
cannot
catch
cats
chuckle
contest
do*
elephant*
family*
foxes
fun
giggle
glitter
hats
have*
in
is
jangle
jingle
join*
juggle
jump
jungle
kick
little
make*
pick
pins
purple
red
ring
run
soon*
sparkle
spin
start
stomp

that
the*
they*
tricks
tumble
turn
who*
wiggle
will
win
you*

**Decodable Book 17: Little Ann's Nap**

a
all
and
animals*
Ann
Ann's
babbles
back
ball
bam
bang
big
bubbles
but
can
chuckle
cuddle
dribbles
Ed
fan
farm
fiddle
first
forth
Frank
Frank's
giggle
gives*
gobbles
good*
gurgles
has
have*
her

his
how*
hug
is
little
marbles
Mom
morning
must
nap
never
pet
pig
play*
purple
rattle
river
rumble
run
she*
slurps
snorts
snuggle
start
starts
stumble
the*
to*
turtle
twins
Uncle
visiting
wants*
will
with

**Get Started Story 18: Shadow in the Snow**

a
all
along
an
and
apple
at
back
black

blows
boat
bowl
branch
chin
coat
crow
day*
drink
eat*
follow
go*
grins
hat
he*
her
hilltop
hunt
I*
in
Jess
let's
look*
me*
milk
muffin
oak
of*
off
on
onto*
play*
pond
rabbit
rests
row
rowboat
Shadow
sings
sits
sled
snack
sniffs
snow
soaks
spring
sun
tells
that
the*
then

tree*
tucks
under
up
we'll*
will
yellow
yells
you*
zips

**Decodable Book 18: The Little Yellow Tugboat**

a
all
and
at
back
big
blows
boat
but
can
chugs
day*
deck
did
do*
dock
ends
fixed
floating
get
go*
good*
hard
has
horn
in
is
it
its
job
little
load
long
low

must
not
on
red
river
shop
sink
slows
still
stops
the*
this
to*
tow
trip
tug
tugboat
tugboat's
up
will
workers*
yellow

# Cumulative Word List: Book 1–3

The following words appear in the *Student Edition* stories, *Get Started Stories*, and *Decodable Books* in Book 1–3.

| | | | | | | |
|---|---|---|---|---|---|---|
| a | bam | brings | chest | curls | ends | from* |
| about* | bang | brother | chick | Curtis | falls | frost |
| act | bark | brush | chickens | cut | family* | fun |
| added | barked | brushed | children | dad | fan | fur |
| again* | barks | bubbles | chill | dad's | far | gaps |
| air* | basket | bucket | chin | dark | farm | gasped |
| all | basketball | bugs | chirp | darling | fast | get |
| along | be* | bumps | chomp | dash | feel* | gets |
| always* | beautiful | bunch | chops | day | fell | getting |
| am | bed | burst | chore | days | felt | giggle |
| an | bells | Burt | chores | deck | Fern | gives* |
| and | Ben | but | chrysalis | desk | fetch | glad |
| animal* | Bert | butterfly | chuckle | did | fiddle | glass |
| animals* | best | buy* | chugs | dipped | fill | glitter |
| Ann | better | by* | clapped | dirt | fills | go |
| Ann's | big | called | claps | dishes | find | gobbles |
| ant | bigger | calls | cling | do* | finishes | going |
| apples | biggest | came | clock | dock | first | good* |
| are | bing | can | cloth | dogs | fish | got |
| arms | Bird | can't | cluck | Dog | fix | grab |
| art | birds | cannot | coat | don't | fixed | grabbed |
| artist | black | car | cold | dot | flaps | Gramps |
| artists | Blanch | Carl | come | dots | flash | grand |
| as | Blanch's | cars | comes | dragged | floating | granddad |
| ask | blast | Carmel | contest | dressed | flowers | Grandpa |
| asked | blinked | carry* | corn | dribbles | fly* | grew* |
| asks | block | cars | Cow's* | drink | follow | |
| at | blow | cat | crash | drops | food | |
| baa | blows | catch | crops | Duck | for | |
| babbles | boat | caterpillar | crossed | eat | forth | |
| back | books* | cats | crow | Ed | foxes | |
| backyard | born | champ | crows | egg | Frank | |
| bad | bowl | charming | crunch | eggs | Frank's | |
| bag | branch | chat | crusts | elephant | friend | |
| ball | Brent | check | cuddle | elephants | friends* | |
| balls | bring | checks | curl | end | Frog | |

**Key:**

\* High-Frequency Word in Book 1–3

*italics* Story Word in Book 1–3

red Word appears for the first time in Book 1–3.

**normal type** Decodable Word or Known Word*

*Known words were taught in the Inventory Unit, in the Kindergarten Program, or in Books 1–1 and 1–2.*

grin
grins
groaned
grow
growing
grunt
gurgles
had
hall
hammock
handed
handle
hands
hang
hangs
happy
hard
has
hat
hatch
hatched
hatching
hats
have
he
head
held
help
helped
helping
hen
her
here
hilltop
him
hint
hints

his
hit
homes
hop
hops
horn
hot
house*
how
huff
hug
hung
hunt
hurt
I
I'll
I'm
idea
if
in
inch
ink
insect
into
is
it
it's
its
jacket
jangle
Jen
Jess
jingle
Joan
job
jobs
join*

juggle
jump
jumped
jumps
jungle
just
kept
kick
kicked
kicking
kindness
king
kit
know*
Lamb
land
landed
last
latch
led
leg
legs
let
let's
library
licks
lift
lifts
like
liked
likes
lines
liquid
little
live*
lived
lives

Liz
load
loaned
logs
long
look*
looked*
looks
lot
lots
loud*
low
luck
Lucky
Lucky's
lunch
mad
made
make
many
map
marbles
Mark
Mark's
marks
Mars
me
Meg
middle
milk
mistake
Mitch
Mitch's
mitt
Mom
money*
more

morning
mouse*
Mrs.*
much
mud
muffin
muffins
munch
munched
must
my
name*
nap
need*
nest
net
never
new
next
nibble
nice*
night
Ning
nipped
no
not
now
nuts
oak
of
off
oh
on
one
onto*
or
other*

others
our*
out
over*
own
ox
pack
packed
paint*
painted
pals
Pam
pants
paper*
parks
part
parts
past
path
patted
pen
people*
perch
perfect
perhaps
pet
pick
picking
picks
picnic
pig
piglets
pigs
pink
pins
plant
plants

play*
please*
plips
plops
pockets
pond
porch
postcard
pretty*
puff
purple
purr
put*
quack
quick
quilt
Quint
Quint's
quit
quiz
rabbit
rain*
ran
ranch
rattle
read*
red
rest
rests
ribbit
Rich
ring
river
Rivera
Rivera's
rocks
rolling

| | | | | | |
|---|---|---|---|---|---|
| room* | sings | sparkle | teacher | trick | we'll |
| row | sink | spend | tell | tricks | went |
| rowboat | sip | spin | telling | trip | were |
| rumble | sips | splashes | tells | tripped | whack |
| run | sir | sport | ten | trouble | wham |
| runs | sister | spot | Texas | trucks | what |
| sad | sit | spots | thank | trunk | when |
| said | sits | spring | thanks | trunks | where* |
| sand | six | squid | that | tuck | whippet |
| sang | skin | squid's | the* | tucks | whispered |
| sat | skips | squids | their | tug | whiz |
| saw | skirt | squirts | them | tugboat | who |
| say* | sled | stack | then | tugboat's | wiggle |
| says | slid | stacked | there* | tumble | will |
| scarf | slinks | stands | there's | turn | win |
| school | slows | starfish | they | turned | wind |
| see | slurps | stars | thick | turtle | wings |
| sees | small | start | thin | twins | wink |
| serving | smell | started | thing | Uncle | wish |
| sets | smelled | starts | things | under | with |
| shade | snack | steps | think | up | wolf |
| Shadow | snacks | sticks | thinking | us | work* |
| sharp | snapshot | still | thinks | use* | worked |
| she | snarl | stomp | third | used | workers* |
| shed | snatched | stop | this | very | would* |
| shelf | sniffs | stops | three* | visit | writing* |
| shelter | snorts | stories | thud | visiting | yard |
| ship | snow | strong | time | want | yelled |
| Shirl | snowballs | stuff | tipped | wanted | yellow |
| shirt | snug | stuffed | to | wants* | yells |
| shirts | snuggle | stumble | toast | warm | yes |
| shop | so | sun | Tomás | was | you* |
| shore | soaks | surprise* | Tomás Rivera | wasn't | you're |
| short | soccer | swim | too | watch* | your* |
| show | soft | swims | top | water | zipped |
| shy | soon | tan | tow | way | zips |
| simple | sorts | tap | trees | we | |

# Cumulative Word List: Books 1–1, 1–2, and 1–3

The following words appear in the *Student Edition* stories, *Get Started Stories*, and *Decodable Books* in Books 1–1, 1–2, and 1–3.

| | | | | | | | |
|---|---|---|---|---|---|---|---|
| a | bark | boss | champ | crack | Dot | find* | fuss |
| about* | barked | bowl | charming | crash | Dot's | finds | gaps |
| act | barks | box | chat | cried | dots | finished | gasped |
| acted | basket | branch | check | crops | down | finishes | get* |
| add | basketball | Brent | checks | crossed | dragged | first | gets |
| added | bat | bring | chest | crows | dressed | fish | getting |
| again* | be* | brings | chick | crunch | dribbles | fit | gift |
| air* | beautiful | brother | chickens | crusts | drink | fits | gifts |
| all | bed | brush | children | cuddle | drops | fix | giggle |
| along | bells | brushed | chill | cup | Duck | fixed | give |
| always* | Ben | bubbles | chin | cups | dug | fizzed | gives* |
| am | bend | bucket | chirp | curl | dump | flag | glad |
| an | bent | bud | chomp | curls | dust | flaps | glass |
| and | Bert | buds | chops | Curtis | eat | flash | Glen |
| animal* | Bess | bugs | chore | cut | Ed | flinging | glitter |
| animals* | best | bumps | chores | dad | Ed's | flip | go |
| Ann | bet | bunch | chrysalis | dad's | egg | floating | goalie |
| Ann's | Beth | burst | chuckle | Dan | eggs | flop | gobbles |
| ant | Beth's | Burt | chugs | dark | elephant | flower | going |
| ants | better | but | clams | darling | elephants | flowers | gold |
| apple | big | butterfly | clang | dash | end | fly* | goo |
| apples | bigger | buy* | clapped | day | ends | fog | good* |
| are | biggest | by* | claps | days | every | follow | got |
| arms | Bill | cab | class | deck | facts | food | grab |
| art | Bill's | called | click | dent | fall | for | grabbed |
| artist | bing | calls | cliffs | desk | falls | form | Gramps |
| artists | bins | came | cling | did | family* | formed | grand |
| as | Bird | can | clinging | dig | fan | fort | granddad |
| ask | birds | can't | clings | digs | fangs | forth | Grandpa |
| asked | black | cannot | clock | dip | far | Fox | grass |
| asks | Blanch | cap | cloth | dipped | farm | Fox's | grew* |
| asleep | Blanch's | car | cluck | dips | fast | foxes | grilled |
| at | blanket | Carl | coat | dirt | fat | Fran | |
| baa | blast | cars | cock-a-doodle-doo | dish | fed | Frank | |
| babbles | blink | Carmel | cold | dishes | feel* | Frank's | |
| back | blinked | carry* | come | do* | feet | fresh | |
| backyard | block | cars | comes | dock | fell | friend | |
| bad | blocked | cash | contest | does | felt | friends* | |
| bag | blow | cast | cord | dog | Fern | Frog | |
| bags | blows | cat | corn | dogs | fetch | frogs | |
| ball | boat | catch | could | doing | fiddle | from* | |
| balls | Bob | caterpillar | Cow's* | don't | fill | frost | |
| bam | books* | catfish | crabs | Doris | filled | fun | |
| bang | born | cats | | dot | fills | fur | |

**Key:**

* High-Frequency Word in Book 1–3

*italics* Story Word in Book 1–3

red Word appears for the first time in Book 1–3

**normal type** Decodable Word or Known Word*

*Known words were taught in the Inventory Unit, in Kindergarten Program, or in Books 1–1, 1–2 and 1–3.*

| | | | | | | | |
|---|---|---|---|---|---|---|---|
| grin | hiss | Jill's | *library* | many | must | paint* | pop |
| grins | hissed | jingle | licked | map | my | painted | pops |
| grip | hit | Joan | licks | maps | name* | pals | porch |
| groaned | hits | job | lift | marbles | nap | Pam | postcard |
| grow | hold* | jobs | lifted | Mark | naps | pan | pot |
| growing | home | jogs | lifts | Mark's | Nat | pants | pots |
| grunt | homes* | join* | like | marks | neck | paper* | pretty* |
| grunted | hop | jug | liked | Mars | need* | parks | princess |
| gurgles | hops | juggle | likes | mat | nest | part* | puff |
| Gus | horn | jump | line | math | nests | parts | puffed |
| had | hot | jumped | lines | mats | net | past | pup |
| hall | house* | jumps | Ling | Max | nets | Pat | purple |
| ham | how* | jungle | lips | me | never | path | purr |
| *hammock* | huff | junk | liquid | Meg | new | patted | put* |
| handed | huffed | just | little | melts | next | pen | quack |
| handle | hug | Ken | live | men | nibble | penguin | queen |
| hands | hung | kept | lived | meow | nice* | penguins | quick |
| hang | hungry | kick | lives | mess | Nick | pens | quilt |
| hangs | hunt | kicked | Liz | Mick | night | perch | Quint |
| happy | hunting | kicking | load | middle | Ning | perfect | Quint's |
| hard | hurt | kicks | loaned | milk | nipped | perhaps | quit |
| has | I | kids | locked | Ming | no* | pet | quiz |
| hat | I'll | Kim | log | Ming's | nods | pick | rabbit |
| hatch | I'm | *kindness* | logs | Miss | north | picked | raft |
| hatched | ice | king | long | mist | not | picking | rags |
| hatching | *idea* | King Midas | look* | *mistake* | now* | picks | rain* |
| hats | if | king's | looked* | Mitch | nut | picnic | ran |
| have | in* | kit | looks | Mitch's | nuts | pig | ranch |
| he | inch | know* | lost | mitt | oak | piglets | rang |
| head | ink | Lad | lot | mixed | octopus | pigs | rattle |
| held | insect | Lad's | lots | Mom | of* | ping | read* |
| help* | into | *Lamb* | loud* | money* | off | pink | red |
| helped | is | land | low | mop | oh* | pins | rest |
| helping | it | landed | luck | more | on | plant | rests |
| helps | it's | laps | *Lucky* | morning | one | plants | ribbit |
| hen | its | last | Lucky's | moths | onto* | play* | Rich |
| hens | Jack | lasting | lug | mouse* | or | please* | Rick |
| her | jacket | latch | lumps | Mr. | other* | plip | rid |
| here | jam | late* | lunch | Mrs.* | others | plips | rig |
| hid | Jan | leaves | lungs | much* | our* | plop | rigs |
| hills | jangle | led | Mack | mud | out | plops | ring |
| hilltop | Jeff | leg | mad | muffin | over* | plump | rips |
| him | Jen | legs | made | muffins | own | plus | river |
| hint | Jess | lend | make | mugs | ox | pockets | Rivera |
| hints | jet | let | makes* | munch | pack | pond | Rivera's |
| his | Jill | let's* | mall | munched | packed | | rock |

rocks
rod
rolling
room*
roots
Ross
row
rowboat
Roz
rug
rumble
run
runs
rush
rushed
rust
sack
sacks
sad
said
Sam
sand
sang
sat
saw
say*
says
scarf
school
scores
sea stars
seal
seals
see
sees
serving
Seth
sets
shack
shade
Shadow
sharp
she
shed
shelf
shelter

ship
Shirl
shirt
shirts
shocked
shop
shore
short
show
shrimp
shy
sick
Sid
sifted
sImple
sing
singing
sings
sink
sip
sips
sir
sister
sit
sits
skid
skim
skin
skips
skirt
sled
slid
slinks
slows
slurps
small
smell
smelled
snack
snacks
snapped
snapshot
snarl
snatched
sniffs

snore
snort
snorts
snow
snowballs
snug
snuggle
so*
soaks
sobs
soccer
socks
soft
some*
song
soon*
sore
sort
sorts
sparkle
spend
spent
spin
splashes
sport
sports
spot
spots
spring
squid
squid's
squids
squirts
stack
stacked
stands
starfish
stars
start
started
starts
stems
steps
sticks
still
sting

stomp
stop
stops
stories
strings
strong
stuck
stuff
stuffed
stumble
sun
surprise*
swim
swims
swing
swung
tacos
tag
tall
tan
tap
task
teacher
tell
telling
tells
ten
Texas
than
thank*
thanks
that
the*
their
them
then
there*
there's
they
thick
thin
thing
things
think
thinking

thinks
third
this
three*
thud
thump
tilted
Tim
time*
tip
tipped
tips
Tip-Top
to
toast
Tom
Tomás
Tomás
   Rivera
too*
top
torn
toss
tossed
tow
town
trash
trees
trick
tricks
trip
tripped
trots
trouble
trucks
trunk
trunks
tub
tuck
tucks
tug
tugboat
tugboat's
tumble
turn
turned

turtle
twigs
twins
Uncle
under
up
us
use*
used
van
very
vet
visit
visiting
wall
want
wanted
wants*
warm
was
wasn't
watch*
water
way
we
we'll
went
were
wet
whack
wham
what
when
where*
whippet
whispered
whiz
who
wiggle
will
win
wind
wings
wink
wish
wished

with
wolf
work*
worked
workers*
worn
would*
writing*
yam
yams
yard
yelled
yellow
yells
yes
yet
you*
you're
your
zipped
zips

# Introducing the Glossary

Explain to children that a glossary is often included in a book so that readers can look up words used in the book. Tell children that the words in a glossary are listed in alphabetical order. Have children say the alphabet aloud. Then ask them questions such as: Would the word *apple* be found near the beginning of the glossary or near the end? Would *monkey* be found at the beginning, in the middle, or at the end of the glossary?

■ Read aloud the introductory paragraph in the *Student Edition* to children. Have them page through the Glossary, and ask them what they notice about the entries. Then choose a word from the Glossary and model using alphabetical order to look it up. Have children read the sentence. Then have them tell how the sentence and the picture help them understand the meaning of the word.

■ Select several other words, with and without accompanying illustrations, and have children practice looking them up, using alphabetical order. Discuss the meanings of the words. Have children explain how using alphabetical order helped them locate the words.

■ Tell children to use the Glossary to check the meanings of new words as they read. Then discuss the differences and similarities between this Glossary and a classroom dictionary, guiding children to recognize that words in a glossary and a dictionary are in alphabetical order. Conclude with the idea that lists in books that people use to look up information are usually arranged in alphabetical order.

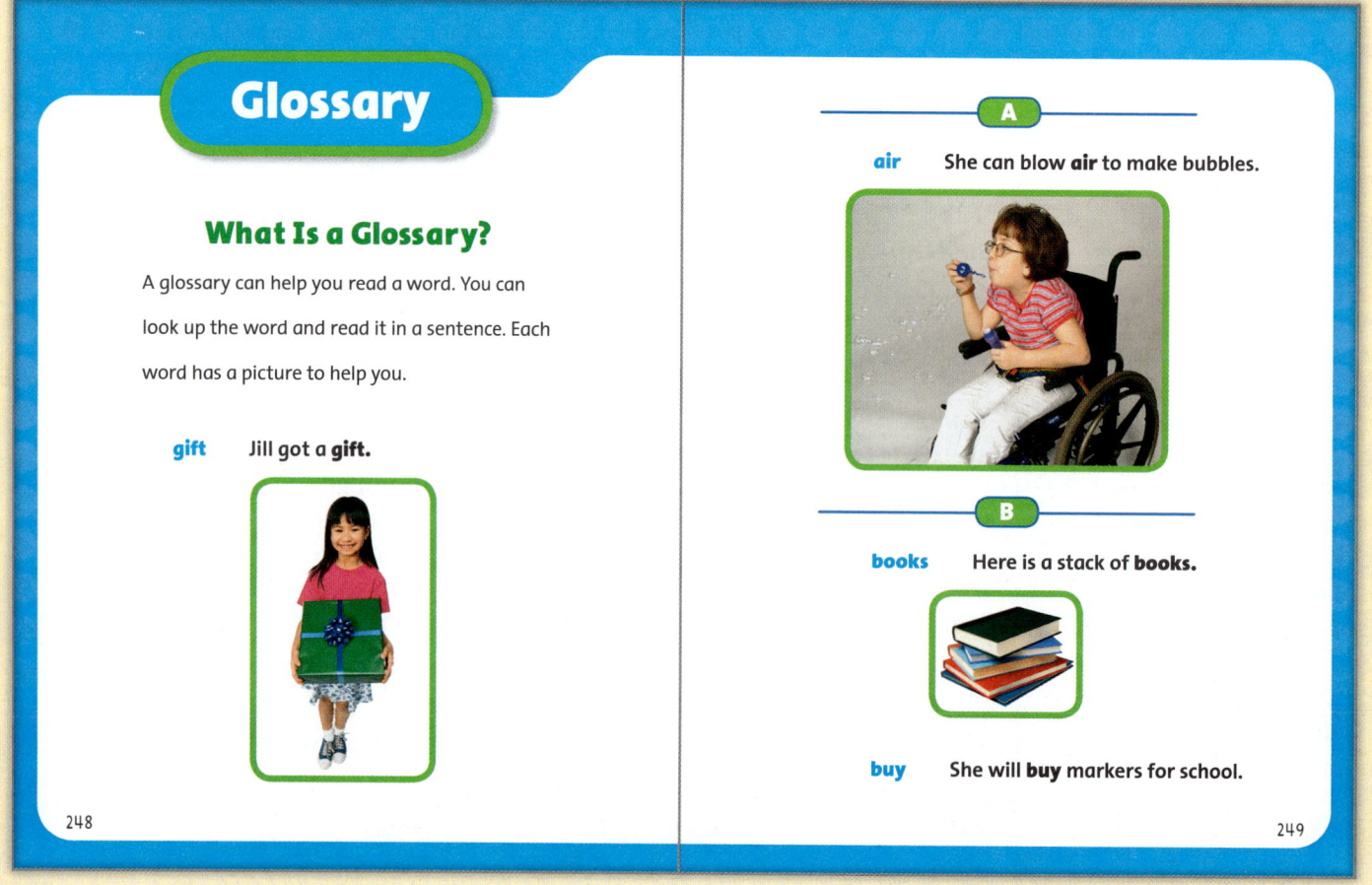

## Glossary

### What Is a Glossary?

A glossary can help you read a word. You can look up the word and read it in a sentence. Each word has a picture to help you.

**gift**　Jill got a **gift**.

**A**

**air**　She can blow **air** to make bubbles.

**B**

**books**　Here is a stack of **books**.

**buy**　She will **buy** markers for school.

248

249

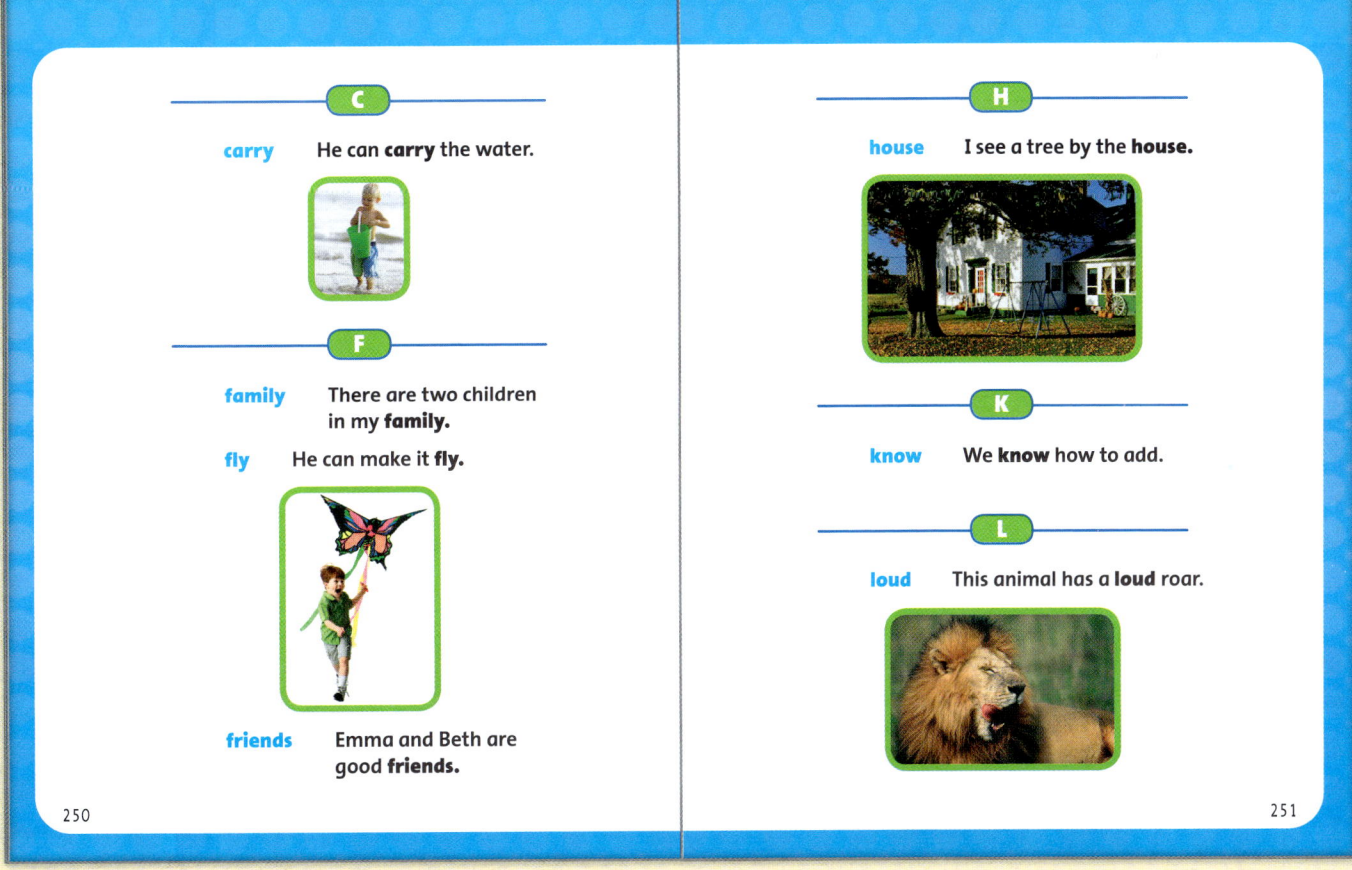

**C**

carry     He can **carry** the water.

**F**

family     There are two children in my **family.**

fly     He can make it **fly.**

friends     Emma and Beth are good **friends.**

**H**

house     I see a tree by the **house.**

**K**

know     We **know** how to add.

**L**

loud     This animal has a **loud** roar.

250

251

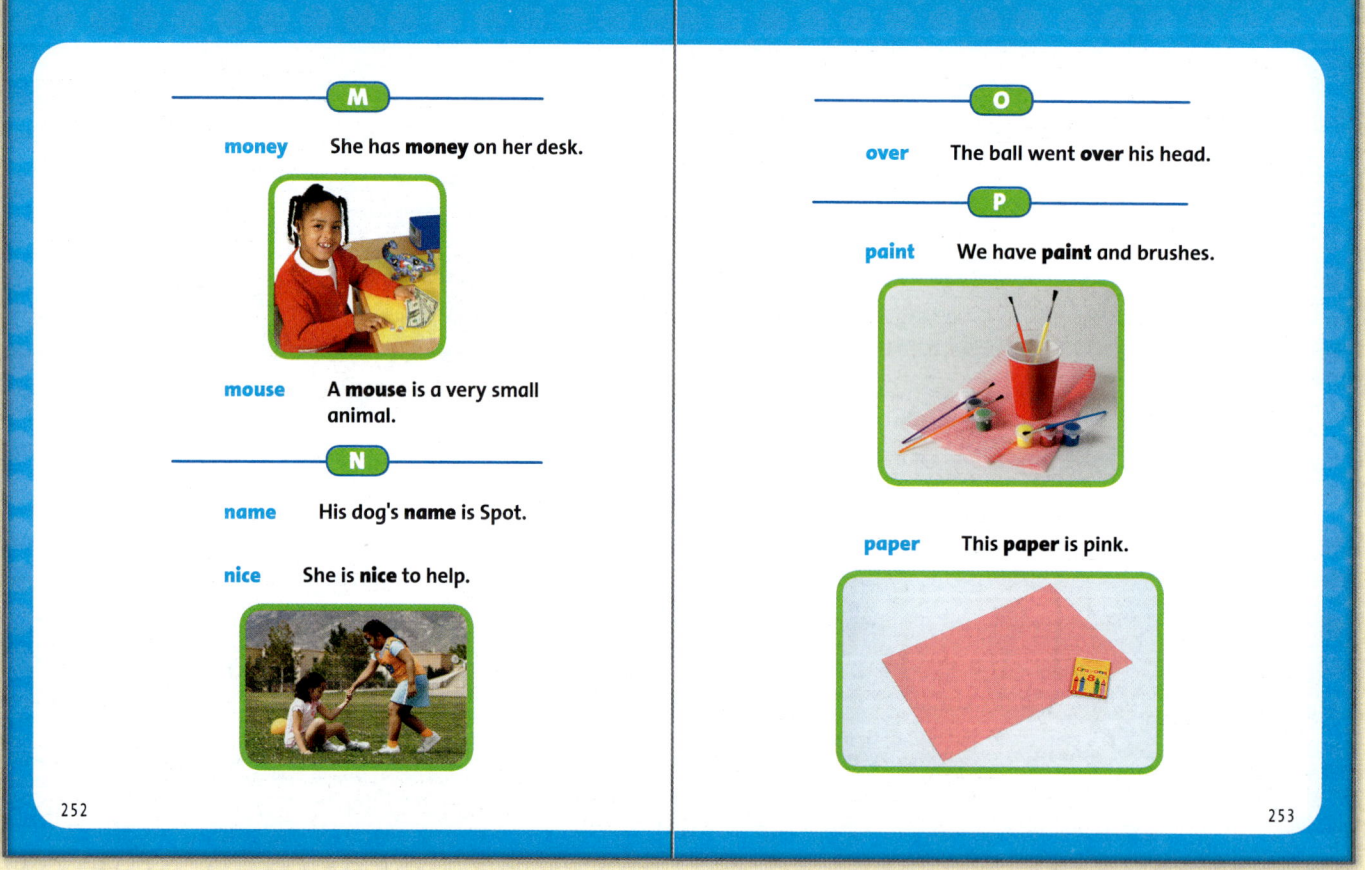

**M**

money    She has **money** on her desk.

mouse    A **mouse** is a very small animal.

**N**

name    His dog's **name** is Spot.

nice    She is **nice** to help.

252

**O**

over    The ball went **over** his head.

**P**

paint    We have **paint** and brushes.

paper    This **paper** is pink.

253

**people**  Many **people** went to the park.

**play**  Sal likes to **play** at the park.

**pretty**  The flowers are **pretty**.

### R

**rain**  The **rain** fell hard.

**read**  I **read** a book with Granddad.

**room**  Jim has a clock in his **room**.

### S

**surprise**  The gift was a **surprise**.

### T

**three**  Here are **three** flowers.

### W

**watch**  They **watch** for the bus to come.

**work**  The birds **work** on their nest.

**writing**  She is **writing** a list.

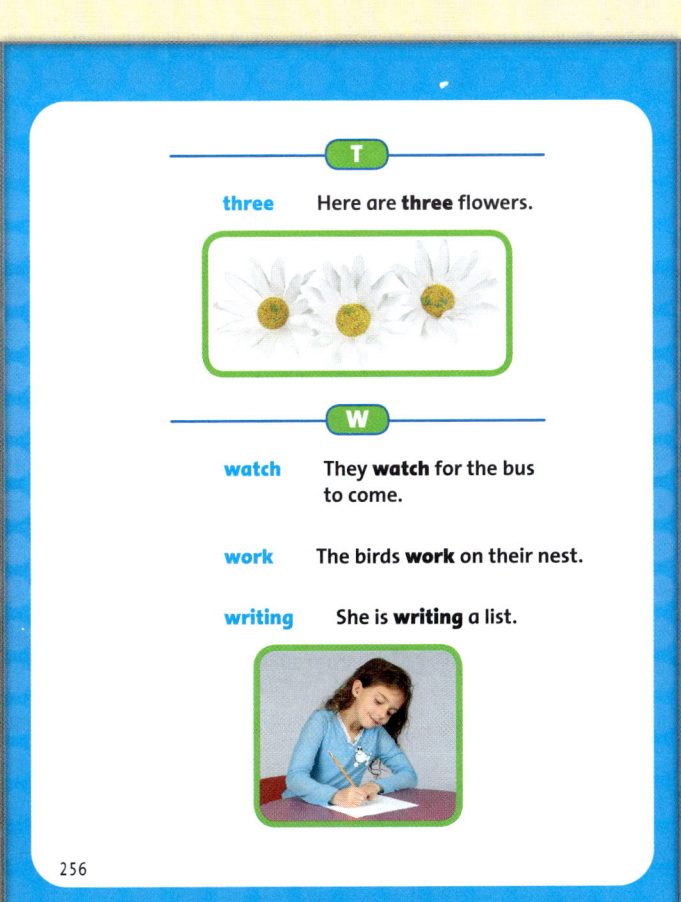

# Professional Bibliography

**Armbruster, B.B., Anderson, T.H., & Ostertag, J.**
(1987). Does text structure/summarization instruction facilitate learning from expository text? *Reading Research Quarterly,* 22 (3), 331–346.

**Ball, E. & Blachman, B.**
(1991). Does phoneme awareness training in kindergarten make a difference in early word recognition and developmental spelling? *Reading Research Quarterly,* 26 (1), 49–66.

**Baumann, J.F. & Bergeron, B.S.**
(1993). Story map instruction using children's literature: effects on first graders' comprehension of central narrative elements. *Journal of Reading Behavior,* 25 (4), 407–437.

**Baumann, J.F., Seifert-Kessell, N., & Jones, L.A.**
(1992). Effect of think-aloud instruction on elementary students' comprehension monitoring abilities. *Journal of Reading Behavior,* 24 (2), 143–172.

**Beck, I.L., Perfetti, C.A., & McKeown, M.G.**
(1982). Effects of long-term vocabulary instruction on lexical access and reading comprehension. *Journal of Educational Psychology,* 74 (4), 506–521.

**Bereiter, C. & Bird, M.**
(1985). Use of thinking aloud in identification and teaching of reading comprehension strategies. *Cognition and Instruction,* 2, 131–156.

**Blachman, B.**
(2000). Phonological awareness. In M. Kamil, P. Mosenthal, P.D. Pearson, & R. Barr (Eds.), *Handbook of Reading Research,* (Vol. 3). Mahwah, NJ: Erlbaum.

**Blachman, B., Ball, E.W., Black, R.S., & Tangel, D.M.**
(1994). Kindergarten teachers develop phoneme awareness in low-income, inner-city classrooms: Does it make a difference? *Reading and Writing: An Interdisciplinary Journal,* 6 (1), 1–18.

**Brown, I.S. & Felton, R.H.**
(1990). Effects of instruction on beginning reading skills in children at risk for reading disability. *Reading and Writing: An Interdisciplinary Journal,* 2 (3), 223–241.

**Chall, J.**
(1996). *Learning to read: The great debate* (revised, with a new foreword). New York: McGraw-Hill.

**Dowhower, S.L.**
(1987). Effects of repeated reading on second-grade transitional readers' fluency and comprehension. *Reading Research Quarterly,* 22 (4), 389–406.

**Ehri, L. & Wilce, L.**
(1987). Does learning to spell help beginners learn to read words? *Reading Research Quarterly,* 22 (1), 48–65.

**Fletcher, J.M. & Lyon, G.R.**
(1998) Reading: A research-based approach. In Evers, W.M. (Ed.) *What's Gone Wrong in America's Classrooms?*, Palo Alto, CA: Hoover Institution Press, Stanford University.

**Foorman, B., Francis, D., Fletcher, J., Schatschneider, C., & Mehta, P.**
(1998). The role of instruction in learning to read: Preventing reading failure in at-risk children. *Journal of Educational Psychology,* 90 (1), 37–55.

**Fukkink, R.G. & de Glopper, K.**
(1998). Effects of instruction in deriving word meaning from context: A meta-analysis. *Review of Educational Research,* 68 (4), 450–469.

**Gipe, J.P. & Arnold, R.D.**
(1979). Teaching vocabulary through familiar associations and contexts. *Journal of Reading Behavior,* 11 (3), 281–285.

**Griffith, P.L., Klesius, J.P., & Kromrey, J.D.**
(1992). The effect of phonemic awareness on the literacy development of first grade children in a traditional or a whole language classroom. *Journal of Research in Childhood Education,* 6 (2), 85–92.

**Juel, C.**
(1988). Learning to read and write: A longitudinal study of fifty-four children from first through fourth grades. *Journal of Educational Psychology,* 80, 437–447.

**Lundberg, I., Frost, J., & Petersen, O.**
(1988). Effects of an extensive program for stimulating phonological awareness in preschool children. *Reading Research Quarterly,* 23 (3), 263–284.

**McKeown, M.G., Beck, I.L., Omanson, R.C., & Pople, M.T.**
(1985). Some effects of the nature and frequency of vocabulary instruction on the knowledge and use of words. *Reading Research Quarterly,* 20 (5), 522–535.

**Nagy, W.E. & Scott, J.A.**
(2000). Vocabulary processes. In M. Kamil, P. Mosenthal, P.D. Pearson, & R. Barr (Eds.), *Handbook of Reading Research,* (Vol. 3) Mahwah, NJ: Erlbaum.

**National Reading Panel**
(2000). *Teaching Children to Read.* National Institute of Child Health and Human Development, National Institutes of Health, Washington, D.C.

**O'Connor, R., Jenkins, J.R., & Slocum, T.A.**
(1995). Transfer among phonological tasks in kindergarten: Essential instructional content. *Journal of Educational Psychology,* 87 (2), 202–217.

**O'Shea, L.J., Sindelar, P.T., & O'Shea, D.J.**
(1985). The effects of repeated readings and attentional cues on reading fluency and comprehension. *Journal of Reading Behavior,* 17 (2), 129–142.

**Paris, S.G., Cross, D.R., & Lipson, M.Y.**
(1984). Informed strategies for learning: A program to improve children's reading awareness and comprehension. *Journal of Educational Psychology,* 76 (6), 1239–1252.

**Payne, B.D. & Manning, B.H.** (1992). Basal reader instruction: Effects of comprehension monitoring training on reading comprehension, strategy use and attitude. *Reading Research and Instruction,* 32 (1), 29–38.

**Rasinski, T.V., Padak, N., Linek, W., & Sturtevant, E.** (1994). Effects of fluency development on urban second-grade readers. *Journal of Educational Research,* 87 (3), 158–165.

**Rinehart, S.D., Stahl, S.A., & Erickson, L.G.** (1986). Some effects of summarization training on reading and studying. *Reading Research Quarterly,* 21 (4), 422–438.

**Robbins, C. & Ehri, L.C.** (1994). Reading storybooks to kindergartners helps them learn new vocabulary words. *Journal of Educational Psychology,* 86 (1), 54–64.

**Rosenshine, B. & Meister, C.** (1994). Reciprocal teaching: A review of research. *Review of Educational Research,* 64 (4), 479–530.

**Rosenshine, B., Meister, C., & Chapman, S.** (1996). Teaching students to generate questions: A review of the intervention studies. *Review of Educational Research,* 66 (2), 181–221.

**Sénéchal, M.** (1997). The differential effect of storybook reading on preschoolers' acquisition of expressive and receptive vocabulary. *Journal of Child Language,* 24 (1), 123–138.

**Shany, M.T. & Biemiller, A.** (1995) Assisted reading practice: Effects on performance for poor readers in grades 3 and 4. *Reading Research Quarterly,* 30 (3), 382–395.

**Sindelar, P.T., Monda, L.E., & O'Shea, L.J.** (1990). Effects of repeated readings on instructional- and mastery-level readers. *Journal of Educational Research,* 83 (4), 220–226.

**Snow, C.E., Burns, S.M., & Griffin, P.** (1998). *Preventing Reading Difficulties in Young Children.* Washington, D.C.: National Academy Press.

**Stahl, S.A. & Fairbanks, M.M.** (1986). The effects of vocabulary instruction: A model-based meta-analysis. *Review of Educational Research,* 56 (1), 72–110.

**Stanovich, K.E.** (1986) Matthew effects in reading: Some consequences of individual differences in the acquisition of literacy. *Reading Research Quarterly,* 21 (4), 360–406.

**Torgesen, J., Morgan, S., & Davis, C.** (1992). Effects of two types of phonological awareness training on word learning in kindergarten children. *Journal of Educational Psychology,* 84 (3), 364–370.

**Torgesen, J., Wagner, R., Rashotte, C., Rose, E., Lindamood, P., Conway, T., & Garvan, C.** (1999). Preventing reading failure in young children with phonological processing disabilities: Group and individual responses to instruction. *Journal of Educational Psychology,* 91(4), 579–593.

**Vellutino, F.R. & Scanlon, D.M.** (1987). Phonological coding, phonological awareness, and reading ability: Evidence from a longitudinal and experimental study. *Merrill-Palmer Quarterly,* 33 (3), 321–363.

**White, T.G., Graves, M.F., & Slater, W.H.** (1990). Growth of reading vocabulary in diverse elementary schools: Decoding and word meaning. *Journal of Educational Psychology,* 82 (2), 281–290.

**Wixson, K.K.** (1986). Vocabulary instruction and children's comprehension of basal stories. *Reading Research Quarterly,* 21 (3), 317–329.

# Program Reviewers & Advisors

**Elizabeth A. Adkins,**
*Teacher*
Ford Middle School
Brook Park, Ohio

**Jean Bell,**
*Principal*
Littleton Elementary School
Avondale, Arizona

**Emily Brown,**
*Teacher*
Orange Center Elementary School
Orlando, Florida

**Stephen Bundy,**
*Teacher*
Ventura Elementary School
Kissimmee, Florida

**Helen Comba,**
*Language Arts Supervisor K-5*
Southern Boulevard School
Chatham, New Jersey

**Marsha Creese,**
*Reading/Language Arts Consultant*
Marlborough Elementary School
Marlborough, Connecticut

**Wyndy M. Crozier,**
*Teacher*
Mary Bryant Elementary School
Tampa, Florida

**Shirley Eyler,**
*Principal*
Martin Luther King School
Piscataway, New Jersey

**Sandy Hoffman,**
*Teacher*
Heights Elementary School
Fort Myers, Florida

**Amy Martin,**
*Reading Coach*
Kingswood Elementary School
Wickenburg, Arizona

**Rachel A. Musser,**
*Reading Coach*
Chumuckla Elementary School
Jay, Florida

**Dr. Carol Newton,**
*Director of Elementary Curriculum*
Millard Public Schools
Omaha, Nebraska

**Alda P. Pill,**
*Teacher*
Mandarin Oaks Elementary School
Jacksonville, Florida

**Dr. Elizabeth V. Primas,**
*Director*
Office of Curriculum and Instruction
Washington, District of Columbia

**Candice Ross,**
*Staff Development Teacher*
A. Mario Loiderman Middle School
Silver Spring, Maryland

**Sharon Sailor,**
*Teacher*
Conrad Fischer Elementary School
Elmhurst, Illinois

**Lucia Schneck,**
*Supervisor/Language Arts, Literacy*
Irvington Board of Education
Irvington, New Jersey

**RuthAnn Shauf,**
*District Resource Teacher*
Hillsborough County Public Schools
Tampa, Florida

**Jolene Topping,**
*Teacher*
Palmetto Ridge High School
Bonita Springs, Florida

**Betty Tubon,**
*Bilingual Teacher*
New Field Primary School
Chicago, Illinois

**Janet White,**
*Assistant Principal*
MacFarlane Park Elementary School
Tampa, Florida

## KINDERGARTEN REVIEWERS

**Denise Bir,**
*Teacher*
Destin Elementary School
Destin, Florida

**Linda H. Butler,**
*Reading First State Director*
Office of Academic Services
Washington, District of Columbia

**Julie Elvers,**
*Teacher*
Aldrich Elementary School
Omaha, Nebraska

**Rosalyn Glavin,**
*Principal*
Walter White Elementary School
River Rouge, Michigan

**Jo Anne M. Kershaw,**
*Language Arts Program Leader, K-5*
Longhill Administration Building
Trumbull, Connecticut

**Beverly Kibbe,**
*Teacher*
Cherry Brook Elementary School
Canton, Connecticut

**Bonnie B. Macintosh,**
*Teacher*
Glenallan Elementary School
Silver Spring, Maryland

**Laurin MacLeish,**
*Teacher*
Orange Center Elementary School
Orlando, Florida

**Mindy Steighner,**
*Teacher*
Randall Elementary School
Waukesha, Wisconsin

**Paula Stutzman,**
*Teacher*
Seven Springs Elementary School
New Port Richey, Florida

**Martha Tully,**
*Teacher*
Fleming Island Elementary School
Orange Park, Florida

## EDITORIAL ADVISORS

**Sharon J. Coburn,**
*National Reading Consultant*

**Hector J. Ramirez,**
*National Reading Consultant*

**Dr. Nancy I. Updegraff,**
*National Reading Consultant*

# Scope and Sequence

| Reading | Gr K | Gr 1 | Gr 2 | Gr 3 | Gr 4 | Gr 5 | Gr 6 |
|---|---|---|---|---|---|---|---|
| **Concepts About Print** | | | | | | | |
| Understand that print provides information | ░ | | | | | | |
| Understand how print is organized and read | ░ | | | | | | |
| Know left-to-right and top-to-bottom directionality | ░ | | | | | | |
| Distinguish letters from words | ░ | | | | | | |
| Recognize name | ░ | | | | | | |
| Name and match all uppercase and lowercase letter forms | ░ | | | | | | |
| Understand the concept of word and construct meaning from shared text, illustrations, graphics, and charts | ░ | | | | | | |
| Identify letters, words, and sentences | ░ | | | | | | |
| Recognize that sentences in print are made up of words | ░ | | | | | | |
| Identify the front cover, back cover, title page, title, and author of a book | ░ | ░ | ░ | | | | |
| Match oral words to printed words | ░ | ░ | | | | | |
| **Phonemic Awareness** | | | | | | | |
| Understand that spoken words and syllables are made up of sequence of sounds | ░ | | | | | | |
| Count and track sounds in a syllable, syllables in words, and words in sentences | • | | | | | | |
| Know the sounds of letters | • | | | | | | |
| Track and represent the number, sameness, difference, and order of two or more isolated phonemes | • | | | | | | |
| Match, identify, distinguish, and segment sounds in initial, final, and medial position in single-syllable spoken words | • | | | | | | |
| Blend sounds (onset=rimes/phonemes) to make words or syllables | • | | | | | | |
| Track and represent changes in syllables and words as target sound is added, substituted, omitted, shifted, or repeated | • | | | | | | |
| Distinguish long- and short-vowel sounds in orally stated words | ░ | ░ | ░ | ░ | | | |
| Identify and produce rhyming words | • | | | | | | |
| **Decoding: Phonic Analysis** | | | | | | | |
| Understand and apply the alphabetic principle | ░ | ░ | | | | | |
| Consonants; single, blends, digraphs in initial, final, medial positions | • | • | • | • | | | |
| Vowels: short, long, digraphs, r-controlled, variant, schwa | • | • | • | • | | | |
| Match all consonant and short-vowel sounds to appropriate letters | • | • | | | | | |
| Understand that as letters in words change, so do the sounds | • | • | | | | | |
| Blend vowel-consonant sounds orally to make words or syllables | • | • | | | | | |
| Blend sounds from letters and letter patterns into recognizable words | • | | | | | | |
| **Decoding: Structural Analysis** | | | | | | | |
| Inflectional endings, with and without spelling changes: plurals, verb tenses, possessives, comparatives-superlatives | | • | • | • | ░ | ░ | ░ |
| Contractions, abbreviations, and compound words | | • | • | • | | | |
| Prefixes, suffixes, derivations, and root words | | | • | • | • | • | • |
| Greek and Latin roots | | | | | • | • | • |
| Letter, spelling, and syllable patterns | ░ | ░ | ░ | ░ | ░ | ░ | ░ |
| Phonograms/word families/onset-rimes | ░ | ░ | | | | | |
| Syllable rules and patterns | | | ░ | ░ | ░ | ░ | ░ |
| **Decoding: Strategies** | | | | | | | |
| Visual cues: sound/symbol relationships, letter patterns, and spelling patterns | ░ | • | | | | | |
| Structural cues: compound words, contractions, inflectional endings, prefixes, suffixes, Greek and Latin roots, root words, spelling patterns, and word families | ░ | • | | | | | |
| Cross check visual and structural cues to confirm meaning | | ░ | ░ | ░ | ░ | ░ | ░ |

Key:

*Shaded area - Explicit Instruction/Modeling/Practice and Application*

- *Tested—Assessment Resources: Weekly Lesson Tests, Theme Tests, Benchmark Assessments*

| | Gr K | Gr 1 | Gr 2 | Gr 3 | Gr 4 | Gr 5 | Gr 6 |
|---|---|---|---|---|---|---|---|
| **Word Recognition** | | | | | | | |
| One-syllable and high-frequency words | • | • | • | | | | |
| Common, irregular sight words | • | • | • | | | | |
| Common abbreviations | | | • | | | | |
| Lesson vocabulary | | • | • | • | • | • | • |
| **Fluency** | | | | | | | |
| Read aloud in a manner that sounds like natural speech | | | | | | | |
| Read aloud accurately and with appropriate intonation and expression | | • | • | • | • | • | • |
| Read aloud narrative and expository text with appropriate pacing, intonation, and expression | | | • | • | • | • | • |
| Read aloud prose and poetry with rhythm and pace, appropriate intonation, and vocal patterns | | | • | • | • | • | • |
| **Vocabulary and Concept Development** | | | | | | | |
| Academic language | | | | | | | |
| Classify-categorize | | • | | | | | |
| Antonyms | | | • | • | • | • | |
| Synonyms | | | • | • | • | • | |
| Homographs | | | | • | | | |
| Homophones | | | | • | | | |
| Multiple-meaning words | | | • | | • | • | • |
| Figurative and idiomatic language | | | | | • | | • |
| Context/context clues | | | • | • | • | • | • |
| Content-area words | | | | | | | |
| Dictionary, glossary, thesaurus | | | | • | • | • | |
| Foreign words | | | | | | | • |
| Connotation-denotation | | | | | | | |
| Word origins (acronyms, clipped and coined words, regional variations, etymologies, jargon, slang) | | | | | | | |
| Analogies | | | | | | | |
| Word structure clues to determine meaning | | | • | • | • | | • |
| Inflected nouns and verbs, comparatives-superlatives, possessives, compound words, prefixes, suffixes, root words | | | • | • | • | • | • |
| Greek and Latin roots, prefixes, suffixes, derivations, and root words | | | | | • | • | • |
| Develop vocabulary | | | | | | | |
|   Listen to and discuss text read aloud | | | | | | | |
|   Read independently | | | | | | | |
|   Use reference books | | | | | | | |
| **Comprehension and Analysis of Text** | | | | | | | |
| Ask/answer questions | | | | | | | |
| Author's purpose | | • | • | • | • | • | |
| Author's perspective | | | | | • | • | |
|   Propaganda/bias | | | | | | | |
| Background knowledge: prior knowledge and experiences | | | | | | | |
| Cause-effect | | | • | • | • | • | |
| Compare-contrast | | | • | • | • | • | • |
| Details | | | • | • | • | • | • |
| Directions: one-, two-, multi-step | | | | • | • | • | • |
| Draw conclusions | • | • | | | • | • | • |
| Fact-fiction | | | | • | • | • | |

Key:

*Shaded area - Explicit Instruction/Modeling/Practice and Application*

    • *Tested—Assessment Resources: Weekly Lesson Tests, Theme Tests, Benchmark Assessments*

| | Gr K | Gr 1 | Gr 2 | Gr 3 | Gr 4 | Gr 5 | Gr 6 |
|---|---|---|---|---|---|---|---|
| Fact-opinion | | | | | • | • | |
| Higher order thinking | | | | | | | |
|     Analyze, critique and evaluate, synthesize, and visualize text and information | | | | | | | |
| Interpret information from graphic aids | | | • | • | | • | |
| Locate information | | | • | | • | | |
|     Book parts | | | | • | • | | |
|     Text features | | | | • | • | | |
|     Alphabetical order | | • | | • | | | |
| Main idea: stated/unstated | | | • | | • | • | • |
| Main idea and supporting details | • | • | • | • | • | • | • |
| Make generalizations | | | | | | • | |
| Make inferences | | | • | • | • | | |
| Make judgments | | | | | | • | • |
| Make predictions/predict outcomes | • | • | • | • | • | | |
| Monitor comprehension | | | | | | | |
|     Adjust reading rate, create mental images, reread, read ahead, set/adjust purpose, self-question, summarize/paraphrase, use graphic aids, text features, and text adjuncts | | | | | • | | |
| Organize information | | | | | | | |
|     Alphabetical order | | | | | | | |
|     Numerical systems/outlines | | | | | | | |
|     Graphic organizers | | | | | | | |
| Paraphrase/restate facts and details | | | | | • | • | |
| Preview | | | | | | | |
| Purpose for reading | | | | | | | |
| Referents | | | | | | | |
| Retell stories and ideas | | | • | • | | | |
| Sequence | | • | | • | • | • | • |
| Summarize | | | • | • | • | • | • |
| Text structure | | | | | | | |
|     Narrative text | | | • | • | • | • | |
|     Informational text (compare and contrast, cause and effect, sequence/chronological order, proposition and support, problem and solution) | | | • | • | • | • | • |

## Study Skills

| | Gr K | Gr 1 | Gr 2 | Gr 3 | Gr 4 | Gr 5 | Gr 6 |
|---|---|---|---|---|---|---|---|
| Follow and give directions | | | • | • | • | | • |
| Apply plans and strategies: KWL, question-answer relationships, skim and scan, note taking, outline, questioning the author, reciprocal teaching | | | | | | | • |
| Practice test-taking strategies | | | | | | | |

## Research and Information

| | Gr K | Gr 1 | Gr 2 | Gr 3 | Gr 4 | Gr 5 | Gr 6 |
|---|---|---|---|---|---|---|---|
| Use resources and references | | | • | | • | • | • |
| Understand the purpose, structure, and organization of various reference materials | | | | | | | |
|     Title page, table of contents, chapter titles, chapter headings, index, glossary, guide words, citations, end notes, bibliography | | | • | • | • | | |
|     Picture dictionary, software, dictionary, thesaurus, atlas, globe, encyclopedia, telephone directory, on-line information, card catalog, electronic search engines and data bases, almanac, newspaper, journals, periodicals | | | • | • | • | • | • |
|     Charts, maps, diagrams, time lines, schedules, calendar, graphs, photos | | | • | | • | | |
|     Choose reference materials appropriate to research purpose | | | | | • | • | • |

## Viewing/Media

| | Gr K | Gr 1 | Gr 2 | Gr 3 | Gr 4 | Gr 5 | Gr 6 |
|---|---|---|---|---|---|---|---|
| Interpret information from visuals (graphics, media, including illustrations, tables, maps, charts, graphs, diagrams, time lines) | | | • | • | | | • |

**Key:**

*Shaded area - Explicit Instruction/Modeling/Practice and Application*

    • *Tested—Assessment Resources: Weekly Lesson Tests, Theme Tests, Benchmark Assessments*

| | Gr K | Gr 1 | Gr 2 | Gr 3 | Gr 4 | Gr 5 | Gr 6 |
|---|---|---|---|---|---|---|---|
| Analyze the ways visuals, graphics, and media represent, contribute to, and support meaning of text | | | | | | | • |
| Select, organize, and produce visuals to complement and extend meaning | | | | | | | |
| Use technology or appropriate media to communicate information and ideas | | | | | | | |
| Use technology or appropriate media to compare ideas, information, and viewpoints | | | | | | | |
| Compare, contrast, and evaluate print and broadcast media | | | | | | | |
|    Distinguish between fact and opinion | | | | | | | |
|    Evaluate the role of media | | | | | | | |
| Analyze media as sources for information, entertainment, persuasion, interpretation of events, and transmission of culture | | | | | | | |
| Identify persuasive and propaganda techniques used in television and identify false and misleading information | | | | | | | |
| Summarize main concept and list supporting details and identify biases, stereotypes, and persuasive techniques in a nonprint message | | | | | | | |
| Support opinions with detailed evidence and with visual or media displays that use appropriate technology | | | | | | | |

## Literary Response and Analysis

### Genre Characteristics

| | Gr K | Gr 1 | Gr 2 | Gr 3 | Gr 4 | Gr 5 | Gr 6 |
|---|---|---|---|---|---|---|---|
| Know a variety of literary genres and their basic characteristics | | | • | • | | | |
| Distinguish between fantasy and realistic text | | | | | | | |
| Distinguish between informational and persuasive texts | | | | | | | |
| Understand the distinguishing features of literary and nonfiction texts: everyday print materials, poetry, drama, fantasies, fables, myths, legends, and fairy tales | | | • | • | | | |
| Explain the appropriateness of the literary forms chosen by an author for a specific purpose | | | | | | | |

### Literary Elements

| | Gr K | Gr 1 | Gr 2 | Gr 3 | Gr 4 | Gr 5 | Gr 6 |
|---|---|---|---|---|---|---|---|
| Plot/Plot Development | | | | | | | |
|    Important events | | • | • | • | | | |
|    Beginning, middle, ending of story | • | • | • | • | | | |
|    Problem/solution | | • | • | • | | | • |
|    Conflict | | | | | • | • | • |
|    Conflict and resolution/causes and effects | | | | | • | • | • |
|    Compare and contrast | | | • | • | • | • | |
| Character | | | | | | | |
|    Identify | • | • | • | | | | |
|    Identify, describe, compare and contrast | | | • | • | • | | |
|    Relate characters and events | | | | | | | • |
|    Traits, actions, motives | | | | | • | • | • |
|    Cause for character's actions | | | | | • | • | |
|    Character's qualities and effect on plot | | | | | • | • | • |
| Setting | | | | | | | |
|    Identify and describe | • | • | • | • | | | |
|    Compare and contrast | | | • | • | | | • |
|    Relate to problem/resolution | | | | | | | • |
| Theme | | | | | | | |
|    Theme/essential message | | | | • | • | • | • |
|    Universal themes | | | | | | | • |
| Mood/Tone | | | | | | | |
|    Identify | | | | | | | • |
|    Compare and contrast | | | | | | | |

**Key:**

*Shaded area - Explicit Instruction/Modeling/Practice and Application*

   • *Tested— Assessment Resources: Weekly Lesson Tests, Theme Tests, Benchmark Assessments*

| Literary Devices/Author's Craft | Gr K | Gr 1 | Gr 2 | Gr 3 | Gr 4 | Gr 5 | Gr 6 |
|---|---|---|---|---|---|---|---|
| Rhythm, rhyme, pattern, and repetition | ░ | ░ | ░ | ░ | ░ | ░ | • |
| Alliteration, onomatopoeia, assonance, imagery | | ░ | ░ | ░ | ░ | • | • |
| Figurative language (similes, metaphors, idioms, personification, hyperbole) | | | | • | • | • | • |
| Characterization/character development | | | ░ | • | • | • | • |
| Dialogue | ░ | ░ | ░ | ░ | ░ | ░ | ░ |
| Narrator/narration | ░ | ░ | ░ | ░ | ░ | ░ | ░ |
| Point of view (first-person, third-person, omniscient) | | | | | | • | • |
| Informal language (idioms, slang, jargon, dialect) | | | | | | | |

| Response to Text | Gr K | Gr 1 | Gr 2 | Gr 3 | Gr 4 | Gr 5 | Gr 6 |
|---|---|---|---|---|---|---|---|
| Relate characters and events to own life | ░ | ░ | ░ | ░ | ░ | ░ | ░ |
| Read to perform a task or learn a new task | ░ | ░ | ░ | ░ | ░ | ░ | ░ |
| Recollect, talk, and write about books read | ░ | ░ | ░ | ░ | ░ | ░ | ░ |
| Describe the roles and contributions of authors and illustrators | ░ | ░ | ░ | ░ | ░ | ░ | ░ |
| Generate alternative endings and identify the reason and impact of the alternatives | | | | ░ | ░ | ░ | ░ |
| Compare and contrast versions of the same stories that reflect different cultures | | | ░ | ░ | ░ | ░ | ░ |
| Make connections between information in texts and stories and historical events | | ░ | ░ | ░ | ░ | ░ | ░ |
| Form ideas about what has been read and use specific information from the text to support these ideas | | | ░ | ░ | ░ | ░ | ░ |
| Know that the attitudes and values that exist in a time period or culture affect stories and informational articles written during that time period | | | | | ░ | ░ | ░ |

| Self-Selected Reading | Gr K | Gr 1 | Gr 2 | Gr 3 | Gr 4 | Gr 5 | Gr 6 |
|---|---|---|---|---|---|---|---|
| Select material to read for pleasure | ░ | ░ | ░ | ░ | ░ | ░ | ░ |
| Read a variety of self-selected and assigned literary and informational texts | ░ | ░ | ░ | ░ | ░ | ░ | ░ |
| Use knowledge of authors' styles, themes, and genres to choose own reading | | | ░ | ░ | ░ | ░ | ░ |
| Read literature by authors from various cultural and historical backgrounds | ░ | ░ | ░ | ░ | ░ | ░ | ░ |

| Cultural Awareness | Gr K | Gr 1 | Gr 2 | Gr 3 | Gr 4 | Gr 5 | Gr 6 |
|---|---|---|---|---|---|---|---|
| Connect information and events in texts to life and life to text experiences | ░ | ░ | ░ | ░ | ░ | ░ | ░ |
| Compare language, oral traditions, and literature that reflect customs, regions, and cultures | ░ | ░ | ░ | ░ | ░ | ░ | ░ |
| Identify how language reflects regions and cultures | | | ░ | ░ | ░ | ░ | ░ |
| View concepts and issues from diverse perspectives | | | | ░ | ░ | ░ | ░ |
| Recognize the universality of literary themes across cultures and language | | | | ░ | ░ | ░ | ░ |

## Writing

### Writing Strategies

| | Gr K | Gr 1 | Gr 2 | Gr 3 | Gr 4 | Gr 5 | Gr 6 |
|---|---|---|---|---|---|---|---|
| Writing process: prewriting, drafting, revising, proofreading, publishing | ░ | ░ | ░ | ░ | ░ | ░ | ░ |
| Collaborative, shared, timed writing, writing to prompts | ░ | • | • | • | • | • | • |
| Evaluate own and others' writing | ░ | ░ | ░ | ░ | ░ | ░ | ░ |
| Proofread writing to correct convention errors in mechanics, usage, and punctuation, using handbooks and references as appropriate | | ░ | ░ | ░ | • | • | • |

### Organization and Focus

| | Gr K | Gr 1 | Gr 2 | Gr 3 | Gr 4 | Gr 5 | Gr 6 |
|---|---|---|---|---|---|---|---|
| Use models and traditional structures for writing | ░ | ░ | ░ | ░ | ░ | ░ | ░ |
| Select a focus, structure, and viewpoint | ░ | ░ | ░ | ░ | ░ | ░ | ░ |
| Address purpose, audience, length, and format requirements | | ░ | ░ | ░ | ░ | ░ | ░ |
| Write single- and multiple-paragraph compositions | | | • | • | • | • | • |

### Revision Skills

| | Gr K | Gr 1 | Gr 2 | Gr 3 | Gr 4 | Gr 5 | Gr 6 |
|---|---|---|---|---|---|---|---|
| Correct sentence fragments and run-ons | ░ | | ░ | ░ | ░ | ░ | ░ |
| Vary sentence structure, word order, and sentence length | ░ | | ░ | ░ | ░ | ░ | ░ |
| Combine sentences | ░ | | ░ | ░ | ░ | ░ | ░ |

**Key:**

*Shaded area - Explicit Instruction/Modeling/Practice and Application*

- *Tested—Assessment Resources: Weekly Lesson Tests, Theme Tests, Benchmark Assessments*

| | Gr K | Gr 1 | Gr 2 | Gr 3 | Gr 4 | Gr 5 | Gr 6 |
|---|---|---|---|---|---|---|---|
| Improve coherence, unity, consistency, and progression of ideas | | | ░ | ░ | ░ | ░ | ░ |
| Add, delete, consolidate, clarify, rearrange text | ░ | ░ | ░ | ░ | ░ | ░ | ░ |
| Choose appropriate and effective words: exact/precise words, vivid words, trite/overused words | ░ | ░ | ░ | ░ | ░ | ░ | ░ |
| Elaborate: details, examples, dialogue, quotations | ░ | ░ | ░ | ░ | ░ | ░ | ░ |
| Revise using a rubric | | ░ | ░ | ░ | ░ | ░ | ░ |

### Penmanship/Handwriting

| | Gr K | Gr 1 | Gr 2 | Gr 3 | Gr 4 | Gr 5 | Gr 6 |
|---|---|---|---|---|---|---|---|
| Write uppercase and lowercase letters | ░ | ░ | ░ | ░ | | | |
| Write legibly, using appropriate word and letter spacing | ░ | ░ | ░ | ░ | | | |
| Write legibly, using spacing, margins, and indention | | | ░ | ░ | ░ | ░ | ░ |

### Writing Applications

| | Gr K | Gr 1 | Gr 2 | Gr 3 | Gr 4 | Gr 5 | Gr 6 |
|---|---|---|---|---|---|---|---|
| Narrative writing (stories, paragraphs, personal narratives, journal, plays, poetry) | ░ | • | • | • | • | • | • |
| Descriptive writing (titles, captions, ads, posters, paragraphs, stories, poems) | ░ | • | • | ░ | ░ | ░ | ░ |
| Expository writing (comparison-contrast, explanation, directions, speech, how-to article, friendly/business letter, news story, essay, report, invitation) | | ░ | ░ | ░ | • | • | • |
| Persuasive writing (paragraph, essay, letter, ad, poster) | | | | | • | • | • |
| Cross-curricular writing (paragraph, report, poster, list, chart) | ░ | ░ | ░ | ░ | ░ | ░ | ░ |
| Everyday writing (journal, message, forms, notes, summary, label, caption) | ░ | ░ | ░ | ░ | ░ | ░ | ░ |

## Written and Oral English Language Conventions

### Sentence Structure

| | Gr K | Gr 1 | Gr 2 | Gr 3 | Gr 4 | Gr 5 | Gr 6 |
|---|---|---|---|---|---|---|---|
| Types (declarative, interrogative, exclamatory, imperative, interjection) | | • | • | • | • | • | • |
| Structure (simple, compound, complex, compound-complex) | | • | • | • | • | • | • |
| Parts (subjects/predicates: complete, simple, compound; clauses: independent, dependent, subordinate; phrase) | | • | • | • | • | • | • |
| Direct/indirect object | | | | | | • | • |
| Word order | | • | ░ | | | | |

### Grammar

| | Gr K | Gr 1 | Gr 2 | Gr 3 | Gr 4 | Gr 5 | Gr 6 |
|---|---|---|---|---|---|---|---|
| Nouns (singular, plural, common, proper, possessive, collective, abstract, concrete, abbreviations, appositives) | ░ | • | • | • | • | • | • |
| Verbs (action, helping, linking, transitive, intransitive, regular, irregular; subject-verb agreement) | | • | • | • | • | • | • |
| Verb tenses (present, past, future; present, past, and future perfect) | | • | • | • | • | • | • |
| Participles; infinitives | | | | | | • | • |
| Adjectives (common, proper; articles; comparative, superlative) | | • | • | • | • | • | • |
| Adverbs (place, time, manner, degree) | | | | • | • | • | • |
| Pronouns (subject, object, possessive, reflexive, demonstrative, antecedents) | | • | • | • | • | • | • |
| Prepositions; prepositional phrases | | | | | • | • | • |
| Conjunctions | | | | | • | • | • |
| Abbreviations, contractions | | | • | • | • | • | • |

### Punctuation

| | Gr K | Gr 1 | Gr 2 | Gr 3 | Gr 4 | Gr 5 | Gr 6 |
|---|---|---|---|---|---|---|---|
| Period, exclamation point, or question mark at end of sentences | ░ | • | • | • | • | • | • |
| Comma | | | | | | | |
|   Greeting and closure of a letter | | ░ | ░ | ░ | ░ | • | • |
|   Dates, locations, and addresses | | | ░ | ░ | ░ | • | • |
|   For items in a series | | | | | • | • | • |
|   Direct quotations | | | | | • | • | • |
|   Link two clauses with a conjunction in compound sentences | | | | | • | • | • |
| Quotation Marks | | | | | | | |
|   Dialogue, exact words of a speaker | ░ | ░ | ░ | ░ | • | • | • |
|   Titles of books, stories, poems, magazines | | | | | • | • | • |

**Key:**

*Shaded area - Explicit Instruction/Modeling/Practice and Application*

- *Tested—Assessment Resources: Weekly Lesson Tests, Theme Tests, Benchmark Assessments*

| | Gr K | Gr 1 | Gr 2 | Gr 3 | Gr 4 | Gr 5 | Gr 6 |
|---|---|---|---|---|---|---|---|
| Parentheses/dash/hyphen | | | | | | • | • |
| Apostrophes in possessive case of nouns and in contractions | | • | • | • | • | • | • |
| Underlining or italics to identify title of documents | | | ■ | | • | • | • |
| Colon | | | | | | | |
|    Separate hours and minutes | | | ■ | | | • | • |
|    Introduce a list | | | | | | • | • |
|    After the salutation in business letters | | | | | | • | • |
| Semicolons to connect dependent clauses | | | | | | | ■ |

## Capitalization

| | Gr K | Gr 1 | Gr 2 | Gr 3 | Gr 4 | Gr 5 | Gr 6 |
|---|---|---|---|---|---|---|---|
| First word of a sentence, names of people, and the pronoun *I* | | • | • | • | • | • | • |
| Proper nouns, words at the beginning of sentences and greetings, months and days of the week, and titles and initials of people | | • | • | • | • | • | • |
| Geographical names, holidays, historical periods, and special events | | | • | • | | | • |
| Names of magazines, newspapers, works of art, musical compositions, organizations, and the first word in quotations when appropriate | | | | | | • | • |
| Use conventions of punctuation and capitalization | | | | • | • | • | • |

## Spelling

| | Gr K | Gr 1 | Gr 2 | Gr 3 | Gr 4 | Gr 5 | Gr 6 |
|---|---|---|---|---|---|---|---|
| Spell independently by using pre-phonetic knowledge, sounds of the alphabet, and knowledge of letter names | ■ | ■ | | | | | |
| Use spelling approximations and some conventional spelling | ■ | ■ | | | | | |
| Common, phonetically regular words | | • | • | • | • | • | • |
| Frequently used, irregular words | | • | • | • | • | • | • |
| One-syllable words with consonant blends | | | • | • | • | • | • |
| Contractions, compounds, orthographic patterns, and common homophones | | | | | • | • | • |
| Greek and Latin roots, inflections, suffixes, prefixes, and syllable constructions | | | | • | • | • | • |
| Use a variety of strategies and resources to spell words | | ■ | | | | | |

## Listening and Speaking

### Listening Skills and Strategies

| | Gr K | Gr 1 | Gr 2 | Gr 3 | Gr 4 | Gr 5 | Gr 6 |
|---|---|---|---|---|---|---|---|
| Listen to a variety of oral presentations such as stories, poems, skits, songs, personal accounts, or informational speeches | ■ | ■ | ■ | ■ | ■ | ■ | ■ |
| Listen attentively to the speaker (make eye contact and demonstrate appropriate body language) | | | ■ | ■ | ■ | ■ | ■ |
| Listen for a purpose | | | | | | | |
|    Follow oral directions (one-, two-, three-, and multi-step) | ■ | ■ | ■ | ■ | ■ | ■ | ■ |
|    For specific information | ■ | ■ | ■ | ■ | ■ | ■ | ■ |
|    For enjoyment | ■ | ■ | ■ | ■ | ■ | ■ | ■ |
|    To distinguish between the speaker's opinions and verifiable facts | | | | ■ | ■ | ■ | ■ |
|    To actively participate in class discussions | ■ | ■ | ■ | ■ | ■ | ■ | ■ |
|    To expand and enhance personal interest and personal preferences | | | | | ■ | ■ | ■ |
|    To identify, analyze, and critique persuasive techniques | | | | | | ■ | ■ |
|    To identify logical fallacies used in oral presentations and media messages | | | | | | ■ | ■ |
|    To make inferences or draw conclusions | | | ■ | ■ | ■ | ■ | ■ |
|    To interpret a speaker's verbal and nonverbal messages, purposes, and perspectives | | | | | ■ | ■ | ■ |
|    To identify the tone, mood, and emotion | | | | | | ■ | ■ |
|    To analyze the use of rhetorical devices for intent and effect | | | | | | | ■ |
|    To evaluate classroom presentations | | | ■ | ■ | ■ | ■ | ■ |
|    To respond to a variety of media and speakers | | | ■ | ■ | ■ | ■ | ■ |
|    To paraphrase/summarize directions and information | | | ■ | ■ | ■ | ■ | ■ |
|    For language reflecting regions and cultures | | | | | ■ | ■ | ■ |

**Key:**

*Shaded area - Explicit Instruction/Modeling/Practice and Application*

- *Tested—Assessment Resources: Weekly Lesson Tests, Theme Tests, Benchmark Assessments*

| | Gr K | Gr 1 | Gr 2 | Gr 3 | Gr 4 | Gr 5 | Gr 6 |
|---|---|---|---|---|---|---|---|
| To recognize emotional and logical arguments | | | | | | ■ | ■ |
| To identify the musical elements of language | | | ■ | ■ | ■ | ■ | ■ |
| Listen critically to relate the speaker's verbal communication to the nonverbal message | | | | | | | |

## Speaking Skills and Strategies

| | Gr K | Gr 1 | Gr 2 | Gr 3 | Gr 4 | Gr 5 | Gr 6 |
|---|---|---|---|---|---|---|---|
| Speak clearly and audibly and use appropriate volume and pace in different settings | ■ | ■ | ■ | ■ | ■ | ■ | ■ |
| Use formal and informal English appropriately | ■ | ■ | ■ | ■ | ■ | ■ | ■ |
| Follow rules of conversation | ■ | ■ | ■ | ■ | ■ | ■ | ■ |
| Stay on the topic when speaking | | ■ | ■ | ■ | ■ | ■ | ■ |
| Use descriptive words | | ■ | ■ | ■ | ■ | ■ | ■ |
| Recount experiences in a logical sequence | | ■ | ■ | ■ | ■ | ■ | ■ |
| Clarify and support spoken ideas with evidence and examples | | | | ■ | ■ | ■ | ■ |
| Use eye contact, appropriate gestures, and props to enhance oral presentations and engage the audience | | | | ■ | ■ | ■ | ■ |
| Give and follow two-, three-, and four-step directions | | ■ | ■ | ■ | ■ | ■ | ■ |
| Recite poems, rhymes, songs, stories, soliloquies, or dramatic dialogues | ■ | ■ | ■ | ■ | ■ | ■ | ■ |
| Plan and present dramatic interpretations with clear diction, pitch, tempo, and tone | | ■ | ■ | ■ | ■ | ■ | ■ |
| Organize presentations to maintain a clear focus | | ■ | ■ | ■ | ■ | ■ | ■ |
| Use language appropriate to situation, purpose, and audience | | ■ | ■ | ■ | ■ | ■ | ■ |
| Make/deliver | | | | | | | |
|    Oral narrative, descriptive, informational, and persuasive presentations | | | ■ | ■ | ■ | ■ | ■ |
|    Oral summaries of articles and books | | | ■ | ■ | ■ | ■ | ■ |
|    Oral responses to literature | | | ■ | ■ | ■ | ■ | ■ |
|    Presentations on problems and solutions | | | ■ | ■ | ■ | ■ | ■ |
|    Presentation or speech for specific occasions, audiences, and purposes | | | | | ■ | ■ | ■ |
| Vary language according to situation, audience, and purpose | | | | ■ | ■ | ■ | ■ |
| Select a focus, organizational structure, and point of view for an oral presentation | | | | ■ | ■ | ■ | ■ |
| Participate in classroom activities and discussions | ■ | ■ | ■ | ■ | ■ | ■ | ■ |

**Key:**

*Shaded area - Explicit Instruction/Modeling/Practice and Application*

- *Tested— Assessment Resources: Weekly Lesson Tests, Theme Tests, Benchmark Assessments*

# Index

S2–S61; **1-3:** T39, T56, T77, T90, T101, T135, T152, T175, T188, T199, T223, T240, T261, T274, T285, T309, T326, T360, T371, T395, T435, T448, T459, T500, T523, T538, T549, S2–S61; **1-4:** T126–T127, T137, T154, T177, T225, T242, T265, T268, T278, T289, T302, T313, T355, T368, T379, T392–T393, T420, T441, T465, T478, T489, T529, T542, T553, T564, S2–S61; **1-5:** T28–T29, T56, T79, T92, T103, T126–T127, T154, T175, T188, T199, T223, T240, T265, T289, T313, T330, T351, T364, T375, T389, T399, T416, T439, T452, T463, T477, T487, T504, T527, T540, T551, S2–S61

Story Events, **1-4:** T366, T452, T540
Talk About the Topic, **1-4:** T85
Titles for People, **1-2:** T492
Using Senses, **1-4:** S20
Visual Cues, **1-4:** T170, T258, T433, T434, T457, T471, T522, S6
*Weekend of Fun, A,* **1-4:** T471
Word Cards
    Categorize Words, **1-4:** T52
Word Meaning, **1-5:** T231
Writing, **1-4:** S10
**English-Language Development** (*See* English Language Learners, Notes)
**Enrichment** (*See* Differentiated Instruction, Advanced Learners, Small-Group Instruction)
**ePlanner** (*See* Technology, Technology Resources)
**Evaluating Writing** (*See* Writing, Process, Evaluating)
**Exclamatory Sentences** (*See* Grammar, Exclamations; Writing, Forms, Exclamatory Sentences)
**Expository Descriptive Writing** (*See* Writing, Forms, Descriptions)
**Expository Texts** (*See* Genre, Nonfiction)
**Expression** (*See* Fluency, Expression)
**Extra Support Copying Masters** (*See* Differentiated Instruction, Extra Support Copying Masters)

**Fact/Fantasy** (*See* Focus Skills, Fact/Fantasy)
**Family Involvement** (*See* Teacher Resource Book, School-Home Connections)
**Fantasy** (*See* Genre, Fantasy)
**Fiction** (*See* Genre, Fiction)
**Fine Art** (*See* Cross-Curricular Connections, Art, Fine Art Connections)
**Flexible Grouping** (*See* Small-Group Planner)
**Fluency, 1-1:** T15, T29, T123, T207, T298, T301, T315, T401, T487; **1-2:** T12, T15; **1-3:** T12, T15. (*See also* Assessment, Oral Reading Fluency Assessment)
    Accuracy, **1-1:** T22, T45, T66, T75, T78, T87, T97, T102, T103, T105, T116, T126, T128, T139, T160, T169, T172, T181, T191, T197, T199, T281, T282, T283, T318, T392, T394, T404, T417, T440, T449, T452, T461, T471, T476, T477, T562, T563, T566, S4–S5, S14–S15; **1-2:** T128, T216, T390, T440, T465, T466, T528; **1-3:** T80, T438, T489; **1-5:** T229, T256, T265, T277, T287, T319, T351, T363, T373, T558, S24–S25, S34–S35
    Choral Reading, **1-4:** T199, T260, T524; **1-5:** T170, T518, T544
    Echo-Read, **1-1:** T244, T354, T526, S5, S15, S25, S35, S45, S55; **1-2:** T68, T141, T293, T317, T467, S5, S15, S25, S35, S45, S55; **1-3:** T77, T107, T166, T252, T426, T547, S5, S15, S25, S35, S45, S55; **1-4:** T70, T138, T256, T314, T346, T404, T432, T520, S5, S15, S25, S35, S45, S55; **1-5:** T40, T70, T138, T166, T224, T256, T314, T342, T400, T482, T488, S5, S15
    Expression, **1-1:** T103, T196, T197, T199, T223, T244, T275, T280, T281, T282, T331, T354, T363, T366, T375, T385, T390, T391, T392, T393, T476, T477, T503, T557, T563, T564, T565, T566, T567, S34–S35, S44–S45; **1-2:** T22, T26, T27, T45, T68, T77, T80, T84, T89, T94, T99, T105, T107, T118, T122, T123, T141, T166, T170, T175,

T178, T182, T187, T197, T202, T203, T205, T280, T290, T293, T352, T377, T378, T464, T465, T468, T472, T473, T491, T516, T525, T528, T537, T547, T552, T554, T556, T557, S4–S5, S14–S15, S34–S35, S54–S55; **1-3:** T104, T105, T107, T128, T175, T178, T202, T204, T205, T264, T288, T289, T291, T347, T463, T553, T554, T557, S14–S15, S24–S25; **1-4:** T65, T91, T231, T256, T260, T265, T277, T282, T287, T319, T346, T355, T367, T377, T560, S24, S34, S44; **1-5:** T363
Group Reading, **1-4:** T358
Intonation, **1-1:** T104, T191, T198, T244, T275, T283, T391, T393, T478, T503, T535, T538, T547, T564, T565, T567, S54–S55; **1-2:** T104, T105, T106, T175, T377, T378, T557; **1-3:** T45, T68, T77, T89, T99, T106, T107, T118, T141, T166, T175, T187, T197, T202, T203, T205, T288, T291, T347, T378, T401, T426, T435, T447, T457, T463, T464, T465, T556, T557, S4–S5, S14–S15, S44–S45; **1-4:** T34; **1-5:** T26–T27, T45, T70, T79, T91, T96, T101, T120–T121, T166, T175, T187, T197, T557, T558, S4–S5, S14–S15
Pace, **1-1:** T567; **1-2:** T557; **1-3:** T106, T290, T462, T464, T552, T553, T554, T555, T557; **1-5:** S34
Partner Reading, **1-4:** T82, T168, T180, T444, T495, T532; **1-5:** T82, T143, T178, T268, T354, T430, T442, T530
Phrasing, **1-2:** T206, T210, T211, T254, T263, T266, T270, T275, T280, T285, T292, T294, T298, T299, T317, T322, T340, T344, T349, T361, T371, T380, T384, T385, T403, T428, T432, T437, T444, T449, T459, T464, T556, S24–S25, S34–S35, S44–S45; **1-4:** T45, T70, T74, T79, T101, T143, T148, T177, T184, T189, T560, S4, S14
Punctuation, **1-1:** T150, T200, T204, T205, T223, T228, T244, T248, T256, T260, T270, T308, T312, T313, T336, T354, T358, T363, T370, T375, T380, T385, T480, T484, T485, T508, T526, T530, T535, T542, T547, T552, T557, T566,

## H

## I

Index • **R57**

T173, T185, T195, T221, T237, T261,
T273, T283, T309, T325, T351, T373,
T383, T399, T415, T437, T449, T459,
T485, T501, T525, T537, T547; **1-5:**
T35, T51, T75, T87, T97, T133, T149,
T171, T183, T193, T219, T235, T261,
T273, T283, T309, T325, T347, T359,
T369, T395, T411, T435, T447, T457,
T483, T499, T523, T535

**Word Webs** (*See* Graphic Organizers, Word
Webs; Vocabulary, Word Webs)

**Word Work** (*See* Decoding/Phonics; High-
Frequency Words)

**Word Work Center** (*See* Literacy Centers,
Word Work Center)

**Writer's Companion, 1-1:** T3, T289; **1-2:** T3;
**1-3:** T3, T517; **1-4:** T3; **1-5:** T3

**Writer's Craft**

Dictating Messages, **1-4:** T72, T270, T290,
T348, T360; **1-5:** T444

Forms

Book Review, **1-5:** T217, T233, T259,
T268, T271, T281, T291, S30, S31

Captions, **1-1:** T319, T335, T357,
T369, T379, T389, T569, S40–
S41; **1-2:** T559; **1-3:** T559; **1-4:**
T290, T563, S59; **1-5:** T377, T561

Charts, **1-5:** T192

Contractions, **1-5:** T194

Descriptions, **1-4:** T7, T33, T49, T73,
T82, T85, T95, T147, T182, T192,
T194, T203, T361, T371, T381,
T397, T413, T434, T447, T457,
T467, S41

Dialogue, **1-2:** T305, T321, T343,
T355, T365, T375, S40–S41; **1-4:**
T259, T529

E-Mail, **1-3:** T129, T145, T169, T181,
T191, T201, S20–S21

Exclamations, **1-1:** T75; **1-2:** T70;
**1-3:** T82, T102; **1-4:** T514

How-To, **1-5:** T307, T323, T345,
T357, T367, T377, S40, S41

Interview Questions, **1-2:** T391, T407,
T431, T443, T453, T463, S21,
S50–S51

Interviews, **1-4:** S29

Invitations, **1-3:** T303, T319, T341,
T353, T363, T373, S40–S41

Journals, **1-1:** T49, T69, T81, T91,
T101, T143, T163, T175, T185,
T195, T227, T247, T259, T269,
T279, T421, T443, T455, T465,
T475; **1-2:** T49, T71, T83, T93,
T103, T145, T169, T181, T191,
T201, T233, T257, T269, T279,
T289, T321, T343, T355, T365,
T375, T407, T431, T443, T453,
T463; **1-3:** T49, T71, T83, T93,
T103, T145, T169, T181, T191,
T201, T233, T255, T267, T277,
T287; **1-4:** T49, T85, T95, T147,
T171, T183, T193, T203, T323,
T349, T361, T371, T381, T413,
T435, T447, T467; **1-5:** T49, T73,
T85, T95, T105, T147, T169, T181,
T191, T201, T291, T409, T433,
T465, T521, T533, T543, T553

Labels, **1-1:** T33, T49, T69, T81, T91,
T101, S10–S11; **1-2:** T266

Letters, **1-3:** T9, T378, T382, T383,
T389, T405, T429, T441, T451,
T461, S50–S51

Lists, **1-2:** T217, T233, T257, T269,
T279, T289; **1-3:** T341; **1-4:**
T358, T535, S11, S52; **1-5:** T233,
T357, T507

Names, **1-2:** T430, T494, T518, T540

Notes, **1-2:** T442, T462; **1-3:** T350

Paragraphs, **1-5:** T249, T323, T345,
T357, T367, T377

Personal Narratives, **1-3:** T217, T233,
T255, T267, T277, T287, S30–S31

Plays, **1-4:** T210, T235, T259, T271,
T277, T281, T291, S30, S31

Poetry, **1-4:** T170, T258, T413, T434,
T435, T447, T457, T467, T483,
T499, T523, T535, T545, T555,
S50, S51, S60, S61

Questions, **1-2:** T80, T129, T145,
T169, T178, T181, T191, T201,
T506; **1-5:** T49, T73, T131

Research Report, **1-5:** T33, T49, T73,
T85, T95, T105, T147, T169, T181,
T191, T201, S10, S11, S20, S21

Respond to a Selection, **1-1:** T65,
T126, T159, T243, T353, T438,
T525; **1-2:** T66, T165; **1-3:** T80;

**1-4:** T130, T167, T178, T320,
T344, T413, T430, T442, T518;
**1-5:** T165, T255, T341, T392,
T429, T480, T517

Rhyming Poem, **1-4:** T483, T499,
T523, T535, T555, S60, S61

Riddles, **1-2:** T479, T495, T519, T531,
T541, T551, S60–S61; **1-4:** S57;
**1-5:** S37

Sentences, **1-1:** T80, T96, T100, T127,
T128, T142, T143, T144, T163,
T164, T175, T176, T185, T186,
T195, T212, T227, T228, T247,
T248, T256, T258, T259, T260,
T269, T270, T279, T285, T334,
T405, T406, T420, T421, T422,
T443, T444, T452, T454, T455,
T456, T465, T466, T474, T475,
T491, T492, T507, T508, T529,
T530, T541, T542, T551, T552,
T561, S2, S20–S21, S30–S31,
S32, S42, S43, S50–S51, S52; **1-2:**
T33, T34, T49, T50, T71, T72,
T83, T84, T93, T94, T103, T232,
T256, T283, T352, T440, S10,
S19, S23, S52; **1-3:** T48, T80,
T82, T180, T254, T266, T286,
T352, T362, T367, T372, T438,
T440, T455, T492, T530, T550;
**1-4:** T72, T100, T170, T180,
T270, T285, T291, T307, T360,
T371, T444, T446, T532, T548,
S9, S59; **1-5:** T72, T84, T99,
T104, T180, T186, T190, T195,
T270, T346, T354, T358, T368,
T371, T408, T458, T459, T464,
T482, T496, T520, T532, T547,
T552

Short Response, **1-5:** T165

Stories, **1-2:** T97, T369; **1-3:** T33, T49,
T71, T83, T93, T103, S10–S11;
**1-4:** T268, T455, S13, S49; **1-5:**
T393, T409, T433, T442, T445,
T455, T465, T481, T497, T521,
T530, T533, T543, T553, S50, S51,
S60, S61

Thank-You Notes, **1-3:** T477, T493,
T517, T528, T531, T541, T551,
S60–S61

# Acknowledgments

**Big Book of Rhymes and Poems:**

For permission to reprint copyrighted material, grateful acknowledgment is made to the following sources:

*Association for Childhood Educational International, 17904 Georgia Avenue, Ste. 215, Olney, MD 20832:* "Fuzzy Wuzzy, Creepy Crawly" by Lillian Schulz from *Sung Under the Silver Umbrella.* Text copyright © 1935 by the Association.

*Curtis Brown, Ltd.:* "The Guppy" from *Versus* by Ogden Nash. Text copyright © 1949 by Ogden Nash. "And There" by Prince Redcloud from *Climb into My Lap: First Poems to Read Together,* selected by Lee Bennett Hopkins. Text copyright © 1998 by Prince Redcloud. Published by Simon & Schuster Books for Young Readers.

*Steven Covey:* "All the People on Our Street" from *City Poems* by Lois Lenski. Text copyright 1954, 1965 by Lois Lenski; text © copyright 1956, 1971 by Lois Lenski.

*The Cricket Magazine Group, a division of Carus Publishing Company:* "Hamstercize" by Lisa Fisher from *Ladybug* Magazine, January 2003. Text copyright © 2003 by Carus Publishing Company. "Poodle Doodles" by Jean Hansen-Novak from *Ladybug* Magazine, March 2003. Text copyright © 2003 by Carus Publishing Company. "A Sound Riddle" by Mary Lafleur from *Ladybug* Magazine, January 1995. Text © 1995 by Mary Lafleur.

*Flint Public Library, 1026 East Kearsley, MI 48502-1994:* "Apple Tree" (Retitled: "Two Little Apples"), "Autumn," "I Dig, Dig, Dig" and "What Am I Baking?" from *Ring a Ring o' Roses: Finger Plays for Pre-School Children,* Ninth Edition.

*Harcourt, Inc.:* "So Many Children" from *Poems of Childhood* by Joan Walsh Anglund. Text copyright © 1996 by Joan Walsh Anglund. "The Inchworm" from *Insectlopedia* by Douglas Florian. Text copyright © 1998 by Douglas Florian. "Way Down Deep" from *The Llama Who Had No Pajama* by Mary Ann Hoberman. Text copyright © 1959 by Mary Ann and Norman Hoberman. "The New Girl" from *Everything Glistens and Everything Sings: New and Selected Poems* by Charlotte Zolotow. Text copyright © 1987 by Charlotte Zolotow.

*HarperCollins Publishers:* "Stop and Go" from *A Pocketful of Poems* by Marie Louise Allen. Text copyright © 1957 by Marie Allen Howarth. "Tommy" from *Bronzeville Boys and Girls* by Gwendolyn Brooks. Text copyright © 1956 by Gwendolyn Brooks Blakely. "Books to the Ceiling" from *Whiskers and Rhymes* by Arnold Lobel. Text copyright © 1985 by Arnold Lobel. Untitled poem (Retitled: "Molly Day's Colors") from *Ride a Purple Pelican* by Jack Prelutsky. Text copyright © 1986 by Jack Prelutsky. "My Fish Can Ride a Bicycle" from *Something BIG Has Been Here* by Jack Prelutsky. Text copyright © 1990 by Jack Prelutsky.

*Elizabeth Hauser:* "Contentment" from *Rhymes About Us* by Marchette Chute. Text copyright © 1974 by Marchette Chute. Published by E. P. Dutton & Co.

*Felice Holman:* "At the Top of My Voice" from *At the Top of My Voice and Other Poems* by Felice Holman. Published by Charles Scribner's Sons.

*Allan Jacobs:* "Elephant" from *Hello, Pleasant Places,* selected by Leland B. Jacobs. Text copyright © 1972 by Leland B. Jacobs. Published by Garrard Publishing Co.

*Bobbi Katz:* "Cat Kisses" by Bobbi Katz. Text copyright © 1974 by Bobbi Katz, renewed 1996 by Bobbi Katz.

*Alfred A. Knopf, a division of Random House, Inc.:* "City" from *The Collected Poems of Langston Hughes* by Langston Hughes. Text copyright © 1994 by the Estate of Langston Hughes.

*Little Brown and Company, Inc.:* "Notice" from *One at a Time* by David McCord. Text copyright © 1965, 1966 by David McCord.

*Marci Ridlon McGill:* "Hamsters" from *That Was Summer* by Marci Ridlon. Text © 1969 by Marci Ridlon.

*G.P. Putnam's Sons, A Division of Penguin Young Readers Group, A Member of Penguin Group (USA) Inc., 345 Hudson St., New York, NY 10014:* "Big" from *All Together* by Dorothy Aldis. Text copyright 1925-28, 1934, 1939, 1952, renewed 1953; text © 1954-1956, 1962 by Dorothy Aldis; text © renewed 1967 by Roy E. Porter. "The Picnic" from *Hop, Skip and Jump!* by Dorothy Aldis. Text copyright 1934 by Dorothy Aldis; text copyright © renewed 1961 by Dorothy Aldis.

*Marian Reiner:* "In the Sand" from *Whispers and Other Poems* by Myra Cohn Livingston. Text copyright © 1958 by Myra Cohn Livingston, text copyright © renewed 1986 by Myra Cohn Livingston. "My Dog" from *The Moon and a Star and Other Poems* by Myra Cohn Livingston. Text copyright © 1965 by Myra Cohn Livingston.

*Marian Reiner, on behalf of the Boulder Public Library Foundation, Inc.:* "Growing Up" from *Always Wondering: Some Favorite Poems of Aileen Fisher* by Aileen Fisher. Text copyright © 1991 by Aileen Fisher. "Something Special" from *In One Door and Out the Other* by Aileen Fisher. Text © 1969, 1997 by Aileen Fisher. Originally titled "At Christmas Time." "Wind" from *Always Wondering: Some favorite Poems of Aileen Fisher* by Aileen Fisher. Text copyright © 1991 by Aileen Fisher.

*Scholastic Inc.:* "Preferred Vehicles" by Leland B. Jacobs from *Poetry Place Anthology.* Text copyright © 1983 by Edgell Communications Inc. Published by Scholastic Teaching Resources. "Searching's End" by Mary Pawlek from *Poetry Place Anthology.* Text copyright © 1983 by Edgell Communications Inc. Published by Scholastic Teaching Resources.

*Michael Strickland:* "Guess What!" by Michael R. Strickland.

*Barbara W. Stuhlmann, Author's Representative:* "Shore" from *Menagerie* by Mary Britton Miller.

*Yale University Press:* "Chanticleer" by John Farrar from *Songs for Parents.*

**Big Books:**

*Barefoot Books, Inc.: Bear At Home* by Stella Blackstone, illustrated by Debbie Harter. Text copyright © 2001 by Stella Blackstone; illustrations copyright © 2001 by Debbie Harter. *There's a Billy Goat in the Garden* by Laurel Dee Gugler, illustrated by Clare Beaton. Text copyright © 2003 by Laurel Dee Gugler; illustrations copyright © 2003 by Clare Beaton.

*Boyds Mills Press Inc.: Go, Go, Go! Kids on the Move* by Stephen R. Swinburne. Copyright © 2002 by Stephen R. Swinburne.

*DK Publishing: Counting on the Woods* by George Ella Lyon, photographs by Ann W. Olson. Text copyright © 1998 by George Ella Lyon; photographs copyright © 1998 by Ann W. Olson.

*Harcourt, Inc.: Market Day* by Lois Elhert. Copyright © 2000 by Lois Elhert. Reprinted by permission of Harcourt, Inc.

*HarperCollins Publishers: It Is the Wind* by Ferida Wolff, illustrated by James Ransome. Text copyright © 2005 by Ferida Wolff; illustrations copyright © 2005 by James Ransome.

*Henry Holt and Company, LLC: We're Going on a Lion Hunt* by David Axtell. Text copyright © 1999 by Macmillan Publishers Limited; illustrations copyright © 1999 by David Axtell.

*Margaret K. McElderry Books, an Imprint of Simon & Schuster Children's Publishing Division: Bear Wants More* by Karma Wilson, illustrated by Jane Chapman. Text copyright © 2003 by Karma Wilson; illustrations copyright © 2003 by Jane Chapman.

*Millbrook Press, a division of Lerner Publishing Group: Ugh! A Bug!* by Ned Crowley. Text copyright © 2006 by Ned Crowley.

*Scholastic Inc.: Here in Space* by David Milgrim. Copyright © 1997 by David Milgrim.

*Viking Children's Books, A Division of Penguin Young Readers Group, A Member of Penguin Group (USA) Inc.: Fireflies, Fireflies, Light My Way* by Jonathan London, illustrated by Linda Messier. Text copyright © 1996 by Jonathan London; illustrations copyright © 1996 by Linda Messier.

# Acknowledgments

*Acknowledgments*

For permission to reprint copyrighted material, grateful acknowledgment is made to the following sources:

*Mari Evans:* "I Can" from *Singing Black* by Mari Evans. Published by Reed Visuals, 1979.

*Marian Reiner, on behalf of the Boulder Public Library Foundation:* "Caterpillars" from *Cricket in a Thicket* by Aileen Fisher. Text copyright © 1963 by Aileen Fisher.

*Photo Credits*

Placement Key: (t) top; (b) bottom; (l) left; (r) right; (c) center; (bg) background; (fg) foreground; (i) inset

12 (c) Images.com/Corbis; 15 (b) Don Farrall / Getty Images; 24 Creatas Images/JupiterImages; 6 Petr RF/Shutterstock; 31 (inset) Peter J Bryant/ BPS/Stone/Getty Images; 41 (bg) Raul Touzon/National Geographic/ Getty Images; 42 (c) Photo 24/Brand X Pictures /JupiterImages; 53 (bl) Royalty Free/Corbis; 62 Ariel Skelley/Corbis; 62 Ingram Publishing /SuperStock; 62 Purestock /SuperStock; 63 Masterfile Royalty Free; 64 (t) image100/SuperStock; 93 (br) RubberBall Productions/PictureQuest; 140 David S April RF/Shutterstock; 102 Christopher Bissell/Stone/Getty Images; 103 Geoff Dann/Dorling Kindersley/Getty Images; 103 Markus Botzek/zefa/Corbis; 129 (br) Ariel Skelley/Blend Images/Picture Quest; 138 BananaStock/Alamy; 161 (c) © Gray Crabbe / Enlightened images; 161 (tc) © Tim Hursley / SuperStock; 161 (c) Ian Dagnall/Alamy; 161 (tc) Jeremy Woodhouse/Digital Vision/Getty Images; 165 (b) Art Wolfe/Getty Images; 176 Katya Arnold; 176 (t) tadija/Shutterstock; 200 (fg) Andy Rouse/NHPA; 201 (cr) Cris Haigh/Alamy; 201 (tr) Matthias Clamer/Getty Images; 201 (br) ZSSD/Minden Pictures; 202 (t) tadija RF/Shutterstock; 205 (l) Stockdisc/Getty Images; 214 (c) Allan Davey / Masterfile; 214 (c) Ray Ooms / Masterfile; 214 Eline Spek/Shutterstock; 215 Royalty-Free/Corbis; 215 SuperStock; 216 (t) Pepe Ramirez/ Shutterstock; 240- 242, 243-245 (t) Peter Wolf/ Wolf Multimedia Studio; 243 (br) Historic NWS Collection/National Oceanic and Atmospheric Administration/Department of Commerce; 246 (t) OlgaLis/Shutterstock. All other photos © Harcourt School Publishers. Harcourt photos provided by Harcourt Index, Harcourt IPR, and Harcourt Photographers: Weronica Ankarorn, Eric Camden, Doug DuKane, Ken Kinsie, April Riehm and Steve Williams.

*Illustration Credits*

Cover Art; Laura and Eric Ovresat, Artlab, Inc.

# Teacher's Notes